— THE —
SABIAN SYMBOLS
— IN —
ASTROLOGY

⌃

BOOKS BY
MARC EDMUND JONES

HOW TO LEARN ASTROLOGY

THE GUIDE TO HOROSCOPE INTERPRETATION

HORARY ASTROLOGY, PROBLEM SOLVING

ASTROLOGY, HOW AND WHY IT WORKS

SABIAN SYMBOLS IN ASTROLOGY

ESSENTIALS OF ASTROLOGICAL ANALYSIS

OCCULT PHILOSOPHY

GANDHI LIVES

GEORGE SYLVESTER MORRIS

THE SABIAN MANUAL

THE SCOPE OF ASTROLOGICAL PREDICTION

MUNDANE PERSPECTIVES IN ASTROLOGY

FUNDAMENTALS OF NUMBER SIGNIFICANCE

⌄

DR. MARC EDMUND JONES

— THE —
SABIAN SYMBOLS
— IN —
ASTROLOGY

ILLUSTRATED BY
1000 HOROSCOPES OF
WELL KNOWN PEOPLE

AURORA PRESS

P.O. BOX 573 SANTA FE, N.M. 87504

First published in 1993 by:
Aurora Press
P.O. Box 573
Santa Fe, N.M. 87504

contents

Marc Edmund Jones
October 1, 1888 — March 8, 1980

Marc Edmund Jones was an original. He dropped out of high school to go into business and years later he completed his formal education with a Ph.D. in philosophy from Columbia University. He participated in the creation of the movie industry by writing scenarios in the very early days and was instrumental in founding what later became the Screen Writer's Guild. He was a Presbyterian clergyman and served in a parish for five years. He was a philosopher, author of the major work, *Occult Philosophy*. However, most people knew him as an astrologer.

Marc Jones began the study of astrology in 1913. In 1922, working with a psychic, Elsie Wheeler, he developed the symbols for each degree of the Zodiac, which have become known as the Sabian Symbols. In 1923 he worked out his Key Principles of Astrology for use with his regular classes. This base was expanded in the following years as he developed 12 sets of lessons for his students, presenting in mimeographed form a comprehensive but condensed version of a variety of approaches to astrology.

While working on his Ph.D. in New York, Marc came out in the open with his ideas on reforming astrology. Some of the problems he saw in the way astrology was usually practiced included assigning rulership to planets, over-personification of symbols, creation of "influences," unnecessary confusion over the distortion of houses, confusion between signs and houses, viewing the signs as quite set in nature, and taking the zodiac as a mystic conglomeration of heavenly influences upon man to which he must submit.

In his increasing efforts to correct such misunderstandings, Marc Jones traveled and lectured in many parts of the country. In these talks he did not refer to "benefics" and "malefics" in the chart. And he challenged the age-old notion that the power is in the stars, that the chart creates the destiny. Instead, he taught that astrology properly used helps clients see more clearly their own tendencies so they can decide for themselves what they want to do with those tendencies.

Beginning with the period in New York, he produced the series of books which had been projected years earlier as the rigorous presentation of techniques worked out in the mimeographed lessons. His plan was reinforced both by the growing public interest in astrology and by his position as occult book editor for the David McKay Book Company. Eleven astrological books were written and published over the years from 1941-1979. His last work, *The Counseling Manual in Astrology,* had been written and most of the type set at the time of his death, and publication was completed posthumously.

In his later years, Marc Jones was widely recognized for his valuable contribution to astrology, and was customarily and affectionately referred to as the dean of American astrology.

FOREWORD

This book probably marks the fruition, for the present life-
time of its author, of a project in astrological research which
has occupied him for more than three decades. The account
of its development has been incorporated in the text itself,
since the details are of general interest and should contribute
to a broader understanding of the symbols and their use.

Every effort has been made to give proper recognition to
the many friends and associates, the ever-widening group of
students and fellow astrologers, who have made their own
whole-souled contribution to this project through the total
of the thirty years, and it is hoped that any unavoidable
ignorance of help given by those who in consequence have
gone unnamed is not to be taken as any lesser measure of
appreciation. It is quite impossible to find felicitousness of
expression to do justice to the interest which these Sabian
symbolizations have awakened, or to the endless hours of effort
volunteered for the difficult tasks arising in the preparation
of these pages. Actually there have been many helpers whose
efforts have no identifiable representation, since they have
worked to build the background of substance and the matrix
of inspiration out of which the book has come. In this
category will be found the long and patient tabulation and
organization of symbolical elements out of other Sabian in-
vestigations, or especially valuable assistance offered by Miss
Alma Lissberger, and the some score of tentative etchings of
the symbols by Robert Miller which served to illuminate the
over-all tone of the interpretations.

Dane Rudhyar, more than any other one person, was responsible for the initial popularization of these degree interpretations, virtually compelling the organization of the project on a scale sufficient to make publication possible. The primary attention to the writing and the continual revision and checking during the past twenty-six months was again the result of the interest of a single individual, Arthur Middleton Young, who caught the vision of the volume-to-be and helped overcome the myriad obstacles arising one after another at the beginning of actual work on the text. His friend, Eric Schroeder, who is preparing a significant and variant interpretation of the symbolizations, was kind enough to read an early draft and to make suggestions of exceptional value. These two men gave freely of their time and advice when the author was working out his first plans for a presentation of the material.

Of the Sabian students not mentioned elsewhere, Miss Mathilde Shapiro was tireless in critical help with the early drafts. James Givens Allen had many clever ideas for the details of exposition and with the Mmes. Mary Bernstein, Minnie Keys and Edna Smith helped carry the extraordinary burden of proofreading in any work of this sort. The Mmes. Sylva Batchelor, Hilda Johnson, Anne Marie Sautour and Dorothy Keeffe have assisted in the special checking of the indices and tabulations. And here, most unfortunately, is a task which is far from reaching completion and in fact has hardly begun. The problem is discussed in the pages following, in the section on the example horoscopes, and a dramatic reminder of its urgency has been provided in the short space of time elapsing between the closing of the forms for the book proper and the writing of this foreword. Out of 113 of the 1000 nativities checked by the author in connection with their citation in the manuscript for the *Essentials of Astrological Analysis,* five cases of wrong position have been found, involving the Mercury of Queen Elizabeth and Sonja Henie, the

Mars of Karl Marx, the moon of Emerson and the Saturn of Benjamin Harrison.

A final contribution to the integrity of the book has been made by the Roberts Studio Press. Erwin Roberts, Jr., is responsible for the rather revolutionary procedures by which it became possible to hold manufacturing costs within the budget without any sacrifice of quality in material and craftsmanship. He suggested and worked out the new and attractive format which this volume brings to the series of which it is a part. Erwin Roberts, Sr., has been more than generous with many suggestions out of his own long experience, and has taken the time to design the end paper and jacket. Mrs. Hadassah Roberts came forward in a last-minute emergency and with a group of astrological students devoted long hours to checking cross references and the data for the example horoscopes.

The great amount of creative work on the manuscript would not have been possible without a generous two-year grant from the Foundation for the Study of Consciousness, and the author's sole strength through the mounting vicissitudes of the project has been in his life-companion through these adventures of inspiration and literary effort, indeed, Priscilla Jones has had some part in virtually every phase of the book's genesis and final completion.

Wilmington, Delaware, March 4, 1953

With the exception of an entirely fresh approach to the horoscopic mathematics in Chapter Fourteen, this third edition has relatively few corrections in addition to those of the second edition published in late 1965.

Stanwood, Washington, May 1, 1969

symbolism in horoscope analysis

CHAPTER ONE

THE POWER OF SYMBOLISM

THE entertaining account of the barber's fifth brother, in the *Arabian Nights,* is in many ways a neat epitome of the life and career of the average person, and of the near-tragic frustrations which seem to be his lot. The hero of the tale, falling heir to the modest legacy of a hundred silver coins, invests this in glassware and goes to the market place to make his start as a merchant. Sitting in the sun, he falls to musing and in his mind begins to pyramid his gains. Two hundred with the first turnover, then four hundred, and at length a diversity of operations until, "Allah willing, I will make my capital an hundred thousand dirhams." Next comes a fine house with white slaves and eunuchs and horses. Following in train is social prestige and a call on the most prominent marriage broker, "demanding for wife the eldest daughter of the Prime Minister." About to become the son-in-law of that gentleman, he is able to make a fine show of his excellence. Indeed, events mount in his imagination until at length, in his haughtiness, he finds himself completely uninterested in his bride on their wedding night. As her charms are pressed upon him with increasing feminine persuasion, he feels a sudden impulsion to kick her "with my foot thus." Actually striking out in his reverie, he overturns his whole initial stock of fragile wares, and so destroys his inheritance and his chance to be of any appreciable importance among his fellows.

Make-believe is a magic which endows man with a genuinely immortal self-confidence, but often it brings self-defeat as surely as in the case of the luckless vender of the glassware. There are hosts of those who bury themselves in their fancies and end up in total maladjustment. They remain out of sympathy with their times, in perhaps the least doleful aspect of human disintegration, and at the worst they become incompetent, unbalanced and even dangerous members of society. Men continue to live in their minds despite the focus of their living in their bodies, and so the latter may take on, in the mental eye, as many amazing and irrational variations as the outside world in general. Here is where life's ever-present symbols become quite personal symptoms. It is the usual rather than the exceptional person who imagines himself suffering from the ailments of which he reads, or which are described to him while a member of some captive audience. If it were not for this self-symbolization the newspaper and magazine advertising and the commercial announcements on radio and television would never support the expensive edifice of modern business promotion.

Psychosomatic medicine, psychiatry and psychoanalysis have well dramatized the fact that most of an individual's ills have their roots in inner conflicts, or in social or occupational uncertainty. The stigmata experienced by St. Francis of Assisi and numerous others—actual physical degeneration of the flesh in reproduction of the crucifixion wounds suffered by Jesus—are beyond dismissal by a mere skeptical disbelief, and this is no less true in the case of many extravagant abnormalities found in the history of hysterics. Children may develop a headache or other pains when it is time for school or a party, or any other phase of life for which at the moment they feel psychologically inadequate. Conversely, the list of bodily malfunctionings which disappear with the onset of excitement, sudden happiness or a broadened understanding is almost endless. Mental or spiritual healing produces many instantaneous results of this sort, and on the whole expects them.

Experience is a continuity of psychological shift and adjustment, involving changes in self and altered relations with others, and it makes full use of inanimate as well as animate factors. This is what life is, as distinguished from mere existence. The child starts out in complete dependence, absorbing nourishment for both his physical and psychological existence in the intra-uterine period, and with birth continuing of necessity in this basic pattern of naïve parasitism and self-obsession. He gains his first satisfactions and sense of self-continuance in the translating of need into demand, and in yielding a conformity to the exactions of others, and this process in time creates the phenomenon of personal relationship and comes to be symbolized as affection and love. What has been a private and automatic matter in the womb takes on larger dimensions, with a continual evolution of choice and character, but the pattern of identity remains what it has been before. There certainly can be no continuity of anything which does not continue to be what it is.

Is whatever it is that continues in such a fashion to be taken as the soul, or the ego? The two words, as far as they identify a spiritual core in man or his experience, have no reference to anything physical or to any indwelling entity of sufficient tangibility to be bound or defined by time and space. If there is a higher principle in the human individual, it cannot with one breath be treated as an object to be fitted into a box—whether compartment of flesh or a structure of idea—and also be taken as something eternal, immutable and ultimately unlimited through some sort of divine nature. There is the god in man, exactly as deity is manifest in the cosmos as a whole, but not spatially in some illogical form of a so-much, nor temporally in the utterly illusive phases of a was-once and a will-be-again. The immortal factor, whether potential or actual, is simply an on-going continuousness like the cord on which beads are strung.

The philosophical problem has been satirized humorously by Oliver Wendell Holmes in the "one-hoss shay" which had no "weakest spot" and which in consequence, after a hundred years, "went to pieces all at once. . .nothing first, just as bubbles do when they burst." The poet's ideal vehicle had that total integrity-in-itself which men like to contemplate in their thinking, or assume in their ordering of the world, but it is something which is never encountered in fact. In the realms of actuality there was once a model-T Ford which in the course of years had every part replaced, until at length not one single piece of metal, wood or fabric was left of the original car. Was it now the same automobile bought some fifteen years before? What is anything, after all, in any absolute way of thinking? Obviously some point of view, rather than a given object as such, always determines any identity in question. Composition or manifestation is stable and intelligible to mind, but unpredictable and a purely metaphysical constant in any detachment from the mental process. Reality after all must be seen in its true nature as a glorified make-believe.

The never-ceasing replacement of the substances in the physical body, dramatized by the necessity to keep on eating after growth has been achieved, is one of the fundamental features of living structures. Thus an organism, which can be defined as that which is capable of self-continuance through its powers of self-replenishment and of adjustive or self-protective movement, might equally well be described as the sort of object of which no particular component, such as may be found embodied in its structure at any specific time, is essential to its existence in any literal sense. Social realities are constituted in this fashion even more strikingly. To illustrate with the case of a merchant of greater pretension than the barber's brother, when did Marshall Field's famous establishment in Chicago become what it is?

The founder was a clerk in Pittsfield, before he went to the Middle West, and thus in one way the commercial activity which still continues began with his very unimportant place behind a Massachusetts counter. Certainly this was a training and a self-realization which contributed to the ultimate success. In 1856 the young man of twenty-one moved to Illinois, but only to start clerking again in another mercantile establishment. It was with the close of the Civil War, and in partnership with Potter Palmer and Levi Leiter, that he formed the firm which later came to be known by his name alone. How much of it was himself then, and how much of it his partners? There is an entity here, of course, but are the buildings and furniture what it is? Hardly, since there have been many changes in eighty-eight years of corporate continuity. Can there be a

single piece left of the stock which was on the shelves in
1865? Obviously the goods passing across its counters are
what makes any store what it can be said to be. But they
are utterly ephemeral. The founder is not alive and his
lineal heir, a grandson, is not active in the company's affairs. None the less, and in the most general sense, Marshall Field and Company is what it always has been.

What primarily is real is an idea, in the Platonic sense
of an entity which can be a universal and a particular one
at the same time. In terms of its constancy it is a tradition,
a morale or an aliveness precisely like that of the human
body through which, in the course of the years, there is
the constant procession of materials. Man not only takes
in physical substance as he remakes himself on the side of
his flesh over and over again, but he also conducts a
continual stream of meanings through the matrix of his
consciousness. There is a cyclic deposit and erasure of
memories. He adjusts himself in a kaleidoscope of reactions as he refines and expands his skills. He establishes
his character as a composite of excellencies, and in general maintains what John Dewey has termed a continuous
reconstruction of experience.

What Plato envisioned as the idea is a symbol which
becomes a focus of imagination, with the whole of its
roots in a magic of make-believe. Here is a power of creativity which makes a very promising start with the child.
He seems always to know, as if by a divine intuition, that
he is nothing of himself. It was long believed that imitation was a primary and ingrained faculty of conscious being, but the sober second-thought of psychologists now
accepts it as almost the first of animal skills to be learned.

There is great reward whenever a youngster, by trial and error, succeeds in shaping himself in some momentary replica of the parental traits. It is prelude to the parallel play of the nursery-school period, then to the nominal or more selective obedience of later childhood, and at length to the orthodoxy or common reliability of the adult. Ultimately the high degree of conformity will facilitate group or social action, and enhance all enjoyment as well as strengthen all sense of security, and so it inevitably will bring some sort of bonus to its practitioner.

Imitation is self-creation or self-discovery in what psychologists recognize as role-playing. The gurgling and belching and breaking of wind of the infant lying at peace, together with its twistings and turnings and grimaces, are not primarily the purposeless exuberance of a healthy and largely unconditioned organism, but rather are ever a revelation of the incipient actor or actress at rehearsal. They are more than purely physical clues for the nurse or doctor, since they constitute an actual beginning of meaning for the emerging psyche. Often they represent a great pyramid of significance, as a parent will discover in disturbing the chain of procedure too unsympathetically. Some of them remain forever solipsistic, passing into the infinity of the discarded and the useless when the child has learned to walk and talk. Most of them, however, fall slowly into pattern, and this is the early substance of character. Meanwhile it is the purest symbolism.

The diaper is comfortable, or the reverse, but in time there is a rhythm with the changing which is also an ebb and flow in the womblike nearness of another's conscious concern. Hence there is an ineradicable significance which

is built into language and habit when adultship and full
personal self-responsibility are gained. A man going forth
to battle symbolically girds his loins. When he comes
home from the struggle and yearns for rest, he seeks his
bed as a species of uterine comfort in which anything that
binds the privates is loosened or made newly fresh and
clean. If it is not time for retirement, there is the easy
chair which in shape and upholstering is a sort of partial
womb, offering bodily comfort in especial case for the
anatomical areas where the reproductive processes are located, indeed encouraging some measure of approach to the
normal position of an unborn babe. This particular complex of implication is only incidentally phallic in nature,
but it dramatizes the process of symbolization as such always has its roots in an everyday experience.

Clothing for the child, together with all the outer manifestations of whatever lies at hand, help produce his first
matrix of symbolical substance, and so contribute to the
very fiber of his make-up. He attains his special identity in
the family circle because those around him tend to
strengthen each particular role through which he may develop a continuity for himself. Thus he has a name, to
which he can respond, long before he has any true appreciation of self or ego, and this possibility becomes a fascinating game. Its sound exacts a certain obedience from him,
but much more important is the fact that this very private
designation is recognized by everybody. Meanwhile parents
and other relatives, their servants and friends, children in
and out of the family, all remember whatever other signal
or stimulus may have brought the reactions and results
they want, and so they repeat them, and the repetition

in its turn creates new symbols in multiplying dimension.

Dressed in his own special habiliments, the youngster is a personage. There is a change in language and in attitude to do homage to the phenomenon, over and over again in satisfying reiteration. And then, undressed, there is another drama to be enacted, and so it is with the bath and all the simple and fundamentally physical rituals of life. The stool has poetry for the nascent intelligence, if not for the adult minds which may have acquired a somewhat sophisticated squeamishness in this area of organic functioning, but the meanings add up to symbolism at both ends of humanity's scale in years. The little fellow's toes are pigs that go to market, and his big sister's carefully pedicured ones appeal to the imagination with quite different connotation, but all is of a piece in the imagery by which human consciousness is able to function. Experience in the raw evolves into comprehension through the refinement which is make-believe at the start and high magic in fulfillment.

The world is very generous in providing the materials for any and all make-believe, together with every opportunity for playing each given role of self-fulfillment. Thus an offspring of underprivileged parents is not handicapped of necessity in any comparsion with more fortunate children. His lot is different, primarily because he has been plunged more directly into a vortex of adult clashes and adjustments. His playground is apt to be the street, and his home devoid of privacy. The symbols of his life are narrow but wholly sophisticated, and there is no softening of an early acquaintance with hunger and deprivation, vice and crime, inhumanity and sordidness. However, his milieu is but one of the many in which the divine spirit of man is refined to advantage, in and through the inevitable call for a personal validation of idealized values. Provided he has the stamina to continue to be himself, together with the grace to do so in a vision such as may transcend the muck or misery around him, he gains sharp and early assurance of his own powers. The youngster of more favored status, contrariwise, builds up his root symbolizations more vicariously by book lore and imaginary excursions, and through what can well become an unhealthy excess of private experience with those whose sole employment is to shape his character in some predetermined manner.

The symbolism of day-by-day living is wholly personal in its significance, with each individual building it variously into the substance of his own being. Hence there is continual impetus to his self-development through his dream life, and his day-dreaming or imaginative excursions among the fancies and ideals by which he rises above the status of a mere animal organism. In this fashion he becomes the self-conscious or spiritual creature. The prime characteristic of these subjective experiences—which, by occurring entirely within the self, are freed of all conditioning responsibility to the world of time and space—is their uninhibited rehearsal of the symbols which dominate the particular consciousness. The repetitive process may not be too obvious, since the images change with the undisciplined scope of their subconscious ramification, but in psychoanalysis — or any similarly thoroughgoing study over an extended period of investigation—the larger self-delimitation of each person begins to reveal itself very clearly. He is seen now in the role he is playing to himself.

He need no longer be judged in the complex of his superficial self-exhibition, or of the confusing versatility he will show in a shifting phantasmagoria of normal relations.

The inner sensitiveness of an individual has its most common outer manifestation—apart from the areas of frustration and compensatory role-playing in amorality and destructive enmity to society as a whole—in the broad field of romance and the arts. It is always the lover who gives the best and simplest dramatization of a world surcharged with promise. Not only is there stimulation through the continued experience of a special nature with a loved one, or a heightened fellow-interest in almost anything either is doing or thinking, but there also is the added and distinctly fetish power of the many mementos which remind each of the other so rapturously. Simple memories are pyramided as both lives are enriched. When symbols gain this completely imaginative dimension they become the substance of a transcendental experience, and the mental catalysis they exert in consequence is a genuine magic.

Man's inner world is always more significant to him than his outer one, despite what may seem to be a much greater stability gained by the latter through its physical make-up or its historical continuity. The battles of life actually are fought, and won or lost, in the purely psychological and intangible areas of being. Make-believe is creativity, therefore, because it has the gift of self-persistence without the by-your-leave of any least figment of reality other than itself, and because also its contribution of a role-being-played and of an idea-being-sustained is a participation in the wholly creative structure of the universe itself. Here, in the individual's ability to create at will, is the dynamic of his being and the essence of his functional or actual identity. It is with this that any effective astrology must have its primary concern.

CHAPTER TWO

THE BASIS OF ASTROLOGY

THERE is an almost inevitable attraction between any creature and another of its kind. "Like to like, jackdaw to jackdaw," says Aristotle. The idea of a consolation through companions in misery—found as early as Publilius Syrus, the Roman dramatist—is merely a variant recognition of this gregariousness. Little girls and boys gravitate to others of their own sex and size with irresistible fascination, and there is fellowship among thieves, scholars, artists and politicians, even when such intimacies take outer and unsocial form as a sort of private vendetta. Men discover and complete themselves in their fellows, and nothing human is so persistent as a curiosity about the how and why of the acts and attitudes of others. The more akin two people may be, in any given classification, the more certainly they are apt to concern themselves over the details of this likeness.

Inquisitiveness has always this mirrorlike function, helping each individuality to obtain a confirmation of itself in the parallels it finds for its experience and its own special make-up. In consequence, a basic theatrical axiom affirms that any play, to be successful, must encourage a full audience assimilation to the characters on the stage. Popular writing achieves a translation of each reader into aspects of himself that he can applaud or find interesting in disapprobation, and thus make the basis of an exciting apprehension. Man has been obsessed with the symbolization of his own being from the first evolution of his conscious life, and out of this urge on his part has come the widely misunderstood, often misapplied and yet curiously promising science of astrology.

How is astrology to be defined? Neither the dictionaries nor the encyclopaedias, at the halfway mark in the twentieth century, are of any particular help. The contemporary astrologers, if anything, are of even less assistance. What there is by way of a genuine psychological organon in the best of current horoscopic practice will be found in a state of complete transition, or of continual clarification and refinement. Any exactness of definition may have to remain an extemporization for some time to come. However, whether the practice is science or pseudo science—that is, whether a valid technique of character analysis or a fascinatingly mechanized fortunetelling—it is as impressively old in its concepts as it is formidably vigorous in its modern recrudescence. There is even a Biblical admonition on the subject, in the words of God addressed to Job out of the storm (chapter 38, verses 32-3).

> *Canst thou bring forth Mazzaroth in his season?*
> *Or canst thou guide Arcturus with his sons?*
> *Knowest thou the ordinances of heaven?*
> *Canst thou set the dominion thereof in the earth?*

The precise meaning of the Hebrew in these couplets is more or less pure conjecture, but they approach the fundamental problem in an understanding of astrology. The *Mazzaroth* are generally supposed to be the signs of the zodiac, or possibly the bright planets which circle the ecliptic against the backdrop of the fainter stars. The next reference is most certainly to the Great Bear, for which Arcturus is an older name. The divine voice seems to be asking whether Job is able to bring about the procession of human differences, such as the zodiacal mansions have come to identify, or to control the over-all orientation of reality as represented by the seasonal shift of the Big Dipper and its undisturbed guiding of the eye to the pole star. In other words, is the patriarch so familiar with the principles operating through the celestial economy that he is competent to trace out stellar or astrological rulerships of life and destiny on earth? Behind the superficial query is a much more important question. Is astrology to be an empty pretension of human pride, and so merely another of the many superstitions which arise from man's assumption of intimacy with the godhead and special insight into divine purpose, or is it to be what any true science must become of necessity, namely, an organization of human knowledge as verified in a normal and everyday fashion?

Symbolism begins to achieve psychological power as it generalizes likenesses, and then proceeds to classify these in some recognizable ordering and reduction of difference. There are the birds of a feather who make common cause, according to the proverb which was old in Aristotle's day, and then there is the problem of the varying kinds of feathering by which, so to speak, the winged creatures are what they are. Land animals and water creatures, men and angels, bacteria and plants, organic variations in every direction, all help form the matrix of totality. These differentiations contribute inwardly and outwardly to the nesting boxes of an illimitable realization, and so call for some functional thread of continuity to lead the mind in and out of the graduated complications which mark each special case. Here is where astrology enters the picture with its fundamental recognition of functions as distinct from things. The whole of manifest creation is ever known through the differences which often may seem to establish a validity of the nondescript and the disconnected, but which really reveal an infinite capacity for the relationship of all existents with all others. The co-operative ramifications of experience, or of the recognizable points of being in its business of continuing to be what it is, are symbolized in their most simple form by the signs of the zodiac.

The twelvefold division of the earth's orbit arises in a common enough realization of the seasons. The heavens have one character in summer, and another in winter, with intermediary variations in the spring and the autumn. The planets contribute a cyclic irregularity to the very orderliness of the cosmos, perhaps annually in the most significant fashion but also daily with a rehearsal of the proposition in a somewhat different sort of significance. The heavenly bodies, however, whether the more distant and relatively fixed stars or the closer and in a sense more restless satellites of the solar system, would have little to bring by way of celestial suggestiveness if it were not for possible and simple parallels to the obvious varieties of human nature.

The rather general influence of the moon must have been recognized very early in human evolution, but this body is almost as much a part of the earth's own physical totality as the oceans and the atmosphere. Its cycles and gravitational pull are much more a matter of ecology than astrology, despite the importance of the lunar movements and aspects in horoscopic analysis. Meanwhile primitive man must have observed also, and long before written history, the species of general rhythm which links, in likeness, the differences evident at once in mankind and in the shifting sky patterns and positions. In a way each could be assumed to support the other, along the lines of the imitative magic developed by all savage tribes. While there was nothing any individual could do about the over-all order, as Job was asked to realize, its calm and eternal dependability was yet an immediate evidence of divinity, and this could be seen to have everyday expression through the constant characteristics of conscious individuality. These were the Godlike stabilities in man. They were his potentials for co-operation with his kind, symbolizing the dominion of heaven in the mundane sphere.

As astrology developed it would tend to reject any idea that God and eternal wisdom are one thing and humanity an outcast something else, with only a blind chance left to say whether human existence would be in concord or discord with the hypothetical greater reality. Hence the stellar science proved attractive to the Stoics, perhaps alone of the Greeks, because it seemed to affirm their pantheism. In any case the lone individual was accepted as no less definitely a part of the cosmic scheme than the deity which contributes form or intelligence to the whole, and this is a relationship which then could be seen to reach down to the least and last particle of inanimate existence. Here was a purely functional interconnection, or what planetary influence must mean in any common-sense terms.

Personality arises in actuality as it brings some one aspect or pattern of its potential to the forefront in a character-istic fashion, meanwhile subordinating or surrendering other and immensely larger proportions of the total, and conscious existence thereupon becomes the sharing of what has come to constitute self and other selves in all the varying modes of distribution.

As the seasons change, so do the reactions of people in their basic distinctions among themselves. There is the one who likes nature's anger in the storm, and who learns im-mortal lessons from mighty voices which speak to him in awe-inspiring fashion. He may be happy only while adven-turing in far places, or searching otherwise for life's illimitable novelties. By contrast a little girl cuddles com-fortably in the nest of pretty things she has made for her-self, and worries not a bit about broader realities. The winter temperament and its direct antithesis are perhaps the seasonal types in too superficial a fashion to be meas-ured in such characteristics by the calendar, but they are found commonly enough in the mass of humanity. The ag-gressive souls have their complementation in the meek and timid, and so on, through endless dichotomies. The intri-cacies of differentiation obviously are more than a matter of the simple aggregation of jackdaws fraternizing with each other. Rather they are a phenomenon of socialized co-operation, or the reaction of men and women to the compatabilities and likenesses which prove to be of service to them in their daily routine.

The division of humanity into twelve totally distinct zodiacal groups is beyond even imaginative possibility. The man who is Aries by birthday classification has a highly varying admixture of the other eleven signs in his make-up, even according to the lore of the most ingenuous of fortunetellers. Often the natives of Libra will share less of likeness among themselves than with those who are wholly different by sun-sign typing. Character is illimitably composite. In consequence no Biblical partriarch—and no philosopher or psychologist of these latter days—can sort humankind for mere intellectual convenience or mental satisfaction. This is the real message of the Scriptural satire. It is a lesson that educators, statisticians and rationalists seem to have difficulty in learning. God and the heavenly order, or the eternal process of putting together and taking apart, cannot be thwarted in its calm and continuing manifestation of a universal intelligence. The cosmos cannot be pushed around, in picturesque everyday terms, and neither can the real man. Does Job, or the superficial astrologer of any passing age, know enough about the bringing forth of the zodiacal signs, or the guiding of the Big Dipper, to be able to speak too surely of anything that has a life and an on-going of its own?

What the primitive mind probably came to appreciate, more by an intuition out of experience than any rational process, is the extent to which life on the smaller or individual scale, and a universally organic being or cosmic order on the larger, are able each to play the prophet for the other. There is no foreordination here, but none the less the true sage, out of his years and the moment's passing signatures (or intuitive indications as they are known in the special language of occultism), has always been able to deduce both the course of human events in general and the fortunes of various individuals in particular with quite reasonable accuracy. Whether by devious ways of self-refinement, or by talent inherent in his make-up from birth, he achieves an articulation of the universal intelligence through his thoughts and words. In this he comes to live the world in himself. His wisdom is his history. He understands above all that everything has its season, and of this his degree of socially significant living is a demonstration.

The course of unfoldment in the case of whatever may be watched, whether by the wise man or the lesser individual, can be seen to be foreshadowed very largely in its first development through the circumstances which sponsor its beginnings and early encouragement. Man's natal day achieves a symbolical importance through the emergence of a parental endowment in the new identity, and also through the auguries implicit in the social complex and the historical situation. Out of the spring, or the winter, and more specifically out of a pattern of positions of planets and the celestial dome for a year and a month, on down to a day and the hour of the clock, comes the sharp focus of the self's physical origin to establish its measure in the perspectives of judicial astrology. However, there is no more possibility of reducing the estimation of a living personality to no more than a strictly mechanical process by astrological analysis than by the scientifically fashionable computations of an intelligence quotient, a professional or business aptitude, and so on. Like the checking of the blood pressure, the acuity tests or urinalysis, the horoscopic indications are highly significant, but they are far from any mysterious or over-all mathematics of the soul.

The concept of the intimacy of relation between the cosmos in its vast reaches and the little spark of life working out its destiny on the surface of the earth—as predicated through the whole development of horoscopic techniques —is known to philosophers as the microcosmic-macrocosmic doctrine. Man is seen as the little world, or as a complete if miniature replica of the total, and the universe is conceived as the greater individuality, or that which carries any least possible reality to its illimitable potential. Actually the microcosm has no existence in solipsistic isolation, and the macrocosm is hardly a remote and unreachable perfection, infinitely regressive from everything here and now. All these conceptions are rational absolutes, and as such they exist only in the mind. Nothing is permanent but change, said Heraclitus of Ephesus, and in his recognition of illimitable extremes reacting continually on each other is to be found the key to a true stellar science. Heat and cold, tall and short, positive and negative, all are ways for getting at a mean or the tangible actuality sustained between them. Hence his divinity and his animal nature forever condition each separate person, leading him to reach for the eternal skies and to seek, concomitantly and with equal zest, for the deepest and stickiest mud in which to mire his feet.

The heavens are man or the microcosm wholly and immortally generalized as macrocosmos, and so the zodiac first of all is the celestial organism with Aries as the head, Taurus as the neck, on down to Aquarius as the ankles and Pisces as the feet. Exactly as a given person may have characteristics that amount to an emphasis on his stomach or his hands, his backbone or his capacity to make a deposit of himself on life around him, so his charting in the skies may show astrological and parallel stress of Cancer or Gemini, Leo or Scorpio (which, in order, are the rulers of the functions mentioned). From all this it may be seen that the zodiacal correlations are made primarily to the human body in an initial and over-all fashion. The twelve personal types, as popularized by superficial birthday readings and ill-trained fortunetellers, are merely a classification of people among their fellows on the basis of the accentuated functions which make them recognizable individuals.

On the unflattering side, therefore, an Aries emphasis gives a headstrong type, Taurus a self-indulgent or sometimes voracious one, Gemini a high-strung sycophant, Cancer a slave to his own appetites and his especially narrow conception of ends, Leo a cheerfully cocksure temperament, Scorpio a self-satisfied and unpleasantly assertive individualism, Aquarius the truckler to convention or devotee of band wagons, and Pisces the fault-finder who is ever critical of the stand taken by himself and others. This of course is the more technical astrology, quite beyond the scope of these pages. The manner in which the twelve signs aid in measuring the potentials of any native for whom a horoscope may be cast is explained in the author's *Astrology, How and Why It Works*. In brief summary, however, the composite individuality is to be recognized in terms of the varying combinations which make up human character in its whole complex. Classification is according to the dominant elements of personality, as they provide a focal emphasis in the pattern of selfhood. Here are individual skills or special characteristics which (1) may be charted by the signs, already given a measure of explanation, (2) identified in the situational involvements shown by the houses, or divisions of the equatorial circle as in contrast with the ecliptic, and (3) correlated to everyday activities through the positions in both celestial circles of the sun, moon and planets.

The zodiac has always been primary in horoscopic symbolism, and it comprises much more than the heavenly man of conventional exposition. It not only gives a measure of each individual by its correlation with his actual physiological and psychical functions, thereby identifying the principal differences which make him unique among his fellows, but it also offers an unlimited insight into his creative self-integration and reveals the real effectiveness of his imaginative powers. Particularly effective in this connection, and a relatively recent development in astrological investigation, is a technique of free association through a special type of symbolization provided by the three hundred and sixty zodiacal degrees. In order to understand this mode of analysis it is necessary to give preliminary attention to the proposition of freedom and compulsion in human experience.

CHAPTER THREE

THE WORLD AND ITS OPPORTUNITIES

"OH THAT one would hear me!" cries Job, in the great poetic drama (chapter 31, verse 35), and there is an over-all intelligence which seems to do so. To the patriarch come answering words from a divine mind, out of the whirling storm which provides a very apt symbol of life. They are found in the familiar couplet which precedes the lines already quoted in criticism of a superficial astro-logy, and they offer an important insight into the nature of life and of the world in which it manifests itself. They also present a therapy which man may develop when he understands the principle involved.

> *Canst thou bind the sweet influences of Pleiades,*
> *Or loose the bands of Orion?*

The meaning of these words of the Almighty is clear enough. There are elements of experience about which it is possible to do something, and also those about which nothing can be done. Did Job think he could bind up the elective or free side of existence? Could he put all reality under necessities which his own mind had conceived, and which he had conjured into being to justify his own un-happy pass? By the same token, did he believe he could loosen the determined or fixed elements of the universe, and so make everything as chaotic as his own inner tur-moil? His sorry state was due, simply enough, to a complete and unnecessary incompatibility with the world in which he found himself. He had mobilized the whole complex of symbols making up his consciousness, not to the end of his own fulfillment and a happy participation in culminations on every hand, but rather for an abject contemplation if not actual enjoyment of his own misery. Job had become everyman, epitomized at the worst.

Primarily Job dramatizes the continuing effort of every individual to achieve a conscious balance between the self and the realities which embrace it. Even an infant has strong reactions not only to the drives which come seated in his organism with birth but to a sense of a need to keep his world well-disposed towards himself. Inattention from the external reality, or deviations in environmental pattern quite removed from the economy of animal function, can be as painful to the little psyche as the pangs of hunger or other wholly bodily discomforts. There is no purely physical explanation for this, and any excursions into theoretical psychology are beyond the scope of this text. Moreover, the various hypotheses of man's make-up offer no single or sure solution for the problems of conscious life and its symbolism. The human individual has a mind and a body, and for these two terms the definition need be no more profound than in the common reference to his inner or personal being on the one hand, and to his outer or social selfhood on the other.

Mind is fundamentally an administrator of body, not unlike an elected official in a democratic society, and it is called on to account for its acts in a host of ways. Indeed, this happens much more frequently than the average person realizes. By the same token, moreover, body ultimately is an actualization of mind, or a recognizable constant of selfhood in its kaleidoscopic ramifications of identity. The two are one, except in this division of labor between them. Body reveals man to himself as he stands existent in his world. Mind interprets the external reality to him as he continues at focus in his personality. All this remains a matter of metaphysical theory in its details. It was the discovery by Job that experience can never really be rationalized, or taken very far out of its immediate context, that brought him to his great agony of soul. His mundane misfortunes, his bereavements and even his physical afflictions of painful and ostracizing disease were events he could take in stride, as long as his heart was at peace with God. Calamity was then a part of himself and his environment conjointly. But when he began to think, and to ask why, and to see the ills as the necessary products of cause—that is, existing in some vacuum of reality—he was caught hopelessly in the net of Satan.

Among the Greeks the idea emerging at this point was put in words effectively by Euripides in the remark that whom the gods would destroy they first made mad. When an individual becomes obsessed with his situation, accepting it as a compulsion upon him, and proceeds to draw within himself until he sees everything other than himself standing off and mobilized against him in bitter and uncompromising warfare, he has surrendered every claim to sanity. His pattern of symbolism has become distorted. Words and mental images are taking him from a bad case to a worse one, and in consequence any therapy must first of all provide reorientation of the symbols in which, by the Stoic imagery, he lives and moves and has his being.

The divine physician, manifest to Job as the voice of God out of the great storm, effects the healing and recovery by just such a process of symbolical manipulation. Happening of itself, this is revelation. Achieved by rational competence, it is the technique to which the present pages will direct themselves. Obviously the resolution of the patriarch's difficulties could not have been through bodily rehabilitation and indemnities, although these followed in course. Had they come first, what had had but little meaning to him before would then merely have had less in any second chapter of parallel experience. Here was a man who had been brought face to face with the vital queries of life itself. Should he ask for bread, a living substance, and receive a stone in the form of mere material restoration? Divinity had to meet his needs on the level of mind. That meant an initial demonstration that symbols are more than fixed marks, or some process of notation by which successive removes of the real might be thought to reach closer and closer to an end perfection. Such a witless regression to infinity would mean a complete loss of both self and its world.

Symbols rather are the actual fact of reality, and Job somehow had to be brought to see this. Deity, becoming articulate, speaks first of all out of the order of nature. Here is the universe, impossibly remote from any individual's experience of its processes in any general or over-all terms. Yet it is found on all hands, as intimately related as anyone might wish in the illimitable potentialities it offers for a rich and rewarding self-existence. Sea and sky stay within their bounds, as a characteristic of their nature. There are the cycles of birth and death, and of the seasons, all indomitable in their orderliness. There is a plethora of animate and inanimate resources for every convenience of man, enhancing as well as limiting his days. Does he have to concern himself with the cosmic economy? He shares the life of the animals, together with all the mysteries of organic integrity, and it is only out of his conscious being that the eternal problem of good and evil arises. There is continuity and fulfillment throughout the total of all life. What of Job's tragic impasse? Need he stand apart from everything, remaining nonparticipant and miserable? Need any individual suffer from the hardships and disillusionments of everyday living when mind is able to bring every diversity into pattern, or when there are immeasurable possibilities to square with the widest and wildest expectations of human imagination?

The crux of the lesson lies in the well-beloved couplet. There is no assurance that these are the particular stars to which the original language refers, but the parallelism of Hebrew poetry makes the general import quite unmistakable. The Pleiades, for reasons beyond any present-day reconstruction, have been taken as symbol for a free motion or a carefree distribution of experience such as no man can hope to constrict, while Orion is seen to represent a limitation or a stability which cannot be upset or thrown out of course by human design. Binding and loosening are the way of life. Nature fixes firmly with one hand and with the other unties or frees for quite unconditional development. Moreover, what is bound in a first instance is released for some·different set of relations in a second, just as the unpredictability of things in any given case is sorted quickly enough into order and its chain of probable

consequences by each shifting exigency of cosmic convenience. The patriarch is asked to realize that sheer indeter-
minacy and absolute integrity are wholly compatible
partners in existence. While he can change the nature of
neither, the implication is that he can enjoy the advantages of both. Man achieves a harmony of being by refusing to favor a single side of nature's coin, either in what he
does or in what he thinks.

He binds and loosens in the organic mechanism of body
itself. There is the intake of food and liquids, and of the
life-giving air, and the complementary elimination or out-
giving of substances either undesired or no longer of use.
The living tissues require the continual balance of assimilation and elimination, and in areas of mind or consciousness the same process should be no more difficult to
understand. Where the difficulty lies, when it comes to the
realms of conscious being, is that the symbols which are
the food, water and air of mental existence are hardly discrete elements with a time-and-space existence. They cannot be weighed or measured, put in a basket with bread
and beef, or coaxed out of a fresh breeze through a venti-
lator at the window. A bodily form has physical bulk, with
consequent limitation in duration and extension, but the
organism provides only the most evanescent boundaries
for conscious experience.

Man is a social animal, and there is little he does alone
or for himself only. He is the whole of his fellows much
more literally and immediately than he is the particularly
separated and identifiable one among them. He cannot
limit the free interchange between human individuals
that constitutes a higher life, although his hours are a con-

tinual establishment of temporary fixities, and neither can he break up the interlacing patterns of general or over-all integrity which comprise the world about him, although he makes the widest and most varying use of them. His differences fit into the sameness of order, and his self-ordering is a contribution of freedom to the whole.

When a baby begins to notice—that is, to organize his instincts and sense impressions on the pattern of the visual images which will provide his intellectual orientation for nearly every detail of his years to come—he first achieves a sort of generalized over-view. There are simple lineaments he is able to recognize on any repetition of impact. A parent's face may be one of these initial symbols, and thereupon include all that is necessary for retention and recollection, despite detailed alterations, additions and subtractions of continuous and almost unlimited degree. Concomitant nonvisual factors, such as a voice or the odor of perfume, may be further variants which again make no difference in the unit of consciousness created by the symbolization. There may be hands that pick up the infant, or a breast against which he can lean for an accustomed warmth or food, but the symbol is what it is, no less and no more. A smile or its absence, differences in clothes or mood, presence alone or with others and in semidarkness or in light, are only pertinent in the symbolical totality as they influence reception in mind or contact in experience. The binding or loosening of life is not dependent on an intellectual reduction of the physical universe to atomic components, or of society to a mere aggregate or matrix of stimulating and conditioning factors in the culture, but rather is a process of imaginative identification and assimi lation of this almost invariably naïve sort. Life is experienced as its meanings are built and rebuilt into particular patterns of selfhood.

The preference of thinkers for objects of thought that stay put has led to a conception of symbols as essentially changeless, that is, as something like building blocks in a fixed structure of understanding. According to such a point of view the complex image must always be broken down or interpreted, and the psychologist is expected to reduce the outer event or the inner dream, the real or the imaginative excursion of self, to a series of consciousness units comprising it. This again can mean pressing on inevitably to more and more minute fragments of signification, ad infinitum. The symbolical impact in human experience is never the result of a combination of fragmented particles of conscious awareness, however, but is the highly personal effect of a whole significance. This is particularly evident in psychoanalysis, in criminal investigation and the work of psychiatry in general.

Consciousness is a law unto itself, far more than the unimaginative individual is apt to realize, and what there may be of binding and loosening in human life is a result of its evolution and its transitions. A person may gain an impression from a work of art out of all sensible context. In drama and oratory the oblique implication is usually much more telling than the direct reference. Reality is ever established by the immediate pattern of participation in what it represents in a very private fashion. Hence a fire may be a calamity to one man, an opportunity to another and an entertaining spectacle to a third.

There is a properly changeless or common symbolism by

which any culture is established, but this is wholly a product of social standardization. Primary in the category is language, or the generalization of pure ideas in everyday living, together with the pictographs and alphabets by which it is written and made available for preservation. Mathematics is the ultimate refinement of this process, leading to the development of logic and a rigorous scientific method. The physical world has stabilities which are universal in all but the most intimate experience, with the result that chemistry and physics have extended the mathematical notation and are responsible for a miracle of symbolization and a complete outer transformation of the globe on which man has found himself. Here may be his greatest achievement, although there are areas in the humanities—such as law and theology—where his works are great in a different way. But it is not in these realms of sophistication, or cultural refinement, that the average individual encounters his problems of insurmountable magnitude. As the divine voice points out to Job, solutions for the issues of living at any desperate pass are not through words and formulas, mathematical and scientific mechanisms, indeed, any sort of mere manipulation of generalities.

Psychological therapy requires an immediate suggestiveness and a high potential of change in its symbolization. When the baby is distraught, the reassuring image of mother can be a resolution of all inharmony. In this most simple of all cases the recognition of the symbol may be all that is needed to resolve the difficulty. Hence the exhausted traveler, at the brow of a hill, sees the town ahead where there will be food and shelter, and finds new energy at his command. The creative artist, reaching a serious block in his work and groping for help, gets the suggestion he needs from a dream or in something he reads or hears. There is little that cannot be ameliorated or started on its way to a full resolution by a basic shift in meaning and value, or by an adjustment in attitude and expectation. The binding and loosening is a basic function of consciousness, primarily, and astrology is most useful in identifying the potentialities of greatest advantage at each step or stage in this self-alignment.

CHAPTER FOUR

THE DIVISIONS OF THE ZODIAC

THE degrees of the zodiac are the primary units by which the position of anything in the horoscope is indicated, or through which any celestial motion is brought to horoscopic significance. The astrologer puts them down according to sign, as Cancer 4° for example, differing from the astronomer who uses an undivided celestial longitude, as 94° for the same point in the ecliptic. The difference is a mere matter of notation. The astrological division into thirty-degree signs may be shown by diagram, and the discussion which follows and comprises the present chapter may be skimmed over very lightly by the casual reader or the nonmathematically-minded inquirer.

There is an important correspondence between the 360 degrees and the 365 or 366 days of the calendar year, but this presents the first of innumerable hurdles for the understanding of any new student of astrology since the inexactness of it can be a very real shock to him. He usually expects to find a mechanical perfection in the horoscopic relationships, although he probably has long since learned that anything of the sort is far from evident in nature's other realms. Nothing comes out quite even in everyday life, and certainly not in the illimitable reaches of rational theory or psychological speculation. Inequality is actually an opportunity for action, if not in fact a *sine qua non* of existence itself. What is needed to fill in a given set of circumstances, or what may have been left over, is precisely what creates the possibility of experience.

The Babylonians and the Sumerians before them—the highly intelligent people with whom history opens in the Mesopotamian valley, and from whom astrology seems to have been derived in principal part—knew well enough that the number of degrees in a circle did not correspond to the number of days in a solar year, that the unit of the day did not come out even in any annual measure, and

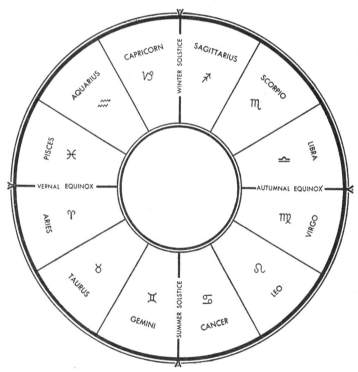

that any charting of the moon produced even more incommensurability when it came to the construction of a calendar. The organization of life, then as now, was on the basis of the wholly practical divisions of time into experience, primarily the twenty-four hours as a solar phenomenon and the week as a lunar manifestation. Twenty-eight days of course is not the moon's revolution, but is a very broad averaging of its orbital period as measured in relation to the sun (about twenty-nine and a half) and the stars (some twenty-seven and a third). The lunar month was more useful than the solar because the phases of the moon gave it a visual measurement, encouraging the ancients to employ it for their reckoning. Various adjustments were required to take up the slack in correspondence to the solar year, and at times the earlier court astronomers apparently would wait for the spring lunation, to find out if an intercalary month were needed. Here was not so much a concern with mathematical niceties as with the task of providing a regularly rectified time scale for everyday living.

The week as a unit of time gave meaning to the procession of days, so that Sunday, Monday and the other five acquired a distinct character, and these distinctions became measurable astrologically. In horoscope practice the sun establishes a symbol for the first day, moon for the second, and so on through the rest. The early astrologers carried the implication of this a little further, developing the planetary hours. To identify them, the heavenly bodies are taken in the order of the orbits from Saturn inward to the center of the system, the sun playing understudy to the earth by assuming its revolution in the geocentric charting, and the moon being left at the innermost end of the scale by what may be no more than a process of sheer elimination. The first hour of any day, taken from sunrise, is identified with the planet ruling that whole twenty-four hours, the following hour with the next planetary symbol in the scaling, and so on, repeating the order over and over again.

The planetary hour is either an even sixty minutes or else a twelfth part of the time from sunrise to sunset and similarly from sunset to sunrise, depending on the astrological school of thought and showing how a neat accuracy can be achieved in one way only by sacrificing it in another. Everything here and elsewhere, in any mechanism of measurement, is arbitrary at root. Thus Sunday is the beginning of the week, but when and how it achieved that pre-eminence is of course beyond knowing. The cycle of planetary hours completes itself three times in each twenty-four-hour period, and then there are three more single-hour units, followed by a fourth which coincides with the rulership for the following day. Thus sunrise progresses through the order of the seven planets from each to a fourth one around the scale, endlessly, as from a Sunday to a Monday (sun as four in position to moon as seven), then to a Tuesday (moon as seven to Mars as three), and so on. The days are seen as assigned to sun, moon, Mars, (Tiu in the Teutonic pantheon), Mercury (Woden), Jupiter (Thor), Venus (Frigg) and Saturn.

The day has an exact astrological correspondence to a degree of the circle in spite of the five and a quarter days left over at the end of a year. Attempts have been made by astrologers to find a way to absorb twenty-one minutes of time in each degree, but the horoscopic significance of the degrees arises from a geometrical division of the circle rather than from any correlation to the calendar units. The symbolism by which such strictly mathematical entities as these are given their application to everyday life and its problems is rooted most fundamentally in theoretical or imaginative manipulations of number, and is hardly a matter of simple arithmetic at any single point. Unquestionably the ancient sexagesimal system was developed as a basis for celestial measurement and theorizing, even while a decimal system with a much more awkward notation was used in trade, and it is probable that sixty was taken as a base because it not only permitted the division into it of all the digits from one through six but also reconciled the decimal and duodecimal relationships. Only the septenary was left out of the consideration, since it is quite characteristically unsocial among the others, and it is probable that seven came to be taken as sacred as a more or less direct consequence of this fact.

A minor puzzle arises from the use of 360 when 720 might have provided a more attractive foundation for the schematism. If the latter is divided by six, five, four, three, two and one in order, the answer is unity. If the same six digits are divided into the former, the answer is a half. There is actually a high symbolical significance in the dichotomized degree, but not in terms of area, that is, a first and then a second thirty minutes of arc. Rather it has a dual aspect which in practical terms becomes the matter of positive and negative indications in a continual complementation of each other. However, the problem here is usually approached in quite a different way. If the zodiacal number twelve be taken as the dividend in which the di-

visors one, two, three and four are all received evenly—
as in contrast with the twenty-four which is the product of
the first four whole numbers—then the bringing of the
five into the scheme, by using it to multiply the twelve,
gives the sixty of the Babylonian scientific numeration,
and the multiplication of this by six provides the 360. The
degree's dichotomy has thus been avoided by some very
left-handed legerdemain, or an obvious ordering of the rational process to produce the desired end in view. Explanation does not exist properly to put the mind at rest, but
rather to release creative potentials, and a failure to realize
the two-way implication of the degrees is to obscure all the
binding and loosening possibilities which they reveal
above everything else.

The most basic ratio inherent in a circle is that of circumference to diameter, the familiar *pi* or 3.14159 . . .
which can never be carried out to exactness. A circle is
really beyond measure because it is too constant in its
curving to have any linear description. Its nature is ap-
proximated by considering it a regular polygon with a
number of sides approaching infinity, up to the point of
accuracy desired. Any circle can be divided into chords of
precise equality, however, and its radius will section its
circumference into six such chords. Here is an important
factor in circular symbolism, and one that has been of
great importance in astrology. A diameter divides the circle into hemispheres, and if this bisection is made twice
by axes perpendicular to each other, the quadrants of the
wheel are established. In the celestial relationship this four-
sectioning provides the equinoctial and solstitial points
in the ecliptic, together with the horizontal and zenith-

nadir meridian points in the celestial equator. By horoscopic language this is Aries-Libra and Capricorn-Cancer
in the zodiac, and the first-seventh and tenth-fourth cusps
among the houses. If six of the chords created by the radius are marked off from both the diameters placed perpendicular to each other, the twelvefold structure of the
signs and houses is created, together with the basis of their
horoscopic significance, and this can be shown by a diagram made for the latter.

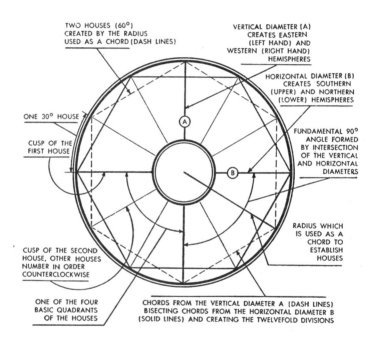

TWO HOUSES (60°)
CREATED BY THE RADIUS
USED AS A CHORD (DASH LINES)

VERTICAL DIAMETER (A)
CREATES EASTERN
(LEFT HAND) AND
WESTERN (RIGHT HAND)
HEMISPHERES

HORIZONTAL DIAMETER (B)
CREATES SOUTHERN
(UPPER) AND NORTHERN
(LOWER) HEMISPHERES

ONE 30° HOUSE

CUSP OF THE
FIRST HOUSE

FUNDAMENTAL 90°
ANGLE FORMED
BY INTERSECTION
OF THE VERTICAL
AND HORIZONTAL
DIAMETERS

RADIUS WHICH
IS USED AS A
CHORD TO
ESTABLISH
HOUSES

CUSP OF THE SECOND
HOUSE, OTHER HOUSES
NUMBER IN ORDER
COUNTERCLOCKWISE

ONE OF THE FOUR
BASIC QUADRANTS
OF THE HOUSES

CHORDS FROM THE VERTICAL DIAMETER A (DASH LINES)
BISECTING CHORDS FROM THE HORIZONTAL DIAMETER B
(SOLID LINES) AND CREATING THE TWELVEFOLD DIVISIONS

The meaning of the degrees, on the mathematical side, comes from the various stages in the progressive divisions of the circle through which the astrological schematism is established. The initial dichotomy produces the factor of hemispheres, and the fractioning of each such division by three gives the two-mansion segments of sixty degrees each, such as are also defined by the chords of the radius. The six groups of two astrological mansions each are of primary importance. Thus Aries-Taurus is a positive-and-negative pair, as is Gemini-Cancer and the rest in order. The first and second houses are a discretion-obligation complementation, as is true of the third-fourth and the others. A dividing of each of these pairings by four gives the half sign—which is not found in the conventional astrological literature, thanks to an entrenched predilection for the decanates or third-parts of the signs—and the division of these fifteen-degree segments by five is responsible for three-degree groups which are divided in turn by six to provide the half-degree emphasis.

The threefold and fourfold factors in the whole circle, or quadratures and triplicities in their functional role, provide the rationale of the signs and houses. They have become the established basis for all astrological charting of character and delimitation of circumstances. The five-fold and sixfold factors provide contrariwise the symbolical outreach to the more unconditioned, nonpatterned and illimitably extensive side of individuality, and so offer an organization of the general human experience through which each person achieves his self-discovery. Dividing the whole circle by six gives the paired signs of sixty-degree segments. These are the chords defined by the radius. They have in consequence a continued and symbolical relationship with both the center and the circumference, and in that fact suggest a species of independence or self-sufficiency different from the mutual dependence on each other of the hemispheres which the diameter establishes and builds into the quadrature and triplicity distinctions.

If the threefold and fourfold factors are used to distribute the sign pairings, the division of sixty by four yields fifteen, and its division by three gives the five-degree sequences in order around the circle. This mathematical irregularity (6, 4, 3, 5, 2) creates a more effective symbolism than the three-degree groups of half signs, or an alternate and possibly more ideal approach to the goal. The displacement of the five factor effects a definition of the basic absoluteness of self-act through a fivefold range of skill or competency in self-manifestation. The emphasis is on man's complete freedom to bind or loose at will, since his self-integration can be charted through any one of the many available patterns disclosed at least in potentiality through the zodical relationships. Alignment may be made with whatever phase of life offers the most immediate and worth-while rewards. It is such a possibility of wholly unfettered choice that the symbolization of the degrees reveals to the creative insight of the astrologer.

CHAPTER FIVE

PLANETS AND CHARACTER TRAITS

"LEAVE it to the gods to decide what is best for us, and most suitable to our circumstances," Juvenal the Roman satirist remarks, and there are in life a multitude of petty divinities to whom the average man will dismiss one and another phase of his affairs with consistent aplomb. The typical individual likes to personify everything around him, and to give an independent character to each detail of his living. In this way he can shed responsibility without losing the occasional and happy fruits of whatever goes well. Meanwhile he creates many an inner conflict. Thus the long-suffering stomach of the gourmand becomes an entity which speaks up and makes it necessary for him to argue endlessly with his own creation. The organ proves itself to be a complex of impulses that can be quite obstreperous, and sometimes quite vindictive in opposition to a particular desire, even if most of the time it remains a well-behaved entity of which he can be very proud. Indeed, he may boast of it among his intimates. It can digest nails, if necessary. It is very appreciative of the hours of close attention given to its indulgence. This is an anthropomorphism which may approach the absurd, but it is a commonplace among human beings.

The process is often much more aesthetic, as in the worship of his playing by the great pianist, or of her superb and lithe grace by the *première danseuse*. The mu-

sician insures his hands for many thousands of dollars, and
shudders at the thought of strong soap or automobile
grease or a careless manicurist. It would not be hard to
look into the special world of a Salvador Dali, and there
see ten fingers and a shock of hair scurrying around with
quite a minuscule man in tow. Meanwhile the dancer, in
her concern over her flesh, may seem in need of ministration by the Freudians, but in all aberrations of this sort
there is no more than the apotheosis of a function. It is
the narcissistic tendency towards this sort of thing that
makes the human individual what he is, i.e., a thoroughly
fanciful creature. It is his weakness, but it is also his power.
Any analysis of his life or any charting or direction of his
acts or his reactions with others becomes, primarily, an
unraveling of the immense snarl of automaticities he has
conjured into being. To these he has given the task of
maintaining his life and keeping him a participant in reality. He knows he continues self-conscious most effort-
lessly in the style of confusion to which he has become
accustomed.

The little anthropomorphic gods of self-activity are
generalized by the planets as greater deities of the sky, able
to absorb all the lesser meanings into themselves and thus
provide man with very effective psychological tools for
grasping and retaining a control of himself and of his
world. As a framework for this self-measurement there is
the heavenly replica of his organism, or the idealized representation of his bodily economy in the zodiac. Then
there are the planetary bodies circling around the earth
in the zodiacal path, offering a suggestive parallel to the
specialized traits of character in their functional orbits

within the self. It is these latter, collectively, which constitute the individual entity, How Saturn, Jupiter and the
other celestial wanderers can in any way identify or measure the multitudinous deifications of organic potentials,
together with the pyramiding structures of human relationship, is hardly something to be accepted as beyond all
answer. Indeed, the proposition involves no more than
everyday and rather common insights.

The concordance of the universe offers a very precise
description of any possible over-all reality. A tantrum
bringing the upset of someone to a head is fundamentally
a functional expression of the individuality involved in the
given relations but, because the person is an integral participant in the situation where he finds himself, the temper
display is also and to no less an extent a manifestation of
the total complex, that is, an activity of the cosmos itself
however minor it may be in such a respect. In religious
terms the sparrow cannot fall without a disruption of
God's consciousness. The environmental integrity is evident in any psychological violence of the moment, although it is the living entity which makes the disturbance
manifest, and it is through a measure of all action or reaction in a consistent and concomitant reference to the
world at large, as well as to the given selfhood in its sepa-
rations of experience and self-awareness, that the astrologer
establishes his planetary indications.

The Sun

The sun, in the astrological role it plays, gives a measure of the days and the seasons, both as these phenomena
remain astronomical with only minor variations and as
the distinctions also move down through a hierarchy of

relationships from the celestial vault to the surface of the earth where topography and latitude make very great changes. Summer is winter below the equator. Night is dav for those who labor when others rest, as well as for those whose inspiration and urge to life is best enhanced by running counter to the usual stream of events in their social relationships. The spread of simple differences here applies to distinctions among people, as between those who are prominent and so receive the physical rewards which enable them to shine among their kind, and those less fortunate individuals whose position in the culture is at nadir. For these latter all opportunity may seem asleep, and they may find no light coming to illuminate their own aspirations.

Does this mean that all is well if the solar orb is high at birth, in the heavens and so in the horoscope which merely maps the celestial position of the earth amid these other bodies? The interpretation at times, and always in part, can be quite that literal. Astrology builds on a curiously naïve symbolism because, first of all, it charts the simple and widespread observations and anthropomorphisms of people at large, and then because these of themselves have primitive roots. Astrological analysis, however, is not unsophisticated to the point of childishness. An elevated sun, in horoscopic terms, indicates the set of temperament that would like to ride the skies, free and wide and ever accepting the homage of all creation, but what is shown is an emphasis or a potentiality and not a fate or an inevitability of living all worked out in advance.

The consequences of character and action have their spread through time and space in direct proportion to the concomitant involvements, since things do not exist by themselves. Nothing can be inevitable *in toto,* or devoid of elements beyond possibility of changing. But there can be no free choice without immediate consequences which are bound, since otherwise there would be no meaning in decision as such. Can a mind choose between one nothing and another, or among things so loose in their relationships as to be beyond all visualization? In New York City a Columbia University professor ended his career by jumping from the roof of an apartment building on Claremont Avenue. He went up the stairs, took off his coat, folded it neatly, went through a considerable number of operations as preparation for the ultimate end before he sat on the parapet and at length leaped off. In the whole chain of events, of which the end consequence was self-destruction, there was no fading away of free will until he had propelled his weight into the air. Then and then only was there inevitability, granting of course no intervening awning, or no passing vehicle with the type of roof to break his fall and save his life. Astrology does not reveal a reality out of context, but rather a complex of the possible in some phase of immediate convenience.

The sun is the central body of the solar system, and in horoscopic symbolism it is correspondingly the core of whatever may be brought under analysis or found at the forefront of attention. The conscious individual stands or exists at center, in respect to the things that fulfill and illuminate or else defeat and destroy him, and the solar orb dramatizes this function of self-centering. It becomes the astrological indication of integration, integrity and identity. The idea is expressed variously as will, ego or pure

selfhood. What is symbolized is the manifestation, not of
something which is in any respect anything other than
itself, but of a completeness of participation and identification by self or identity in whatever lies at hand and becomes pertinent. The concept is so simple that some minds
balk at accepting it, but it is nothing more difficult than
the mathematician's notion of a point. It is continuum as
source, or existence as entirely self-explanatory. It is the
primary clue to life in horoscopy because it reveals the living entity behind the screen of all superficial deviations.

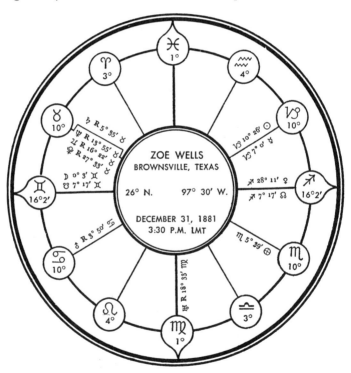

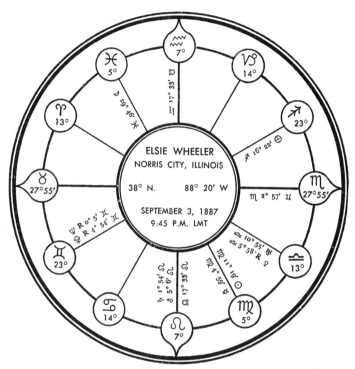

An illustration of astrological procedures, as these may be based in considerable part on the symbolism of the zodiacal degrees, is provided by the horoscopes of two gifted women. Both possessed unusual capacities for transcendental insight, and also had a significant part in events coming to a culmination in the degree symbolizations. Zoë Wells was a recognized artist in the commercial field. Elsie Wheeler, crippled by arthritis to a point of almost immobility and forced in consequence to spend the principal years of her life in a wheel chair, was a professional

medium of considerable reputation. Miss Wheeler died in
1938, and Miss Wells not long afterwards. If the astrological
sun reveals a potential individuality of great intuitive
power, in the case of these natives, then the whole horoscope should show the basic integration of this special capacity, that is, both the manner in which each of them
would be most capable of capitalizing on it and the extent
to which others would be most apt to have satisfactory
results in any appeal to their spiritualistic gifts.

Either of these horoscopes might be examined in the
light of innumerable other inquiries, ranging from the
deepest frustrations of private life to the simple and over-
all problems of any American individual going his usual
and lawful way as a member of society, but neither of the
cases would have much interest for the reader apart from
the symbolical degrees and the questions of imagination
or the powers of make-believe through which the zodiacal
symbolizations and the lives of the two women are intimately and inextricably linked. Indeed, it is impossible to
go very far in astrological analysis without a rather complete factual knowledge of the subject. Otherwise there is
no substance in which the basic insights can be expressed.
Here, however, are personalities who continue to live in
their achievement, and who can be known as thoroughly
in this respect as a brother in terms of family life, or an
associate in business matters of common concern.

Miss Wells' sun is found in Capricorn, 10° 26′, and since
these zodiacal divisions are mathematical entities in a
geometry of the heavens—rather than a point of emphasis
that might be thought to be determined by the stars, or by
peaks of influence in the universal gravitation—any frac-

tions indicate the next degree as the one symbolically significant. Thus the minutes of arc in the ecliptic, from its precise beginning at Aries 0° 0′ 0″ up to an even 60, are Aries 1. Those from 61 through 120 are Aries 2, and so on. The symbolization of Capricorn 11 is a large group of pheasants, and its emphasis is on the reduplications and multiplications of every facet of existence. The continuous variations are a dramatization of the infinite potential in the whole, and the keyword is illimitability.

The type of astrological judgment following at this point is an adaptation of the psychologist's free association, that is, utilizing an affinity of ideas for a spontaneous and imaginative conclusion of the sort often identified as intuition, and frequently made unnecessarily mysterious. The symbol gives a clue to what the world at large may have been expected to provide, in normal course, by way of aid to Miss Wells in her fundamental self-expression through her spiritistic gifts, and to what particular examples of this would have a primary encouragement in her self-discovery. The pheasants, in their multiplying presentation of themselves and their illimitability of self-being, suggest that this highly sensitive artist was at her best in her psychic outreach as she allowed herself an untrammeled sweep of exploratory vision, or sought a complete spread of transcendental understanding. There was in her make-up a self-glorification or almost vain egotism of which the birds are also a symbol, and this was a high asset for her mediumship although a considerable handicap in other ways.

In the chart of Miss Wheeler the sun is found at Virgo, 11° 19′, and the twelfth degree of that sign is symbolized by a bride with her veil snatched away. The emphasis is on life's demand that man continue at all times to prove himself in full accordance with whatever claims he has made for himself. The keyword is invitation. Thus while Miss Wells, the senior of these women by her birth in 1881 in comparison with 1887, was much more centered in her own self-confidence, and was a superb clairvoyant because of this utter independence of spirit, the younger of the two, with her years of exceptional physical handicap, was sensitive by contrast to her own nothingness in the terms of herself alone. She was eager for a spiritual justification which for long she was unable to obtain on her own account and to her own satisfaction. Her struggle was heroic. By gradual stages she brought herself up to the point where she was entirely self-supporting, and no longer dependent on the good will or kind offices of others. Indeed, in her last years she helped her fellows, continually. Meanwhile she had expressed the desire, over and over again, to use her intuitive gifts for something more worthwhile than answering the petty and selfish questions brought in usual course to the professional medium. The alacrity with which she moved to assist in developing the Sabian degrees was not unlike a bride's eagerness. Because her claims for herself were insistent, she was able to invite an exceptional opportunity to substantiate them.

The Moon

The moon in astrology, second of the two lights in horoscopic language, complements the sun and the recognition of the self in terms of will, and reveals the native's outer or practical self-centering in the world at large. The lunar orb as the one actual or proper satellite of the earth, and exhibiting a thoroughly physical influence on the tides and various fluid cycles in the living organism, might be expected to have a symbolical reference to man's everyday milieu, especially in its immediate co-operation with his inner or private nature. What is emphasized is a side of his personal self which does not have the broad recognition given to discrete individuality, such as is identified so conveniently in the sun's symbolism and seen to be so much a law unto itself. The lesser light measures the distribution of individual activity through all phases of organic functioning. By its position in the zodiac it establishes the point of reference for answering questions concerning not so much the basic or central characteristic of selfhood as the equally important social or commonly shared potentials by which each person has his contact with others. What is shown most importantly is his capacity for human fellowship, as in contrast with the more subjective integration. Here is indication of his personal warmth, his feelings or emotional nature and his ability to throw himself into experience thoroughly and completely.

Zoë Wells' moon is in Gemini 1, and the symbol is a glass-bottomed boat in still water. The emphasis is on an alertness to the deeper potentials of experience, and on a poise which lends intelligence to act. The keyword is curiosity, suggesting that this native was not inclined at any time to plunge into the immediate activities of human existence, but that rather she found in them a passing phantasmagoria to be considered by reflection and observed from a distance or through a glass as in the employment of her inner faculties. Thus she was the true artist, living to interpret and reproduce dispassionately whatever might go into the complex of realities around her. This is quite different in signification from the high self-awareness and almost necessary self-disclosure which the pheasants dramatize. As a personality and in immediate human relationship, as indicated by the sun, she was perhaps too aggressively self-centered. She always seemed to be seeking recognition for her talents. But when it came to the subject matter of consciousness or to the broad fields of aesthetic expression, under the moon's symbolization, she was just as assiduous in subtracting herself. Then she became impersonal to the point of high gestative detachment, somehow becoming as nothing when there was anything of the outside reality for which she could be a channel. This balance of uninhibited self-drive and exceptional catholicity of response to her world at large was the bottom reason for the excellence of her psychic gifts, as well as for the major troubles which beset her.

Miss Wheeler's moon is in Pisces 30, and the symbol is the Great Stone Face or the natural formation on Profile Mountain in New Hampshire dramatized in the well-known story by Nathaniel Hawthorne. The emphasis is on an immortality of the soul through its success in becoming a living manifestation of its own ideal. This is a call on every man to select that image of reality into which he can mold himself, and the keyword is discernment. Here is a self-detachment comparable to Miss Wells' interpretive aloofness from life, as far as any personal interest is concerned, but also an insatiable desire to be of real worth, and there is in consequence a genuine co-operation with the utter self-giving shown by the sun's symbolization, or the bride with her veil snatched way. The astrological indications so far have shown the older woman almost hermetically sealed up within herself, and it was in such a fashion that she lived and died. The younger woman, contrariwise, could not reach out far enough nor distribute herself broadly enough, from the limitations of her invalid's chair, to meet the challenges she accepted. It is in this manner that the symbols, as they are brought into functional relation with each other through specific horoscopes or other astrological techniques, reveal their power of catalysis for the understanding. Each meaning flows into every other one, and thereupon gives an expanded perspective on the nature and immediate promise of any given personality or issue, both as taken by itself and as seen in larger context.

Jupiter and Saturn

The astrologer employs eight true solar satellites in his analysis, in addition to the sun and moon which for convenience he classifies with the others. The physical character of these bodies has little to do with their astrological significance, which arises primarily from mathematical factors such as the relative positions of their orbits and related details of a purely geometric symbolism. The names come from the gods of the Greco-Roman world, with only minor correspondence between the traditional personalities of the deities and the planets to which they are assigned. In the course of the long development in horoscopic techniques it has been found advantageous to consider these eight bodies in pairs, along the lines of the approach to the two lights in the preceding paragraphs. The first two of them, in a sequence of psychological importance among the original five known to Claudius Ptolemy, are those whose orbits were then the most distant ones. Jupiter is the nearest of this pair, and its astrological nature is the function of bringing the more remote elements of experience into the fiber of selfhood or of giving a self-significance to everything which can be said to exist separately from self. This is simple ensoulment, or an entering into the different substances and various phases of an indefinite reality to give them form and meaning. It facilitates the self's acquisition of a personal being or a conscious personality, and is the manifestation of soul and character as in distinction from the basic identity or nascent and unconditioned vitality shown by the sun. It is enthusiasm as in contrast with will. it is an emphasis of spontaneity rather than ego.

Saturn as the farthest distant of the original planets reveals the over-all delimitation of personality, primarily in the form of wisdom and an ultimate orderliness. Because its period in years roughly approximates that of the moon in days, it has been used to indicate the factor of time as well as space in this all-encompassing delineation of selfhood. Astrologically it describes a sensitiveness to enduring things, in direct complementation of the lunar awareness of an everyday milieu or of the interaction of self with everything more immediately at hand and in terms of feeling rather than knowing. The greater infortune, as the medieval astrologers identified it, presents a mode of reality quite the reverse of the jovial benevolence attributed to Jupiter as the greater fortune. The Saturnine indication has been conventionalized in a concept of destiny, and thus seen to chart the superficial limitations of personal life through such various ills as bad health.

The horoscope of Zoë Wells presents Jupiter in Taurus 17, and the symbol is a battle between the swords and the torches. The emphasis is on the conflict between the practical necessities and the motives or meanings in life, and the keyword is resolution. Her personality or fundamental self-direction of character was marked by a continual unrest in the face of the great moral and ethical issues of the day. For her there was no peace in any acceptance of things as they were, and she did not have any tolerance for humanity's easy surrender of its true self-interest at so many of the major turning points in history. Her Saturn lies nearby in the sixth degree of the same zodiacal sign, and it is symbolized by a bridge being built across a gorge. This emphasizes the conquest of natural difficulties by conscious means, and the keyword is channelship. Here is indication of her scorn for any dependence on primitive resource or nascent wit, or for halfway measures and soul-wearying detours. The artist must live passionately, never loath to be caught up in a battle to the death, ever striving in the lists of honor for the exaltation of the soul's powers and so ready to risk all in order to achieve a genuinely creative role in life's affairs. Obviously this type of personal self-orientation gave the native the greatest possible challenge in developing her gift of insight, and in refining her spiritual or occult talents. She had found an area of experience offering her a real self-quickening.

Elsie Wheeler's Jupiter is in Scorpio 3, and the symbol is a house-raising. The emphasis is on the joy of common enterprise for the enhancement of a personal fulfillment, and the keyword is helpfulness. As already evident in the comparison with the artist and her strictly amateur psy-

chism, the professional medium was equipped with an ideal
temperament for the role of counselor and for offering
adjunct eyes and a wider judgment to others. The symbolism of her sun and moon, showing that all privacy or
chance for retreat into herself was denied to her from
birth, had its continual re-emphasis in her cripped condition through the principal years of her life, and this led
to her finding herself by proxy in her service to her clients.
Her personality had its fullness in the spiritualism which
in her case became a calling of the highest order, enabling
her to offer a literal assistance in completing those edifices
of the understanding in which her fellows might dwell.
This was her enthusiasm. Her Saturn lies in Leo 2 and the
symbol is an epidemic of the mumps. The emphasis here
is on the necessity that every living spirit retain an accentuated sensitiveness to the import and usefulness of whatever it may encounter, and the keyword is infection. She
was permitted no relaxation into a mere knowing, and no
surcease of intensified and personal realizations by any simple dismissal of realities to their own due course. She
could not shrug off what in one sense was none of her business because her particular role in life was to make anything and everything her very special concern. She was the
sensitive per se, and her being had its sole consummation
as she could share the troubles of others to as complete an
extent as possible.

Mars and Venus

With the remaining planets the horoscope gets down
to the more petty gods of everyday living, and uses them
to chart life's immediate demands or rewards and its relatively superficial struggles. The first pair among these

six provides the indications of adjacency, or of the passing contiguities of existence. The positive side in this perspective has its measure through the cycles of Mars as that body, in an orbit lying next outwardly in relation to the earth's path, has become the significator of war, pestilence and all current forms of everyday excitement. The planet primarily is the indicator of simple initiative, or of the manner in which anyone starts things. Hence it shows how he throws himself into conscious action, or continues any particular activity. This is in distinction from the enthusiasm or spontaneity of Jupiter, which is a psychological and subjective proposition, and from the basic self-integration or expression of pure will and ego which is measured by the sun. The planetary bodies in this third pairing become the representatives of surface affairs and common human relations. They are concerned with the tangible objects and discrete aggregates which can be moved around, put together and taken apart, or in any or all ways given a place and meaning in time and space. Venus, with its orbit situated next inwardly from the earth, is the converse of Mars in its astrological implication. It charts the conventional coming to an end or climax of all elements going into the make-up of human life and relationships. The simple completions of day-by-day existence, or its ordinary accumulations and satisfactions, are in contrast with the education and refinement of self which are implicit in Saturn's indications, and with the basic capacity for reaction to others or assimilation into their experience which the moon measures.

Mars has special emphasis in the chart of Zoë Wells because it is the rising planet in a case where there is no

elevated one. It is situated in Cancer 4, and the symbol
is a cat arguing with a mouse. The emphasis is on man's
need for a definite set in mind as a prelude for everything
he does, and the keyword is justification. It was on the
level of everyday affairs that this native experienced the
most bitter of her struggles, meeting what to most points
of view would be considered high frustration followed
by complete defeat. Despite her genius as a sensitive, she
was unable to initiate anything that bore any ultimate
fruits in any practical terms, and instead was ever quarreling in spirit with the conditions of each opportunity as it
opened up before her. Her unreasoning demand for recognition in advance of performance, in order to justify herself as a personality, blocked all possibility of achievement.

Her Venus lies in Sagittarius 29, and the symbol is a
fat boy mowing the lawn. The emphasis is on the over-
balancing of primitive appetites by social incentives, and
the keyword is participation. Had she been able to come
down out of the grandstand, so to speak, and to take a direct and creative part in the affairs of the world, the story of
her life might have been written quite differently. But
all the magnificent struggling of her personality, all her
inner and personal desire to do something significant,
were diverted into a flight from reality. If this was not
always into fantasy, at least it was too often into perverse
and unrewarding superficialities of interest and effort. Her
daily routine always mocked her deeper aspiration. She
allowed herself to become overweight, and thereupon became discouraged in any real attention to her appearance.
She was at peace only in the fullness of her mediumistic
gifts, but even when it came to these she was never able

to bring herself to dedicate them to any general or public service. Instead she trimmed and trimmed away at the grass of her intentions.

Elsie Wheeler's Mars is in Leo 6, and its symbol is an old-fashioned woman and an up-to-date girl. The emphasis is on the stimulus to each other of conventionality and uninhibited self-expression, and the keyword is contrast. Here is a stress on the need of the old to be challenged by the changes which may invalidate its standards, and of the new to be tested and confirmed by some measure of broad acceptance. The crippled little woman in her wheel chair, gazing daily into her crystal, could hardly meet the usual conventions of California life or exhibit much by way of an actual or outer free choice in a physical world of time and space. However, an especially strong aspect of favorable nature between her two planets of this department shows the extent to which she was spared any sharp struggle in connection with the superficialities of her existence. She was able to bring everyday events pretty much under her control because her initiative functioned best in maintaining a balance between the extremes she found around her, and because she was able to establish this poise or equilibrium for others.

Venus in her horoscope is found in Libra 6, and the symbol is in the ideals of a man abundantly crystallized. The emphasis is on the meanings in which all being has its effective beginning, and the keyword is personification. Her consummations, therefore, were very properly within her own personality, as far as she was concerned herself, and her life story becomes very different from the bitter psychological battle through which Miss Wells was torn to pieces and at length destroyed. Miss Wheeler found the embodiment of her achievements in the lives of those she helped. Her fulfillment was in the purest make-believe, facilitated as it was by her role as a practicing spiritualist, and in this fact she provides a most useful demonstration of the fundamental principles of therapy put down at various points in these pages.

Uranus and Neptune

In 1781 a new planet was discovered by Sir William Herschel, and for a while it bore his name, although now it is known almost universally as Uranus. This and the other bodies added to astrology's original septenary are hardly to be considered necessary for accurate judgment prior to their possession by the practitioners of a stellar art, but rather they are the indicators of elements which have come into history with their initial identification. Thus Herchel's discovery is remarkably close to the Declaration of Independence of the American colonies in 1776. The finding of Neptune in 1846, in triumphant vindication of the new celestial mathematics which predicted the event and gave the place where it would be found, has even closer correspondence to the focal developments of the great nineteenth-century socio-economic revolution in 1848. The first and positive one of this new pair of planets shows today's truly social independence of the individual through a freeing of his talents and an expanding of his personal skills in a modern or industrialized world. There has been nothing similar to it in earlier historical periods, by even the broadest of parallels. It is quite distinct from the initiative of Mars, the enthusiasm or spontaneity of Jupiter and the will or ego of the sun.

The second and correspondingly negative body in this pairing, contrariwise, gives the measure of each man's bondage through the rising complexities of the new and global culture. This is quite different from the everyday desires of Venus, the psychological and physical limitations of Saturn and the simple or commonplace involvements of the moon. It is an ideological delimitation of self quite unknown to any ancient or medieval community.

Miss Wells has Uranus in Virgo 19, and the symbol is a swimming race. The emphasis is on the necessity to bring each special capacity of selfhood in leash and the key-word is elimination. Never able to uproot the superficial standards of an exceptionally proper upbringing, she yet was drawn irresistibly to New York's Greenwich Village of the twenties, and so she made a compromise and lived her best years on the uptown or indomitably respectable edge of Washington Square. The race was on, but she was afraid to swim. She held the whole world in her hand through her psychic gifts, but she dared not use them to the full of her powers. The planet is nadir and retrograde, so that her spiritual foundations for participation in the new era literally were superb, but the independence which lay at her hand in this direction was not what she desired most. Her Neptune is in Taurus 14, and the symbolization is shellfish groping and children playing. This emphasizes the self-sufficiency of life in each of its characteristic spheres, and the keyword is emergence. She had the power to bring the depths of human potentials out into the life of everyday, so that even the youngsters could see and know eternal stability and significance, but the deep-seated struggle within her left her self-obsessed or hopelessly self-divided. Like the children she was gay when it meant nothing, and like the shellfish she continued groping until the very end.

Miss Wheeler has Uranus in Libra 11, and the symbol is a professor peering over his glasses. The emphasis is on the subordination of all other considerations to some major pattern of responsibility, and the keyword is specialization. Her personality, in the new social perspective of modern times, was wholly insulated from all destructive taints of the self-pity or the self-indulgence which would have betrayed any higher or spiritual impulses. She did not have the cultural background or opportunities of Miss Wells, but she was far more able to project herself into the consciousness of others and thus share the enduring values of a global society. Her dispassion here built to the impersonality needed for her role as the professional medium, and furthered her real opportunity for personal achievement. Her Neptune is found in Gemini 1, or the place of Zoë Well's moon, and the glass-bottomed boat symbolizes the detachment in which her freedom of the spirit actually was guaranteed to her. In the older woman's case this degree emphasizes a weakness, since it encourages a retreat from contact with others, but for the younger psychic it shows a strength, since her involvements were of the spirit and of necessity nurtured in a physical aloofness. There was no corner of reality to which she could not be taken for the fulfillment of her professorial or impersonal inquiry, and her life was rich because it took its focus on a transcendental level.

Mercury and Pluto

The two remaining planets of the ten now in common

use do not normally constitute a pair on their own account, although they may be conceived in such a fashion. Each rather is a supernumerary body, with functions of supplementation for the other pairings. They have much in common, however, in respect to their celestial behavior and relations. Both of them are indicators of individual points of view or orientation, as well as of the generalized meanings and abstract relationships in which all human thinking is framed. Here are elements quite distinct in implication from the charting of literal experience for which the other eight primarily are employed. Mercury has association with Mars and Venus in the area of everyday affairs, and in the simplest of possible terms is the astrologer's representative of mind, that is, the focus of awareness or the immediate threshold of consciousness. Thus it is fundamental in any estimation of the intellectual situation, or in any determination of an individual's capacity for hewing to his line of intention whenever he seeks to carry out some plan or project. Pluto, by contrast, gives the measure of what might be termed a cosmic mentality or a group ideation. Discovered in 1930, this curiously small body with as many astronomical eccentricities as the undersized Mercury, gains much of its significance through the reconstitution of human society after the great 1929 depression. It shows the immediate applicability of any native's philosophy of life, and in general charts the potential response of each individual to the new and still unsettled patterns of a global culture. In both the good and bad senses of the term it is the obsession by which someone is caught up completely in a cause or conception to which he can dedicate himself.

The Mercury of Zoë Wells is in Capricorn 7, and the symbol is a veiled prophet of power. The emphasis is on the untapped resources inherent in all personality, and the keyword is supremacy. In the matter of her psychic gifts, therefore, the horoscope provides every suggestion of their extraordinary range and their really superb capacity. In the outworking of her everyday life, however, the focus of mind or the general awareness was a tragic stress of a futile and almost naïve self-affirmation. There was altogether too much encouragement for the near megalomaniac pattern under which the gradual and final disintegration of body and understanding took place. Her Pluto—with the general reservation that must be made in its case for all its positions prior to its discovery, thanks to a questionable reliability of the tables available for its movements—lies in Taurus 28. The symbolization is a woman pursued by mature romance, and the keyword is persuasion. Thus Miss Wells' later years were emphasized, in respect to the over-all orientation she had achieved in the socio-economic scheme of things from the time of the great depression onward, in values that might very well have been hers in especial case since she was then approaching the heightened appreciation of her fifties. It is part of the general debacle of her life that her intuitive brilliance, which actually reached its peak just before the new planet came into astrological activity, was caught up in her spreading dissatisfaction with the world and all its ways. Hence her talent dissipated and destroyed itself before it could achieve its highest potentiality.

In the horoscope of Elsie Wheeler the position of Mercury is in Virgo 5, and the symbol is a man dreaming of fairies. The emphasis is on his ability to use the coin of experience with real wisdom or insight, and the keyword is outlook. The operation of Miss Wheeler's mind was buttressed by its continual inner communion with the personified powers of the outer world. This would have proved to be a considerable handicap in the case of a more prosaic situation in life, but it was an additional qualification for her career as the professional spiritualist. What might have been a retreat from reality in other circumstances became a deepening touch with the unsuspected factors which in their turn could provide a solution for many a problem and an answer for many a misgiving. Her Pluto is found in Gemini 5, and the symbolization is a radical magazine. This emphasizes man's power to give high exaltation and dramatic force to whatever may have stirred him deeply within himself, and the keyword is tangency. What there was of sharp deviation from normal activities and interests in her years, after her first critical illness and incapacity, became a high potential for which the new order of things had a special frame. This was hers with the emergence of the Plutonian influence, following on the events of which the planet becomes the special measure in astrology. In consequence she gained the wish to which she had held above all else, or a chance to make some sort of permanent contribution to the transcendental reality in which she felt she had found her place.

CHAPTER SIX

MOTIVES AND THEIR MEASURE

It is an axiom of everyday life that the human animal does precisely what it wants to do. Advertising techniques are based on the happy psychology by which, in the ancient fable, the wind failed to blow off the coat which the sun removed by the mere persuasion of its warmth. The old saw has it that more bears are caught by honey than by steel traps. Whether by creating a species of fright or shame, or by an appeal to selfishness or to the self-gratification of a righteous impulse, anyone who is able to conjure up a real want in the consciousness of his fellows will find himself well-equipped to bend them to his will. People always are activated by their own wholly private desires. Thus a millionaire, for the satisfaction of a monument to his name, endowed the medical school and hospital through which a certain young man had the chance which otherwise would have been impossible. And then there was a poetic youth who climbed a wall each day to revel in the beauty of rambling gardens created and maintained by a wealthy gentleman who never even looked at them. The trespasser probably enjoyed a much more actual possession of the loveliness than the owner, despite the fact his intrusion had no moral sanction of society. He risked all possible penalties because the driving impulse was strong upon him. Meanwhile the student, taking equally impersonal advantage of the endowment set up for the study of medicine in no less a context of vanity, is applauded for his enterprise. It should be very evident that meanings are always as important as facts, and that astrology of necessity must give a very real attention to this subjective factor and all its illogical ramifications.

The study of the two women in the preceding chapter, although limited to the horoscopic analysis of their exceptional psychic gifts, dramatized what should be almost a self-evident proposition, namely, that what becomes an asset in one respect easily proves to be a handicap in another, or vice versa. Astrological therapy is based on the simple realization following from this. It is seen that any really inadequate perspective or gross misapplication of effort can be avoided very easily, if only the consequences are faced in time. Elsie Wheeler came to live a life which at the end was certainly more rewarding to her than any conventional interpretation of the indications could have promised, whereas Zoë Wells gradually brought her years to an end in a hopeless snarl of frustrations. There was nothing in their horoscopes—or in the ramification of what astrology designates technically as the directions or progressions—to show that such an outcome in either case was at all written in the stars as irrevocably necessary, or that the one native would improve her fundamental capacities while the other would depreciate hers. It is what an individual actually does with his potentials in any one instance that determines the more precise probability of their outworking in the next. Change or redirection may then become more difficult, but beginnings are never a cancellation of the chance to begin.

The horoscope, because of the fundamentally ambivalent tendencies developed by all people, presents a potential of personality that can lean in either of two ways, that is in everyday language, towards good or evil. The soul is not an absolute, either god or devil in terms of any necessity, but is a living continuum which partakes of both extremes. The human creature is of the earth and of the skies, and this is a mixture of natures which is hardly to be resolved to any rational simplicity by a legerdemain of logic. No individual by fine resolution can cut himself off from the soil which like his mother's womb cradles him forever in the depth of his own roots, and by the same token it is impossible for him to debase himself to the point where he is unable to hold himself inviolate in his very anarchistic divinity and to know thereupon that the tie to heaven remains unbroken. Job on the dung heap could talk to the Almighty, and so may the most hopeless of derelicts in the Bowery gutter or on Skid Row if ever he chooses to get around to it.

Since no conscious entity can be identified or explained in the terms of any irrevocable fixity, but instead can become virtually anything at all for as broad and long a fixed state as suits its prevailing mood or impulse, the more therapeutic method of astrological interpretation does not concern itself too much with the social environment and other physical situations of man, nor even with the character given to him by his world and accepted by him as a convenience along with all the other externalities entering into his experience. Rather it gives primary consideration to his self-indulgences, the rebellious moments of his social conduct, the lapses towards solipsism especially evident in his dream or subconscious life, the abstract or verbal ideals he tends to hold and express, and so on. All these represent the native as he relaxes into himself and finds in his mind's eye the justifications and satisfactions which become a creative substitute for such superficial verdicts as are pronounced on him by his fellows. His various flights from major lines of current reality, whenever he finds events too generally unappreciative of himself and his works, are wonderfully self-revealing.

The symbols for the degrees have implications to fit this subjective side of the coin no less than the social and functioning characteristics to which attention has been given thus far. In order to assist the interpretation of these human ambivalences, the symbolism has been given negative as well as positive meanings, thus bringing consideration down to the true significance of the half degree and its emphasis of the functional fluidity in all conscious being. For an example of the type of judgment now to be illustrated, some individual is needed who is well enough known to the average person to give point to the astrological delineations, and preferably one whose career has been characterized by an obvious and personal preference for evil in its more common manifestations. Almost ideal for this purpose is the recent Nazi leader of Germany, Adolf Hitler. His extreme frustration, his absurd fanaticism, his dramatic megalomania, all show the significance of the planets on the negative or self-defeating side.

Hitler's horoscope is not particularly impressive at first glance, as might be expected to be the case with someone able for a few years to set the whole world dancing to his tune. Most individuals of outstanding stature tend to suggest what they will come to be, at least to the discerning

eye if as yet they have been unable to make any demonstration of their special genius, but there are also those who
never do this to any appreciable extent. There are no absolutes in astrological configurations, any more than in
everyday's normal lineaments, and so astrology offers no
fortuneteller's inside information except as it utilizes supplementary insights of a psychic and not too reliable sort.
At the beginning the German would-be dictator seemed a
rather laughable imitation of Benito Mussolini in Italy,
a half-baked agitator not to be taken too seriously. This

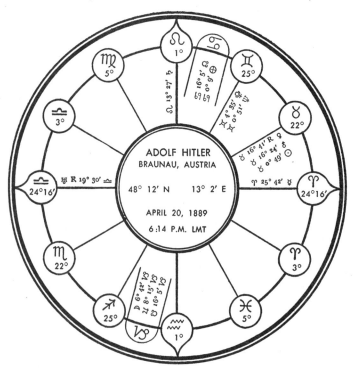

verdict would have been reversed immediately, however, on any consideration of the degree symbols for his planets in connection with his widely publicized characteristics.

The veteran astrologer begins his analysis of a horoscope by giving attention to feaures which are revealing on an initial inspection by the eye of experience. This is a matter of parallel to life itself. An individual encountered in the course of any particular relationship will always project certain phases of himself as against other possible ones, and this is a key to his character as it comes to immediate focus in the common milieu. In astrological techniques, therefore, the significance of any obvious correspondence between a native and his chart, and between it in turn and the total situation, is always a matter of primary and careful note. Uranus in Hitler's case lies to the east well apart from the other planets in the circle of the houses, and it is emphasized further because it is close upon the ascendant. As the significator of the independence of the individual in modern and mechanized society, it is of course, also and importantly, the mark of the neurotic and eccentric. Retrograde in its geocentric motion, and placed in the house of subjective sustainment, it shows the extent to which the native can be conditioned and perhaps utterly limited by his own aberrations. The Sabian symbol for Libra 20 is a Jewish rabbi, exceptionally suggestive in upside-down fashion because of the Nazis' primary appeal to racial and other discrimination. The negative interpretation of the psychological freedom here is an unhealthy sense of inherent self-superiority.

Any dramatic aptness in astrological indication is the factor of concordance or of signature strength which, by and large, is a suggestion of the native's potential importance to his own particular circumstances. Added to the testimony of Uranus is the elevated and stationary Saturn in Leo 14. The mid-heaven position of this planet of destiny has long been known as the Napoleonic aspect, interpreted generally by nineteenth-century astrologers as testimony of great rise followed by great fall. There are other similarities in the horoscopes of the two dictators, if reliance is to be placed on the one traditionally accepted for Napoleon, such as the Libra ascendant and Capricorn moon in both. Even without this parallel there seemed to be every possibility, in the early Thirties, that the ridiculous fanatic of the "beer hall putsch" in 1923, who actually became Chancellor as a result of the 1932 plotting of the Junkers and their associates, might make a very appreciable impact on history. The symbolism for Saturn's degree is the human soul awaiting opportunity for expression, and this is a splendid personal potentiality in any normal implication. On the negative side, however, it is naïve procrastination and a lack of all genuine interest or enthusiasm, and hence a clue to the self-defeating weakness.

If the Austrian megalomaniac had received even the slightest appreciation or known the least amount of genuine and normal human affection in his younger and impressionable years, he might have played a role closer to a true messiah. Taken on the constructive side, the zodiacal degree of his Uranus shows the extraordinary power of insight given to those who stand on the shoulders of giants who have gone before, thus establishing its keyword as heritage. The slanting of his life had long since become destructive when he reached his mid-forties, however, and the potentials revealed by the symbolism of Saturn's place were hopelessly warped. The chance for any species of messiahship had been dissipated beyond recapture, but his unusually tragic case reveals the high possibilities of an altered emphasis and ensuing rich rewards for those individuals who are not so thoroughly caught up in the sweep of their own inadequacy. Personality serves history always, in small areas if not on any large scale, and whatever is strong in its contribution to destructive developments can well be of very sturdy significance on the more enduring side of things.

In the view of a genuinely modern astrology there are no irrevocable blacks and whites. Whatever comes into being may always be continued if it seems worth while. Similarly, it may be changed if it proves unworthy or unprofitable. While some therapy may achieve its results almost instantly, and other involvements arrive at disentanglement only after years or even a sequence of lifetimes, nothing is either fixed completely or beyond all possibility. The stellar science deals with reality in process, and reaches its judgments by a balancing of relations in an actuality of context which is both psychological and physical. The chancellor of the Third Reich had a dramatic power of accomplishment, however erratically he made it manifest. It is shown in his chart by the splaylike gathering of the planets in little groups established and linked by close aspects—i.e., showing exceptional concentrations of potential—but since these stand in over-all disjunction from each other there was less than normal integration from birth, and as a deviate he was unusually free to create something new and outstanding or to contribute spectacularly to the disintegration of his fellows. His tragedy was that he didn't make a proper use of his potentialities, not that he was born with some sort of Satanic stamp upon him.

Character of real worth has its charting in the horoscope through those planetary relations which an older astrology always designated as adverse, primarily as these bodies are situated opposite or in square to each other. The sole opposition in Hitler's case is Mercury to Uranus. The indicator of mind thus stands as special handmaiden to his eccentricity, and ,it is in Aries 26, for which the symbol is a man possessed of more gifts than he can hold. The keyword is equipment. There is every promise of an inexhaustible self-discovery, such as might indeed have gone into the development of a messiah, but instead it operated negatively through an obsession by ideas of no practical worth. The marked horizontal axis created by these two planets in this chart is an indication of the native's excitable personality, or his psychological dependence on crisis after crisis, but this characteristic could have equipped him for assimilating the woes of the world into himself in a happier employment of each special potential. Meanwhile the squares of the midheaven Saturn provide the dynamic for the spiritual opportunity he handled so ineptly. Here principally is a functional link to the two planets, Mars and Venus, which always must be taken in connection with each other for any over-all delineation of life's everyday circumstances, and the closeness of their conjunction deprives the Nazi leader of all perspective in the practical immediacies of life. Both are found in Taurus 17, and the symbolization is the battle of the swords and torches seen in the case of Zoë Wells' Jupiter.

What in the refinement of Miss Wells' psychic talents was a continual sensitiveness to the great moral and ethical issues of existence can now be seen on its out-and-out evil rather than merely frustrated side. Here is a complete loss of self between the confused compulsions of necessity and desire, taking ugly form as the administration of a cosmic horror. The German dictator was the prey of such deep and strong forces at war within him that outwardly he became almost a literal pillar of fire by night and of cloud by day to lead his people out of their political and economic impasse. There was a touch of Moses in him, but by burlesque. Only the panzer divisions gave any approximation to the spiritual legerdemain or dramatic exaltations the world might have known again.

The sun, as basic continuum for the sadistic daydreamer who took the Nazis to power, is a clue to all this at core. The greater light, accentuated in its relationship to his political destiny through its wide square to Saturn, is found in Taurus 1. The symbol, a clear mountain stream, has all the beauty of the ideal figure the native might have been, but it also suggests his personal coldness or utter incapacity for even the simplest human ties. He could have given an undiluted purity of inspiration to his fellows, but he conformed to the negative implication in his tendency to waste the potentialities of his being by his eccentric self-ramifications. Instead of challenging others to their best efforts, he drew a scum of malcontents around him and capitalized on depravity.

The four remaining planets of Hitler's horoscope are found in two groups. None of them have the square or opposition relationships, so valuable in developing a genuinely human character, either among themselves or with any of the other six. This emphasizes the extent to which the German leader was essentially the deviate. However, what ends up here as an over-all pattern of weakness in social orientation, with the consequences an ultimate downfall, none the less could have been rare opportunity had his life been framed in the strength of a real vision. Potentially devoid of personal integrations of any normal sort, he could hardly have made a conventional place for himself in some more settled period of history. But the times were unusual in every respect, and their upset called to him. He felt himself cradled in their turmoil. Where his destiny failed him was in the fact that the evils around him became his nourishment rather than a challenge to his more worthy potentials. He might as easily have given articulation to the latent good. A great spiritual figure in human evolution is always a voice for humanity's aspirations of the moment. The Nazi prophet launched an ultimate destructiveness because he sought to give exposition to a private philosophy or a personal insight without the slightest real orientation in his fellow man. The true messiah is an instrument, a clear mountain stream in which all men are cleansed.

The moon is one of the planets standing aloof from most of the others, in Capricorn 7, and the symbol, a veiled prophet of power, suggests the inspired figure who can command the hearts and minds of men and call them to action by dramatizing their most remote dreams and aspirations. What on the positive side is an unerring insight into motives and a consequent gift for organizing effort—the measure of achievement by Zoë Wells through her Mercury in this degree—is negatively a complete inability to distinguish true values from false. The tremendous impact of the native's oratory and self-display on the German people, and his success in remaining the figure of hope for as long as he did in the expectations of as many as held their faith, show the power he achieved through this lunar focus of his life, but his allegiances were with the unspeakable rather than the elevating and as a result the whole Third Reich fell to pieces the moment it needed a genuine strength within itself.

Close to the lunar position in an astrological pairing is Jupiter, in Capricorn 9, and this planet is to be taken as especially significant because like Saturn it is stationary. However, it is about to go retrograde rather than direct, and it is intercepted with the lesser light, these factors indicating a character-pattern of restraint rather than of any sincerity of self-projection into passing affairs. The owl gained a reputation for wisdom by motionless silence, and often a hesitant man will impress others because his uncertainty is mistaken for an intelligent weighing of considerations. Once the momentum of events began to serve the Nazis, the leader's vagaries became a part of the vain display and were admired. His planet of enthusiasm and spontaneity is symbolized by an angel carrying a harp, and thus what could have been a bringing of the music of the spheres to man in an additional aspect of messianic wonder became evident instead as idle fantasy and a wholly naïve self-superiority.

Hitler's Neptune, indicating his over-all obligation to

a modern or industrialized society, is found in Gemini 1. Miss Wheeler has the same planet here, and it is the degree of Miss Wells' moon. The symbol is the glass-bottomed boat, and the detachment from everyday reality which was a professional asset for both the medium and the artist was for the Nazi leader an exaggeration, ultimately, of his status as the social pariah. Any possibility of an outreach on his part toward a genuine messianic potential must have been knocked out of the neurotic youngster long before he achieved any measure of discrimination, but a high spiritual interest was no more impossible to him than to the two women. However, decisions grounded in any strength of inner character had long been beyond him by the time he reached adulthood. He had come to exhibit the callousness of a boat-riding which observes without concern or responsibility, and to achieve a lordly disdain for all possible participation in any bottom richness of living.

Pluto provides a final note of testimony to the consistently negative direction of all potentials in the Hitler horoscope. Its position in Gemini 5 duplicates the potentiality it brought to Elsie Wheeler. The symbolization through the radical publication, which with her was the positive capacity for putting her own direct stamp upon everything she touched, was in his case the negatory determination to stand apart from all true communion with others. His philosophy of life was to hate his fellows, and to play Procrustes to the limit. He seems to have liked the bed he made for himself, and it is probable that he even enjoyed his tragedy as he brought it to its grand if petulant climax.

CHAPTER SEVEN

HISTORY AND ITS MEANINGS

A special department of astrology has been developed for the interpretation of events on the world stage, or the charting of trends in global affairs. The simplest procedure of the mundane astrologers is to consider the horoscope of a country's ruler or chief administrative officer as a figure for its destiny as well as for his own. Thus the fortunes of Adolf Hitler through the thirties and into the forties were taken as those of the German people as a whole, and also in very considerable part of the hapless populations overrun by the Nazi armies. A much more rewarding method of analysis, however, is based on a study of the great cycles and configurations of the major planets. Attention is given to the zodiacal places of these bodies—taken directly from the ephemeris—and the positions are significant when they are found to correspond by the astrological symbolism to some important historical development with which the given planet has a special relationship, or when there is a culmination of some phase of its movement in the zodiac through (1) its change in direction, (2) its ingress into a sign or (3) its arrival at an exact aspect of importance to one or more of its fellows.

Pluto is that one of the astrologer's indicators which has the most direct correspondence with the wholly unique socio-economic structure of modern life. It entered man's world of actuality with its discovery on January 18, 1930,

and on that day was retrograde in Cancer 19. The symbol
for the degree is a priest performing a marriage ceremony,
and this can be seen to describe the spiritual stewardship
of man, especially in the terms of his conscious responsibility for the integrity of human society and for those
everyday institutions through which the racial ideals have
a continued embodiment. The globe-wide depression of
1929 has resulted in the complete disappearance of individual equities in property as any sort of inalienable
right, since confiscatory taxes and various regulations by
governmental agencies do not hesitate to cancel them out
whenever the group welfare suggests such a step. Indeed,
any privacy of self-expression, as well as of tangible possessions, is becoming more and more an immediate dis-
pensation of the community at large. Mankind, like the
bride, is leaving the home of his forebears forever, and
like the groom, is taking on responsibilities quite new
and strange to his experience. The world is bringing its
children into a cosmic matrimony these days, and demanding that each make living a sacrament for the common good.

The first great step in world economic adjustment along
these lines was the abandonment of the long-established
policy of national currencies stabilized by reserves of pre-
cious metal. England went off the gold standard on September 21, 1931, when Pluto was slowing to stationary
and getting ready to go retrograde in Cancer 22. The
dramatic action of Franklin D. Roosevelt in declaring a
bank holiday on March 6, 1933—as a prelude to the new
sort of stabilization for the American monetary system,
calling in all gold to become a purely governmental or

static asset—occurred when Pluto was back in exactly the same degree, slowing to stationary and preparing to go direct. The symbol is a woman awaiting a sailboat, that is, watching for her ship to come in by the old figure of speech, and she is quite unperturbed that she must suit her convenience to the vagaries of the wind. This well dramatizes the reaction of the average individual unquickened to the real potentialities of the new order of things. In too many instances he has accepted the notion that it is a function of government to look after him, and that in consequence it is not a result of his own inadequacies if anything untoward happens to him. The point is not that there is anything wrong with the conception of social security, which indeed is one of the major advances of modern times, but that a senselesss dependence on the accidents of fortune is the negative aspect of this degree.

The United States stands upon its championship of an international free enterprise, with only very general controls, and the major challenge to this ideal came with the surprise attack by Japan, directed principally at Pearl Harbor, on December 7, 1941. Pluto was then in Leo 6, and had been stationary going retrograde just a month before at the same point. The symbol is an old-fashioned woman and an up-to-date girl, already encountered in these pages in connection with the Mars of Miss Elsie Wheeler. Here two utterly incompatible world views are seen coming into armed clash with each other. There is the way of tradition in which the individual is asked to be grateful for a regimented well-being, and an alternative road of self-advancement in which the resourceful spirit of an open frontier has its culmination. World War II and the events that continue its conflicts are a result of the unresolved rivalry, and each way of life already has undergone revolutionary alterations which Pluto has measured very dramatically. This does not imply that Western democracy is becoming a planned society, but it does foreshadow a social structure in which both dictatorial and individualistic emphases must continue their broadening readjustment to each other. Nations cannot live for themselves alone, any more than people can.

Franklin D. Roosevelt, architect of the new American order as it took various forms at center in Washington, came to the end of his career on April 12, 1945, and his successor had been chosen almost inevitably for this role when he was nominated for the vice-presidency on July 21st of the year before. Pluto went direct in Leo 7 in mid-April, 1944, was in Leo 9 at the time of the Democratic convention, and was stationary turning direct in Leo 8 almost at the moment when Harry S. Truman became president of the country. The significant symbol is not for Leo 9, when the relative inevitability of the thirty-third chief executive was determined in the summer of 1944, but rather at the time of Pluto's preceding station in April and its stronger indication then for the general period in this area of over-all cosmic patterns and their out-working. Leo 7 is symbolized by the constellations in the sky. This supplements the suggestiveness of a cosmic matrimony, and shows the shaping of all individual destiny to the requirements of a universal wholeness as such may have its particular application to the United States.

The stationary position of Pluto going direct in 1945,

and giving the probable slanting of the Truman administration, was in Leo 8. The symbolization is a Bolshevik propagandist, that is, a demagogue or a dictator in the making but yet also an individual who dramatizes the indomitable expectation of the human spirit. Here is the over-all orientation of Franklin D. Roosevelt's political heir as he struggles along in the midst of the globe-wide economic and political revolution, and epitomizes the dominant spirit of the land. On the positive side there is an unconquerable determination to bring great ideals to pass and perhaps make a permanent impress on history. The motivation is not unlike Hitler's, but with a fortunate and complete reversal of attitude toward human individuals and their rights. Negatively the degree is futile ranting against the various superficial ills of the day, and the extent to which this is manifest in so much American writing and public statement at the moment is an index of the country's weakness in the face of its exceptional opportunity. It is rather significant that on December 2, 1942, when man first initiated the controlled release of atomic energy at Chicago, this newest of the planets was situated in Leo 8, and also had been stationary at this point on November 8th, less than four weeks before. The atomic bomb thus has come into existence with an implication not too happy for the spiritual destiny of the United States, if ever the American vision allows itself to get out of hand.

The stations of the great planets, as their places are designated when they stop to turn retrograde or to go direct again in their geocentric motion, are the zodiacal points giving an over-all orientation for events and meanings in the areas of life for which each heavenly body provides a special delineation. Beginning with Jupiter, and moving outwardly from the earth's orbit, each of them has two stationary positions each year. Neptune is particularly important because it charts the highly socialized and industrial developments of the modern world. This fact can even be used rather strikingly to identify the anticipations of this development for many centuries before the planet was discovered in late September, 1846. It was then in Aquarius 26, retrograde and slowing down for its station during early November in the same degree. The symbol is a hydrometer, or an instrument for measuring the specific gravity of a liquid, and this is pre-eminent dramatization of utilitarianism or mechanical efficiency. Across the face of history came the great political revolution in which the control of events passed from an aristocracy of lineage, or of an inherited privilege, to the dynasty of the entrepreneur and to the forms of governmental administration where big business and organized manufacture began to pull the strings behind the scene.

With the end of all ruling classes in the old sense, it became relatively easy for anyone with initiative and staying qualities to indulge his lust for power. Society no longer rested primarily on a family basis, with its roots in the land and a settled group tradition. Workers increasingly became itinerant with the development of the giant factories and the change of nearly all home functions into community-wide activities. This social reshuffling of mankind, to be complicated further by the new economic structure due to take form at the time of Pluto's discovery, was inaugurated rather formally by the revolutionary events of 1848, when Neptune re-entered Pisces. Its first station in that year, epochal in so many directions, was in Pisces 3, and the symbol of a petrified forest emphasizes the crystallization of human mores for all the thousands of years before the complete transformation about to be effected now in the short span of a century and a half. Thus the symbolism is suggestive, initially, through an inversion of meaning such as has been encountered in the case of the Jewish rabbi for Hitler's Uranus.

The meaning of the new planet is actually revealed very strikingly by this symbolism, no less than in the hydrometer, since the Neptunian epoch is really to be dated from 1848 on the grounds of the actual historical demarcations. Characteristic of the trees preserved forever in rock is the stability of life itself whenever it is manifest in imaginative creativity rather than in any literal changelessness. Reality is not perceived directly by the senses, but reveals itself through the intangible steadiness of a continued experience. Anything is as real as the utilization of the fact of itself will permit outwardly and objectively, and as its being so can be accepted in a personal realization inwardly and subjectively. Neptune is that one of the astrologer's ten zodiacal pointers which pre-eminently is the indicator of make-believe, and often it shows delusion, self-deception and all the chicanery that comes with a false perspective and a warping self-indulgence. There is eternal potentiality as long as the illusion holds, so that it can be a magic of faith on the constructive side. Whatever any individual persists in seeing, or recognizing, is precisely what continues to dominate his life.

Hence Neptune measures the individual's obligation to

the world he has made his own, and also and equally his capacity to make this precisely as he would like to have it. The new society is man-made for better or worse. Thus the ninth planet in many respects has become the most important of the ten. Its value is particularly evident in connection with the larger or defining cycles of current history. This is illustrated by the second of its stations in 1848, in Aquarius 30, for which the symbol is a moonlit field of prehistoric Babylon with its night blooms. Here is complementation for the petrified trees in a depth of intuitive or psychic potential, and in addition there is a stress of another of Neptune's most characteristic indications. Perhaps fundamentally the social hydrometer—in the way Pluto by comparison is the cosmic advisor or eternal priest—it balances the petrifying process, which it at once attacks and supports, with an inner rehearsal of life and its meanings. It is through this constant psychological inventory that each person ultimately finds himself. It is the creative sensitiveness by which modern genius endlessly expands the boundaries of its being. Unfortunately it also can be human make-believe out of all worth-while orientation.

Neptune's ingresses give an over-all perspective of primary importance in mundane astrology. Its first of these, after its discovery, was into Pisces for a brief two months in 1847, at about the time Marx and Friedrich Engels were preparing the *Communist Manifesto*. It re-entered that sign in February, 1848, the month when revolution broke out in France. The symbol of Pisces 1 is the public market, in which a free and spontaneous intercourse among men enables them to buy and sell the fruits of their mutual skills. This represents the domination of life by the expanded divisions of labor in all modern social structure, or the communal organization of functions which in time promises to break down and eliminate the tribal or feudal state forever. The emphasis on the producer of life's necessities, and the presumed practicality of his direct relation with the consumer without any middleman exploitation or profit, has long been the core of Communist propaganda.

Next of the signs to be entered by Neptune was Aries, on April 14, 1861, exactly coincident with the surrender of Fort Sumter in Charleston harbor. General Beauregard had begun the bombardment two days before, thus launching the American Civil War. This fundamentally was an armed struggle to the death between the older plantation or feudal order, and the newer factory or town-meeting society, and thus a further step in the Neptunian transformation of the globe. The symbolization for Aries 1 is a woman rising from the waters and a seal following to embrace her. The receptive and assertive principles of human individuality must emerge in a common and conscious responsibility for each person's welfare, and so also for the well-being of the national or cultural group. There must be a sense of illimitable source in the roots from which anything in question may have sprung, and also a willing and immediate co-operation among all possible facets of self-expression. Mechanical productivity took the reins from husbandry more firmly than ever. The agricultural culture had reached every apparent possibility of expansion or imaginative self-projection, and the machine promised endless multiplication for the potentialities of everyday living. Life was rising from the ocean once more, in an entirely new dimension.

The third ingress of Neptune in the great new sweep of history was into Taurus on June 7, 1874, with a re-entry to stay on April 7, 1875. A varied spread of events might be taken as key indications of the ferment at work. The failure of Jay Cooke and Company, in Philadelphia on September 18, 1873, precipitated one of America's greatest panics and practically compelled government regulation of big business. The Granger decisions, delivered by the Supreme Court in 1876, gave permanent establishment for the principle that financial transactions clothed with pub lic interest may be controlled under society's normal police powers. There was a real start toward social reorganiza tion along free trading or functional lines rather than on any continuing pattern of protection for established prop erty and entrenched privilege. The symbol for Taurus is the clear mountain stream analyzed in connection with Hitler's sun. What in his case became a solipsistic and ill founded self-sufficiency proved for the United States in general a triumph of man's pure outflow of self-discovering and self-developing resources.

Neptune's entrance into Gemini was on August 15, 1887, for a brief stay, again on May 26, 1888, and then finally on March 21, 1889. The Haymarket Square riot in Chicago, on May 4, 1886, brought about the necessity for a more effective organization of skilled labor and led to the establishment of the American Federation of Labor in December of that year (out of the earlier group formed by Samuel Gompers in 1881), and on February 4, 1887 the Interstate Commerce Act was passed (following the long struggle beginning with the passage of the McCrary Bill in the House of Representatives in 1874). Actually the trend of things-to-be is marked with little variation on the outer face of history. The symbolization for Gemini 1 is the glass-botttomed boat found significant in the Neptunian conditioning of Adolf Hitler and Elsie Wheeler, as well as in the emotional set of Zoë Wells, and the important developments were more intellectual than otherwise. Rather than a mental detachment from the world of facts, there was a complete assimilation into the new activities through mind and its powers of functional make-believe. It was from this point forward that America was destined to produce a body of seminal thinking unmatched since the early Greeks. William Torrey Harris became United States Commissioner of Education in 1889 and achieved a prestige for the philosophical ideals for which he had been a channel through his *Journal of Speculative Philosophy* ever since 1867. William James completed his epochal *Principles of Psychology* in 1890. George Sylvester Morris died in 1889 with his insights not quite at culmination, and in that year bequeathed his mantle to John Dewey.

Neptune's fifth ingress, into Cancer, was on July 19, 1901, and on May 21, 1902. The assassination of President William McKinley, who died on September 14, 1901, led to the administration of Theodore Roosevelt and the inauguration of a program for restraint of the corporations paralleled by the nation's first full-scale attempt at a conservation of its natural resources. The symbol for Cancer 1 is a ship with two flags, one flying for all to see and the other furled and hidden, thus dramatizing the need for some effective approach to those problems of multiple citizenships and clashing allegiances which have become the increasing plague of modern society. People in general began to sense the need for open covenants arrived at openly, and there was a great preliminary stirring toward a political righteousness. The rise of muck-raking exposés was unpleasant but salutary.

The entrance of Neptune into Leo on September 23, 1914, for the first time, and its approach to within a bare seven minutes of arc from entering Libra on January 1, 1942, give interestingly close measure to the outbreak of World War I on August 4, 1914, and to the drawing of the United States into World War II with the Japanese attack at Pearl Harbor on December 7, 1941. These conflicts have arisen in the course of the strains and adjustments in the socio-economic structure of global relations, very suggestively symbolized, for Leo 1, by the case of apoplexy which is apt representation of the pressures breaking out of bounds in 1914, and for Libra 1 by the butterfly which lives its career so swiftly and with such a vain beauty and hence so bitterly caricatures the Utopian propaganda and promises of the Mussolinis, Hitlers and the other megalomaniac world planners. The planet meanwhile had entered Virgo on September 21, 1928, and re-entered on July 24, 1929, and the degree is represented by a man's head as a cosmic testimony to individual character. The great depression of 1929 was the historical event which brought significance to personality on its own terms, and it was this major transition in history which astrology now is able to measure so strikingly through Pluto.

When Uranus was discovered, March 13, 1781, it was

responsible for the first real break from the past on the part of astrologers in general, since the stellar science could no longer remain a tight little system based on the seven planets (that is, five and the two lights). The traditional lore, which had come down in basic detail from antiquity, began to lose much of the authority of its long past. Meanwhile the thralldom to empty claims out of the night of time had long since disappeared in other intellectual fields, thanks to the contributions of Copernicus, Galileo, Kepler, Newton and an almost interminable list of modern pioneers in astronomy, physics, chemistry, medicine and every other sphere of scientific investigation. The eighth planet came to typify this spirit of inquiry, and for a while it was used to indicate the revivified astrology.

The real clue to astrology's modern ordering of life under Uranus is in the great transitions of the social order as these at bottom have been political and a matter of spiritual stirrings. The ferment had been coming to be more and more evident in the New World, where it had been given every opportunity to experiment with itself through the illimitable resources of an open frontier. Man before had always been forced to live under an economy of scarcity, with little actual chance to think of eternal values. His daily wage for untold centuries had been almost constant in terms of its purchasing power. There was no previous time in history when he had had even the dream of an everyday plenty, all for the mere enterprise of making it his own. But the old situation began to seem outrageous with the sudden broadening of knowledge. Men were quickened with the discovery of endless new worlds, and began to strike out blindly in their own

behalf in economics, religion and every other area of experience. For two centuries the great unrest was without
much over-all patterning, and then all at once everything
became genuinely articulate with the Declaration of Independence by the American colonies in 1776. The position of Uranus on that particular July 4th, in Gemini 9
gives real insight into the meaning of the planet. The
symbol is a quiver filled with arrows, and this is prophecy
of the new age and of a complete unleashing of personality
and its powers.

The more rapid movement of Uranus, in comparison
with Neptune and Pluto, means that the symbolical significance of its stations in the heavens, and of its ingresses into
the signs, has a lesser general importance. The planet is
valuable rather in charting the more common cycles of
group impetus, or the shift in social individuality as this
is manifest in rhythms of war, political dynasty, moral
fashions and other phases of widely shared experience.
Thus during the final events leading to the declaration
of war on England in 1812, on June 18th, Uranus was
retrograde in Scorpio 20, and the symbol is a woman
drawing two dark curtains aside. This suggests the groping stage of humanity's outreach before the development
of the key insights which later could lead to the atomic
age. The preceding station in Scorpio 24, with its symbolization in the crowds coming down the mountain to
listen to one man, tended to accentuate the heroic figure
of William Henry Harrison and to strengthen the demands of the War Hawks on President James Madison.
There was a sense of some great message from Sinaitic
heights, but there was also too much ill-determined enthu-

siasm or even actual gullibility, and too little tangible effort directed toward a definite and really worthy goal.

Warfare with Mexico had its identifiable beginning with the battle of Palo Alto on May 8, 1846. The Uranian degree was Aries 13. This is symbolized by an unsuccessful bomb explosion, which can be interpreted as leading to results much happier than might have been expected. Texas had already been annexed and New Mexico was coveted. California, Arizona, Nevada, Utah and more, a wonderful empire-to-be, came along in train through the aggrandizement. Somehow all seemed to be forgiven, although there was little basis for overlooking the wrong. With the Civil War the emphasis through Uranus, which on April 12, 1861, was in Gemini 10, is dramatized by a falling airplane. Actually the saving of the Union was far more than an adjustment of difficulties, but was instead an unanticipated re-creation of the original vision. This is suggested by the previous station of the planet, on February 17, 1861, at Gemini 9 or its position at the time the Declaration of Independence was signed.

The Spanish-American war had its practical inception with the still unsolved blowing up of the battleship *Maine* in Havana harbor on February 15, 1898. The new planet was in Sagittarius 4, slowing as it prepared to go retrograde. The symbolism is a little child learning to walk, and it was now a nation that was beginning its role as a world power but very timidly on the whole. April 6, 1917, brought the declaration of war on Germany by the United States in World War I. Uranus was in Aquarius 23. The symbol is a big bear seated and waving all four paws. In the lives of far too many Americans the adventure was a lark, with slogans and songs and no disposition to take any responsibility of international scope. There was no national adultship as yet. Pearl Harbor gave Uranian emphasis to Taurus 28, the degree of Zoë Wells' Pluto. The country at last had reached a certain maturity, and was called on to learn that the fullness of life is ageless and that there are always beginnings in whatever may be worth while. However, the rewards are as yet ahead, not on hand as something over which to quarrel.

Indeed, history has hardly begun to write itself for the republic with its roots in the open frontier and in its vision of an ever-generous democracy among men. The astrological indicators have charted the early developments, and can set the future potentials to a convenient scale for those alert enough to respond to the key events. This technique can be applied in any land and for any people, and of course can be supplemented by all the other methods of mundane astrology. In any case the view should ever be forward, and as at least a footnote on American destiny it might be well to note the Uranus station immediately preceding the death of Franklin D. Roosevelt in 1945. It was then again, as when the Civil War broke out—this time within eighteen minutes of arc in exactness—at the place in Gemini it occupied when the Declaration of Independence was signed. In many respects, therefore, the nation's third birth (in these terms of Uranus) may be indicated through present events and the perspective they have provided for the preparation of these pages.

CHAPTER EIGHT

DAY-BY-DAY GUIDANCE

THE astrologer is tempted at times to quote from Seneca. "As long as you live, keep learning how to live. . . Let us balance life's account each day . . . count each day as a separate life." It is the spirit of a true zest in self, a reaching out for the real in living with something like the enthusiasm of the Dauphin in *King John*. "The day shall not be up as soon as I, to try the fair adventure of tomorrow." Awakening is ever a rebirth, a regrasping of destiny's threads, and astrology offers a daily guidance which makes the flavor and color of each twenty-four hours as explicit in advance as the departure of trains to be learned from a railway timetable, or the schedule of radio and television broadcasts to be taken from the newspaper. It is a phase of the stellar art which can be misused to the point of absurdity or purest superstition, as when someone consults the aspectarian in his ephemeris before deciding whether to stop for a cup of coffee or to buy a necktie. However, the trouble here is not that he is anxious to be sure the aspects are right but that he is willing to tailor his judgment to the limited intelligence represented by a machine, i.e., the mathematical tabulation of purely material tensions and relationships. To build a house it is necessary to measure the lot, obviously, and to prepare plans, but the structure is not the blueprint nor the slave of limitations put down by the architect.

Conscious existence is essentially fluid, though only poets and sensitives seem to understand this to any appreciable extent. Guidance toward life's fulfillment must begin as anything organic always does, through an emergence of meaning out of a vast complex of convenient and converging realities. To posit a single line of cause in any or all of this—for the intellectual satisfaction of viewing the point of crisis or the focus of observation as a consequent effect—is to set up an infinite regression and so to get nowhere at all ultimately. Such reasoning degenerates into more and more of less and less. Actually each day is a separate life in a quite literal sense, and living quite truly is learning how to live. Hence one of the most effective of all possible approaches to any human problem is through framing it, first of all, in the common potentials of whichever twenty-four hours are about to entertain it in a time and space world. There is a highly reliable clue, through this procedure, to the pertinence or implication of every factor involved in the whole issue of the moment, whether it be other people, the arrangement of immediate events, disturbance through the lack or the presence of inanimate objects, the favorable or unfavorable state of the weather and other aspects of nature, or anything else identifiable in experience.

The astrological day begins with sunrise, and its most general or over-all character is shown by the degree in which the sun arrives above the horizon at any particular place on the earth's surface. The calculations seldom need to be carried to a fine point of minutes and seconds of arc, since normally it will be obvious to the eye whether the planet is changing degrees. On the day these lines were written, February 8, 1951, in New York City, the sun rose at 7:04 a.m. by local mean time, which was 7:00 by the clock. At the eastern-standard midnight beginning the whole twenty-four-hour period, the sun's position was Aquarius 18° 37′ 22″, and its hourly motion was 2′ 32″. Adding 17′ 44″ to the zero-hour position gives 18° 55′ 6″, hence the zodiacal point identifying this solar day is Aquarius 19°.

The symbol is a forest fire quenched. Presumably it was brought under control by co-ordinated effort on the part of the many agencies rallied for a common interest, and this situation by free association should suggest something relative to the general tendency of events through the hours ending with the following sunrise. The author, as a fairly convenient example, was in the course of working out the first draft of his ten chapters, but he had been engaged at the task for many preceding days and so no fresh beginning was involved. Outside the weather was cold, a record for the winter and with a bitterly sharp wind, but it was clear and all vistas from the Riverside Drive corner were brilliant in their outline. This was true for everyone in the vicinity, as was the indication of that one of the degrees in which the sun rose. What then was made explicit in the special case? Obviously there could be no local forest fire, and there was no word of any conflagration of any appreciable magnitude in the city.

Zodiacal symbolization is literal only in the exceptional instance. The author's lady on her arrival home, between the composition of the preceding paragraph and this, was happy to report that her beauty salon, which had understood it would have to go out of business because the fire department had condemned the building, had just learned that it might continue in its present location indefinitely. However, this quite oblique contribution to a literal implicitness in the symbol would concern very few from among the many millions living in the metropolitan area. Here certainly is not the quality of interpretation desired, although the occasional exact parallel between the symbols and events is always exciting. Rather what must be seen is that woods or forest lands in the general tenor of symbolism are always representative of life itself, suggesting a compacting of living creatures into a reality where they associate in varying fashion with their fellows in order to share the water and minerals from the earth, the oxygen and carbon-dioxide from the air and so on through the ramifying details of organic existence. Each individual is identified in the fire which is himself, and when this sweeps out to play the tyrant, history can become a Hitleresque horror. And when the megalomaniac conflagration is stopped, by better and more effective realizations, peace comes again to the face of the earth. February 8th seemed to demand that the author make this sort of proposition especially clear.

The day, as defined by the sun from one morning to the next, is a passing frame for self-realization and practical self-assertion. There is, supplementing the more objective climate of the moment as such, a division of the twenty-four hours from one moonrise to another. The time of Luna's appearance is given in the general almanacs which are available everywhere, and the computation is as before except that any simple approximation is apt to be unreliable. On February 8th, on Manhattan Island, the lesser light rose in Pisces 18, shortly after the sun. The symbol is a gigantic tent which suggests the circus and the universal actuality there entertained with animals and performers from all over the world. When the human heart is taken to any sort of carnival, it instinctively allows itself to become wonderfully at one with all its kind. The daily lunar period provides a rhythm for the emotional side of self, and the momentary framework for every fresh adventure in self-discovery. Since this eighth chapter was begun almost precisely at the moon's rising, the reader is asked through its exposition to realize that each special episode of his conscious on-going can be a fascinating spectacle of self-consummation. The make-believe and magic which mark the source of all real joyousness in living are ever given a very real encouragement beneath the big top of the universe itself.

A more precise or genuinely personal species of daily guidance requires a consideration of the transits, or the momentary positions of the heavenly bodies, in their relation to the natal horoscope. The major planets, through their stations and ingresses, their current configurations and the other celestial emphases which measure the turns and critical points in history for all people collectively, come to a high focus in over-all significance for a particular person when any one of them lies in the zodiacal place of itself or its fellows in the birth chart, or is situated directly opposite in the zodiac, in either case within 60 to 90 minutes of arc in exactness. Indications of this sort tend to be sharper in the case of individuals with a measure of real cosmic stature. Hence the *de facto* ruler or recognized central executive of a country is often the best of possible examples, since the concerns of a total people are epitomized in his person. This was pointed out in Chapter Seven, and a consideration of Harry S. Truman in this connection is not primarily an analysis of the man but is rather a survey of current events as given perspective through his official actions.

At the time of writing it is apparent that the most vital events of President Truman's term of office have their roots in the outbreak of the Korean war on June 25, 1950. The moon was approaching its own natal position and Pluto

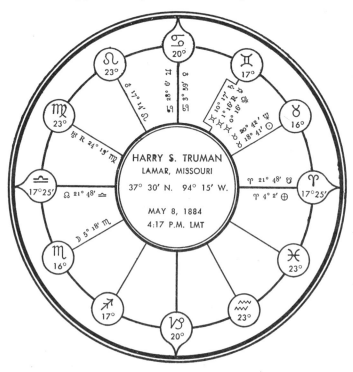

HARRY S. TRUMAN
LAMAR, MISSOURI
37° 30′ N.   94° 15′ W.

MAY 8, 1884
4:17 P.M. LMT

was situated in the degree of its station at the time of the
1948 election, but what was immediately significant was
the position of the sun on the president's Venus, within
77 minutes of arc in exactness at the moment of the first
hostilities. Cancer 4 is symbolized by the cat engaged in
argument with the mouse, encountered in a preceding
chapter in connection with Zoë Wells' Mars, and here it
offers an obvious indication that the Communist strategy
was very largely a matter of feeling out the temper of the
Western democracies. In terms of horoscopic advisement,
this would suggest that it was necessary to act decisively, in
one place if not in another, if a more or less complete surrender to the enemy's aims were not desired. As it happened, such a conclusion gained a rather rapid and general
acceptance. Of all the planets in the Truman horoscope,
the one thus given a primary emphasis is fundamentally
the significator of completions and the resolution of energy and activity to value. There was nothing to imply
that the intervention in Korea with military force could
have any necessary consequences in global war, or that
the prestige of the country would suffer or that its real
welfare would be impeded. The greater light was the body
acting out of the over-all reality, and its point of impact
was in high elevation and so had effective dignity in the
birth figure.

This is the simplest form of daily guidance through
the reference of the transits to a natal chart, and it depends on events important enough to establish a time
and give a degree emphasis to the day-by-day positions.
The zodiacal points thus brought to momentary promi-
nence are the basis of interpretation as they also have a

fixed or constant stress in the personal horoscope. Much more vital, however, as a basis for astrological advice along these lines, are the stations of the great planets, since they identify general rhythms of significance in which all people participate. Their over-all charting of history itself has had special consideration in a prior chapter, and it is when they fall on natal positions or opposition points that the native has his greatest opportunities and may proceed to carry out his dreams with the fullest assurance. Of the two different modes of impact, the conjunction measures the more practical developments and is usually taken as the more favorable in its indications. It calls for a direct and immediate concern over the interests of self, and for activities of an open-and-above-board nature in order to obtain a maximum of possible co-operation from others. The opposition operates more subjectively, and for the major part indicates an increased sensitiveness and a subtle awareness or a capacity for feeling things through and thus achieving any results by more roundabout or less overt measures. There is no real choice between these two types of intensification in experience. The one tends to be up and at things, but thereupon to burn itself out and so lose its enthusiasm, whereas the other moves into action more slowly and thereby holds its realization and refines its understanding over longer periods of time.

If the career of Harry S. Truman be taken in its long-range perspective, its real start or its essentially political orientation came with his election as county judge in 1922. Neptune went retrograde on November 21st in that year, and did so within 58 minutes of arc in exactness of conjunction with his radical Mars. The latter, in Leo 18, has for its symbol a teacher of chemistry, and in his basic initiative the president represents the forward-going genius of the country on the technical side, together with the widespread determination to penetrate to the deepest mysteries of an everyday reality. The Neptunian symbolization, in Leo 19, is a houseboat party, and thus an indication of a creative relaxation and a desire for a rather private congeniality. In these early years of his struggle, anxious to pay off twenty thousand dollars of debt as a result of his business failure in 1921, the way ahead had potentiality for him as he gave first attention to his friends, built up his fences in terms of personal contacts and connections, and in every way kept an eager eye on the political future offered him under the auspices of the Pendergast machine. Advisement at the period, with the nature of the planets taken into full account, would have suggested a playing of the game very much as this native actually played it, and an encouragement to conduct himself in the manner expected of office-seekers then and now. There was no transcendental vision, no messianic potential and no ready-made dedication to the solution of social problems with any sort of statesmanly aplomb.

Neptune was destined to be of continued help to the ambitious politician and in 1941, now a United States senator, he proposed the committee for investigating the national defense program and became its chairman. The planet on June 7th went direct on his radical Uranus within 42 minutes of arc in exactness. The symbol for Virgo 25, applying to both the natal position and the station, is a flag at half-mast, suggesting the inevitable accounting which life requires from every part of itself. The man from

Missouri was now called to genuine public service. Circumstances demanded that he win a high respect from the entire country. In the light of this it is interesting to return for a moment to the more simple technique illustrated in connection with the outbreak of war in Korea. When Franklin D. Roosevelt died on April 12, 1945, the transiting Uranus rested on the Saturn of the Vice-President within a bare six minutes of arc in deviation from exactness, and the symbolization for Gemini 11 is a new path of realism in experience. Here an independence or higher actuality of self-expression is required of the native, in terms of his wisdom or inner sensitiveness, and the transition from the earlier way of going could have been explained to him in very great detail by an astrologer.

Meanwhile the sun by transit was in conjunction with his dragon's tail with only the same six minutes of arc away from exactness, and the symbolism of Aries 22 is the gate to the garden of desire. These Arabian points have a high suggestiveness in astrology, although they are used rather infrequently, and this south or descending node of the moon identifies a focus of self-undoing which also, and more happily, can be a spiritual opportunity. Here are the details in a life attitude where horoscopic advice has its greatest value. Fortunately Mr. Truman did not go the way of Hitler, or fall short of all the more constructive potentials in his nativity. There are sharp dangers here which have revealed themselves through his years in the White House, but on the whole he has held to the higher vision opening before him. The climax of personal opportunity thus far has been the 1948 election, which he won against the expectations of practically all the political prophets, and it was on November 17th of that year that Pluto went retrograde on his Mars. This time Leo 17 is emphasized, and the symbolization of a nonvested church choir shows the growth in stature of the man Tom Pendergast put in a county judgeship under so very similar a planetary emphasis. With the next campaign looming up, the Neptune station (January 24, 1952) was on his dragon's head within the six minutes of arc which has been significant before. This one of the nodes indicates high protection, and the symbol is a child giving birds a drink at a fountain. In the President's case this evidently was a call to less exacting responsibilities, since he decided not to be a candidate for re-election.

The configurations of the great planets, to no less appreciable extent than their stations, are of major importance in both mundane astrology and the daily guidance which arises out of the global perspectives. The planet which moves to a conjunction, opposition or any other primary aspect in the heavens is significant at the moment and in the place where this relationship becomes exact, and the basic implication is precisely the same as when it arrives at one of its stationary points. However, there are more general ramifications, as should be obvious enough. The recurring conjunctions and oppositions between various of the heavenly bodies are especially valuable to the astrologer, and in this category the lunations and particularly the solar eclipses are most important. Thus the eclipse of August 10th, when Mr. Truman first ran for U.S. Senator in 1934, was within eleven minutes of arc in exactness of conjunction with his Mars, emphasizing Leo 18 and the ideals implicit in the chemistry teacher. This links the two elections of 1922 and 1934 as the most vital ones in his public career, and dramatizes further the real possibilities of astrological advice. Additionally illuminating are the indications in 1944, when he was Roosevelt's running mate in the presidential campaign, and when the July eclipse was within 44 minutes of arc in exactness of conjunction with his elevated Jupiter in Cancer 29. The basic symbol here is a muse weighing twins, suggesting that this native can go plummeting to relative oblivion or climb to enduring heights, and the configuration itself is symbolized by a modern Pocahontas, who represents his opportunity for linking the primitive and the more modern sides of America's whole destiny.

The eclipse in 1948 on Truman's radical sun, within 19 minutes of arc from exact, is perhaps the most dramatic indication in connection with this horoscope. The nineteenth-century astrologers regarded all eclipses as unfortunate, especially when one fell on the place of the greater light at birth. Actually the emphasis of some significant point in the zodiac by the transits is an over-all intensification. While a general stirring-up would necessarily be rather bad for the thoroughly crystallized individual, in modern times the stimulation seems consistently helpful. The symbol of Taurus 19 is a newly forming continent. This native was chief administrative officer of a land in which atomic power and many of the intellectual and practical outworkings of the new age seem to have a principal centering. Epitomizing the nation and the epoch, his election under this configuration pointed forward to great promise indeed. It is too soon to decide the degree to which his own contribution will be remembered in history, but for his term of office he was light-bearer of importance in new and untrodden ways.

CHAPTER NINE

HORARY ASTROLOGY

"DARE to be wise: begin!" This is the advice of Horace. "He who postpones the hour of living rightly is like the rustic who waits for the river to run out before he crosses." As for the great stream of reality, it flows on, never the same, and yet ever dependable in continuing to sustain the differences which comprise its existence. Here is life, and words can hardly catch the wonder of its endless manifestation. Of itself, it remains a commonplace, and yet it eludes definition if not actually resenting all defining terms. It is a kaleidoscopic immediacy in which all things participate, and through which they either take on consequence or else accept dismissal to a relative nonentity, but does this say what it is? Jackdaws make common cause with jackdaws as a condition of remaining what they are, externally and objectively at least, namely, jackdaws. Each of them, however, additionally and contrariwise, is something else, with infinite variations. Indeed, there is no living creature that must not be a myriad of other things as well as what it is of itself in these outward terms. As a result there is no discrete existent that acts in even a remotely predictable fashion, if ever it is viewed in isolation from its patterns of involvement.

The young boy on his way home from school, in an underprivileged neighborhood, is engaged in the internal and organic operations consequent upon wolfing an apple.

Meanwhile the skin of his scalp is providing pasture for his ringworm fungus, quite unwittingly as far as he is concerned. He is distressed at vague stirrings precipitated within himself by his desk neighbor of the opposite sex, both of them gravitating helplessly into the glandular responses of preadolescence. His conscious mind is dealing with a problem at home, since his father drinks and his mother is a subject of neighborhood gossip, and he has been punished previously for stealing pocket money as the only means he knows for getting it. He has the pressing question of the bully a year older than himself, with whom he hesitates to engage in any fistic expression of their mutual dislike. All in all his outlook is clouded in every normal direction. But suddenly he encounters his special intimates, with whom he shares a passion for athletic prowess, and of these juniors he is quite the best baseball player anywhere around. In an instant the make-believe and magic of an idealized and relatively private reality are at work to transform him. He has achieved a gratifying here-and-now in which everything other than the game to be pitched is completely inconsequential. There may be certain and sure reckoning of an unpleasant sort in the other areas excluded from his consciousness for the moment, because he yet is little for all his brave inches of height and the really superb muscles of his throwing arm, but he is discovering the fact that he may center himself in the universe quite effectively on the basis of his better potentials.

The ugly duckling story, or its variant in Cinderella, is folklore deeply rooted in the night of time. An individual in the wrong place is defeated, not by his inadequacies or even by the indifference and cruelty of the world at large, but by the improper placing or orientation of himself in his total milieu. Thus it is that astrology presents a very effective therapy, since it measures all human potentialities in the terms of their widest application through all possible areas of experience. When the imaginative astrol-oger, aided by his quite unconditioned or free association of ideas, is able to suggest a miraculous open-sesame and thereupon launch some lucky native on his way to great rewards, what may be grounded in very blind insight is yet paying high dividends. A special branch of horoscopic art has been developed for just such a creatively untrammeled analysis of the immediate consequences in a life situation—out of all necessary connection with anything at all—and it has its regular if usually rather minor miracles because it is here that there is touch with the real or inner and unpredictable man at root.

The technique comes down directly from William Lilly (1602-1681), and it has been expanded and clarified for modern practice in the author's *Horary Astrology, Problem Solving by*. The judgments are based on a chart erected for the particular moment of identifiable action or mental reaction in each given case, and while the method does not have the everyday reliability of natal horoscopy it yet produces spectacular results at its best because of the extent to which it can eliminate elements of no pertinency from the consideration. A case history is essential for any competent interpretation of a birth figure, since past performance must be scaled against the astrological indications if the astrologer is to achieve any predictive accuracy in respect to a present potential, but the essence of skill in the special horary art is an ability to distinguish the things at hand from their hampering involvements. After all, any little duck may prove to be a swan. Who can tell? However, since the procedures are worked out in the relative vacuum of immediacies, its practice develops a sharp need for correctives such as the rigid demand for certain horoscopic conditions to be met before making any deductions. This determines whether or not the time-and-space complex is a proper frame for the individual problem. As an additional safeguard, in making sure the analysis is shaped to the real and fluid pertinencies of which advantage can be taken, the symbolic degrees are invaluable.

Example horoscopes for illustrating the horary techniques are seldom satisfactory. Troubles and issues are always present in life, but when they are shared it is as they present differing phases of themselves to different participants. What is needed is the rare sort of event which has a relatively identical significance for each possible reader. One that may be ideal in such a category is the first example in history of the controlled release of atomic energy. This took place in extemporized quarters under the seats at the University of Chicago athletic field, on December 2, 1942, at 3:01 p.m. local mean time. What first would catch the eye of anyone experienced in horary judgments, examining a chart erected for this time and place, is the close conjunction of the moon and Neptune in the house ruling military activities. Although the project was brought to its first point of success almost a full year after Pearl Harbor, it is part and parcel of the completely revolutionary events of which the Neptunian ingress into Libra had been a prophecy. The actual entrance of the planet into the sign

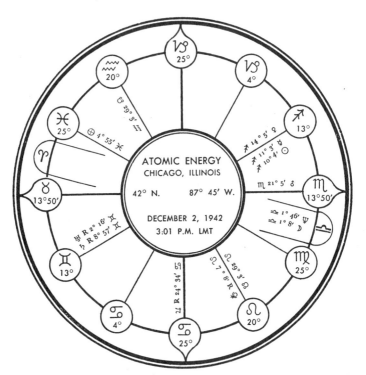

occurred on October 4, 1942, or less than two months before this key achievement in harnessing the atom.

The lunar position is always exceptionally significant in
horary astrology because the swift movement of the lesser
light, in comparison with the other bodies, gives a greater
flexibility of indication in day-by-day adjustments among
people in general. While the birth of a child or the emergence of a new organism is a phenomenon of convergence
and endowment, the focus at a point in time and space of
some critical integration of man's efforts and aspirations is

by contrast more an orientation or actual readjustment. It has no life of its own but instead represents a distribution or a discovery, that is, a release of energy and a call to living reaction and personal interest on the part of whatever may be concerned. This is not continuum, for which the sun is a significator in the fashion that makes the greater light of prime importance in natal horoscopy, but is basic or simple participation in any given complex of convenient or immediate reality, and such essentially and transiently is measured by the moon. Thus Luna, of primary significance in the special technique, is always the point of contact with external potentialities.

The degree of the two planets is Libra 2, and the symbolism is the light of the sixth race transmuted to the seventh. This suggests a wholly epochal transition, and is a real key to what has happened with man's achievement of his new powers over nature. Neptune indicates the over-all social obligation of the individual, and the moon represents his intimate or effective touch with the public. Since these planetary bodies are intercepted and cadent, it can be said that what they show in this chart is highly secret, and that their basic impact on everyday living is through covert and relatively indirect means. Their close trine to the rising and retrograde Uranus, and their quintile to Venus as ruler of the ascendant, together with the complete absence of any so-called adverse aspect to either of them, suggests an ultimate contribution of a peaceful rather than warlike nature. Despite the atomic bombs dropped on Hiroshima and Nagasaki, the astrological judgment from this horary chart would seem to be fundamentally favorable for mankind.

There is war, none the less, in the picture presented to the astrologer's eye. Mars, indicator of aggression and violence as well as a more pleasant and everyday initiative and energy, is the only planetary body of the ten in its own sign. Also, this planet is situated in the house of open conflict or warfare per se. However, the next aspect it makes is a pleasant one to Jupiter at the nadir—or the end of any matter in horoscopic indication—and this trine, by the timetable used for these charts of actual events as well as for the more conventional type of horary analysis, measures to a rough three and a half years of atomic development (taking the sixth as the subsidiary first). This gives a fairly accurate prediction of Japan's surrender in two years and nine months as a direct result of the A-bomb development. The degree occupied by the significator of the bombing is Scorpio 22 and the symbol is hunters starting out for ducks. By free association in a present afterview, the symbolization suggests first of all that it is the pressures of armed conflict or really bitter competition that always speed up the scientific advances of man. There must be the special incentives of the hunt. It might have required a century or more of purely peaceful initiative to provide the equivalent of the two billion dollars spent, together with the vast mobilization of necessary and special talents.

Astrology encourages a larger view also in the fact that the seventh house not only rules battles and the resources of the military but opportunity in general, including all the hosts of tête-à-tête relationships from marriage to business partnership. There are three planets here, more than in any of the other mansions, and this suggests a weighting of events towards some broad outreaching of greater scope than a mere open enmity. The symbol for the seventh cusp is telephone linemen at work. They represent the efforts of modern science to provide lines of relationship such as will integrate every new ramification of global living, and this is a clue to the whole picture of atomic energy in terms of the astrological promise. What has come into man's reality is not so much a physical force as a means for socio-economic elbowroom, enabling him to live on a less competitive basis and to share what he has to a greater extent in an equally exciting contest of emulations.

Both sun and Mercury are found in this angle of the horoscope, in addition to Mars. They are in trine with Pluto, whose position in Leo 8 already has been discussed at length, and they have an equally close conjunction with Venus in the adjoining house. More important than these aspects of momentum and co-operation, however, are the oppositions with the rising Uranus and Saturn. These latter are the only configurations of the nature of structural strength or genuine character development, a matter of great importance in a natal chart, and it is this planetary axis which establishes the type of the whole wheel as that of fundamental containment, in a bowl typing. Suggested is the development of a distinct contribution of some sort, and also revealed is the exceptional degree of awareness or sharpened sensitivity through which the uranium fission comes to represent a spirit or a morale for a new age. The five planets concerned (sun, Mercury, Venus, Uranus and Saturn) represent the five major departments of life outlined in earlier pages. This is exceptional symmetry in astrological distribution, and hence an indication that the chart possesses more than normal significance and reliability. Actually what occurred on December 2, 1942, was more than another event in the several recent centuries of scientific marvels. Here is indeed the threshold of a major epoch in human history.

The sun in Sagittarius 11 has for a symbol the lamp of physical enlightenment at the left temple. This suggests the nature of the underlying stability which may well characterize the new epoch. What has come to pass is not so much a new dimension added to a materialistic reality— that is, providing more competitive horrors and greater all-round weapons for ruthless aggrandizement—but is instead a remarkable quickening of all men to the practical and everyday powers inherent in their own being. Mercury is particularly significant in this connection because it rises behind the sun while the moon tends to be slow by mean daily motion. In consequence the mental set apt to distinguish the atomic culture is the intuitive one, or the form of thinking which moves to its conclusions by bringing wholes into a focus of immediate pertinency rather than manipulating or aggregating components in the manner of a machine or a mathematical mechanism. The method of imaginative analysis illustrated in these pages is quite possibly an anticipation of its powers.

Mercury is in Sagittarius 12, symbolized by a flag that turns into an eagle that crows. The loyalties of life tend always to awaken the free or soaring spirit of man, but the great birds of prey with their nest on the high crags and their life in the storm are indomitably isolationistic. The real supremacy through the coming age may have the lowly characteristics of the barnyard, where chanticleer symbolizes the self-responsibilities of a true human society and

forever calls man to the outwardly dull business of giving
a seminal impulse to everyday affairs. Rationalism has had
its fling, and the flag-waving of superficial allegiances may
well be ready to yield to something better. Hence it is not
surprising that Venus, lord of the ascendant, should be
found in the place of rebirth and regeneration. The symbol
for Sagittarius 15 is the ground hog looking for its shadow,
and in present-day culminations it seems that man's personality is becoming more and more the measure of all
things. The image of his hopes and desires begins to drape
itself quite significantly over the outer face of history.
Today he has begun to make his own world in very large
measure, whether he is pleased with the results or not.

The altogether unique conception of a global society, or
the characteristic trend of human personality as given new
direction through the coming of the A-bomb and the dramatic denouements following on its perfection, is indicated
by Uranus and Saturn in the house of personality or fundamental self-focus. The first of these significators is found
in Gemini 3, for which the garden of the Tuileries is a
symbol. When royalty is viewed in a sympathetic retro-
spect, at its point of studied magnificence just prior to the
French Revolution, emphasis falls on the accentuated
graciousness which once held high importance. This is the
element of the old most worthy of acceptance by the new.
The planet is retrograde, and so its testimony is on the subjective or spiritual as in contrast with the material side.
The real or immortal man, whom events are calling into a
practical and everyday existence, is above all else to be
regal in his sense of stewardship for the values which have
begun to prove themselves to him and his fellows.

The rising Saturn, also retrograde, is significant mainly through the prodigality always indicated by its position in this one of the twelve houses. So situated in a natal horoscope, it would indicate that the native was inclined to give too much for too little, and the atomic developments actually have contributed to a wasteful and indiscreet period. However, humanity cannot be expected to grow into its new lineaments overnight, or without long and at times unpleasant interludes of regression into its old vindictive and recriminative attitudes. Only in the willingness of each individual to throw himself wholeheartedly into the enlarged dimensions of his living, helping himself through the expanded make-believe which will release his true capacities, is there genuine hope for the new world spirit. The planet's degree, Gemini 9, has for a symbol the quiver filled with arrows, and this has long typified the open frontier and the great American achievement.

The final implication for the atomic age, through this astrological chart, is found in connection with its point of special nadir emphasis. Any planet on a horary cusp, within less than sixty minutes of arc in orb, gains a particular significance, and there is added testimony of importance when both are symbolized by the same degree, as is true for Jupiter and the fourth cusp in Cancer 25. The symbol is a dark shadow or mantle thrown suddenly over the right shoulder, and it often identifies a leader of men launched somewhat startlingly on his way. Here of course is not so much a personality as a cosmic potential in which every individual may find himself sustained or re-established. The fourth house is the end of the matter, or the home and what there may be of a personal estate, and the future security of humanity is here vested in a psychological and spiritual reality of a much greater and more enduring promise than the land and buildings, credits and cash or other external tokens of today's material privileges or wholly superficial good fortune.

CHAPTER TEN

RECTIFICATION BY SYMBOLS

THE horizon at the instant of an organism's birth int
an independent physical actuality, as established by the
place of that event on the surface of the earth and as deter
mined by the necessary astronomical calculations, become
the ascendant of the astrological chart and so the mathe
matical representation of the nascent personality. It is i
this fashion that an individual is framed in a pattern o
illimitable generalizations, derived from all human ex
perience, for the sake of a particular and detailed psychc
logical examination. Everything in the astrologer's map
ping of the life evolves from this simple base, and sinc
a new degree of the zodiac rises at approximately each fou
minutes of time, the precise moment of the baby's firs
breath—its initial act of sharply identifiable nature in th
world outside the uterus—must be found as the fundamer
tal condition for a reliable horoscope. Because this seldor
can be known to a point of requisite accuracy, it must b
established by deduction through the process known a
rectification. There are innumerable systems for the de
termination of the ascending point, and they range i
merit from complete worthlessness to practical and hig
reliability. Some are fancy theories, like schemes for breal
ing the bank at a gambling casino. All are beyond rea
proof of the sort characterizing the physical sciences, sinc
what is gained in the end is no more than a dependabl

correspondence between the horoscopic indications and the known facts in a given native's case, and this involves a fallible human judgment at all stages.

First of all methods, in the sense that it has been entrenched for generations, is the prenatal technique based on the general hypothesis that the places occupied by the moon and ascendant at birth are identical with those held at the moment of conception, but interchanged in accordance with various patterns of modification. Other arbitrary assumptions of a similar sort have become very common. In actual astrological practice, however, there can be but one appreciably reliable procedure, and this rests on a proposition which holds throughout the psychological sciences. Whenever there is a duplication of measurable conditions, what has happened before is a prediction of what may be expected to happen again. All analysis of character is an application of this principle, that is, the identification of constants which are significant in a given case and which in consequence yield an expectancy. Hence the more careful practitioners of the stellar art make use of events in the past, primarily, for checking the ascending degree. Once a native's horizon has been adjusted to a point of concordance with prior experience —whatever the detailed and convenient mode of measuring the correspondences—the astrologer has a chart which will give him a generally accurate outline of potentialities in any pertinent area of experience.

The symbolical degrees of the zodiac, of the sort interpreting the geometrical divisions of the zodiac and presented in these pages, were pioneered in major part by Charubel (John Thomas) for the sole purpose of dramatizing the nature of the ascendant. In this role they constituted an utterly simple type of rectification, and they may always be used profitably for that purpose. A more effective technique, however, involves the familiar part of fortune as well as the zodiacal point ascending at birth, and it can be expanded to include others of the Arabian parts also. These provide unlimited refinements of personal horizon through the two areas of each individual's experience, that is, the subjective as shown by the signs and the objective as indicated by the houses. Of the many thousands of such derivative ascendants which may be calculated, however, only the one is at all in general use. It is a function of the moon, and it identifies the quality of co-operation towards his own ends which any native may expect to receive from society at large.

The part of fortune is a purely mathematical entity, such as has little parallel in the planetary bodies with their mass and movement in the solar system. The distance in arc of the movement by the lesser light forward through the zodiac from the greater is the geometrical factor which establishes it, and the projection of this segment of the circle counterclockwise from the ascending rim of the celestial vault at birth is the given point in the heavens. What happens in rectification is that it moves its position in the zodiac whenever the ascendant is moved. In consequence the astrologer, wishing to employ the symbolizations of the degrees for help in determining an exact birth time, has two shifting points to take into account on the basis of their mutual suggestiveness.

The procedure may be illustrated with the horoscope of Adolf Hitler. As accepted in this text, the ascendant

of the Nazi leader is Libra 25. The picturization is information in the symbol of an autumn leaf. The Nazi movement was indeed as ephemeral as the leaves of a tree, and
the rich coloring of the autumnal foliage was a mirage of
transient and very elusive beauty. The part of fortune in
Cancer 1 is symbolized by the two flags, one flown for all to
see and the other kept from recognition. The implication
here, and in comparison with the delineation of the Neptune ingress for 1901 in earlier pages, is the chicanery
and shrewd cunning with which the German dictator was
able to appeal to his dupes, making continuous false repre-
sentations of himself. This of course is interpretation of the
unhappy fact rather than the idealized promise. The messianic potential would have been a bringing of all life to
the soft warmth and satisfaction of a harvest time, together
with the achievement of a self-restraint as well as a self-
projection in day-by-day loyalties or displaying the allegiances of self as some of these have pertinency and as others
may best be held in reserve. In any case the combination
of interpretations tends to confirm the time accepted for
his nativity.

Rupert Gleadow, the British astrologer who made a fea-
ture of Hitler's horoscope in his book, *Astrology in Everyday Life,* uses Libra 26 for a rising degree. The imaginative representation is an eagle and a large white dove
which keep turning one into the other continuously, thus
dramatizing literally a proffering now of peace and now of
war as a method of political aggrandizement. Normally
associated with this would be Cancer 2, symbolizing a man
in levitation over a vast level place, or dependent on nothing other than himself for support, and this certainly could

identify the megalomaniac who proceeded wholly on the
basis of his own intuitions. Actually Mr. Gleadow's chart
does not move the ascendant enough to change the part of
fortune from Cancer 1, so that the ambivalence of the two
degrees (Libra 26 and Cancer 1) might seem to many the
better of the alternatives. Such a possibility remains a second preference in this text because the impact of the man
on his day and age would seem to require a greater one-
pointedness at root, as well as a more definite identification of the messianic potential. Evil is a good turned inside
out, ultimately, and there is little dynamic for history in
either an uncertain ill-will or a confusing vacillation of
malevolence.

There are other possibilities, of course. A Libra 24 and
Gemini 30 pairing links a butterfly, which has a third or
supernumerary wing on the left side, with bathing beauties. This rectifying towards an earlier birth moment
would emphasize a more completely schizophrenic and ex-
hibitionistic individual, hardly squaring with the potentialities of the wheel as a whole or with the historical
horrors of World War II. A Libra 27 and Cancer 3 coup-
ling presents an airplane, which can be suggestive of the
English bombings, and a man all bundled up in furs as he
leads a shaggy deer, not unreminiscent of two great de-
bacles of dictatorial ambition in Russian winters, but here
the applicability of the symbols, so neat in one direction,
is faulty through a real lack of significance in the larger
perspective.

The problem of decision in response to these essentially
subjective correctives for the judgment is illustrated with
great sharpness in the case of President Truman. The

birth hour obtained by the astrologers in 1944 was rectified by somewhat general agreement from 4:00 p.m., standard time, to 4:14 p.m. in local mean measure, and the chart as published in various astrological journals gives Libra 17 for the ascendant and Aries 4 for the part of fortune. The symbolizations, a retired sea captain and two lovers strolling through a secluded walk, are hardly typical of the country's recent executive. However, by adding three minutes to the hypothetical moment of a first breath, the ascending degree becomes Libra 18 and the moon's part then lies in Aries 5. For these points the symbolism first presents two men placed under arrest, dramatizing the extent to which the native has been called on to submerge his private identity in a role to be played on both personal and public counts, and secondly, a triangle with wings, typifying the great dream of the new age.

Thus the symbolical degrees have revealed themselves as an instrument of great power, primarily of course in their stimulation to the imagination. From the many examples in these chapters of their possible application it may be seen that their strength is directly proportionate to the intelligence with which they are used. There is no substitute for good judgment in any area of man's conscious existence, but at the same time there is no mind short of complete incapacity which cannot be aided in its insights and thereupon encouraged in its development and range of understanding by a free and fearless response to the symbolism which speaks to it on every hand.

the sabian symbols

CHAPTER ELEVEN

THE SABIAN SYMBOLS

The Sabian symbols for the degrees of the zodiac were obtained by clairvoyant means in 1925. By then a good ten years had been given to experiment with the delineations of John Thomas, a Welsh seer who used the pseudonym of Charubel (*The Degrees of the Zodiac Symbolized*, London, Fowler, 1898). These had demonstrated a reliability of suggestive insight in their application to the horoscope, but it had become apparent that more effective results might follow if each degree were not so strongly moralized, that is, presented as essentially good or evil in its own nature. A tentative attempt to rework the earlier symbolism proved impractical, and a new start was made instead.

Most of the symbols then obtained were found to hold rather closely to the criteria put down, namely, that they should reflect modern life in a way which would be clear to any person of average background, that they should be neutral in the fact that no one of them in its application would seem favorable or unfavorable by necessity and that, while Charubel's interpretations had been shaped primarily for the ascendant of a birth figure, these new ones were to be no less significant when a degree was occupied by a planet, any other cusp, any part or node and so on, including the day-by-day place of the heavenly bodies and their positions in astrological progression. However, many of them are negative in the sense that they portray tragedy and ill luck, such as "an automobile wrecked by a train" or "a large disappointed audience." Others are intangible, as "lost opportunity regained in the imagination," or obscure in terms of any obvious reference, as " a cameo profile of a man in the outline of his country." Some are highly formalized in their symbolism, as "a triangle with wings" and "a square brightly lighted on one side," or definitely ambiguous, as "a sleigh without snow," or even ridiculous as "a flag that turns into an eagle that crows." Because no over-all pattern or unifying quality of insight seemed to characterize the picturizations as a whole, they were put aside in disappointment.

Within the next year the word of these symbols had spread among a small group of Los Angeles students, awakening considerable interest, and a number of typescripts were made and distributed for the test of actual application. The unsuspected real worth of the interpretations then began to make itself evident, and in consequence an initial step was taken to ready them for public trial through the issuance (from May to November, 1931) of the mimeographed lessons known as *Symbolical Astrology*. These have been in fairly wide circulation ever since, and they remain available for research purposes precisely as first released for experimental use. In this version the original roughly penciled notes on loose cards were expanded into basic descriptions for each degree, followed by fifty to sixty words of interpretation and analysis. Careful comparison was made with Charubel's work, which alone of other attempts along this line has seemed to meet the needs for an extension of the technique beyond the ascendant or perhaps the sun, and it was from this presentation that Dane Rudhyar was given permission to make an abridgment for his *Astrology of Personality* (New York, Lucis, 1936).

There was much about the mimeographed version of the Sabian degrees which fell far short of the original goal. While they continued to make friends, and were met at times with an almost extravagant commendation, the interpretations in nearly every case were too grooved in a single mood—no less objectionable than the older identification as good or bad—and it soon became obvious that the keywords were none too serviceable and that the formulas conveyed little if any meaning to anybody. A new version was made in 1948, reworking the delineations on the basis of the seventeen years of general reaction and the near quarter-century of continued experimentation since the first notes were made. There was improvement but not enough, and much of the intuitive force of the initial descriptions was lost. In consequence all attempts to prepare the material for book publication were dropped until early in 1951. Since then some two years of steady work have gone into the presentation which now makes its appearance in print, and it is probable that any further refinements will have to be the work of fresh minds in another generation.

In the beginning a fully rounded-out vignette of life was envisioned for each symbol, and the original penciled notes on cards were never intended to be more than a sort of shorthand memorandum for the creative authorship to follow. What has happened over the years is that the requisite genius has not been available, and that no effort has proved adequate enough to get the ideas in the universal form needed for the astrological techniques. Since the first notations are at least the crude stuff of pure insight, produced at high speed and with great inspirational heat, there probably is no better recourse than to use these just as they were first put down. This has been the procedure in the present pages, and there have been very few changes.

Minor matters of punctuation and some corrections in spelling need no comment. Abbreviations have been spelled out, as in the case of gymnasium for gym and automobile for auto. Airplane is used for aeroplane. In a few cases the pencil is impossible to decipher with certainty, so that Capricorn 6 could be two instead of ten logs. Gem was read for germ (Cancer 17) and parts for paths (Libra 15) in preparing the 1931 interpretations. A serpent is coiling, not circling (Aries 14). Side comments have been ignored. Thus the Tuileries card had Paris on the margin. Taurus 19 was marked tangible, and this idea has been incorporated in the description. In Sagittarius 17 the word sunrise is inserted, since a notation that it was early a.m. had been jotted down at the edge. In Cancer 10 the diamond is said to be not quite cut instead of not quite carved, as was written on the card. In Leo 6 the word flapper is replaced with the phrase up-to-date girl, and in Gemini 16 the suffragist is said to be haranguing rather than orating, as the pencil notes have it. Chocolate is changed to colored in Virgo 4. There is a great mystery, which may be part of what occultists know as the necessary twist in any series of relations of spiritual import, since the cards for Libra 18 and 19 were first in reverse of their present order, and then the descriptions were scratched and repenciled as they are found in all the various versions of the Sabian degrees, and as indeed they seem correctly placed. There is neither record nor recollection of what happened in this connection, whether originally in San Diego's Balboa Park or when the first typescripts were made.

There are unlimited ways in which these Sabian symbols can be interpreted, and the practiced student or professional astrologer need not confine himself to any one mode of approach. However, of all the many choices for a basic delineation, the one which here should be of the greatest value if for no other reason than that it is the point of view taken in dealing with the horoscope in the author's companion volume, *The Essentials of Astrological Analysis,* is a first consideration of opposites or of the axes of balance as the heavenly wheels are taken at one place or another for their measure of man. The degrees which lie face to face across the circle will be found to complement each other in a fashion that is mutually illuminating, and this fact has been of the greatest assistance in working out the detailed symbolism. Thus there are abstract ideas which of themselves might have little meaning, as in the case of Aries 7 and the man expressing himself successfully in two realms at once. Libra 7 is represented by a woman feeding chickens and protecting them from hawks. In both instances there is an obvious division of labor, and so this can be taken as subjective on the one side and objective on the other. In nearly every instance the interpretations are keyed through this sort of diametrical relationship.

Many of the symbols are wholly ambiguous if taken by themselves. Taurus 8, a sleigh without snow, could mean either its effective functioning in any kind of weather or else its complete inability to move. Cancer 22, a woman

awaiting a sailboat, can suggest unprofitable attendance
on chance or a very sure reward of expectation. Beautifully gowned wax figures, Aquarius 8, might be a waxworks or the manikins in a department store window. An
aviator in the clouds, Pisces 10, implies a state of complete
muddle as easily as an advantage of perspective or protection. There are cases of close duplication as the sea cap-
tains of Leo 13 and Libra 17, and the moons of Scorpio 8,
Pisces 27 and Pisces 28. When it comes to the crosses of
Virgo 2 and Pisces 7, there is nothing in the imagery itself
to suggest that the latter is not placed in position deliber-
ately and effectively. The slight distinction between Sagittarius 12 and Aquarius 9 is curious in as bizarre a conception as that of a flag which becomes an eagle. There are
the pictures of frustration or disillusionment as the audience in Aries 28, and the old man attempting to reveal the
Mysteries in Taurus 16, and the women in Capricorn 24
and Aquarius 21.

The greatest problem of interpretation, in view of the
arbitrary requirement that there be no choice between degrees as better or worse in any general or absolute way,
has been the many instances of reversed symbolism, that is,
presentation of a wholly unencouraging or negative picture. However, the widow at the open grave, Taurus 5,
can be seen to be an emphasis on the possible stabilities in
human life when taken in connection with Scorpio 5, a
massive, rocky shore. A woman of Samaria, Taurus 7, becomes an illustration of one kind of depth to which experience may plunge when compared with the deep-sea
divers, Scorpio 7. The sleigh without snow, Taurus 8, is
explained through a distinction in sustainments when its

complement, the moon shining across the lake, Scorpio 8, is taken into account. The labor upsets of Gemini 8 and 21, the bankruptcy of Gemini 28, the automobile wreck of Cancer 5, the intoxicated chickens of Leo 21, the boat landing washed away of Libra 16, the men under arrest of Libra 18, the gang of robbers of Libra 19, and the soldier and sailor derelict in duty of Scorpio 21 and Aquarius 3, afford further examples of the clarifications provided by a consideration of the relations across the wheel. It is to facilitate a practical or everyday use of the diametrical indications in this manner that the symbols are printed on facing pages, the signs Aries through Virgo on the left and Libra through Pisces on the right.

The interpretations follow a rather rigid formula. First are the sign and degree, with the original short notation for the symbol following in italics. Next comes a philosophical exposition of the over-all type of functioning called forth by any emphasis of human activity or character through the position of a planet, cusp, node or part in the given sixty-minute segment of the zodiac. It is to be noted again that these are geometrical divisions, and not areas of influence or proclivity with a peak of effect graduating out in either direction. Measurement is from Aries 0° 1′ to Aries 1° 0′ for Aries 1, from 1° 1′ to 2° 0′ for Aries 2, and so on around the circle. When consideration is given to moving bodies, as in astrological progressions or directions, the indication is to be seen as in full force from the crossing of any 1′ point to the arrival at the threshold of the next 1′. The mode of description, characteristically consisting of three sentences but occasionally put down in two, is the result of long experimentation ranging through the three versions. It is a highly stylized and often very oblique depiction. Here are speculative vignettes designed to fall into place in any possible connection of experience or potentiality, and to resist all attempts to use them as statements of direct or specific probability in any sort of mechanical fortunetelling. They have been conceived as a species of poetry, working with the symbolical notations as a catalyst for the creative inspiration and remaining forever fresh and unique in every single instance of their employment.

The keywords, which are presented in small capitals, have been revised completely no less than five times in as many recent years, to supplement the basic pictograph and descriptive matter and also to give important expression to the suggestive complementation of insights from the opposite points of the zodiac. For some types of mind this single expression may be much more useful than either the original picture or the philosophical scrim of words prepared to be dropped theatrelike across the face of a situation. Each pair of these concepts is designed to afford additional intimation concerning whatever may be brought to focus by zodiacal position in the horoscope. Thus for Aries-Libra 1 the terms are realization and articulation, or character as it comes to a singleness inwardly and a pointedness outwardly. With Aries-Libra 2 there is release as immediate or transitory self-projection and threshold as self poised ready to project itself more significantly in some enlarged or superior dimension of being. There is no over-all rhythm in the possible dominance of one symbol over its partner in the pairing, whether in terms of initiative or advantage or anything else, since this is a matter of each shifting perspective. Active and passive, or other such fixed dichotomies, are always an expression of a narrow or superficial view such as has no ultimate validity. The woman of Aries 1 is a creature of events, and so is the butterfly of Libra 1. But the effectiveness with which they both are equipped, whether practically or imaginatively, has its fruits in the experience revealed in suggestive outline by the planets, points or cusps emphasized at these particular points in the zodiac.

The positive and negative delineations provide the most simple procedure of interpretation, and they may be of the most service to the younger student or less experienced astrologer. In a very general way they are shaped for (1) the sun, (2) the other planets except the moon as representative of selfhood in various aspects, (3) the moon as showing how the self is best able to present itself in its public activities and (4) the ascendant as representing the being in its simple or direct capacity for co-operation with others. They offer the easiest of all ways to check the efficacy of this free-association technique on the one hand and to develop a sensitiveness to the deeper nuances of insight on the other. In the preceding pages there has been no employment of the constructive suggestiveness, since the analysis of Zoë Wells and Elsie Wheeler was made on the basis of the original symbolism and the philosophical vignettes. However, the tragic misdirection of his messianic potentialities by Adolf Hitler was shown primarily through the adverse implication provided by the negative indications.

The formulas, which follow next in smaller type and italics, are for the specialist or research-minded astrologer, and are a basis for any deliberate or intellectual as against an intuitive or wholly imaginative creation or validation of symbols for the degress. Indeed, they may be used toward that purpose at any future time, or may be employed for further light on any problem of interpretation.

The positive signs (fire and air) are MANIPULATING and extensional as in contrast with the negative ones (water and earth), which are SUSTAINING and intensive. Thus a comedian entertaining a group (Aries 2) and the light of the sixth race transmuted to the seventh (Libra 2) are of the former order, while a man suspended over a vast level place (Cancer 2) and three stained glass windows, one damaged by bombardment (Capricorn 2) are of the latter. The distinctions generally have quite literal confirmation by the symbolism, but their value is the other way around or in the extent to which they illuminate the symbols significantly. Thus an epidemic of mumps (Leo 2) might seem more negative than positive, and an electrical storm (Taurus 2) more manipulating than sustaining, but the spread of sickness, and the unexpected violence of weather which is its complement (Aquarius 2), are better taken as high potentiality out of control, and the display of lightning, with the broken bottle and spilled perfume which is its opposite (Scorpio 2), as an effectiveness of impact by a catalytic rather than a direct influence.

The distinctions of quadrature and triplicity, providing the second and third terms of the formula for each degree, are of foundation importance in all astrology. They are the measure at root of man's mode of participation in experience on the one hand and of his manner of self-integration on the other.

Cardinal signs are CRITICAL in the sense that under their emphasis life remains at all points a problem or challenge to the self, as in the cases of the comedian, the man suspended, the light of the race and the three windows (Aries 2, Cancer 2, Libra 2 and Capricorn 2). Fixed signs are IDEAL in the fact that the individual in any identification through them is quickened to pertinent meanings and values, or seems to be concerned more with the ideas than the facts involved in any immediate issue. The epidemic, the spilled perfume and the two storms (Leo 2, Scorpio 2, Aquarius 2, and Taurus 2) are of this order, all presenting an implication of a pervasive significance rather than a direct call to specific action. There is a subjective mediation, whereas cardinal stress rejects any mediating factors. Common signs are PRACTICAL in calling for adjustment to others or to relationships with them in meeting a need to mediate all experience in social terms, that is, to utilize the culture and develop the resources of a civilization. Santa Claus filling stockings furtively (Gemini 2) with its complement, the ocean covered with whitecaps (Sagittarius 2), and a large white cross upraised (Virgo 2) linked with a squirrel hiding from hunters (Pisces 2), are of this sort. If the personal inference seems somewhat indirect in connection with the waves keeping cheerful company with each other across the expanse of water, as in contrast with the Christmas symbolization and its suggestion that all men should love and cherish each other, or when it comes to the frightened little animal which reveals the associative necessities of life in reverse in the balance of concepts with the clear religious challenge, the ordering pattern helps the astrological mind in grasping the ultimate import of its insights.

The fire triplicity is always ORIGINAL in the sense of a creative self-adequacy at root, illustrated in the comedian (Aries 2), the epidemic (Leo 2) and the whitecaps (Sagittarius 2). A phase of indomitable spontaneity is seen in its rising-to-an-immediate-occasion, ideal-stimulating and socially eager forms. The air signs (also positive or manipulating) are INGENIOUS primarily, shown in the transmuted light of the race (Libra 2), the unexpected thunderstorm (Aquarius 2) and Santa Claus (Gemini 2) as a resourcefulness in improving a present situation, in adjusting to the conception of it and as sharing its fruits. The water triplicity is always UNIVERSAL in its scope or make-up, as in the case of the man suspended (Cancer 2), the perfume (Scorpio 2) and the squirrel (Pisces 2). They symbolize an illimitable perspective in simple directness, an unlimited spread of associative ideas in memory and the broadest possible awareness of personal relations or social responsibility. The earth signs (also negative or sustaining) are always EFFICIENT through a great gift for holding things in the given reality, dramatized by the stained-glass windows of which one is damaged (Capricorn 2), the electrical storm (Taurus 2) and the cross (Virgo 2). Revealed here is a characteristically human genius for continuing on under handicap, for self-realization in the midst of outside pressure and for a personal exaltation of fundamentally social potentials.

The fourth term of the formula for each degree is an identification of the first half of each sign as SPECIALIZING and the other as GENERALIZING. This is a distinction between what is more objective or to the point and what is more cumulative or ultimately a matter of contribution by indirection. When a comedian entertains a group, the directness is obvious, but two prim spinsters (Aries 17 as corresponding with Aries 2 in this comparison) are effective much more subjectively in their symbolism, even if their manner of living is also manipulating, critical and original. The specialized impact of the electrical storm is matched by the generalized battle between the swords and torches (Taurus 2 and 17), i.e., a sustaining-ideal-efficient working to resolution through vicarious and imaginative considerations coming into conflict with each other. Santa Claus in this fashion can be compared with the head of health dissolving into the head of mentality (Gemini 2 and 17) as a manipulating-practical-ingenious organization of effort and interest in close and remote terms. While a man is suspended over a vast level place more specifically, the germ grows into knowledge and life more generally (Cancer 2 and 17). The epidemic of mumps is much more to a point in comprehension than the nonvested church choir (Leo 2 and 17) and the large white cross has sharper implication than the volcano in eruption (Virgo 2 and 17). The similar distinctions are fairly obvious through the 2nd and 17th degree comparisions of the other six signs, or the redirected light of the race and the inactive sea captain (Libra), the spilled perfume and the idealized or virgin birth (Scorpio), the white caps and the stylized impact of the Easter sunrise service (Sagittarius), the stained-glass windows and the surreptitiousness of the bather (Capricorn), the thunderstorm and the watchdog waiting for eventualities (Aquarius) and the squirrel and .the ritualized promenade (Pisces).

The first five degrees of each half sign are PHYSICAL, as the comedian and the spinsters (Aries 2 and 17), the next are SOCIAL, as a man expressing himself successfully in two realms at once (Aries 7) and the gate to the garden of desire (Aries 22), and the remaining ones SPIRITUAL, as a flock of wild geese (Aries 12) and lost opportunity regained in the imagination (Aries 27). The comedian has an audience but what he presents and maintains is himself. The man with expression in two forms is anchored of necessity in a social situation which he is able to approach in more than one aspect of himself, thereby furthering his self-fulfillment no less than the entertainer with whom he is linked in this phase of the patterns underlying the symbolism. It can then be seen that as a result of the achievement in self-integration there is the broader freedom or simple transcendence of limitation represented by the flock of wild geese. Similarly the spinsters, who represent a simple capacity for weighing immediate pros and cons, dramatize a phase of self-expression which on the social level is the gate to the garden of all things desired, or is the visualization of broader and more sharable rewards for everyday living, and in the transcendental aspect of this symbolical strand of patterning there is an utterly untrammeled power of visualization, such as can serve man by recapturing whatever aspects of reality he has allowed to slip away from him.

The sixth and final term of the degree formula gives the distribution of the fivefold dimension of self-expression around the circle, and may be illustrated at the end of the zodiac where three lunar vignettes in succession give a marked similarity in the picturization and exhibit the progression more sharply. The new moon that divides its influences (Pisces 26) is EXPERIMENTAL, as naïve and first outreaching in any or all experience. A harvest moon (Pisces 27) is SENSITIVE in the sense that reality is faced or stood against, here in the consummation of crop-gathering or life fulfillment in its sustaining-practical-universal-generalizing-spiritual aspect. A fertile garden under the full moon (Pisces 28) is RECEPTIVE in a responsiveness to the potentials of being, together with a willingness to permit the flow of self into every realization of life's real complementation of a personal identity. A prism (Pisces 29) is RESPONSIBLE in an illustration of the reliability of man's conscious awareness of his state, and of his ability to measure its potentialities and attack its problems. The Great Stone Face (Pisces 30) is INSPIRED because it is here in each of these little cycles that the individual, at first concerned over his outreach into the separation of self-reality, is now turned back to the cosmic certainty in which he finds himself in union and partnership with the over-all fact of existence.

Reference to the example horoscopes is by number, and the essential data for all of them will be found in the listing of the names and tabulation of the cusps and planets. The original vision was to present a case of the position of every planet in every degree of every sign, but nothing of this scope is possible on the basis of a thousand charts alone. The two outermost and most recently discovered planets, Neptune and Pluto, do not make a complete circuit of the zodiac within the range of years for which astrological tables are available, as far as the average student or investigator is concerned, and so they are not cited as examples although their positions are tabulated. The places of the other eight bodies are given in reference to each symbol, and in general the distribution has been fairly even through the signs, especially in the case of the sun. Mars is curiously deficient in its representation in Pisces. Scorpio comes closest to the original ideal in that instances of the sun, Mercury, Mars, Saturn and Uranus are found in every degree. This is true of Virgo in reference to Mercury, Mars and Uranus, and of Libra with Mercury, Mars and Saturn. Cases of Venus are found in every degree of Taurus and Pisces, of the moon in Cancer, and of Jupiter in Aries. Within the signs the distribution of planetary representation through the degrees tends to be quite irregular, as will be obvious to the eye.

There is great danger in drawing any very precise conclusions from the example cases, primarily because of the over-all unreliability of the astrological data with which a present generation of researchers must work. Equally a problem is the very obvious handicap of small actual acquaintance with the private life or real nature of the average public figure. There are times where a degree symbol will prove dramatically apt in a very literal fashion, but there are fully as many instances where it may seem most inapt. Actually the symbolism is mediative to the mind, and not descriptive except most incidentally and unpredictably as already has been brought out in detail.

ARIES 1   *A woman rises out of water, a seal rises and embraces her.* This is a symbol of completely unconditioned potentiality, as this may be grasped on the practical side of life. Here are elements of soul emerging from primordial nonexistence, and of an essentially feminine receptivity calling up a more masculine or personal and self-seeking initiative. There is an implicit emphasis on the mutual interdependence of the emotional and purposeful aspects of self. The keyword is REALIZATION. When positive, the degree is an illimitability of experience of which anyone can take advantage under any or all circumstances, and when negative, a failure to find a place in life because the self cannot separate itself from its own private obsessions.

The formula is: manipulating-critical-original-specializing-physical-experimental. Examples are: sun, 921; moon 102, 225, 896; Mercury, 423, 463, 872; Venus, 75, 81, 427; Mars, 10, 73, 77, 325, 797, 983; Jupiter, 755, 953; Uranus, 30, 411.

ARIES 2   *A comedian entertaining a group*   This is a symbol of the mirror which life holds up to itself recurrently, and so facilitates an everyday understanding of itself. The identity of each individual is projected back into the wholly naïve potentials of his experience, thereby providing a fresh and transcendent self-perspective. Here is man's heightened individuality as he discovers he may play whatever role he finds useful in each momentary contact with others, together with the continual self-reassurance he gains in self-rehearsal. The keyword is RELEASE. When positive, the degree is the power of personality through a full and completely uninhibited self-expression, and when negative, a neglect of common responsibility through idle diversions of interest.

The formula is: manipulating-critical-original-specializing-physical-sensitive. Examples are: sun, 289, 340; moon, 141, 293, 670, 744; Mercury, 300, 548, 807, 871, 927; Mars, 61, 319, 380; Jupiter, 968, 980; Saturn, 77, 301, 624, 780; Uranus, 356, 489, 793.

LIBRA 1 *A butterfly made perfect by a dart through it* This is a symbol of completely unconditioned potentiality, as this may be grasped on the imaginative side of life. Here are elements of individual consciousness emerging from a primordial formlessness, and of wisdom developing through the human spirit's continual determination to project itself into experience. Each person comes into identifiable being through the nature which has been molded for him, and thereupon refines this for his own self-expression. The keyword is ARTICULATION. When positive, the degree is man's awakening to the need for some more whole-souled focus of character, and when negative, the loss of all true selfhood by a needless surrender to the world and conformity to its ways.

The formula is: manipulating-critical-ingenious-specializing-physical-experimental. Examples are: sun, 230, 803, 892; moon, 56, 382, 389, 604, 867; Mercury, 294, 792,; Venus, 86, 453, 652; Mars, 519, 684, 938; Jupiter, 394, 474, 557, 634, 840; Saturn, 372, 989; Uranus, 923.

LIBRA 2 *The light of the sixth race transmuted to the seventh* This is a symbol of the mirror which history provides for mankind, so that each new generation may see itself reflected in its own past and therefore may be challenged to its real future. The characteristics of a modern and global society (identified by occultists as the sixth root manifestation of human culture) are idealized in the vision ahead (a seventh and climactic manifestation) and every individual is seen within full reach of his own ultimate potential. The keyword is THRESHOLD. When positive, the degree is the imaginative sweep of man's vision and an eagerness to execute its promise, and when negative, a loss of reality in an infinitely regressive otherworldliness or a total lack of all practicality.

The formula is: manipulating-critical-ingenious-specializing-physical-sensitive. Examples are: sun, 7, 45; moon, 257, 325, 467; Mercury, 534, 556, 741, 764; Venus, 908; Mars, 50; Jupiter, 146, 452, 664, 786, 850; Saturn, 8, 290, 347, 932; Uranus, 204.

ARIES 3 *A cameo profile of a man in the outline of his country*
This is a symbol of a real breadth of participation in everyday
affairs, and of the extent to which every individual tends to
epitomize the tradition and culture from which he has emerged.
There is here the suggestion of both an impersonal self-dedication to broader community interests and a highly personal
dramatization of the self as a focus for group actuality. The
keyword is EXPLOITATION. When positive, the degree is man's
capacity for giving full play to every ramification of the reality
he has created for himself, and when negative, an unimaginative conventionality which leaves him in bondage to every current stereotype of human relations.

*The formula is: manipulating-critical-original-specializing-physical-recep-
tive.* Examples are: sun, 658, 685, 701, 810; moon 42, 243, 719, 947;
Mercury, 53, 125, 154, 228, 714; Venus, 154, 216, 714; Mars, 201, 351, 572,
988; Jupiter, 412; Saturn, 252, 467, 594, 649, 929; Uranus, 22, 927.

ARIES 4 *Two lovers strolling through a secluded walk* This is
a symbol of the first innocent rounding out of conscious experience, and of an unspoiled assurance of personal potentialities for which no immediate sense of responsibility is necessary.
Implicit here is the fact that reality is ever without meaning
or power except as it stimulates the self to move in its own
interest persistently and continuously whenever the least opportunity offers. The keyword is ENJOYMENT. When positive,
the degree is an utterly naïve assimilation of self into its world
and a complete flow of all effort towards some proper end, and
when negative, the indiscriminate loss of the self's real assets
in pure self-indulgence.

*The formula is: manipulating-critical-original-specializing-physical-respon-
sible.* Examples are: sun, 42, 115, 271, 773; moon, 637, 690, 765; Mercury
138, 439, 836; Venus, 884, 956; Mars, 225, 809; Jupiter, 28, 620; Uranus
131, 722.

LIBRA 3   *The dawn of a new day, everything changed*   This is a symbol of the illimitable potentialities to be found when it comes to any personal participation in everyday affairs, and of the thoroughness with which each individual remains the recurrent expression of his own self-consistencies. There is here the necessity for an ultimate self-dependence, and the consequent need to blaze a path of special recognition for each particular characteristic of selfhood. The keyword is INNOVATION. When positive, the degree is man's insatiable appetite for experiment and continuing self-discovery in every possible area of human experience, and when negative, inability to catch the challenge of living in even the most trivial matters.

The formula is: manipulating-critical-ingenious-specializing-physical-receptive. Examples are: sun, 93, 341, 837; Mercury, 495, 725, 804, 822; Venus, 7, 103, 194, 478, 748; Mars, 173, 364, 426, 542, 641; Jupiter, 603, 612; Saturn, 92, 678, 916; Uranus, 226, 719.

LIBRA 4   *A group around a campfire*   This is a symbol of an initial or uncritical consummation of group experience, and of the totally unconditioned capacity of each individual to associate himself with his kind without exaction or inhibition. Implicit here is the fact that any reality broader than a simple self-concern must have its origin in common functions where any responsibility becomes the expression of identity rather than of a divergence in interest. The keyword is AMIABILITY. When positive, the degree is special skill in building an everyday morale and in sustaining an effective structure for further and greater objectives in life, and when negative, a lazing away of opportunity and an idle dependence on others.

The formula is: manipulating-critical-ingenious-specializing-physical-responsible. Examples are: sun, 384, 835; Mercury, 111, 691; Venus, 39, 904; Mars, 131, 359, 535, 759; Jupiter, 101; Saturn, 244, 609, 720; Uranus, 26, 299, 745, 875, 960.

ARIES 5 *A triangle with wings* This is a symbol of the inviolability of man's essential nature throughout every ramification of his experience, as long as he holds to the purity of
his original impulses. There is here a very practical balance
in his self-fulfillment, thanks to his threefold individuality in
terms of skills, loyalties and values. Light rather than darkness remains the goal of his life, and his personal capacities
become a continual refinement of every baser metal in selfhood. The keyword is ZEAL. When positive, the degree is the
creative transformation of everything into an expression of
enduring idea and a reflection of the real vision ahead, and
when negative, blissful obliviousness to all normal or every
day considerations.

*The formula is: manipulating-critical-original-specializing-physical-in-
spired.* Examples are: sun, 905; Mercury, 318, 471, 728, 884; Venus, 11, 134,
261; Mars, 271, 366, 826, 840; Jupiter, 156, 287; Saturn, 602; Uranus, 21,
64, 93.

ARIES 6 *A square brightly lighted on one side* This is a symbol of experience as the over-all sustainment of any personal
or conscious being. A materialistic reality is found to be sheer
illusion when taken of itself or given any power on its own
account, but it also is discovered to be the servant of every
human impulse whenever life becomes red-blooded or achieves
a motivation and an effective appreciation of its own nature.
Implicit here is the realization that things are given their
fundamental ordering as they are accepted in consciousness.
The keyword is SET. When positive, the degree is the absolute
unimpeachability of a genuine self-direction, and when negative, complete loss of self-efficacy in a surrender to frustrations.

*The formula is: manipulating-critical-original-specializing-social-experi-
mental:* Examples are: moon, 159, 653, 706; Mercury, 545; Venus, 15,
433, 623, 976; Mars, 275, 452; Jupiter, 64, 721, 767, 898; Saturn, 390, 493;
Uranus, 1, 892.

LIBRA 5 *A man teaching the true inner knowledge* This is a symbol of the inviolability of all genuine inspiration, and of the opportunity offered every individual to reach out to his fellows through his participation with them in everyday experience, and thereupon to communicate his deeper insights to them through common responsibilities. His integrity of being lies in his continual self-orientation to both man and the world in terms of ultimate potentialities. The keyword is AFFINITY. When positive, the degree is a genius for understanding and calling out the underlying realizations by which human character comes to know itself at its best, and when negative, fatuous pride in the self's acumen and subtle or underhanded attempts to dominate everyone.

The formula is: manipulating-critical-ingenious-specializing-physical-inspired. Examples are: sun, 166, 609, 676, 829, 878; moon, 586, 663; Mercury, 722; Venus, 544; Mars, 550, 620, 671, 958; Jupiter, 99, 321, 815, 882; Saturn, 284; Uranus, 455, 549.

LIBRA 6 *The ideals of a man abundantly crystallized* This is a symbol of experience as the practical or everyday substantiation of inner insight and conscious understanding. Idealistic reality is found to be sheer escapism if ever taken by itself or given any authority on its own account, but is the sole dynamic for the human spirit whenever any individual actually stands face to face with his opportunity. Implicit here is the realization that man's being has its beginning in the meanings with which it is endowed. The keyword is PERSONIFICATION. When positive, the degree is power through the full employment of imagination for the discovery and development of human potentiality, and when negative, self-defeat through inadequate expectation and superficial allegiances.

The formula is: manipulating-critical-ingenious-specializing-social-experimental. Examples are: sun, 34, 111, 209, 358, 690, 706, 971; moon, 602, 760; Mercury, 161, 502; Venus, 166, 535, 676, 678, 961; Mars, 761, 894; Jupiter, 96, 591; Saturn, 207, 265, 386, 584, 937, 949.

ARIES 7   *A man successfully expressing himself in two realm.
at once*   This is a symbol of a creative division of labor withir
the self, such as distinguishes human kind from the lowe:
orders of life and enables any individual to participate in the
experience of many interpenetrating realms of reality. There
is capacity here for a complete control of events by shifting
from one to another focus of emphasis whenever it proves con
venient or expedient. The keyword is PROFICIENCY. Wher
positive, the degree is unlimited versatility and a special gif
for divorcing the things of issue from whatever lacks immediate
pertinence, and when negative, a tendency to defeat all self
competence in an unintelligent scattering of interest.

The formula is: manipulating-critical-original-specializing-social-sensitive
Examples are: sun, 53, 323, 883; moon, 61; Mercury, 265, 905, 929;˙Venus
651, 701; Mars, 38, 104,˙327, 715, 743; Jupiter, 483; Saturn, 215, 587
Uranus, 10, 28, 380.

ARIES 8   *A large hat with streamers flying, facing east*   This i
a symbol of naïve creativity, or the fundamentally phalli
stirrings of man as these keep him forever responsive for bette
or worse to the general potentialities of an everyday being
and as they also enable him to realize and utilize the eve
emerging novelties and variations of human relationship
Implicit here is an unconditioned and complete co-operatio
with every immediate trend of events, whether consciousl
or otherwise. The keyword is EXCITATION. When positive, th
degree is continual self-orientation to the nascent potentialitie
of all life and experience, and when negative, a tendency t
idle posing or an empty pretense of good will and interest.

The formula is: manipulating-critical-original-specializing-social-receptiv
Examples are: sun, 127, 412, 562, 965; moon, 114, 123, 572, 948; Mercur
651; Venus, 66, 73, 579, 669, 773, 947; Mars, 274, 297, 683; Jupiter, 418, 49
528; Saturn, 55, 190, 657, 708, 856, 863; Uranus, 90.

LIBRA 7 *A woman feeding chickens and protecting them from the hawks* This is a symbol of the creative division of labor between the functions of man and nature, and of the dual constitution of the soul in its responsibilities of conservation on the one hand and of development on the other. There is here every capacity for a control of events through a nurturing of the things which are desirable and a rejection of those which have no immediate value. The keyword is SHREWDNESS. When positive, the degree is a high competence in administering the duties of normal experience and a very special skill in protecting the self's real interests, and when negative, a complete personal ineptitude in the face of life's everyday and recurrent complexities.

The formula is: manipulating-critical-ingenious-specializing-social-sensitive. Examples are: sun, 912; moon, 224, 379, 883; Mercury, 432, 706; Venus, 182; Mars, 166, 310, 455, 799, 890; Jupiter, 678; Saturn, 405, 738, 871; Uranus, 101, 146, 487.

LIBRA 8 *A blazing fireplace in a deserted home* This is a symbol of naïve reality, or of the basic law of the cosmos whereby all things tend to continue steadily in their accustomed function. Implicit here is the burning desire or capacity for passion which establishes man's loyalty to each object of his self-projection and instruments his more consistent self-orientation through each phase of personal responsibility to the world in which he finds himself. The keyword is GUARDIANSHIP. When positive, the degree is an exceptional gift for enlisting both men and the natural forces of life in the service of self and its dominating vision, and when negative, a witless dismissal of all affairs to their own devices.

The formula is: manipulating-critical-ingenious-specializing-social-receptive. Examples are: sun, 95, 97; moon, 471, 482, 499, 682, 837, 919; Mercury, 97, 284, 355, 820; Venus, 211, 671, 737; Mars, 25; Saturn, 109, 128, 379, 701, 773, 790; Uranus, 320, 611.

ARIES 9   *A crystal gazer*   This is a symbol of man's capacity
for bringing an entire universe within the purview of his
mind. There are higher faculties of human understanding,
but as no more than the illimitable possibilities of personal
experience in the realms of potentiality. Implicit is the concept of the world and the individual as irrevocably in partnership, each reflecting the other and thereby providing a
foreview of every possible mood or situation. The keyword is
ACUTENESS. When positive, the degree is consummate insight
in planning the course of events or organizing them in the
light of immediate convenience, and when negative, an idle
curiosity and a surrender of all reality to the vagaries of the
moment.

*The formula is: manipulating-critical-original-specializing-social-responsi-
ble.* Examples are: sun, 439; moon, 98, 650, 721, 979; Mercury, 144, 156,
342, 949; Venus, 572; Mars, 292, 567, 606; Jupiter, 122, 895; Saturn, 160,
565, 729, 825.

ARIES 10   *A man teaching new forms for old symbols*   This is
a symbol of the continuous and necessary rectification of understanding through direct and everyday experience, such as
brings every factor of inner realization into immediate and
personal significance. Here the wisdom of the race is revivified
and made available for all through its recurrent and continual validation in human affairs. There is a serving of the
many by the one who provides a momentary dramatization for
each special phase of a total reality. The keyword is INTERPRE-
TATION. When positive, the degree is an exceptional capacity
for putting every part of an individual's heritage to work, and
when negative, witless distortion of values and twisted perspective in general events.

The formula is: manipulating-critical-original-specializing-social-inspired.
Examples are: sun, 75, 396; moon, 259, 446, 591; Mercury, 465, 479, 643;
Venus, 745; Mars, 323, 399, 720, 827; Jupiter, 21, 73, 258, 421, 632, 842;
Saturn, 751, 859, 908; Uranus, 165, 596.

LIBRA 9 *Three old masters hanging in an art gallery* This is a symbol of man's capacity for embracing a universal reality within his own personal experience. Here is representation of the fundamental faculties of self-expression as they may be established in effective alignment with each other, thereby furthering every pertinent aspect of human potentiality. Implicit is the concept of the past and the present as irrevocably in partnership, every individual's heritage providing him with a foundation for the achievement he desires. The keyword is ACCORD. When positive, the degree is a gift for bringing people and events together in high appreciation of the greater values of life, and when negative, idle worship of tradition and destructive self-contemplation.

The formula is: manipulating-critical-ingenious-specializing-social-responsible. Examples are: sun, 58, 367, 459, 488, 509, 524, 736; Mercury, 18, 93, 145, 473, 690; Venus, 335, 355, 458, 590, 985, 991; Mars, 172, 306, 639, 897; Jupiter, 372, 473, 904; Saturn, 166, 222.

LIBRA 10 *A canoe approaching safety through dangerous waters* This is a symbol of the necessary validation of all experience through an acceptance of risk, and of the refinement of personal skills through a direct contact with the recurrent exigencies of everyday living. Here the genius of the race is preserved by a fresh and constant participation in life's transient situations. There is always the goal through which man is led to develop his powers. The keyword is COMPETENCY. When positive, the degree is conscious and skilled resort to the course of action which leads most surely to success, and when negative, a primitive love of adventure and a wholly unintelligent faith in sheer good luck.

The formula is: manipulating-critical-ingenious-specializing-social-inspired. Examples are: sun, 303, 344; moon, 103, 281; Mercury, 105, 699, 762, 791; Venus, 104, 229, 294, 344, 556, 788; Mars, 499; Jupiter, 229, 337, 617; Saturn, 75, 300, 956; Uranus, 137, 194, 610, 872.

ARIES 11 *The president of the country* This is a symbol c
high ego on the impersonal side, evident in the complete an
naïve dedication of the individual to some part he chooses t
play among his fellows. Implicit here is the selection of suc
a role as will have a maximum breadth of recognition, so tha
the player may be established in a reality which he would b
quite unable to sustain by himself. There is a subordinatio
of all other considerations to one primary act of individu a
assurance. The keyword is IDEALIZATION. When positive, th
degree is the self-sacrifice required of anybody who would b
come the creative representative of eternal value, and whe
negative, an often well-meaning but usually destructive asse
tiveness or vain pretense.

The formula is: manipulating-critical-original-specializing-spiritual-exper
mental. Examples are: sun, 99, 370, 391, 927; moon, 358, 860, 940; Mercur
255, 773; Mars, 42, 214, 231, 874, 947; Jupiter, 54, 679, 681; Saturn, 111, 61
749, 802.

ARIES 12 *A flock of wild geese* This is a symbol of the irr
sistible aspiration and indomitable desire for freedom whic
represent the real core of personality, and which in everyda
affairs are often the sole manifestation of an individual's in
mortal potential. Here there are vagaries of immediate capri c
to the point of irresponsibility, but through them is the u a
deviating course characteristic of the migratory fowl and s
a promise of obligations to be met and ideals to be realize
The keyword is INSOUCIANCE. When positive, the degree is
completely naïve independence or an ever-immediate capaci
for rising above any given involvement in experience, an
when negative, thoughtless disinterest in anything of real val u
to the self.

The formula is: manipulating-critical-original-specializing-spiritual-sen
tive. Examples are: sun, 189, 807, 836, 956; moon, 223, 336, 900; Mercu a
379, 701, 866, 956; Venus, 26, 321, 761; Mars, 456, 625; Jupiter, 225, 74
Saturn, 695; Uranus, 312.

LIBRA 11 *A professor peering over his glasses* This is a symbol of high ego on the personal side, or of the naïve self-confidence by which an individual is enabled to continue the role of superiority he has elected to play among his fellows. Implicit here is the refinement of self in whatever particular phase of excellence will promise recognition for itself, and also the acceptance of the form in which it is manifest. There is a subordination of all other considerations to the immediate dramatization of responsibility. The keyword is SPECIALIZATION. When positive, the degree is a quiet mastery of events through a developed insight or depth of understanding, and when negative, a joy in depreciating others and compelling their subservience.

The formula is: manipulating-critical-ingenious-specializing-spiritual-experimental. Examples are: sun, 180, 441, 684; Mercury, 582, 708; Venus, 459, 495, 725, 811; Mars, 171, 304, 483, 687; Jupiter, 327, 799; Saturn, 4, 352, 658, 707; Uranus, 42, 533, 961.

LIBRA 12 *Miners emerging from a mine* This is a symbol of the irresistible curiosity and indomitable self-confidence which represent the real strength of personality, and which in everyday affairs are sometimes the sole manifestation of an individual's broader potentials. There is here all his transient involvement in hampering and unattractive phases of experience, but there is also a persistent doggedness of effort which has its ultimate fruits in a better world and in happier relationships among men. The keyword is ESCAPE. When positive, the degree is inexhaustible resources of self with a consequent uncompromising strength of character, and when negative, complete inability to develop personal potentials or rise above dull nonentity.

The formula is: manipulating-critical-ingenious-specializing-spiritual-sensitive. Examples are: sun, 284, 936; moon, 140, 156, 201, 577, 755, 956; Mercury, 454, 803; Venus, 95, 97, 394, 490, 881; Mars, 418, 778; Jupiter, 436, 606, 959; Saturn, 129, 179, 426, 454, 590, 874; Uranus, 222, 349, 882.

ARIES 13 *An unsuccessful bomb explosion* This is a symbol of the survival of good through evil intention and effort, and of the infinite capacity of the world to absorb and nullify the destructive acts of man. Implicit in the reversed symbolism is not so much the fruitlessness of ill deed as the need for a better instrumentation of the action springing from the deeper sources in selfhood. There is here an almost complete exemption from the normal penalties for unsocial results of a hapless initiative. The keyword is IMPETUOUSNESS. When positive, the degree is a dramatic rejection of any accomplishment falling at all short of very deep or hallowed purpose, and when negative, a waste of opportunity and a futile expenditure of self through vanity or petulance.

The formula is: manipulating-critical-original-specializing-spiritual-receptive. Examples are: sun, 157, 205, 293, 366; moon, 301; Mercury, 345; Venus, 283; Mars, 460, 902, 942; Jupiter, 857, 931; Saturn, 286, 576; Uranus, 81, 958.

ARIES 14 *A serpent coiling near a man and a woman* This is a symbol of the threefold nature of man, in its aspect of a high competency on the subjective side. There are here the emotional and rational elements of selfhood as they achieve their unity through the creative ordering of a universal wisdom. Implicit in the phallic significance is a fullness of being following on the everyday satisfaction of ordinary human appetites, but only as these are made a manifestation of a higher appreciation and a greater self-dedication. The keyword is REVELATION. When positive, the degree is exceptional self-discipline in the continual acquisition of a very real understanding, and when negative, a surrender to lower or transient impulses in every area of personal experience.

The formula is: manipulating-critical-original-specializing-spiritual-responsible. Examples are: sun, 154, 695, 999; moon, 496, 884, 887, 890; Mercury, 75, 790; Venus, 114, 203, 244, 600; Mars, 974; Jupiter, 978; Saturn, 531, 835; Uranus, 150, 523.

LIBRA 13 *Children blowing soap bubbles* This is a symbol of man's reassurance through the presence of the beautiful and the good in every least promising form of human relationship. People are disposed kindly toward their fellows, but there is no growth in the mere rhythm of everyday routine, and human individuality knows it must be up and at the business of self-hood whether constructively or otherwise. Implicit in the symbolism is the challenge to rise above childish things while yet clinging to childlike ways. The keyword is ENCHANTMENT. When positive, the degree is a consistent simplicity of character which enables anyone to maintain his touch with a transcendental magic of being, and when negative, a constant and idle daydreaming.

The formula is: manipulating-critical-ingenious-specializing-spiritual-receptive. Examples are: sun, 377, 504, 977; moon, 50, 694, 937, 982; Mercury, 958; Venus, 430, 606, 644; Mars, 272, 608, 926; Saturn, 399, 613, 758, 852; Uranus 176, 397, 504, 818, 854.

LIBRA 14 *A noon siesta* This is a symbol of man's basic competency, dramatized on the objective side as he is able to organize his responsibilities and withdraw his attention for a moment of inner reorientation. Implicit in the symbolism is a fullness of being through the everyday satisfactions which come as a reward of effort, or through a realization that it is possible to participate with profit in the common business of living. Here a subconscious fellowship with the eternal has its fruits in a freedom from unnecessary involvement in ephemeral affairs. The keyword is RECUPERATION. When positive, the degree is an incisiveness of thought or reaction and an effective directness of act, and when negative, a fundamental and self-defeating disinterest in life.

The formula is: manipulating-critical-ingenious-specializing-spiritual-responsible. Examples are: sun, 542, 585, 587, 958; moon, 10, 895; Venus, 371, 435, 476; Mars, 718, 788; Jupiter, 14, 29, 87, 130, 280, 559, 869; Saturn, 211; Uranus, 74, 336, 393, 934.

ARIES 15　*An Indian weaving a blanket*　This is a symbol of personal fulfillment through a simple excellence of self-expression, and it presents the basic skills of being as a means for bringing all desired things to center in a true self-possession. The ego is stabilized through the individual's gift for preserving or enhancing some one of the arts or values which comprise the culture in which he finds himself. The business of life becomes a meeting of human needs as a means of enduring self-gratification. The keyword is DILIGENCE. When positive, the degree is the quiet persistence of each proper act of self in the interest of its own genius, and when negative, an acceptance of the dull routine of everyday as a species of transient security.

The formula is: manipulating-critical-original-specializing-spiritual-inspired. Examples are: sun, 41; moon, 239, 553, 899; Mars, 428, 457, 557, 566; Jupiter, 232, 307, 625, 675; Saturn, 156, 182, 218, 335, 846, 985, 991; Uranus, 644.

ARIES 16　*Brownies dancing in the setting sun*　This is a symbol of the essentially friendly relationships which exist between man as a person and the totally impersonal forces of nature. The cosmic integrity demands a continual reversion to pure source in the case of each segment of reality, and the universal activity provides a continual sorting and sifting of all things into convenience and order. Implicit here is the dance of life as an unending rehearsal and exhibition of every special capacity of selfhood. The keyword is INVIGORATION. When positive, the degree is simple good fortune together with unlimited opportunity as the direct fruitage of effort, and when negative, delusions of adequacy with a complete inability to act in real self-interest.

The formula is: manipulating-critical-original-generalizing-physical-experimental. Examples are: sun, 252, 569, 871, 884, 906; moon, 14, 80, 115, 417, 590, 568, 914; Mercury, 376, 562, 639; Venus, 27, 545, 862; Mars, 107; Jupiter, 56, 216, 352, 389, 663, 750, 945; Saturn, 428, 869.

LIBRA 15 *Circular paths* This is a symbol of subjective fulfillment through a thoroughness of participation in experience, here dramatized by every individual's gift for remaining true to himself at center. There are interminable repetitions in the events of personal life, but the consciousness ever holds to its orbit and the realization must remain constant. Man and his world may seem completely at variance with each other at some point of crisis, but inevitably everything falls into place. The keyword is CONGRUITY. When positive, the degree is a rather extraordinary facility in self-adjustment or practical reorientation, and when negative, a tendency to think in circles and to lose all perspective in inconsequentialities.

The formula is: manipulating-critical-ingenious-specializing-spiritual-inspired. Examples are: sun, 518; moon, 271, 689; Mercury, 296, 549; Mars, 132, 528; Jupiter, 738; Saturn, 58, 881; Uranus, 57, 427, 554, 651, 670.

LIBRA 16 *A boat landing washed away* This is a symbol of the superficially unfriendly relations which exist between man as a person and the totally impersonal forces of nature. The reversed symbolism emphasizes the cosmic integrity as a continual attempt on the part of its over-all ordering to restore each phase of reality to pristine conditions. Here is not so much a thwarting of human effort as a stimulation to new accomplishment, and a freedom from whatever has exceeded its usefulness. Implicit here is a challenge to pure individuality. The keyword is RESPITE. When positive, the degree is a joy in bringing every self-competence to the recurrent emergencies of life, and when negative, frustration as an excuse for inaction.

The formula is: manipulating-critical-ingenious-generalizing-physical-experimental. Examples are: sun, 296, 478, 502, 741, 764, 792, 816, 944; moon, 941; Mercury, 131, 788; Venus, 165; Mars, 11, 393, 739; Jupiter, 38; Saturn, 282, 542, 925; Uranus, 92.

ARIES 17   *Two prim spinsters*   This is a symbol of what ultimately becomes an entirely private sustainment of reality, or
a characteristically personal creation of his world in its varying
aspects on the part of each participant in its events. There are
here the two sides of self in an eternal pro and con, rejecting
all outside judgments in the issues of everyday living and
rejoicing in a complete insulation from the passing rewards
as well as the unprofitable and self-diffusing superficialities of
normal relationships. The keyword is DIVORCEMENT. When positive, the degree is an utter fidelity to self and all its special
idealizations of its own capacities, and when negative, an increasing exaltation of shallow interests and a witless pretense
of distinction and great virtue.

*The formula is: manipulating-critical-original-generalizing-physical-sensi-
tive.* Examples are: sun, 324, 345, 480; moon, 110, 168, 784; Mercury, 48,
98, 134, 148, 366, 658, 856; Venus, 445; Jupiter, 243, 399, 514; Saturn, 73,
234, 327, 511, 559; Uranus, 374, 459, 808.

ARIES 18   *An empty hammock*   This is a symbol of self-
adequacy at its maximum potential for inner reorientation
and outer readjustment, and of an utter absoluteness of non-
compulsion on man as far as any essential conditioning or
self-irrevocability is concerned. Implicit in the symbol's static-
ism is the poise or balance of personal reality between the
extremes of pure impulse and act which in each man's given
case would limit the individual and deny his conscious existence. The keyword is RUMINATION. When positive, the degree
is a thoroughgoing integrity established by the inner reconciliation of outer inharmonies, and when negative, inability to
comprehend the conflicts of life and a consistent effort to
dodge them.

*The formula is: manipulating-critical-original-generalizing-physical-recep-
tive.* Examples are: sun, 197, 202, 287, 376, 572, 828, 898, 981; moon, 21,
391, 702, 729, 924, 999; Mercury, 151, 191, 566; Venus, 466, 484, 851, 965;
Mars, 933; Jupiter, 128, 289, 314, 535, 550, 671; Uranus, 43, 95, 500.

LIBRA 17 *A retired sea captain* This is a symbol of what ultimately must be an entirely personal enjoyment of reality, or an indomitable sustainment of man's world in the precise terms of his own special participation in its varying aspects. There is here a completeness of self-consummation through a gift for bringing all prior factors of realization to focus in the present moment. The self is secure because it has made its peace with every separate potentiality of its being. The keyword is RELAXATION. When positive, the degree is an utter fidelity to the lessons learned from experience and a consequent unshakeable poise in embarking on any new enterprise, and when negative, idle contemplation of past achievement.

The formula is: manipulating-critical-ingenious-generalizing-physical-sensitive. Examples are: sun, 18, 440, 498, 534, 631; moon, 865; Mercury, 95, 886; Venus, 195, 328, 500, 585, 619, 718, 816, 971; Mars, 91, 206, 355, 429, 709; Jupiter, 384, 595; Saturn, 5, 105, 172, 823; Uranus, 47, 173.

LIBRA 18 *Two men placed under arrest* This is a symbol of the maximum demand that may be made of any individual for self-consistency, and of the absoluteness of compulsions on human nature to provide a balance between inner and outer capacities. Implicit in the reversed symbolism is the importance of the self's responsibility to its own essential characteristics, not as a limitation arising from the role it plays in life but as the necessity that the potentials of value in any given situation be brought to some point of immediate and effective function. The keyword is CONSEQUENCE. When positive, the degree is a heightened challenge to every special talent, and when negative, total inappropriateness of impulse and act.

The formula is: manipulating-critical-ingenious-generalizing-physical-receptive. Examples are: sun, 549, 926; moon, 87, 728; Mercury, 58, 78, 821, 926, 967; Venus, 129; Mars, 705, 777; Jupiter, 435; Saturn, 16, 269, 302; Uranus, 279, 426, 509, 529, 555, 640, 740, 944.

ARIES 19   *The magic carpet*   This is a symbol of the periodic expansion of man's freedom of spirit and soul through his widely winging interest in potentialities far removed from his normal promise, dramatized here on the side of a vicarious or imaginative self-fulfillment. There is in consequence a revelation of the mind's infinite capacity for an overview of experience, or for a participation in the idealistic possibilities without any necessary self-involvement. Human affairs become personal only to the precise extent desired. The keyword is PANORAMA. When positive, the degree is full realization of the broad endowment which every man may make his own, and when negative, detachment from ordinary living and a scorn for its responsibilities.

The formula is: manipulating-critical-original-generalizing-physical-responsible. Examples are: sun, 13, 451, 867; moon, 39; Mercury, 115, 406; Venus, 460, 696; Mars, 621; Jupiter, 521, 969; Uranus, 902.

ARIES 20   *A young girl feeding birds in winter*   This is a symbol of man's self-assurance as regained by giving nourishment to forms of life other than his own. The social nature of the inner being is stressed here by a receptivity to experience which becomes the characteristic of youth and of femininity, and by a deep generosity of spirit which marks maturity and the more masculine aspiration which has its expression in the more barren periods of everyday being. The keyword is HOSPITALITY. When positive, the degree is a naïve genius in the administration of both the powers of nature and the potentialities of selfhood, and when negative, an overzealous and wasteful use of the self's resources in an effort to win approval by bread alone.

The formula is: manipulating-critical-original-generalizing-physical-inspired. Examples are: sun, 73, 570, 604, 730, 767; moon, 469; Mercury, 839; Venus, 54, 770, 831, 866; Mars, 634, 664; Jupiter, 102, 207, 370, 782, 864; Saturn, 71, 527.

LIBRA 19 *A gang of robbers in hiding* This is a symbol of the periodic exercise of man's freedom of spirit and soul in a complete if often unhappy deviation from his normal impulses or attitudes, dramatized here on the side of a practical or everyday self-fulfillment. Emphasis is on every person's disturbing capacity for antisocial or even self-perverted practices, or for self-involvement in potentials which may have imaginative but hardly intelligent sustainment in his consciousness. The reversed symbolism reveals his need for initiative, and for a more challenging perspective. The keyword is DIVERGENCE. When positive, the degree is alertness to every threat against a true individuality, and when negative, abnormal mistrust of everything worth while.

The formula is: manipulating-critical-ingenious-generalizing-physical-responsible. Examples are: sun, 804; moon, 36, 752, 824, 834; Mercury, 222, 459, 679; Venus, 296, 563, 668; Mars, 34, 106, 555, 651, 895; Jupiter, 50, 185, 277, 630, 989; Saturn, 762, 983; Uranus, 158, 339, 785, 970.

LIBRA 20 *A Jewish rabbi* This is a symbol of man's self-assurance as gained by bringing a deeper understanding to his fellows. The social nature of the inner being is stressed here by an interest in eternal values such as is characteristic of years and masculinity, and by a feminine receptivity of soul which has its expression in the warmer contacts of a ministration to everyday human needs. Here is the potential of high dedication by which an individual or a group may become a special channel for the aspirations of all. The keyword is HERITAGE. When positive, the degree is the extraordinary insight which comes to those who are able to stand on the shoulders of the giants who have gone before, and when negative, an unhealthy sense of self-superiority.

The formula is: manipulating-critical-ingenious-generalizing-physical-inspired. Examples are: sun, 618, 791; moon, 575; Mercury, 209, 411; Venus, 313; Mars, 552, 738; Jupiter, 720; Saturn, 570; Uranus, 191, 342, 462, 717.

ARIES 21   *A pugilist entering the ring*   This is a symbol of a complete lack of personal sensitiveness. There are here the raw elements of experience, primarily on the side of self-realization as man exhibits full confidence in his own powers and seeks the support of that audience the world will always provide for the spectacle when anyone is willing to risk his major fruits of achievement. Implicit in the symbolism is a need to be up and at the business of life. The keyword is EXERTION. When positive, the degree is a mobilization of the self's capacities in a concentrated attempt at self-establishment, and when negative, blind rebellion and a willingness to squander every resource on pseudo values.

The formula is: manipulating-critical-original-generalizing-social-experimental. Examples are: sun, 44, 297, 566; moon, 63, 350, 557, 631; Mercury, 333, 808, 891; Mars, 159, 999; Jupiter, 71, 124, 187, 278; Saturn, 51, 87, 652, 661; Uranus, 142, 150.

ARIES 22   *The gate to the garden of desire*   This is a symbol of man's uncompromising faith in the fact of his being, and of his naïve optimism as life opens up one or another of its opportunities before him. Here is self-fulfillment in the realization that there are always unlimited days ahead and that immeasurable frontiers are yet to be crossed. Personality forever reassures itself by an enhancement of its dreams and a strengthening of its deeper expectations. The keyword is PROSPECT. When positive, the degree is a high quickening to every possibility of individual discovery and experience, and when negative, a tendency to while away the years in contemplating the things which might be claimed for the self rather than making any real effort to gain them.

The formula is: manipulating-critical-original-generalizing-social-sensitive. Examples are: sun, 250, 460, 486; moon, 242, 433, 715, 847; Mercury, 124, 493, 496, 999; Venus, 301, 516, 695; Mars, 289, 982; Jupiter, 51, 284, 609, 954; Saturn, 343.

LIBRA 21 *A crowd upon the beach* This is a symbol of a complete lack of social sensitiveness. There are here the raw elements of experience, primarily on the side of a basic self-awareness and with man exhibiting the unconditioned friendliness through which he brings new facets of himself to a point of immediate expression. Implicit in the symbolism is a need to release the pyramiding tensions of personality whenever it is held too closely in rein, and to enjoy a wider self-realization through whatever fellowship may lie at hand. The keyword is EXHILARATION. When positive, the degree is naïve assurance and a basic delight in every possible aspect of human relationship, and when negative, a look to others for fulfillment without any willingness to give at all of self.

The formula is: manipulating-critical-ingenious-generalizing-social-experimental. Examples are: moon, 415, 771, 910; Mercury, 2, 613, 684; Venus, 162, 830; Mars, 110, 427; Jupiter, 290, 347, 360, 444, 911; Saturn, 144; Uranus, 282.

LIBRA 22 *A child giving birds a drink at a fountain* This is a symbol of man's uncompromising faith in the friendly relationships characterizing the world at large, or of his naïve optimism as he finds that he can take advantage of one or another of life's opportunities whenever he chooses to do so. Here is self-fulfillment in the discovery that there are always the fruits of everyday to justify the simple fact of selfhood, and that there are also the responsibilities which provide a consummation for the ideals and the inner nature. The keyword is SOLICITUDE. When positive, the degree is the creative concern for others by which any individual comes to experience his own immortality, and when negative, superficial effort for transient popularity.

The formula is: manipulating-critical-ingenious-generalizing-social-sensitive. Examples are: sun, 29, 172, 267, 640, 968; moon, 400: Mercury, 377, 977; Mars, 192, 278; Jupiter, 217, 222, 635, 638, 916; Saturn, 96; Uranus, 96, 631, 837, 974.

ARIES 23 *A woman in pastel colors carrying a heavy and valuable but veiled load* This is a symbol of the soul's basic anchorage in the privacy of its own functioning, and of the centering of real personality in the elements of its own particular genius. Implicit in the symbolism is the ultimate unimportance of purely superficial distinctions among various individuals, and the enduring worth of any experience for which the self accepts a complete responsibility. The keyword is RETICENCE. When positive, the degree is the unimpeachable integrity of the man whose fullness of life becomes a practical contribution to the circumstances in which he dwells, and when negative, a disinclination to participate at all fairly in everyday living.

The formula is: manipulating-critical-original-generalizing-social-receptive. Examples are: sun, 342, 545; moon, 166; Mercury, 66, 250, 461; Venus, 19, 836, 871; Mars, 559, 650, 853; Jupiter, 76, 250, 711; Saturn, 104, 241, 365, 496, 681; Uranus, 60, 594, 624.

ARIES 24 *An open window and a net curtain blowing into a cornucopia* This is a symbol of the mutual prodigality of man and his world whenever he retains his uninhibited enthusiasm and so welcomes every varying and recurrent opportunity opening up before him. There are here the continued outer manifestations of what at times may seem to be an unmerited good fortune, but they merely show the human and cosmic facets of reality in a convenient and joyful realization of each other. The keyword is MUNIFICENCE. When positive, the degree is an irrepressible genius for capturing the richer rewards of life and providing a wider distribution for the higher realities, and when negative, a smug and petty self-importance in dispensing favors to others.

The formula is: manipulating-critical-original-generalizing-social-responsible. Examples are: sun, 427, 470; Mercury, 65, 202, 572, 862, 981; Venus, 178, 225, 548; Mars, 662, 812, 824; Jupiter, 201, 245, 510, 932; Saturn, 632, 750, 945; Uranus, 911.

LIBRA 23   *Chanticleer*   This is a symbol of the soul's ultimate self-realization through a basic integrity of its own insights or judgments, and of the unchallenged acceptance it is able to gain for its particular role in human affairs. Implicit in the symbolism are the practical rewards which come from the more effectively dramatized distinctions of everyday living, and the enduring significance which the self achieves for itself through the place in life it succeeds in making its own. The keyword is FERVOR. When positive, the degree is a fearless self-affirmation which gains a sympathetic attention and wins immediate allegiance from the hearts and minds of everybody, and when negative, ill-starred conceit and ineffective bombast.

The formula is: manipulating-critical-ingenious-generalizing-social-receptive. Examples are: sun, 722, 788, 979; moon, 139, 248, 758; Mercury, 498; Venus, 45, 143, 692, 803, 993; Mars, 454; Jupiter, 52, 885; Saturn, 375, 796; Uranus, 260, 381, 530.

LIBRA 24   *A third wing on the left side of a butterfly*   This is a symbol of the illimitable potentiality of both man and his world, and of the practical fruits of his efforts whenever he retains his own unconditioned uniqueness of make-up and is alert to whatever opportunities arise in his particular milieu and permit his own special destiny to fulfill itself. There are here the fundamental affinities of all differentiation as these are able to make their particular contribution to human experience. The keyword is DISTINCTIVENESS. When positive, the degree is an idealistic originality and a high facility in quick analysis, and when negative, an interest in the worthless or an obsession with the improbable and ridiculous.

The formula is: manipulating-critical-ingenious-generalizing-social-responsible. Examples are: sun, 207, 740; moon, 345; Mercury, 629, 775, 843; Venus, 341, 724, 892; Mars, 529; Jupiter, 19, 206, 429, 512, 971; Saturn, 198, 485, 508, 546, 593, 665, 726, 776, 794, 990; Uranus, 446, 798.

ARIES 25 *A double promise* This is a symbol of man's stark resourcefulness on the side of everyday experience. For each potentiality that life may offer him there are alternatives of equal or supplementary value which he is able to recognize, and within himself there is always the symbolical as well as the literal pertinence of everything that comes to his attention. Here is unlimited capacity for seeing the world and self both inwardly and outwardly. The keyword is SENSIBILITY. When positive, the degree is a facility of adjustment by which everything in a given situation may be brought into the fullest co-operation with everything else, and when negative, compromising insincerity and a lean to chicanery in all human relationships.

The formula is: manipulating-critical-original-generalizing-social-inspired. Examples are: sun, 160, 203, 228, 255; moon, 219, 545, 726; Mercury, 729, 883; Venus, 202, 232, 280, 288, 569; Jupiter, 69, 133, 567, 873, 893, 917; Saturn, 857; Uranus, 657.

ARIES 26 *A man possessed of more gifts than he can hold* This is a symbol of exceptional personal endowment on the side of social capacity and of an individual's ever-potential value to his fellows, here marked by an abnormal spread of interest and a tendency to attempt all things. Implicit in the symbolism is the risk of frustration or even self-betrayal through an uncontrollable restlessness and exaggerated self-confidence, but there is also a prodigality of ambition and effort which can lead to a very genuine self-fulfillment. The keyword is EQUIPMENT. When positive, the degree is an uncompromising independence and an inexhaustible drive toward self-discovery, and when negative, an obsession by ideas of no practical worth.

The formula is: manipulating-critical-original-generalizing-spiritual-experimental. Examples are: sun, 76, 639; moon, 479, 493; Mercury, 396, 412, 462; Venus, 359, 891; Mars, 326, 468; Jupiter, 707, 1000; Uranus, 695.

LIBRA 25 *Information in the symbol of an autumn leaf* This is a symbol of man's stark resourcefulness on the side of imagination or inner experience. Human intelligence becomes a fundamental sensitiveness to the final ends that may be served, and to the efficient means that may be shaped for the welfare of self and others. There is here a capacity to see the world and the individual in continual interdependence, and to understand the mutual contribution to each other of all the varying aspects of life. The keyword is TACT. When positive, the degree is spontaneous adaptability and an unswerving and instinctive fidelity to ultimate goals and meanings, and when negative, fascination with the trivial and delight in unbridled fancy.

The formula is: manipulating-critical-ingenious-generalizing-social-inspired. Examples are: sun, 355, 476; moon, 91; Mercury, 45, 341, 912, 979; Venus, 109, 574; Mars, 387, 524, 795; Jupiter, 533; Saturn, 382, 449, 816; Uranus, 297, 376, 641, 896.

LIBRA 26 *An eagle and a large white dove turning one into the other* This is a symbol of exceptional personal endowment on the side of an individual capacity to meet each particular situation, here revealed in a creative or purposive approach to all aspects of human experience. Implicit in the symbolism is the self's responsibility for the general state of affairs in each immediate reality, and also the risk of very real frustration whenever the face of events cannot be shaped along more idealized lines. Man is the master of his fate to the extent his action is in his own true interest. The keyword is ADEPTNES:. When positive, the degree is unusually effective self-discipline, and when negative, unhappy vacillation between ultimate ideals and momentary desires.

The formula is: manipulating-critical-ingenious-generalizing-spiritual-experimental. Examples are: sun, 606, 820; moon, 647, 745; Mercury, 542, 889, 892; Venus, 223, 758; Mars, 579, 692; Jupiter, 387; Saturn, 89, 112, 935; Uranus, 12, 140, 345, 669, 690, 706, 836, 965.

ARIES 27 *Lost opportunity regained in the imagination* This is a symbol of the psychological maturity of man on the practical side of life, and of the all-important and creative fluidity of character which makes him an immortal being. Here is emphasis on experience as a means by which he may become the author of his own destiny rather than a pawn of purely superficial events, and on his capacity to re-establish himself in his own world by his own efforts whenever he desires a better foundation for whatever he may be set to accomplish. The keyword is REFORMULATION. When positive, the degree is the self's effective command of itself in any situation brought to immediate issue, and when negative, self-pity as a retreat from reality.

The formula is: manipulating-critical-original-generalizing-spiritual-sensitive. Examples are: sun, 191, 423, 463, 866; moon, 285, 620, 622, 818; Mercury, 569; Venus, 480, 578, 611, 759, 933; Mars, 403; Jupiter, 4, 162, 365, 545, 866, 986; Saturn, 56, 308; Uranus, 863.

ARIES 28 *A large disappointed audience* This is a symbol of the transiency of the rewards in a life taken too literally and narrowly in its more superficial terms. Implicit in the reversed symbolism is the disillusionment that comes when an individual learns that he cannot depend on the applause of his fellows, or make the momentary mood of the masses any proper guide for the values he should pursue. There is here the call to a selfhood which can rest secure in its own creative potentiality, catering to nothing exterior to itself. The keyword is DISJUNCTION. When positive, the degree is complete spiritual independence, and when negative, a destructive assimilation of the self to every defeat or frustration of human kind.

The formula is: manipulating-critical-original-generalizing-spiritual-receptive. Examples are: sun, 696, 872, 896; moon, 2, 27, 322, 926; Mercury, 847; Venus, 139, 291, 320, 333, 345, 496; Mars, 370, 668, 721; Jupiter, 109, 673; Saturn, 514, 550, 671, 711; Uranus, 218, 234, 869, 877.

LIBRA 27 *An airplane hovering overhead* This is a symbol of the psychological maturity of man on the ideal side of life, and of the imaginative resourcefulness of character which makes him an immortal being. Here is emphasis on experience as a means for achieving an over-all view of the world at large, and on the self-satisfaction which follows from seeing things in terms of their consequences and relationships. The individual finds himself the momentary epitome of every human potential. The keyword is REFLECTION. When positive, the degree is high effectiveness in self-adjustment or real skill in meeting the crises of life, and when negative, complete inability to get down into immediate realities.

The formula is: manipulating-critical-ingenious-generalizing-spiritual-sensitive. Examples are: sun, 699; Mercury, 166, 476, 618, 968; Venus, 603, 791; Mars, 46, 721; Jupiter, 211, 319, 584, 818; Saturn, 256, 297; Uranus, 672, 689, 723, 792.

LIBRA 28 *A man in the midst of brightening influences* This is a symbol of the enduring rewards of life whenever it is taken seriously in its own fundamental terms or accepted with a realization of the underlying friendliness of the world at large. Implicit in the intangible symbolization is an encouragement on which any individual may count, knowing that his unflagging courage in pressing forward on his pilgrimage from darkness to light is the best of all guarantees of his achievement. Circumstances here are seen as they dramatize his mood and confirm his potentiality. The keyword is RESPONSIVENESS. When positive, the degree is a complete spiritual fellowship with human kind, and when negative, self-stultification through wishful thinking.

The formula is: manipulating-critical-ingenious-generalizing-spiritual-receptive. Examples are: sun, 270, 346, 582, 605; moon, 634, 942; Mercury, 38, 207, 779; Venus, 912; Mars, 22, 279, 842, 860; Jupiter, 13, 336, 915; Saturn, 12, 140, 604, 867; Uranus, 136, 420, 583.

ARIES 29   *A celestial choir singing*   This is a symbol of man's
capacity to make himself an immortal instrument for the enduring visions and aspirations which have created and now
hallow the world in which he lives. There are overtones here
which transform every lesser aspect of experience, calling on
the individual to give a spiritual dramatization to his daily
living for himself and his fellows within every range of his
powers and skills. The keyword is VENERATION. When positive,
the degree is a gift for the effective articulation or manifestation of those eternal realities through which all people find
themselves at one, and when negative, self-deception and an
acceptance of every fantasy which will flatter the ego.

*The formula is: manipulating-critical-original-generalizing-spiritual-re-
sponsible.* Examples are: sun, 66, 245, 688; moon, 45, 298, 403; Mercury,
76, 248, 322; Venus, 224, 340, 810, 960; Mars, 937, 940; Jupiter, 308;
Saturn, 521, 535, 591, 674, 864, 969.

ARIES 30   *A duck pond and its brood*   This is a symbol of
the eternal fitness of things, provided the individual take the
fullest advantage of the cosmic ordering. Implicit in the symbolism is man's ability to establish his world of experience
according to his own needs, and to function effectively because
he has the acumen to align himself with his own genius and
to seek a personal satisfaction in a simple efficacy of being
himself. The keyword is RELIABILITY. When positive, the degree
is an accustomed competency or ease in dealing with immediate
circumstances, and when negative, a tendency toward provincialism or an acceptance of life with an altogether uncritical
complacency.

*The formula is: manipulating-critical-original-generalizing-spiritual-in-
spired.* Examples are: sun, 465, 651, 714, 729; moon, 261, 262; Mercury,
160, 224, 288, 486, 696; Venus, 96, 376, 408, 493, 828, 929; Mars, 236, 240,
410, 714, 872; Jupiter, 262, 490, 658; Uranus, 280, 527.

LIBRA 29 *Humanity seeking to bridge the span of knowledge* This is a symbol of man's capacity to make himself a very practical instrument for the accumulated experience or perfected wisdom which has built and now supports the world in which he lives. There is here a universal desire for achievement and realization, and this calls for the fullest dramatization of life's potential in every possible direction of effort. The faith of the individual in his own reasoning powers must have every chance to prove itself. The keyword is RATIONALITY. When positive, the degree is a gift for every inspiring or unusual contribution to human well-being, and when negative, an egotism which belittles or defeats even normal accomplishment.

The formula is: manipulating-critical-ingenious-generalizing-spiritual-responsible. Examples are: sun, 86, 454, 843; moon, 19; Mercury, 585, 676, 837; Venus, 152, 558, 629, 699; Mars, 332, 613; Jupiter, 74, 92, 137, 205, 344; Saturn, 186, 668; Uranus, 139, 781, 996.

LIBRA 30 *Three mounds of knowledge on a philosopher's head* This is a symbol of the eternal fitness of things, as it lies within man's power to comprehend this for his own special guidance. Implicit in the symbolism is a challenge to each individual to develop full and equal potentialities of skills, allegiances and ideals, and to recognize cosmic order through its manifestation in his own person and affairs. In this fashion he comes to know the world, and thereupon is able to anticipate the ways of its going. The keyword is PRESCIENCE. When positive, the degree is a perfected integrity of self and an exceptional gift for furthering all progress, and when negative, a fatuous pride in mere intellect.

The formula is: manipulating-critical-ingenious-generalizing-spiritual-inspired. Examples are: sun, 668; moon, 329, 662, 688, 730; Mercury, 295, 631; Mars, 47, 421, 564; Jupiter, 772; Saturn, 34, 400, 667, 812; Uranus, 7, 259.

TAURUS 1 *A clear mountain stream* This is a symbol of the individual spirit in its irrepressibility, and of the purity and excellence of its real sources of strength. Here man is freed from any necessity to meet the superficial limitations of life in any particular way or to conform to any pattern of events except as there is genuine contribution to an ultimate goal. The self possesses illimitable depths on which to draw in any special emergency, and holds to an over-all consistency in its self-expression. The keyword is RESOURCEFULNESS. When positive the degree is high achievement through an unswerving fidelity to some definite course of action, and when negative, a tendency to waste the potentialities of being by aimless self-ramifications.

The formula is: sustaining-ideal-efficient-specializing-physical-experimental. Examples are: sun, 138, 318, 462; moon, 25, 195, 902; Mercury, 745; Venus, 42, 326, 472, 682; Mars, 400, 475, 801; Jupiter, 10, 24, 380, 800; Saturn, 321, 406, 783; Uranus, 14, 652, 661.

TAURUS 2 *An electrical storm* This is a symbol of man's real power for making an effective impact on events, dramatized at each moment of issue and crisis by the completeness of his inward self-mobilization. There is here a catharsis of nature, mirroring the capacity of every individual for discharging the whole complex of strain in his affairs and so clearing the way for a more genuine progress ahead. Implicit in the symbolism is a terror in the loss of aplomb whenever human personality rises to a moment of union with the universal forces. The keyword is TRANSFORMATION. When positive, the degree is a genius for dramatizing both the values at hand and the potentials ahead, and when negative, unreasoning timidity in all self-expression.

The formula is: sustaining-ideal-efficient-specializing-physical-sensitive. Examples are: sun, 134; moon, 12, 120, 398, 749, 780; Mercury, 293, 774; Venus, 323, 489, 815; Mars, 90, 584; Jupiter, 75, 423, 481, 956; Saturn, 423, 731; Uranus, 674.

SCORPIO 1 *A sight-seeing bus* This is a symbol of the individual spirit in its catholicity, and of the naïveté and indomitability of its interest in life as a whole. Here man is freed
from all artificial boundaries of experience, and is encouraged
to reach out widely and profitably in sharing his realizations
with his fellows. There is an exceptional range of understanding and sympathy, and a gift for developing varying avenues
of self-expression. The keyword is FRIENDLINESS. When positive,
the degree is a basic impersonality which capitalizes on the opportunity of the moment and helps reorder the situation
whenever there is difficulty or dissatisfaction, and when negative, a genius for avoiding any and every actual expenditure
of self.

*The formula is: sustaining-ideal-universal-specializing-physical-experi-
mental.* Examples are: sun, 131, 899, 934, 941; moon, 735, 820; Mercury, 394,
414, 504, 739; Venus, 22, 215, 509, 582, 641; Mars, 174, 233, 779, 822; Jupiter,
166, 194, 645; Saturn, 170, 264, 445, 448, 622, 650, 914; Uranus, 401, 410,
561, 950.

SCORPIO 2 *A broken bottle and spilled perfume* This is a
symbol of man's real power in making his permanent impact
on others, dramatized at each moment of issue and crisis by a
completeness of the self's flow out and into every last ramification of the given experience. There is in the reversed symbolism an irrevocability of self-expression which marks every individual's divine determination to be significant at all costs.
The chrysalis of being is burst open in what may well be
tragedy for anything short of a supreme self-dedication. The
keyword is PERMEATION. When positive, the degree is persistence in creative effort and utter fidelity to the inner essence
of selfhood, and when negative, witless dissipation of every
resource of self and society.

The formula is: sustaining-ideal-universal-specializing-physical-sensitive.
Examples are: sun, 678, 718; moon, 265, 353, 976; Mercury, 736; Venus,
159, 907; Mars, 258, 686, 888; Jupiter, 397, 872, 913; Saturn, 164; Uranus,
214, 791, 824, 843.

TAURUS 3 *Steps up to a lawn blooming with clover*   This is a symbol of the indomitable outreaching of the human spirit on the side of a possible and profitable co-operation with the natural universe, and of man's intuition of divine reality as he entrenches himself in beauty and order. There is restraint in act as a contribution of self-realization, but yet a steady questing for all worth-while fruits of living. Here the upward vision is held completely in leash. The keyword is HOPEFULNESS. When positive, the degree is a creative optimism brought to embrace every facet of everyday striving, and when negative, an unwarranted self-indulgence and a disregard of all practical reality through a concern over the phantasmal and impossible.

The formula is: sustaining-ideal-efficient-specializing-physical-receptive. Examples are: sun, 265; moon, 254, 346, 430, 548; Mercury, 26, 761; Venus, 5, 974; Mars, 437, 770; Saturn, 344, 433, 815.

TAURUS 4 *The rainbow's pot of gold*   This is a symbol of the true incentives of an outer and physical world, and of the rewards which are guaranteed by an eternal covenant between the least of individuality and the universal matrix of life itself. There is always the promise of a treasure which at the end proves to be a gratifying complementation in physical tokens of whatever spirituality the self has brought into manifestation through its own efforts. The keyword is FAITH. When positive, the degree is an inner assurance which enables man to hold steady in every course of his choosing, and when negative, a loss of all opportunity through futile expectation and an unintelligent wandering off in the quests of pure fancy.

The formula is: sustaining-ideal-efficient-specializing-physical-responsible. Examples are: sun, 144, 288, 648; moon, 236, 437, 516, 703; Mercury, 27; Venus, 85, 117, 150, 248, 471, 536, 656, 847; Jupiter, 121, 769; Saturn, 116, 484, 533, 753, 763, 943; Uranus, 344.

SCORPIO 3 *A house-raising* This is a symbol of the indomitable outreaching of the human spirit on the side of simple co-operations in everyday living, and of the individual's realization of his own inherent divinity as he seeks his fulfillment through his fellows. There is a joy in common enterprise which strengthens his efforts for personal gain, and also a sense of well-being in the sure dependence he may place on family and neighbors whenever an emergency arises. The keyword is HELP-FULNESS. When positive, the degree is an exceptional power of accomplishment through a consistent success in winning the good will and enlisting the services of others, and when negative, a complete inability to fit into any pattern of shared relationships.

The formula is: sustaining-ideal-universal-specializing-physical-receptive.
Examples are: sun, 158, 220, 775; moon, 15, 57, 856; Mercury, 518, 546, 505, 806, 930; Venus, 130, 173, 432; Mars, 844; Jupiter, 159, 578, 854, 961; Saturn, 70, 161, 532, 637, 910; Uranus, 69, 133, 314, 782, 879, 917.

SCORPIO 4 *A youth holding a lighted candle* This is a symbol of a true contact with inner and transcendental realms of reality, and of the rewards to the spirit which come from a realization of the continuing ties between the least of individuality and universal life as such. There are always evidences of higher meaning and immortal value in each moment's detail of everyday living, and there is an enthusiasm which arises from an ever-clear vision to bring every possible sustainment to man in his outer and practical world. The keyword is RELI-ANCE. When positive, the degree is an unquenchable and irresistible confidence in the goodness and integrity of all things, and when negative, a simple-minded impracticality if not a very unhealthy self-obsession.

The formula is: sustaining-ideal-universal-specializing-physical-responsible.
Examples are: sun, 806; moon, 275, 434; Mercury, 270, 367, 509; Venus, 49, 270, 647, 686; Mars, 330; Jupiter, 544, 676, 862; Saturn, 853, 919; Uranus, 714, 932, 966.

TAURUS 5 *A widow at an open grave* This is a symbol of the impermanence of physical things whenever man permits reality to come to center in the static representation, and thus neglects the creative contribution through which he has responsibility for the larger whole. Implicit in the reversed symbolism is the need for an inner and constant return to every enduring value achieved by the self, and for a complete and immediate release from all outworn elements of experience. The keyword is REORIENTATION. When positive, the degree is man's genius for personal aplomb or an effective transcendence of disappointment and delay in an ever-spiraling self-discovery, and when negative, surrender to frustration or descent to ineptitude.

The formula is: sustaining-ideal-efficient-specializing-physical-inspired. Examples are: sun, 30, 643, 761; moon, 11, 181, 307, 341, 564; Mercury, 30, 287, 385, 578, 767, 898; Venus, 99, 125, 142, 243, 913; Mars, 776, 848; Jupiter, 90, 300; Saturn, 213, 360, 797; Uranus, 94, 360, 518, 636, 648.

TAURUS 6 *A bridge being built across a gorge* This is a symbol of the conquest of natural difficulties by conscious means, and of any individual's essential independence of nature's accidents or inconveniences. There are always ways in which physical limitations may be transformed into personal or social assets, thus contributing a dependability on the outer side to a consistency on the inner and so giving every possibility of continuance and intelligence to human experience. The keyword is CHANNELSHIP. When positive, the degree is the directness and the practical instinct by which personality achieves ultimate benefit of its powers, and when negative, a love of short cuts and every possible escape from the obligations of daily living.

The formula is: sustaining-ideal-efficient-specializing-social-experimental. Examples are: sun, 655, 949; moon, 96, 1000; Mercury, 268, 291, 324, 557, 632, 688, 939; Venus, 14, 573, 625, 728; Mars, 863; Jupiter, 304, 434, 795; Saturn, 957.

SCORPIO 5 *A massive, rocky shore* This is a symbol of the dependability of the physical universe whenever man holds the center of reality within himself and uses the static constituents in nature as a sustainment for his essentially dynamic being. Implicit in the symbolism is the need for a direct and continual attention to the over-all interests of the self at every point in life. Here is an exaltation of pure experience in its eternal and universal lineaments. The keyword is STABILIZATION. When positive, the degree is a poised spirit and a firmness of personality which enable every individual to prepare himself and his fellows for any possible contingency, and when negative, blind stubbornness or unreasoning conservatism.

The formula is: sustaining-ideal-universal-specializing-physical-inspired.
Examples are: sun, 503; moon, 121, 191, 790, 918, 963; Mercury, 440, 441, 478; Venus, 36; Mars, 111, 435; Jupiter, 42, 151, 801; Saturn, 430; Uranus, 133, 284, 287, 609, 767, 898.

SCORPIO 6 *A gold rush* This is a symbol of the exploitation of natural resources through personal initiative or intelligence, and of every individual's essential independence of the commonplace limitations or superficial inadequacies of life. There are always high rewards awaiting any genuine enterprise, and as man dramatizes the opportunities of the world at large he is able to improve his own immediate condition in all possible directions. Human skills are forever challenged to their own good fortune. The keyword is AMBITION. When positive, the degree is instinctive self-dedication to the unseen potentials of everyday existence, and when negative, a lack of practical discrimination and an irresistible desire for easy money.

The formula is: sustaining-ideal-universal-specializing-social-experimental.
Examples are: sun, 646; moon, 530, 652, 909; Mercury, 86, 703, 737, 920; Venus, 38, 383; Mars, 471, 517, 816; Jupiter, 134, 176, 454; Saturn, 261, 476, 475; Uranus, 207, 412, 516, 728, 893.

TAURUS 7   *A woman of Samaria*   This is a symbol of the unimpeachable divinity which characterizes man's nature at root,
represented here by his instinct for higher things as he yet
plumbs all experience to the depths and welcomes life almost
indiscriminately into the uttermost inner reaches of his being.
Implicit in the reversed symbolism of this famous amoral
figure of Biblical times is an indomitability of striving for
real and gratifying self-fulfillments. The keyword is AWAKEN-
ING. When positive, the degree is absolute and wholly impersonal self-giving in the hope of an honest self-realization
and when negative, a debasing and carefree dissoluteness accepted in compensation for the unattained and more enduring
satisfactions.

The formula is: sustaining-ideal-efficient-specializing-social-sensitive. Examples are: sun, 406, 636; moon, 35, 388, 815, 958; Mercury, 197, 460, 896;
Venus, 96, 228, 379, 711, 793; Mars, 250, 852, 865; Saturn, 68, 507, 648, 716,
805, 948; Uranus, 396, 712.

TAURUS 8   *A sleigh without snow*   This is a symbol of the
magic which man always may summon to his assistance in facing the problems of everyday living. Implicit in the static
stress of the symbolism is a needless acceptance of the contingent relationships by which the defeats of life are facilitated.
Snow is only necessary for this vehicle under the most unimaginative circumstances, since nature is ever prodigal in her
means for supporting reality. The keyword is SUSTAINMENT.
When positive, the degree is a complete and effective alignment of self with whatever greater possibilities may remain
unrealized in a given milieu, and when negative, a cheerful
tolerance of today's frustrations in the vague hope of a better
tomorrow.

The formula is: sustaining-ideal-efficient-specializing-social-receptive. Ex-
amples are: sun, 856, 962; moon, 176; Mercury, 245; Venus, 240, 586, 797;
Mars, 489, 950; Jupiter, 25, 197, 379, 701, 773, 797; Saturn, 331, 636;
Uranus, 63, 358, 572.

SCORPIO 7 *Deep-sea divers* This is a symbol of the absolute integrity of man's nature at root, dramatized here by his insatiable determination to plumb all experience to the depths and to uncover the illimitable reaches of potentiality in his world of everyday relationships. Implicit in the symbolism is a challenge to self-refinement through a subjection of the skills of self to every possible test or opportunity for a further perfection. Self-fulfillment is through an ever-increasing interest in day-by-day problems. The keyword is INVOLVEMENT. When positive, the degree is a persistent penetration to the very vital core of human motive and make-up, and when negative, fundamentally unsocial instincts and a resort to wholly absurd escapism.

The formula is: sustaining-ideal-universal-specializing-social-sensitive. Examples are: sun, 394, 920; moon, 380, 731; Mercury, 195, 458; Venus, 346, 843, 875; Mars, 97, 122, 893; Saturn, 123, 340, 810; Uranus, 88, 128, 163, 422, 469, 765, 873, 976.

SCORPIO 8 *The moon shining across a lake* This is a symbol of the magic on which man always may call in facing any problems of inner or psychological adjustment. Implicit in the static symbolism is a fellowship of feeling which leads to all romance and which enables human hearts to gain their moments of release from the outer compulsions upon them and thus achieve their inner and more enduring orientation. Natural events here tend to shape themselves to meet the individual's real yearning for a deeper experince. The keyword is RAPPORT. When positive, the degree is an absolute and usually unsuspected mastery over the forces and exigencies of life and nature, and when negative, witless joy in the sheer vagaries of imagination.

The formula is: sustaining-ideal-universal-specializing-social-receptive. Examples are: sun, 128, 613, 629, 779, 951; moon, 327, 667, 825; Mercury, 267, 646; Venus, 352, 565, 703, 812, 823, 941, 998; Mars, 211, 348, 358, 371, 510, 585; Jupiter, 560, 613; Saturn, 183; Uranus, 129, 405, 590.

TAURUS 9 *A Christmas tree decorated* This is a symbol of a self-renewal through a sharing with others, or a remaking of ties and a regathering of visions through the recurrent birth of a world spirit. Here individual reciprocity is given added dimensions as both a practical fact and an idealistic pattern or ritualization. Possessions are enhanced as they are exhibited, and as the enjoyment becomes increasingly vicarious and spiritual. The keyword is SYMBOLIZATION. When positive, the degree is man's achievement of complete self-satisfaction through a simple sharing of his potentials with his fellows, and when negative, a desire to place people under obligation and to enjoy life's riches without payment in kind.

The formula is: sustaining-ideal-efficient-specializing-social-responsible. Examples are: sun, 20, 117, 379, 444, 461, 468; moon, 968; Mercury, 452, 604, 867, 933; Venus, 461, 632; Mars, 76, 276, 401, 682; Jupiter, 790; Saturn, 441, 940; Uranus, 46, 388, 894.

TAURUS 10 *A Red Cross nurse* This is a symbol of human service on the ideal or spiritual side and it emphasizes the greatest of all roads to self-realization. The steadiness of concern for the more extreme needs of others is dramatization of the most consistent opportunity for self to become momentarily a phase of all-self, and through that universal experience to become more satisfactorily whatever it wishes to be on its own account. The keyword is ENLISTMENT. When positive, the degree is a complete dedication of the self to the worth-while and enduring projects through which it can lose all sense of separativeness, and when negative, a superficial pretense of humanitarianism in order to gain transient importance.

The formula is: sustaining-ideal-efficient-specializing-social-inspired. Examples are: sun, 236, 511; moon, 785; Mercury, 297; Venus, 148, 311, 382, 468, 511, 790; Mars, 735, 793; Jupiter, 688, 892; Uranus, 77.

SCORPIO 9 *Dental work* This is a symbol of self-renewal through a continuous and conscientious attention to the needs of the being on all planes of effort, and of that stewardship of an inner and divine spark through which individuality sustains its spiritual citizenship in the symbolical community of its kind. Here are high personal rewards for every proper concern over one's own potentialities and possessions. Man fulfills his highest mission as he dramatizes himself and his excellencies for his fellows. The keyword is PRACTICALITY. When positive, the degree is a creative ingenuity brought to a real service for others, and when negative, a thoughtless acceptance of life's makeshifts and an unhealthy admiration for artificiality.

The formula is: sustaining-ideal-universal-specializing-social-responsible. Examples are: sun, 546, 970; moon, 173, 551, 646; Mercury, 172, 587, 816, 924; Venus, 222, 944, 966; Mars, 267, 586, 814; Jupiter, 302, 730, 883; Saturn, 907; Uranus, 352, 379, 758, 790.

SCORPIO 10 *A fellowship supper* This is a symbol of human service on the practical side of everyday reality, and of the need of man for the company of his fellows in every phase of outer existence. Here the emphasis is on the physical and bodily essentials of life as the simplest possible factors in any social intercourse. What all men understand best in their own terms is what each may make the convenient basis for his appreciation of the others in his recurrent relations with them. The keyword is FRATERNITY. When positive, the degree is an effective channeling of personal aspirations into the commonplace grooves of a shared experience, and when negative, a surrender of individual distinction and exaltation of naïve animality.

The formula is: sustaining-ideal-universal-specializing-social-inspired. Examples are: sun, 610; moon, 255; Mercury, 593, 941; Venus, 564; Mars, 294, 775; Jupiter, 504, 674; Saturn, 955; Uranus, 58, 75, 172, 542, 579, 777, 956.

TAURUS 11   *A woman sprinkling flowers*   This is a symbol of the soul's determination to give constant and tangible manifestation of its creative powers, and of its eagerness to pour itself into every potentiality of living. There is here an easy and rewarding partnership between man and nature, so that a natural profusion tends to match his inner generosity of spirit. He feels responsible for the welfare of his world, and its rewards for his interest are very great. The keyword is CARE. When positive, the degree is the high stewardship by which man builds everything around him into an enduring organism for his own fulfillment, and when negative, superficial satisfactions and a wasteful truckling to petty concerns.

The formula is: sustaining-ideal-efficient-specializing-spiritual-experimental. Examples are: sun, 218, 790; moon, 216, 654; Mercury, 730, 831; Venus, 32, 356, 655; Mars, 342, 577; Jupiter, 165, 596, 871; Uranus, 964

TAURUS 12   *Window-shoppers*   This is a symbol of human imagination as the real corrective for man's experience, enabling each individual to know in advance whether the choices he will make are in line with his desires. Implicit in the passive symbolism is the continual demand that action follow each tentative examination of life's possibilities, and that some latent phase of self-awareness be quickened in consciousness as a result. The keyword is VISUALIZATION. When positive, the degree is high ability in presenting the immediate potentialities of human achievement and the consequent self-realizations, and when negative, self-depreciation and a dismissal of all really desirable things as beyond actual acquisition.

The formula is: sustaining-ideal-efficient-specializing-spiritual-sensitive. Examples are: sun, 151, 847, 848; moon, 440, 476, 502; Venus, 136, 451, 463, 688, 769, 896; Mars, 245, 480, 786; Jupiter, 350, 406, 460; Saturn, 94, 730; Uranus, 789.

SCORPIO 11 *A drowning man rescued* This is a symbol of the soul's personal immortality, and of its unabated eagerness in returning to the various phases of its experience again and again. There is here a consistent partnership between man and nature, so that the very accidents of circumstance can be counted on to serve him as long as he maintains his underlying enthusiasm of being. His consciousness has a continuity through his sense of responsibility for his own creative powers. The keyword is SAFETY. When positive, the degree is the inherent courage which constitutes a protection from the vicissitudes of life, and when negative, a tendency to hysteria on the least occasion and a lean on transient excitement for all self-realization.

The formula is: sustaining-ideal-universal-specializing-spiritual-experimental. Examples are: sun, 430, 571, 712; moon, 541, 691, 737; Mercury, 641, 944, 970; Mars, 465, 556; Jupiter, 138, 167, 211, 431, 646; Saturn, 525, 561; Uranus, 399, 658.

SCORPIO 12 *An embassy ball* This is a symbol of human imagination as the most effective corrective for man's allegiances, and of the social dramatizations which enable each person to know whether his over-all loyalties are bringing him the self-fulfillment to which he aspires. Implicit in the symbolism is an emphasis on the practical values of life, and on the political organization of society as either a consummation or exploitation of personal potentialities. Civilization exhibits the individuality as it frames itself in the general scheme. The keyword is DISPLAY. When positive, the degree is an absolute stability of self as a contribution to group integrity, and when negative, a smug demand for special privilege.

The formula is: sustaining-ideal-universal-specializing-spiritual-sensitive. Examples are: sun, 253; Mercury, 211, 540, 606; Venus, 354, 417; Mars, 253, 255, 495, 513, 605, 737, 881; Jupiter, 97, 881; Saturn, 36, 152, 171, 338, 458, 618, 737, 922; Uranus 832, 983.

TAURUS 13 *A man handling baggage* This is a symbol of the joy in effort put forth on the practical or everyday side of life, and of the adjustment by which the human individual is able to make his niche for himself in each available sphere of activity. Here is an extreme of dependence on the strength and resources of self, and an emphasis on the fact that there is no function in society which is not of equal importance with every other in fulfilling a person's need to be useful. The key word is INDUSTRY. When positive, the degree is an effective self-competence and virility of interest in normal living, and when negative, a dissipation of selfhood and a depreciation of all ambition through the performance of drudgery without protest.

The formula is: sustaining-ideal-efficient-specializing-spiritual-receptive
Examples are: sun, 48, 98, 232, 515; moon, 66, 155, 184, 186, 615; Mercury 636; Venus, 437, 990; Mars, 500; Jupiter, 642, 746, 817, 847, 868; Saturn 828, 876; Uranus, 80.

TAURUS 14 *Shellfish groping and children playing* This is a symbol of the self-sufficiency of existence on each separate level of being, thus preserving the lower orders and facilitating the progressive development of higher ones. Implicit in the symbolism is the connection between that life which is reaching out on a broad evolutionary scale, and that which comes to its immediate maturity through a genuine individuality. Here is an emphasis on self-discovery as the basic mode of greater reality. The keyword is EMERGENCE. When positive, the degree is the integrity of selfhood through its absoluteness of attention to its own business of continuing to be, and when negative, hopeless self-diffusion through unnecessary concern over divergent potentials of experience.

The formula is: sustaining-ideal-efficient-specializing-spiritual-responsible
Examples are: sun, 492, 654, 947; moon, 451, 816; Mercury, 301, 648, 915 Venus, 115, 685, 921; Mars, 149, 191, 565; Jupiter, 628, 660, 820, 870; Saturn 63, 126, 354, 992; Uranus, 600.

SCORPIO 13 *An inventor experimenting* This is a symbol of the joy in effort put forth on the imaginative or intellectual side of life, and of the creative achievement by which the human individual is able to make a special niche for himself in some particular sphere of activity. Here is a complete dependence on the ingenuity and resources of selfhood and an emphasis on the fact that there is no area of reality in which it is not possible to expand man's usefulness and to facilitate some unique contribution. The keyword is CLEVERNESS. When positive, the degree is a capacity for accomplishment beyond all normal expectation, and when negative, a superficial dawdling over things to be done and futile dreams of great genius.

The formula is: sustaining-ideal-universal-specializing-spiritual-receptive.
Examples are: sun, 563, 593, 802, 879; moon, 215, 677; Mercury, 170, 869; Venus, 650; Mars, 57, 178, 458, 506; Jupiter, 248, 934; Saturn, 577, 757, 982; Uranus, 776.

SCORPIO 14 *Telephone linemen at work* This is a symbol of the interconnection which links all phases of existence with all others, and of man's special genius for expanding the relationship between the most widely separated and distinctive aspects of experience. Implicit in the symbolism is a responsibility on the part of all higher life for all lower, and a faithfulness of all lesser things to the requirements of the greater. Here is emphasis on self-specialization as the root mode of all individual being. The keyword is ATTACHMENT. When positive, the degree is an effective penetration of human competence into each pertinent complex of everyday living, and when negative, unnecessary concern over the affairs of others.

The formula is: sustaining-ideal-universal-specializing-spiritual-responsible.
Examples are: sun, 38, 50, 328, 812; moon, 764; Mercury, 571; Mars, 394, 408, 430, 554; Jupiter, 783, 891; Saturn, 503; Uranus, 144, 389, 796.

TAURUS 15   *A man muffled up, with a rakish silk hat*   This is a symbol of absolute self-integrity at a simple extreme of self-consciousness, or of the human spirit in its inherent supremacy over all possible limitations or embarrassments. There is here a sure dramatization of self, or a continual and effective aware-ness of a role to be played in life. The individual is willing to utilize whatever arises in experience, but he refuses to accept any dictation from any least part of it. The keyword is SOPHIS-TICATION. When positive, the degree is a superb aplomb arising from the constant rediscovery of greater powers latent in self-hood, and when negative, marked insensibility to all deeper impulses and complete surrender to superficial self-interest.

The formula is: sustaining-ideal-efficient-specializing-spiritual-inspired. Ex-amples are: sun, 322, 333, 774; moon, 28, 485, 626; Mercury, 139; Venus, 197, 265; Mars, 155, 293, 859; Jupiter, 265, 373, 924; Saturn, 712; Uranus, 82, 323.

TAURUS 16   *An old man attempting vainly to reveal the Mys-teries*   This is a symbol of the need to share whatever may be the ultimate substance of selfhood, as here brought to a per-sonal realization on the intellectual side. Implicit in the nega-tive symbolism is an awakening to a transient inadequacy, and a stirring to the effort which of itself is a promise of fulfill-ment once the proper conditions have been established. There is revolt against an inertia which threatens the very core of selfhood. The keyword is PERTINACITY. When positive, the de-gree is the uncompromising integrity of higher vision and an unshakeable determination to dramatize it, and when nega-tive, a failure in accomplishment through a loss of touch with everyday practicality.

The formula is: sustaining-ideal-efficient-generalizing-physical-experi-mental. Examples are: sun, 359, 452, 591, 698, 808, 839, 919; moon, 143, 512, 683; Venus, 289, 439, 887, 940; Mars, 95, 228, 459, 526; Jupiter, 224, 295, 468, 886, 930, 940, 949; Saturn, 113, 357.

SCORPIO 15 *Children playing around five mounds of sand*
This is a symbol of absolute self-integrity at a simple extreme
of social consciousness, or of the human spirit in its nascent
competence for meeting all possible eventualities. There is
here a dramatization of the psychological faculties as a means
for contact with other people, and of the illimitable capacity
for experience in any situation where man may find himself.
The individual is able to deal with whatever may arise in the
circumstances of his being, and to commit himself to whatever proves to be worth while. The keyword is NAÏVETÉ. When
positive, the degree is a gift for a continual discovery of new
and effective facets of selfhood, and when negative, wholly
purposeless ineptitude.

The formula is: sustaining-ideal-universal-specializing-spiritual-inspired.
Examples are: sun, 237, 703, 908; moon, 51, 273, 928; Mercury, 29, 678;
Venus, 2, 25, 473, 646, 955, 968; Mars, 125, 180, 322, 547; Jupiter, 63, 433,
484, 731, 762, 894; Saturn, 325, 383, 526, 558, 647; Uranus, 198, 201, 567,
668, 794.

SCORPIO 16 *A girl's face breaking into a smile* This is a
symbol of the need to share any true essence of selfhood, as
here brought to an immediate actuality in everyday living. No
ultimate values can be cloistered forever in the depths of self,
and implicit in the symbolism is the gregarious nature of the
human soul as revealed in the naïve friendliness it shows for
all other creatures. Here is a magic of personality by which
any desired reality may be conjured into being. The keyword
is ACQUIESCENCE. When positive, the degree is man's ingratiating gift for employing the simple things of life for surmount-
ing any momentary obstacles to his self-fulfillment, and when
negative, self-betrayal through a lack of all discrimination.

*The formula is: sustaining-ideal-universal-generalizing-physical-experi-
mental.* Examples are: sun, 739; moon, 250, 311, 376, 399, 741, 988; Mercury, 158, 640; Venus, 3; Mars, 725; Jupiter, 224, 928; Saturn, 18, 154,
696, 880, 884; Uranus, 89, 112, 508, 650, 667, 812, 935.

TAURUS 17 *A battle between the swords and the torches* This is a symbol of the eternal struggle between the practical necessities or transient competitions of life on the one hand and the motives and meanings which give them direction and order on the other, as here emphasized on the world stage. Man survives and gains a genuine self-fulfillment as he aligns himself with the cause of enlightenment while yet respecting the manifestations of might. The keyword is RESOLUTION. When positive, the degree is high organizational skill and an ability to bring the magic of understanding to any specific difficulty, and when negative, a loss of self-competence through the conflicting compulsions of necessity and desire.

The formula is: sustaining-ideal-efficient-generalizing-physical-sensitive. Examples are: sun, 124, 357, 496, 759, 887, 891, 910; moon, 38, 226, 332, 408, 708, 925, 995; Mercury, 848, 919; Venus, 33, 385, 462, 485, 638, 981; Mars, 266, 462, 851, 891; Jupiter, 405, 507, 805, 957, 987; Saturn, 396, 499, 572; Uranus, 310.

TAURUS 18 *A woman holding a bag out of a window* This is a symbol of the soul's high ministry of service to every purpose and function of living, and of the individual's self-fulfillment as he furthers the over-all ends of men in general. There is here an exaltation of every commonplace activity. Life comes to its ultimate fruition as a community realization, with everyone increasingly aware of his fellows and ever seeking to encourage them in their daily routine. The keyword is FACILITATION. When positive, the degree is high personal effectiveness in commandeering the elements of experience for any particular purpose, and when negative, dissatisfaction with things as they are and complete ineptness in handling them.

The formula is: sustaining-ideal-efficient-generalizing-physical-receptive. Examples are: sun, 141; moon, 427, 783; Mercury, 136, 597, 797; Venus, 588, 727, 986; Jupiter, 832; Saturn, 46, 358, 894, 952; Uranus, 106, 110.

SCORPIO 17 *A woman the father of her own child* This is a symbol of the eternal conflict between the practical involvements and the ideal potentialities of human nature, as here emphasized in man's conscious individuality. The soul feels the weight of its transient responsibilities while the indwelling and immortal spirit is sensitive to its need for an enduring place in the scheme of things. The recurrent virgin birth of self is its reconciliation with its world through their common center of reality. The keyword is NUCLEATION. When positive, the degree is an illimitable self-potentiality with effective spiritual or ideal as well as practical or everyday orientations, and when negative, a characteristically anarchistic self-sufficiency.

The formula is: sustaining-ideal-universal-generalizing-physical-sensitive. Examples are: sun, 192, 196, 313, 540, 564, 830; moon, 188, 256; Mercury, 740, 879; Venus, 8, 94, 367, 640, 979; Mars, 395, 413, 768, 796; Jupiter, 502; Saturn, 45, 210, 341, 592, 912; Uranus, 264, 622, 709.

SCORPIO 18 *A woods rich in autumn coloring* This is a symbol of nature's high ministry of service to every function and purpose of individual living, and of the varying manifestations of a reality supported and brought to its genuine fruitage by the eternal and illimitable resources on every hand. There is here an exaltation of every ideal potentiality, dramatized in the form of inevitable and universal consummations of order and beauty. Life achieves its ultimate promise in a personal excellence, which may be found compounded a thousandfold. The keyword is FULFILLMENT. When positive, the degree is high success in every area of true self-interest, and when negative, a perverse delight in permitting worth-while things to go to seed.

The formula is: sustaining-ideal-universal-generalizing-physical-receptive. Examples are: sun, 223, 295, 650, 677, 964; moon, 62, 452; Mercury, 206, 430; Venus, 58, 736; Mars, 109, 145, 697; Jupiter, 779, 823, 852, 999; Saturn, 59, 193, 364, 966; Uranus, 70, 164, 532, 582, 637, 699, 853, 910.

TAURUS 19 *A newly formed continent* This is a symbol of
the raw substance of existence, and it suggests that experience
may shape its own ground in full conformity with its desires.
Inherent in the symbolism is an awareness of the constant reworking of all reality through the course of successive over-
all cycles, and it dramatizes the fact that man re-establishes
himself continuously within the lineaments of each new realization of his powers and of the opportunities of his world. The
keyword is ORIGINALITY. When positive, the degree is a revolutionary potentiality by which each individual is enabled to
remodel the entire face of the universe, and when negative, a
genius for futile turmoil and persistent upset.

The formula is: sustaining-ideal-efficient-generalizing-physical-responsible.
Examples are: sun, 27, 65, 70, 363, 536, 909; moon, 202, 876; Mercury, 382,
444, 511, 910; Venus, 53, 191, 325; Mars, 927; Jupiter, 68, 569, 716, 890,
948; Saturn, 801.

TAURUS 20 *Wind clouds and haste* This is a symbol of the
transiency which characterizes life for the average individual,
and of the instability which results from the disinclination of
most people to give very much of themselves to their experience. Implicit in the negative symbolism is the divine aplomb
of the ego, ever able to hold to its course through superficial
excitement. There is a real spiritual lightness here as an outer
mark of the soul's fundamental freedom. The keyword is EX-
ALTATION. When positive, the degree is efficiency in control-
ling events at any point of transition or crisis, and when negative, a diffusion of self and waste of energy in an attempt to
grasp the myriad facets of the unessential.

The formula is: sustaining-ideal-efficient-generalizing-physical-inspired.
Examples are: sun, 862; moon, 133, 157, 371; Mercury, 954; Venus, 179,
342, 412, 949; Mars, 232, 492; Saturn, 334, 482, 502, 626; Uranus, 639, 761,
899.

SCORPIO 19 *A parrot listening and then talking* This is a symbol of the raw substance of intelligence, and it suggests that conscious existence can be shaped according to any desired lineaments. Inherent in the symbolism is a sensitiveness to the continual reworking of reality on the ideal or imaginative side, and to the opportunity the individual may have for selecting or rejecting every essential element of his make-up. Man continually projects the image in which he creates himself. The keyword is CONVENTIONALITY. When positive, the degree is exceptional skill in bringing the whole tenor of transient circumstances to the service of a personal aspiration, and when negative, idle mimicry and self-gratifying pretense.

The formula is: sustaining-ideal-universal-generalizing-physical-responsible. Examples are: sun, 3, 732, 756; moon, 428, 531, 838; Mercury, 373, 429, 702, 720, 900, 914; Venus, 740; Mars, 118, 220, 367, 627, 670, 747; Jupiter, 46; Saturn, 464; Uranus, 475, 713, 819, 919.

SCORPIO 20 *A woman drawing two dark curtains aside* This is a symbol of the enduring values which the average individual visualizes behind the outer façade of everyday existence, and of his desire to penetrate to more worthy dimensions of experience. Implicit in the symbolism is the essential courage of the soul, and the vital concept of life as unrewarding except as it provides a way to cross every threshold of common limitation. Man's being is not his own unless he can gamble on its continuance. The keyword is DARING. When positive, the degree is the psychological indomitability with which the human spirit plunges ahead in every new adventure of accomplishment, and when negative, a personality debased by fatuous self-exhibition.

The formula is: sustaining-ideal-universal-generalizing-physical-inspired. Examples are: sun, 414, 603, 880, 930; moon, 26, 693, 944; Mercury, 503, 650, 881, 899, 901, 948; Venus, 384, 936, 948; Mars, 491, 804, 847; Jupiter, 636, 874, 925; Saturn, 85, 656, 697; Uranus, 132, 340, 810.

TAURUS 21   *A finger pointing in an open book*   This is a symbol of the rectification of experience on the side of ends and meanings, and of the fine discrimination of which man is capable. There is here a dramatization of the racial wisdom as this becomes incarnate in conscious individuality. Purpose and interest sharpen the attention, which in turn quickens the insight and permits an outreach into events which thereupon are ordered by the self's potentials. The keyword is CONFIRMA-TION. When positive, the degree is a sensitiveness to the enduring significance of each special complex in human affairs, and when negative, a loss of integrity through blind obedience to others and a tendency to do things by rote.

The formula is: sustaining-ideal-efficient-generalizing-social-experimental. Examples are: sun, 243, 268, 392, 532, 659; moon, 9, 187, 368, 488; Venus, 20, 415, 423, 635, 643, 927; Mars, 335, 991; Jupiter, 331, 367; Saturn, 66, 84, 538, 693; Uranus, 359, 453, 759.

TAURUS 22   *White dove over troubled waters*   This is a symbol of the clear direction or absolute orientation which comes to man from birth as a consequence of his indwelling spirit or divine heritage, whether or not there is any conscious co-operation with it on his part. Here willy-nilly is freedom of understanding, and the strength which the possession of a real mission or a genuine reason for being will give to any individual. There is also a wholly practical protection, to the precise extent it is accepted. The keyword is GUIDANCE. When positive, the degree is a skillful reconciliation of difficulties in the light of over-all potentials, and when negative, an ineffectiveness of mind through habitual woolgathering.

The formula is: sustaining-ideal-efficient-generalizing-social-sensitive. Examples are: sun, 597, 630; moon, 561, 842; Mercury, 141, 314, 357; Venus, 370; Mars, 87, 248, 299, 553, 612; Jupiter, 112; Saturn, 520; Uranus, 54, 225, 625, 755, 953, 980.

SCORPIO 21 *A soldier derelict in duty* This is a symbol of the necessary adjustments of life on the side of decisions and consequences, and of the penalties for man's lack of discrimination in any given set of circumstances. The reversed symbolism dramatizes the tragedy when obligations and desires come into conflict with each other, but suggests that the inherent divinity of the individual makes it ever impossible for him to continue in any course which does not prove rewarding. The keyword is DEVIATION. When positive, the degree is effective responsibility to the inner stirrings of self and a willingness to face the consequence of true self-assertion, and when negative, complete faithlessness to the common welfare.

The formula is: sustaining-ideal-universal-generalizing-social-experimental. Examples are: sun, 153, 869; moon, 92, 276, 317, 506, 546, 797; Mercury, 128, 712, 749; Venus, 533; Mars, 18; Jupiter, 505, 648, 732; Saturn, 714; Uranus, 577, 737.

SCORPIO 22 *Hunters starting out for ducks* This is a symbol of the simplicity of self-expression and the straightforward honesty of desire which men tend to exhibit from birth in nearly every realm of normal or everyday activity, and of the average individual's need for genuine psychological elbow-room in his dealing with the world about him. Here is freedom of action willy-nilly, as marked in the frequent determination of the human spirit to have this by one means if not by another. The keyword is ENTERPRISE. When positive, the degree is a complete lack of personal frustration and a constant refinement of special and practical skills in the approach to daily problems, and when negative, a callous exploitation of all life.

The formula is: sustaining-ideal-universal-generalizing-social-sensitive. Examples are: sun, 109, 211, 778; moon, 272, 330, 409, 423, 549, 903; Mercury, 718; Venus, 183, 706; Mars, 736; Jupiter, 16, 105, 179, 269, 358, 615; Saturn, 31, 585; Uranus, 45, 141, 341, 558, 982.

TAURUS 23 *A jewelry shop* This is a symbol of the practical values of everyday living, and of the personal display by which man may cherish the rewards of his effort and so seek to give them an effective durability. Implicit in the symbolism is the kaleidoscopic capacity of the world at large for producing and reproducing whatever an individual may require in the way of immediate realities with which to deal. Here is the luxury which mirrors any marked achievement in character or skills. The keyword is PRESERVATION. When positive, the degree is a happy gift for shaping all vision to larger dimensions and directing all aspiration to more than trivial ends, and when negative, a greediness which betrays the soul with trifles.

The formula is: sustaining-ideal-efficient-generalizing-social-receptive. Examples are: sun, 248, 831, 877; moon, 13, 369; Mercury, 83, 659; Venus, 174; 208, 465; Mars, 100, 614, 802, 818, 908; Jupiter, 89, 198, 586, 794, 935; Saturn, 333, 414, 522, 616; Uranus, 289, 370, 620.

TAURUS 24 *A mounted Indian with scalp locks* This is a symbol of pride in personal prowess, and it suggests an exceptional capacity for gaining and administering authority among men. There is here an appreciation of the potentials in nature herself, and of the senses as they can be brought to the full service of an individual's aspiration and ambition. The conquest of an enemy becomes not so much a momentary supremacy over him as an acquisition and subsequent use of his particular genius. The keyword is COMMAND. When positive, the degree is an unimpeachable control over life through a discipline of the self and its powers, and when negative, a ruthlessness or complete inhumanity in dealing with others.

The formula is: sustaining-ideal-efficient-generalizing-social-responsible. Examples are: sun, 224, 234, 797; moon, 862, 922, 967, 998; Mercury, 70, 117, 243, 515; Venus, 255, 391, 983; Mars, 985; Jupiter, 566, 709, 796, 819; Saturn, 39, 189; Uranus, 76, 245, 250, 418, 483, 528, 895.

SCORPIO 23   *A bunny metamorphosed into a fairy*   This is a symbol of the inner or creative values of everyday living, and of the personal or more dynamic meanings with which man may endow the least of the things around him. Implicit in the symbolism is the kaleidoscopic capacity of his imagination, or the extent to which he may mold and remold the everyday reality with which he deals. Here is poetry of soul as it mirrors each person's ongoing achievement in character and skills. The keyword is TRANSITION. When positive, the degree is the thorough self-conquest by which an individual subordinates his naïve and animal impulses to his ideals and aspirations, and when negative, undisciplined escapism and complete distortion of attitude.

The formula is: sustaining-ideal-universal-generalizing-social-receptive. Examples are: sun, 195, 491; moon, 267, 419, 674, 897; Mercury, 220, 346, 603, 668, 781, 998; Venus, 282, 926; Mars, 441, 603, 744, 849; Jupiter, 407; Saturn, 203, 263, 470, 702, 752, 900, 946, 959, 997; Uranus, 325, 383, 592, 647, 912.

SCORPIO 24   *Crowds coming down the mountain to listen to one man*   This is a symbol of recognition for intellectual attainment, and of the supremacy of spiritual over other and more tangible forms of authority among men. There is here an emphasis on the fact that any higher realization must be brought to earth both for its initial confirmation and its ultimate sharing among the many, and that aspiration is meaningless until it achieves some practical focus in those realms and events with which people in general are familiar. The keyword is APPEAL. When positive, the degree is an almost spectacular ability to enlist the higher potentialities of everyone for some practical need of the moment, and when negative, indiscriminate and carefree gullibility.

The formula is: sustaining-ideal-universal-generalizing-social-responsible. Examples are: sun, 132, 615, 641, 700, 737, 781; moon, 241, 868; Mercury, 82, 610, 814, 853; Venus, 18, 82, 436, 542, 592; Mars, 688, 819, 873, 918; Jupiter, 173, 212, 247, 438, 518; Saturn, 200, 494, 598, 807, 905; Uranus, 274.

TAURUS 25 *A large well-kept public park* This is a symbol of the everyday integrity of society at large, and of the community divisions of labor through which each person gains the resources for well-being and self-enjoyment which obviously he could never create for himself through his own isolated efforts. There is here an emphasis on the common experience of mankind as the setting for an individual's worth and achievement in their more characteristic lineaments, and for his consequent self-discovery and self-realization. The keyword is RECREATION. When positive, the degree is a high devotion to the practical welfare of all people collectively, and when negative, a complete surrender of personality to mass judgments and transient superficialities.

The formula is: sustaining-ideal-efficient-generalizing-social-inspired. Examples are: sun, 632, 745; moon, 197, 537; Venus, 160, 604, 867; Mars, 41, 96, 182, 354, 386, 643, 992; Jupiter, 667; Saturn, 267, 385, 605; Uranus, 122, 258, 421, 842, 968.

TAURUS 26 *A Spaniard serenading his senorita* This is a symbol of man's unlimited capacity for self-establishment and for finding everything he desires immediately at hand, as here given emphasis on the ideal side. Reality is seen as the product of every least element the individual contributes to its overall effectiveness, rather than as the end result of whatever he may discover and pre-empt for himself privately. A poetry of living and a music of desire become the final touchstones for a true self-fulfillment. The keyword is CONSTANCY. When positive, the degree is the continual reassurance by which the will of man coaxes the depths of his soul into his experience, and when negative, futile attempts to control life by empty blandishment.

The formula is: sustaining-ideal-efficient-generalizing-spiritual-experimental. Examples are: moon, 377, 974; Mercury, 23, 218, 655, 877; Venus, 218, 620; Mars, 17, 243, 658, 749, 984; Saturn, 388; Uranus, 769, 795.

SCORPIO 25 *An X ray* This is a symbol of man's organic integrity, or of the unvarying structures of nature on which all intelligence depends. There is here an emphasis on the well-being of each individual as a foundation for his self-realization in the world he shares with his fellows, and on his responsibility to keep himself fit for the performance of his part in the common functioning. He recognizes himself as the measure of all effective reality, and sees everything around him as a continual revelation or validation of his own capacity. The keyword is INVESTIGATION. When positive, the degree is an exceptional power of analysis, and when negative, uncritical over-sensitiveness to both the condition of self and the state of society.

The formula is: sustaining-ideal-universal-generalizing-social-inspired. Examples are: sun, 49, 249, 458, 533, 924; moon, 44, 70, 383; Mercury, 192, 660, 692, 812, 934; Venus, 879; Mars, 197, 298; Jupiter, 424; Saturn, 208, 273, 305, 316, 318, 704; Uranus, 464, 702, 900.

SCORPIO 26 *Indians making camp* This is a symbol of man's inexhaustible capacity for self-establishment and for finding everything he needs immediately at hand, as here given emphasis on the practical side. Reality is the result of each individual's choices and rejections in his everyday dealings with the world at large, and the wide range of possible experience provides him with every facility he may need for the moment. His alertness to the potentialities of his being becomes the secret of his true self-fulfillment. The keyword is EXTEMPORIZATION. When positive, the degree is unusual resourcefulness and a gift for finding real opportunity in the least promising of situations, and when negative, unambitious acceptance of things as they are.

The formula is: sustaining-ideal-universal-generalizing-spiritual-experimental. Examples are: sun, 702, 900; moon 458; Mercury, 132, 162, 213, 564; Mars, 198, 672, 794, 869, 994; Jupiter, 282; Saturn, 32, 237, 285, 287, 311; Uranus, 32, 208, 273, 305, 494, 704, 926, 939.

TAURUS 27 *A squaw selling beads* This is a symbol of the soul's fundamental disinterest in everyday superficialities, and of its characteristic anchorage in an inner reality. The exterior squalor here indicates a great satiety of experience, with petty excellencies of person dismissed as inconsequential in comparison with the fruitage of skills. Individual existence is justified in a fidelity to the recognized tokens of the cultural heritage. The keyword is DETACHMENT. When positive, the degree is creative aplomb or the ability of humankind to dramatize itself effectively in even the least of situations, and when negative, a retreat within and an acceptance of the sterilities of life as the manifestation of selfhood.

The formula is: sustaining-ideal-efficient-generalizing-spiritual-sensitive. Examples are: sun, 19, 26, 321, 557; moon, 362, 916, 977; Mercury, 232, 236; Venus, 41, 149, 250, 857; Mars, 280; Jupiter, 450, 508, 539, 828, 876, 943; Saturn, 432; Uranus, 25, 569.

TAURUS 28 *A woman pursued by mature romance* This is a symbol of the eternal promise underlying all objective existence, since the fullness of life is ageless and the human spirit immortal in its functioning. Implicit in the symbolism is the danger of disappointment whenever any deprivation is taken as final, or when an individual no longer can be stimulated to the effort able to bring him his rewards. There is here the heightening of appreciation which comes with genuine maturity. The keyword is PERSUASION. When positive, the degree is the soul's effective capitalization on its more enduring potentials, and when negative, a tendency to lose heart and accept lesser things when greater ones lie at hand.

The formula is: sustaining-ideal-efficient-generalizing-spiritual-receptive. Examples are: sun, 721; moon, 60, 504, 756, 850; Mercury, 359, 363, 468, 492, 759, 962; Venus, 76, 245, 431, 654; Mars, 398; Jupiter, 116, 236, 713, 753, 763; Saturn, 789, 947.

SCORPIO 27 *A military band on the march* This is a symbol of the human spirit's continual desire to avoid everyday trivialities and drabness, ever pressing on toward some goal which can become a basis for a more enduring and individual reality. The blare of self-affirmation is a rejection of the lesser experience which brings only a self-satiety, and its martial nature arises from the realization that things of worth must be gained at the price of a thoroughly self-mobilized effort. The keyword is INTREPIDITY. When positive, the degree is a dramatic capacity for drawing events to a focus and directing their course successfully to what might have seemed impossible ends, and when negative, foolhardy self-exploitation.

The formula is: sustaining-ideal-universal-generalizing-spiritual-sensitive. Examples are: sun, 371, 881; moon, 889; Mercury, 552, 724; Venus, 237, 302, 303, 859; Mars, 558; Jupiter, 78, 426, 589, 756; Saturn, 249, 705; Uranus, 285, 288, 311, 524, 705, 768.

SCORPIO 28 *The king of the fairies approaching his domain* This is a symbol of the eternal promise underlying all inner self-realization, since any actual fullness of life is altogether independent of the passing state of affairs in a world of time and space. Implicit in the symbolism is the futility of man's common reliance on people and things through some mere accident of contact. Outer reality takes the form with which he endows it as he exercises his sovereignty over its various potentials in the creative realms of his own imagination. The keyword is ALLEGIANCE. When positive, the degree is a special competence of inward vision and a consequent outward perspective of high effectiveness, and when negative, capricious self-indulgence.

The formula is: sustaining-ideal-universal-generalizing-spiritual-receptive. Examples are: sun, 162, 744, 901; moon, 112, 316, 414, 839, 972; Mercury, 281, 694; Venus, 377, 547, 977; Mars, 414, 971; Jupiter, 57, 227, 554, 670, 889; Saturn, 251, 524, 893; Uranus, 251, 394, 536, 655.

TAURUS 29   *Two cobblers working at a table*   This is a symbol of the co-operative wisdom by which men make their world their own, solving all its special problems through the simple communion of functions performed in a genuine division of labor. Here is emphasis on man's discursive reason, or the balancing of the pros and cons in his mind as he works out his ideas with the general assistance of his fellows. There is high reward for the creative operations he is able to claim as peculiarly his own. The keyword is CAPABILITY. When positive, the degree is a recognized integrity as an outer sign of exceptional talents, and when negative, a willingness to putter the years away at tasks devoid of all personal meaning.

The formula is: sustaining-ideal-efficient-generalizing-spiritual-responsible.
Examples are: sun, 578, 637; moon, 299, 466; Mercury, 532, 698, 986; Venus, 322, 863; Mars, 286, 576, 835, 925; Jupiter, 506; Uranus, 817, 820.

TAURUS 30   *A peacock parading on an ancient lawn*   This is a symbol of the proper dignification which can be given to superficial excellencies, and of the momentary elevation of the individual beyond his capacity or worth as he is able to exhibit the various ideals of others in his own person. There is an insouciance of vulgar display that serves a purpose here, encouraging men to strive for outer ornament when they are as yet unquickened to inner or eternal values. The keyword is ALOOFNESS. When positive, the degree is a special flair for dramatizing the heritage of the race or for capitalizing on the lessons of history in some special fashion, and when negative, a wholly unrewarding if not destructive self-contemplation.

The formula is: sustaining-ideal-efficient-generalizing-spiritual-inspired.
Examples are: sun, 139, 385, 952; moon, 770, 861; Mercury, 20, 311, 656, 874, 887; Venus, 252, 872, 906, 939; Mars, 252; Saturn, 80, 326, 964; Uranus, 239, 319, 403, 409, 683, 886, 972.

SCORPIO 29 *An Indian squaw pleading to the chief for the lives of her children* This is a symbol of the stark sacrifices the self must make in the common interest and of the high responsibilities the group must accept for the welfare of each individual, as these factors together create a functioning society and enable man to control his everyday world. Here is emphasis on the give-and-take in human allegiances, and a call for a balancing of rights and wrongs as a result of direct experience with the problems of self-fulfillment. The keyword is EFFECTIVENESS. When positive, the degree is personal accomplishment and satisfaction through an exceptional gift for holding first things first, and when negative, naïve willingness to truckle to others.

The formula is: sustaining-ideal-universal-generalizing-spiritual-responsible. Examples are: sun, 82, 537; moon, 33, 165, 882, 905; Mercury, 152, 153; Venus, 549; Mars, 540; Jupiter, 393, 700, 712, 827; Saturn, 366, 497, 536, 873; Uranus, 188, 283, 439, 603, 981.

SCORPIO 30 *The Halloween jester* This is a symbol of a proper informality in the release of the buoyant energies through which an individual gains refreshment, or is freed for the moment from life's insistent demand on him that he live according to some ideal beyond his potentiality. The dignification of what often becomes an overbroad humor here serves its purpose by encouraging man to attempt new and various modes of contact with his fellows, and thus ultimately to achieve a more genuine spiritual sensitiveness. The keyword is SPONTANEOUSNESS. When positive, the degree is a gift for making the desires and ambitions of self not only of interest but of actual value to others, and when negative, ineptness of self-expression and contempt for established values.

The formula is: sustaining-ideal-universal-generalizing-spiritual-inspired. Examples are: sun, 298, 315, 353, 436, 674; moon, 269, 280, 517, 623, 943; Mercury, 253, 371, 796, 802, 878; Venus, 720, 888; Mars, 237, 381, 647, 723, 823; Jupiter, 353, 515; Saturn, 188, 307, 655, 675, 931; Uranus, 130, 229, 612, 684, 904.

GEMINI 1 *A glass-bottomed boat in still water* This is a symbol of man's alertness to every ramification of experience open to him, and of the necessity that he take definite action on his own account if he is to capitalize on any particular opportunity. The emphasis is on an objective inactivity of value to the individual as it becomes a poise through which he is able to regrasp his destiny at each point of advantage, and as it gives him a readiness of touch with the transient stream of everyday affairs. The keyword is CURIOSITY. When positive, the degree is high competence in the estimation of life's potentialities, and when negative, a lack of effective participation in reality because of continual indecisiveness.

The formula is: manipulating-practical-ingenious-specializing-physical-experimental. Examples are: sun, 291, 939; moon, 339, 441, 658, 957; Mercury, 85, 392, 960; Mars, 75, 573; Jupiter, 172, 213, 542, 590; Saturn, 240, 298, 744; Uranus, 293, 413.

GEMINI 2 *Santa Claus filling stockings furtively* This is a symbol of the illimitable source of everything ever needed for life and experience, emphasized on the practical side of everyday rewards and individual compensations. Implicit in the symbolism is the necessity for complementing nature's largess and society's favors with high personal appreciation, as in helping maintain the enduring ritual by which spiritual values may be kept alive in human hearts. The keyword is PRODIGALITY. When positive, the degree is an unusual capacity for bringing man's possessions into a wide acceptance and for heightening every proper joy in worldly goods, and when negative, a childish or clandestine futility in seeking any normal richness of living.

The formula is: manipulating-practical-ingenious-specializing-physical-sensitive. Examples are: sun, 277, 325; moon, 72, 74; Mercury, 32, 179, 362, 431, 721, 909, 947; Venus, 124, 169, 287, 898; Mars, 186, 244; Jupiter, 58, 118, 129, 758; Saturn, 437, 451, 491; Uranus, 153, 395, 537.

SAGITTARIUS 1 *A Grand Army of the Republic campfire*
This is a symbol of man's continuing appreciation of every
phase of experience that ever has opened up for him, and his
desire to live worthily as a basis for every present or future
well-being. Here is an emphasis on a subjective passivity of value to the individual as it becomes the inner strength by which
he may sustain himself at critical points in his affairs. In his
periodic and symbolical return to center he regrasps each special potentiality of his being. The keyword is REMINISCENCE.
When positive, the degree is accomplishment through the cultivation and preservation of enduring ties with others, and
when negative, superficial idleness and unhealthy veneration
for the past.

*The formula is: manipulating-practical-original-specializing-physical-ex-
perimental.* Examples are: sun, 259, 373, 692, 772; moon, 105; Mercury,
50, 159, 173, 677; Venus, 158, 269, 738, 792; Mars, 530, 928; Jupiter, 555;
Saturn, 283, 394, 439, 963, 981; Uranus, 384, 718, 786.

SAGITTARIUS 2 *The ocean covered with whitecaps* This is a
symbol of the unending availability of everything ever needed
for life and experience, emphasized subjectively through the
tireless anticipations of the human soul. Implicit in the symbolism is the necessity for giving direction to the restlessness
of an over-all consciousness in which man's immortal being is
cradled, and for channeling this into a manifestation of personal energy. The individual prospers as he is self-quickened
to his own potentialities. The keyword is IRREPRESSIBILITY.
When positive, the degree is an indomitable resourcefulness
and a naïve delight in the problems of everyday living,
and when negative, pointless irritability and nervous self-
exhaustion.

*The formula is: manipulating-practical-original-specializing-physical-sen-
sitive.* Examples are: moon, 132; Mercury, 313, 494, 951; Venus, 147, 779,
838; Mars, 120, 383; Jupiter, 41, 317, 541, 546, 682, 770; Saturn, 436, 603,
679, 777; Uranus, 557.

GEMINI 3 *The garden of the Tuileries* This is a symbol of the self-confidence and authority which come to man through social position and wealth, and of his ability to bring all his capabilities to some graceful and exquisite self-expression. Here are the more exalted or immortal constants of everyday values, evident as they are given a solid foundation in human achievement or are preserved through a concern for them by people in general. The keyword is LUXURY. When positive, the degree is the creative stability which enables each individual to participate in the full gamut of satisfactions developed and cherished by his fellows as well as himself, and when negative, complete selfishness and a joy in lording it over others.

The formula is: manipulating-practical-ingenious-specializing-physical-receptive. Examples are: sun, 1, 326, 851, 933; moon, 736, 994; Mercury, 402, 442; Venus, 48, 273, 729, 954; Mars, 126, 956; Jupiter, 49, 938; Saturn, 253; Uranus, 747, 806, 994.

GEMINI 4 *Holly and mistletoe* This is a symbol of the maximum possible encouragement of human personality on the inner or subjective side, or of life's continual stimulus to every resource of imagination and spiritual appreciation. Here is a universal richness of experience through which man may substantiate the dignity of his order and learn to share the magic of his own self-renewal on every occasion. He responds quickly and enthusiastically to the frequent and cyclic manifestation of life's eternal overtones. The keyword is RITUALIZATION. When positive, the degree is a gift for fellow participation in every rewarding expression of individuality on all levels of human relationship, and when negative, complete obsession with superficialities.

The formula is: manipulating-practical-ingenious-specializing-physical-responsible. Examples are: sun, 320, 611; moon, 190, 725, 933; Mercury, 63, 169, 413, 654, 990; Venus, 44, 167, 506; Mars, 14, 48, 659, 931; Jupiter, 357, 375, 851; Saturn, 40, 623, 766; Uranus, 291, 303, 734, 741, 764, 811.

SAGITTARIUS 3 *Two men playing chess* This is a symbol of the self-confidence and authority which come to man through his refinement of skills and discipline of understanding, and of his capacity for mobilizing every potentiality of self at any point of challenge in events. Here is emphasis on the individual's effective and profitable participation in a reality which he has been able to approach and master through the completeness of his perspective. His gift of concentration is his genius of self-fulfillment. The keyword is ABILITY. When positive, the degree is high sensitiveness to every possibility of accomplishment or broadened self-discovery, and when negative, unsuspected bigotry or foolish exactitude.

The formula is: manipulating-practical-original-specializing-physical-receptive. Examples are: sun, 170, 724; moon, 246, 392, 559; Mercury, 196, 328, 575; Venus, 132, 719, 741, 764, 992; Mars, 260, 569, 602, 619, 712; Jupiter, 354, 529, 593; Saturn, 721; Uranus, 337, 452.

SAGITTARIUS 4 *A little child learning to walk* This is a symbol of the maximum possible encouragement of human personality on the practical or objective side, or of life's continual stimulus to every potentiality of skill and character. Here is the universal fellowship which enables man to share the various privileges of his state with other members of his order. There is a constant rehearsal and perfecting of function through which the conscious being gains and strengthens its powers. The keyword is INDIVIDUALITY. When positive, the degree is exceptional facility for entering experience on its own immediate terms while yet preserving the full genius of selfhood, and when negative, inability to take any real initiative.

The formula is: manipulating-practical-original-specializing-physical-responsible. Examples are: sun, 494, 575, 660, 720; moon, 175, 445, 698; Mercury, 259, 868, 908; Venus, 16, 172, 349, 732, 778; Mars, 488, 689; Jupiter, 509; Saturn, 435, 579; Uranus, 772.

GEMINI 5   *A radical magazine*   This is a symbol of the necessary element of change in human affairs, and of the extent to which the remote or the nonpossessed and entirely potential will have its full and functioning part in any immediate reality with which an individual may be seeking to come to terms. Here is the power of man to give high exaltation and dramatic force to whatever succeeds in stirring him deeply within himself. Emphasized in principal and important part is the supremacy of inner over outer compulsions. The keyword is TANGENCY. When positive, the degree is personality in its highly effective capacity for putting its stamp on everything it touches, and when negative, a perverse determination to quarrel with everybody.

The formula is: manipulating-practical-ingenious-specializing-physical-inspired. Examples are: sun, 179, 450, 913; moon, 456, 596, 920, 985; Mercury, 96, 260, 378, 415, 536, 857; Venus, 23, 767; Mars, 431, 448, 877; Jupiter, 144, 386; Saturn, 98, 472, 553; Uranus, 115, 148, 415, 517.

GEMINI 6   *Drilling for oil*   This is a symbol of man's indomitable efforts to discover every last resource of the world in which he finds himself, and of his desire to endow his experience with every possible enhancement on the physical side of things. Here is his capacity for penetrating to the uttermost depths of whatever potentiality may be of immediate concern to him, and for opening new dimensions of being by his willingness to undergo every possible risk in pursuing even the most uncertain of objectives. The keyword is SPECULATION. When positive, the degree is achievement through an exceptional concentration or specialization of effort, and when negative, long-range or foolish gambling and ill-considered self-exploitation.

The formula is: manipulating-practical-ingenious-specializing-social-experimental. Examples are: sun, 85, 301, 656, 798; moon, 526, 962; Mercury, 219, 242, 586, 591; Venus, 357, 452, 492, 774; Mars, 123, 562; Jupiter, 86, 413; Saturn, 53, 921; Uranus, 501.

SAGITTARIUS 5 *An old owl up in a tree* This is a symbol of the necessary element of steadiness in human affairs, and of the extent to which the demonstrated and widely accepted values of life must have their full and functioning part in the immediate reality with which an individual may be seeking to come to terms. Here is the power of man to give an eternal stability or a universal compulsion to whatever seems to call to his own deeper and private potentialities. Emphasized especially is the real dignity of self-respect. The keyword is NOR-MALITY. When positive, the degree is exceptional wisdom or effective self-restraint in each detail of personal accomplishment, and when negative, self-betraying intellectual and emotional smugness.

The formula is: *manipulating-practical-original-specializing-physical-inspired.* Examples are: sun, 146, 349, 438; moon, 402, 464, 480; Mercury, , 966; Venus, 513; Mars, 163, 446, 477, 713, 811; Jupiter, 279, 944; Saturn, , 799; Uranus, 645.

SAGITTARIUS 6 *A game of cricket* This is a symbol of man's insatiable desire to refine and strengthen every last potentiality of his own personal character and skills, and of his need to gain recognition for his success in this from each area of life in which he finds himself. Here is his capacity for holding steady in any given milieu of confusion in which he may participate, and for bringing a measure of stability to every situation in which he may be involved. Man is here at his best when he is most seriously challenged to be himself, and to play his part in strict accordance with the rules. The keyword is SPORTS-MANSHIP. When positive, the degree is exceptional competency in crisis, and when negative, false pretense to personal excellence.

The formula is: *manipulating-practical-original-specializing-social-experimental.* Examples are: moon, 608; Mercury, 79, 227, 249, 387, 563, 738; Venus, 618; Mars, 183, 732, 765; Jupiter, 47, 427, 640, 651, 740, 992; Saturn, 4, 114, 229, 466, 595, 685, 904, 971; Uranus, 97.

GEMINI 7 *An old-fashioned well* This is a symbol of the un
impeachable source of life on the side of personal self-renewa
and simple organic integrity. Implicit in the symbolism is th
purity of everything adding up to any individual character
and the curious capacity of man to remain himself wheneve
he enters into relationship with others and encourages the as
similation of their reality into his own. He draws in and give
out the substance of himself continuously, and is rewarded b
nature as he expends himself in this process of continuing t
be. The keyword is RECOMPENSE. When positive, the degree i
absolute self-reliance and uncompromising faithfulness, an
when negative, insensibility and ineptness in all human con
tact.

The formula is: manipulating-practical-ingenious-specializing-social-sens
tive. Examples are: sun, 5, 280, 400; moon, 544, 583, 603; Mercury, 1
Venus, 467, 997; Mars, 105, 268; Jupiter, 312, 368, 441, 829, 952; Saturr
575; Uranus, 65, 607, 778, 839.

GEMINI 8 *An industrial strike* This is a symbol of the ne
cessity that man act in his own interest whenever his genera
situation fails to provide him with the creative outlet he need
or proves inadequate for his relations with his fellows. Implici
in the reversed symbolism is an emphasis on the instabilitie
of life as a dynamic for accomplishment, calling on the huma
spirit for constructive reorganization. There is here the dignit
of a personality which may be exalted but never exploitec
The keyword is PROTEST. When positive, the degree is undev
ating self-assertiveness and a refusal to accept any lesser in lie
of a greater, and when negative, a dissatisfaction which su
renders rather than regrasps the self's potential.

The formula is: manipulating-practical-ingenious-specializing-social-recep
tive. Examples are: sun, 83, 164, 240, 680; moon, 628; Mercury, 321, 47
Venus, 726; Mars, 33, 67, 846; Jupiter, 395; Saturn, 145, 492, 710; Uranu
35, 199, 230, 235, 270, 296, 941.

SAGITTARIUS 7   *Cupid knocking at the door*   This is a symbol of the unimpeachable resources of life on the side of social self-renewals and psychological self-fulfillment. Implicit in the symbolism are the incurably romantic leanings of mankind, and the consequent willingness of the individual to refine or alter every aspect of his own being as a means for entering into self-quickening relations with others. He associates with his fellows and then breaks the ties he makes with them, but in time he achieves a spiritual integrity. The keyword is AL-LUREMENT. When positive, the degree is an insatiable appetite for enlarged experience and highly self-consummative intimacies, and when negative, self-exaltation and unbridled desire.

The formula is: manipulating-practical-original-specializing-social-sensitive. Examples are: sun, 8, 25, 31; moon, 492, 618, 828; Mercury, 237, 624, 642, 888; Venus, 213, 226, 267, 546; Mars, 249, 469, 784, 798; Jupiter, 739; Saturn, 130, 612, 984; Uranus, 99, 560, 578, 862, 913.

SAGITTARIUS 8   *Rocks and things forming therein*   This is a symbol of the necessity that man create his own reality out of the actual situations in which he becomes involved, and that he do so by taking control of the circumstances which provide the matrix for his everyday existence. Implicit in this symbolism of nature's processes is the demand that the stabilities thereby established be taken as a foundation for all consequent and individual initiative. Each person in accepting his roots and capitalizing on his own endowment is enabled to proceed to high achievement. The keyword is COMPOSITION. When positive, the degree is exceptional ability to mold or remold the course of events, and when negative, persisting inner confusion.

The formula is: manipulating-practical-original-specializing-social-recep-tive. Examples are: sun, 17, 152, 914; moon, 699; Mercury, 558, 674; Venus, 29, 249, 482, 970; Mars, 669; Jupiter, 158; Saturn, 185, 384, 786; Uranus, 151, 159, 615, 732, 883.

GEMINI 9 *A quiver filled with arrows*   This is a symbol of
extreme alertness to the interests and needs of selfhood, and
of high competency in pursuing any and all practical ends in
view. There is a basic emphasis on the inalienable right of man
to make demands on his fellows, or to bring to his service
whatever may help him hold his place in the scheme of things.
Here are the fruits of the self-discipline and training which
equip an individual with the skills for which he will have continual use. The keyword is PREPARATION. When positive, the
degree is unlimited personal capacity for rising to the issue of
the moment on any level of experience, and when negative,
querulous overconfidence and quixotic notions.

The formula is: manipulating-practical-ingenious-specializing-social-respon
sible. Examples are: sun, 378, 857; moon, 89, 450, 528, 788; Venus, 659
Mars, 167, 531, 588, 789; Jupiter, 81, 324; Saturn, 962; Uranus, 456, 760, 865

GEMINI 10 *An airplane falling*   This is a symbol of the capacity of man to plunge into experience with a complete disregard of consequences, or to act in full independence of those
sustainments which his fellows have accepted as limitation
Implicit in the reversed symbolism is an expectation of right
ing the dive, thus re-establishing control of the flight as suit
a conscious purpose. The individual certifies his divine birth
right as he remembers that whatever he releases in one aspect
he may regrasp in another. The keyword is CRISIS. When posi
tive, the degree is the highly advantageous reorientation of self
hood through every issue, and when negative, defeat through
disinclination to lift even a finger in decent self-interest.

The formula is: manipulating-practical-ingenious-specializing-social-in
spired. Examples are: sun, 620, 769; moon, 116, 359, 574, 710; Mercury
231, 450; Venus, 231; Jupiter, 570; Saturn, 254, 600; Uranus, 443.

SAGITTARIUS 9 *A mother with her children on stairs* This is a symbol of extreme alertness to the interests and needs of others, and of high competency in pursuing any and all ideal ends in view. There is a basic emphasis on the inescapable duty of man to remember that he is his brother's keeper, and that he must develop and demonstrate a genuine social conscience. Here are the fine fruits of service to humanity, evident in the individual's continual rounding-out of his community usefulness and the increasing recompense he gains through the approbation of his fellows. The keyword is EDUCATION. When positive, the degree is effective response to every personal challenge in everyday affairs, and when negative, immature act and reaction.

The formula is: manipulating-practical-original-specializing-social-responsible. Examples are: sun, 206, 429, 948; moon, 510, 609, 913, 953; Mercury, 223, 686, 830, 964; Venus, 560; Mars, 390; Jupiter, 94, 440, 743, 970; Saturn, 337; Uranus, 317, 438, 541.

SAGITTARIUS 10 *A golden-haired goddess of opportunity* This is a symbol of the sure protection afforded every individual who enters experience with a genuine self-expenditure, and of the inevitable good fortune coming to those who refuse to be dependent on encouragement or support from others. Implicit in the symbolism is the principle that nature always takes care of her own, and that potentiality best fulfills itself in its sure grasp of itself. Man is prospered as his expectation remains wholly unconditioned. The keyword is REWARD. When positive, the degree is an irresistible confidence in self and a tireless outreaching to all the wonders of an everyday world, and when negative, consistent diversion of effort to worthless ends.

The formula is: manipulating-practical-original-specializing-social-inspired. Examples are: sun, 22, 143; moon, 722, 748; Mercury, 31; Venus, 220, 615, 768, 809; Mars, 170, 615, 965; Saturn, 389, 557; Uranus, 227, 440, 779.

GEMINI 11   *A new path of realism in experience*   This is a symbol of the enlarged understanding which comes from a personal and immediate participation in the affairs of an everyday world, and of the continuing rewards which result from trying one and another way of doing things. Here is self-orientation as a consequence of a persistent weighing of the pros and cons in normal life relations, and a determination of values on the basis of their demonstrated usefulness. Selfhood is refined through its constant self-analysis. The keyword is IDENTIFICATION. When positive, the degree is effective mobilization of the self's practical resources for the role it must play in daily living, and when negative, self-delusion through sheer fantasy.

The formula is: manipulating-practical-ingenious-specializing-spiritual-experimental. Examples are: sun, 136, 442; moon, 659; Mercury, 1, 798, 858; Venus, 217, 268, 665, 874, 877, 946; Mars, 23, 502; Jupiter, 48; Saturn, 323, 392, 909, 821; Uranus, 887.

GEMINI 12   *A Topsy saucily asserting herself*   This is symbol of the balance which every individual must maintain between the compulsions of the social milieu on which his well-being depends and the necessity that he exercise his fledgling wings on every possible occasion. Like the slave girl trying the patience of her mistress as far as she dares, man must speak out to life with an almost spiritual impudence in order to have any character at all. Personality here is refined as it risks its very being to be what it as yet has still to become. The keyword is GROWTH. When positive, the degree is a high gift for taking personal advantage of every new situation in experience, and when negative, a joy in pure dissatisfaction.

The formula is: manipulating-practical-ingenious-specializing-spiritual-sensitive. Examples are: sun, 314, 431, 437, 477, 954, 960; moon, 831; Mercury 167, 769; Venus, 444, 680, 817; Mars, 141, 336, 340, 445, 769, 954; Jupiter 319, 409, 683, 747, 972; Saturn, 310; Uranus, 568, 680, 771.

SAGITTARIUS 11   *The lamp of physical enlightenment at the left temple*   This is a symbol of the enlarged understanding which comes from an inner and spiritual outreaching, and of the rewards following on a ceaseless experiment with one or another mode of self-expression. Here is self-orientation through a continual balancing of consequences and meanings in everyday activity and relationship. The world is seen as a laboratory for the soul, able to provide each individual with the reality he seeks for himself. The keyword is RECONCILIATION. When positive, the degree is personal effectiveness through an intelligent capitalization on past achievement, and when negative, witless trial and error leading to an utter confusion of ideas.

The formula is: manipulating-practical-original-specializing-spiritual-experimental. Examples are: sun, 79, 617, 686, 868; moon, 113, 144, 554; Mercury, 436, 537, 732, 756, 778, 880, 963; Venus, 315, 404, 605; Mars, 88, 422, 836; Jupiter, 126, 391, 548, 692, 724, 906; Saturn, 452, 890; Uranus, 134, 951.

SAGITTARIUS 12   *A flag that turns into an eagle that crows*   This is a symbol of the balance which every individual must maintain between the established allegiances which create the substance of his conscious selfhood and the idealized ambitions by which he is self-sustained as an identity in his own right. He must present his own version of himself in order to have any character at all, but his personality must conform to what comes to be expected of it in order to survive. Understanding is refined through the tireless struggles of the self with its situation. The keyword is ADJUSTMENT. When positive, the degree is successful self-establishment through genuine self-expression, and when negative, idle prejudices and unsubstantiated claims.

The formula is: manipulating-practical-original-specializing-spiritual-sensitive. Examples are: sun, 213, 215, 302, 574, 642; moon, 29, 588; Mercury, 8, 25, 302, 565, 693; Venus, 79, 84, 538, 593, 760; Mars, 345, 376, 841; Saturn, 832.

GEMINI 13   *A great musician at his piano*   This is a symbol of individual artistry as the property of all, with its expression both its strength and the means whereby others are encouraged to like accomplishment. Here is experience at a climax on the side of self-refinement in skills and talent, and at a peak in its gratification and its promise of continuing effort and sharing of rewards. A continually expanded dimension of being becomes the constant revelation of man's true estate. The keyword is ACHIEVEMENT. When positive, the degree is the creative assurance which contributes enduring overtones to human understanding, and when negative, self-defeat through a delight in momentary attention or superficial adulation.

The formula is: manipulating-practical-ingenious-specializing-spiritual-receptive. Examples are: sun, 356, 382; moon, 5, 305, 858, 866, 960; Mercury, 276, 630; Venus, 645, 785; Mars, 43, 188, 251, 308, 810; Jupiter, 239; Saturn, 83; Uranus, 9, 127, 833, 834.

GEMINI 14   *A conversation by telepathy*   This is a symbol of the transcendent level on which human experience has its truest focus, here at the extreme of personal realization. There are illimitable ties between each individual and every one of his fellows, providing the fabric for a fellowship of invisible sympathies or co-operations and making him sensitive at all times and at all points to the potentialities in which he may have a self-fulfillment. The keyword is INTIMATION. When positive, the degree is an exceptional capacity for achievement through the more organic relationships of personality in given and pertinent connections, and when negative, attempted accomplishment through innuendo or underhanded means.

The formula is: manipulating-practical-ingenious-specializing-spiritual-responsible. Examples are: sun, 815; moon, 227, 352, 665, 893; Mercury, 783; Venus, 138, 553; Mars, 74, 515, 710; Jupiter, 403, 520; Saturn, 82; Uranus, 120, 157, 419, 486, 666, 918.

SAGITTARIUS 13 *A widow's past brought to light* This is a symbol of an individual agony of soul as the property of all, its public revelation becoming both a personal clearance and an encouragement to others in their own ordeals of the spirit. Here is experience at a climax on the side of self-protection in spiritual or inner realization. The reversed symbolism is an emphasis on the better chance ahead rather than on any present or future penalties to be suffered. The keyword is RECTIFICATION. When positive, the degree is a successful employment of past failure as well as prior accomplishment in the effective integration of the personality, and when negative, callous repudiation of the self's responsibilities.

The formula is: manipulating-practical-original-specializing-spiritual-receptive. Examples are: sun, 183, 281, 352, 694, 809, 814, 853, 998; moon, 82, 404; Mercury, 109, 397; Venus, 540, 555; Mars, 592, 803, 896, 914; Jupiter, 385, 686, 951; Saturn, 367, 746; Uranus, 391, 548, 906, 998.

SAGITTARIUS 14 *The Pyramids and the Sphinx* This is a symbol of the ultimate criterion of reality provided by the common or physical world of normal experience, here at the extreme of man's enduring works in material substance. There are myriads of testimonials to human genius across the surface of the globe, and these provide the fabric for a fellowship of creative capacity and give even the least of individuals an assurance and a self-sustainment as he continues to make his new or better mark on the face of events. The keyword is CERTIFICATION. When positive, the degree is effective practicality through a gift for bringing real imagination to everyday living, and when negative, ridiculous efforts to fill the shoes of giants.

The formula is: manipulating-practical-original-specializing-spiritual-responsible. Examples are: moon, 349, 535; Mercury, 491, 809; Venus, 253, 674, 693, 853; 1000; Jupiter, 332, 333, 860; Saturn, 772, 892; Uranus, 147, 309, 736.

GEMINI 15 *Two Dutch children talking* This is a symbol of the creative interest of man in the broad range of potentialities on which he may draw. His rehearsal of experience here becomes vicarious and a matter of childlike or unconditioned familiarity with the simple contributions of the self to its milieu at root, thus facilitating a more effective grasp of life on every practical or everyday level. All relationships are reduced to common elements of background and skills. The keyword is CLARIFICATION. When positive, the degree is a self-confidence of spirit by which man is able to establish himself advantageously at ease in any possible situation, and when negative extreme provincialism and inability to communicate ideas on any moment.

The formula is: manipulating-practical-ingenious-specializing-spiritual-inspired. Examples are: sun, 405, 986; moon, 23, 759; Mercury, 405, 485, 527, 637, 680; Venus, 339, 378, 449, 455, 597; Saturn, 463; Uranus, 814.

GEMINI 16 *A woman suffragist haranguing* This is a symbol of the soul's demand for a full participation in the responsibilities of human society, and of the realization that the values of life are maintained only as there is a mutual give-and-take in respect to every real difference in point of view. There is here the necessity for substantiating right with a reasoned conviction, and for enlarging the privileges of man through a broad extension of all common or community functions. The keyword is INDIGNATION. When positive, the degree is an unswerving determination to expand every potential of being and take part in every possible detail of world-wide reconstruction and when negative, a bias forever exalting itself.

The formula is: manipulating-practical-ingenious-generalizing-physical-experimental. Examples are: sun, 14, 23, 638; moon, 525, 932; Mercury 234, 553; Venus, 121; Mars, 997; Jupiter, 734, 994; Saturn, 219, 242, 858, Uranus, 192, 552.

SAGITTARIUS 15 *The ground hog looking for its shadow* This is a symbol of the creative interest of man in the immediate set or drift of the potentialities on which he must depend. Here is his direct rehearsal of experience through an anticipation of eventualities, or an unhesitating and thoroughly practical trial and error. Implicit in the symbolism is a consistent sensitiveness to straws in the wind, and a willingness to make any amount of self-adjustment in order to capitalize on the situation of the moment. The keyword is REASSURANCE. When positive, the degree is a natural talent for determining the proper course of action or reaction in any given issue, and when negative, lack of self-stability and ingrained timidity.

The formula is: manipulating-practical-original-specializing-spiritual-inspired. Examples are: sun, 552, 624; moon, 244, 455, 490; Mercury, 49, 92, 98, 517, 647; Venus, 387, 626, 772; Mars, 209, 269, 509, 571; Jupiter, 66, 13, 209; Saturn, 201, 567; Uranus, 37, 571.

SAGITTARIUS 16 *Sea gulls watching a ship* This is a symbol of the spirit's demand for its full share in the privileges and rewards of human society, and of the individual's realization that his personal interests are served only as he maintains an inceasing vigilance in his own behalf. There is a continual and wholly impersonal give-and-take in every phase of life's over-all economy, so that what loses its usefulness in one respect will gain an immediate high potentiality in another. Moreover, what man fails to claim definitely for himself is promptly surrendered to the devices of someone else. The keyword is ALERTNESS. When positive, the degree is a gift for recognizing every opportunity at hand, and when negative, aimless expectation.

The formula is: manipulating-practical-original-generalizing-physical-experimental. Examples are: sun, 100, 233, 558, 738; moon, 274; Mercury, 43, 700, 794, 911; Venus, 170, 239, 499; Mars, 518, 976; Jupiter, 80; Saturn, 295, 742, 978; Uranus, 361, 447.

GEMINI 17 *The head of health dissolved into the head of mentality* This is a symbol of man's achievement on the level of spiritual or eternal fellowship with his kind, here emphasized subjectively as a focus of selfhood in conscious self-awareness and as a capacity to live the lives of all men in imagination and appreciation. Implicit in the symbolism is the foundation of any human well-being in everyday or immediate and practical fact, with well-rounded individuality made the condition of all real progress. The keyword is DEVELOPMENT. When positive, the degree is the effective orientation of selfhood in an over-all vision, and when negative, a defeat of accomplishment by a senseless clinging to the illusions of youth.

The formula is: manipulating-practical-ingenious-generalizing-physical-sensitive. Examples are: sun, 167, 169, 424, 573; moon, 302, 795, 981; Mercury, 687, 982; Mars, 113, 283; Jupiter, 293, 306, 523, 616, 897, 958; Saturn, 223, 774; Uranus, 244, 993.

GEMINI 18 *Two Chinese men talking Chinese* This is a symbol of an everyday exclusiveness on the intellectual side of experience, the individual strengthened not as much by actual distinctiveness as by a continual co-operation with fellow enthusiasts in various special areas of interest. A species of uniqueness is idealized as a corrective for self-diffusion. There are here the potentials of high erudition and of an exceptional refinement of the personality along original or unusual lines. The keyword is DIFFERENCE. When positive, the degree is the effective mobilization of self and others for life's more specialized objectives, and when negative, a thorough dissipation of selfhood through alien relationships.

The formula is: manipulating-practical-ingenious-generalizing-physical-receptive. Examples are: sun, 832; moon, 100, 753; Venus, 56, 305, 44?, 648; Mars, 593, 904; Jupiter, 39, 522, 811; Saturn, 563, 597; Uranus, 584, 93?

SAGITTARIUS 17   *An Easter sunrise service*   This is a symbol of man's achievement on the level of spiritual or eternal fellowship with others, here emphasized objectively by the enduring values he is able to dramatize for himself in everyday religious terms. The lives of all are seen in their common contribution to the total worth of a human estate, rather than as set off against each other in a senseless struggle for ephemeral rewards. Implicit in the symbolism is individual fulfillment through the quickening of humanity as a whole. The keyword is REBIRTH. When positive, the degree is an unusual realization of immortal resources and an ability to employ them wisely, and when negative, overconcern with superficial form and ceremony.

The formula is: manipulating-practical-original-generalizing-physical-sensitive. Examples are: sun, 327, 693; moon, 309, 338, 424, 879, 973; Mercury, 147, 315, 533, 538, 615; Venus, 275, 756; Mars, 16, 295, 356, 693; Jupiter, 253, 547, 789; Saturn, 545, 663, 866, 924, 930; Uranus, 135, 281, 425, 461, 694.

SAGITTARIUS 18   *Tiny children in sunbonnets*   This is a symbol of man's very common self-cloistering on the practical side of experience, or of the individual's capacity to give primary and needed attention to his own personal affairs. Normality is idealized as a corrective for the self-diffusion or frustration which follows from any inadequacy of contact with others. Here is a happy and full participation in everyday living, aided by some suitable and chosen role in life. The keyword is INNOCENCE. When positive, the degree is a continual and complete protection of self through its exploration of its own potentials and its exploitation of its opportunities, and when negative, witless retreat to a wholly infantile self-assertiveness.

The formula is: manipulating-practical-original-generalizing-physical-receptive. Examples are: sun, 159; moon, 642; Mercury, 22, 71, 84, 561, 707; Venus, 263, 503, 806; Mars, 92, 368, 438, 930; Saturn, 102, 187, 373, 660, 709; Uranus, 402, 775, 878.

GEMINI 19 *A large archaic volume* This is a symbol of the ultimate indestructibility of experience, so that any path once traversed may be taken again with a greater ease and a broader self-discovery. There is here the assurance of illimitable resources in wisdom, and the suggestion that this heritage may be made manifest at any time in an immediate and practical guidance. The past always provides an illumination of the present, and man achieves best as he cultures a real sense of obligation to his own roots. The keyword is BACKGROUND. When positive, the degree is a special capacity for the recovery of prior advantages or the effective disentanglement of present involvements, and when negative, a slavish worship of tradition and authority.

The formula is: manipulating-practical-ingenious-generalizing-physical-responsible. Examples are: sun, 260, 372, 415, 635; moon, 252, 310, 971; Mercury, 5, 818, 851, 952; Venus, 393, 885; Mars, 285, 291, 501, 546, 594, 946; Jupiter, 537, 808, 983; Uranus, 444, 715.

GEMINI 20 *A cafeteria* This is a symbol of the facility with which men organize their own special experience for the benefit of the community at large. The divisions of labor which constitute a civilization are refined to the point where each individual has the largest possible part in the total reality, and the resultant ease of function provides a continual reassurance of the self's competence. Here a prodigality of resources in general becomes a very immediate realization. The keyword is SUPPLY. When positive, the degree is a fullness of contribution and an effectiveness of requisition in all personal relationships, and when negative, a chronic inability to make decisions or a hopelessly dilettante spirit.

The formula is: manipulating-practical-ingenious-generalizing-physical-inspired. Examples are: moon, 200, 592, 648, 684; Mercury, 241, 437; Venus, 483, 557, 715, 808; Mars, 379, 832; Jupiter, 5, 153, 551; Saturn, 226, 501, 719; Uranus, 107, 277, 630, 720, 942.

SAGITTARIUS 19 *Pelicans moving their habitat* This is a symbol of the ultimate integrity of individual character, with each particular skill and capacity incorporated in selfhood as a potential of self-competency for subsequent refinement. There are here illimitable resources of experience, so that when life becomes unprofitable in one phase there are always additional areas of realization in which the being may have its prompt re-establishment. Man achieves best as he makes the fullest use of his own immediate genius. The keyword is FRONTIER. When positive, the degree is the indomitable originality by which the human spirit remains at a forefront of everyday accomplishment, and when negative, an unreasonable attitude and fundamentally unsocial instincts.

The formula is: manipulating-practical-original-generalizing-physical-responsible. Examples are: sun, 92, 275, 709; moon, 172, 354; Mercury, 215, 349, 353, 383, 505, 543, 574, 854, 859; Venus, 259, 389, 959; Mars, 64, 238, 372, 944; Jupiter, 471, 491; Saturn, 97, 167, 431, 560, 642, 868; Uranus, 33, 476, 478, 588.

SAGITTARIUS 20 *Men cutting through ice* This is a symbol of the facility with which men organize the processes of nature for the benefit of the community at large. The potentialities of the individuals who make up a civilization are given their natural distribution by the availability of natural resources and social opportunities, and the self must establish itself initially through the recognition given its competency. A common waste of personal endowment is avoided only by organized effort. The keyword is PROCUREMENT. When positive, the degree is exceptional capacity for overcoming obstacles and capitalizing on every possible eventuality, and when negative, lack of perspective and wholly unnecessary acceptance of hardship.

The formula is: manipulating-practical-original-generalizing-physical-inspired. Examples are: sun, 173, 538, 647; moon, 326, 460, 582, 679; Mercury, 709, 744, 850; Venus, 575, 775, 781; Mars, 112, 538, 968; Jupiter, 256, 998; Saturn, 645; Uranus, 20, 573, 633, 654.

GEMINI 21 *A labor demonstration* This is a symbol of man's unimpeachably universal spirit, and of his realization that the lines of property and private rights which he finds entrenched all around him are limitations without validity except as they constitute a social stewardship. Implicit in the reversed symbolism is the fact that right and justice only prevail to the exact extent a conscious effort is made to establish and maintain them. Individuals and groups will prosper as they dramatize their own justification effectively. The keyword is REPRESENTATION. When positive, the degree is a consistent courage in attacking major problems at any cost of minor well-being or inconvenience, and when negative, futile ill-will and bluster.

The formula is: manipulating-practical-ingenious-generalizing-social-experimental. Examples are: sun, 586, 874; moon, 508; Mercury, 208, 326, 343; Venus, 698; Mars, 45, 139, 229, 341; Saturn, 322; Uranus, 38, 606, 621, 664.

GEMINI 22 *A barn dance* This is a symbol of complete self-fulfillment through the established or normal activities of the community at large, and of a consummation of self by the broadest possible participation in the divisions of labor which constitute a human society. Richness of living comes from an uninhibited sharing of everyday potentialities, together with a maximum of happy give-and-take between any one individual and any other. The keyword is GREGARIOUSNESS. When positive, the degree is an ability to plunge into major and rewarding experiences without the least self-reservation, and when negative, a dependence on superficialities for self-satisfaction and on petty indulgences for self-assurance.

The formula is: manipulating-practical-ingenious-generalizing-social-sensitive. Examples are: sun, 63, 96, 149, 311; moon, 686, 989; Mercury, 212, 240, 407; Venus, 118, 636, 856, 919, 952; Mars, 790; Jupiter, 72, 303, 334, 580, 741, 764, 806; Saturn, 534.

SAGITTARIUS 21 *A child and a dog with borrowed eyeglasses* This is a symbol of man's unimpeachably universal spirit, and of his realization that there are no absolute lines of demarcation between higher and lower life or between the varying stages of competency to be found in each. Self-consciousness requires a supplementation of its capacities in the structures and materials of each particular plane of being, and individuality develops as it enters into reality through its own characteristic modes of insight. The keyword is EXAMINATION. When positive, the degree is an exceptional skill in the analysis of personal opportunity throughout the many dimensions of experience, and when negative, distorted vision and self-defeating prejudice.

The formula is: manipulating-practical-original-generalizing-social-experimental. Examples are: sun, 84, 796; moon, 76, 109, 171, 232, 396; Mercury, 327; Venus, 677; Mars, 84, 195, 681; Jupiter, 298, 328, 448, 665, 726, 744; Saturn, 248, 700, 756; Uranus, 15, 62, 79, 202, 581, 848.

SAGITTARIUS 22 *A Chinese laundry* This is a symbol of complete self-refinement through the unsuspected or even generally unaccepted activities of the community, and of a consummation of the being through specialized interests which may tend to deny man his more superficial communion with his fellows. A richness of living comes from a concentration on goals with remote reward, and from an association in spirit with souls of very high achievement. Here is imaginative self-sustainment through unremitting hard labor. The keyword is SECLUSION. When positive, the degree is an unusual gift for maintaining poise and self-perspective in every unfamiliar or alien situation, and when negative, unnecessary acceptance of self-inferiority.

The formula is: manipulating-practical-original-generalizing-social-sensitive. Examples are: sun, 383, 387; moon, 524, 846; Mercury, 298; Venus, 50, 206, 334, 414, 429, 914; Mars, 30, 162, 215, 512, 707; Jupiter, 34, 313; Saturn, 72, 353, 691, 732, 913, 999; Uranus, 271, 519, 844.

GEMINI 23 *Three fledglings in a nest high in a tree* This is a symbol of potentiality caught and held through an initial and effective appreciation, here dramatized by man's capacity for giving each nascent possibility of character a chance to prove itself. The human soul is a consistent manifestation of its own special genius from the very beginning, and the individual first finds himself in the early and transcendental perspectives of immaturity. The keyword is ELEVATION. When positive, the degree is an unconditioned creativity exalted to the point of complete freedom from any immediate involvement, and when negative, psychological witlessness and a false sense of release from responsibility.

The formula is: manipulating-practical-ingenious-generalizing-social-receptive. Examples are: sun, 782, 990; Mercury, 325, 786; Venus, 310, 910; Mars, 80, 887, 912; Jupiter, 626; Uranus, 16, 269, 989.

GEMINI 24 *Children skating on ice* This is a symbol of the persisting imminence of adventure in experience, and of the constant danger to self in failing to sustain or order the complex of things as they are. Implicit in the symbolism is the value of an established reality as a foundation for further refinement of personal capacity and skill. The satisfaction of a successful self-expression always must remain a dynamic impetus to further achievement, and so never become a static aplomb or a surrender to self as it stands. The keyword is FUN. When positive, the degree is soul-satisfying experiment in the infinitely varying channels of possible self-discovery, and when negative, a tendency to live for momentary excitement.

The formula is: manipulating-practical-ingenious-generalizing-social-responsible. Examples are: sun, 119, 177, 362; moon, 733, 799, 843; Mercury, 277, 280; Venus, 52, 405, 418, 962, 982; Mars, 15, 876; Jupiter, 691; Saturn, 106, 110, 822; Uranus, 179, 290, 347, 823, 916.

SAGITTARIUS 23 *Immigrants entering* This is a symbol of opportunity caught and held through its effective recognition in advance, here dramatized by the creative faith of those who risk their well-being in bringing their skills into pioneer areas of self-expression. The human soul must be a consistent manifestation of its own special genius, and the individual escapes any major impasse in his life when he is able to transplant his roots. Reality is never more sure than when regrasped in a radical reorientation. The keyword is ENTRANCE. When positive, the degree is courage in crossing new frontiers and skill in repeating or improving on prior achievement, and when negative, a surrender of the real in a pursuit of the false.

The formula is: manipulating-practical-original-generalizing-social-receptive. Examples are: sun, 94; moon, 31, 742; Mercury, 275, 438; Venus, 190, 438, 700; Jupiter, 12; Saturn, 151, 350, 551, 578, 582, 615, 699, 862.

SAGITTARIUS 24 *A bluebird standing at the door of the house* This is a symbol of the persisting imminence of real rewards in experience, and of an ever-immediate danger of failing to see or welcome them. Implicit in the symbolism is the need for a conscious worthiness of selfhood as the foundation for any self-fulfillment, or for any capitalization on the opportunities to be found in everyday reality. There must be a creative alertness to the signs and portents by which the world speaks to man, or else all personality is lost in an eventual nonentity. The keyword is FORTUNE. When positive, the degree is radiant good will and an ingratiating proficiency of self-interest, and when negative, carelessness and impracticality.

The formula is: manipulating-practical-original-generalizing-social-responsible. Examples are: sun, 285, 565, 823; Venus, 175, 409, 624, 795; Mars, 52, 369, 516, 640, 829; Jupiter, 257, 485; Saturn, 438, 883; Uranus, 272, 315, 599, 608, 687, 813, 933.

GEMINI 25   *A man trimming palms*   This is a symbol of the
pride in effort by which man seeks to leave his immortal stamp
on the world around him. There is here the bending of all
natural resources to the will of the individual, and an enlistment of every beauty and capacity of nature for a continuing
revelation of the self's aesthetic sense. The harmony between
the workman and his materials becomes gratifying evidence of
the soul's powers on the more objective side of a self-justification. The keyword is ENHANCEMENT. When positive, the degree is an exceptional gift for bringing all things to an effective
service in some special aspect of over-all achievement, and
when negative, an empty display of trivial excellencies.

*The formula is: manipulating-practical-ingenious-generalizing-social-in-
spired.* Examples are: sun, 32, 413, 833; moon, 58, 177, 370; Mercury, 320,
611; Venus, 363, 861; Mars, 360, 675; Jupiter, 189, 482, 973; Saturn, 180, 804;
Uranus, 211, 454, 613, 874, 881.

GEMINI 26   *Winter frost in the woods*   This is a symbol of
the cosmic significance in any momentary cancellation of the
more immediate interests and private concerns, and the emphasis is on the supremacy of the needs and powers of nature
over the aspirations and conveniences of man. Implicit in the
static symbolism is the call for a reorientation in the individual's point of view, and for some further discovery of the
self's potentials. Normal life is brought to a point of sharp
suspension so that the larger magic may be manifest. The keyword is SPLENDOR. When positive, the degree is the creative
transformation by which older cycles give way to newer ones,
and when negative, a reduction of the useless to a total anni-
hilation.

*The formula is: manipulating-practical-ingenious-generalizing-spiritual-
experimental.* Examples are: sun, 37, 56, 393, 402; moon, 709; Venus, 70;
Mars, 1, 494, 541, 644, 882; Jupiter, 291, 703; Saturn, 639; Uranus, 166, 445.

SAGITTARIUS 25 *A chubby boy on a hobbyhorse* This is a symbol of the ambition by which man ultimately manages to leave his immortal stamp on the world around him, here dramatized in his desire for a fullness of living and a perfection of accomplishment. The individual employs whatever means are available for trying his hand at the skills through which he would know his expanding self-fulfillment, and in his days of play and training he learns to fix his eyes steadily on the pyramid of goals ahead. The keyword is EMULATION. When positive, the degree is an indomitable determination to give the lesser potentialities of existence a more effective dimension, and when negative, idle self-indulgence and ingenuous claims of merit.

The formula is: manipulating-practical-original-generalizing-social-inspired. Examples are: sun, 227, 505, 966; moon, 124, 584, 949; Mercury, 525, 992; Venus, 707, 972; Mars, 205, 525, 740, 885, 920; Jupiter, 147, 396, 445, 572; Uranus, 91, 143, 574.

SAGITTARIUS 26 *A flag-bearer* This is a symbol of the enduring significance which tends to overshadow the more immediate interests or wholly selfish concerns of man, and the emphasis is on the natural supremacy of common ideals over mere individual ambitions. Implicit in the symbolism is the call for a high self-sacrifice, and for the development of such new dimensions of experience as will permit the self to realize its transcendental aspirations. Every resource of normal life is commandeered for the greater potentiality. The keyword is NOBILITY. When positive, the degree is spiritual exaltation through some dramatic or vital service to all, and when negative, a resort to empty show or a demand for false credit.

The formula is: manipulating-practical-original-generalizing-spiritual-experimental. Examples are: moon, 304, 487, 532, 581; Mercury, 146; Venus, 399, 491, 525, 571, 610, 614, 850, 880; Mars, 55, 175, 373; Jupiter, 382, 841, 964; Saturn, 132, 227, 629, 703, 819; Uranus, 11, 111.

GEMINI 27 *A gypsy coming out of the forest* This is a symbol of human enthusiasm or of self-consciousness mobilized in a freshness or naïveté of self-realization and dramatized by an irresistible desire for success and recognition in an everyday world. Here are the enlarged horizons which follow from the individual's faith in his own potentialities and his willingness to draw on them prodigally and in generous co-operation with his fellows. Man thus finds the resources of all nature available for his exploitation. The keyword is EXPENDITURE. When positive, the degree is self-release through a joy in the accomplishments of the moment, and when negative, complete disinclination to enter into the ordinary relationships of society.

The formula is: manipulating-practical-ingenious-generalizing-spiritual-sensitive. Examples are: sun, 33, 231, 622; moon, 360, 754, 894, 912; Mercury, 395, 528, 906; Mars, 317, 396, 892; Jupiter, 274, 629, 698; Saturn, 453, 761; Uranus, 448, 604, 867.

GEMINI 28 *A man declared bankrupt* This is a symbol of the eternal individuality of the human spirit, able to enter new paths of opportunity and thereupon achieve a further self-refinement whenever its particular involvements in everyday affairs have come to some point of futility. Implicit in the reversed symbolism is the realization of the ultimate transiency of both the rewards and penalties in life, and of the unreality of consequences if ever taken as other than a convenient converging of relationships. The keyword is DELIVERANCE. When positive, the degree is an effective and over-all resourcefulness in even the worst of situations, and when negative, a willingness to dodge every responsibility and betray the very core of self.

The formula is: manipulating-practical-ingenious-generalizing-spiritual-receptive. Examples are: sun, 219, 242, 588; moon, 7, 507, 906, 917; Venus, 515, 730, 893; Mars, 68, 307, 507, 657, 702, 716, 805, 900; Jupiter, 84, 340, 363, 538, 693, 733, 810; Saturn, 348, 359, 759; Uranus, 852.

SAGITTARIUS 27 *A sculptor* This is a symbol of creative ability as the manifestation of self-consciousness in its maturity of realization, dramatized by an irresistible desire to endow all life with some enduring potentiality. Here are the enlarged horizons which follow from an individual's mastery of his own particular talents, and from the expanded vision which he must develop and share with his fellows if he is to possess it for himself. He is able to idealize nature because he has brought her to subjection. The keyword is IMMORTALIZATION. When positive, the degree is exceptional self-expression through a gift for building all experience into a personal fulfillment, and when negative, callous impersonality and overambitious pretensions.

The formula is: manipulating-practical-original-generalizing-spiritual-sensitive. Examples are: sun, 354; moon, 32, 527; Mercury, 17, 681, 918; Venus, 602; Mars, 13, 31, 217, 935; Jupiter, 936, 995; Saturn, 628, 713, 851, 870; Uranus, 24, 262, 490, 800.

SAGITTARIUS 28 *An old bridge over a beautiful stream* This is a symbol of the eternal stability of the world at large, and of each person's ability to preserve its form and function in full accordance with his own convenience. Implicit in the static symbolism is the complete dependability of man-made structures at their best, and the joy of nature in making them an enduring part of herself in every respect. What is ephemeral in any possible phase of the real is merely that which serves no purpose in its transient state of existence. The keyword is CONSERVATION. When positive, the degree is an individual genius for fitting all needs and ideals into the universal patterns, and when negative, total lack of initiative.

The formula is: manipulating-practical-original-generalizing-spiritual-receptive. Examples are: sun, 888; moon, 169, 365, 761; Mercury, 560, 760; Venus, 153, 627; Mars, 108, 915; Jupiter, 238, 430, 988; Saturn, 209, 987; Uranus, 215, 404.

GEMINI 29 *The first mockingbird in spring* This is a symbol of the contribution of aesthetic experience to the strengthening of self at core, given emphasis by the skill in imitation through which any vicarious participation in life is enhanced. Here man's aspiration becomes articulate far in advance of his self-refinement, and as a result the promise in his given case may be manifest in achievements of which he would be quite incapable in normal course. At the least he is called to attempt a self-revelation which will add real stature to his role in everyday living. The keyword is QUICKENING. When positive, the degree is consistent stimulation to others in all human affairs, and when negative, annoying self-assertiveness.

The formula is: manipulating-practical-ingenious-generalizing-spiritual-responsible. Examples are: sun, 343, 419, 483, 485, 940, 982; moon, 149; Mercury, 400, 895; Venus, 532, 630; Mars, 134, 136; Jupiter, 432; Uranus, 382, 925, 990.

GEMINI 30 *Bathing beauties* This is a symbol of human excellence on the side of purely natural endowment, and of the soul as wholly inadequate except as it is able to meet some need of everyday experience with the elements inherent in its make-up and so free from any or all responsibility to anything other than itself. Here individuality gains a needed assurance through the phases of its being which prove immune from change or loss. A person becomes himself as he is able thus to stand radiant and reliant among the total of his fellows. The keyword is CHARM. When positive, the degree is a special capacity for bringing the familiar desires and interests to an enduring representation of worthiness, and when negative, regression to childish vanities.

The formula is: manipulating-practical-ingenious-generalizing-spiritual-inspired. Examples are: sun, 443, 520; moon, 221, 503, 621, 915; Mercury, 424, 815, 995; Venus, 234, 798; Mars, 119, 177, 254, 907; Jupiter, 475, 903, 947; Saturn, 899; Uranus, 105, 195, 485, 546, 593, 757.

SAGITTARIUS 29   *A fat boy mowing the lawn*   This is a symbol of the contribution of familiar experience to the refinement of selfhood, given emphasis by the full self-expenditure required for any satisfactory acceptance into a fellowship with others. Here a practical attention to the immediate needs of the individual as a member of his group is the effective evidence of the broader competency. Social incentives inevitably come to overbalance the more primitive instincts and appetites. The keyword is PARTICIPATION. When positive, the degree is the calm efficiency which enables man to pour all of himself into the mastery of any situation arising to challenge him, and when negative, complete perfunctoriness of thinking and doing.

The formula is: manipulating-practical-original-generalizing-spiritual-responsible. Examples are: sun, 417, 519, 755, 963; moon, 333, 477; **Mercury**, 352, 388, 513; Venus, 319, 529, 552, 702, 855, 900, 957; Mars, 148, 660; Jupiter, 369, 604, 717,867, 990; Saturn, 236, 566, 860; Uranus, 856, 929, 954.

SAGITTARIUS 30   *The Pope*   This is a symbol of human excellence on the side of the special values exalted in the various social and political hierarchies of modern civilization, and of man's ambition as entirely inadequate except as he is able to meet some exceptional need of everyday experience and so proceed to dramatize whatever abilities he may have developed in climbing to the position in which he finds himself. A person is strengthened within himself by the appreciation he succeeds in winning from his fellows. The keyword is SANCTITY. When positive, the degree is an effective and spectacular sacrifice of self in some enduring service to the race at large, and when negative, inordinate love of self-display and surrender to a lust for power.

The formula is: manipulating-practical-original-generalizing-spiritual-inspired. Examples are: sun, 282, 517; moon, 357, 372; Mercury, 239, 338; Venus, 196, 353, 537, 869; Mars, 4, 834; Jupiter, 108, 195, 837, 849; Saturn, 317, 328, 332, 440, 541; Uranus, 232, 243.

CANCER 1   *A furled and an unfurled flag displayed from a vessel*   This is a symbol of the extremes to which an individual will go in the practical allegiances with which he meets the various situations in life, and of his capacity to compromise or reverse any stand he may take whenever this suits his ultimate ends. Here is his inflexible determination to further every ambition, and his consistent preparation for every eventuality that might be anticipated. He is unhappy except as he somehow can feel himself safely a step ahead of himself. The keyword is ADAPTABILITY. When positive, the degree is a gift for highly profitable adjustment in every developing relationship with others, and when negative, vacillation if not complete instability.

The formula is: sustaining-critical-universal-specializing-physical-experimental. Examples are: sun, 418, 580, 858; moon, 118, 183, 411, 501; Mercury, 164, 372, 989; Mars, 221, 331, 444, 624; Jupiter, 414, 415; Saturn, 620; Uranus, 922.

CANCER 2   *A man suspended over a vast level place*   This is a symbol of man's capacity for an illimitable overview of his experience in advance of his involvement in its details, and of the infinite ramification of possibilities he is able to uncover in the world he seeks to make his own. Implicit in the negative symbolism is the poise in act by which he escapes the bondage of any random compulsions, and a leisure in perspective which preserves his free choice. The keyword is CONTEMPLATION. When positive, the degree is an exceptional spread of comprehension and a continual self-orientation of understanding, and when negative, a flighty transcendence or an impatience with all immediate or down-to-earth considerations.

The formula is: sustaining-critical-universal-specializing-physical-sensitive. Examples are: sun, 786; moon, 208, 723; Mercury, 186, 356, 483, 620; Venus, 141, 839; Mars, 415; Jupiter, 267, 605; Saturn, 101, 540; Uranus, 338, 449, 525, 665, 726.

CAPRICORN 1 *An Indian chief demanding recognition* This is a symbol of the extreme fidelity of the normal individual to the everyday or accepted values of life, and of his uncompromising inner integrity when it comes to meeting any situation of the moment. Here is his determination to maintain every advantage gained by birth or through experience, and to grasp every opportunity for genuine self-expression. He is unhappy except as he can feel secure in the place he has made for himself. The keyword is INFLEXIBILITY. When positive, the degree is an ever-effective authority following from a single eye of vision and a consistent dignity of character, and when negative, idle pompousness and a senseless raising of minor issues.

The formula is: sustaining-critical-efficient-specializing-physical-experimental. Examples are: sun, 10, 547, 911; moon, 543; Mercury, 4, 116, 617, 753, 768; Venus, 192, 964; Mars, 3, 21, 82, 89, 115, 303, 411, 533, 728; Jupiter, 339, 785; Saturn, 313; Uranus, 118, 190, 278, 308, 368, 829.

CAPRICORN 2 *Three stained-glass windows, one damaged by bombardment* This is a symbol of man's illimitable capacity for memorializing his experience by the record he leaves in history, and of the necessity that he protect his handiwork from the superficial destructiveness of a life without vision or pride. Implicit in the negative symbolism is the irrevocable narrowing of all things to their point of greatest personal significance, and the responsibility of the individual for exalting whatever he may draw to pertinence in his own case. The keyword is COMMEMORATION. When positive, the degree is effective self-dramatization in some vital service to human affairs, and when negative, overconservatism and unwarranted fearfulness.

The formula is: sustaining-critical-efficient-specializing-physical-sensitive. Examples are: moon, 394, 538; Mercury, 399; Venus, 743; Mars, 158, 222, 227, 312, 635, 963; Jupiter, 378, 442, 479, 601, 631; Saturn, 951; Uranus, 86, 506.

CANCER 3 *A man all bundled up in fur leading a shaggy deer* This is a symbol of the pioneer or trail-blazing instinct in the human heart, and of the self's insistent determination to strengthen itself in its own highly individual roots. Here is a repudiation of most normal experience as unnecessarily self-limiting in its accepted opportunities and boundaries. Life is taken as real or rewarding only as it can be carried on from something known to some unknown which will provide a real challenge ahead. The keyword is INDOMITABILITY. When positive, the degree is unlimited self-reliance in and through every possible phase of self-expression, and when negative, self-imposed handicaps and a needless acceptance of everyday restrictions.

The formula is: sustaining-critical-universal-specializing-physical-receptive. Examples are: sun, 212, 264, 276, 527, 983; moon, 119, 877, 885; Mercury, 39, 67, 522, 746; Venus, 193, 514, 528; Jupiter, 902; Saturn, 220, 483; Uranus, 183.

CANCER 4 *A cat arguing with a mouse* This is a symbol of man's necessary establishment of a set in mind or realization as a preliminary to any entrance into personal experience, and of his tendency to enjoy the preparatory more than the consummatory phases of his participation in reality. Here also is the eternal effort of human nature to get outer acceptance or social sanction for its inborn desires, as well as inner or intelligent and practical confirmations for the values it has made its own. The keyword is JUSTIFICATION. When positive, the degree is a gift for persuading others to accept the motives of self and to co-operate with its ends, and when negative, interminable quarreling with the nature of things.

The formula is: sustaining-critical-universal-specializing-physical-responsible. Examples are: sun, 727; moon, 984; Mercury, 588, 616, 832; Venus, 833, 909; Mars, 439, 591, 957; Jupiter, 326, 499, 776, 853; Saturn, 149, 418, 619; Uranus, 34, 256, 430.

CAPRICORN 3 *The human soul receptive to growth and understanding* This is a symbol of mankind's fundamentally naïve capacity for experience, and of every individual's equally fundamental dependence on the understanding and support of fellow participants in each moment of self-discovery. Here is a delight in normal living, not through its limitation but rather through a reiterated release of selfhood. Life is found to be real and rewarding because it may be encountered in such infinite ramifications of itself. The keyword is AVIDITY. When positive, the degree is a gift for entering into the kaleidoscopic patterns of personal relationship with an unbounded enthusiasm, and when negative, simple shiftlessness or abandon.

The formula is: sustaining-critical-efficient-specializing-physical-receptive. Examples are: sun, 147, 316, 380; Mercury, 183, 285, 519, 823; Venus, 295, 744, 901; Mars, 638; Jupiter, 184, 361, 447; Saturn, 471; Uranus, 49, 156, 510, 586.

CAPRICORN 4 *A party entering a large canoe* This is a symbol of man's necessary adjustment of the practical details in his immediate environment as a preliminary to any personal participation in experience, and of his greater concern with these at times than with the real ends in view. Here also is his desire for the approval of his fellows before he commits himself, and his determination to involve them in whatever commands his own attention. The individual is sure of himself as he acts with others. The keyword is ORDERING. When positive, the degree is exceptional capacity for bringing all proper relationships to a point of effectiveness in any given exigency of everyday affairs, and when negative, inability to get along with anybody.

The formula is: sustaining-critical-efficient-specializing-physical-responsible. Examples are: sun, 71, 198, 397, 719, 953; moon, 211, 695; Venus, 92, 519; Mars, 94, 690, 706, 868; Saturn, 294, 488, 495, 548, 556, 725; Uranus, 71, 73, 224, 441, 847.

CANCER 5 *An automobile wrecked by a train* This is a symbol of the irresistible power of completion inherent in the very make-up of man's world whenever a sequence of events once is set in motion, as is evident continually on the objective side of things. Implicit in the reversed symbolism is the concept of control, or the assurance that it is not necessary to continue any given action to the point of self-cancellation. The ultimate obligation of the individual is to himself, and not to the narrow and momentary direction of circumstances. The keyword is DISPERSION. When positive, the degree is a special genius for a creative reorganization of all experience, and when negative, an insensitive recklessness.

The formula is: sustaining-critical-universal-specializing-physical-inspired. Examples are: sun, 217, 645, 746; moon, 595, 757, 870; Mercury, 33; Venus, 65, 649; Mars, 130, 375, 604, 727, 867; Jupiter, 70, 141, 240, 362, 513, 910, 919; Saturn, 528, 617; 923; Uranus, 200, 203, 276, 470, 598, 807, 905.

CANCER 6 *Game birds feathering their nests* This is a symbol of the unlimited degree to which the spirit of man may develop and preserve its initiative by utilizing the natural course of things in the world at large, and of the satisfaction anyone may know through his conscious participation in a group destiny. Individuality flourishes whenever it is able to establish its personal rights over some desirable segment of reality, and thereupon justify its own being by fulfilling the expectation of others. The keyword is METICULOUSNESS. When positive, the degree is high intelligence and skill in enlisting the potentials of experience for the service of self, and when negative, unnecessary concern over everyday security.

The formula is: sustaining-critical-universal-specializing-social-experimental. Examples are: moon, 111, 130, 348, 717, 805; Mercury, 573, 863; Mars, 923; Jupiter, 132, 437, 532, 650; Saturn, 196, 204, 745, 895; Uranus, 263, 959.

CAPRICORN 5 *Indians rowing a canoe and dancing a war dance* This is a symbol of the irresistible impulse to action inherent in the very fact of conscious being, and of the powers of accomplishment brought to their personal focus as some pattern of motives takes form on the subjective side of things. Implicit in the symbolism is the ever-primitive nature of life at root, and the necessity that thoroughly practical and immediate considerations prevail whenever the inner or ideal ordering proves inadequate. The keyword is MOBILIZATION. When positive, the degree is a capacity for aggressive leadership and an unusual effectiveness in sidetracking minor issues for the sake of major achievement, and when negative, unnecessary moods and tantrums.

The formula is: sustaining-critical-efficient-specializing-physical-inspired. Examples are: sun, 116, 292, 753, 794; moon, 921, 993; Mercury, 755; Venus, 116, 214, 298, 930; Mars, 19, 482, 642, 741, 764, 783; Jupiter, 96, 135, 140, 183, 736, 974; Saturn, 274, 391, 906, 998; Uranus, 51, 197, 377, 688, 977.

CAPRICORN 6 *A dark archway and ten logs at the bottom* This is a symbol of the illimitable resources of self in preserving its own integrity through the varying fortunes of everyday living, and of the satisfaction anyone may know through a conscious direction of his own destiny. Personality comes to fulfillment as it realizes that its function is an unending exploration of its own potentialities. Man remains unimpeachably himself because he is able to extend himself indefinitely. The keyword is THOROUGHNESS. When positive, the degree is high competence in the interpretation of life's purposes or unusual persistence in employing its ramifying potentials effectively, and when negative, fear of experience and bondage to mystery.

The formula is: sustaining-critical-efficient-specializing-social-experimental. Examples are: sun, 278, 918; moon, 819; Mercury, 94, 185, 475, 838; Venus, 456, 683, 753, 754, 813; Mars, 337, 338, 970; Saturn, 306, 644, 920; Uranus, 733, 903.

CANCER 7 *Two fairies on a moonlit night* This is a symbol of nature's illimitable potentialities on the side of the release she offers man from his physical or psychological involvement, and of the necessity that he achieve some measure of lightness in self-expression as a balance for the strain of everyday existence. Here is an exaltation of fancy as a dynamic factor in all self-realization, and of the quiet moments of experience as a real opportunity for self-orientation. The magic of selfhood lies in its ability to rise above whatever may threaten its well-being. The keyword is ASCENDANCY. When positive, the degree is a transforming sensitivity or a healing imagination, and when negative, a senseless retreat to make-believe.

The formula is: sustaining-critical-universal-specializing-social-sensitive. Examples are: sun, 407, 514, 553; moon, 158, 234, 373, 613, 661, 789, 873, 952; Venus, 67, 392; Mars, 202, 551, 680, 955; Jupiter, 261, 582, 637, 668, 699, 812; Saturn, 26; Uranus, 85, 123, 656.

CANCER 8 *Rabbits dressed in clothes and on parade* This is a symbol of the upward reach of consciousness towards spirit, or of the necessity in all worth-while experience that events in some fashion make their continual and stimulating contribution to whatever values the self may be building into its own nature. The habiliments of higher implication are always available for a lower life to wear experimentally, thus sharing in what as yet it has not been able to assimilate to itself. The real is established as it is dramatized. The keyword is APPROPRIATION. When positive, the degree is unlimited assurance in any projection of self into a superior dimension of reality, and when negative, an ingenuous substitution of affirmation for accomplishment.

The formula is: sustaining-critical-universal-specializing-social-receptive. Examples are: sun, 174, 241, 309, 395, 666; moon, 69, 845, 965; Mercury, 715; Venus, 304, 477, 541, 637, 662, 942; Mars, 66, 424, 580; Jupiter, 169, 888; Saturn, 54, 146, 225, 289, 370, 625, 842, 875, 960; Uranus, 907.

CAPRICORN 7 *A veiled prophet of power* This is a symbol of nature's illimitable potentialities on the side of her readiness to meet the physical and psychological demands of man, and of the necessity that he exercise his mastery of natural forces as a basis for his self-assurance in meeting everyday strain and turmoil. Here is an exaltation of the untapped resources inherent in all personality, and a dramatization of life achievement as the essence of self-fulfillment. The keyword is SUPREMACY. When positive, the degree is unerring insight into the motives of men and a consequent gift for organizing their efforts along any given line of accomplishment, and when negative, inability to distinguish true values from false.

The formula is: *sustaining-critical-efficient-specializing-social-sensitive.* Examples are: moon, 218, 374, 378, 462, 781; Mercury, 100, 233, 389, 628, 957; Venus, 4; Mars, 138, 213, 601; Saturn, 147, 897; Uranus, 213, 365, 580, 973.

CAPRICORN 8 *Birds in the house singing happily* This is a symbol of the descent of spirit or intelligence into every last ramification of everyday reality, and of man's self-fulfillment as he is successful in shaping circumstances or precipitating events so that they become the ultimate and outward revelation of that higher vision by which he continues to be himself at core. Here is the actual and impregnable independence of the individual, evident as at length he is able to make his world his own and call on all to share it with him. The keyword is ESTABLISHMENT. When positive, the degree is an insatiable urge to put everything to use and to employ every least talent of self, and when negative, idle narcissism.

The formula is: *sustaining-critical-efficient-specializing-social-receptive.* Examples are: sun, 168, 226, 389, 795, 854, 980; moon, 34, 101, 193, 266, 569, 564; Mercury, 190; Mars, 246, 667; Jupiter, 297, 641, 775; Saturn, 2, 141, 562; Uranus, 116, 406, 753, 763, 888.

CANCER 9 *A tiny nude miss reaching in the water for a fish*
This is a symbol of the eternal and unsullied freshness of soul
as it enters every new experience with an unabated enthusiasm
and thereby both substantiates its divine estate and brings enduring significance to whatever it may touch. Here is the absolute lack of inhibition which enables man to grasp the reins of
control in every realm he decides to make his own, and the un-
quenched and simple curiosity which virtually makes it impossible for any potentiality of being ever to escape him. The
keyword is INCLINATION. When positive, the degree is ingratiating and irresistible capacity for self-expression, and when
negative, continual indiscretion as a bar to any appreciable
achievement.

The formula is: sustaining-critical-universal-specializing-social-responsible
Examples are: sun, 208, 428, 528, 687; moon, 135, 580, 822, 830, 904; Mercury, 14, 577; Venus, 37, 317; Mars, 450, 695, 910, 919, 981; Jupiter, 27
164; Saturn, 67, 76, 245, 250, 258, 421, 549; Uranus, 466, 503, 618, 685, 880
955.

CANCER 10 *A large diamond not completely cut* This is a
symbol of man's basic self-justification on the cultural or intellectual side, and of the complete dependence of the world
around him on his arts and skills for any values that may be
built or sustained in its eternal promise. Here all progress
turns out to be primarily the endowment of reality with expanded dimensions of significance, and man's pilgrimage
through the lower planes of being is revealed as a continual
service to higher meanings through which he knows himself.
The keyword is LATENCY. When positive, the degree is an effective gift for dramatizing the potentialities of everything at
hand, and when negative, a futile lean on purely static merit.

The formula is: sustaining-critical-universal-specializing-social-inspired. Examples are: sun, 818; moon, 222; Mercury, 149, 638; Venus, 221, 277, 419
551, 832; Mars, 630; Jupiter, 831; Saturn, 122; Uranus, 6, 44, 114, 193.

CAPRICORN 9   *An angel carrying a harp*   This is a symbol of
the eternal and unabated interest of the human spirit in the
simple potentialities of experience, and of the unconditioned
enthusiasm of all human motives in their original inception.
Here is a continuing sense of spiritual source as it pervades
man's consciousness, enabling him to avoid the limitations in
any given situation and so to drive ahead to a point of self-
fulfillment. There is an over-all harmony of which each individual remains essentially a part. The keyword is ATTUNEMENT.
When positive, the degree is a special gift for inspiring others
to accomplishment and for realizing the ultimate dreams of
self as a consequence, and when negative, simple fantasy and
uncritical self-superiority.

The formula is: sustaining-critical-efficient-specializing-social-responsible.
Examples are: sun, 12, 525, 592, 595, 850; moon, 65, 68, 99, 671, 697; Mercury, 763; Venus, 17, 126, 200, 390, 494; Mars, 281, 349, 412, 694; Jupiter,
91, 309, 342, 351, 388, 462; Uranus, 48, 513, 787, 943.

CAPRICORN 10   *An albatross feeding from the hand*   This is
a symbol of man's basic self-justification on the practical or
commonplace side, and of his complete dependence on the co-
operation of the world at large for any actuality of personal
experience. He must ever take the initiative in meeting the
needs of others if he is to expect them to stir appreciably and
similarly in his own behalf. If he reaps in life he must sow
abundantly, and he establishes himself as he expends himself
and thereby encourages his fellows to do the same. The keyword is NURTURE. When positive, the degree is unusual success
in dramatizing the potentialities of human nature and its ramifying achievements, and when negative, overconcern with side
issues.

The formula is: sustaining-critical-efficient-specializing-social-inspired.   Examples are: sun, 763; moon, 122, 478, 863, 880; Mercury, 354, 380, 547;
Venus, 397, 617, 673, 924; Mars, 792; Jupiter, 37, 402, 498, 571; Saturn, 363,
898; Uranus, 246, 346, 539.

CANCER 11 *A clown making grimaces* This is a symbol of the continual self-rehearsal by which the everyday personality of man is able to sustain its particular characteristics, and of the tentative side of experience through which the uncertainties of life can be dramatized for acceptance or rejection without incurring any penalties. Here is an emphasis on the ridiculous as an instructive exaggeration of human nature, or as an exhibition of its inadequacies in a direct stimulation to better self-realizations. The keyword is INIMITABILITY. When positive the degree is effective sharpening of an individual's dominant or everyday impact on others, and when negative, a loss of personal influence through aimless self-exploitation.

The formula is: sustaining-critical-universal-specializing-spiritual-experimental. Examples are: sun, 885; moon, 64, 138, 431, 619; Mercury, 520, 785, 997; Venus, 372, 704; Mars, 70, 321; Jupiter, 43, 377, 543, 977; Saturn 980; Uranus, 59, 721.

CANCER 12 *A Chinese woman nursing a baby with a message* This is a symbol of the wide ramification in experience by which man achieves his greater opportunities, emphasized on the wholly personal side as he is able to include the far-flung capabilities of the race itself in his own individual complex of talents and skills. Life gains significance to the extent that each person embraces the totality of his kind in his own make-up or seeks to embody universal values in his everyday consciousness. The keyword is MATERIALIZATION. When positive, the degree is a gift for bringing the more Godlike resources or superior powers of self to a point of real community service, and when negative, completely unreasonable demands for recognition.

The formula is: sustaining-critical-universal-specializing-spiritual-sensitive. Examples are: sun, 973; moon, 762, 806; Mercury, 56, 273; Venus, 917, Mars, 161, 200, 532, 598, 610; Jupiter, 553, 607, 644; Saturn, 755, 953; Uranus, 364, 963.

CAPRICORN 11 *A large group of pheasants* This is a symbol of the social ritualization by which man's everyday personality is able to maintain and refine its particular characteristics, and of the common expression of self through which life endows each individual with his fundamental inner certainty and his convenient outer reality. Here is an emphasis on the reduplications and multiplications of every facet of existence, so that the continuous variations come to dramatize an infinite potential inherent in the whole. The keyword is ILLIMITABILITY. When positive, the degree is a tireless pursuit of every personal aspiration, and when negative, egotistic satisfaction in matching the mediocrity of others.

The formula is: *sustaining-critical-efficient-specializing-spiritual-experimental*. Examples are: sun, 475, 482, 543, 707, 849, 957; moon, 397, 657; Venus, 337, 464; Mars, 86, 479, 787; Jupiter, 425, 525; Saturn, 417, 736, 768; Uranus, 861.

CAPRICORN 12 *A student of nature lecturing* This is a symbol of the wide ramification in experience by which man achieves his greater opportunities, emphasized on the vicarious or intellectual side as he participates in events and shares meanings through the mind's eye alone. Here is direct fulfillment in consciousness. Life gains its illimitability as the individual discovers that he can master its endless facets through ever-expanding facilities of the reason. The keyword is EXPLANATION. When positive, the degree is self-confidence through the acquisition of knowledge and effective self-direction through the practical application of all values, and when negative, psychological smugness and an unreasonable pride of intellect.

The formula is: *sustaining-critical-efficient-specializing-spiritual-sensitive*. Examples are: sun, 681, 859, 1000; moon, 16, 552, 560, 597; Mercury, 10; Venus, 595, 763; Mars, 184, 464; Jupiter, 292; Saturn, 361, 447, 571; Uranus, 145.

CANCER 13 *One hand slightly flexed with a very prominen* *thumb* This is a symbol of that belief in his inherent suprem acy over all other orders of nature by which man is chara terized most fundamentally, dramatized by his quite norma confidence in his ability to deal with every eventuality of day by-day activity and relationship. Any individual must rul his environment or surrender his own potentialities forevei Here is practicality brought to the point of ruthlessnes The keyword is DETERMINATION. When positive, the degre is exceptional steadiness and a high sense of self-responsibi ity in every issue of the moment, and when negative, unnece sary aggressiveness and a self-defeating shortsightedness.

The formula is: sustaining-critical-universal-specializing-spiritual-receptiv Examples are: sun, 221, 348, 616, 751; moon, 95; Mercury, 635, 751; Ven 721; Jupiter, 622; Saturn, 769; Uranus, 237, 249, 585, 697.

CANCER 14 *A very old man facing a vast dark space to th* *northeast* This is a symbol of the immeasurable reaches c past experience as a strengthening of the human spirit for i immediate destiny, and of the eternal rebirth through whic man may discover that present aspiration and future achiev ment are without the slightest limitation in any terms of even to come. Here is an absoluteness of self as a completeness c expectation. There are no dark moments of outlook that ca not yield inspiration or assurance. The keyword is SANCTIOI When positive, the degree is a highly effective enlistment c deeper and hidden elements of life for some momentary en and when negative, lack of purpose and utter chaos in unde standing.

The formula is: sustaining-critical-universal-specializing-spiritual-respo sible. Examples are: sun, 522, 653, 789, 861, 863, 902; moon, 37, 778; Me cury, 264, 339, 512; Venus, 133, 343, 434; Mars, 204, 301, 384, 653, 82 Saturn, 455; Uranus, 102, 187, 545, 663, 866, 931, 978.

CAPRICORN 13 *A fire worshiper* This is a symbol of man's inner strength through his realization of an inviolable tie with the creative power of the universe itself, dramatized by his continual outreach to the divine in a spiritualizing of his aspiration and a dedication of his talents and possessions to the over-all reality. He knows he must demonstrate his ultimate independence of his circumstances or else surrender his own potentialities forever. Here is ideality brought to the point of miracle. The keyword is MAGIC. When positive, the degree is extraordinary skill in enlisting every resource of the world for the exaltation of self and the consummation of its ambitions, and when negative, consistent overestimation of personal capacity.

The formula is: sustaining-critical-efficient-specializing-spiritual-receptive. Examples are: moon, 550; Mercury, 175, 282, 409, 953; Venus, 338, 594, 882; Jupiter, 20, 36, 202, 654; Saturn, 838; Uranus, 27, 499, 587, 708, 831.

CAPRICORN 14 *An ancient bas-relief carved in granite* This is a symbol of the immeasurable potentiality of the present moment as a recurrent manifestation of all that ever has been or that ever can be, and of the ability of man to capitalize on opportunities thus brought to focus in himself and his world at large again and again. Here is an absoluteness of self as it proceeds to express itself with a true conviction, and a completeness of its achievement as it acts with the over-all perspective of which it is capable. The keyword is FOUNDATION. When positive, the degree is a gift for bringing all things into a pattern of convenience and thereupon precipitating an inevitability of desired results, and when negative, meaningless imitation.

The formula is:sustaining-critical-efficient-specializing-spiritual-responsible. Examples are: sun, 251, 760, 768; moon, 40, 55, 79, 84, 521, 716, 986; Mercury, 337, 448, 922, 972; Venus, 286; Mars, 287, 328, 676, 731, 750, 861, 922; Jupiter, 2, 338, 461, 563; Saturn, 309, 926; Uranus, 825.

CANCER 15 *A group of people who have overeaten and en*
joyed it This is a symbol of the inescapable richness of life
in any normal manifestation of itself, here given emphasis on
the side of the rewards which come to man as a result of his
own efforts. There are penalties whenever he attempts to freeze
the present as a promise for the future or seeks to overindulge
himself in one direction as compensation for the consequence
of inadequacy in another, but individuality in its fullness has
recurrent and consistent assurance that its potentials will not
be dissipated. The keyword is SATIETY. When positive, the de
gree is an effective and smooth demonstration of human com
petence, and when negative, a self-disintegrating surrender to
appetite.

The formula is: sustaining-critical-universal-specializing-spiritual-inspired
Examples are: sun, 52, 467, 612, 662, 931, 995; moon, 453; Mercury, 5?
119, 177, 622; Venus, 420, 751, 895; Mars, 137, 181, 405, 496, 828, 948, 97?
Jupiter, 199, 264, 500, 816, 914; Saturn, 138, 928, 968; Uranus, 675, 74?

CANCER 16 *A man before a square with a manuscript scroll*
before him This is a symbol of intellectual experience as
primarily an exercise in self-competency, or of life as a never
ending adjustment of practical realities to their ideal po
tentials. Man's conscious realizations require continual ex
amination by logical or judicial criteria, whether this proces
takes place wittingly or otherwise. Here is the individual
exaggerated sensitiveness to things of possible concern to him
The keyword is PROFUNDITY. When positive, the degree is a
absolute and personal control and organization of self for th
purposes of each special situation, and when negative, sel
limitation through unimaginative perspective.

The formula is: sustaining-critical-universal-generalizing-physical-exper
mental. Examples are: sun, 39, 181, 186, 997; moon, 263; Mercury, 44
580; Venus, 69; Mars, 277, 453, 817; Jupiter, 3, 35, 115, 148, 170, 40?
Saturn, 42; Uranus, 307.

CAPRICORN 15   *Many toys in the children's ward of a hospital*
This is a symbol of the inescapable richness of life in any normal manifestation of itself, here given emphasis through its
ample rewards on the social and ideal side. There are physical
and psychological limitations which come to all humankind
without apparent reason, and which often seem a travesty of
divine justice, but they are always an unrealized opportunity
for a deeper fellowship. Experience is real in its fruits, rather
than in the means to its ends. The keyword is ABUNDANCE.
When positive, the degree is man's ability to develop the real
potentialities of himself and his fellows despite every transient
accident of circumstance, and when negative, hypocritical sympathy and childish self-pampering.

The formula is: sustaining-critical-efficient-specializing-spiritual-inspired.
Examples are: sun, 269, 513: moon, 483, 593; Mercury, 263, 278, 592, 849,
855; Venus, 598, 709, 819; Mars, 81, 898, 945, 967; Jupiter, 223; Saturn,
37, 281, 659, 694, 748, 877, 967; Uranus, 457, 751.

CAPRICORN 16   *Boys and girls in gymnasium suits*   This is a
symbol of practical experience as at root a matter of developing self-competency, and of life as a never-ending adjustment
of ideals and motives to the everyday potentials of human society. The individual is called on to co-operate in a continual
estimation and re-estimation of his powers and capacities by
his fellows, and to bring an aliveness of interest to everything
in which he would participate. A disciplined self-responsibility
is demanded for a common achievement. The keyword is ANI-
MATION. When positive, the degree is an effective appreciation
of joint action and a high skill in supervising group effort,
and when negative, self-betrayal through unimaginative conventionality.

The formula is: sustaining-critical-efficient-generalizing-physical-experi-
mental. Examples are: sun, 838, 992; Venus, 505, 576, 854; Mars, 27, 313,
719, 767; Jupiter, 281, 526, 694; Saturn, 425, 855, 979.

CANCER 17 *The germ grows into knowledge and life.* This is a symbol of the irresistible determination of living substance to press forward indefinitely and uncompromisingly in the expansion and refinement of its own special genius and identity, and thus to establish every possible phase of self-existence in more eternal lineaments. Implicit in the symbolism is the concept of the philosopher's stone, or of that sure core of immutable distinctiveness which actually constitutes self as such. The keyword is UNFOLDMENT. When positive, the degree is a completeness of personal realization and self-consummation in every context of immediate concern, and when negative, an assumption of self-integrity neither appreciated nor possessed.

The formula is: sustaining-critical-universal-generalizing-physical-sensitive.
Examples are: sun, 799; moon, 802; Mercury, 467; Venus, 247, 260, 307, 675; Mars, 124, 263, 333, 637, 959; Saturn, 872; Uranus, 746.

CANCER 18 *A hen scratching for her chicks* This is a symbol of the maximum protection which life at large will provide for the individual in general, here given emphasis on the personal side. There are always high rewards for any effort which is self-consistent or industrious at base, and by the reverse implication of the symbolism it is always possible for human creativity to endow its own manifestations with a gift of self continuousness. Normality is exalted in the simple business of self-being. The keyword is PROVISION. When positive, the degree is a marked capacity for meeting every demand of existence advantageously and with a persisting self-fulfillment, and when negative, idle bustle and unprofitable labor.

The formula is: sustaining-critical-universal-generalizing-physical-receptive.
Examples are: sun, 895; moon, 283, 385, 817; Mercury, 645, 662, 833, 885, 946; Venus, 1, 107, 512, 717, 975; Mars, 20, 72, 618, 655, 752, 833, 905; Saturn, 176; Uranus, 679.

CAPRICORN 17 *A girl surreptitiously bathing in the nude* This is a symbol of the irresistible desire of all life to strip back to essentials, and to gain self-renewal by some immediate and close intimacy with the accepted roots of all-being. Implicit in the symbolism is the spiritual significance of the human body as a temple of the spirit, or as the archetype representing the total potentiality in a personal existence. Here is successful resort to self-sacrifice or psychological renunciation in order to achieve a new dimension of conscious reality. The keyword is IMMERSION. When positive, the degree is a highly effective dramatization of the basic characteristics and potentials of self, and when negative, furtiveness or eccentricity.

The formula is: sustaining-critical-efficient-generalizing-physical-sensitive.
Examples are: sun, 943; moon, 71, 251, 297; Mercury, 120, 510, 959; Venus, 227, 233, 279, 330, 373; Mars, 216, 316, 582, 677, 699, 831; Jupiter, 451, 922; Saturn, 416, 461; Uranus, 252, 534.

CAPRICORN 18 *The Union Jack* This is a symbol of the maximum protection which life at large will provide for the individual in general, here given emphasis on the social or political side. There are always high rewards for common effort, since the organized nation is able to bring benefits to man beyond anything any person or group could ever win in a lesser dimension of enterprise. A greater community of interest is exalted through every possible phase of normal and everyday being. The keyword is SUPERVISION. When positive, the degree is the self's ever-widening spread of interest in its insatiable desire to leave some permanent imprint of itself on everything it touches, and when negative, smug or strong-armed paternalism.

The formula is: sustaining-critical-efficient-generalizing-physical-receptive.
Examples are: sun, 16, 388; moon, 600, 852; Mercury, 398, 417, 595, 980; Venus, 599; Mars, 12, 226, 626, 746, 806; Jupiter, 98; Uranus, 104, 390, 602.

CANCER 19 *A priest performing a marriage ceremony* This is a symbol of the spiritual stewardship of man as expressed in his conscious concern for the integrity of human society and for the everyday institutions through which all racial ideals must have their continued embodiment. There are very full rewards awaiting the individual who is willing to live the life of his fellows through his consistent shaping of his own acts and opinions to dramatize the current aspirations of his kind. His service to the established rituals becomes a special self-fulfillment. The keyword is CONFORMITY. When positive, the degree is a genius for bringing various facets of life into organic unity, and when negative, bondage to outer form.

The formula is: sustaining-critical-universal-generalizing-physical-responsible. Examples are: sun, 273; moon, 712, 804; Mercury, 842; Venus, 164, 450, 568, 746; Mars, 212, 570, 785, 929; Jupiter, 95, 439, 710, Uranus, 236, 566, 628, 870, 890, 987.

CANCER 20 *Gondoliers in a serenade* This is a symbol of the ever-exuberant music of life itself, and is an emphasis on experience as a symphony of co-operative relationships. The divisions of labor which create a human society are here brought to high consummation in the expanding development of selfhood and its functions. The capacity of the individual spirit for participation in the basic stream of events is exalted momentarily in a contribution to the imagination and the hunger of the soul. The keyword is SENTIMENT. When positive, the degree is a perfecting of those personal traits and inclinations which bring an enduring satisfaction to every immediate situation, and when negative, a retreat of self from all worth-while reality.

The formula is: sustaining-critical-universal-generalizing-physical-inspired. Examples are: sun, 506, 946; moon, 443, 497, 573; Mercury, 217, 393; Venus, 83; Mars, 339, 344, 632, 807; Jupiter, 235, 826, 839; Saturn, 817, 854; Uranus, 851.

CAPRICORN 19 *A child of about five with a huge shopping bag* This is a symbol of the spiritual stewardship of man as expressed in his inherent sense of responsibility for the welfare of others, and in his desire to serve his community to the extreme of his particular range of skills. There is wonderful recompense for the individual willing to share the total of his potentialities, and to enjoy those of his fellows to the limit of his understanding. His quickening to every opportunity of common function becomes a special self-fulfillment. The keyword is EXPECTATION. When positive, the degree is an effective breadth of participation in everyday living, and when negative, indiscriminate conformity to every passing fad.

The formula is: sustaining-critical-efficient-generalizing-physical-responsible.
Examples are: sun, 120; moon, 344; Mercury, 77; Venus, 475; Saturn, 221, 939.

CAPRICORN 20 *A hidden choir singing* This is a symbol of the eternal music of the spheres, and is an emphasis on the ideality of experience as at root a symphony of cosmic reconciliations. The differences of individual character which have contributed to a person's initiative and a conscious selfhood are here brought to their point of ultimate and single source in an over-all existence, and each and every element of inharmony is reordered as a participating distinctiveness of the whole. All men are at one in the universal pattern. The keyword is WORSHIP. When positive, the degree is a unique gift for establishing a common interest and making it a power for the good of all, and when negative, personal aloofness and lukewarm loyalties.

The formula is: sustaining-critical-efficient-generalizing-physical-inspired.
Examples are: sun, 4, 337, 350, 559; moon, 179; Mercury, 168, 316, 482; Venus, 100, 543, 841; Mars, 771, 830; Jupiter, 809; Saturn, 288, 411, 627, 826; Uranus, 55, 241, 327, 343, 492.

CANCER 21 *A prima donna singing* This is a symbol of an inevitable culmination for individual opportunity, and of an enduring contribution of skill and talent to whatever may entertain the soul's recurrent and constant rediscovery of itself. Here the popularization of human values becomes a creative encouragement for the common man, enabling him to lose himself for the moment and live vicariously in what he cannot yet establish for himself. Perfection is sought as a certainty of self-continuance. The keyword is EXCELLENCE. When positive, the degree is an overflowing richness of self through its full command of its own deep and genuine potentials, and when negative, superficial self-affirmation and unseemly display.

The formula is: sustaining-critical-universal-generalizing-social-experimental. Examples are: sun, 455, 989; moon, 638, 651; Mercury, 37, 428, 727; Venus, 400, 402, 666, 771, 894; Mars, 407, 416, 419, 654; Jupiter, 65, 294, 861; Saturn, 397; Uranus, 350.

CANCER 22 *A woman awaiting a sailboat* This is a symbol of the creative poise and quiet range of perspective which give real power to the human soul, endowing it with its gift for sustained interest in the present situation and its constructive attitude towards each ramifying potentiality of things to be. Here man exalts his destiny as he is aware of the ships that may come in for him, and he learns that it is through the consummation of idea and not the pyramiding of facts that life achieves its more enduring reality. The keyword is EQUANIMITY. When positive, the degree is a sure insight into the meaning of chance events and the current drift of circumstance, and when negative, senseless dependence on accidents of fortune.

The formula is: sustaining-critical-universal-generalizing-social-sensitive. Examples are: sun, 747; moon, 331, 950; Venus, 119, 177, 314, 607, 710; Mars, 563, 815; Jupiter, 230, 495, 556; Saturn, 569; Uranus, 295, 367, 373, 642, 660, 868, 924, 930.

CAPRICORN 21 *A relay race* This is a symbol of an inevitable culmination for group opportunity, and of a continual enhancement of the individual's skills and talents through his thoroughgoing co-operation with others in some vital phase of experience. Human values are established as they become the coin of effective relationship between one person and another, and their dramatization is the means through which man best discovers and refines his own latent potentialities. His importance to his fellows is his certainty of self-continuance. The keyword is FITNESS. When positive, the degree is exceptional skill in bringing the elements of any given situation to a functional wholeness, and when negative, complete inadequacy of self-resource.

The formula is: sustaining-critical-efficient-generalizing-social-experimental. Examples are: sun, 560; moon, 189, 463; Mercury, 12, 163, 226, 306, 319, 943; Venus, 361, 447, 517, 660, 943, 963; Mars, 288, 508; Jupiter, 275; Saturn, 23, 633, 754; Uranus, 196, 619.

CAPRICORN 22 *A general accepting defeat gracefully* This is a symbol of the immediate opportunism by which the human will develops its real power, and of its underlying and uncompromising loyalty to the long-range ends in view. A realistic practicality is made effective through a self-disciplined grace of spirit, so that men are won over very often by the enemy they have defeated. The individual exalts his destiny as he finds its roots established in values accepted by his fellows as well as himself. The keyword is EXPEDIENCY. When positive, the degree is a genius for learning from experience and transforming setback into accomplishment, and when negative, irresponsible acceptance of the worst and insensibility to self-inadequacy.

The formula is: sustaining-critical-efficient-generalizing-social-sensitive. Examples are: sun, 239, 937; moon, 465, 777, 782; Mercury, 719, 765, 783; Venus, 146, 375; Mars, 9, 839; Jupiter, 310; Saturn, 62, 476, 478, 581, 878; Uranus, 511, 559, 617.

CANCER 23 *Meeting of a literary society*   This is a symbol of man's resourcefulness in developing new areas of experience on the imaginative side, and of his genius for widening his interests and stimulating everybody to broader ideals and more rewarding goals in everyday living. The continual re-examination of a general intellectual and aesthetic inheritance becomes a heightening of personal identity, and the individual achieves a very genuine estimation of his fellows. The keyword is CRITICISM. When positive, the degree is accomplishment through an exacting appreciation of common effort and a rigorous revaluation of private acts and attitudes, and when negative, a substitution of idle discussion for actual participation in reality.

The formula is: sustaining-critical-universal-generalizing-social-receptive. Examples are: sun, 67, 193, 801; moon, 83, 421, 366; Mercury, 299, 381, 612, 817, 890, 942; Venus, 256, 413; Mars, 164, 218, 223, 262, 463; Jupiter, 517, 725; Saturn, 349, 533.

CANCER 24 *A woman and two men on a bit of sunlit land facing south*   This is a symbol of the soul's necessary decisiveness in the basic allegiances of life, here emphasized in the terms of practical or everyday relations. There must be a mediation between the competing demands for immediate attention to various transient needs, and for some consistent or over-all goal which will bring an individual's efforts into a cohesive pattern. The inner capacities must be disciplined continually for the sake of a plethora of outer opportunities. The keyword is INCEPTION. When positive, the degree is an unusual gift for organizing and exploiting the self's potentials, and when negative, a devastating sense of ineptitude and estrangement from reality.

The formula is: sustaining-critical-universal-generalizing-social-responsible. Examples are: sun, 308, 726; moon, 73, 129, 247, 361, 447, 459, 969; Mercury, 60, 221, 348, 419, 675, 940; Venus, 28, 309, 351, 583, 825; Mars, 194, 503, 883; Jupiter, 254, 296; Saturn, 304, 460; Uranus, 306, 363, 551, 698, 897.

CAPRICORN 23 *Two awards for bravery in war* This is a symbol of man's resourcefulness in developing new areas of experience on the practical side, and of his genius for dramatizing the fruits of an everyday aliveness and thereby stimulating a broadened self-expenditure. The continual effort of an idealistic leadership to hold social and political gains demands an exaltation of personal vision and character, and in the course of time every individual is brought to a broader understanding of his fellows. The goal of living becomes a preservation of values. The keyword is RECOGNITION. When positive, the degree is the social stewardship which demands a continual self-dedication, and when negative, strutting self-exploitation.

The formula is: sustaining - critical - efficient-generalizing-social - receptive. Examples are: sun, 399, 404, 589, 602; moon, 204; 473; Mercury, 51, 274, 497, 555, 766, 777; Venus, 31, 824; Mars, 65, 143, 196, 433; Jupiter, 659, 757, 877, 907, 955; Uranus, 348.

CAPRICORN 24 *A woman entering a convent* This is a symbol of the soul's characteristic dependence on some deep-stirring challenge to its potentialities, and of the fact that life can have no satisfaction for the individual unless he is able to develop and maintain some enduring allegiance of an over-all significance. Here is a measure of that cosmic insight through which the self knows that of itself it is nothing, and that it can find itself only as it somehow can feel itself a participant in all-self. Man's talents are exalted only by a dedication to eternal ends. The keyword is CONSECRATION. When positive, the degree is the irresistible power of a true inner vision, and when negative, abject surrender to weakness.

The formula is: sustaining-critical-efficient-generalizing-social-responsible. Examples are: sun, 190, 338; moon, 681; Mercury, 40, 469, 614, 673; Mars, 190, 574, 966; Jupiter, 618; Uranus, 87.

CANCER 25 *A dark shadow or mantle thrown suddenly over the right shoulder* This is a symbol of the irrevocability of man's obligation to the reality of which he is a part, with the emphasis on his capacities of leadership as a revelation of racial stewardship on the more personal or spiritual side. Self-expression here is a release of his inner potentialities, and it becomes both an individual gratification and an expanding responsibility to all other individuals making up the social complex. The keyword is DESTINY. When positive, the degree is some dramatic manifestation of genius vital to the general welfare of man, and when negative, a tendency to unwarranted presumption if not outright megalomania.

The formula is: sustaining-critical-universal-generalizing-social-inspired. Examples are: sun, 577; moon, 78, 212, 264, 500, 533, 644; Venus, 241, Mars, 203, 470, 536, 679, 691, 733; Jupiter, 53, 186, 270, 472, 921, 941; Saturn, 468, 481, 886; Uranus, 72, 362, 691.

CANCER 26 *Contentment and happiness in luxury, people reading on davenports* This is a symbol of a pure mastery of experience in its outer aspect, and of a full capitalization on the potentials of all being in a personal and ultimately immortal realization. The static symbolism is a warning against idle self-indulgence, and an emphasis on the fact that any lessening of practical responsibility is primarily a call to self-strengthening and a prelude to some greater outreaching. The keyword is REPOSE. When positive, the degree is a relaxation valuable for the momentary sustainment of human aspiration whenever it is strained beyond its powers of self-regeneration, and when negative, the loss of all reality in a needless softness of living.

The formula is: sustaining-critical-universal-generalizing-spiritual-experimental. Examples are: sun, 715, 733; moon, 88, 106, 125, 406, 938; Mercury, 309, 893; Venus, 782; Mars, 385; Jupiter, 623, 778.

CAPRICORN 25 *An oriental-rug dealer* This is a symbol of the irrevocability of man's obligation to the reality of which he is a part, with the emphasis on his accumulated knowledge or acquired skills as an indication of his enduring competency on the more immediate or practical side. Self-expression here is the use of various advantages and resources as actually a commerce in human potentialities, and this becomes an individual's real service to his fellows. Eternal values are meaningless until they are woven into the fabric of humanity's familiar transactions. The keyword is CONSIGNMENT. When positive, the degree is an effective employment of the facilities and goods of a modern society, and when negative, concern over trivialities.

The formula is: sustaining-critical-efficient-generalizing-social-inspired. Examples are: sun, 555, 594; moon, 4, 145, 892; Mercury, 292, 813; Venus, 742; Mars, 116, 334, 753, 901, 1000; Jupiter, 82, 503; Saturn, 79, 684, 718; Uranus, 322, 815.

CAPRICORN 26 *A water sprite* This is a symbol of a pure mastery of experience in its inner or spiritual aspect, and of the possession of every richness of outer reality in a highly imaginative or personal form. Here the pure integrity of self asserts itself as a protection against blind or inept participation in the current course of events, and calls for a conscious self-idealization in even the most unimportant or transient functions of life. Spontaneity is demanded as a necessary quickening to values. The keyword is RESTLESSNESS. When positive, the degree is an exceptional sensitiveness to over-all implications and high skill in avoiding drab or commonplace involvements, and when negative, carefree irresponsibility and a dislike of intimacies.

The formula is: sustaining-critical-efficient-generalizing-spiritual-experimental. Examples are: sun, 777; moon, 481, 585, 814; Mercury, 214, 456; Mars, 127, 911; Jupiter, 123; Saturn, 30, 168, 356; Uranus, 321, 502, 591.

CANCER 27 *A storm in a canyon* This is a symbol of a pyramiding reality on the side of external circumstances, or of violence and terror as divine in their capacity for lifting man out of his aplomb and demanding some manifestation of his inner ideals and enduring values. Here is the indomitable integrity of everything to be taken as of consequence in its own right, shown in the energy with which it preserves itself. Nature ever dramatizes man's unleashed powers, or his ability to rise in supremacy over each momentary crisis. The keyword is INTENSIFICATION. When positive, the degree is an enlistment of every resource in life for a heightened expression of self, and when negative, fatuous enjoyment of turmoil.

The formula is: sustaining-critical-universal-generalizing-spiritual-sensitive.
Examples are: sun, 381, 665, 852; moon, 49, 228, 632, 636, 813, 966; Mercury, 421, 931; Venus, 59, 424, 577, 852; Mars, 666; Jupiter, 488, 962; Saturn, 673, 795; Uranus, 629, 703.

CANCER 28 *A modern Pocahontas* This is a symbol of effective co-operation between various phases of human culture, such as those which have become crystallized in a faithfulness to the special values they have held intact and those which provide the new potentials of a genuine frontier spirit. These differences as brought to unity are a stimulus to a greater differentiation of the self in its own illimitable capacity for expanded relationships. The keyword is COMPATIBILITY. When positive, the degree is high skill in bringing older or neglected reality to the service of fresher and more vital self-fulfillments, and when negative, an inability to make personal adjustments and a stupid exaltation of conservatism.

The formula is: sustaining-critical-universal-generalizing-spiritual-receptive.
Examples are: sun, 817; moon, 614; Mercury, 174, 852, 983; Venus, 789; Mars, 880; Jupiter, 821; Saturn, 25, 413, 820; Uranus, 826.

CAPRICORN 27 *A mountain pilgrimage* This is a symbol of a pyramiding reality on the side of inner or spiritual realization in a complete harmony of all the ideals and values ever developed by man. Here is an indomitable integrity of human comprehension, and an intensification of every vision to which intelligence might aspire. The individual is encouraged to hold unswervingly to the ultimate course he has chosen for himself. The keyword is PERSEVERANCE. When positive, the degree is a total reconciliation of mind and heart in an unquestioned devotion to some worth-while task at hand, and when negative, satisfaction in superficial allegiances and a parade of false virtue.

The formula is: sustaining-critical-efficient-generalizing-spiritual-sensitive.
Examples are: sun, 51, 626; moon, 363, 997; Venus, 868; Mars, 813; Jupiter, 266, 838, 880; Saturn, 33, 271, 519, 588, 784; Uranus, 783.

CAPRICORN 28 *A large aviary* This is a symbol of the ramifying differentiation of interest to be found in the many areas of normal life, and of man's gift for bringing any one special line of effort to the immediate services of any other. His wide spread of aspiration is encompassed in the over-all realization by which he has organized himself, and his everyday problems have their solution in his breadth of resources. His administration of human potentialities on this social level is his self-fulfillment. The keyword is COMMUNITY. When positive, the degree is exceptional success in making all personal concerns a matter of common welfare, and when negative, loss of all character in sheer officiousness.

The formula is: sustaining-critical-efficient-generalizing-spiritual-receptive.
Examples are: sun, 584; moon, 579, 811; Mercury, 374, 795, 897; Venus, 922; Jupiter, 633, 845; Saturn, 374, 573, 830, 848; Uranus, 354, 433, 731, 801.

CANCER 29   *A Muse weighing twins*   This is a symbol of man's continual if not always evident relationship with the over-reality in which he lives and moves and has his being, here given an emphasis on the side of inner reconciliations. Individual existence is always manifest as personality in the world of the senses and as reason in a realm of eternalities, and the effective union of these complementary functions is found in the immortal insights of a spiritual wholeness. A person knows himself now one way and now another, and thereby realizes his integrity of selfhood. The keyword is VALUE. When positive, the degree is an effectiveness of judgment irrespective of momentary contradictions on every hand, and when negative, an undisciplined perfectionism.

The formula is: sustaining-critical-universal-generalizing-spiritual-responsible. Examples are: sun, 310, 521, 785; moon, 323, 422, 611, 739, 891, 923; Mercury, 500, 747; Venus, 72, 219, 242, 621, 780, 858, 873; Mars, 24, 751, 857; Jupiter, 23, 40, 392, 417, 443, 766, 855, 909; Saturn, 137, 395, 1000; Uranus, 23, 855.

CANCER 30   *A Daughter of the American Revolution*   This is a symbol of the enduring background in human relations as essentially dependent on an established tradition, and of a willingness to maintain it through a sharp rejection of any modifying influence of unsympathetic times or events. The emphasis here on an outer conservatism carries with it an implicit warning against any mere resistance to change, and also stresses the need for a life which is exemplary through its faithfulness to standards of proved worth. The keyword is INHERITANCE. When positive, the degree is an infectious pride in leadership through which a group is able to act as a unit, and when negative, the ultimate betrayal of selfhood by a false assumption of superiority.

The formula is: sustaining-critical-universal-generalizing-spiritual-inspired. Examples are: sun, 339, 917; moon, 194, 198, 668; Mercury, 418, 747, 799; Mars, 234, 357, 800; Jupiter, 246, 920; Saturn, 194, 427, 651; Uranus, 294, 495, 556, 725, 838.

CAPRICORN 29   *A woman reading tea leaves*   This is a symbol of man's persistent desire to establish conscious relationship with an invisible world of over-reality, given an emphasis here on the side of outer or everyday self-encouragement. The mind has its ultimate focus in eternal and universal co-ordinates, and ever tends to fit the exigencies of practical living into some pattern of possible consummations. Conscious experience therefore comes to be supplemented by intuition as a direct realization of pure potentiality. The keyword is SIGNATURE. When positive, the degree is naïve insight as brought to high intelligence in meeting the recurrent issues of life, and when negative, superstitious dependence on the unknown.

The formula is: sustaining-critical-efficient-generalizing-spiritual-responsible. Examples are: sun, 185, 263; moon, 151, 294, 300, 315, 457, 491, 565, 931; Mercury, 126, 188; Venus, 168, 642; Mars, 157, 763; Jupiter, 62, 561, 788; Saturn, 8, 61, 178; Uranus, 484, 992.

CAPRICORN 30   *A secret business conference*   This is a symbol of the momentary background in human relations as essentially the product of current activities and attitudes, and of a determination to capitalize on any given situation through effective allegiances among the principal personalities involved. The emphasis here is on man's desire for an inner circle of associates through whom he may exercise a real control over immediate eventualities, and on his realization that in this fashion he may monopolize the resources of his fellows. The keyword is OPPORTUNITY. When positive, the degree is a gift for clever planning and successful administration in every area of life, and when negative, rampant selfishness and rank exploitation of others.

The formula is: sustaining-critical-efficient-generalizing-spiritual-inspired. Examples are: sun, 988; moon, 147, 489, 768; Mercury, 238, 283; Venus, 814, 937; Mars, 49, 484; Jupiter, 581, 672, 780; Saturn, 125, 408; Uranus, 253, 730, 928.

LEO 1 *A case of apoplexy* This is a symbol of an overwhelming potentiality, and of an ever-pressing necessity for genuine self-establishment and personal stability. Implicit in the reversed symbolism is man's complete lack of inhibition in his everyday make-up, together with his ability to mobilize all his powers and even risk his own existence rather than accept any thwarting of his desires. Here is emphasis on the unbroken continuity between being and doing, or between identity and its continual manifestation of itself. The keyword is IRRESISTIBILITY. When positive, the degree is creativity in the day-by-day expression of the self's real possibilities, and when negative, thoroughgoing self-indulgence and imposition on others.

The formula is: manipulating-ideal-original-specializing-physical-experimental. Examples are: sun, 121, 299, 386, 420, 449; moon, 249, 494; Mercury, 307, 453, 514; Venus, 9, 212, 407, 520, 521, 527, 931, 995; Jupiter, 288; Saturn, 47, 162, 743, 747; Uranus, 221, 417, 488.

LEO 2 *An epidemic of mumps* This is a symbol of personal capacities wholly out of hand, and of the momentary appeal of escapist ideas whenever the self fails to remain alive to its own immediate needs or ultimate interests. The reversed symbolism emphasizes the absolute necessity laid on every living spirit, that somehow it retain a passionate sensitiveness to the practical import or organic usefulness of everything it encounters in its everyday situation. Here is life poised in sharp susceptibility. The keyword is INFECTION. When positive, the degree is continual self-dramatization as the basis for participation in current affairs, and when negative, retreat to self-deficiencies in a frantic effort to avoid experience.

The formula is: manipulating-ideal-original-specializing-physical-sensitive. Examples are: Venus, 63, 752; Mars, 560, 903; Jupiter, 83; Saturn, 279 961; Uranus, 255, 465, 920.

AQUARIUS 1 *An old adobe mission* This is a symbol of ever-lasting sustainment, and of the necessity for both an over-all orientation and an underlying stability in all personal existence. Implicit in the static symbolism is man's heritage of enduring ties which he must neither neglect nor underrate, and so a call on him to remember his own true state at all times. Here is emphasis on the unbroken continuity between the psychological and physical certainties of his being, and a reminder of their continuing value to him. The keyword is DURABILITY. When positive, the degree is effective breadth of vision and a respect-compelling depth of character, and when negative, lack of ambition and blind adherence to superficialities.

The formula is: manipulating-ideal-ingenious-specializing-physical-experimental. Examples are: sun, 499, 743, 959; moon, 291, 673, 980; Mercury, 404, 1000; Venus, 410, 694; Mars, 153, 443; Jupiter, 276, 564, 813; Saturn, 93, 131, 272, 608, 722; Uranus, 126, 298, 491, 744.

AQUARIUS 2 *An unexpected thunderstorm* This is a symbol of nature's potentialities as they lie beyond any individual control, as well as of the tendency of all things to come to some dramatic head in either physical or psychological terms. The primitive symbolism emphasizes the necessity that every living spirit remain wholly self-quickened within itself, and be alert to its more or less inevitable participation in every shifting pattern of events. The convergence of relations in some climax of experience is man's real opportunity for self-fulfillment. The keyword is ACCIDENT. When positive, the degree is creative opportunism and a genius for shaping all eventualities to some desired end, and when negative, complete temperamental instability.

The formula is: manipulating-ideal-ingenious-specializing-physical-sensitive. Examples are: sun, 390; moon, 410, 436, 610, 713; Mercury, 841; Venus, 403; Mars, 99, 397, 487; Jupiter, 649, 723; Saturn, 174.

LEO 3 *A woman having her hair bobbed* This is a symbol of human independence carried to a point of extreme self-examination, here emphasized in a desire for greater participation in the momentary trends and heightened values of the social milieu. There is open invitation to every possibility of personal experience, and a willingness to grasp the least promising opportunity in order to achieve an enlarged significance. The soul accepts every minor modification of itself in order to perfect the channels of its self-expression. The keyword is DECISION. When positive, the degree is exceptionally effective self-mobilization for the sake of personal ambition, and when negative, wholly inadequate appreciation for the self and its destiny.

The formula is: manipulating-ideal-original-specializing-physical-receptive. Examples are: sun, 60, 305, 530; moon, 146, 182, 306, 401, 540, 864; Mercury, 137, 336, 666; Venus, 276, 580; Mars, 420, 472, 774, 921; Jupiter, 60, 464, 787; Saturn, 529, 544; Uranus, 125, 178, 408, 416.

LEO 4 *A man formally dressed and a deer with its horns folded* This is a symbol of self-assertion at a point of effective impact on the world, dramatized here on the side of an established and everyday reality. Formality becomes a magical ordering of the automatisms of lesser things, enlisting them in an enduring service to each individual's more outstanding talents. His achievements become evident in the trophies by which he makes his consistent contribution of the real essence of himself to his fellows. The keyword is MORALE. When positive, the degree is exceptional capacity for winning and holding the esteem of men, and when negative, dependence on applause and a playing to the gallery to get it.

The formula is: manipulating-ideal-original-specializing-physical-responsible. Examples are: sun, 80, 512, 842; moon, 320, 337, 416, 705; Mercury, 347; Venus, 60, 161, 443, 786; Mars, 53, 856, 875, 986; Jupiter, 145, 252, 325, 939; Saturn, 555, 734, 994.

AQUARIUS 3 *A deserter from the navy* This is a symbol of human independence carried to a point of extreme rebellion against things as they are, here emphasized in a disregard of all consequences for the sake of an immediate liberation of the spirit. There is a demand for a more rewarding expression of individuality, and the reversed symbolism suggests that any late acceptance of full and personal responsibility for life is better than none at all. Except as man creates his own allegiances, his destiny holds no depth. The keyword is DEFIANCE. When positive, the degree is genuine psychological courage in a repudiation of all meaningless loyalties, and when negative, complete inability to follow the rules of any game.

The formula is: manipulating-ideal-ingenious-specializing-physical-receptive. Examples are: sun, 456, 608, 673; moon, 288, 567, 617, 840; Mercury, 155, 251, 683, 860; Venus, 238, 285; Mars, 350, 417; Jupiter, 562, 689, 690, 706, 792; Saturn, 255, 465, 850; Uranus, 113, 138, 743.

AQUARIUS 4 *A Hindu healer* This is a symbol of self-assertion at a point of effective impact on the world, dramatized here on the side of an inner and transcendental reality. A spiritualized self-discipline achieves a magical ordering of the whole course of events, and in its perfecting it provides a spectacular ministry for the minds and bodies of all. The individual ever dramatizes his immortal capacities as he translates these into his tangible achievements on one or another level of life. The keyword is THERAPY. When positive, the degree is high personal skill in bringing the least of human potentials to some ultimate consummation, and when negative, false claims of psychological power in an effort to impress others.

The formula is: manipulating-ideal-ingenious-specializing-physical-responsible. Examples are: sun, 272; moon, 720; Mercury, 88, 91, 269, 589, 819; Venus, 327; Mars, 646, 939, 943; Jupiter, 599; Saturn, 22, 28, 91; Uranus, 66, 223, 333, 385, 563.

LEO 5 *Rock formations at the edge of a precipice* This is a symbol of the constitution of reality in crisis, offering a challenge to man as it pyramids in ramifying involvements until action or decision becomes an immediate necessity. There is no possible sustainment of individuality without an acceptance of difficulty as significant and an accompanying realization that every shift in orientation is a demand for some enlarged self-discovery. Personality only achieves its stability at the threshold of the risks it is willing to take. The keyword is ENDURANCE. When positive, the degree is man's genius for initial aplomb and ultimate competency in the face of all danger, and when negative, pure bullheadedness.

The formula is: *manipulating-ideal-original-specializing-physical-inspired.* Examples are: sun, 336; moon, 343, 449, 536; Mercury, 258; Venus, 842; Mars, 315, 607, 622; Jupiter, 219, 221, 242, 575; Saturn, 393, 504; Uranus, 174, 748, 967.

LEO 6 *An old-fashioned woman and an up-to-date girl* This is a symbol of the essentially dramatic function of the soul as it plays its various roles in a human society, here brought out in a practical aspect of everyday values. There is at once a co-operation and a competition between those ways of life which protect the contribution of the past on the one hand and administer the promise of the future on the other. Conventionality and initiative are a continual stimulus to each other. The keyword is CONTRAST. When positive, the degree is personal achievement through a creative appreciation and adaptation of the values established by others, and when negative, overemphasis of individualistic traits and a psychological timidity.

The formula is: *manipulating-ideal-original-specializing-social-experimental.* Examples are: sun, 118, 710, 903; moon, 277, 996; Mercury, 194, 246, 364, 530, 710, 789, 973; Venus, 46, 78, 329, 708, 822, 932; Mars, 382, 597, 623, 961; Jupiter, 492, 858; Saturn, 293, 811, 934; Uranus, 979.

AQUARIUS 5 *A council of ancestors* This is a symbol of the enduring reality which man creates in the over-all ideal he accepts for himself, and of his immortal dependence on the characteristics which have proved their value and hence have their continual re-embodiment in the hearts and minds of one generation after another. The emphasis here is on the individual as a challenge to the world at large, since the whole of his background mobilizes itself continually to serve him and to facilitate a further refinement of potentialities incarnate in his person. Self ultimately must fulfill itself. The keyword is ANTE-CEDENCE. When positive, the degree is power through absolute self-integrity, and when negative, sterile conservatism.

The formula is: manipulating-ideal-ingenious-specializing-physical-inspired. Examples are: sun, 61, 633; moon, 54, 160, 563, 605, 680; Mercury, 90, 422, 481, 602, 623, 672, 937; Venus, 47, 978; Mars, 8, 132, 346, 493; Jupiter, 467, 669; Saturn, 11, 489, 793; Uranus, 849.

AQUARIUS 6 *A performer of a mystery play* This is a symbol of the mediating function of the mind as it is called on to interpret the individual and his world to each other, and as the everyday values of experience thereby are heightened in personality on the one side and in life itself on the other. The conventional aspect of reality is found to be a convenient backdrop for man's self-realization, and his particular characteristics are exalted as variant and ever-stimulating potentialities of living relationship in general. The keyword is SUBTLETY. When positive, the degree is a gift for dramatizing the deeper or real opportunities of a human society, and when negative, consistent self-mystification and marked impracticability.

The formula is: manipulating-ideal-ingenious-specializing-social-experimental. Examples are: sun, 40, 922; moon, 319, 594, 627, 629, 808; Mercury, 350, 369, 743, 870; Venus, 507, 584; Mars, 150, 486, 537, 854; Jupiter, 627, 781; Saturn, 143, 574, 844, 927.

LEO 7 *The constellations in the sky*   This is a symbol of the infinite regression in all universal reality, not as a fact of some unreachable end in knowledge but rather as a demonstration that any abandonment of the known for the sake of the unknown is fruitless. The cosmos is illimitable in the sense that man's questing may ramify in time and space to the extent of any given pertinence, but his assurance lies within his own being and experience. The stars are his confirmation, never his explanation. The keyword is SURETY. When positive, the degree is consistent effectiveness in understanding and self-ordering, and when negative, a loss of all present integrity through an unnecessary retreat to the remote or mysterious.

The formula is: manipulating-ideal-original-specializing-social-sensitive. Examples are: sun, 104, 135, 583, 649, 890; moon, 498; Mercury, 317, 541, 801, 861; Venus, 362; Mars, 151, 583, 648, 772, 952; Jupiter, 768; Saturn, 169, 173, 403; Uranus, 268, 480, 643.

LEO 8 *A Bolshevik propagandist*   This is a symbol of the indomitable expectation of the human spirit as it gathers strength from the innermost reaches of man's own or enduring nature, here emphasized by the recurrent battles over social and political concepts. The exceptional dynamic involved is seen in the selfless energy developed to an extreme by the revolutionists of each new age. Implicit in the reversed symbolism is the need of the human community for a worthy cause to which to rally in every aspect of its potentials. The keyword is LEAVEN. When positive, the degree is a determination to share the soul's vision and to make a permanent impact on history, and when negative, futile ranting against a multitude of superficial ills.

The formula is: manipulating-ideal-original-specializing-social-receptive. Examples are: sun, 347, 421, 607; moon, 41, 474, 649, 734; Mercury, 290, 506, 653; Venus, 784; Mars, 210, 320, 440, 474, 611, 636; Jupiter, 161, 592; Saturn, 291, 324, 683; Uranus, 840.

AQUARIUS 7 *A child born of an eggshell* This is a symbol of the infinite regression in all personal reality, not as a fact of some mysterious loss of self either in source or in final dissolution but as a demonstration of the illimitable potentialities to be found in each immediate moment of self-realization. For his own enlightenment a man may project himself indefinitely into what has been or what may be but his assurance is in the ever-present sustainment of the auric egg or self-matrix in which existence continues to create itself in its own image. The keyword is ESSENTIALITY. When positive, the degree is a highly individual and completely unlimited resourcefulness, and when negative, naïve reliance on external accident.

The formula is: manipulating-ideal-ingenious-specializing-social-sensitive.
Examples are: sun, 175, 188, 334, 409, 539, 614; moon, 295, 442, 599, 746, 954; Mercury, 16, 54, 64, 332; Venus, 185, 755, 805, 846; Mars, 142, 757, 781; Jupiter, 155, 259, 446, 965; Uranus, 498.

AQUARIUS 8 *Beautifully gowned wax figures* This is a symbol of the ineradicable vanity of the human spirit as it gathers strength not only from the finery it wears but from a superficial display of woman's form and man's reputation, here emphasized through personal idealizations. A strong psychological dynamic for individual effort comes from the direct influence of outstanding and even notorious people, and implicit in the static symbolism of the waxworks is a necessity to recognize and identify the values worthy of emulation. The keyword is IMPACT. When positive, the degree is achievement through the effective dramatization of human character on some level of everyday understanding, and when negative, futile effort to recapture outworn experience.

The formula is: manipulating-ideal-ingenious-specializing-social-receptive.
Examples are: sun, 972; moon, 796; Mercury, 176; Venus, 64, 796; Mars, 599, 932; Jupiter, 301, 345, 376, 476, 478, 530, 836, 878; Saturn, 1, 29, 840; Uranus, 98, 220, 275, 351, 451, 540, 809.

LEO 9 *Glass blowers* This is a symbol of man's inexhaustibly creative skill of hand and genius of self-application, and of
his inherent urge to perform the tasks to be done and to have
justification in the ideals to which he would give expression.
Here is his contribution of enduring form to things through a
private manifestation of the divine breath, and a manipulation of the baser materials of life through a heat that represents his living enthusiasm. The arts and crafts of a culture are
both its first beginnings and its final testimony. The keyword
is DEFTNESS. When positive, the degree is an effectiveness of
personal participation in everyday existence, and when negative, willful or unintelligent distortion of reality.

The formula is: manipulating-ideal-original-specializing-social-responsible.
Examples are: sun, 74, 123; moon, 90, 529; Mercury, 181, 726; Venus, 199,
308, 395; Mars, 56, 154, 264, 467, 544; Jupiter, 154, 210, 383, 457, 558, 568,
647, 696, 737, 884, 982; Saturn, 319, 415; Uranus, 119, 177, 784.

LEO 10 *Early morning dew* This is a symbol of the eternal
refreshment which comes to the individual with every recurrent cycle of his experience, and of nature's continual endorsement of his aims or benediction on his efforts. There are
unexpected resources which man can find at hand when life
otherwise may seem to have defeated him, and these are often
revealed to him despite his lack of expectation. He reaps real
fruits as he develops a genuine alertness to the unexpected,
and denies all personal limitation. The keyword is REJUVENA-
TION. When positive, the degree is a special talent for finding
the better in every situation where a worse may threaten dis-
aster, and when negative, procrastination and total insensibility
to the real powers of selfhood.

The formula is: manipulating-ideal-original-specializing-social-inspired. Examples are: sun, 290, 942; moon, 86; Mercury, 57, 74, 107, 902; Venus, 364,
634; Mars, 717, 884; Jupiter, 117, 458; Saturn, 409, 938, 972; Uranus, 181,
653, 850.

AQUARIUS 9 *A flag turned into an eagle* This is a symbol of man's inexhaustibly fertile imagination or genius for significant self-representation, and of his capacity for rising to every situation in the terms of its most rewarding potentials. Here is his contribution of enduring purpose to all things by his vision of their worth, and his determination to make this evident through every ramification of his own personal living. The loyalties of human beings are the foundation of any possible society, and any individual prospers as he springs to action in their defense. The keyword is DRAMATIZATION. When positive, the degree is accomplishment through utter self-dedication, and when negative, vindictive pride.

The formula is: manipulating-ideal-ingenious-specializing-social-responsible. Examples are: sun, 398, 448, 529, 766, 855, 860; moon, 77, 94, 170, 220, 238, 390, 562, 803; Mercury, 559, 731; Venus, 531; Mars, 69; Jupiter, 381, 754; Saturn, 50, 159, 404, 473, 687.

AQUARIUS 10 *A popularity that proves ephemeral* This is a symbol of the eternal challenge which comes to an individual at every point of climax in his experience, and of the swing of the pendulum between an endorsement and a repudiation of his efforts by his social group. He must learn to accept the applause as encouragement in his self-strengthening, but to look for any continued sustainment from his own stability of being. A courageous self-confidence and an unflagging faith are worthy of recognition, but only in their moment of significance. The keyword is APPROBATION. When positive, the degree is a gift for bringing the issues of life to a dramatic consummation at a time of crisis, and when negative, prodigal opportunism.

The formula is: manipulating-ideal-ingenious-specializing-social-inspired. Examples are: sun, 510, 627, 827; Mercury, 594; Venus, 77; Mars, 133, 543; Jupiter, 15, 77, 271, 896; Saturn, 206, 429.

LEO 11   *Children on a swing in a huge oak tree*   This is a symbol of satisfaction in the normal exercise of selfhood, and of a new realization of the high dependability exhibited by man's physical and social sustainments. Implicit in the symbolism is a special refreshment of the spirit, but only through a continual development of its responsibilities to its own manifestation of itself. As each individual accepts the overshadowing of a universal life and order he achieves an ever-better conception of personal reality. The keyword is DELIGHT. When positive, the degree is a consistent zest for every possible phase of living and a real generosity of self-expenditure, and when negative, laziness exalted as a virtue.

The formula is: manipulating-ideal-original-specializing-spiritual-experimental. Examples are: sun, 59, 262, 541, 735; moon, 161, 523, 566; Mercury, 59; Venus, 186, 421, 622; Mars, 674, 862; Saturn, 239, 303, 741, 764; Uranus, 8, 830.

LEO 12   *An evening lawn party*   This is a symbol of the common enhancement of individual experience on the side of its more superficial or everyday gratifications, and of the inherent normality through which man shares the fruits of his personal accomplishment with his intimates and neighbors at every opportunity. There are limitless forms of self-expression by which he may come to discover himself as a distinct personality, but what he achieves is meaningless unless there is some definite recognition of its worth from his fellows. The keyword is COMPANIONSHIP. When positive, the degree is a genuine social maturity and an effective capacity for working with others, and when negative, a lack of all appreciation for the underlying reality of life itself.

The formula is: manipulating-ideal-original-specializing-spiritual-sensitive. Examples are: sun, 137, 258, 317, 416, 426, 551, 994; moon, 432, 468, 743, 786; Venus, 876; Mars, 975, 990; Jupiter, 346, 416, 771; Saturn, 57, 554, 806; Uranus, 13, 19, 205, 474, 544.

AQUARIUS 11 *Man tête-à-tête with his inspiration* This is a symbol of satisfaction in the transcendental experiences of selfhood, and of a new realization that each individual lives in a consistent intimacy with spiritual verities of every sort and on every hand. Implicit in the symbolism is the need to act continually in personal self-interest, and to translate every vision into practical consummation. As man accepts the overshadowing of a universal life and order, he must demonstrate his own special capacities and rededicate his own individual achievements. The keyword is ECSTASY. When positive, the degree is an enthusiastic idealism and a tireless desire to serve others, and when negative, complete self-obsession.

The formula is: manipulating-ideal-ingenious-specializing-spiritual-experimental. Examples are: sun, 77, 112, 332, 507; moon, 137, 289, 347, 951; Mercury, 225, 445; Venus, 55; Mars, 6, 300, 314, 609, 617, 673, 755; Jupiter, 263; Saturn, 99, 387, 474; Uranus, 355, 371.

AQUARIUS 12 *People on stairs graduated upwards* This is a symbol of the common enhancement of individual experience on the side of its inner gratification, and of the inherent differences among human kind which enable man to share any endeavor with his fellows whenever they prove either more or less competent than himself. There are limitless levels on which he may bring his aspiration to a momentary consummation, but no one of these alone can ever offer him sufficient ground for his own ultimate self-fulfillment. The keyword is PROGRESSION. When positive, the degree is an effective forward point of view and a genuine capitalization on all prior accomplishment, and when negative, frantic efforts to keep ahead of others.

The formula is: manipulating-ideal-ingenious-specializing-spiritual-sensitive. Examples are: sun, 62, 163, 176, 457, 805; moon, 364, 601, 934; Mercury, 108, 112; Mars, 259; Jupiter, 315, 966; Saturn, 64; Uranus, 155, 263, 597, 774.

LEO 13 *An old sea captain rocking* This is a symbol of man's great love for reliving his experiences in memory, and of his gift for achieving a mastery in advance of whatever new situations he may face by bringing all the ramifying relationships to a focus in a personal and competent grasp of their more pertinent potentialities. He fights the battles of the world in his imagination, over and over again. He knows that events repeat themselves, and so may be brought in leash. The keyword is RETRÓSPECT. When positive, the degree in each person's unlimited capacity for calling up afresh the powers he has gained in his struggle toward self-fulfillment, and when negative, insensibility to present reality in a full surrender to the past.

The formula is: manipulating-ideal-original-specializing-spiritual-receptive Examples are: sun, 446, 661, 675; moon, 287, 318; Mercury, 305, 771; Venus, 348, 691, 735; Mars, 5, 696; Jupiter, 330; Saturn, 153, 537, 670; Uranus, 635, 638.

LEO 14 *The human soul awaiting opportunity for expression* This is a symbol of life's normal expectation on the personal or subjective side, and of the totally unconditioned potential of self at its point of entrance into each new complex of activity with its fellows. Here all the ramifications of man's promise are made ready for any or every refinement of immediate value and his skills and talents are given a special sensitiveness to the momentary nuances of his individual aspiration. The key word is INGENUOUSNESS. When positive, the degree is a genius for an absolute wholeheartedness of participation in the everyday adventures of personality, and when negative, naïve procrastination and a lack of all genuine interest or enthusiasm.

The formula is: manipulating-ideal-original-specializing-spiritual-responsible. Examples are: sun, 864, 893; moon, 164; Mercury, 310, 864; Venus, 74, 679, 886, 889; Mars, 28, 199, 766; Jupiter, 142, 150; Saturn, 191, 342, 462; Uranus, 52, 217, 473, 885.

AQUARIUS 13 *A barometer* This is a symbol of man's great love for living his experience in advance, and of his gift for meeting every possible contingency by an effective estimation of his own potentials. He uses the power of the human mind for broad generalization or abstract insight, and balances this with the tendency of nature to operate at all points through quite specific and measurable dependabilities. He knows that life can always be made to reveal any pertinent details of its fundamental ordering. The keyword is INDICATION. When positive, the degree is unusual keenness of observation and exceptional competence in judgment, and when negative, superficial uncertainty and a continual trimming to passing events.

The formula is: manipulating-ideal-ingenious-specializing-spiritual-receptive. Examples are: sun, 361, 447, 750, 841; moon, 192; Mercury, 87, 584; Venus, 369, 713, 953; Mars, 284, 374; Jupiter, 79, 220, 260, 355, 477, 798; Saturn, 181, 480, 653; Uranus, 103.

AQUARIUS 14 *A train entering a tunnel* This is a symbol of life's normal expectation in the performance of community services or in the refinement of social divisions of labor, and of the utterly natural participation of self in its more impersonal relationships with others. Here is the basic generosity of human personality in an eagerness for any or every new path of experience, or in a readiness to share its skills or its talents as these have been sharpened by actual employment and thus are fit for further usefulness. The keyword is COURTESY. When positive, the degree is man's gift for meeting the most exacting of demands on his various potentialities, and when negative, uninspired conformity to limitation.

The formula is: manipulating-ideal-ingenious-specializing-spiritual-responsible. Examples are: sun, 319, 374, 765, 945; moon, 178, 640, 645; Mercury, 61, 723; Venus, 481, 501; Mars, 511, 711, 953; Saturn, 21, 119, 165, 377, 643, 911.

LEO 15 *A pageant* This is a symbol of man's constant de light in exhibiting the fruits of his achievement, and of naïveté dramatized in the world of everyday through a ver human pride in common works and co-operative accomplish ment. There is high magic in the public display of all th things in which the least of individuals may have had som minor part, and out of it comes a sense of fellowship throug which the whole is revealed in an over-all excellence and ever last inarticulate ideal somehow is exalted. The keyword i DEMONSTRATION. When positive, the degree is an irresistibl heightening of self-significance across the whole face of experi ence, and when negative, unconvincing claims and embarras ing self-assertion.

The formula is: manipulating-ideal-original-specializing-spiritual-inspirec Examples are: sun, 28, 568, 916; moon, 571, 792, 959; Mercury, 554, 66 Venus, 258; Mars, 40, 311, 549, 748, 878; Jupiter, 9, 577; Saturn, 607, 97 Uranus, 29, 512.

LEO 16 *Sunshine just after a storm* This is a symbol of pe sonal stability through man's recuperative powers, emphasize in terms of his psychological or inner orientation. Here is na ture's inevitable return to enduring values as this occurs afte every major issue of life, and the consequent opportunity fo self to regrasp itself and to enlist every element of its enviro ment in some new effort or fresh approach to experienc Everyday stress and strain are found of high use, either as clearance or a reconstruction in all human affairs. The ke word is RECOVERY. When positive, the degree is exceptiona steadiness of perspective and fidelity to individual responsibi ity, and when negative, continual upset over petty issues.

The formula is: manipulating-ideal-original-generalizing-physical-exper mental. Examples are: sun, 734; moon, 1, 108, 678, 700, 794, 992; Mercur 308; Venus, 35, 246, 336, 616, 664; Mars, 32, 85, 117, 187, 402, 485, 514, 57 656; Jupiter, 751; Uranus, 50, 206, 387, 429, 515.

AQUARIUS 15 *Two lovebirds sitting on a fence* This is a symbol of nature's delight in exhibiting the fruits of simple self-fulfillment, dramatized most effectively as a natural consummation of a shared richness or tenderness in human personality. There is high magic in any inner or psychological completeness, so that in consequence the whole world loves a lover and the average individual is usually much more interested in the romantic than the practical rewards of life. Man achieves his true destiny as he embraces his fellows in a reality he has made his own. The keyword is AFFIRMATION. When positive, the degree is a self-consistency which wins an absolute loyalty and a complete co-operation, and when negative, unreasoning jealousy.

The formula is: manipulating-ideal-ingenious-specializing-spiritual-inspired. Examples are: sun, 469, 581; moon, 153, 231, 387, 405; Mercury, 626, 988; Venus, 110, 911, 938, 950; Mars, 782; Jupiter, 540; Saturn, 268, 596; Uranus, 67, 175.

AQUARIUS 16 *A big-business man at his desk* This is a symbol of personal stability through organizational powers, emphasized in terms of an efficient participation in everyday affairs. The maintenance of the position or advantage an individual may win among his fellows requires a constant attention to his fundamental interests through the continual ebb and flow of circumstances, and he is genuinely successful as he remains undisturbed within himself throughout the ramifying vicissitudes. Personality is developed as it is challenged to prove itself. The keyword is ACCOMPLISHMENT. When positive, the degree is effective self-realization through achievement of consequence, and when negative, ambitious superficiality.

The formula is: manipulating-ideal-ingenious-generalizing-physical-experimental. Examples are: sun, 306; moon, 3, 439, 448, 692, 812, 939; Mercury, 11, 529, 599, 987; Venus, 87, 401, 539, 608, 826, 980; Mars, 917; Jupiter, 371, 848; Saturn, 10, 490; Uranus, 17, 100, 149.

LEO 17 *A nonvested church choir* This is a symbol of the inviolability of experience as dramatized for each individual through his participation in the broader or community functions of life. The common activity of group effort apart from any or all social and spiritual regimentation is a necessary exercise in respect for others, and an encouragement to an ordered self-expression. Here is high appreciation of reality through an enhanced and normal enjoyment of everyday living. The keyword is COMMUNION. When positive, the degree is the effective quickening of man's heart through interests which have been expanded to a point of real concern for his fellows, and when negative, unimaginative striving for undeserved popularity.

The formula is: manipulating-ideal-original-generalizing-physical-sensitive
Examples are: sun, 304, 453, 844, 923; moon, 505, 509, 589, 641, 711; Mercury, 193, 420, 455; Venus, 93, 416, 973; Mars, 102, 117, 545; Saturn, 199; Uranus, 41, 424, 682, 770, 915.

LEO 18 *A teacher of chemistry* This is a symbol of the human mind's illimitable power for penetrating into the deeper mysteries of an everyday world, and of the growing ambition of man to gain an effective control over all the processes of nature. Here is high organization of the intellectual faculties and a special skill in the practical adaptation of scientific principles to commonplace problems. The individual is given a full sense of his creative responsibilities. The keyword is INSTRUCTION. When positive, the degree is exceptional self-confidence and a delight in subjecting all experience to the test of immediate application, and when negative, unintelligent dependence on supposition or rules of the book.

The formula is: manipulating-ideal-original-generalizing-physical-receptive
Examples are: sun, 307; moon, 22, 210, 898; Mercury, 661; Venus, 264, 522, 653, 818; Mars, 35, 575, 866, 909, 989; Jupiter, 887; Saturn, 35, 509, 849, 944; Uranus, 212, 407.

AQUARIUS 17 *A watchdog standing guard* This is a symbol of the inviolability of experience as dramatized for each individual through the social sanctions and legal rights on which he may count in his own personal affairs. Community integrity requires the strengthening of each separate participant in its common functions, so that he may stand ready to protect and reinforce his fellows to the extent of his capacity in each moment of crisis. Effective living is a co-operative activity such as will stimulate the highest response from all. The keyword is PROBITY. When positive, the degree is unswerving faithfulness to ideals and a real determination to achieve them, and when negative, unfriendly instincts and groundless suspicion.

The formula is: manipulating-ideal-ingenious-generalizing-physical-sensitive. Examples are: sun, 126, 216, 783; moon, 235, 308, 821; Mercury, 55, 770, 976; Mars, 261, 838, 980; Jupiter, 200, 519, 588, 933; Saturn, 380; Uranus, 162, 735.

AQUARIUS 18 *A man unmasked* This is a symbol of the human mind's illimitable power for penetrating into the deeper stirrings and underlying motivations of human nature, and of a very modern determination to gain a scientific mastery of every psychological process. Here is a repudiation of all individualism as other than the common divisions of labor in a social reality, and a demand that each person make a public accounting of himself whenever the general welfare requires it. Life becomes a laboratory for an immortal curiosity. The keyword is ANALYSIS. When positive, the degree is a considered self-dedication to greater or more wonderful reasons for being, and when negative, self-betrayal through exceptional ineptitude.

The formula is: manipulating-ideal-ingenious-generalizing-physical-receptive. Examples are: sun, 497, 742; moon, 245, 766; Mercury, 750; Venus, 272, 278; Mars, 207; Jupiter, 33, 103, 463, 573; Saturn, 24, 779, 800; Uranus, 304, 398, 662, 1000.

LEO 19 *A houseboat party* This is a symbol of creative relaxation as a prelude to effective effort, and of man's normal
capacity for achievement through an everyday rehearsal of
co-operative relationships with his fellows. There is here a seal
ing off of some pleasant pocket of life for an intensified cul
ture of the skills and inspiration which can implement a
contribution to the world at large. Any dull routine of exist
ence may be exalted as a common adventure in self-expendi
ture. The keyword is CONGENIALITY. When positive, the degree
is a gracious eagerness of participation in the more worth
while or enduring aspects of human affairs, and when negative
thoughtless self-indulgence and contempt for the general wel
fare.

The formula is: manipulating-ideal-original-generalizing-physical-respon
sible. Examples are: sun, 103, 107, 171, 474, 894; moon, 558; Mercury, 386
916; Venus, 262, 360, 609; Mars, 392, 913; Jupiter, 152, 374; Saturn, 640
740; Uranus, 676, 827, 988.

LEO 20 *The Zuni sun worshipers* This is a symbol of man's
recognition of higher and natural forces from which he receive
his life and strength, emphasized here in his everyday ritualiza
tion of his loyalties and in his self-buttressing through a pres
ervation of older values in any evolution of new ones. The
normal individual is endowed by custom with an effective as
surance which is centered in his fellows as well as in himself
and he has self-fulfillment as he is true to his group tradition
The keyword is FIDELITY. When positive, the degree is an in
ner and absolute realization of the self's illimitable resource
in situation and background, and when negative, a surrender
of all personal reality to meaningless ceremonies.

The formula is: manipulating-ideal-original-generalizing-physical-inspired
Examples are: sun, 24, 257, 652; moon, 303, 328, 539; Mercury, 551, 590
Venus, 111, 181, 358, 368, 864; Mars, 282, 663, 951; Jupiter, 501, 680, 748
865; Saturn, 65, 115, 158, 235, 839, 970; Uranus, 505, 589, 646.

AQUARIUS 19 *A forest fire quenched* This is a symbol of regenerative relaxation after extraordinary effort, and of man's exceptional capacity for achievement through the whole-giving of himself in an emergency. Here is the dynamic co-operation by which the individual gains a high peak of self-expenditure, and in the moment's intensification rehearses potentialities he would never discover otherwise. What can be misfortune to be suffered can as easily become a successful adventure in broad social responsibility. The keyword is CONCERN. When positive, the degree is special skill in bringing personal interests to some larger point of effectiveness, and when negative, a fear of experience and a subtle delight in calamity.

The formula is: manipulating-ideal-ingenious-generalizing-physical-responsible. Examples are: sun, 274, 464, 813, 928; moon, 18, 395, 418, 555; Mercury, 286, 499, 567, 938; Venus, 10, 113; Mars, 144, 633; Jupiter, 411, 598; Saturn, 262, 278; Uranus, 109, 231, 673.

AQUARIUS 20 *A big white dove, a message bearer* This is a symbol of man's recognition of a transcendental or superior wisdom from which he may always receive his inspiration and assurance, emphasized here by his inner faith and his self-strengthening through an ever-constructive attitude of mind. There are always secret signs of divine favor for a faithful heart, and they are no less real because the reason is able to dismiss them as a mere oversensitiveness to the prompting of a wholly naïve insight. The keyword is CONVICTION. When positive, the degree is a facility for ordering all personal desires in a cosmic framework and a gift for knowing when to act and what to do, and when negative, sanctimonious self-deception.

The formula is: manipulating-ideal-ingenious-generalizing-physical-inspired. Examples are: sun, 6, 935; moon, 990; Mercury, 272, 312, 390, 608, 633, 657, 824, 945; Venus, 198, 589, 794; Mars, 160, 389, 539, 568; Jupiter, 600; Saturn, 646, 676; Uranus, 707.

LEO 21 *Chickens intoxicated* This is a symbol of the inevitable distress of the human soul whenever it seeks stimulation from elements essentially alien to its own nature, dramatized in the reversed symbolism by the futility of a dependence
on physical agency for spiritual results. There are limitations in
man's basic make-up which he must learn to put to use other
than as a justification for his various inadequacies. They are
a reason for achievement, not a cancellation of potentials. The
keyword is ACCENTUATION. When positive, the degree is the
individual's capacity for a creative self-mobilization which
will enable him to rise to the needs of every possible situation,
and when negative, unnecessary bondage to externals.

*The formula is: manipulating-ideal-original-generalizing-social-experimen-
tal.* Examples are: sun, 57, 122, 199, 800, 904; moon, 152, 356, 367, 470,
607, 639; Mercury, 135, 521, 568; Venus, 15, 39, 612; Mars, 490; Saturn, 148,
339, 785; Uranus, 247, 458.

LEO 22 *A carrier pigeon* This is a symbol of the unlimited
service of life at large to the special requirements of an individual's intelligence or understanding. Implicit in the symbolism is the extraordinary extent to which man may count on
learning whatever he may need to know whenever he faces any
unfamiliar or critical issue. Here is a universal sensitiveness
of mind which in a sense commands all-knowledge, and re-
ceives messages of immediate pertinence through sheer intuition whenever its rational capacity has been developed. The
keyword is ENLIGHTENMENT. When positive, the degree is a complete mastery of all things through the normal processes of
thought, and when negative, a lack of simple good sense.

The formula is: manipulating-ideal-original-generalizing-social-sensitive.
Examples are: sun, 364; moon, 6, 270, 351, 381, 878; Mercury, 449, 733;
Venus, 254, 967; Mars, 329, 478; Jupiter, 255, 465, 967; Saturn, 230; Uranus,
184, 378, 442, 479, 601.

AQUARIUS 21 *A woman disappointed and disillusioned* This is a symbol of the inevitable distress of the human soul whenever it seeks any enduring sustainment from elements without anchorage in its own nature, dramatized in the negative symbolism by the futility of its attempted fulfillment through a capitalization on purely physical assets of self. The deeper potentials of the being afford the real possibilities of self-discovery, and personal frustrations are a challenge to a genuine self-realization rather than a denial of opportunity. The keyword is CLEARANCE. When positive, the degree is the self's inherent gift for pressing on and gaining increased powers with every setback, and when negative, the acceptance of all defeat as final.

The formula is: manipulating-ideal-ingenious-generalizing-social-experimental. Examples are: sun, 214; moon, 340, 384, 955; Mercury, 201, 266, 361, 447, 974; Venus, 71, 108, 316, 380, 508, 865, 905; Mars, 318; Jupiter, 774; Saturn, 232, 243, 510, 954; Uranus, 4, 434, 481.

AQUARIUS 22 *A rug placed on a floor for children to play* This is a symbol of the unlimited service of life at large to the special requirements of an individual's comfort or everyday convenience. Implicit in the symbolism is the extraordinary extent to which man may count on finding the facilities he needs in his self-development. He is ever discovering himself in situations where he may concentrate his efforts to the best possible advantage on the perfection and employment of his personal skills. The keyword is REFINEMENT. When positive, the degree is unusual capacity for the exploitation of immediate resources and the deepening of every potential of selfhood, and when negative, carefree self-indulgence and meaningless luxury.

The formula is: manipulating-ideal-ingenious-generalizing-social-sensitive. Examples are: sun, 88, 90, 286, 330, 422, 628, 683, 754; moon, 324; Mercury, 110, 464, 576; Venus, 292, 663; Mars, 165, 497; Saturn, 90, 505, 915; Uranus, 121.

LEO 23   *A bareback rider*   This is a symbol of man's absolute mastery of his immediate world of experience, and of his ability to capitalize on any special function of life with which he is concerned. There are illimitable opportunities for the human spirit to dramatize its personal achievement or individual aspiration, and to do this is the way of most effective self-refinement if only it is pursued assiduously and valiantly enough. The keyword is AUDACITY. When positive, the degree is uncompromising courage in the everyday business of living and a carefree assurance in meeting the problems of a modern society, and when negative, idle self-display and intemperate desire for applause.

The formula is: manipulating-ideal-original-generalizing-social-receptive. Examples are: sun, 133, 704; moon, 886, 908; Venus, 428; Mars, 152, 527, 886; Jupiter, 833, 863; Saturn, 351, 443; Uranus, 78, 108, 238, 369, 889, 995.

LEO 24   *An untidy, unkempt man*   This is a symbol of the complete self-obsession which human individuality may exhibit, emphasized here on the side of an insensitiveness to every exaction or reward of the world. Implicit in the reversed symbolism are the values of an inner refining of self and a need to use and exalt rather than hoard the physical and psychological possessions of the being. Paradoxically enough the bringing of reality to center is a development and sharing of its potentialities. The keyword is IMPERTURBABILITY. When positive, the degree is an ease of outer accomplishment thanks to the inner intensification and increasing sensibility, and when negative, perverse satisfaction in a neglect of self.

The formula is: manipulating-ideal-original-generalizing-social-responsible. Examples are: sun, 246, 554; moon, 174, 927; Mercury, 122, 969; Venus, 80, 687; Mars, 247, 406, 649; Jupiter, 125, 419, 822; Saturn, 296; Uranus, 547, 841.

AQUARIUS 23   *A big bear sitting down and waving all its paws*
This is a symbol of man's absolute mastery of his own lower
nature, and of his ability to bring every function of life to a
high personal fulfillment. There are illimitable channels
through which he may further each separate phase of his self-
discovery, but he always must demonstrate the worth of his
own individual gifts before he can participate adequately in
any larger reality. His soul finds itself through the excellencies
it makes the very fabric of itself. The keyword is APTITUDE.
When positive, the degree is a consistent desire for genuinely
significant experience and a willingness to dramatize the self's
potentials to any necessary extent, and when negative, frantic
efforts to gain and hold attention.

The formula is: manipulating-ideal-ingenious-generalizing-social-receptive.
Examples are: sun, 312, 576, 984; moon, 17, 335, 616, 791; Mercury, 539,
928; Venus, 271, 667, 681, 918; Jupiter, 203, 318, 323, 899; Saturn, 134, 205;
Uranus, 124, 460, 477, 986.

AQUARIUS 24   *A man turning his back on his passions and
teaching from his experience*   This is a symbol of the complete self-obsession which human individuality may exhibit,
emphasized here on the side of a sensitiveness to the world and
its exactions. Implicit in the symbolism are the values of a
generous and broad participation in everyday life, and the
necessity that any personal refinement be preserved through the
sharing of its rewards. The self assimilates itself to its own
higher vision and so achieves an outer selflessness. The keyword is SERENITY. When positive, the degree is effective accomplishment through a genuine peace of inner understanding,
and when negative, thorough dissatisfaction with the normal
fruits of living.

*The formula is: manipulating-ideal-ingenious-generalizing-social-respon-
sible.* Examples are: sun, 238, 579, 870, 897; moon, 128, 286, 853, 857;
Mercury, 334, 457, 663, 682; Venus, 106, 883; Mars, 62, 596; Jupiter, 30,
214, 272, 608; Saturn, 13; Uranus, 3, 300, 468.

LEO 25 *A large camel crossing the desert* This is a symbol of man's capacity to overcome the handicaps imposed on him by the normal limitations of the world in which he elects to function, and of his underlying and basically inexhaustible endurance. Here is a psychological integration of human character, revealing an effective self-mobilization which the least of men may accomplish. His achievements in the face of the difficulties to be overcome are the real foundation of his self-refinement and ultimate self-discovery. The keyword is ADEQUACY. When positive, the degree is uncompromising persistence and uncomplaining self-expenditure in any course to be followed, and when negative, ruthlessness in an unintelligent self-interest.

The formula is: manipulating-ideal-original-generalizing-social-inspired. Examples are: sun, 194, 247, 351; moon, 660; Mercury, 917; Venus, 180, 705, 915; Mars, 208, 425, 520, 978; Jupiter, 408, 456, 666; Saturn, 270, 717, 941; Uranus, 257, 686, 692, 724, 739.

LEO 26 *A rainbow* This is a symbol of the over-all realization which comes to man for his guidance whenever he strives to reach his goals of a more enduring sort. Here is assurance of divine participation in the most unpromising of human relationships. The individual learns that there is a consistent ordering throughout the world in which he finds himself, and that nature will co-operate effectively with every vision he chooses to keep alive on his own account. The keyword is SIGNIFICANCE. When positive, the degree is a sense of very real spiritual power and presence in all personal effort and desire, and when negative, an uncritical acceptance of every passing hope or dream as something on which to depend.

The formula is: manipulating-ideal-original-generalizing-spiritual-experimental. Examples are: sun, 69, 780; moon, 633, 643, 809; Mercury, 335, 446, 975, 991; Venus, 284; Mars, 504; Jupiter, 178, 979; Saturn, 517, 778; Uranus, 301, 562.

AQUARIUS 25 *A butterfly with the right wing more perfectly formed* This is a symbol of man's capacity to overcome any handicap imposed on him by the abnormalities which at times become an inevitable part of his own nature, and of his underlying stamina or psychological integrity. Here is a functional integration of conscious existence, with the variations which constitute an individual remaining the basis of all self-knowing on any or every level of experience. The self mobilizes its powers effectively as it takes full advantage of the significant differences in both itself and its world. The keyword is UNIQUENESS. When positive, the degree is a genius for turning deficiency into a real asset, and when negative, unhappy and rebellious conceit.

The formula is: manipulating-ideal-ingenious-generalizing-social-inspired. Examples are: sun, 200, 279; moon, 714, 810; Mercury, 216, 244, 625, 689; Venus, 68, 101, 716, 840; Mars, 114, 128, 701, 729, 773; Saturn, 512. 958; Uranus, 701, 773, 938.

AQUARIUS 26 *A hydrometer* This is a symbol of the powers of immediate analysis which enable man to achieve his commonplace or practical goals. Here he has full assurance of an intelligence and order to be found throughout the world of everyday realities, and he comes to see that a very real co-operation of natural conditions and forces may be enlisted for any project of special concern. The individual learns that when he will take responsibility for events he may shape them to his own convenience, and thus find ways to capitalize on any difficulties that arise. The keyword is EFFICIENCY. When positive, the degree is exceptional ability in manipulating the fundamental complexities of living, and when negative, self-defeating worry over trifles.

The formula is: manipulating-ideal-ingenious-generalizing-spiritual-experimental. Examples are: sun, 68, 89, 283, 561, 882, 978; moon, 134, 199, 205, 420, 425, 672; Venus, 43, 176, 251; Mars, 302, 378, 404; Jupiter, 905, 937; Saturn, 19, 52, 217, 885, 988; Uranus, 386, 543, 871.

LEO 27 *Daybreak*   This is a symbol of the cycles of change as
an ultimate assurance to the human heart, with an emphasis on
reason as the means by which man knows the nature of his own
continuance. No matter what may be the course of events in
their over-all unpredictability, there is always dawn or spring-
time as the promise of resurgence or a new potential in every
manifestation of self and its world. Reality is ever a beginning
in the sense of the immediacy it offers the individual. The
keyword is GENESIS. When positive, the degree is an untiring
capture and recapture of life throughout the constant and confusing shifts of being, and when negative, wishful thinking
and satisfaction in a vague tomorrow.

The formula is: manipulating-ideal-original-generalizing-spiritual-sensitive.
Examples are: sun, 35, 72, 229; moon, 213, 836; Mercury, 903; Venus, 122,
747; Mars, 83, 461, 476, 964; Jupiter, 171, 760; Uranus, 266.

LEO 28 *Many little birds on the limb of a large tree*   This
is a symbol of the transcendence of the lesser things in life by
a continual expansion of higher considerations, or of the individual's ability in a crisis to center his attention on the enduring orientations through which he gains his own assurance.
Here is a happy lightness of the human spirit as it rejoices in
its infinitely varying relations with the beautiful and the good,
or as its experience is poised at a point of highest satisfaction.
The keyword is RAMIFICATION. When positive, the degree is
man's effective mobilization of all the unrealized possibilities
of his destiny, and when negative, an enjoyment of confusion
or the momentary self-importance it brings.

The formula is: manipulating-ideal-original-generalizing-spiritual-receptive.
Examples are: sun, 434, 621, 644, 771, 975; moon, 282; Mercury, 985;
Mars, 742, 996; Jupiter, 180, 825; Saturn, 3, 345, 376, 543, 568, 798, 836, 896,
965; Uranus, 467, 936.

AQUARIUS 27 *An ancient pottery bowl filled with violets* This is a symbol of the permanence or changelessness of the real as an ultimate assurance to the human heart. No matter how many shifting forms the face of life may present to man, there are always the surviving tokens of an enduring stability on which the ephemeral and the superficial are unable to make any impact. Where there is replacement of substance and variety of structure there is also an over-all continuance of meaning and identity in which self may anchor itself. The keyword is TRADITION. When positive, the degree is a high realization of values and a real gift for using them, and when negative, a loss of self in conventionality and its meaningless trappings.

The formula is: manipulating-ideal-ingenious-generalizing-spiritual-sensitive. Examples are: sun, 91, 716, 840; moon, 117, 655, 835; Mercury, 102, 142, 150, 200, 330, 507; Venus, 12; Mars, 442, 581; Jupiter, 168; Saturn, 49, 86, 523, 635, 638, 827; Uranus, 170, 265, 321, 816, 914, 919.

AQUARIUS 28 *A tree felled and sawed* This is a symbol of the employment of a lesser reality for the development and sustainment of a greater, and of the individual's ability in a crisis to center his attention on the pressing functions and necessities of a very practical well-being. Here is the human spirit's joy in energy expended and satisfaction in the efficient use of skills and materials, with its experience poised in the fluidity of its self-expression. The keyword is IMMEDIACY. When positive, the degree is man's uninhibited and enthusiastic desire to be at work or to mobilize everything around him in his own interest, and when negative, unnecessary surrender to hard or unrewarding effort through a total lack of imagination.

The formula is: manipulating-ideal-ingenious-generalizing-spiritual-receptive. Examples are: sun, 55, 365; moon, 148, 556, 991; Mercury, 331, 627, 805, 935; Venus, 526, 559, 849, 988; Mars, 466, 628; Jupiter, 356, 807, 824; Saturn, 368, 829; Uranus, 375.

LEO 29 *A mermaid* This is a symbol of humanity's insatiable appetite for experience on the side of psychological self-assurance, and of the nascent eagerness of the soul for a private and personal participation in every possible facet of self-fulfillment. There is an ineradicable purity of man's make-up at core, and in consequence an ultimate repudiation of all the compromises which seem to be demanded in everyday relationships. The individual forever seeks and responds to the creative needs of life itself. The keyword is IMPORTUNITY. When positive, the degree is a completeness of quickening to inner instincts of the being and a real willingness to trust them, and when negative, a lack of discrimination and an awkward insensitivity.

The formula is: manipulating-ideal-original-generalizing-spiritual-responsible. Examples are: sun, 360, 717, 811; moon, 230, 515; Mercury, 121, 583, 621, 907; Venus, 24, 209, 587, 837, 890, 902; Mars, 347; Jupiter, 174, 804; Saturn, 155, 260, 477, 498, 669, 837; Uranus, 649.

LEO 30 *An unsealed letter* This is a symbol of the spiritual integrity of all things in and of themselves, dramatized here by the remarkable extent to which reliance may be placed on the discretion of others in even the most trivial details of day-by-day living. Suspicion is a poison to the mind whenever it becomes a set of temperament rather than a normal competency in applying the lessons of experience, and in consequence man must trust his fellows in general and in spite of his frequent disillusionments in order to discover how far he may do so in every given case. The keyword is CONFIDENCE. When positive, the degree is exceptional skill in winning and holding the respect of everybody, and when negative, a genius for indiscreetness.

The formula is: manipulating-ideal-original-generalizing-spiritual-inspired. Examples are: sun, 204, 254; moon, 97, 763; Mercury, 28, 80, 235, 304, 649; Venus, 34, 57, 426; Mars, 60, 290, 521; Jupiter, 45, 341, 487; Saturn, 689, 723, 771; Uranus, 292, 780.

AQUARIUS 29 *Butterfly emerging from chrysalis* This is a symbol of humanity's insatiable appetite for experience on the side of an intellectual self-assurance, and of the nascent eagerness of the conscious self for a complete or effective grasp of all possible knowledge. There is a continually self-renewing purity of man's mind at root, and he somehow feels that nature herself springs from her over-all potential as spontaneously as his own ideas come forth from the formless matrix of his inner being. The keyword is EMANATION. When positive, the degree is uncompromising faith in the promise of existence itself and in the wonders of a continuing creation, and when negative, utterly sluggish response to reality.

The formula is: manipulating-ideal-ingenious-generalizing-spiritual-responsible. Examples are: moon, 930, 732; Mercury, 106, 433, 827; Venus, 89, 201, 293, 562, 807; Mars, 850; Jupiter, 175, 237, 249, 585; Saturn, 14, 280.

AQUARIUS 30 *The field of Ardath in bloom* This is a symbol of the spiritual integrity of nature herself, dramatized by Marie Corelli's mystic meadow of ancient Babylon as an ageless and special challenge to modern life. Everyone may count on the inherent friendliness of the universe, and in consequence on the capacity of man's destiny to endow him with fruits of his good rather than his bad works. The individual ultimately must rely on the world in which he finds himself, and so should live in such fashion that a reliance on him in turn is both possible and inviting. The keyword is CONTINUITY. When positive, the degree is self-illumination through exceptional service to others, and when negative, witless reaction to fantasy.

The formula is: manipulating-ideal-ingenious-generalizing-spiritual-inspired. Examples are: sun, 64, 155, 623, 731, 819, 834, 976; moon, 612, 675, 776; Mercury, 62, 187; Venus, 189, 266, 306; Mars, 870; Jupiter, 91, 410, 453, 470, 493; Saturn, 197; Uranus, 570.

VIRGO 1 *A man's head* This is a symbol of full maturity in human estate, with an emphasis on the personal integrity which represents in general what all men are asked to be in particular. The ideals of an inner life are given their outer manifestation through some self-accepted responsibility on which others can count. Ambition has its high dignity here in the distinction with which it endows those who remain most faithful to its exactions and thereupon become most conscious of its rewards. The keyword is CHARACTER. When positive, the degree is an effective self-assurance and an ever-clear vision of each emerging opportunity in life, and when negative, inordinate vanity and a consistent overestimation of individual capacities.

The formula is: sustaining-practical-efficient-specializing-physical-experimental. Examples are: sun, 752, 925; moon, 52, 207, 413, 798, 832; Mercury, 9, 426; Venus, 523, 776; Mars, 2, 63, 235; Jupiter, 536, 655, 708, 912, 981; Saturn, 631, 672; Uranus, 160, 493, 729.

VIRGO 2 *A large white cross upraised* This is a symbol of the conscious stewardship through which man sustains his more enduring values, here emphasized by an uncompromising testimony to his deeper allegiances. His moral courage is a dynamic for all transcendental achievement, and his psychological fearlessness is a corrective for the maladjustments of both individual and society. A sense of spiritual belonging is exalted as the greatest of human satisfactions. The keyword is GLORIFICATION. When positive, the degree is an utterly selfless enlistment in some dramatic service for the ultimate welfare of humankind, and when negative, witless dogmatism and misdirected efforts for causes of great pretension but little real worth.

The formula is: sustaining-practical-efficient-specializing-physical-sensitive. Examples are: sun, 435, 596, 670; moon, 24, 314, 484; Mercury, 129, 182, 434, 670, 844; Venus, 440, 799, 800, 829; Mars, 273, 365, 629, 726, 837; Jupiter, 439; Saturn, 9, 275, 809; Uranus, 428, 845.

PISCES 1 *A public market* This is a symbol of full maturity in man's social estate, with an emphasis on the group integrity which facilitates the development of each individual in his own special pattern. The common ideals of a community life are given their everyday manifestation through the willingness of each participant to do his part. Ambition has its effective refinement here as it combines a consistent generosity toward the aims of others with a real intensity of effort directed toward its own ends. The keyword is COMMERCE. When positive, the degree is an exceptional capacity for organizing the converging and conflicting interests of many people in practical arrangements of mutual benefit, and when negative, complete insensibility to any over-all welfare.

The formula is: sustaining-practical-universal-specializing-physical-experimental. Examples are: sun, 445, 481, 672; moon, 20, 214, 518; Mercury, 6, 601, 754; Venus, 205, 672, 987; Mars, 176; Jupiter, 697; Saturn, 450, 688, 770; Uranus, 5, 152, 261.

PISCES 2 *A squirrel hiding from hunters* This is a symbol of the conscious conservatism through which man preserves his more enduring values, here emphasized by an uncompromising loyalty to his own self-interest. Implicit in the negative symbolism is a species of high courage in refusing to enter any phase of experience where the risks are out of proportion to probable rewards. A sense of illimitable self-adequacy is contingent on good judgment as the highest of human potentialities. The keyword is CAUTION. When positive, the degree is an intelligent independence of spirit and a consequent real gift for setting the conditions for all personal participation in events, and when negative, self-debasing timidity.

The formula is: sustaining-practical-universal-specializing-physical-sensitive. Examples are: sun, 369, 598; moon, 386, 587, 724, 872, 888; Mercury, 501, 757; Venus, 61, 127, 324, 581; Mars, 808; Jupiter, 61; Saturn, 118, 682, 692, 724, 739, 847; Uranus, 330, 677, 901.

VIRGO 3 *Two angels bringing protection* This is a symbol of the absolute certainty which any individual may develop in the terms of his conscious faith, and of the power in human character which becomes the hallmark of his spiritual orientation. There are the traditional legions of heavenly forces which ever move to sustain the soul in its outreaching to eternal values, facilitating the simple and consistent convergence of all good things toward their own kind. High-mindedness here pays very pleasant dividends. The keyword is SECURITY. When positive, the degree is a sure conviction which enables man to proceed to an effective fulfillment of his dreams, and when negative, vain pretense and self-importance.

The formula is: sustaining-practical-efficient-specializing-physical-receptive. Examples are: sun, 15, 915; moon, 570; Mercury, 118, 171, 652, 748, 784; Venus, 996; Mars, 103, 522, 616, 899, 916; Jupiter, 926; Saturn, 103, 381, 530, 887; Uranus, 788.

VIRGO 4 *A colored child playing with white children* This is a symbol of the actual illimitability of human relationships, dramatized here in the more personal and wholly specialized environment of everyday affairs. There are no facets of man's character that cannot be built into the fabric of both a whole self and an integrated group, but each one of them must always have its own unconditioned manifestation. These are differences which as embraced in mutual appreciation become the basis of all conscious being or individual satisfaction. The keyword is INTIMACY. When positive, the degree is successful participation in every possible variety of experience, and when negative, lack of capacity for psychological adjustment.

The formula is: sustaining-practical-efficient-specializing-physical-responsible. Examples are: sun, 294; moon, 203, 342, 520, 635, 859; Mercury, 262, 787; Venus, 299, 381, 554, 733, 804; Mars, 121, 473, 665, 762; Jupiter, 32, 311; Saturn, 487, 641, 680; Uranus, 564.

PISCES 3 *A petrified forest* This is a symbol of the absolute certainty which any individual may develop in the terms of his conscious knowledge, and of the power in human character which becomes the hallmark of his intellectual orientation. The static symbolism is a warning against any reliance on stabilities to which no immediate or personal contribution is made, and which in consequence may become obstacles to progress. Here rather is dramatization of an eternal stout-heartedness, and of its very practical dividends in spiritual continuance. The keyword is SURVIVAL. When positive, the degree is effective continuity and breadth of resource in all human effort, and when negative, complete immobilization in superficial reality.

The formula is: sustaining-practical-universal-specializing-physical-receptive. Examples are: sun, 261; moon, 547, 854; Mercury, 410, 581; Venus, 21, 62, 388, 487, 935; Mars, 481; Jupiter, 11, 401, 749, 802, 950, 963; Saturn, 224, 312, 506, 586, 686, 889; Uranus, 161, 803.

PISCES 4 *Heavy traffic on a narrow isthmus* This is a symbol of the ultimate illimitability of human relationships, dramatized here in the more personal and ever-ramifying environment of everyday affairs. There are no potentialities of common self-interest that man cannot shape for the convenience and encouragement of a whole selfhood and a well-integrated community, but a high discipline is always necessary for both the individual and the group in each particular development of immediate reality. The keyword is CONVERGENCE. When positive, the degree is an unusual gift for organizing all transient enterprise in patterns of a rewarding and overall effectiveness, and when negative, stubborn blindness to the general welfare.

The formula is: sustaining-practical-universal-specializing-physical-responsible. Examples are: sun, 54, 201, 493, 599, 938; moon, 727, 826, 983; Mercury, 261, 489, 984; Venus, 120, 157, 350, 633, 783; Mars, 548; Jupiter, 908; Saturn, 41, 78, 547.

VIRGO 5 *A man dreaming of fairies* This is a symbol of the imaginative resources of life as manifest in the folklore of the race, and of man's ability to use the coin of his inner and eternal experience with a practical wisdom and insight. Here is his effective communion with the personified powers of the everyday world, as this instruments his efforts whenever he moves toward his goal and reorders his perspective whenever he gives voice to his vision. The dreams of men are always the foretaste of human achievement. The keyword is OUTLOOK. When positive, the degree is subtle persuasiveness by which real support is gained for any given end, and when negative, lack of all appreciation for enduring realities.

The formula is: sustaining-practical-efficient-specializing-physical-inspired. Examples are: sun, 256, 619; moon, 206; Mercury, 123, 607, 961, 994; Venus, 386; Mars, 39, 534, 998; Jupiter, 322, 511, 587; Saturn, 419, 446, 833; Uranus, 335, 496, 632, 857, 991.

VIRGO 6 *A merry-go-round* This is a symbol of a cyclic and necessary intensification of any personal being, as emphasized on the side of normal or everyday experience. Pleasure is the simplest possible form of creative exchange, and it always encourages and refines the individual's range of potentiality. Here is a receptiveness to every turn of opportunity to be found in the immediate situation, and a willingness to attempt its demonstration. The keyword is DIVERSION. When positive, the degree is endless and happy resourcefulness in a constant reorientation of self to meet varying exigencies of life, and when negative, a continuous and senseless ricochet from one to another meaningless phase of self-expression.

The formula is: sustaining-practical-efficient-specializing-social-experimental. Examples are: sun, 556, 634; moon, 429, 606; Mercury, 735; Venus, 787, 989; Mars, 449, 645, 703, 780, 825; Jupiter, 208, 226, 534, 719, 803; Saturn, 195, 299, 666, 865; Uranus, 56, 182, 514, 985.

PISCES 5 *A church bazaar* This is a symbol of the instinctive loyalties of life as manifest in community institutions, and of man's ability to capitalize on the enduring allegiances he develops among his kind. Here is his everyday communion with the warmth of personality and its pyramiding powers of accomplishment, and his consequent instrumentation of every individual effort. He makes his over-all contribution to human achievement through his ever-revivifying contacts with his fellows. The keyword is BENEFIT. When positive, the degree is a special genius for philanthropy and the organization of society's real concern for the well-being of men in general, and when negative, social exclusiveness and smug self-satisfaction.

The formula is: sustaining-practical-universal-specializing-physical-inspired. Examples are: moon, 104, 807; Mercury, 340, 472, 810; Venus, 777; Mars, 855, 871; Jupiter, 160, 364, 835; Saturn, 81, 518; Uranus, 31, 186, 400.

PISCES 6 *Officers on dress parade* This is a symbol of a cyclic and necessary intensification of any personal being, as emphasized on the side of ritualized or ideal experience. Dignity and protocol always provide a dramatic and valuable rehearsal of cultural or group values, exalting each individual in some one respect for the strengthening of all in their total pattern. Here is an investment of selfhood for the long-range potentialities of life, made possible by some immediate and self-fulfilling demonstration of personal skill or capacity. The keyword is DISCIPLINE. When positive, the degree is schooled self-assurance and absolute responsibility, and when negative, unimaginative exercise of special privilege.

The formula is: sustaining-practical-universal-specializing-social-experimental. Examples are: sun, 749, 757; Mercury, 210, 742, 840, 978; Venus, 112, 757; Mars, 343; Jupiter, 59, 729, 929, 984; Saturn, 247; Uranus, 18, 210, 316, 678, 738.

VIRGO 7 *A harem* This is a symbol of the withdrawal from reality in one aspect as a means for regrasping it in another, here dramatized by an acceptance of regimentation as a species of insulation against life's demand for some more dynamic manifestation of the self. Implicit in the static symbolism is the necessity for using any fellowship in lesser values as a self-strengthening in a definite and renewed struggle towards the greater. An enforced conservation of energies need not encourage a surrender of basic ideals. The keyword is RESTRAINT. When positive, the degree is a courageous and complete disregard of limitation by the rejection of its terms at any cost, and when negative, self-betrayal for momentary ease.

The formula is: sustaining-practical-efficient-specializing-social-sensitive. Examples are: sun, 335; moon, 625, 874; Mercury, 46, 247, 523, 915; Venus, 524, 722; Mars, 934, 979; Jupiter, 283, 299; Uranus, 521, 531, 835, 846.

VIRGO 8 *First dancing instruction* This is a symbol of the self-perfecting required for the many different forms of man's participation in the experience of his fellows, illustrated here in a potential excellence of special skill. The dance of life includes infinite versions of its rhythm and provides illimitable variations on the theme of its melody, but there must be some specific encouragement of individual ability as a stimulus to effective endeavor. Necessary always is that initial trial of self which in time leads to a continuity of effort. The keyword is ASSISTANCE. When positive, the degree is achievement through a personal competence and a high gift for co-operation, and when negative, cheerful acceptance of ineptitude.

The formula is: sustaining-practical-efficient-specializing-social-receptive. Examples are: sun, 495, 590, 691, 991, 996; moon, 46, 47, 67, 150, 542, 624, 936; Mercury, 351, 368, 697; Venus, 550, 801; Mars, 219, 242; Jupiter, 273, 702, 900; Uranus, 286, 576, 864.

PISCES 7   *A cross lying on rocks*   This is a symbol of with-drawal from reality in one aspect as means for regrasping it in another, here dramatized by a wholly unnecessary accept-ance of the world's common repudiation or neglect of an individual's higher ideals. Implicit in the static symbolism is the need to be active in the cause of every standard or alle-giance through which life has been made worth while, and the insistent stirring of an inner voice which seeks to quicken the soul to the paramount necessities of its existence. The key-word is CONSCIENCE. When positive, the degree is a rugged independence of inner spirit and a courageous rejection of all outer compromise, and when negative, utter timidity of self-interest.

The formula is: sustaining-practical-universal-specializing-social-sensitive.
Examples are: sun, 178, 667; moon, 107, 454, 848, 875; Mercury, 271; Venus, 13, 40, 312, 570, 601; Jupiter, 85, 182, 193, 565, 656, 985; Saturn, 515; Uranus, 154, 884.

PISCES 8   *A girl blowing a bugle*   This is a symbol of the self-perfecting required for the many different forms of man's participation in the experience of his fellows, illustrated here in his successful achievement and discharge of group respon-sibility. Life's activities may have a myriad modifications, but human personality must make one of these its special charge as a basis for its own fulfillment. The individual chal-lenges his fellows and is challenged by them in turn at each recurring point of special potentiality. The keyword is SUM-MONS. When positive, the degree is an eagerness for self-expres-sion and an alertness to every opportunity for self-justification, and when negative, officiousness and delight in regimentation.

The formula is: sustaining-practical-universal-specializing-social-receptive.
Examples are: sun, 108, 114, 225, 266, 487; Mercury, 140, 526; Venus, 366, 561, 566; Mars, 451, 505; Jupiter, 335, 991; Saturn, 95, 407, 424, 459, 841; Uranus, 117, 171, 329, 497, 696.

VIRGO 9   *A man making a futurist drawing*   This is a symbol
of the originality an individual must show in any true asser-
tion of himself, and of the importance of the aesthetic or more
spiritual areas of his experience. It is only through an identifiable and personal uniqueness that man is able to establish
himself among his fellows, and the risk he takes is that if this
becomes too extreme it may repel rather than attract. Implicit
in the symbolism is a challenge to a distinctiveness which will
release the creative capacities of others as well as self. The
keyword is EXPERIMENT. When positive, the degree is a gift
for the illimitable expansion of the human mind and a consequent extension of its powers, and when negative, complete
and continuous confusion of ideas.

The formula is: sustaining-practical-efficient-specializing-social-responsible.
Examples are: sun, 787, 825, 969; Mercury, 416, 619; Venus, 207, 518, 845;
Mars, 71, 146, 590; Jupiter, 188, 343, 494; Saturn, 456; Uranus, 565, 614,
749, 802, 859, 908.

VIRGO 10   *Two heads looking out and beyond the shadows*
This is a symbol of man's transcendental powers of comprehension, emphasized here in his ability to reduce all knowledge
to exact and efficient formulas. His stereoscopic reason gives
him an intellectual genius on the one hand and endows him
with an exceptional mechanical sense in everyday or practical
realms on the other. The inner and outer facets of reality are
merged in the effectiveness of his judgment. The keyword is IN-
TELLIGENCE. When positive, the degree is a superb capacity for
seeing both sides in every given issue and so bringing all the
various phases of human enterprise to some unity of common
purpose, and when negative, hopeless fragmentation of self
within itself.

The formula is: sustaining-practical-efficient-specializing-social-inspired.
Examples are: moon, 258; Mercury, 69, 103, 130; Venus, 697; Mars, 51,
230, 361, 436, 447, 858, 864; Jupiter, 18, 228, 241, 348, 923; Saturn, 231,
330, 760; Uranus, 797, 969.

PISCES 9 *A jockey* This is a symbol of the eagerness for life an individual must show in any true revelation of himself, and of the concern he must have for the struggles and competitions of everyday experience. It is only through thoroughly consistent performance of his skills and talents that man establishes himself among his fellows, and as this develops in excellence he is under increasing obligation to be successful in exhibiting them. Implicit in the symbolism are very harsh penalties for any failure to drive the capabilities of self to the limit. The keyword is PRACTICE. When positive, the degree is a spectacular gift for rising to any occasion, and when negative, witless gambling of every resource and potentiality.

The formula is: sustaining-practical-universal-specializing-social-respon-sible. Examples are: sun, 47, 87, 375, 824; moon, 240, 656, 869, 871, 964; Mercury, 21, 89, 425, 598; Venus, 102, 486, 567; Mars, 936; Jupiter, 791, 843, 879; Saturn, 212, 238; Uranus, 228, 436, 975.

PISCES 10 *An aviator in the clouds* This is a symbol of man's transcendental powers of comprehension, emphasized here in his exploratory genius and his gift for creating the endless hypotheses he needs for solving the problems of a modern world. He is able to take a perspective superior to any involvement or pattern of limitation, and to examine any special complex of human affairs with a consistent thoroughness of over-view. The inner and outer realms of reality are brought to a point of effective revelation of each other. The keyword is OBSERVATION. When positive, the degree is special competence in whole judgment and long-range planning, and when negative, insensate otherworldliness or irresponsible isolationism.

The formula is: sustaining-practical-universal-specializing-social-inspired. Examples are: sun, 101, 331, 663, 723, 865; moon, 279, 284, 475, 901; Mercury, 68, 127, 323, 516, 600, 716, 793; Venus, 766, 897; Mars, 140; Jupiter, 714, 859; Saturn, 369, 377, 500, 888, 977; Uranus, 302, 595, 727.

VIRGO 11 *A boy molded in his mother's aspiration for him* This is a symbol of the immortality of man as dramatized in his physical heredity, or in a succession of tangible achievements and possessions down through a family line. The soul is fundamentally a matrix of itself, since in a sense the ideals it holds create its outer habiliments among its kind and contribute to its embodiment on some congenial plane of human affairs. The coming of the self into experience is always in response to these inner and almost irrevocable compulsions. The keyword is EXACTION. When positive, the degree is personal excellence sustained in its own creative consciousness, and when negative, insensitive conformity to superficialities.

The formula is: sustaining-practical-efficient-specializing-spiritual-experimental. Examples are: sun, 664; moon, 43, 48, 253; Mercury, 133, 257, 734; Venus, 925; Mars, 26, 78, 147, 305, 631, 745; Jupiter, 251, 285 ,305, 366, 993; Saturn, 136, 139, 662, 690, 706; Uranus, 423, 535, 550, 671, 940.

VIRGO 12 *A bride with her veil snatched away* This is a symbol of life's demand that man continue at all times to prove himself in full accordance with the claims he has made for himself, emphasized here on the side of his everyday relationships with his fellows. Implicit in the phallic symbolism is the necessity that an individual continue along the path of experience he has once chosen for his own, since the fact of his choice indicates a capacity for profiting from the consequences. The keyword is INVITATION. When positive, the degree is absolute purity in motive and a completely unconditioned fullness of self-giving as a prophecy of high reward, and when negative, unfounded self-esteem or contempt for moral values.

The formula is: sustaining-practical-efficient-specializing-spiritual-sensitive. Examples are: sun, 145, 873, 961; Mercury, 35, 845; Venus, 171, 235, 530, 534, 762; Mars, 135; Jupiter, 55; Saturn, 355; Uranus, 711.

PISCES 11 *Men seeking illumination* This is a symbol of the immortality of man as dramatized in some form of an apostolic succession, or a living tradition of spiritual achievement. The divine spirit is fundamentally a matrix of itself, since its continuance depends on its unswerving maintenance of the purity in motive and expression which it has contributed to the humanity it has created in its own image. The emergence of the human self into experience is similarly a manifestation of the potentialities to which it must devote itself to be itself. The keyword is DEDICATION. When positive, the degree is high accomplishment in an effective alignment with ultimate reality, and when negative, obvious hypocrisy.

The formula is: sustaining-practical-universal-specializing-spiritual-experimental. Examples are: sun, 466, 526, 846; moon, 260, 375; Mercury, 178, 579, 685, 713, 882; Venus, 827; Mars, 423; Jupiter, 7, 233; Saturn, 108, 513; Uranus, 185, 366, 752.

PISCES 12 *An examination of initiates* This is a symbol of life's demand that man continue at all times to prove himself in full accordance with the claims he has made for himself, emphasized here on the side of his ideals and spiritual aspiration. Every seeker for immortal understanding must be self-dedicated to values far removed from the gross appetites and transient jealousies of his fellows, and he reveals himself ultimately through the potentialities he develops to the point where he can share them with others. The keyword is QUALIFICATION. When positive, the degree is instinctive conformity to the highest expectation of everybody concerned in each new situation of consequence, and when negative, embittered self-solicitude.

The formula is: sustaining-practical-universal-specializing-spiritual-sensitive. Examples are: sun, 11, 567; moon, 233, 844; Mercury, 184, 279; Venus, 51, 331, 628, 834, 870; Saturn, 601, 775, 808.

VIRGO 13 *A strong hand supplanting political hysteria* This is a symbol of the real weight of human personality as emphasized here by the direct intervention of outstanding individuals in the affairs of their follows. They must provide an over-all ordering for each moment of history if it is to count for much in the lives of the others around them, since there is always a counsel of confusion to take over when events are allowed to drift or when the immediate leadership proves deficient. The greatest opportunity for self-discovery lies in the transient crises of everyday living. The keyword is POWER. When positive, the degree is consistent effectiveness in dramatizing personal potentials, and when negative, loss of all opportunity by timid action.

The formula is: sustaining-practical-efficient-specializing-spiritual-receptive. Examples are: sun, 329, 500, 762; moon, 472, 511, 676; Mercury, 36, 199, 717, 875; Venus, 135, 923; Mars, 7, 820; Jupiter, 204, 727; Saturn, 401, 792, 950, 982; Uranus, 216, 750, 945.

VIRGO 14 *A family tree* This is a symbol of the ever-effective dynamic with which an established tradition endows mankind, dramatized here by the extent to which an individual will live the lives of his forebears or accept the guidance stemming from them through their spiritual presence in his blood. Men are swayed and torn by the demands of the interweaving relationships which form among them or hold them in varying complexes of common experience, but yet each person looking to his endowment may reveal an integrity peculiarly his own. The keyword is GENTILITY. When positive, the degree is exceptional fidelity to some unique promise of self and so an ultimate achievement of distinction, and when negative, a false sense of heritage.

The formula is: sustaining-practical-efficient-specializing-spiritual-responsible. Examples are: sun, 9, 129, 725; moon, 278, 486; Mercury, 535, 758, 923; Venus, 502, 670; Mars, 129, 193, 708; Jupiter, 218, 234, 390, 784; Saturn, 320, 371, 410, 611, 735, 993; Uranus, 681.

PISCES 13 *A sword in a museum* This is a symbol of the real weight of human personality, emphasized here by the surviving influence of great figures out of the past. The tradition of the race helps bring history to center in some outstanding individual of real promise at each point of crisis in human affairs, and the wisdom which thus becomes reincarnate in the new leadership is always available to counter any counsel of confusion arising from a moment's uncertainty. The dramatization of prior achievement is the greatest of all possible present encouragement. The keyword is EXAMPLE. When positive, the degree is personal power in living common ideals, and when negative, ridiculous pretense of epic merit.

The formula is: sustaining-practical-universal-specializing-spiritual-receptive. Examples are: sun, 81, 433, 501, 516, 531, 770, 987; moon, 290, 740, 779; Mercury, 101, 669; Venus, 156, 210, 470, 723, 984; Mars, 168; Jupiter, 6, 428; Saturn, 48, 184, 479, 902; Uranus 946, 997.

PISCES 14 *A lady in fox fur* This is a symbol of the ever-effective dynamic with which everyday custom endows mankind, dramatized here by an individual's desire to be in style and to express opinions of momentary weight. Men are strengthened through whatever they are able to possess or do and think in common, but this is their bondage unless they are able also to contribute a creative content to their own experience. The self gains integrity as it learns never to surrender its initiative, and so it adds its touch to all reality. The keyword is TASTEFULNESS. When positive, the degree is high accomplishment through a consistent representation of the self's assets in the best possible light, and when negative, amoral opportunism.

The formula is: sustaining-practical-universal-specializing-spiritual-responsible. Examples are: sun, 408, 548; moon, 85, 185; Mercury, 289, 834; Venus, 155, 318, 999; Mars, 730, 995; Jupiter, 489, 996; Saturn, 202; Uranus, 372, 971.

VIRGO 15 *An ornamental handkerchief* This is a symbol of
man's self-quickening desire for allegiance to a reality higher
or finer than himself, evident on the side of his aesthetic instincts. The knight in theory at least could never enter the
lists of chivalry without his lady's bit of lace as a talisman of
the spirit, and every normal person feels rather lost without
some continual reminder of his better impulses. Objects therefore are of value as they preserve meaning and help perfect
action. The keyword is GRACEFULNESS. When positive, the degree is an effective refinement of personal manner and a high
achievement through an exceptional charm, and when negative, insinuating self-pretense and a pompous interest in trifles.

The formula is: sustaining-practical-efficient-specializing-spiritual-inspired.
Examples are: sun, 697, 985; moon, 696, 970; Mercury, 7; Mars, 224, 993;
Jupiter, 602, 677, 704, 946, 997; Saturn, 175, 420, 824; Uranus, 357, 520,
876, 952.

VIRGO 16 *An orangutan* This is a symbol of the primitive
power which the processes of evolution have brought into leash
with the development of mankind, and which each person
must refine for his own use in meeting the demands of higher
life. There are always unmobilized resources in self to meet
the exigencies of any unique situation in which an individual
may unwittingly be involved, and maturity at root is a continual discovery of these and a consequent increasing facility
for rising to any possible occasion. The keyword is DEXTERITY.
When positive, the degree is man's ability to strip himself to
fundamentals and there stand proudly on his own, and when
negative, self-justification in crudity or violence.

*The formula is: sustaining-practical-efficient-generalizing-physical-experi-
mental.* Examples are: sun, 105, 161, 165; moon, 75, 167, 519, 701; Mercury, 24, 435, 544, 634, 894; Venus, 131, 257, 631; Mars, 93, 377, 977;
Jupiter, 527, 695, 901; Saturn, 214, 583, 781; Uranus, 39, 522, 616, 828.

PISCES 15 *An officer preparing to drill his men* This is a symbol of man's self-betraying desire for a hierarchy of allegiances in which he can lose himself, evident on the side of the superficial life of everyday and its dismissal of all responsibility of consequence. Implicit in the symbolism is a challenge to make the best of the situations from which there is no immediate extrication, but to do so only with a determination to participate in some reality of more enduring importance. Living is vital to the extent each individual decides to motivate it. The keyword is PRECISENESS. When positive, the degree is a gift for bringing genuine efficiency and real adventure to common objectives, and when negative, uninspiring drudgery.

The formula is: sustaining-practical-universal-specializing-spiritual-inspired. Examples are: moon, 30, 163, 135, 522, 881; Venus, 163, 187, 300, 457, 479; Mars, 156, 239, 352, 685, 987; Jupiter, 139, 143, 215, 574, 614, 793, 856; Saturn, 292, 733, 903, 973; Uranus, 435.

PISCES 16 *The flow of inspiration* This is a symbol of the spiritual power which the development of civilization has brought to a point of practical potentiality, and on which each person may draw in meeting any or all critical issues of everyday living. There are illimitable resources in the world of reality around him, and maturity at root is a conscious and disciplined sensitiveness to these. Man is himself as he puts his talents and skills to a real test, welcoming each new challenge to their competency. The keyword is INGENUITY. When positive, the degree is exceptional capacity for meeting the unusual developments on every level of human experience, and when negative, delusions of cleverness and contempt for real effort.

The formula is: sustaining-practical-universal-generalizing-physical-experimental. Examples are: sun, 140, 300; moon, 127, 209, 355, 576, 929; Mercury, 205, 365, 484, 826; Venus, 91, 184, 425, 765; Mars, 189; Jupiter, 111, 136; Saturn, 20, 580, 654; Uranus, 762.

VIRGO 17   *A volcano in eruption*   This is a symbol of that constant expansion of self and nature which constitutes reality in its most fundamental terms, emphasized here on the side of physical force and the blind urge of life to continue to be. Implicit in the wonder and destructiveness is man's ease of self-recovery in the critical phases of his experience, often aided by the sheer violence with which he acts to meet some major issue. His irresistible outbursts may be merely the total mobilization of his deeper potentials. The keyword is EXPLOSION. When positive, the degree is creative passion as a rejection of superficiality and a genuine ordering of self, and when negative, petulance and tantrums.

The formula is: sustaining-practical-efficient-generalizing-physical-sensitive.
Examples are: sun, 130, 235, 432, 544, 784, 907; moon, 747; Mercury, 671; Venus, 903; Mars, 37, 324, 388, 889, 960; Jupiter, 31, 497; Saturn, 259, 486, 803; Uranus, 331.

VIRGO 18   *An ouija board*   This is a symbol of the completeness with which man is able to see his experience both steadily and whole, dramatized here by the planchette as representative of effective anticipation or a true rational divination. The inner comprehension becomes articulate in outer form whenever a practical judgment is allowed to order it, and the individual then begins to realize that coming events have a myriad of signatures on which he can count. He masters life through his creative sensitiveness to the illimitable potentials. The keyword is ACUMEN. When positive, the degree is cleverness in making use of everyday insights and intimations, and when negative, a bondage to superstition and a surrender to the unknown.

The formula is: sustaining-practical-efficient-generalizing-physical-receptive.
Examples are: sun, 748; moon, 229, 393, 438, 444; Mercury, 72, 230, 384, 550, 704, 800, 904; Venus, 123; Mars, 29, 758; Saturn, 127, 157, 610; Uranus, 68, 507, 716. 805.

PISCES 17 *An Easter promenade* This is a symbol of that constant expansion of self and experience which characterizes reality on its conscious levels, emphasized here on the side of humanity's utterly individualistic self-expression. Implicit in all the ridiculous extremes of man's vanity and self-exhibition is a realization that each least manifestation of his personal excellencies must be shared widely and generously as the basic condition of their development. A human society exists only as one person is able to dramatize himself satisfactorily to all. The keyword is CELEBRATION. When positive, the degree is tireless self-refinement in an effective inspiration of others, and when negative, a craving for attention.

The formula is: sustaining-practical-universal-generalizing-physical-sensitive. Examples are: sun, 410; moon, 196; Mercury, 99, 157, 403; Venus, 274, 297; Mars, 265; Jupiter, 110, 777; Uranus, 353, 700, 756, 799.

PISCES 18 *A gigantic tent* This is a symbol of the completeness with which man is able to see his experience both steadily and whole, dramatized here by the circus as representing an utterly naïve intensification of self-consciousness. The totality of life is brought to some single center in every moment of true excitement or total sharing of skills and risks, and each individual at such times has a renewed insight into his capacity for putting his world in order for his ultimate on-going as well as for his immediate entertainment. The keyword is APPORTIONMENT. When positive, the degree is a genius for organizing divergent capabilities in a common cause, and when negative, delusions of grandeur and unamusing bombast.

The formula is: sustaining-practical-universal-generalizing-physical-receptive. Examples are: sun, 150, 403, 657, 974; moon, 801; Mercury, 43; Venus, 144, 469; Jupiter, 106, 114, 286, 420, 576, 583, 927; Saturn, 43, 135, 813; Uranus, 999.

VIRGO 19 *A swimming race* This is a symbol of the utter impartiality of existence in any larger dimension, and of the stimulus of direct competition whenever an individual seeks to perfect or enjoy some one of the special skills comprising his individuality. He discovers that it is necessary to control every separate factor of his being, or else be ruled by the divergencies which make them up apart from their function within himself. Life superficially remains in unstable balance, and survival is in the terms of that effectiveness or excellency which is best able to prove itself. The keyword is ELIMINATION. When positive, the degree is man's capacity for any extreme of self-pointedness he may find valuable in a given case, and when negative, inadequate self-dramatization.

The formula is: sustaining-practical-efficient-generalizing-physical-responsible. Examples are: sun, 535; moon, 142, 321, 767, 769, 907; Mercury, 34, 204, 772; Venus, 878; Mars, 101, 661, 756; Jupiter, 316, 657; Saturn, 228, 715, 882, 996; Uranus, 432, 948, 957.

VIRGO 20 *An automobile caravan* This is a symbol of nature's prodigality as revealed through man's genius for multiplying the facilities of modern life, and for pyramiding the expectancies which will interest an enlightened individual. Experience is on the move in a civilized society, since everyone has been encouraged to heed his visions and to claim increasing rewards for the skill he develops. Self goes out very courageously to meet its world, and as a result finds it has brought a cosmos to its doorstep. The keyword is VARIETY. When positive, the degree is an exceptional capacity for creating a greater promise and producing expanded dividends in every area of human activity, and when negative, improvidence and restlessness.

The formula is: sustaining-practical-efficient-generalizing-physical-inspired Examples are: sun, 182, 876, 993; moon, 578, 598, 774; Mercury, 825, 955; Venus, 411, 821; Mars, 296, 363, 561, 698; Jupiter, 486, 875; Saturn, 552, 727; Uranus, 240, 326, 437, 553, 947.

PISCES 19 *A master instructing his pupil* This is a symbol of the unlimited potentiality of existence in any larger dimension, and of the demand of human intelligence for the self-refinement and self-orientation by which a greater understanding is possible. Life entreats the individual to employ its privileges and enjoy its bounty, and gives every encouragement to that initiative of spirit by which he may be led to do so. He finds that personality comes into its own as it is able to direct its own destiny. The keyword is ELUCIDATION. When positive, the degree is high executive ability through patient investigation and genuine psychological insight, and when negative, a desire to live by rule and a conceit of empty knowledge.

The formula is: sustaining-practical-universal-generalizing-physical-responsible. Examples are: sun, 110, 125, 142, 471, 625, 826, 689; moon, 514, 750, 911, 946; Mercury, 47; Venus, 374, 657, 928; Mars, 257; Jupiter, 466; Saturn, 257, 402, 599; Uranus, 332, 860.

PISCES 20 *A table set for an evening meal* This is a symbol of nature's prodigality as revealed through the normal satisfactions for which modern man seldom has to exert himself, and as these take on significance through his instinct for finding every phase of reality a special revelation of his own potentials. Every individual discovers that there is no part of the universe he cannot enlist for the fulfillment of his own desires, and in making every such potentiality an expression of his own genius he achieves its promise in a thorough self-gratification. The keyword is FAMILIARITY. When positive, the degree is an effective sensitiveness to every passing need of mankind, and when negative, naïve selfishness and a wholly witless optimism.

The formula is: sustaining-practical-universal-generalizing-physical-inspired. Examples are: sun, 21, 113; moon, 296, 685, 935; Mercury, 711; Venus, 731; Jupiter, 17, 100, 163, 404, 765; Saturn, 378, 442; Uranus, 891.

VIRGO 21 *A girls' basketball team* This is a symbol of the
integrated divisions of labor by which any higher reality is
manifest in everyday terms, and of the opportunity which the
wide variations of modern life have provided for individual
specialization and personal refinement. The self cannot exist
in a vacuum, and there is no satisfaction in any effort expended
for ends in which others are not vitally concerned. Man's fulfillment is primarily a continued participation in common
goals, with rewards to which his fellows contribute as consistently as himself. The keyword is EXPRESSION. When positive
the degree is effective self-consummation through exceptional
co-operation and adaptability, and when negative, listless conformity.

*The formula is: sustaining-practical-efficient-generalizing-social-experimen
tal.* Examples are: sun, 46, 671, 758, 776, 932; Mercury, 229, 254, 488, 873,
932; Venus, 441, 661, 684, 994; Mars, 434; Jupiter, 127, 157, 619; Saturn,
192, 834, 942; Uranus, 189, 267, 710.

VIRGO 22 *A royal coat of arms* This is a symbol of the eternal authority implicit in the very fact of existence, and of the
consequent dignification of experience through the laws and
customs by which man organizes the conduct of his own affairs.
The elders of the tribe were long the custodians of this
common-sense regulation of life, and an aristocracy of blood
or of the inherited stewardship of social function has continued to re-enact these values and to enforce their observance.
Right is dramatized as a privilege worthy of sustainment. The
keyword is PREROGATIVE. When positive, the degree is a gift
for bringing all men together in common purpose and unified
stability, and when negative, subtle exploitation of the unwary.

The formula is: sustaining-practical-efficient-generalizing-social-sensitive.
Examples are: sun, 78, 550, 708, 821, 822; moon, 334, 534, 707, 855; Mercury, 15, 358, 971; Venus, 145, 504, 690; Mars, 79, 523, 700; Jupiter, 104,
192, 268, 552, 624; Saturn, 7, 107, 124, 814, 986; Uranus, 605.

PISCES 21   *A little white lamb, a child and a Chinese servant*
This is a symbol of the scattered divisions of labor through
which any over-all reality is encountered by man in his everyday or more haphazard existence, and of the necessity that he
brings the threads of his diffusion into a skein of meaning
and opportunity. He must learn that nothing acts alone or
persists in a vacuum, and that in consequence there is an in-
tegrating significance throughout his own experience. He must
find this and draw it to single focus in some special design of
self-expression. The keyword is TALENT. When positive, the
degree is completely unconditioned self-discovery out of wholly
unlimited potentialities, and when negative, groping aimless-
ness.

*The formula is: sustaining-practical-universal-generalizing-social-experi-
mental.* Examples are: sun, 472; moon, 268, 412, 718, 793; Mercury, 252;
Venus, 90; Mars, 241, 949; Jupiter, 190, 469; Saturn, 995; Uranus, 167, 248,
313, 328, 431, 471, 526.   ,,

PISCES 22   *A man bringing down the new law from Sinai*
This is a symbol of the eternal authority implicit in the very
act of man's ideals, and of a spiritualization of experience
through the religious insights of human society and the institutions it has created for the common welfare. The inspired
prophets of each age have been custodians of an enduring
morality, and this has its embodiment in the mountain-top
aspiration of even the least of individuals. Right is dramatized
as a personal responsibility for the course of events. The keyword is MANDATE. When positive, the degree is self-sacrifice
and a determination to further the ultimate upliftment of all
men, and when negative, self-exploitation and impenetrable
egotism.

The formula is: sustaining-practical-universal-generalizing-social-sensitive.
Examples are: sun, 244, 484, 601, 682; moon, 180, 237; Mercury, 480, 570;
Venus, 6, 398, 497, 658, 860; Mars, 498; Jupiter, 88, 422, 846; Saturn,
266, 346; Uranus, 209.

VIRGO 23 *An animal trainer* This is a symbol of the organic integrity of the world at large, evident here in man's gift for using all its interweaving relationships to impose his ideas and desires on lesser forms of life. Implicit in the symbolism is the fact that an individual will be conditioned more and more hopelessly by his environment and experience if he fails to give continual attention to his own potentials and to the self-discipline he must have to develop them. He finds that he can do everything for which he is able to enlist the whole of himself. The keyword is RESOLUTENESS. When positive, the degree is illimitable patience and adroitness in personal accomplishment, and when negative, futile show-off and idle boasting.

The formula is: sustaining-practical-efficient-generalizing-social-receptive. Examples are: sun, 222, 490, 886; moon, 407, 461; Mercury, 180, 256, 344, 490, 780; Venus, 347, 934, 969; Mars, 309, 678; Jupiter, 119, 177, 594, 643, 661, 705, 752, 975; Saturn, 120, 621, 677, 901, 918; Uranus, 254, 334, 414.

VIRGO 24 *Mary and her white lamb* This is a symbol of the self-adequacy of experience on the inner or subjective side, or of that fullness of life which comes through a cherishing of young ideas. The healthy approach to heaven through a child's wide-eyed expectation is a clue to the adult's responsibility for his potentials. These he must take with him in a very conscious fashion wherever he goes if he is not to find himself divided within himself and so defeated by his own confusion. The keyword is ARTLESSNESS. When positive, the degree is a highly ingenuous creativity by which an individual is able to make all contact with others a worth-while relationship of self, and when negative, happy-go-lucky vacuity of spirit and understanding.

The formula is: sustaining-practical-efficient-generalizing-social-responsible. Examples are: sun, 411, 523; Mercury, 165, 303, 524, 664, 829; Venus, 446, 820; Mars, 652, 704; Jupiter, 549, 715; Saturn, 314, 634, 664, 782; Uranus, 84, 169, 482, 538, 626, 693, 821.

PISCES 23 *Spiritist phenomena* This is a symbol of the organic integrity of the world at large, evident here in man's facility for actual and conscious co-operation with the potentials of an immortal reality. Implicit in the symbolism is the fact that the individual will be conditioned increasingly by the caprice of his ideas and the mishaps of his experience unless he gives continual attention to the realms of reality he has thought to make particularly his own. He achieves as he holds a clear picture of the end results he desires. The keyword is SENSITIVITY. When positive, the degree is exceptional ability in shaping every immediate aspect of life to a personal convenience, and when negative, instability and confused perspective.

The formula is: sustaining-practical-universal-generalizing-social-receptive.
Examples are: sun, 600, 711; Mercury, 13, 408, 846; Venus, 188, 406, 448; Jupiter, 531, 579, 844.

PISCES 24 *An inhabited island* This is a symbol of the self-adequacy of experience on the objective side of everyday reality, and of man's gift for the organization of his own private world in any area of his special interest. He is always able to function in a complete independence of the alien or the unfriendly, and to develop adequate resources for his need in what at the beginning might seem to be the most barren of situations. He capitalizes on the potentials among which he finds himself, and nurses the least of promise to its fruits. The keyword is CULTIVATION. When positive, the degree is achievement through a creative opportunism or inventiveness of exceptional order, and when negative, snobbish complacency and self-indulgence.

The formula is: sustaining-practical-universal-generalizing-social-responsible. Examples are: sun, 102, 489, 508, 929; moon, 851, 978; Mercury, 44, 114, 466, 508; Venus, 236, 689; Mars, 391; Jupiter, 685, 687, 976; Saturn, 315; Uranus, 36.

VIRGO 25   *A flag at half-mast*   This is a symbol of the inevitable judgment which life must pronounce on itself, and of the sure rewards that stand ready for whatever proves of worth in the course of effort. The highest of everyday values for the common man are created in a public service which has its first compensation in the individual's self-fulfillment, and its ultimate justification in some measure of immortal contribution to history. Reputation is the subtle coin by which personality creates an enduring wealth for everyone, to be preserved no less in death than life. The keyword is RESPECT. When positive, the degree is achievement in a full transcendence of selfhood, and when negative, superficial self-dramatization.

The formula is: sustaining-practical-efficient-generalizing-social-inspired. Examples are: moon, 81, 513, 841; Mercury, 329, 644; Venus, 137, 290; Mars, 36, 353, 595, 754, 791; Jupiter, 181, 480, 524, 652; Saturn, 121, 767, 791, 975; Uranus, 83, 219, 242, 392, 858, 909, 962.

VIRGO 26   *A boy with a censer*   This is a symbol of individual initiative as a basic dynamic in the universal scheme of things, and it reveals itself most simply in man's positive and necessarily self-seeking outreach to the world he would claim for himself. He makes his conscious appeal to God, since it is a divine being which provides the over-all unity he recognizes and would enlist for his aspiration. His motive is spiritual because he knows he must share any reality he would care to possess. The keyword is RAPTURE. When positive, the degree is a completeness of self-dedication and an achievement grounded in a consistent worthiness of living, and when negative, a resort to empty motions in order to avoid any appreciable self-expenditure.

The formula is: sustaining-practical-efficient-generalizing-spiritual-experimental. Examples are: sun, 368; moon, 292, 751, 775; Mercury, 360, 609, 811; Venus, 128, 734, 958; Mars, 59; Jupiter, 329, 653, 684, 814, 830, 834, 942; Saturn, 412, 843, 898, 917; Uranus, 53, 921.

PISCES 25 *The purging of the priesthood* This is a symbol of the inevitable judgment which life must pronounce on itself, and of the sure penalties that await whatever may fail to prove its worth. Man demands an absolute integrity for his spiritual or immortal insights, and will have no falling short of his ideals in those who elect to be custodians of his higher and invisible treasures. He approaches the problems of his own regeneration through a dramatization of potentials he recognizes but cannot altogether instrument, and he will not tolerate their depreciation. The keyword is REFORMATION. When positive, the degree is revolt against all superficial exaltation of human nature, and when negative, blind bigotry and vindictiveness.

The formula is: sustaining-practical-universal-generalizing-social-inspired. Examples are: moon, 53, 93, 669, 987; Mercury, 81, 375, 667, 921, 950; Venus, 30, 332; Jupiter, 22, 639; Saturn, 27, 60, 457, 562, 831.

PISCES 26 *A new moon that divides its influences* This is a symbol of universal initiative as a basic dynamic in any personal scheme of things, and it reveals itself most simply in man's instinctive and often blind outreach to the reality in which he participates. His action must be tentative until he achieves his own true self-discovery, but he makes a fine skill of his uncertainty and refuses to commit himself except as he encounters a full response to his deeper realization and ultimate motives. The keyword is FINESSE. When positive, the degree is a thoroughgoing capitalization on life's transitions and an effective development of every emerging potentiality of self, and when negative, a completely disruptive vacillation,

The formula is: sustaining-practical-universal-generalizing-spiritual-experimental. Examples are: sun, 106, 728; moon, 154, 495, 738, 827, 849, 975; Mercury, 41, 401, 487, 828; Venus, 88, 510, 848; Jupiter, 131; Saturn, 787; Uranus, 627.

VIRGO 27 *Grande dames at tea*   This is a symbol of life's maturity as a threshold of new discovery rather than as any canceling out of personal reality, and it emphasizes the fact that each individual may pass on what he has gained and thereby have an effective continuance of himself through others. Here are the highly concentrated values of selfhood as the reservoir of racial assets, since the traditions of one generation are always the ever-ready strength of the next. The keyword is APLOMB. When positive, the degree is an efficient administration of inheritance or position and a full capitalization on the opportunities of common experience, and when negative, a selfish delight in special privileges of any sort.

The formula is: sustaining-practical-efficient-generalizing-spiritual-sensitive. Examples are: sun, 36; moon, 162, 773; Mercury, 596, 835, 925, 993; Venus, 749, 844, 951; Mars, 270, 845, 969; Jupiter, 26, 320, 611, 745, 960; Saturn, 17, 329, 728, 879; Uranus, 472.

VIRGO 28 *A bald-headed man*   This is a symbol of a simple satisfaction in the inner rather than outer manifestations of reality, and of the challenge to any purely personal attainment to become more than a visible proof of the special excellency. Man is not called on to make himself a scourge of his fellows any more than he is to be encouraged to neglect them, but there are illimitable areas in which the driving power of his personality can create or advance widespread opportunities for a richer and more enjoyable living. The keyword is DOMINANCE. When positive, the degree is accomplishment through a completeness of self-mastery and a rigid control of others, and when negative, a sadistic sophistication.

The formula is: sustaining-practical-efficient-generalizing-spiritual-receptive. Examples are: sun, 473, 845; moon, 687; Mercury, 936; Venus, 454, 712, 920; Mars, 587, 722, 734; Jupiter, 107, 120, 610, 918; Saturn, 100, 398, 434, 516, 818; Uranus, 40, 575, 623, 766.

PISCES 27 *A harvest moon* This is a symbol of life's moments of culmination as the threshold of new achievement rather than as any canceling out of experience in the given aspect, and it emphasizes the fact that nature in her immeasurable prodigality is forever showering man with the products of her untiring creativeness. She is saying to him that his productivity is as rich as hers, and that the highly concentrated resources of the world are at the immediate service of anyone who will put them to use and so facilitate their replacement. The keyword is BENEDICTION. When positive, the degree is self-consummation which is successful beyond any possibility of measure, and when negative, loss of self in a welter of opportunity.

The formula is: sustaining-practical-universal-generalizing-spiritual-sensitive. Examples are: sun, 425; moon, 772; Mercury, 113, 531, 965; Venus, 422; Mars, 98, 409; Jupiter, 149, 516, 722; Saturn, 142, 150, 246, 564; Uranus, 2, 754.

PISCES 28 *A fertile garden under the full moon* This is a symbol of a simple satisfaction through outer rather than inner manifestations of reality, or of a normal self-dedication to purely conventional accomplishment. Man is blessed as he is more the average than the exceptional individual, since he then is legion in his service to his kind. His struggles have the common note in which the race survives, and in his archetypal make-up there is room to salvage all the failures and embody all the contributions of the far more lonely genius. The keyword is ULTIMACY. When positive, the degree is high reward in worldly goods and exceptional self-integrity in using them, and when negative, irritating pride of possessions.

The formula is: sustaining-practical-universal-generalizing-spiritual-receptive. Examples are: sun, 43, 187, 210, 479, 793; Mercury, 73, 189, 865; Venus, 365; Mars, 44, 179, 589, 906, 972; Jupiter, 44, 231, 398, 761; Saturn, 788, 861; Uranus, 318, 659, 984.

VIRGO 29 *A man gaining secret knowledge from a paper he is reading* This is a symbol of the world's conservatism, and of the refusal of nature to surrender any part of her heritage unnecessarily. The fixity of idea by which human beings preserve their culture is also a protection for all hidden wisdom and unsuspected ways of knowing, since the deeper awareness is merely a broader reference or a further application of stabilities which constitute a universe at large. The possibilities of greater experience lie in embryo throughout the lesser. The keyword is DISCOVERY. When positive, the degree is imagination brought to the full of its powers through conscious effort, and when negative, loss of common sense in pure supposition.

The formula is: sustaining-practical-efficient-generalizing-spiritual-responsible. Examples are: sun, 2, 955, 967; moon, 800, 829; Mercury, 104, 752, 996; Venus, 204, 596, 835, 916; Mars, 256, 941; Jupiter, 8; Saturn, 69, 133, 277, 976; Uranus, 822.

VIRGO 30 *A false call unheard in attention to immediate service* This is a symbol of human responsibility as an immortality of the soul, and of a way of living which has achieved an absoluteness of attitude or understanding and is able in consequence to dramatize a high personal competency in everyday problem solving. Each individual creates his place for himself among his fellows, and thereafter all life tends to protect him in his way of going and all circumstances somehow seem to shape themselves for his convenience and encouragement. The keyword is SAFEGUARD. When positive, the degree is exceptionally gratifying self-fulfillment through the development of a genuine integrity, and when negative, consistently witless indiscretion.

The formula is: sustaining-practical-efficient-generalizing-spiritual-inspired. Examples are: sun, 679, 705, 875, 889; moon, 59, 126, 313; Mercury, 705, 776, 876; Venus, 105, 230, 474, 488, 498, 613, 802, 899; Mars, 58, 185, 362, 843; Jupiter, 455, 621, 718; Saturn, 74, 88, 163, 233, 336, 422, 444, 469, 606, 630, 765; Uranus, 180, 804.

PISCES 29 *A prism* This is a symbol of the world's stability, and of the refusal of nature to change any aspect of herself unnecessarily. The reliability of normal processes and the consistency of true intelligence are the foundation of a common knowledge which man has been expanding through the centuries, and his continuance of the control he has gained over his environment is promise of much more wonderful achievement ahead. He is able to take any convenient facet of the reality at his hand and fashion it into an effective instrument for a measure of the whole potential. The keyword is VALIDATION. When positive, the degree is exceptional accomplishment through judgment of unusual accuracy, and when negative, fatuous pride of intellect.

The formula is: sustaining-practical-universal-generalizing-spiritual-responsible. Examples are: sun: 156, 184, 713, 950; moon, 8, 131, 704, 945; Mercury, 42; Venus, 140, 396, 750; Mars, 169, 600; Jupiter, 1, 67, 93, 662, 735; Saturn, 933; Uranus, 168.

PISCES 30 *The Great Stone Face* This is a symbol of human responsibility as an immortality of the soul, and of a way of living which has become a continual manifestation of its ideal and so a constant dramatization of its self-discovery to others as an encouragement to them in their own alignment to eternal reality. Each individual selects the image within himself to which he would shape himself outwardly, and this he comes to resemble as in Nathaniel Hawthorne's tale. Destiny is character as it most persistently constitutes itself. The keyword is DISCERNMENT. When positive, the degree is self-integrity in its irresistible impact on the course of events, and when negative, wholly inarticulate and ineffectual self-realization.

The formula is: sustaining-practical-universal-generalizing-spiritual-inspired. Examples are: sun, 148, 401, 669; moon, 136, 217, 630, 666, 961; Mercury, 203, 370, 391, 427, 451, 470, 695; Venus, 591, 639, 945; Mars, 54, 760; Jupiter, 359, 728, 759; Saturn, 15, 845; Uranus, 61.

CHAPTER TWELVE

THE CLAIRVOYANT FACTOR

The greatest difficulty in any discussion of spiritistic phenomena is the meaning of terms. Added to this is the widespread doubt of any validity in a type of experience which seems restricted by necessity to the small group of sensitives to be found under any given set of circumstances. The author is not within years of readiness to report on long and continued investigation in this field, primarily for the lack of language adequate for the purpose. However, the Sabian symbols are a fact and they may be examined or employed by anybody who wishes. They have entered the realm of common reality and become subject to the universal logic of man's mind. The problem is in explaining them, whether by putting the story of their origin on record or by attempting to give an intelligent picture of the aberrant sort of rational insight of which they are a part. Hence the opening chapters of the book have approached the whole proposition very obliquely, and what follows is pure extemporization.

The possibility of any reach into the past, or out into any phase of the unknown or as yet unmanifest, is a faculty of consciousness which ultimately may come to be explained by assuming mind to be devoid of the sort of discrete boundaries which are characteristic of body, and by recognizing individuality as merging into individuality to the varying degrees necessary to constitute the framework of a culture and a human society. The whole Sabian enterprise, whether in its identifiable thirty years of existence or in the near double that time of the special curiosity which led to its establishment, has been primarily a species of tapping back into early Mesopotamian and allied roots or of utilizing a matrix of reasoned conclusions from which so much of language and its notation, or of mathematical abstraction and scientific achievement, seems to have streamed. The technique which has been refined in this connection has been a proposition of borrowing or reconstructing mind-complexes out of the continuing heritage—particularly those of Ibn Gabirol, Plotinus, Plato and Aristotle in that order among the philosophers, and a long list of others in the traditions of Christian theology and occult techniques—with an accumulation of about four million words of research material preserved in the form of mimeographed lecture-lessons.

A fundamental clue to the whole problem of man's understanding or psychological orientation has been found in the doctrine of theism, or in the theory of the nontime-and-space nature of the self. This has been found in the *Bhagavad Gita* and the incomplete contribution of George Sylvester Morris and has a significant development in the contribution of Ibn Gabirol. God and man exist in a very effective intimacy, such as can be described through a frank anthropomorphism on the one hand and an equally useful apotheosis on the other. The former is a commonplace of today's evangelical Christianity, and as stripped of unnecessarily fantastic features is possibly the real hope of Western culture. The latter is strange to the average person, in any familiar terms of current life and values, but has been brought to a point of signal usefulness by the Theosophists in their conception of Masters, Brothers or members of the Great White Lodge. The nonoccultist must understand, however, that these personalities of spiritual realms reveal not so much the transcendent reality of a discrete person as the living but unembodied mind of the sort represented in a sense, and of course as a purely convenient example, by an Albert Einstein of the present age. It is not difficult to conceive of him as less an individual than a universally accepted and utilized matrix or chrysalis of thought and theorization. Research psychism seems to deal with this sort of group entity, or with an intelligence which is immortal in the fact that it can be revivified and consulted at will.

In late 1922 the author shared a large amount of spiritistic activity with Miss Zoë Wells, who was then a neighbor. She was especially anxious to try her superphysical gifts on matters more worth while than the usual questions of love and money, or the petty suspicions and selfish desires, with which her friends were plaguing her. As a result it became necessary to delve into various occult books and even intuitive sources to find loose ends of this and that for examination by clairvoyant means. There are a host of rigid rules in connection with work of this sort, such as seem to have come down from a remote antiquity. Thus there can be no consistent reliability of result unless the object of investigation has an intimate and personal concern. The corrective here, more often neglected than not, was observed rigorously in these sessions, as were a great many others, and as a result there soon was a dearth of leads for further inquiry. It was at this time, in an experimental paralleling of Charubel's interpretation of the zodiacal degrees, that a series of fifty-two symbols for a pack of ordinary playing cards was obtained. At the end of this session an ancient seal was described by Miss Wells, as a mode of certification for what had been put down, but no record was made and later attempts to reproduce it were uncertain. However, this was the beginning of a conscious recognition of the ancient sources as a self-contained and living integrity available for use.

The next step, in Southern California a little over two years later, was the creation of the new set of symbols for the zodiacal degrees. Miss Elsie Wheeler was very anxious to start, and on the visible side of things it was necessary to provide uninterrupted hours, with a problem of inevitable fatigue to be taken into account. She had to be carried, no others could be present and conditions in general had to enable her to function in her accustomed manner. Balboa Park in San Diego offered a spot where a driveway was a matter of a very few yards from one of the city's busiest traffic intersections, fortuitously meeting the necessity that work of this sort be done in the turmoil of some metropolitan center or other unusually dense aggregation of people active in the business of being. There was a screen of trees and bushes, and during the day no one would show any interest in a car parked here for a few hours. Special blank cards were prepared for the 360 degrees, so that they could be shuffled continuously. A quarter of the pile was taken at random for the first session. One card was put face down before the medium, and she reported on the picture she saw by inward vision. This was noted hurriedly in pencil on the card itself. The process continued steadily for nearly two hours, and then after a brief rest another ninety symbols were recorded.

After a drive well out into the country, where there was little chance for any intrusion of alien interest but an opportunity for a pleasant and leisurely noon dinner, the sessions were resumed at the same spot in the park and the other degrees interpreted in a similar fashion.

The author had three tasks in addition to the physical care of his student sensitive. These were (1) the shuffling which maintained the immediate synchronization with the source material, (2) making pencil notations of the psychic pictures with critical rejection and selection at each point of progress, and (3) sustaining the ancient mind-matrix which made the whole procedure possible. The third task had its expression, in terms of any human experience to be captured in words, through the presence and co-operation on the invisible side of life of that one of the Brothers (to use the term by which he would be identified in Theosophy) who has been concerned in every spiritistic phase of Sabian investigation.

The pictures which Miss Wheeler saw came from various sources, as far as their substance was concerned. Some were directly out of her own experience, or as she reached out to take them from other minds directly available to her. Some were beyond her range of comprehension and were impressed upon her consciousness, and so were received in distorted fashion or with an overlay of detail which had to be screened out. As events have shown, her total contribution was an exceptional achievement, and this one of the author's volumes is dedicated to her memory, in the hope that it may in time become a monument to the beauty of her character and the immortal quality of her ideals.

the example horoscopes

CHAPTER THIRTEEN

THE EXAMPLE HOROSCOPES

The present collection of charts of prominent people, as a basis for reference in astrological writing and lecturing, began as a labor of love on the part of Miss Ida Hine about 1927. She put down all possible information concerning the source and validity of the data, and supplemented this with rather full biographical material. Already available at the time was the Alan Leo manual, *1001 Notable Nativities* (London, Fowler, 1911), and this was being supplemented by Maurice Wemyss with more than four hundred additional cases. The author, preparing his first astrological books in 1940-5, drew on these sources for illustration of horoscopic points.

With the beginnings of preparation for this text, in 1948, Mrs. Lena Sutcliffe undertook the task of enlarging the collection in the light of its particular standards. This meant primarily a known moment of birth, since the degree symbolism could be unreliable in the case of the moon if this were in error by any appreciable part of an hour, and in the case of house cusps if a precise rectification had not brought the time fairly close to within the minute of accuracy. Horoscopes for years prior to 1800 would not permit student research in future efforts towards a greater reliability, because of the general lack of planetary tables and the necessity to resort to approximations not possibly accurate enough for any use of the symbols. By the same token, individuals were needed who were sufficiently prominent or otherwise significant to assure any inquirer of adequate information concerning their lives and attitudes if he had to seek this in an average library. The goal was a better ground for future study and for a continued refinement of the intuitive technique. An appeal in the astrological periodicals brought some response, but Mrs. Sutcliffe and her co-workers, Mrs. Ruth Gerry and Mr. Robert Hartley in particular, were able to make only very slow progress.

At this point the project of more than seventeen years of special search and investigation on the part of Miss Lilian Polk, whose long-projected book *A Time To Be Born, Accurate Birth Data of 3000 Notable Persons and Events* will provide a genuinely thorough and scholarly presentation of the evidence, supplied a real bottom for exhibiting the implication of the degree symbols. The full use of her collection was offered, graciously and generously and without limitation, and at a conference it was decided that whatever additional charts were acquired for the present text would be given to her to supplement her efforts, and also that all matters of source of information and discussion of validity of evidence would be left as the basic function of her volume. A careful check showed that some nine hundred of her cases had potential value for this exposition, and Mrs. Ethel Strange made the trip from Kansas City to Shreveport to copy the horoscopes. More than two hundred of them were duplications of those already possessed, but at the end about a hundred and seventy have been added to her list. In the meanwhile machinery has been set up to continue the collecting and verifying process, and to provide more material for the future use of astrological scholars.

It usually comes as a very real shock to the devotee of the stellar art to discover the extraordinary and discouraging unreliability of the horoscopes of public figures on which he must depend for his broader generalities. There is untold work here for astrologers yet to be born. Often this fact is ignored, or given righteous denial, neither of which procedures is any help towards any real recognition of astrology. The question might well be asked, however, why any attempt should be made to proceed with material so suspect in the matter of its validity, and the answer is that there are effective approximations that may be used safely as long as they are not mistaken for precise indications. Generalizations from single instances are wholly worthless, of course, and always there are too few cases available for any broad certainty when it comes to any specific principle or procedure. Because horoscopy is a social science, like other branches of psychology or medicine where individual differences preclude any open and shut conclusions, there is an effective suggestiveness which can be disciplined and brought to a point of very practical reliability, and in the meanwhile the sights may be set on the more exact ideals of a future accomplishment.

There are three factors behind the general unreliability of astrological data. First is the question of the birth information itself. In the cases which follow there are two where the difference of opinion in biographical authorities is as great as eleven years, and two where it is ten. The policy here has been to follow the astrologer, since often he has access to inside information or has been able to make his rectification with the aid of the native or relatives, but this is no guarantee of anything since four of

America's leading practitioners of the art, responsible for a very large number of the horoscopes becoming public property, not only have long had a reputation for mathematical carelessness but the charts attributed to them have exhibited a disproportionately large number of errors. To narrow material of this sort down to fewer cases would solve nothing because the chances of inaccuracies are just as great in instances where the circumstances of original calculation are less a matter of record. Astrology has been an intuitive science for the major part, and in the transition to a better day, when a fuller record and a more thorough verification will be demanded as a matter of course, there is little to do but provide the greatest possible spread of examples, thus permitting the general averages to establish the principles which in time will contribute to a surer verification. Indeed, it was only with the greatest difficulty that it was possible to present a full thousand charts coming at all close to the criteria laid down. The present text in consequence is shaped to aid the intuition and general critical faculties in any stellar analysis, recognizing frankly that this is a generation in which there is no real alternative to methods of approximation.

Second of the factors in astrological unreliability is the deficiency of the tables the astrologer has available for his use. There are four published sets of these in current wide use, and the longest established of these, Raphael's, goes back to 1800 and in general is the basis for the planetary positions used in this text. Pluto is only given approximately for the years prior to its discovery, and the positions of Neptune are approximate prior to 1848. The calculations in the various publications do not always agree with each other. Thus the positions for one horoscope were computed from the various sources for comparison, and the differences changed the symbolical significance at four points. Since neither the original data for a chart, nor the astronomical factors from which it is erected, are of a known dependability in any given case, an astrologer must depend on internal consistencies in the given birth wheel, and on the heightening significance which it lends to known facts in the particular life, if he is not to lean rather foolishly on the intuitive factor or on a supposed but non-existent mathematical exactness. Dependable advisement must always be based on the determination of potentials through a careful charting of events in the past as an indication of what any future potentialities may be. It is in this area of horoscopy that the symbolical degrees have value, since their reference is directly to experience and its immediate meaning. In this, for the skilled practitioner, they provide a useful corrective for his judgment at nearly all points.

Third of the factors of unreliability is the common carelessness in computation and recording data. Eliminating the type of correction made necessary by the rigorous requirements of the symbolical degrees of the Charubel or Sabian sort, so that rounded positions would have to be recalculated (i.e, 20° possibly meaning 19° 45′, which symbolically is Aries 20, or 20° 15′, which symbolically is Aries 21), and also the common omission of the retrograde sign, better than twenty out of each hundred horoscopes in the collection had one or more errors that made appreciable difference. In the matter of the cusps of the

chart, the serious errors ran higher, and none of the cusps
as listed are to be considered reliable for the degree symbolism. Each case will have to be treated individually.
Many charts are rectified carefully, but there is no way of
being sure this is so except through special research and
rerectification. Because of this fact, the cusps were only
checked most incidentally in preparing the tabulations.
There has been consistent confusion relative to Old Style
dates, but as far as possible these cases have been checked
to make sure the information is given in New Style terms
(with the horoscope of Lenin remaining questionable).
The data listed is as it has been obtained from the astrologer, with birth place or other information left out if not
given in the astrological source. It is always possible to
reconstruct most of a horoscope's data from the wheel
itself, and this has been done in the checking, but what
has been thus obtained is not put down since it then would
imply a greater degree of original information than actually is possessed.

The preparation of the biographical material and its
listing has been a labor of love on the part of Mrs. Grace
Lobanov, with the assistance of Mrs. Dorothy Keeffe, and
both of these students have rendered other and most valuable assistance to the author in the preparation of the
manuscript. There were innumerable errors in the names
and titles, and all have been compared with the best
authorities available. Space limitation has made it impossible to give much more than a single word of identification to an individual, and there probably is great room for
quarreling with the term selected. The criterion has been
the greatest possible service to the astrologer or student

making use of the book, not to pass any judgment on any person or on his place in the scheme of things.

The mathematical verification has involved the examination of every chart once and questionable ones at least twice. Checking was carried only to the point where a planetary position rounded to the even degree could be seen actually no more than the exact sixty minutes of arc, and where recalculation was made the positions were generally rounded to half and full degrees, depending on which was the next larger value. This most laborious chore was the contribution of a group of the author's students, including the Mmes. Hannah Baker, Rosamond Bradshaw, Leonora Camner, Marian Collins, Virginia Diffenbacher, Annis Freeman, Elba Lebrecht, Pauline Messina, Minnie Keys, Gertrude Kramer, Edna Smith, Lena Sutcliffe and unquestionably many others whose efforts were not reported. The tabulations were prepared for the printer by Richard Stanewick.

It is to be noted, in consulting this second or 1966 edition of the *Sabian Symbols,* that the year is disputed for chart 872, the month for 892 and the hour for 343, 425, 527 and 980. In general charts 320, 579, 654 and 696 are to be preferred as here listed over the versions employed in *How to Learn Astrology* and the *Guide to Horoscope Interpretation,* but charts 1, 348, 806, 884 and 908 are probably preferable as found in the two earlier books. Nearly two hundred corrections have been made in the astrological data, but minor differences that do not affect the symbolism of planetary position are left unchanged for the moon in charts 60, 73, 118, 156, 267, 525, 538, 584, 589, 599, 640, 662, 735, 805, 842 and 905; the sun in 163, 584, 640, 662, 710, 719, 747 and 833; Mercury in 59, 122, 140, 197, 461, 571, 589, 747, 905, 921, 968 and 980; Venus in 175, 185, 282, 394, 483, 640, 661, 662, 735, 799, 886, 905, 921 and 980; Mars in 21, 42, 122, 205, 225, 369, 640, 662, 735, 768, 921 and 980; Jupiter in 21, 104, 128, 197, 348, 475 and 806; Saturn in 21, 103, 396, 510 and 886; and Uranus in 21, 22, 68, 95, 104, 175, 282, 313, 576 and 933.

1   Abdul Baha, mystic, Teheran, 1844, May 23-4, midnight
2   Adbul-Hamid II, Sultan, Constantinople, 1842, Sept. 22
3   Abrams, George, pugilist, 1918, Nov. 11, 11:00 a.m.
4   Acton, John E. E. Dalberg, 1st Baron, historian, Naples, 1834, Jan. 10
5   Adams, Charles Francis, author, Boston, 1835, May 27, 9-11 p.m.
6   Adams, Evangeline, astrologer, Jersey City, 1868, Feb. 8, 8:30 a.m.
7   Adams, J. Donald, author, New York City, 1891, Sept. 24, 10:44 a.m.
8   Adams, Mary, numerologist, Brooklyn, N.Y., 1873, Nov. 28, 6:15 p.m.
9   Addams, Jane, social worker, Cedarville, Ill., 1860, Sept. 6, 3:39 a.m.
10 Ador, Gustave, statesman, Geneva, 1845, Dec. 23, 1:00 a.m.
11 Adrian, Gilbert, designer, Naugatuck, Conn., 1903, Mar. 3, 11:05 a.m.
12 Agoult, Comtesse d', author, Frankfurt-am-Main, 1805, Dec. 30, 11:55 p.m.
13 Albert I, King of the Belgians, Brussels, 1875, Apr. 8, 5:30 p.m.
14 Albert, s. of Leopold III, Brussels, 1934, June 6, 10:45 p.m.
15 Albert, Prince Consort of England, Coburg, 1819, Aug. 26, 6:00 a.m.
16 Albert Victor, Prince, s. of Edward VII, Windsor, 1864, Jan. 8, 8:58 p.m.
17 Alcott, Louisa May, author, Germantown, Pa., 1832, Nov. 29, 12:20 a.m.
18 Alden, William Livingstone, author, Williamstown, Mass., 1837, Oct. 9
19 Aldrich, Elizabeth, astrologer, Des Moines, 1875, May 17, 11:55 a.m.
20 Alexander II, Emperor of Russia, Moscow, 1818, Apr. 29, 10:00 a.m.
21 Alexander III, Emperor of Russia, St. Petersburg, 1845, Mar. 10
22 Alexandra, Queen Consort of Edward VII, Copenhagen, 1844, Dec. 1
23 Alexandra Feodorovna, Empress of Russia, Darmstadt, Hesse, 1872, June 6
24 Alexis Nikolaevich, Czarevitch, s. of Nicolas II, 1904, Aug. 12, noon
25 Alfonso XII, King of Spain, Madrid, 1857, Nov. 28
26 Alfonso XIII, King of Spain, Madrid, 1886, May 17, 12:30 p.m.
27 Alfonso, Prince of Covadonga, Madrid, 1907, May 10, 12:35 p.m.
28 Alfred, Prince, s. of Queen Victoria, Windsor, 1844, Aug. 6, 7:50 a.m.
29 Alfred, Prince of Saxe-Coburg-Gotha, London, 1874, Oct. 15, 2:45 a.m.
30 Alice, Princess, d. of Queen Victoria, London, 1843, Apr. 25, 4:00 a.m.
31 Allen, Sir William, M.P., Dundee, 1837, Nov. 29, 7:00 a.m.
32 Allison, May, actress, Riding Farm, Ga., 1897, June 14, 11:29 p.m.
33 Alter, Louis, composer, Haverhill, Mass., 1902, June 18, 7:00 a.m.
34 Amélia, Queen of Portugal, Twickenham, Eng., 1865, Sept. 28, 7:05 a.m.
35 Amulree, 1st Baron, statesman, Scone, Scot., 1859, Aug. 19, 11:25 p.m.
36 Ananda Mahidol, King of Thailand, Heidelberg, 1925, Sept. 20, 1:45 a.m.
37 Anastasia, Grand Duchess, d. of Nicholas II, Peterhof, 1901, June 17
38 Anderson, Andrew Macbeth, jurist, Coupar Angus, Scot., 1862, Nov. 6, 7:00 p.m.
39 Anderson, Sir John, cabinet official, Edinburgh, 1882, July 8, 3:00 a.m.
40 Andrews, Roy Chapman, explorer, Beloit, Wis., 1884, Jan. 26, 2:00 a.m.
41 Anglin, Margaret Mary, actress, Ottawa, 1876, Apr. 3
42 Arbuckle, Roscoe, comedian, Smith Center, Kans., 1887, Mar. 24
43 Argyll, Princess Louise, Duchess of, London, 1848, Mar. 18, 8:00 a.m.
44 Arliss, George, actor, London, 1868, Apr. 10, 12:06 a.m.
45 Armour, Thomas Dickson, golfer, Edinburgh, 1896, Sept. 24, 8:30 a.m.
46 Asquith, 1st Earl of Oxford and, statesman, Morley, York, 1852, Sept. 12
47 Assagioli, Roberto, psychologist, Venice, 1888, Feb. 27, noon
48 Astor, Mary, actress, 1906, May 3, 8:10 p.m. CST
49 Astrid, Queen of the Belgians, Stockholm, 1905, Nov. 17
50 Atholl, Duchess of, politician, Edinburgh, 1874, Nov. 6, 8:25 a.m.

51 Aumale, Duc d', s. of Louis Philippe, Paris, 1822, Jan. 16
52 Babson, Roger, statistician, Gloucester, Mass., 1875, July 6, 12:05 p.m.
53 Bachaus, Wilhelm, pianist, Leipzig, 1884, Mar. 26
54 Baden-Powell of Gilwell, 1st Baron, soldier, London, 1857, Feb. 22
55 Baer, Max, pugilist, 1909, Feb. 16, 11:00 p.m. CST
56 Bailey, Alice, Theosophist, 1880, June 16, 7:32 a.m.
57 Baird, John, inventor, Helensburgh, Scot., 1888, Aug. 13, 8:00 a.m.
58 Baldwin, Faith, author, New Rochelle, N.Y., 1893, Oct. 1, 8:00 a.m.
59 Baldwin, Stanley, statesman, Worchestershire, 1867, Aug. 3, 7:43 p.m.
60 Balfour, Arthur James, statesman, Haddingtonshire, 1848, July 25, 9:30 a.m.
61 Banerji, Sir Goorooder, jurist, Narikeldanga, Calcutta, 1844, Jan. 25
62 Bankhead, Tallulah, actress, Huntsville, Ala., 1902, Jan. 31
63 Barnato, Barney, speculator, London, 1852, June 12, 7:35 a.m.
64 Barrett, Wilson, actor, Essex, 1845, Feb. 18
65 Barrie, Sir James, dramatist, Kirriemuir, Scot., 1860, May 9, 6:30 a.m.
66 Barrie, Wendy, actress, London, 1912, Apr. 18, 3:15 p.m.
67 Barry, Elaine, actress, New York City, 1915, July 16, 1:15 a.m.
68 Barrymore, John, actor, Philadelphia, 1882, Feb. 14
69 Bart, Belle, astrologer, New York City, 1892, Aug. 18, 7:45 a.m.
70 Barthelmess, Richard, actor, 1895, May 9, 7:07 a.m.
71 Barton, Clara, Red Cross founder, Oxford, Mass., 1821, Dec. 25
72 Baruch, Bernard, financier, Camden, S.C., 1870, Aug. 19, 1:50 p.m.
73 Baudelaire, Pierre Charles, poet, Paris, 1821, April 9
74 Baxter, George, artist, Lewes, Eng., 1804, July 31, 2:30 p.m.
75 Baxter, Warner, actor, 1893, Mar. 29
76 Beatrice, Princess, d. of Queen Victoria, London, 1857, Apr. 14, 1:45 p.m.
77 Beatrix, Princess, d. of Queen Juliana, Amsterdam, 1938, Jan. 31, 9:47 a.m.
78 Becker, William Dee, politician, E. St. Louis, 1876, Sept. 13, 9:38 a.m.
79 Beebe, Lucius, journalist, Wakefield, Mass., 1902, Dec. 3, 1:04 a.m.
80 Belasco, Richard, actor, San Francisco, 1853, July 25, 11:40 p.m.
81 Bell, Alexander Graham, inventor, Edinburgh, 1847, Mar. 3, 7:00 a.m.
82 Benedict XV, Pope, Genoa, 1854, Nov. 21, 9:45 a.m.
83 Beneš, Eduard, statesman, Kožlany, Bohemia, 1884, May 28, 5:08 a.m.
84 Benjamine, Elbert, astrologer, Des Moines, 1882, Dec. 12, 5:55 a.m.
85 Bennett, Arnold, author, Hanley, Eng., 1867, May 27, 9:36 a.m.
86 Bennett, Constance, actress, New York City, 1905, Oct. 22
87 Bennett, Joan, actress, Palisades, N. J., 1910, Feb. 27, 11:45 a.m.
88 Bennett, Sidney K., astrologer, 1892, Feb. 10, 9:00 a.m.
89 Benny, Jack, comedian, Waukegan, Ill., 1894, Feb. 14, 4:04 a.m.
90 Beresford, Lord Charles, admiral, Waterford, Ire., 1846, Feb. 10, 5:00 a.m.
91 Bergen, Edgar, ventriloquist, Chicago, 1903, Feb. 16, 5:30 a.m.
92 Berlioz, Louis Hector, composer, near Grenoble, 1803, Dec. 11, 5:00 p.m.
93 Bernhardt, Sarah, actress, Paris, 1844, Sept. 25, 8:00 p.m.
94 Berry, Charles Albert, churchman, Lancashire, 1852, Dec. 14
95 Besant, Annie, Theosophist, London, 1847, Oct. 1, 5:20 p.m.
96 Bidder, George Parker, engineer, Hampstead, 1806, June 13
97 Binnie, A. W., aviator, Edinburgh, 1889, Oct. 1, 7:15 a.m.
98 Birkenhead, Sheila, author, Weybridge, Eng., 1913, May 3, 9:50 a.m.
99 Bismarck, Prince Otto von, statesman, Kneipholf, 1815, Apr. 1, 1:00 p.m.
100 Björnson, Björnstjerne, author, Kvikne, Norway, 1832, Dec. 8, 12:05 a.m.

101 Black, Hugo L., jurist, Harlan, Ala., 1886, Feb. 27, 11:57 p.m.
102 Blackwood, Algernon, author, Kent, Eng., 1869, Mar. 14, 12:02 a.m.
103 Blavatsky, Helena, Theosophist, Ekaterinoslav, 1831, Aug. 12, 2:17 a.m.
104 Blondell, Joan, actress, New York City, 1909, Aug. 30, 7:55 p.m.
105 Bollenbacher, Jennie, Theosophist, Peoria, Ill., 1864, Sept. 7, 6:40 p.m.
106 Bonaparte, Prince Eugene, s. of Napoleon III, Paris, 1856, Mar. 16, 3:30 a.m.
107 Bond, Carrie Jacobs, composer, Janesville, Wis., 1862, Aug. 11, 1:57 a.m.
108 Boninsegna, Celestina, singer, Emilia, Italy, 1877, Feb. 26, 6:33 a.m.
109 Booth, Edwin, actor, Hartford, Co., Md., 1833, Nov. 13
110 Booth, William Bramwell, evangelist, Halifax, 1856, Mar. 8, 8.30 p.m.
111 Bordeaux, Duc de, last elder Bourbon, Paris, 1820, Sept. 29, 2.35 a.m.
112 Boris III, King of Bulgaria, Sofia, 1894, Jan. 30
113 Borris, Siegfried, musician, Münster, 1912, Mar. 10, 2:00 a.m.
114 Borwich, Leonard, pianist, Walthamstow, Eng., 1868, Feb. 26, 7:00 a.m.
115 Bottomley, Horatio, journalist, Birmingham, 1860, Mar. 23, 5:08 p.m.
116 Boucicault, Dion, dramatist, Dublin, 1822, Dec. 26
117 Boulanger, Georges Ernest, soldier, Rennes, 1837, Apr. 29, 8:15 a.m.
118 Bow, Clara, actress, Brooklyn, N.Y., 1905, July 29
119 Bowes, Edward, showman, San Francisco, 1874, June 14, 3:00 p.m.
120 Bozanno, Ernest, Spiritualist, Genoa, 1862, Jan. 9, 4:08 a.m.
121 Brabant, Duke of, s. of Leopold I, Brussles, 1833, July 24, 4:30 a.m.
122 Brady, Diamond Jim, gourmet, New York City, 1856, Aug. 12, 9.57 p.m.
123 Bragdon, Claude, architect, Oberlin, O., 1866, Aug. 1, 4:39 a.m.
124 Brahms, Johannes, composer, Hamburg, 1833, May 7, 3:41 p.m.
125 Braithwaite, Lillian, actress, Ramsgate, Eng., 1873, Mar. 9, 8:39 a.m.
126 Braun, Eva, mistress of Adolf Hitler, Munich, 1912, Feb. 6, 5.31 a.m.
127 Brand, Aristide, statesman, Nantes, Fr., 1862, Mar. 28, 10:35 a.m.
128 Brice, Fanny, actress, New York City, 1892, Oct. 30
129 Bricker, John W., politician, Madison Co., O., 1893, Sept. 6
130 Bridges, Henry Styles, politician, W. Pembroke, Me., 1898, Sept. 9, 10:39 a.m.
131 Bridges, Robert Seymour, poet, Walner, Kent, 1844, Oct. 23, 10:49 a.m.
132 Bright, John, M.P., Rochdale, Eng., 1811, Nov. 16, 8:00 p.m.
133 Broglie, Prince Louis Victor dt, physicist, Dieppe, 1892, Aug. 15, 1:00 a.m.
134 Brontë, Charlotte, author, Thornton, Yorks, 1816, Apr. 21, 2:41 p.m.
135 Brontë, Emily, author, Thornton, Yorks, 1818, July 30, 2:49 p.m.
136 Brook, Clive, actor, London, 1891, June 1
137 Brooke, Rupert, poet, Rugby, Eng., 1887, Aug. 3
138 Broughton, Luke, astrologer, Leeds, Eng., 1828, Apr. 20, 10:00 a.m.
139 Browder, Earl Russell, politician, Wichita, Kans., 1891, May 20
140 Browning, Elizabeth Barrett, poet, Durham, Eng., 1806, Mar. 6, 7:00 p.m.
141 Browning, Robert, poet, London, 1812, May 7
142 Browning, Robert Wiedemann, artist, Florence, 1849, Mar. 9, 2:15 a.m.
143 Bruce, Billy, singer, 1903, Dec. 2, 4:00 p.m.
144 Bruce, Charles W., aviator, Sutton, Surrey, 1894, Apr. 23, 9:00 a.m.
145 Bruckner, Anton, composer, Ansfelden, Aus., 1824, Sept. 4, 4:00 a.m.
146 Brüning, Heinrich, statesman, Münster, Ger., 1885, Nov. 26, 5:00 p.m.
147 Bruns, Paul H., jurist, Terre Haute, Ind., 1900, Dec. 24, 12:05 a.m.
148 Bryan, William Jennings, politician, Salem, Ill., 1860, Mar. 19, 9:04 a.m.
149 Budge, Donald, tennis player, Oakland, Cal., 1915, June 13, 1:45 a.m.
150 Burbank, Luther, naturalist, Lancaster, Mass., 1849, Mar. 7, 11:57 p.m.

151 Burgess, John L., astrologer, Ozark, Mo., 1899, May 1, 12:09 p.m.
152 Burnand, Sir Francis Cowley, editor, London, 1836, Nov. 29
153 Burns, John, labor leader, London, 1858, Nov. 13
154 Burroughs, John, naturalist, Roxbury, N.Y., 1837, Apr. 3
155 Burton, Lady Isabel, wife of Sir Richard, London, 1831, Feb. 18, 8:50 a.m.
156 Burton, Sir Richard, Orientalist, Hertfordshire, 1821, Mar. 19, 9:30 p.m.
157 Butler, Nicholas Murray, educator, Elizabeth, N.J., 1862, Apr. 2, 10:30 a.m.
158 Byrd, Richard Evelyn, explorer, Winchester, Va., 1888, Oct. 25, noon
159 Byron, Augusta Ada, d. of Lord Byron, London, 1815, Dec. 10, 1:00 p.m.
160 Cabell, James Branch, author, Richmond, Va., 1879, Apr. 14, 6:30 a.m.
161 Campbell-Bannerman, Sir Henry, statesman, Glasgow, Scot., 1836, Sept. 7
162 Canova, Judy, comedienne, Jacksonville, Fla., 1916, Nov. 20, 7:00 a.m.
163 Cantor, Eddie, comedian, New York City, 1892, Jan. 31
164 Cárdenas, Lázaro, statesman, Michoacán, Mex., 1895, May 29
165 Carey, George, occultist, 1845, Sept. 7, 4:45 p.m.
166 Carlos I, King of Portugal, Lisbon, 1863, Sept. 28, 1:35 p.m.
167 Carlota, Empress of Mexico, near Brussels, 1840, June 7, 1:00 a.m.
168 Carmen Sylva, Queen of Rumania, Neuwied, Ger., 1843, Dec. 29, noon
169 Carnarvon, 3d Earl of, traveler, Highclere, Berkshire, 1800, June 8
170 Carnegie, Andrew, industrialist, Dunfermline, 1835, Nov. 25, 6:00 a.m.
171 Carnot, Sadi, statesman, Limoges, Fr., 1837, Aug. 11, 6:00 p.m.
172 Carol II, King of Rumania, Sinaia, Rumania, 1893, Oct. 15, 1:00 a.m.
173 Carr, Ralph, politician, Rosita, Colo., 1887, Dec. 11, noon
174 Carrel, Alexis, biologist, Ste. Foy-lès-Lyons, 1873, June 28, 11:30 p.m.
175 Carroll, Lewis, author, Daresbury, Eng., 1832, Jan. 27, 3:48 a.m.
176 Carter, C. E. O., astrologer, Parkstone, Dorset, 1887, Jan. 31, 10:58 p.m.
177 Carter the Great, magician, 1874, June 14, 4:00 a.m.
178 Caruso, Enrico, singer, Naples, 1873, Feb. 25, 12:14 p.m.
179 Carver, George W., botanist, Diamond Grove, Mo., 1864, May 24, 7:10 p.m.
180 Case, Paul Foster, occultist, Fairport, N.Y., 1884, Oct. 3, 6:00 a.m.
181 Castelot, Jollivet, alchemist, Douai, Fr., 1874, July 8, 4:30 a.m.
182 Caswell, Edward C., traveler, New York City, 1879, Sept. 12, 9:00 a.m.
183 Cavell, Edith, nurse, Swardston, Norfolk, Eng., 1865, Dec. 4, 2:30 a.m.
184 Cayce, Edgar, spiritualist, Hopkinsville, Ky., 1877, Mar. 18, 3:30 p.m.
185 Cézanne, Paul, artist, Aix-en-Provence, Fr., 1839, Jan. 19, 1:00 a.m.
186 Chamberlain, Joseph, statesman, London, 1836, July 8, 2:36 a.m.
187 Chamberlain, Neville, statesman, Birmingham, 1869, Mar. 18, 2:21 a.m.
188 Champion, Maude, astrologer, Emporia, Kans., 1897, Jan. 26, 6:30 a.m.
189 Chaney, Lon, actor, Colorado Springs, Colo., 1883, Apr. 1, 7:19 a.m.
190 Chaney, W. H., astrologer, near Augusta, Me., 1821, Jan. 13, 11:31 p.m.
191 Chaplin, Charles Spencer, actor, near London, 1889, Apr. 16
192 Charbonnet, Victor Marc, statesman, Geneva, 1861, Nov. 9, 3:00 a.m.
193 Charcot, Jean B., explorer, Neuilly-sur-Seine, 1867, July 15, 10:40 a.m.
194 Charles I, Emperor of Austria, Castle of Persenberg, 1887, Aug. 17
195 Charles, Prince, s. of Queen Elizabeth II, London, 1948, Nov. 14, 9:14 p.m.
196 Charubel, seer, Castle Caereinion, Montgomery, Wales, 1826, Nov. 9, 7:00 a.m.
197 Chase, Ilka, author, New York City, 1905, Apr. 8, 2:00 a.m.
198 Chatterton, Ruth, actress, New York City, 1893, Dec. 24, 7:30 p.m.
199 Chitnis, J. T., astrologer, Bombay, 1859, Aug. 14
200 Choisnard, Paul, astrologer, Tours, Fr., 1867, Feb. 13, 11:00 p.m.

201 Chopin, Frédéric, composer, near Warsaw, 1810, Feb. 22, 6:00 p.m.
202 Christian IX, King of Denmark and Norway, Gottorp, 1818, Apr. 8
203 Christian, Prince, grandson of Victoria, Windsor, 1867, Apr. 14, 5:00 p.m.
204 Christiansen, W. A., Seeing Eye dogs, 1885, Aug. 22, 7:22 a.m.
205 Chrysler, Walter P., industrialist, Wamego, Kans., 1875, Apr. 2, 12:02 p.m.
206 Churchill, Winston L. S., statesman, Woodstock, 1874, Nov. 30, 10:58 a.m.
207 Claire, Ina, actress, Washington, D.C., 1892, Oct. 15
208 Clancy, Paul G., astrologer, Toronto, 1897, June 29, 8:40 a.m.
209 Clemenceau, Georges, statesman, Chateau de l'Aubraie, Vendée, 1841, Sept. 28
210 Cleveland, Grover, statesman, Caldwell, N.J., 1837, Mar. 18, 11:32 a.m.
211 Clyde, James Avon, Lord, jurist, Dollar, Scot., 1863, Nov. 14, 12:20 p.m.
212 Cobb, Irwin S., humorist, Paducah, Ky., 1876, June 23, 5:15 a.m.
213 Cobbe, Frances Power, anti-vivisectionist, near Dublin, 1822, Dec. 4
214 Coleman, Ronald, actor, 1891, Feb. 9, 6:00 p.m.
215 Coleridge, 1st Baron, jurist, Ottery St. Mary, Eng., 1820, Dec. 3
216 Coli, François, aviator, Marseille, 1881, Feb. 5, 11:00 a.m.
217 Collins, Sir Godfrey P., politician, Glasgow, 1875, June 26, 4:55 a.m.
218 Connaught, Arthur, Duke of, soldier, London, 1850, May 1, 8:17 a.m.
219 Conwell, Lenora, astrologer, 1884, June 18, 10:02 a.m.
220 Coogan, Jackie, actor, 1914, Oct. 26, 2:45 a.m.
221 Coolidge, Calvin, statesman, Plymouth, Vt., 1872, July 4, 9:00 a.m.
222 Cooper, Jackie, actor, Los Angeles, Cal., 1922, Sept. 15, 12:05 p.m.
223 Corns, Edith Mary, nurse, 1913, Nov. 10, noon
224 Cotton, Joseph, actor, Petersburg, Va., 1905, May 15, 7:00 a.m.
225 Coué, Émile, psychotherapist, Troyes, Fr., 1857, Feb. 26, 4:00 a.m.
226 Councel, Paul, astrologer, Danville, Va., 1884, Dec. 28, 9:29 a.m.
227 Coward, Noel, dramatist, Middlesex, Eng., 1899, Dec. 16, 4:24 a.m.
228 Cox, Danny, pugilist, Washington, D.C., 1921, Apr. 15, 7:30 a.m.
229 Crawford, Laurel, mass murderer, 1898, Aug. 18-19, midnight
230 Crockett, Samuel Rutherford, author, Galloway, 1859, Sept. 24, 5:20 a.m.
231 Crookes, Sir William, scientist, London, 1832, June 17, 5:30 p.m.
232 Crosby, Bing, entertainer, Spokane, Wash., 1904, May 2, 4:00 p.m.
233 Crosby, Percy Lee, cartoonist, Brooklyn, N. Y., 1891, Dec. 8, 4:00 a.m.
234 Cross, Robert, astrologer, East Anglia, Eng., 1850, May 15, 2:35 a.m.
235 Cullen, William James, jurist, Edinburgh, 1859, Sept. 9, 3:30 p.m.
236 Cummings, Homer S., attorney-general, Chicago, 1870, Apr. 30, 12:10 a.m.
237 Curie, Marie, physical chemist, Warsaw, 1867, Nov. 7, 8:44 p.m.
238 Curtius, Julius, statesman, 1877, Feb. 11, 11:45 p.m.
239 Curzon of Kedleston, Marquess, statesman, Kedleston, 1859, Jan. 11, 5:20 p.m.
240 Defoe, Allan Ray, physician, 1883, May 29, 9:30 p.m.
241 Dahl, Harold Edward, aviator, Sidney, Ill., 1909, June 29, 3:30 p.m.
242 Daladier, Édouard, statesman, Carpentras, Fr., 1884, June 18, 10:45 a.m.
243 Dali, Salvador, artist, Cadaques, Garona, Spain, 1904, May 11, 8:45 a.m.
244 D'Annunzio, Gabriele, poet, Pescara, Italy, 1863, Mar. 12, 8:00 a.m.
245 Darrow, Clarence, attorney, Farmdale, O., 1857, Apr. 18
246 Dart, Justin W., executive, Evanston, Ill., 1907, Aug. 17, 7:06 a.m.
247 Däubler, Theodor, author, Trieste, 1876, Aug. 17, 6:45 a.m.
248 Daudet, Alphonse, author, Nîmes, Fr., 1840, May 13
249 Daudet, Léon, journalist, Paris, 1867, Nov. 16, 9:00 p.m.
250 Davidson, John, poet, Barrhead, Scot., 1857, Apr. 11, 2:30 p.m.

251 Davies, Marion, actress, Brooklyn, N.Y., 1897, Jan. 3
252 Davis, Bette, actress, Lowell, Mass., 1908, Apr. 5, 11:50 p.m.
253 Davis, Humphrey, actor, Meriden, Conn., 1912, Nov. 4, 4:00 a.m.
254 Davis, Jeff, hobo king, Cincinnati, O., 1883, Aug. 22, 10:24 p.m.
255 Davis, John W., attorney, Clarksburg, W. Va., 1873, Apr. 13, 11:40 p.m.
256 Dawes, Charles G., politician, Marietta, O., 1865, Aug. 27, 3:32 p.m.
257 De, Harinath, linguist, 1877, Aug. 12
258 Deakin, Alfred, statesman, Melbourne, Australia, 1856, Aug. 3
259 de Gaulle, Charles, soldier, Lille, Fr., 1890, Nov. 22, 11:54 a.m.
260 Delafield, E. M., author, Hove, Sussex, Eng., 1890, June 9, 8:00 a.m.
261 Delibes, Léo, composer, St. Germain du Val, 1836, Feb. 21, 2:00 p.m.
262 Del Rio, Dolores, actress, Durango, Mexico, 1904, Aug. 3, 7:20 a.m.
263 Delville, Jean, artist, 1867, Jan. 19
264 Dempsey, Jack, pugilist, 1895, June 24, 5:30 a.m.
265 Depew, Chauncy, attorney, Peekskill, N. Y., 1834, Apr. 23
266 Destinn, Emmy, singer, Prague, 1878, Feb. 26, 3:58 p.m.
267 de Valera, Eamon, statesman, New York City, 1882, Oct. 14, 5:11 p.m.
268 DeVoe, Walter, healer, 1874, May 11, 6:46 a.m.
269 Dewar, Thomas Robert, Baron, distiller, Perth, 1864, Jan. 6, 12:05 a.m.
270 Dewey, John, philosopher, Burlington, Vt., 1859, Oct. 20, 9:52 p.m.
271 Dewey, Thomas E., politician, Owosso, Mich., 1902, Mar. 24, 7:45 p.m.
272 DeWohl, Louis, astrologer, 1903, Jan. 24, 7:45 p.m.
273 Diamond, Legs, gangster, 1897, July 10, 2:00 a.m.
274 Dickens, Charles, author, near Portmouth, Eng., 1812, Feb. 7
275 Dickinson, Emily, poet, Amherst, Mass., 1830, Dec. 10
276 Dickson, Henry Morton, meteorologist, Edinburgh, 1866, June 24, 8:00 a.m.
277 Dickson, J. G., churchman, Edinburgh, 1863, May 23, 11:00 a.m.
278 Dietrich, Marlene, actress, Berlin, 1904, Dec. 27
279 Di Frasso, Countess, Watertown, N.Y., 1888, Feb. 13, 3:30 a.m.
280 Dionne, Yvonne, eldest quintuplet, Callander, Ont., 1934, May 28, 3:56 a.m.
281 Disney, Walt, cartoonist, Chicago, 1901, Dec. 5, 12:30 a.m.
282 Disraeli, Benjamin, statesman, London, 1804, Dec. 21, 5:30 a.m.
283 Diviner, astrologer, Berlin, 1897, Feb. 14, 9:00 a.m.
284 Dollfuss, Engelbert, statesman, Texing, Aus., 1892, Oct. 4, 12:30 a.m.
285 Doolittle, James, aviator, Alameda, Cal., 1896, Dec. 14, 4:25 p.m.
286 Dorten, Johann, statesman, near Bonn, Ger., 1880, Feb. 10, 3:00 p.m.
287 Douglas, D. W., airplane builder, 1892, April 6, 6:00 a.m.
288 Douglas, Stephen A., politician, Brandon, Vt., 1813, Apr. 23, 11:50 a.m.
289 Doumer, Paul, statesman, Aurillac, Fr., 1857, Mar. 22, 3:00 a.m.
290 Doumergue, Gaston, statesman, Aigues-Vives, Fr., 1863, Aug. 1, 11:00 p.m.
291 Doyle, Sir Arthur Conan, author, Edinburgh, 1859, May 22, 4:55 a.m.
292 Doyle, Jack, sports promoter, 1877, Dec. 26, 5:00 a.m.
293 Drayton, Edward Raoule, statesman, 1859, Apr. 2
294 Dreiser, Theodore, author, Terre Haute, Ind., 1871, Aug. 27, 8:27 a.m.
295 Dressler, Marie, actress, Cobourg, Ont., 1869, Nov. 9, 7:57 p.m.
296 Dreyfus, Alfred, soldier, Mulhouse, Alsace, 1859, Oct. 9
297 Drouet, Juliette, mistress of Victor Hugo, 1806, Apr. 10, 3:00 p.m.
298 Duke, Doris, heiress, 1912, Nov. 22
299 Dumas, Alexandre, author, Villers-Cotterets, 1802, July 24, 5:30 a.m.
300 du Maurier, George, author, Paris, 1834, Mar. 6, 5:47 a.m.

301 Duncan, Isadora, dancer, San Francisco, 1878, May 27, 2:25 a.m.
302 Durbin, Deanna, actress, Winnipeg, 1922, Dec. 4, 2:00 p.m.
303 Duse, Eleonora, actress, Vigevano, Italy, 1858, Oct. 3, 2:00 a.m.
304 Dyess, William Edward, aviator, Albany, Tex., 1916, Aug. 9
305 Earhart, Amelia, aviator, Atchison, Kans., 1897, July 24-25, midnight
306 Ebert, Friedrich, statesman, Heidelberg, 1871, Feb. 4, noon
307 Eckener, Hugo, aeronaut, Flensburg, Ger., 1868, Aug. 10, 10:30 a.m.
308 Eddy, ·Mary Baker, mystic, near Concord, N. H., 1821, July 16, 5:33 p.m.
309 Eddy, Nelson, singer, Providence, R.I., 1901, June 29
310 Edelfelt, Albert, artist, Helsingfors, 1854, July 21
311 Eden, Anthony, statesman, Windlestone, Eng., 1897, June 12, 8:14 a.m.
312 Edison, Thomas Alva, inventor, Milan, O., 1847, Feb. 11
313 Edward VII, King of England, London, 1841, Nov. 9, 10:48 a.m.
314 Ekstrom, Gustave, astrologer, Chicago, 1892, June 1, 7:28 a.m.
315 Eliot, George, author, Warwickshire, Eng., 1819, Nov. 22, 5:00 a.m.
316 Elizabeth, Empress of Austria, Munich, Ger., 1837, Dec. 24, 10:43 a.m.
317 Elizabeth, Queen Consort of George VI, Waldenbury, 1900, Aug. 4, 11:31 a.m.
318 Elizabeth II, Queen of England, London, 1926, Apr. 21, 1:40 a.m.
319 Ellis, Havelock, psychologist, Croydon, Surrey, 1859, Feb. 2, 8:15 a.m.
320 Emerson, Ralph Waldo, philosopher, Concord, Mass., 1803, May 25, 1:16 p.m.
321 English, Richard, author, 1910, May 18
322 Eugénie, Empress of the French, Granada, Sp., 1826, May 5, 1:1:55 a.m.
323 Ewing, Sir Alfred, educator, Dundee, 1855, Mar. 27, 12:30 p.m.
324 Eythe, William, actor, Mars, Pa., 1918, Apr. 7, 2:00 a.m.
325 Fagan, Cyril, astrologer, Dublin, 1896, May 22, 11:45 a.m.
326 Fairbanks, Douglas, actor, Denver, Colo., 1883, May 23, 9:00 a.m.
327 Fairbanks, Douglas Jr., actor, New York City, 1909, Dec. 9, 3:45 a.m.
328 Fallières, Clément Armand, statesman, Mézin, Fr., 1841, Nov. 6
329 Farida, former Queen of Egypt, 1921, Sept. 5, 5:00 p.m.
330 Farouk I, King of Egypt, Cairo, 1920, Feb. 11, 10:30 p.m.
331 Farrar, Geraldine, singer, Melrose, Mass., 1882, Feb. 28, 9:40 a.m.
332 Faure, François, Félix, statesman, Paris, 1841, Jan. 30
333 Faye, Alice, actress, New York City, 1912, May 4-5, midnight
334 Feder, Gottfried, economist, Würzburg, Ger., 1883, Jan. 27, 6:00 a.m.
335 Ferrière, Adolph, educator, Geneva, 1879, Aug. 30, 2:35 p.m.
336 Feuerbach, Ludwig, philosopher, Bavaria, 1804, July 28, 1:35 a.m.
337 Fields, Gracie, actress, Rochdale, Eng., 1898, Jan. 9, 7:00 a.m.
338 Findlay, Sir John Ritchie, publisher, Edinburgh, 1866, Jan. 13, 6:00 p.m.
339 Fishbein, Morris, author, St. Louis, Mo., 1889, July 22, 7:06 a.m.
340 Fitts, Buron, politician, Belcherville, Tex., 1895, Mar. 22, 11:00 a.m.
341 Fitzgerald, F. Scott, author, St. Paul, Minn., 1896, Sept. 24, 3:30 p.m.
342 Flandin, Pierre Étienne, statesman, Paris, 1889, Apr. 12, 4:00 a.m.
343 Flynn, Errol, actor, Autrim, Ireland, 1909, June 20, 9:25 p.m.
344 Foch, Ferdinand, soldier, Tarbes, Fr., 1851, Oct. 2, 10:00 p.m.
345 Fokker, Anthony, aircraft builder, Kediri, Java, 1890, Apr. 6, 7:00 a.m.
346 Fontaine, Joan, actress, Tokyo, Japan, 1907, Oct. 22
347 Ford, Henry, industrialist, Greenfield, Mich., 1863, July 30, 2:22 p.m.
348 Foster, Stephen Collins, song writer, Pittsburg, 1826, July 4, 12:30 p.m.
349 Foujita, artist, Tokyo, Japan, 1886, Nov. 27, 3:00 a.m.
350 Francis, Prince of Teck, London, 1870, Jan. 9, 11:00 p.m.

351 Francis Joseph I, Emperor of Austria, Vienna, 1830, Aug. 18, 8:23 a.m.
352 Franco, Francisco, soldier, El Ferrol, Spain, 1892, Dec. 4, 4:30 a.m.
353 Frederick, Empress of Germany, London, 1840, Nov. 21, 1:50 p.m.
354 Frederick, Prince, grandson William II, 1911, Dec. 19, 10:00 p.m.
355 Frederick III, Emperor of Germany, Potsdam, 1831, Oct. 18
356 Frederick VIII, King of Denmark, Copenhagen, 1843, June 3
357 Frederick William, Crown Prince, Potsdam, 1882, May 6, 9:45 p.m.
358 French, John Denton P., soldier, Ripple Vale, Kent, 1852, Sept. 28, 4:30 p.m.
359 Freud, Sigmund, psychologist, Frieberg, Ger., 1856, May 6, 9:00 a.m.
360 Frohman, Daniel, producer, Sandusky, O., 1851, Aug. 22, 2:00 a.m.
361 Gable, Clark, actor, Meadville, Pa., 1901, Feb. 1, 9:00 p.m.
362 Gadski, Johanna, singer, Anklam, Ger., 1871, June 15, 2:27 p.m.
363 Galigher, Maud Fletcher, occultist, St. Louis, Mo., 1871, May 9, 3:30 p.m.
364 Galsworthy, John, author, Parkfield, Kingston, 1867, Aug. 14, 2:30 p.m.
365 Galton, Sir Francis, scientist, Birmingham, 1822, Feb. 16, 9:00 p.m.
366 Gambetta, Léon, statesman, Cahors, Fr., 1838, Apr. 2, 8:00 p.m.
367 Gandhi, Mohandas, reformer, Porbandar, India, 1869, Oct. 2, 7:33 a.m.
368 Garbo, Greta, actress, Stockholm, 1905, Sept. 18, 9:00 p.m.
369 Garden, Mary, singer, Aberdeen, Scot., 1877, Feb. 20, 9:24 a.m.
370 Gardner, F. L., book collector, London, 1857, Mar. 31, 6:45 a.m.
371 Garfield, James A., statesman, Orange Township, O., 1831, Nov. 19
372 Garland, Judy, actress, Grand Rapids, Mich., 1922, June 10, 6:00 a.m.
373 Garner, John, politician, Red River Co., Tex., 1869, Nov. 22, 2:59 a.m.
374 Garner, Peggy Ann, actress, Canton, O., 1932, Feb. 3, 8:00 a.m.
375 Garnett, Richard, author, Litchfield, Eng., 1835, Feb. 27, 5:30 p.m.
376 Gavin, Sanford, aviator, Romsey, Hants, 1890, Apr. 7, 5:15 p.m.
377 Gaynor, Janet, actress, Philadelphia, 1906, Oct. 6, 4:00 a.m.
378 Gebuhr, Otto, actor, 1877, May 29, 2:00 p.m.
379 Geddes, Norman Bel, stage designer, Adrian, Mich., 1893, Apr. 27
380 George I, King of Greece, Copenhagen, 1845, Dec. 24, 7:30 p.m.
381 George II, King of Greece, Athens, 1890, July 19, 9:00 a.m.
382 George V, King of England, London, 1865, June 3, 1:18 a.m.
383 George VI, King of England, London, 1895, Dec. 14, 3:05 a.m.
384 Gershwin, George, composer, Brooklyn, N.Y., 1898, Sept. 26, 11:09 a.m.
385 Gibb, Mary-Margaret, Siamese twins, Holyoke, Mass., 1912, May 20, 6:30 a.m.
386 Gibbons, James, churchman, Baltimore, 1834, July 23
387 Gilbert, Clarence H., jurist, 1874, Dec. 13, noon
388 Gladstone, Herbert John, statesman, London, 1854, Jan. 7, 9:06 p.m.
389 Gladstone, William Ewart, statesman, Liverpool, 1809, Dec. 29, 9:00 a.m.
390 Gleadow, Rupert S., astrologer, Leicester, Eng., 1909, Jan. 22, noon
391 Gloucester, Henry, Duke of, s. of George V, Sandringham, 1900, Mar. 31
392 Gluck, Alma, singer, Bucharest, 1884, May 11
393 Godwin, Grace, tearoom proprietress, Philadelphia, 1888, June 16, 10:00 a.m.
394 Goebbels, Joseph Paul, politician, Rheydt, 1897, Oct. 29, 10:30 p.m.
395 Goethals, George Washington, engineer, Brooklyn, N.Y., 1858, June 29
396 Gogh, Vincent van, artist, Groot-Zundert, 1853, Mar. 30, 11:00 a.m.
397 Gömbös, Julius von, statesman, Tolna Co., Hung., 1886, Dec. 25-26 midnight
398 Gordon, Charles George, soldier, Woolwich, Eng., 1833, Jan. 28, 9:30 a.m.
399 Göring, Hermann, politician, Rosenheim, Bavaria, 1893, Jan. 12, 3:13 a.m.
400 Gould, Jay, financier, Roxbury, N.Y., 1836, May 27, 5:35 a.m.

401 Goulding, Edmund, cinema director, London, 1891, Mar. 20, 8:45 a.m.
402 Gounod, Charles François, composer, Paris, 1818, June 17, 4:00 a.m.
403 Grahame, Kenneth, author, Edinburgh, 1859, Mar. 8, 10:15 a.m.
404 Grant, Cary, actor, Bristol, Eng., 1904, Jan. 14, 1:07 a.m.
405 Grant, Ernest, astrologer, Detroit, 1893, June 4, 6:28 p.m.
406 Grant, Ulysses S., soldier, Point Pleasant, O., 1822, Apr. 27, 5:00 a.m.
407 Grant, William Thomas, merchant, Stevensville, Pa., 1876, June 27, 7:47 a.m.
408 Green, William, labor leader, Coshocton, O., 1873, Mar. 3, 2:06 p.m.
409 Grierson, Sir James, soldier, Glasgow, 1859, Jan. 27, 3:50 a.m.
410 Griffin, Colby, astrologer, Clear Lake, Ia., 1891, Mar. 7, 1:00 a.m.
411 Griffis, William Elliot, author, Philadelphia, 1843, Sept. 17, 7:30 a.m.
412 Grofé, Ferde, composer, New York City, 1892, March 27
413 Gustavus V, King of Sweden, Drottningholm, 1858, June 16, 10:00 a.m.
414 Gustavus Adolphus, Crown Prince, Stockholm, 1882, Nov. 11.
415 Guthrie, Sir James, artist, Greenock, Scot., 1859, June 10, 11:00 a.m.
416 Haakon VII, King of Norway, Copenhagen, 1872, Aug. 3, 4:00 p.m.
417 Hadley, Henry K., composer, Somerville, Mass., 1871, Dec. 20, 2:30 a.m.
418 Haggard, Sir Henry Rider, author, Woodsfarm, Norfolk, 1856, June 22
419 Haig, Douglas, 1st Earl, soldier, Edinburgh, 1861, June 19, 9:36 p.m.
420 Haile Selassie, Emperor of Ethopia, Addis Ababa, 1891, July 23, 11:15 a.m.
421 Haldane of Cloan, Viscount, statesman, Edinburgh, 1856, July 30, 3:30 p.m.
422 Hale, Alan, actor, Washington, D.C., 1892, Feb. 10, 3:00 p.m.
423 Halifax, 1st Earl of, statesman, Garrowby, Yorks., 1881, Apr. 16
424 Hall, J. J., astrologer, Washington, D.C., 1876, June 6, 7:00 p.m.
425 Hall, Manly Palmer, occultist, 1901, Mar. 18
426 Hamilton, Sir William, mathematician, Dublin, 1805, Aug. 3-4, midnight
427 Hammond, John Hays, inventor, San Francisco, 1888, Apr. 13, 4:15 a.m.
428 Hampden, Walter, actor, Brooklyn, N.Y., 1879, June 30, 12:30 a.m.
429 Hankins, Chela, physician, S. Margaret, Herts, 1874, Nov. 30, 9:30 a.m.
430 Harding, Warren G., statesman, Blooming Grove, O., 1865, Nov. 2, 2:00 p.m.
431 Hardy, Thomas, author, Dorset, Eng., 1840, June 2, 8:00 a.m.
432 Harewood, 6th Earl of, soldier, London, 1882, Sept. 9, 7:00 a.m.
433 Harlow, Jean, actress, Kansas City, Mo., 1911, Mar. 3, 7:30 p.m.
434 Harrison, Benjamin, statesman, North Bend, O., 1833, Aug. 20, 4:04 a.m.
435 Harte, Francis Brett, author, Albany, N.Y., 1839, Aug. 25
436 Hartmann, Franz, Theosophist, Bavaria, 1838, Nov. 22, 2:32 p.m.
437 Harwick, Samuel, engineer, 1883, June 2, 1:00 p.m.
438 Hauptmann, Bruno, kidnapper, Kamenz, Ger., 1899, Nov. 26, 1:10 p.m.
439 Hawks, Frank M., aviator, Marshalltown, Ia., 1897, Mar. 28
440 Hayes, Helen, actress, Washington, D.C., 1900, Oct. 10
441 Hayes, Rutherford B., statesman, Delaware, O., 1822, Oct. 4
442 Haynes, Gideon Pillow, occultist, Memphis, Tenn., 1877, May 31, 7:00 p.m.
443 Hazelrigg, John, astrologer, Hazelrigg, Ind., 1860, June 20, 1:07 p.m.
444 Hearst, W. Randolph, publisher, San Francisco, 1863, Apr. 29, 5:58 a.m.
445 Hedin, Sven Anders, explorer, Stockholm, 1865, Feb. 19, 4:02 a.m.
446 Heidelberg, Anna, nurse, 1890, Aug. 4
447 Heifetz, Jascha, violinist, Vilna, Russia, 1901, Feb. 2
448 Heindel, Augusta Foss, occultist, Mansfield, O., 1865, Jan. 27, 5:20 p.m.
449 Heindel, Max, occultist, Copenhagen, 1865, July 23, 4:45 a.m.
450 Helena, Princess, d. of Queen Victoria, London, 1846, May 25, 2:55 p.m.

451 Henie, Sonja, skater, Oslo, Norway, 1913, Apr. 8
452 Henlein, Konrad, politician, Asch, Ger., 1898, May 6, 11:00 a.m.
453 Herkless, Sir John, educator, Glasgow, 1855, Aug. 9, 8:30 p.m.
454 Herschell, astrologer, Frome, Eng., 1863, Oct. 22, 4:30 p.m.
455 Hersholt, Jean, actor, Copenhagen, 1886, July 12
456 Hewlett, Maurice, author, London, 1861, Jan. 22, 1:57 a.m.
457 Hickman, William E., murderer, Hartford, Ark., 1908, Feb. 1, 4:45 a.m.
458 Hindemith, Paul, composer, Hanau, Ger., 1895, Nov. 16
459 Hindenburg, Paul von, soldier, Posen, 1847, Oct. 2, 2:59 p.m.
460 Hines, Arthur, dancer, 1917, Apr. 12
461 Hirohito, Emperor of Japan, Tokyo, 1901, Apr. 29, 10:10 p.m.
462 Hitler, Adolf, statesman, Braunau, Austria, 1889, Apr. 20, 6:14 p.m.
463 Hodiak, John, actor, Pittsburgh, Pa., 1914, Apr. 16, 4:30 p.m.
464 Hoffman, Harold, politician, South Amboy, N.J., 1896, Feb. 7, 3:00 a.m.
465 Hogge, James Myles, M.P., Edinburgh, 1873, Apr. 19, 4:15 p.m.
466 Hohenberg, Duchess of, morganatic wife of Francis Ferdinand, 1868, Mar. 1
467 Holbrooke, Josef, composer, Croydon, Eng., 1878, July 6
468 Holm, Celeste, actress, New York City, 1917, Apr. 29, 6:00 a.m.
469 Holmes, Blanca, astrologer, 1892, Feb. 3, 5:00 a.m.
470 Holmes, Marion, reformer, 1867, Apr. 13
471 Holmes, Oliver Wendell, jurist, s. of author, Boston, 1841, Mar. 8
472 Holmes, Stuart, actor, Chicago, 1884, Mar. 10, 4:45 p.m.
473 Holst, Gustave von, composer, Cheltenham, 1874, Sept. 21, 12:30 a.m.
474 Hoover, Herbert, statesman, West Branch, Ia., 1874, Aug. 10-11, midnight
475 Hoover, J. Edgar, criminologist, Washington, D.C., 1895, Jan. 1, 7:00 a.m.
476 Hopkins, Miriam, actress, Bainbridge, Ga., 1902, Oct. 18, 7:38 a.m.
477 Hopper, Hedda, journalist, Altoona, Pa., 1890, June 2, 2:00 a.m.
478 Horton, Louis P., sea captain, E. Providence, R.I., 1902, Oct. 9, 1:09 a.m.
479 Hotson, Sir John Ernest, statesman, Edinburgh, 1877, Mar. 17, 1:30 p.m.
480 Houdini, Harry, magician, Appleton, Wis., 1874, Apr. 6, 2:24 a.m.
481 Howard, Frank, entertainer, 1917, Feb. 19
482 Howard, Roy W., publisher, Gano, O., 1882-83, midnight
483 Hubbard, Elbert, author, Bloomington, Ill., 1856, June 19, 1:03 p.m.
484 Hubbard, L. Ron, author, Tilden, Nebr., 1911, Mar. 13, 2:01 a.m.
485 Hugenberg, Alfred, publisher, Hanover, Ger., 1865, June 19, 11:45 p.m.
486 Hughes, Charles Evans, statesman, Glens Falls, N.Y., 1862, Apr. 11
487 Hugo, Victor, author, Besançon, Fr., 1802, Feb. 26, 10:30 p.m.
488 Hull, Cordell, statesman, Overton Co., Tenn., 1871, Oct. 2
489 Humbert I, King of Italy, Turin, 1844, Mar. 14, 10:30 a.m.
490 Humbert, Prince of Piedmont, Racconigi, Italy, 1904, Sept. 15
491 Hutton, Barbara, heiress, New York City, 1912, Nov. 14, 2:25 p.m.
492 Huxley, Thomas, biologist, Ealing, Middlesex, 1825, May 4, 8:00 a.m.
493 Hyer, H. Warren, singer, 1879, Mar. 24
494 Ingersoll, Margery, singer, Bridgeport, Conn., 1896, Nov. 25, 4:00 a.m.
495 Innes, Laurence, engineer, West Calder, Scot., 1871, Aug. 31, 4:00 p.m.
496 Ironside, William Edmund, soldier, Aberdeen, 1880, May 6, 8:00 a.m.
497 Irving, Sir Henry, actor, Glastonbury, Eng., 1838, Feb. 6
498 Isabella II, Queen of Spain, mother of Alfonso XII, Madrid, 1830, Oct. 10
499 Jackson, Stonewall, soldier, Clarksburg, W.Va., 1824, Jan. 20-21, midnight
500 James, Jesse, outlaw, Centerville, Mo., 1847, Sept. 4-5, midnight

501 James, Victoria, d. of Betty Grable, Los Angeles, 1944, Mar. 3, 3:35 a.m.
502 Jayne, Charles A., astrologer, Philadelphia, 1911, Oct. 9, 10:43 p.m.
503 Jelliffe, Ely Smith, neurologist, New York City, 1866, Oct. 27, 6:00 p.m.
504 Jeritza, Maria, singer, Brünn, Austria, 1887, Oct. 6, 7:00 a.m.
505 Jinarajadasa, C., Theosophist, Colombo, 1875, Dec. 16, 6:45 p.m.
506 John, Prince, s. of George V, Sandringham, 1905, July 12, 3:05 a.m.
507 Johndro, L.E., astrologer, 1882, Jan. 30
508 Johnson, Osa, explorer, Chanute, Kans., 1894, Mar. 14
509 Jones, Marc Edmund, occultist, St. Louis, Mo., 1888, Oct. 1, 8:37 a.m.
510 Judd, Winnie Ruth, murderess, Oxford, Ind., 1905, Jan. 30, 12:38 a.m.
511 Juliana, Queen of Holland, The Hague, 1909, Apr. 30
512 Jung, Carl, psychologist, Basel, 1875, July 26, 7:20 p.m.
513 Kane, John Riley, aviator, near Waco, Tex., 1907, Jan. 5, 5:22 p.m.
514 Keller, Helen, blind and deaf, Tuscumbia, Ala., 1880, June 27
515 Kelley, Edward J., politician, Chicago, 1876, May 1, 11:50 p.m.
516 Kennedy, A. C., churchman, 1892, Mar. 2, 8:00 p.m.
517 Kennedy, A. R. S., educator, Boyndie, Scot., 1859, Dec. 21, 5:30 p.m.
518 Kent, Edward, Duke of, s. of George, Duke of Kent, London, 1935, Oct. 9
519 Kent, George, Duke of, s. of George V, Sandringham, 1902, Dec. 20
520 Kent, Rockwell, artist, Tarrytown Heights, N.Y., 1882, June 21, 4:00 a.m.
521 Keyserling, Count Hermann, philosopher, Livonia, 1880, July 20, 9:41 p.m.
522 Khan, Murshid Inayat, musician, Baroda, India, 1882, July 5, 11:00 p.m.
523 Kingsford, Anna Bonus, mystic, Stratford, Essex, 1846, Sept. 16, 5:00 p.m.
524 Kingsley, Myra, astrologer, Westport, Conn., 1897, Oct. 1, 4:15 p.m.
525 Kipling, Rudyard, author, Bombay, India, 1865, Dec. 30, 4:53 p.m.
526 Kirby, Alice Bell, psychic, 1925, Mar. 1, 7:00 p.m.
527 Kitchener, Field Marshall Lord, Ballylongford, Ire., 1850, June 24, 12:37 a.m.
528 Knott, Cargill, meteorologist, Penicuick, Scot., 1856, June 30, 1:30 a.m.
529 Koo, Vi Kyuin Wellington, statesman, Shanghai, 1888, Jan. 29, 8:00 a.m.
530 Kraum, Ralph Emerson, astrologer, 1890, July 25, 3:00 a.m.
531 Kreuger, Ivar, industrialist, Kalmar, Sweden, 1880, Mar. 2, 5:30 a.m.
532 Krishnamurti, Jeddu, mystic, Madanapalle, Madras, 1895, May 12, 12:25 a.m.
533 Krock, Arthur, journalist, Glasgow, Ky., 1886, Nov. 16
534 Kruger, Oom Paul, statesman, Colesberg, Cape Colony, 1825, Oct. 10
535 Kung, H. H., statesman, Shansi Province, China, 1880, Sept. 11, 4:00 p.m.
536 La Follette, Philip, politician, Madison, Wis., 1897, May 8
537 Lagerlöf, Selma, author, Värmland, Sweden, 1858, Nov. 20, 9:00 p.m.
538 La Guardia, Fiorello, politician, New York City, 1882, Dec. 11
539 Lalo, Édouard, composer, Lille, Fr., 1823, Jan. 27, 3:00 p.m.
540 Lamarr, Hedy, actress, Vienna, 1914, Nov. 9, 7:30 p.m.
541 Lamont, André, occultist, 1900, Aug. 3, 7:33 p.m.
542 Lamothe, Julian, author, New Orleans, 1893, Oct. 6, 2:00 p.m.
543 Landis, Carole, actress, Fairchild, Wis., 1919, Jan. 1, 6:36 a.m.
544 Landon, Alfred, politician, West Middlesex, Pa., 1887, Sept. 9
545 Landru, Henri Desiré, murderer, 1869, April 12, 6:00 a.m.
546 Lang, Cosmo Gordon, churchman, Aberdeen, 1864, Oct. 31, 3:55 p.m.
547 Lang, J. P., politician, Sydney, Australia, 1876, Dec. 21
548 Larison, Ruth Hooper, advertising, Suffern, N.Y., 1900, Mar. 4, 5:30 p.m.
549 Lash, Franziska, astrologer, Bornhofen, Ger., 1885, Oct. 11, 2:18 a.m.
550 Lasky, Jesse L., cinema producer, San Francisco, 1880, Sept. 13

601 Lowenstein, Alfred, financier, Brussels, 1877, Mar. 11, 2:00 p.m.
602 Lubbe, Marinus van der, Nazi scapegoat, Leiden, 1909, Jan. 13, 5:30 a.m.
603 Luciano, Lucky, gangster, 1897, Nov. 11
604 Ludendorff, Erich, soldier, Posen, 1865, Apr. 9, 11:00 a.m.
605 Lugosi, Bella, actor, 1882, Oct. 20, 3:30 p.m.
606 Lumière, Auguste, inventor, Besançon, Fr., 1862, Oct. 19, 9:30 a.m.
607 Lunn, Sir Henry, politician, Horncastle, Eng., 1895, July 30
608 Lycett, Mrs. Randolph, tennis player, Norwood, Eng., 1903, Jan. 23, noon
609 Lynd, Robert S., sociologist, New Albany, Ind., 1892, Sept. 26, 5:10 p.m.
610 Lytton, Lady, wife of author, near Limerick, 1802, Nov. 2, 10:00 a.m.
611 Lytton, Edward Bulwer-, 1st Baron, author, London, 1803, May 25, 8:00 a.m
612 Mabbot, Thomas Oliver, educator, New York City, 1898, July 6, 10:00 p.m.
613 McAdoo, William Gibbs, lawyer, Marietta, Ga., 1863, Oct. 31, 12:30 p.m.
614 MacArthur, Douglas, soldier, Little Rock, Ark., 1880, Jan. 26, 10:13 a.m.
615 McBride, Mary Margaret, commentator, Paris, Mo., 1899, Nov. 16, 6:46 a.m
616 MacCarthy, Maud, violinist, Clonmel, Ireland, 1882, July 4
617 McClellan, George B., soldier, Philadelphia, 1826, Dec. 3, 12:15 a.m.
618 MacDonald, Ramsay, statesman, Lossiemouth, Scot., 1866, Oct. 12, 11:24 p.m
619 MacFarren, Walter, musician, London, 1826, Aug. 28, 8:05 p.m.
620 MacGillivray, James, sculptor, Kintore, Scot., 1856, May 30, 7:00 p.m.
621 McGroarty, John Stephen, poet, 1862, Aug. 20, 4:00 a.m.
622 MacIntyre, David Lowe, govt. official, Portnahaven, 1895, June 18, 3:00 a.m.
623 McIntyre, Oscar Odd, journalist, Plattsburg, Mo., 1884, Feb. 18
624 Mackensen, August von, soldier, Saxony, 1849, Dec. 6, 7:00 a.m.
625 Mackenzie, Lord Charles Kincaid, jurist, Edinburgh, 1857, Mar. 9, 2:00 p.m.
626 Mackenzie, Compton, author, W. Hartlepool, Eng., 1883, Jan. 17, 9:49 a.m.
627 McKinley, William, statesman, Niles, O., 1843, Jan. 29, 10:00 p.m.
628 McKinnell, Norman, actor, Maxwellton, Scot., 1870, Feb. 10, 3:30 a.m.
629 Mackintosh, Hugh R., churchman, Paisley, Scot., 1870, Oct. 31, 3:00 a.m.
630 MacLean, Sir Donald, M. P., Tyree, Scot., 1863, May 13
631 McPherson, Aimee Semple, evangelist, Ingersoll, Ont., 1889, Oct. 9
632 MacPherson, J. J., statesman, Newtonmore, Scot., 1880, May 14, 10:30 p.m
633 Madsden, Norma, singer, Sydney, Aust., 1902, Jan. 26, 1:00 a.m.
634 Maeterlinck, Count Maurice, dramatist, Ghent, 1862, Aug. 29, 12:20 p.m.
635 Mair, Alexander W., educator, Banffshire, Scot., 1875, June 9, 2:15 p.m.
636 Malloy, Joseph Fitzgerald, historian, Wexford, Ireland, 1852, Apr. 26
637 Malotte, Albert Hay, composer, Philadelphia, 1895, May 19, 4:00 p.m.
638 Mann, Thomas, author, Lübeck, Ger., 1875, June 6, noon
639 Mann, Tom, labor leader, Warwickshire, Eng., 1856, Apr. 15
640 Mansfield, Katherine, author, Wellington, N.Z., 1888, Oct. 14, 8:00 a.m.
641 Manuel II, King of Portugal, Lisbon, 1889, Nov. 15
642 Mapleton, Hugh, manufacturer, 1869, Dec. 3
643 Marconi, Marchese Guglielmo, inventor, Bologna, 1874, Apr. 25, 9:00 a.m.
644 Margaret Rose, Princess, d. of George VI, Angus, Scot., 1930, Aug. 21
645 Marie, Grand Duchess, d. of Nicholas II, 1899, June 26
646 Marie, Queen of Rumania, Kent, Eng., 1875, Oct. 29, 10:28 a.m.
647 Markey, Gene, journalist, Jackson, Mich., 1895, Dec. 11, 7:06 p.m.
648 Markham, Edwin, poet, Oregon City, Ore., 1852, Apr. 23, 6:00 a.m.
649 Marquis, Don, humorist, Walnut, Ill., 1878, July 29, 4:30 p.m.
650 Marsh, Mae, actress, Madrid, N.M., 1894, Nov. 9, 8:40 p.m.

651 Marsh, Marguerite, actress, Lawrence, Kans., 1888, Apr. 18, 11:24 a.m.
652 Marston, Philip Bourke, poet, London, 1850, Aug. 13
653 Martin, Wyndham, author, near London, 1874, July 6, 3:00 a.m.
654 Marx, Karl, political philosopher, Treves, Prus., 1818, May 5, 1:30 a.m.
655 Mary, Princess, d. of George V, Sandringham, 1897, Apr. 25, 3:30 p.m.
656 Mary, Queen Consort of George V, London, 1867, May 26, 11:59 p.m.
657 Masaryk, Thomas, statesman, Houdonin, Moravia, 1850, Mar. 7, 11:40 p.m.
658 Mason, Edith, singer, St. Louis, Mo., 1893, Mar. 22
659 Massenet, Jules Frédéric, composer, Montaud, Fr., 1842, May 12, 1:00 a.m.
660 Maud, Queen of Norway, London, 1869, Nov. 26, 12:20 a.m.
661 Maupassant, Guy de, author, Dieppe, Fr., 1850, Aug. 5, 8:00 a.m.
662 Maximilian, Emperor of Mexico, Vienna, 1832, July 6, 4:00 a.m.
663 Maybank, Thomas, artist, 1869, Feb. 28
664 Maybrick, Florence, murderess, Mobile, Ala., 1862, Sept. 3
665 Mayo, Charles, physician, Rochester, Minn., 1865, July 19, 2:00 a.m.
666 Mayo, William, physician, Le Sueur, Minn., 1861, June 29
667 Meher Baba, mystic, near Bombay, India, 1894, Feb. 25, 4:35 a.m.
668 Mei Lan-fang, actor, Kiangsu, China, 1894, Oct. 22, 6:00 a.m.
669 Melchior, Lauritz, singer, Copenhagen, 1890, Mar. 20, 12:51 p.m.
670 Mellenthin, Herman E., dog breeder, 1888, Aug. 23
671 Mencken, H. L., author, Baltimore, Md., 1880, Sept. 12
672 Menjou, Adolphe, actor, Pittsburgh, Pa., 1890, Feb. 18, 8:30 p.m.
673 Menuhin, Yehudi, violinist, New York City, 1917, Jan. 22, 11:30 p.m.
674 Mercier, Désiré J., churchman, Braine l'Alleud, Bel., 1851, Nov. 22, 1:00 p.m.
675 Merikanto, Oskar, composer, Helsingfors, Fin., 1868, Aug. 5
676 Mérode, Cleo de, dancer, San Francisco, 1875, Sept. 27, 5:10 p.m.
677 Meyer, Cord Jr., reformer, Washington, D.C., 1920, Nov. 10, 12:30 a.m.
678 Michael, King of Rumania, Sinaia, Rumania, 1921, Oct. 25
679 Miles, Eustace H., tennis player, Hampstead, Eng., 1868, Sept. 22
680 Mill, Hugh Robert, meteorologist, Caithness, Scot., 1861, May 28, 3:00 p.m.
681 Miller, Addie, astrologer, Tunico, Miss., 1881, Jan. 1, 2:00 a.m.
682 Miller, Kenneth Hayes, artist, Oneida, N.Y., 1876, Mar. 11, 9:00 a.m.
683 Millerand, Alexandre, statesman, Paris, 1859, Feb. 10, 9:20 a.m.
684 Millet, Jean Francois, artist, Gruchy, Fr., 1814, Oct. 4, 8:00 p.m.
685 Millikan, Robert Andrews, physicist, Morrison, Ill., 1868, Mar. 22
686 Moldenhauer, Paul, economist, Cologne, 1876, Dec. 2, 3:01 a.m.
687 Mollison, Amy, aviator, Hull, Eng., 1903, July 1, 1:30 a.m.
688 Mollison, James, aviator, Glasgow, Scot., 1905, Apr. 19, 2:45 p.m.
689 Molotov, Vyacheslav, statesman, Bialystok, 1890, Mar. 9
690 Monteath, J. G., statesman, Edinburgh, 1890, Sept. 28, 11:00 a.m.
691 Montessori, Marie, educator, Chiaravalle, It., 1870, Aug. 31, 1:20 p.m.
692 Monzie, Anatole de, politician, 1876, Nov. 22, 7:00 p.m.
693 Mooney, Tom, labor leader, Chicago, 1882, Dec. 8, 4:00 a.m.
694 Moore, Grace, singer, Slabtown, Tenn., 1901, Dec. 5
695 Moores, Mark, phrenologist, 1850, Apr. 3
696 Morgan, J. Pierpont, financier, Hartford, Conn., 1837, Apr. 17, 3:00 a.m.
697 Morgan, J. Pierpont Jr., financier, Irvington, N.Y., 1867, Sept. 7, 9:15 p.m.
698 Morgenstern, Christian, poet, Munich, Ger., 1871, May 6, 6:30 a.m.
699 Morny, Duc de, politician, Paris, 1811, Oct. 21, 2:00 a.m.
700 Morris, George S., philosopher, Norwich, Vt., 1840, Nov. 15, 1:46 p.m.

701 Morris, William, poet, Walthamstow, 1834, Mar. 24
702 Mosley, Sir Oswald, M. P., London, 1896, Nov. 16, 11:15 p.m.
703 Mossman, Robert Cockburn, meteorologist, Edinburgh, 1870 Nov. 7, 7:00 a.m.
704 Mowbray, Norman Wiggin, mountain climber, 1897, Aug. 15, 10:30 a.m.
705 Muni, Paul, actor, Lemberg, Aus., 1897, Sept. 22, 5:00 a.m.
706 Munro, Roy de L., aviator, W. Port, N.Z., 1890, Sept. 29, 1:30 a.m.
707 Murat, Princess Caroline, Bordentown, N.J., 1833-4, Dec. 31, midnight.
708 Murray, Kenneth George, aviator, Edinburgh, 1908, Sept. 14, 1:15 p.m.
709 Mussett, Alfred de, poet, Paris, 1810, Dec. 11
710 Mussolini, Benito, Fascist leader, Dovia, It., 1883, July 29, 2:00 p.m.
711 Mustafa Kemal, soldier, Salonika, 1881, Mar. 12
712 Mutsuhito, Emperor of Japan, Kyoto, 1852, Nov. 3, 12:48 p.m.
713 Napoleon II, l'Aiglon, s. of Napoleon I, Paris, 1811, Mar. 20, 9:20 a.m.
714 Napoleon III, nephew of Napoleon I, Paris, 1808, Apr. 20, 1:00 a.m.
715 Napoleon, Prince Victor, grandnephew of Napoleon I, Paris, 1862, July 18
716 Nathan, George Jean, critic, Fort Wayne, Ind., 1882, Feb. 14
717 Neblett, William H., attorney, Lunenburg Co., Va., 1889, Aug. 21, 2:00 p.m.
718 Nemours, Duc de, s. of Louis Philippe, Paris, 1814, Oct. 25
719 Nesbitt, Evelyn, actress, 1884, Dec. 25
720 Nevin, Ethelbert, composer, Edgeworth, Pa., 1862, Nov. 25, 8:00 p.m.
721 Nicholas II, Emperor of Russia, St. Petersburg, 1868, May 18, 12:02 p.m.
722 Nietzsche, Friedrich, philosopher, near Lützen, 1844, Oct. 15, 10:07 a.m.
723 Nijinsky, Vaslav, dancer, Kiev, Russia, 1890, Feb. 28, 2:45 p.m.
724 Noguchi, Hideyo, bacteriologist, North Japan, 1876, Nov. 24
725 Norman, Montague Collet, banker, Hertfordshire, 1871, Sept. 6, 1:56 a.m.
726 Northcliffe, Viscount, publisher, County Dublin, Ireland, 1865, July 15
727 Nourrit, Jacqueline, musical prodigy, Asnières, Fr., 1921, June 25
728 Nungesser, Charles, aviator, Paris, 1892, Mar. 15, 2:00 p.m.
729 Nusselein, Henry, spiritualist, Nuremberg, Ger., 1879, Apr. 20, noon
730 Nuthall, Betty, tennis player, Surbiton, Sur., 1911, May 11, 10:30 a.m.
731 Oberon, Merle, actress, Bombay, 1911, Feb. 19, 6:00 a.m.
732 O'Brien, Pat, actor, 1899, Nov. 11, 1:30 a.m.
733 Odets, Clifford, dramatist, Philadelphia, 1906, July 18
734 Ogilvy, Sir Francis, geologist, Aberdeenshire, 1858, Aug. 8, 2:15 p.m.
735 Olcott, Henry Steel, Theosophist, Orange, N.J., 1832, Aug. 2
736 Old, Sydney George, astrologer, Bristol, Eng., 1901, Oct. 2, 3:47 a.m.
737 Olga, Grand Duchess, d. of Nicholas II, 1895, Nov. 15
738 Oliphant, John, H., aviator, Hemphill, Tex., 1921, Dec. 8, 4:30 a.m.
739 Olsen, Cuthbert, politician, Fillmore, Utah, 1876, Nov. 7, 3:40 a.m.
740 O'Neill, Eugene, dramatist, New York City, 1888, Oct. 16
741 Orion, astrologer, Melton, Eng., 1858, Oct. 9, 12:50 p.m.
742 Orléans, Duc d', Louis Philippe Robert, London, 1869, Feb. 6, 1:50 p.m.
743 Oscar II, King of Sweden and Norway, Stockholm, 1829, Jan. 21
744 Otto, Archduke, s. of Charles I, Schwarzan, 1912, Nov. 20, 2:36 a.m.
745 Ousta, John, silkworm breeder, Turkey, 1886, May 15
746 Owen, G. Vale, spiritualist, Birmingham, Eng., 1869, June 26, 6:00 p.m.
747 Pankhurst, Emmeline, suffragist, Manchester, Eng., 1858, July 14
748 Pantaky, Norman, occultist, Bombay, 1872, Sept. 10, 4:00 a.m.
749 Papen, Franz von, statesman, Werl, Ger., 1879, Oct. 29, 3:00 p.m.
750 Parchment, S. R., occultist, Jamaica, B.W.I., 1881, Feb. 1, 9:30 a.m.

751 Paris, Henri, Comte de, Aisne, Fr., 1908, July 5, 7:11 a.m.
752 Paris, Louis Philippe Albert, Comte de, s. of Ferdinand, Paris, 1838, Aug. 24
753 Pasteur, Louis, chemist, Dôle, Fr., 1822, Dec. 27, 2:00 a.m.
754 Patti, Adelina, singer, Madrid, Spain, 1843, Feb. 10, 4:00 p.m.
755 Pattison, A. Seth Pringle-, philosopher, Edinburgh, 1856, Dec. 20, 11:20 a.m.
756 Pearce, Alfred J., astrologer, 1840, Nov. 10
757 Pearson, Sir C. Arthur, publisher, Somerset, 1866, Feb. 24, 11:00 a.m.
758 Peary, Marie, d. of explorer, Greenland, 1893, Sept. 12, 6:45 p.m.
759 Peary, Robert E., explorer, Cresson, Pa., 1856, May 6, 12:04 p.m.
760 Peck, Sir William, astronomer, Kirkoud, Scot., 1861, Jan. 3, 12:10 p.m.
761 Pétain, Henri Philippe, soldier, Clauchy-le-Tour, 1856, Apr. 24, 10:30 p.m.
762 Peter II, King of Yugoslavia, Belgrade, 1923, Sept. 6, 2:52 a.m.
763 Petöfi, Sandro, poet Kiskörös, Hungary, 1822-3, Dec. 31, midnight
764 Phillips, G. F. L., manufacturer, 1858, Oct. 9, 9:00 a.m.
765 Phillips, Norma, actress, Baltimore, Md., 1892, Feb. 2, 4:25 a.m.
766 Piccard, Jean and Auguste, balloonists, Basle, 1884, Jan. 28, 11:00 p.m.
767 Pickford, Mary, actress, Toronto, Ont., 1892, Apr. 9, 3:00 a.m.
768 Pitman, Sir Isaac, shorthand inventor, Trowbridge, 1813, Jan. 4, 12:40 a.m.
769 Pius XI, Pope, Milan, 1857, May 31, 8:00 a.m.
770 Pius XII, Pope, Rome, 1876, Mar. 2, noon
771 Poincaré, Raymond, statesman, Bar-le-Duc, Fr., 1860, Aug. 20, 5:00 p.m.
772 Post, Wiley, aviator, Grand Saline, Tex., 1898, Nov. 22, 11:00 a.m.
773 Powell, John Wesley, ethnologist, Mount Morris, N.Y., 1834, Mar. 24
774 Power, Tyrone, actor, Cincinnati, O., 1914, May 5, 5:30 p.m.
775 Prentiss, Elizabeth, author, Portland, Me., 1818, Oct. 26, 3:00 p.m.
776 Priestly, J. B., dramatist, Bradford, Eng., 1894, Sept. 13, 8:00 a.m.
777 Proudhon, Pierre Joseph, journalist, Besançon, Fr., 1809, Jan. 15
778 Pryse, James M., occultist, Cincinnati, O., 1859, Nov. 14, 9:30 a.m.
779 Quain, Sir Richard, physician, Mallow, Ireland, 1816, Oct. 30
780 Quezon y Molina, Manuel, statesman, Baler, P.I., 1878, Aug. 19, 7:00 a.m.
781 Quirino, Elpidio, statesman, 1890, Nov. 16, 6:00 a.m.
782 Rathbone, Basil, actor, Johannesburg, Transvaal, S.A., 1892, June 13
783 Reagan, Ronald, actor, Tampico, Ill., 1911, Feb. 6
784 Reinhardt, Max, theatrical producer, near Vienna, 1873, Sept. 9, 1:00 a.m.
785 Reith, John C. W., Baron, govt. official, Stonehaven, 1889, July 20, 4:30 p.m.
786 Remarque, Erich Maria, author, Osnabrück, Ger., 1898, June 22, 8:15 p.m.
787 Reuther, Walter, labor leader, Wheeling, W.Va., 1907, Sept. 1, 10:04 p.m.
788 Reynaud, Paul, statesman, Barcelonette, Fr., 1878, Oct. 15, 2:00 p.m.
789 Rhodes, Cecil, empire builder, Hertfordshire, 1853, July 5, 7:00 p.m.
790 Ribbentrop, Joachim von, statesman, Wesel on Rhine, 1893, Apr. 30, 10:35 a.m.
791 Rich, Irene, actress, Buffalo, N.Y., 1891, Oct. 13, 5:34 a.m.
792 Rickenbacher, Eddie, aviator, Columbus, O., 1890, Oct. 8, 8:00 a.m.
793 Rimski-Korsakov, Nikolai, composer, Novgorod, 1844, Mar. 18, 10:30 a.m.
794 Ripley, Robert, cartoonist, Santa Rosa, Cal., 1893, Dec. 25
795 Roberts, Morley, author, London, 1857, Dec. 29, 10:00 a.m.
796 Robinson, Edward G., actor, Bucharest, Rumania, 1893, Dec. 12, 5:00 p.m.
797 Robinson, Hugh A., aviator, 1881, May 13, 11:15 a.m.
798 Robson, Vivian, astrologer, Birmingham, Eng., 1890, May 26, 11:56 a.m.
799 Rockefeller, John D., oil magnate, Richford, N.Y., 1839, July 8-9, midnight
800 Rogers, Charles, band leader, Olathe, Kans., 1904, Aug. 13

801 Rogers, Ginger, actress, Independence, Mo., 1911, July 16, 2:00 a.m.
802 Rogers, Will, humorist, Oologah, Okla., 1879, Nov. 4
803 Rooney, Mickey, actor, Brooklyn, N.Y., 1920, Sept. 23, noon
804 Roosevelt, Eleanor, stateswoman, New York City, 1884, Oct. 11
805 Roosevelt, Franklin, statesman, Hyde Park, N.Y., 1882, Jan. 30, 8:46 p.m.
806 Roosevelt, Theodore, statesman, New York City, 1858, Oct. 27, 11:03 a.m.
807 Roper, Daniel Calhoun, politician, Marlboro Co., S.C., 1867, Apr. 1, 6:00 p.m.
808 Rosebery, 5th Earl of, statesman, London, 1847, May 7, 3:00 a.m.
809 Rossetti, Christina, poet, London, 1830, Dec. 5, 3:10 p.m.
810 Rudhyar, Dane, astrologer, Paris, 1895, Mar. 23, 12:42 a.m.
811 Rudolf, Archduke, s. of Francis Joseph, Vienna, 1858, Aug. 21, 10:15 a.m.
812 Ruml, Beardsley, financier, Cedar Rapids, Ia., 1894, Nov. 5, 1:30 p.m.
813 Ruskin, John, critic, London, 1819, Feb. 8, 7:30 a.m.
814 Russell, Lillian, actress, Clinton, Ia., 1861, Dec. 4, 10:50 p.m.
815 Russell, Rosalind, actress, Waterbury, Conn., 1910, June 4, 4:15 p.m.
816 Saint-Saëns, Camille, composer, Paris, 1835, Oct. 9, 6:45 a.m.
817 Salvesen, Lord, jurist, South Leith, Scot., 1857, July 20, 11:15 a.m.
818 Sand, George, author, Paris, 1804, July 1
819 Sandeau, Jules, author, Aubusson, Fr., 1811, Feb. 19
820 Sands, Lord, jurist, County Perth, Scot., 1857, Oct. 18, 10:15 a.m.
821 Sanger, Margaret, reformer, Corning, N.Y., 1883, Sept. 14
822 San Martin, Grau, statesman, 1884, Sept. 13, 10:39 a.m.
823 Santayana, George, philosopher, Madrid, 1863, Dec. 16, 9:00 a.m.
824 Sarnoff, David, radio executive, Minsk, Russia, 1891, Feb. 27
825 Saroyan, William, dramatist, Fresno, Cal., 1908, Aug. 31, 10:00 p.m.
826 Savage, R. S., statesman, 1872, Mar. 8, 8:00 p.m.
827 Schacht, Hjalmar, financier, Tingleff, Schleswig, 1876, Jan. 30, 11:40 a.m.
828 Schleicher, Kurt von, soldier, Brandenburg, 1882, Apr. 7, 11:30 p.m.
829 Schmeling, Max, pugilist, 1905, Sept. 28, noon
830 Schneevoigt, Georg, conductor, Viborg, Russia, 1873, Nov. 8
831 Schulze, Karl, pugilist, 1907, May 14, 3:30 a.m.
832 Schumann, Robert, composer, Zwickau, Ger., 1810, June 8, 9:30 p.m.
833 Schumann-Heink, Ernestine, singer, near Prague, 1861, June 15, 1:30 a.m.
834 Schwab, Charles, industrialist, Williamsburg, Pa., 1862, Feb. 18
835 Scott, Cyril Meir, composer, Oxton, Eng., 1879, Sept. 27, 3:58 a.m.
836 Scott, Howard, reformer, Charlottesville, Va., 1890, Apr. 1, 7:11 a.m.
837 Scott-Moncrieff, C. K. M., translator, Polmont, Scot., 1889, Sept. 25, 11:30 a.m.
838 Scriabin, Alexander, composer, Moscow, 1872, Jan. 6, 2:00 p.m.
839 Seth, James, philosopher, Edinburgh, 1860, May 6, 4:00 a.m.
840 Shackleton, Sir Ernest, explorer, Kilkee, Ireland, 1874, Feb. 15, 2:30 a.m.
841 Shaw, Frank P., politician, N. Warwick, Ont., 1877, Feb. 1, 4:00 a.m.
842 Shaw, George Bernard, dramatist, Dublin, 1856, July 26, 12:15 a.m.
843 Shawn, Ted, dancer, Kansas City, Mo., 1891, Oct. 21, 10:39 a.m.
844 Shearer, Norma, actress, Montreal, 1903, Aug. 10, 10:00 a.m.
845 Sinclair, Upton, author, Baltimore, Md., 1878, Sept. 20, 9:00 a.m.
846 Sison Teofilo, statesman, 1880, Feb. 29, 8:00 a.m.
847 Skolsky, Sydney, columnist, New York City, 1905, May 2, 3:00 p.m.
848 Slezak, Walter, comedian, Vienna, 1902, May 3, 2:00 a.m.
849 Smith, Alexander, poet, Kilmarnock, Scot., 1829-30, Dec. 31, midnight
850 Smith, Alfred E., politician, New York City, 1873, Dec. 30, 6:00 a.m.

851 Smuts, Jan Christiaan, statesman, Cape Town, S.A., 1870, May 24, 4:45 a.m.
852 Snowden, Philip, statesman, Cowling, Yorks., 1864, July 18, 3:00 p.m.
853 Soong, T. V., financier, Kiangsu, 1894, Dec. 4, 4:00 a.m.
854 Spare, Austin O., artist, 1886, Dec. 30
855 Spenceley, Frederick, occultist, Boston, Mass., 1872, Jan. 29, 6:44 a.m.
856 Spencer, Herbert, philosopher, Derby, Eng., 1820, Apr. 27
857 Spengler, Oswald, philosopher, Blankenburg, Ger., 1880, May 29, 6:40 p.m.
858 Stacy-Judd, Robert B., architect, London, 1884, June 21, 11:00 p.m.
859 Stalin, Joseph, statesman, Gori, Georgia, 1880, Jan. 2, 8:15 a.m.
860 Stanley, Sir Henry Morton, explorer, Denbigh, Wales, 1841, Jan. 28
861 Stanwick, Barbara, actress, Brooklyn, N.Y., 1907, July 6, 9:00 a.m.
862 Starhemberg, Prince Ernst-Rüdiger von, statesman, 1899, May 10, 3:37 a.m.
863 Stead, William T., journalist, Embelton, Eng., 1849, July 5
864 Steigner, Henry, occultist, Zeil-am-Main, 1880, Aug. 5, 5:07 a.m.
865 Steiner, Rudolf, occultist, Kraljevic, Aus., 1861, Feb. 27
866 Steinheil, Marguerite, tried for murder, Beaucourt, Fr., 1869, Apr. 16
867 Steinmetz, Charles, inventor, Breslau, Ger., 1865, Apr. 9, noon
868 Sterling, George, poet, Sag Harbor, N.Y., 1869, Dec. 1, 11:48 p.m.
869 Stevenson, Robert Louis, author, Edinburgh, 1850, Nov. 13, 1:30 p.m.
870 Stinnes, Hugo, industrialist, Mulheim, Ger., 1870, Feb. 12, 8:00 a.m.
871 Stockton, Frank R., author, Philadelphia, 1834, Apr. 5
872 Stokowski, Leopold, conductor, London, 1887, Apr. 18, 4:00 a.m.
873 Stowacki, L., author, 1809, Sept. 4, 7:00 a.m.
874 Strauss, Richard, composer, Munich, 1864, June 11
875 Stroheim, Eric von, actor, Vienna, 1885, Sept. 22, 8:47 a.m.
876 Stuart, Alec, astrologer, 1881, Sept. 12
877 Sullivan, Sir Arthur, composer, London, 1842, May 13, 4:47 p.m.
878 Sullivan, Ed, columnist, New York City, 1902, Sept. 28
879 Sun Fo, s. of Sun Yat-sen, Kwangtung, 1891, Nov. 5, 4:00 a.m.
880 Sun Yat-sen, statesman, near Canton, 1866, Nov. 12
881 Sunday, Billy, revivalist, Ames, Ia., 1863, Nov. 19, 6:05 a.m.
882 Sutter, John Augustus, pioneer, Kandern, Ger., 1803, Feb. 15, 5:00 a.m.
883 Swanson, Gloria, actress, Chicago, 1899, Mar. 27, 12:45 a.m.
884 Swinburne, Algernon, poet, London, 1837, Apr. 5, 5:00 a.m.
885 Sylva, Marguerite, singer, Brussels, 1875, July 2, 4:00 p.m.
886 Taft, William Howard, statesman, Cincinnati, 1857, Sept. 15, 9:46 a.m.
887 Tagore, Sir Rabindranath, poet, Calcutta, 1861, May 7, 4:02 a.m.
888 Tally, Marion, singer, 1906, Dec. 20
889 Tardieu, André, statesman, Paris, 1876, Sept. 22, 1:00 p.m.
890 Tarkington, Booth, author, Indianapolis, 1869, July 29, 10:00 a.m.
891 Tchaikovsky, Pëtr Ilich, composer, Vitkinsk, Russia, 1840, May 7
892 Temple, Shirley, actress, Santa Monica, Cal., 1928, Sept. 23, 9:00 p.m.
893 Tennyson, Alfred, poet, Somersby, Eng., 1809, Aug. 6, 12:05 a.m.
894 Tennyson, Hallam, s. of above, Twickenham, 1852, Aug. 11, 9:30 a.m.
895 Tesla, Nikola, inventor, Smiljan, Yug., 1856, July 9-10, midnight
896 Teyte, Maggie, singer, Wolverhampton, Eng., 1890, Apr. 17
897 Thaw, Harry K., murderer, Pittsburgh, 1871, Feb. 12
898 Thomas, Lowell, commentator, Woodington, O., 1892, Apr. 6
899 Thomson, David Croal, art expert, Edinburgh, 1855, Oct. 24, 4:30 a.m.
900 Tibbett, Lawrence, singer, Bakersfield, Cal., 1896, Nov. 16

901 Tierney, Gene, actress, Brooklyn, N.Y., 1920, Nov. 19, 5:15 p.m.
902 Tingley, Katherine, Theosophist, New York City, 1847, July 6, 10:00 a.m.
903 Todd, Thelma, comedienne, 1906, July 29
904 Toomey, Regis, actor, Pittsburgh, 1898, Aug. 13, 9:00 a.m.
905 Toscanini, Arturo, conductor, Parma, Italy, 1867, Mar. 25, 2:00 a.m.
906 Tracy, Spencer, actor, Milwaukee, 1900, Apr. 5, 1:57 a.m.
907 Trine, Ralph Waldo, mystic, Mt. Morris, Ill., 1866, Sept. 9, 1:00 a.m.
908 Trotsky, Leon, revolutionary, Yanavka, Russia, 1879, Nov. 7, 10:09 p.m.
909 Truman, Harry S., statesman, Lamar, Mo., 1884, May 8, 4:17 p.m.
910 Tschiffely, A. T., traveler, 1895, May 7, 12:46 a.m.
911 Tsugu, Prince, s. of Hirohito, Tokyo, 1933, Dec. 23, 6:39 a.m.
912 Tuck, William M., politician, 1896, Sept. 28-29, midnight
913 Tunney, Gene, pugilist, New York City, 1899, May 25, 8:00 a.m.
914 Twain, Mark, author, Florida, Mo., 1835, Nov. 30, 4:45 a.m.
915 Tweedsmuir, Lord, author, Perth, Scot., 1875, Aug. 26, 3:00 a.m.
916 Twigg, Thomas, police inspector, 1863, Aug. 7
917 Ulric, Lenore, actress, New Ulm, Minn., 1892, July 21
918 Vaillant, Auguste, anarchist, 1861, Dec. 27
919 Valentino, Rudolph, actor, Castellaneta, It., 1895, May 6, 3:00 a.m.
920 Valéry, Paul Ambroise, author, Cette, Fr., 1871, Oct. 30, 7:00 p.m.
921 Vandenberg, Arthur, politician, Grand Rapids, Mich., 1884, Mar. 20, 3:10 a.m.
922 Vandervelde, Émile, statesman, Ixelles, Belgium, 1866, Jan. 25, 6:00 a.m.
923 Van Maasdijk, Clement, aviator, 1885, Aug. 8
924 Vecher, Joseph, murderer, Beaufort, Fr., 1869, Nov. 16, 1:00 a.m.
925 Venizelos, Eleutherios, statesman, Crete, 1864, Aug. 23, 5:00 a.m.
926 Verdi, Giuseppe, composer, Parma, Italy, 1813, Oct. 10, 8:00 p.m.
927 Verlaine, Paul, poet, Metz, France, 1844, Mar. 30, 9:00 p.m.
928 Verne, Jules, author, Nantes, France, 1828, Feb. 8, noon
929 Victor Emmanuel II, King of Italy, Turin, 1820, Mar. 14, 12:30 a.m.
930 Victor Emmanuel III, King of Italy, Naples, 1869, Nov. 11, 10:15 p.m.
931 Victoria, Princess, d. of Edward VII, London, 1868, July 6, 4:25 a.m.
932 Victoria, Princess, d. of William II, 1892, Sept. 13
933 Victoria, Queen of England, London, 1819, May 24, 4:15 a.m.
934 Victoria Ena, Queen of Spain, Balmoral, Scot., 1887, Oct. 24
935 Vidor, King, cinema director, Galveston, Tex., 1894, Feb. 8, 6:00 p.m.
936 Villa, Pancho, Mexican rebel, Rio Grande, Tex., 1877, Oct. 4, 4:19 a.m.
937 Vivekanada, Swami, Vedantist, 1863, Jan. 12
938 Wadlow, Robert, giant, Alton, Ill., 1918, Feb. 22, 6:00 a.m.
939 Wagner, Richard, composer, Leipzig, 1813, May 22, 4:00 a.m.
940 Walker, James, politician, New York City, 1881, June 19, 3:30 p.m.
941 Walker, Jane, physician, Dewsbury, Eng., 1859, Oct. 24, 8:30 p.m.
942 Walker, Sir Norman, physician, Dysart, Scot., 1862, Aug. 2, 7:00 a.m.
943 Wallace, Alfred Russell, naturalist, Monmouthshire, 1823, Jan. 8
944 Wallace, Henry A., politician, Adair Co., Ia., 1888, Oct. 7, 7:12 p.m.
945 Walton, Evarts C., astrologer, Philadelphia, 1881, Feb. 2, 2:30 a.m.
946 Wanamaker, John, merchant, Philadelphia, 1838, July 11
947 Wang Ching-wei, politician, Canton, 1883, May 4, 10:00 a.m.
948 Wang Chung-hui, statesman, Kuantung, 1881, Dec. 1, 2:00 a.m.
949 Ward, Artemus, humorist, Waterford, Me., 1834, April 26
950 Warren, Earl, politician, Los Angeles, 1891, Mar. 19, 2:00 a.m.

951 Waters, Ethel, actress, Chester, Pa., 1900, Oct. 31, 9:15 a.m.
952 Watson, Robert, author, Glasgow, 1882, May 20, 8:00 a.m.
953 Wavertree, Lord, sportsman, 1856, Dec. 25, 5:00 a.m.
954 Weissmuller, Johnny, actor, 1904, June 2, 6:30 p.m.
955 Wells, H. G., author, Bromley, Eng., 1866, Sept. 21
956 Wells, Linton, author, Louisville, Ky., 1893, Apr. 1, 3:06 a.m.
957 Wells, Zoë, artist, Brownsville, Tex., 1881, Dec. 31, 3:30 p.m.
958 Westinghouse, G., inventor, Central Bridge, N.Y., 1846, Oct. 6, 11:20 a.m.
959 Weygand, Maxime, soldier, Brussels, 1867, Jan. 21
960 Whalen, Grover, politician, New York City, 1886, June 2
961 Wheeler, Elsie, spiritualist, Norris City, Ill., 1887, Sept. 3, 9:45 p.m.
962 White, Felix H., composer, London, 1884, Apr. 27
963 White, John, churchman, Glasgow, 1867, Dec. 21, 2:30 a.m.
964 White, Stanford, architect, New York City, 1853, Nov. 9
965 Whiteman, Paul, band leader, Denver, Colo., 1890, Mar. 28
966 Whittier, John Greenleaf, poet, Haverhill, Mass., 1807, Dec. 17, 9:00 a.m.
967 Wilde, H. T., seaman, 1872, Sept. 21
968 Wilde, Oscar, author, Dublin, 1856, Oct. 15, 2:37 a.m.
969 Wilhelmina, Queen of Holland, The Hague, 1880, Aug. 31, 6:15 p.m.
970 Wilkins, Sir George, explorer, S. Australia, 1888, Oct. 31, 11:00 a.m.
971 Willard, Frances Elizabeth, reformer, Churchville, N.Y., 1839, Sept. 28
972 William II, Emperor of Germany, Potsdam, 1859, Jan. 27, 2:45 p.m.
973 William, Prince, grandson of William II, Potsdam, 1906, July 4, 9:15 a.m.
974 Williams, Ben Ames, author, Macon, Miss., 1889, Mar. 7, 11:30 a.m.
975 Williams, Esther, actress, 1921, Aug. 20, 9:00 p.m.
976 Willkie, Wendell, politician, Elmwood, Ind., 1892, Feb. 18, 5:00 a.m.
977 Wills, Helen, tennis player, Centerville, Cal., 1906, Oct. 6
978 Wilson, C. T. R., meteorologist, Glencorse, Scot., 1869, Feb. 14, 4:00 a.m.
979 Wilson, Edith, wife of president, Wytheville, Va., 1872, Oct. 15, 9:00 a.m.
980 Wilson, Woodrow, statesman, Staunton, Va., 1856, Dec. 28, 11:45 p.m.
981 Winchell, Walter, commentator, New York City, 1897, Apr. 7
982 Windsor, Duchess of, Monterey, Pa., 1896, June 19, 7:00 a.m.
983 Windsor, Duke of, Surrey, 1894, June 23, 10:00 p.m.
984 Winkler, Robert, actor, 1927, Feb. 12
985 Wirth, Karl Joseph, statesman, Freiburg, Ger., 1879, Sept. 7, 9:30 p.m.
986 Wolseley, Viscount, soldier, near Dublin, 1833, June 4, 11:55 p.m.
987 Wood, Sir Henry Joseph, conductor, London, 1870, Mar. 3
988 Woollcott, Alexander, journalist, Phalanx, N.J., 1876, Jan. 19, 3:30 p.m.
989 Woolley, Mary E., educator, S. Norwalk, Conn., 1863, July 13
990 Yeats, William Butler, poet, near Dublin, 1865, June 13
991 Yoshihito, Emperor of Japan, Tokyo, 1879, Aug. 31, 8:10 a.m.
992 Young, Loretta, actress, Salt Lake City, 1912, Jan. 6
993 Younger, Sir Robert, jurist, Alloa, Scot., 1861, Sept. 12, 5:00 p.m.
994 Yule, Sir David, merchant, Edinburgh, 1858, Aug. 4, 4:00 a.m.
995 Zamora, Niceto Alcalá-, statesman, Preigo, Spain, 1877, July 6, 1:10 p.m.
996 Zeigler, Adrian M., astrologer, Philadelphia, 1891, Aug. 31, 5:50 a.m.
997 Zeppelin, Count Ferdinand von, aeronaut, Constance, Ger., 1838, July 8
998 Zionchek, Marion, politician, 1900, Dec. 5, 5:00 a.m.
999 Zola, Émile, author, Paris, 1840, Apr. 2, 11:00 p.m.
1000 Zorina, Vera, dancer, Berlin, 1917, Jan. 2, noon

	10	11	12	Asc.	2	3	☉	☽	☿
	°	°	°	° ′	°	°	° ′	° ′	° ′
1	♐ 5	♐ 27	♑ 20	19 ♒ 0	♈ 4	♉ 9	3 ♊ 0	15 ♌ 30	10 ♊ 18R
2	♍ 9	♎ 10	♏ 5	25 ♏ 0	♐ 26	♒ 2	29 ♍ 0	27 ♈ 30	21 ♎ 0
3	♏ 7	♐ 1	♐ 23	15 ♑ 0	♒ 25	♈ 5	18 ♏ 30	16 ♒ 0	4 ♐ 10
4	♑ 9	♒ 2	♓ 2	17 ♈ 30	♉ 24	♊ 18	20 ♑ 0	25 ♑ 0	0 ♑ 30
5	♏ 7	♐ 1	♐ 20	10 ♑ 38	♒ 24	♈ 6	6 ♊ 3	12 ♊ 4	18 ♊ 15
6	♐ 25	♑ 16	♒ 12	20 ♓ 35	♉ 5	♊ 3	19 ♒ 7	21 ♌ 20	0 ♓ 40
7	♍ 13	♎ 14	♏ 8	28 ♏ 29	♑ 0	♒ 6	1 ♎ 18	27 ♊ 44	14 ♍ 41
8	♓ 11	♈ 15	♉ 26	3 ♋ 15	♋ 24	♌ 15	6 ♐ 58	28 ♓ 17	11 ♐ 9
9	♉ 13	♊ 19	♋ 23	21 ♌ 35	♍ 13	♎ 10	13 ♍ 52	20 ♉ 9	0 ♍ 11
10	♍ 18	♎ 16	♏ 7	22 ♏ 0	♐ 23	♒ 6	0 ♑ 5	13 ♎ 10	11 ♑ 30R
11	♒ 26	♓ 29	♉ 10	21 ♊ 41	♋ 12	♌ 2	11 ♓ 54	4 ♉ 27	15 ♒ 13
12	♋ 7	♌ 12	♍ 12	5 ♎ 33	♏ 0	♐ 1	9 ♑ 0	1 ♉ 9	20 ♑ 14R
13	♋ 13	♌ 18	♍ 17	9 ♎ 17	♏ 5	♐ 6	18 ♈ 14	22 ♉ 41	22 ♓ 39
14	♏ 25	♐ 14	♑ 2	22 ♑ 40	♓ 26	♉ 6	15 ♊ 30	15 ♈ 21	8 ♋ 22
15	♊ 6	♋ 13	♌ 16	12 ♍ 0	♎ 4	♏ 2	2 ♍ 6	2 ♏ 32	21 ♍ 53R
16	♊ 4	♋ 11	♌ 14	10 ♍ 0	♎ 2	♎ 29	17 ♑ 54	11 ♑ 35	6 ♒ 56
17	♊ 17	♋ 21	♌ 22	18 ♍ 30	♎ 14	♏ 14	7 ♐ 2	22 ♒ 32	26 ♐ 6
18	♏ 2	♏ 26	♐ 17	7 ♑ 30	♒ 18	♈ 0	16 ♎ 14	18 ♒ 49	8 ♎ 30
19	♉ 26	♋ 1	♌ 3	1 ♍ 38	♍ 24	♎ 22	26 ♉ 23	28 ♎ 1	6 ♊ 28
20	♈ 7	♉ 19	♋ 3	5 ♌ 0	♌ 20	♍ 9	8 ♉ 23	0 ♓ 11	29 ♉ 5
21	♉ 9	♊ 23	♌ 1	26 ♌ 0	♍ 14	♎ 6	19 ♓ 30	18 ♈ 0	9 ♓ 0
22	♍ 16	♎ 15	♏ 6	21 ♏ 0	♐ 22	♒ 4	9 ♐ 30	17 ♌ 30	17 ♐ 42
23	♒ 1	♒ 25	♈ 4	0 ♊ 44	♊ 24	♋ 12	16 ♊ 0	14 ♊ 39	26 ♉ 0
24	♌ 26	♍ 28	♎ 21	7 ♏ 0	♐ 6	♑ 12	19 ♌ 15	1 ♍ 45	15 ♍ 20
25	♉ 14	♊ 22	♋ 27	25 ♌ 0	♍ 15	♎ 11	6 ♐ 30	0 ♉ 45	11 ♐ 57
26	♊ 19	♋ 23	♌ 24	20 ♍ 27	♎ 16	♏ 16	26 ♉ 27	19 ♏ 5	2 ♉ 43
27	♉ 29	♋ 3	♌ 5	3 ♍ 33	♍ 27	♎ 25	18 ♉ 40	27 ♈ 30	3 ♉ 30
28	♊ 11	♋ 18	♌ 20	16 ♍ 0	♎ 8	♏ 6	15 ♌ 0	15 ♉ 0	29 ♌ 30
29	♊ 6	♋ 13	♌ 16	12 ♍ 0	♎ 3	♏ 1	21 ♎ 30	12 ♐ 0	14 ♏ 10
30	♑ 3	♑ 22	♒ 18	9 ♈ 0	♉ 22	♊ 15	4 ♉ 30	15 ♓ 0	4 ♉ 30
31	♍ 23	♎ 21	♏ 10	24 ♏ 18	♐ 26	♒ 12	6 ♐ 55	22 ♐ 35	9 ♐ 19
32	♐ 17	♑ 16	♒ 5	9 ♓ 13	♈ 21	♉ 23	24 ♊ 20	26 ♐ 51	1 ♊ 22
33	♈ 16	♉ 23	♋ 0	1 ♌ 50	♌ 21	♍ 15	26 ♊ 17	28 ♏ 3	4 ♋ 19R
34	♋ 22	♌ 27	♍ 26	16 ♎ 40	♏ 13	♐ 15	5 ♎ 10	7 ♑ 18	18 ♍ 35
35	♒ 13	♓ 9	♈ 27	25 ♊ 0	♋ 10	♋ 25	26 ♌ 23	6 ♉ 54	11 ♍ 52R
36	♈ 20	♉ 28	♋ 8	8 ♌ 30	♌ 26	♍ 18	26 ♍ 30	18 ♎ 30	12 ♍ 30
37	♐ 13	♐ 27	♑ 12	3 ♒ 20	♈ 24	♉ 26	26 ♊ 0	13 ♋ 30	20 ♋ 30
38	♑ 26	♒ 17	♓ 27	2 ♊ 46	♊ 24	♋ 10	13 ♏ 51	17 ♉ 0	27 ♎ 1
39	♒ 26	♓ 28	♉ 20	6 ♋ 30	♋ 21	♌ 6	15 ♋ 50	18 ♈ 30	2 ♋ 9R
40	♌ 29	♎ 1	♎ 26	17 ♏ 5	♐ 17	♑ 22	5 ♒ 59	13 ♑ 30	23 ♑ 55R
41	♑ 7	♑ 28	♒ 26	12 ♈ 2	♉ 23	♊ 17	14 ♈ 4	7 ♌ 12	25 ♓ 56
42	♑ 19	♒ 13	♓ 17	4 ♉ 0	♊ 5	♊ 28	3 ♈ 30	3 ♈ 0	29 ♓ 0R
43	♑ 24	♒ 17	♓ 23	24 ♉ 0	♊ 19	♋ 7	28 ♓ 0	10 ♍ 45	18 ♓ 0R
44	♎ 22	♏ 16	♐ 4	19 ♐ 0	♒ 0	♓ 17	20 ♈ 24	24 ♏ 28	23 ♓ 32
45	♌ 6	♍ 6	♎ 7	25 ♎ 30	♏ 22	♐ 26	1 ♎ 47	28 ♈ 7	24 ♎ 43
46	♓ 19	♈ 27	♊ 14	21 ♋ 0	♌ 6	♌ 24	20 ♍ 19	7 ♍ 18	6 ♍ 32R
47	♓ 5	♈ 9	♉ 23	3 ♋ 0	♋ 24	♌ 11	8 ♓ 21	7 ♍ 54	18 ♓ 10R
48	♍ 11	♎ 12	♏ 6	27 ♏ 26	♐ 28	♒ 4	12 ♉ 42	10 ♍ 52	16 ♈ 6
49	♑ 27	♒ 17	♓ 28	13 ♊ 57	♊ 29	♋ 13	24 ♏ 44	26 ♋ 55	14 ♐ 18
50	♍ 18	♎ 17	♏ 8	21 ♏ 45	♐ 23	♒ 7	13 ♏ 48	12 ♎ 30	1 ♐ 0R

	♀	♂	♃	♄	♅	♆	♇
	° ′	° ′	° ′	° ′	° ′	° ′	° ′
1	18 ♋ 0	25 ♊ 5	28 ♓ 36	7 ♒ 17 R	5 ♈ 30	24 ♒ 0	23 ♈ 15
2	15 ♏ 0	1 ♍ 0	13 ♑ 30	8 ♑ 0	26 ♓ 30 R	17 ♒ 0 R	21 ♈ 16 R
3	15 ♏ 30	0 ♑ 10	15 ♋ 12	27 ♌ 31	23 ♒ 49	9 ♌ 20	6 ♋ 20 R
4	6 ♑ 30	29 ♐ 30	26 ♈ 30	11 ♎ 0	21 ♒ 0	29 ♑ 0	12 ♈ 0
5	2 ♉ 24	12 ♌ 26	19 ♊ 35	16 ♎ 50 R	0 ♓ 31	3 ♒ 43 R	14 ♈ 0
6	21 ♓ 30	10 ♒ 10	12 ♓ 57	4 ♐ 40	9 ♋ 26 R	12 ♈ 55	14 ♉ 5
7	2 ♎ 53	12 ♍ 41	10 ♓ 39 R	21 ♍ 50	29 ♎ 53	9 ♊ 2 R	8 ♊ 42 R
8	16 ♏ 8	4 ♒ 25	28 ♍ 20	28 ♑ 52	10 ♌ 32 R	26 ♈ 11 R	20 ♉ 42 R
9	0 ♌ 2	21 ♑ 4	14 ♌ 54	1 ♍ 26	12 ♊ 3	28 ♓ 22 R	9 ♉ 15 R
10	18 ♒ 20	0 ♈ 30	0 ♉ 51 R	15 ♒ 51	6 ♈ 20	23 ♒ 48	22 ♈ 55 R
11	4 ♈ 23	15 ♎ 12 R	2 ♓ 43	4 ♒ 52	25 ♐ 18	0 ♋ 56 R	17 ♊ 38 R
12	26 ♒ 8	18 ♑ 0	22 ♐ 13	27 ♎ 17	25 ♎ 15	28 ♏ 18	9 ♓ 30
13	6 ♓ 45	26 ♐ 12	28 ♎ 0 R	23 ♒ 25 R	11 ♌ 13 R	0 ♉ 2	21 ♉ 59
14	5 ♉ 9	3 ♊ 2	13 ♎ 18 R	28 ♒ 11	0 ♉ 1	9 ♍ 40	23 ♋ 30
15	20 ♌ 13	23 ♊ 27	9 ♒ 43 R	29 ♓ 13 R	20 ♐ 30 R	25 ♐ 56 R	27 ♓ 18 R
16	3 ♐ 24	16 ♐ 11	21 ♏ 46	17 ♎ 45	22 ♊ 5 R	3 ♈ 29	10 ♉ 19 R
17	8 ♑ 42	25 ♉ 20 R	19 ♓ 11	26 ♍ 45	15 ♒ 8	25 ♑ 12	10 ♈ 30
18	23 ♏ 30	20 ♏ 17	9 ♍ 2	16 ♏ 0	5 ♓ 6 R	5 ♒ 30	16 ♈ 30 R
19	22 ♈ 59	4 ♑ 32	23 ♎ 16 R	25 ♒ 46	11 ♌ 32	1 ♉ 28	22 ♉ 8
20	20 ♉ 33	17 ♋ 42	12 ♑ 59	15 ♓ 21	19 ♐ 39 R	26 ♐ 30 R	26 ♓ 30
21	3 ♓ 0	1 ♑ 0	10 ♈ 0	14 ♒ 0	5 ♈ 0	24 ♒ 0	22 ♈ 40
22	0 ♏ 7	28 ♎ 0	24 ♓ 30	3 ♒ 30	2 ♈ 30	21 ♒ 30	22 ♈ 5
23	4 ♊ 30	11 ♊ 0	29 ♋ 0	21 ♑ 0	29 ♋ 0	25 ♈ 30	20 ♉ 0
24	28 ♌ 50	28 ♋ 15	0 ♉ 7	17 ♒ 30 R	26 ♐ 11 R	7 ♋ 14	21 ♊ 18
25	14 ♏ 40	7 ♎ 21	7 ♉ 44 R	28 ♋ 0 R	26 ♉ 53 R	19 ♓ 53 R	5 ♉ 17 R
26	11 ♈ 16	10 ♍ 54	26 ♍ 6 R	6 ♋ 7	3 ♎ 50 R	25 ♉ 20	1 ♊ 41
27	15 ♈ 30	15 ♑ 10	8 ♋ 30	24 ♓ 30	12 ♑ 30 R	10 ♋ 30	22 ♊ 30
28	24 ♋ 0 R	13 ♌ 30	4 ♈ 0 R	3 ♒ 13 R	6 ♈ 30 R	23 ♒ 0 R	23 ♈ 50 R
29	7 ♐ 8	18 ♍ 0	14 ♎ 0	8 ♒ 0	15 ♌ 0	29 ♈ 30 R	19 ♉ 45 R
30	24 ♓ 30	21 ♐ 30	23 ♒ 30	26 ♑ 0	0 ♈ 30	21 ♒ 30	21 ♈ 45
31	22 ♑ 37	27 ♐ 0	16 ♍ 52	21 ♏ 47	4 ♓ 42	5 ♒ 57	15 ♈ 0 R
32	10 ♉ 59	15 ♌ 53	3 ♍ 43	25 ♏ 32 R	25 ♏ 57 R	20 ♊ 8	13 ♊ 21
33	16 ♉ 25	7 ♊ 49	17 ♒ 1 R	26 ♑ 31 R	19 ♐ 0 R	1 ♋ 0	18 ♊ 16
34	29 ♌ 45	18 ♎ 56	21 ♐ 58	29 ♎ 45	3 ♋ 55	9 ♈ 17 R	13 ♉ 15 R
35	15 ♌ 51	17 ♌ 3	15 ♋ 35	17 ♌ 17	7 ♊ 31	26 ♓ 31 R	6 ♉ 0 R
36	4 ♏ 45	24 ♍ 30	12 ♑ 52	11 ♏ 20	23 ♓ 22 R	23 ♌ 34	15 ♋ 38
37	8 ♋ 50	16 ♍ 5	9 ♑ 54 R	14 ♑ 30	14 ♐ 30	28 ♊ 48	17 ♊ 20
38	5 ♏ 32	6 ♈ 52	15 ♎ 31	1 ♎ 35	20 ♊ 4 R	1 ♈ 26 R	10 ♉ 22 R
39	20 ♌ 11	4 ♍ 30	17 ♊ 30	23 ♉ 2	15 ♍ 30	18 ♉ 30	29 ♉ 43
40	6 ♓ 41	14 ♌ 28 R	28 ♋ 41	3 ♊ 16 R	27 ♍ 54 R	18 ♉ 17 R	29 ♉ 2 R
41	26 ♉ 59	24 ♉ 38	1 ♐ 34 R	3 ♓ 49	16 ♌ 3 R	2 ♉ 4	22 ♉ 12
42	0 ♉ 15	11 ♈ 0 R	4 ♏ 16 R	15 ♋ 30	11 ♎ 0 R	26 ♉ 0	2 ♊ 13
43	25 ♒ 19	12 ♊ 19	11 ♋ 0	17 ♓ 3	17 ♈ 5	1 ♓ 12	25 ♈ 30
44	3 ♊ 59	27 ♓ 24	27 ♓ 38	5 ♐ 6 R	9 ♋ 9	15 ♈ 1	15 ♉ 0
45	22 ♎ 34	20 ♊ 51	29 ♌ 15	16 ♏ 10	21 ♏ 49	20 ♊ 19 R	13 ♊ 37 R
46	5 ♌ 30	26 ♎ 48	18 ♏ 58	17 ♉ 47 R	8 ♉ 9 R	9 ♓ 49 R	1 ♉ 26 R
47	4 ♒ 16	29 ♎ 54	5 ♐ 30	0 ♌ 33 R	16 ♎ 39 R	27 ♉ 33	2 ♊ 58
48	2 ♊ 22	3 ♊ 44	10 ♊ 16	12 ♓ 47	8 ♑ 18 R	8 ♋ 11	22 ♊ 0
49	3 ♏ 30	29 ♑ 40	2 ♊ 19 R	26 ♒ 28	2 ♑ 9	10 ♋ 6 R	22 ♊ 5 R
50	22 ♐ 0	2 ♎ 0	19 ♎ 0	8 ♒ 10	15 ♌ 13	29 ♈ 1 R	21 ♉ 50 R

	10 °	11 °	12 °	Asc. ° ′	2 °	3 °	☉ ° ′	☽ ° ′	☿ ° ′
51	♊ 16	♋ 22	♌ 23	19 ♍ 0	♎ 12	♏ 11	26 ♑ 30	15 ♏ 0	23 ♑ 0
52	♋ 14	♌ 17	♍ 16	11 ♎ 30	♏ 8	♐ 9	14 ♋ 11	0 ♍ 9	14 ♋ 30R
53	♓ 5	♈ 9	♉ 26	9 ♋ 30	♋ 24	♌ 12	6 ♈ 7	24 ♓ 55	2 ♈ 6
54	♐ 9	♐ 27	♑ 16	12 ♒ 0	♈ 12	♉ 17	3 ♓ 39	4 ♒ 45	6 ♒ 57
55	♌ 4	♍ 7	♎ 5	28 ♎ 1	♏ 26	♐ 29	27 ♒ 54	13 ♑ 8	16 ♒ 14R
56	♈ 20	♊ 0	♋ 11	11 ♌ 0	♌ 28	♍ 19	25 ♊ 28	0 ♎ 29	11 ♋ 3
57	♊ 19	♋ 26	♌ 27	21 ♍ 30	♎ 15	♏ 14	20 ♌ 56	2 ♏ 55	9 ♌ 50
58	♌ 9	♍ 12	♎ 10	2 ♏ 40	♐ 1	♑ 4	8 ♎ 34	24 ♊ 3	17 ♎ 2
59	♐ 9	♐ 27	♑ 16	11 ♒ 30	♈ 12	♉ 17	10 ♌ 57	29 ♍ 28	10 ♌ 6R
60	♊ 25	♌ 3	♍ 3	26 ♍ 0	♎ 18	♏ 18	2 ♌ 30	27 ♉ 45	23 ♋ 35R
61	♏ 22	♐ 17	♑ 12	9 ♒ 0	♓ 17	♈ 23	4 ♒ 10	6 ♈ 34	13 ♒ 41R
62	♊ 28	♌ 0	♍ 1	28 ♍ 0	♎ 25	♏ 26	11 ♒ 20	17 ♏ 30	29 ♒ 25
63	♈ 16	♉ 25	♋ 6	7 ♌ 0	♌ 24	♍ 16	21 ♊ 24	20 ♈ 48	3 ♊ 23
64	♍ 12	♎ 12	♏ 4	20 ♏ 0	♐ 21	♒ 1	29 ♒ 20	10 ♋ 50	6 ♒ 30
65	♒ 22	♓ 18	♉ 11	2 ♋ 30	♋ 17	♌ 1	18 ♉ 48	8 ♑ 47	23 ♈ 49
66	♊ 17	♋ 24	♌ 25	19 ♍ 16	♎ 12	♏ 10	28 ♈ 12	12 ♉ 46	22 ♈ 57R
67	♒ 9	♓ 7	♈ 16	2 ♊ 29	♊ 26	♋ 17	22 ♋ 38	7 ♍ 28	2 ♋ 51
68	♒ 23	♓ 24	♉ 5	17 ♊ 10	♋ 9	♌ 0	25 ♒ 57	8 ♑ 49	9 ♓ 40R
69	♉ 27	♋ 2	♌ 4	2 ♍ 11	♍ 25	♎ 23	25 ♌ 58	7 ♋ 53	9 ♍ 26R
70	♓ 3	♈ 6	♉ 18	27 ♊ 8	♋ 17	♌ 8	18 ♉ 35	24 ♏ 51	23 ♉ 58
71	♑ 2	♑ 23	♒ 20	2 ♈ 30	♉ 15	♊ 11	3 ♑ 37	16 ♑ 50	17 ♐ 50
72	♍ 20	♎ 25	♏ 20	10 ♐ 55	♑ 13	♒ 19	26 ♌ 33	1 ♊ 45	17 ♍ 8
73	♊ 4	♋ 11	♌ 13	10 ♍ 0	♎ 21	♏ 0	19 ♈ 30	23 ♋ 30	27 ♓ 30
74	♍ 14	♎ 14	♏ 7	24 ♏ 27	♐ 26	♒ 5	8 ♌ 04	1 ♊ 30	9 ♌ 30
75	♋ 26	♌ 29	♍ 28	22 ♎ 20	♏ 20	♐ 22	9 ♈ 34	15 ♍ 18	13 ♈ 10R
76	♉ 21	♊ 29	♌ 3	1 ♍ 4	♍ 21	♎ 14	25 ♈ 33	20 ♐ 52	28 ♈ 42
77	♑ 6	♑ 25	♒ 22	15 ♈ 36	♉ 26	♊ 18	10 ♒ 51	8 ♒ 55	18 ♑ 30
78	♌ 15	♍ 18	♎ 15	7 ♏ 38	♐ 7	♑ 10	21 ♍ 19	24 ♋ 6	17 ♎ 6
79	♋ 1	♌ 4	♍ 5	0 ♎ 53	♎ 26	♏ 27	10 ♐ 10	13 ♑ 39	5 ♐ 1
80	♑ 27	♒ 23	♓ 28	14 ♉ 17	♊ 13	♋ 5	3 ♌ 10	15 ♈ 15	29 ♌ 26
81	♑ 0	♑ 16	♒ 8	0 ♈ 0	♉ 22	♊ 14	12 ♓ 7	24 ♍ 38	25 ♓ 0
82	♎ 28	♏ 23	♐ 12	1 ♑ 8	♒ 12	♓ 25	28 ♏ 43	12 ♐ 3	23 ♏ 56R
83	♒ 20	♓ 20	♉ 6	24 ♊ 0	♋ 12	♋ 29	7 ♊ 10	22 ♋ 29	22 ♉ 53R
84	♍ 19	♎ 19	♏ 12	2 ♐ 26	♑ 4	♒ 12	20 ♐ 25	13 ♑ 19	17 ♐ 48
85	♉ 1	♊ 12	♋ 17	15 ♌ 48	♍ 6	♍ 29	5 ♊ 35	13 ♓ 35	0 ♊ 12
86	♋ 8	♌ 11	♍ 11	7 ♎ 0	♏ 3	♐ 4	28 ♎ 20	9 ♌ 2	5 ♏ 1
87	♓ 2	♈ 5	♉ 16	26 ♊ 25	♋ 17	♌ 7	8 ♓ 13	17 ♎ 54	12 ♒ 45
88	♑ 5	♑ 27	♒ 25	8 ♈ 54	♉ 19	♊ 14	21 ♒ 22	25 ♋ 46	3 ♒ 54
89	♎ 27	♏ 22	♐ 13	3 ♑ 27	♒ 12	♓ 23	25 ♒ 59	8 ♊ 23	8 ♓ 16
90	♏ 3	♏ 25	♐ 12	27 ♐ 20	♒ 13	♈ 1	21 ♒ 30	8 ♌ 32	4 ♒ 12
91	♏ 20	♐ 12	♑ 2	24 ♑ 6	♓ 12	♈ 21	26 ♒ 38	24 ♎ 24	3 ♒ 40
92	♓ 2	♈ 5	♉ 19	1 ♋ 34	♋ 20	♌ 9	18 ♐ 47	20 ♏ 30	14 ♐ 30
93	♒ 0	♒ 24	♈ 4	29 ♉ 0	♊ 22	♋ 11	3 ♎ 0	24 ♓ 30	8 ♎ 52R
94	♑ 15	♒ 5	♓ 3	8 ♉ 0	♊ 9	♊ 28	22 ♐ 52	8 ♒ 49	5 ♑ 48R
95	♐ 28	♑ 15	♒ 8	23 ♓ 36	♉ 14	♊ 8	7 ♎ 54	12 ♋ 41	17 ♎ 0
96	♒ 15	♓ 13	♈ 29	21 ♊ 0	♋ 8	♋ 25	21 ♊ 30	5 ♉ 11	4 ♊ 6
97	♌ 28	♎ 1	♎ 24	9 ♏ 24	♐ 8	♑ 16	7 ♎ 57	29 ♌ 6	7 ♎ 55
98	♈ 9	♉ 18	♋ 0	2 ♌ 0	♌ 19	♍ 10	12 ♉ 21	8 ♈ 9	16 ♈ 48
99	♉ 4	♊ 14	♋ 20	19 ♌ 0	♍ 8	♎ 2	10 ♈ 55	8 ♑ 53	16 ♓ 56
100	♊ 19	♌ 1	♍ 1	23 ♍ 0	♎ 14	♏ 11	16 ♐ 0	17 ♊ 30	6 ♑ 30

	♀ ° ′	♂ ° ′	♃ ° ′	♄ ° ′	♅ ° ′	♆ ° ′	♇ ° ′
51	12 ♓ 0	9 ♍ 30 R	22 ♈ 0	20 ♈ 30	4 ♑ 30	3 ♑ 30	27 ♓ 30
52	23 ♊ 2	23 ♐ 48 R	22 ♎ 13	25 ♒ 22 R	13 ♌ 38	2 ♉ 50	23 ♉ 10
53	18 ♉ 10	3 ♌ 30	24 ♋ 36	5 ♊ 30	25 ♍ 30 R	19 ♉ 12	29 ♉ 29
54	19 ♈ 59	29 ♓ 56	10 ♈ 49	7 ♋ 30 R	21 ♉ 20	19 ♓ 30	3 ♉ 50
55	10 ♒ 13	25 ♐ 24	11 ♍ 6 R	7 ♈ 38	19 ♑ 15	14 ♋ 41 R	23 ♊ 51 R
56	17 ♊ 52	8 ♌ 43	15 ♈ 16	26 ♈ 30	5 ♍ 24	13 ♉ 21	27 ♉ 26
57	29 ♌ 55	12 ♏ 6	27 ♏ 8	11 ♌ 30	14 ♎ 30	2 ♊ 12	5 ♊ 40
58	17 ♏ 24	29 ♍ 27	1 ♊ 14 R	14 ♎ 54	9 ♏ 5	13 ♊ 30 R	10 ♊ 37 R
59	26 ♋ 40	25 ♍ 30	5 ♓ 30 R	17 ♏ 30	10 ♋ 30	15 ♈ 1 R	15 ♉ 59 R
60	3 ♌ 11	30 ♌ 0	2 ♌ 30	25 ♓ 0 R	22 ♈ 17	2 ♓ 0 R	27 ♈ 40
61	2 ♓ 0	2 ♈ 0	2 ♓ 0	29 ♑ 0	29 ♓ 19	21 ♒ 0	21 ♈ 0
62	2 ♓ 20 R	23 ♒ 40	28 ♑ 45	21 ♑ 21	20 ♐ 3	29 ♊ 3 R	16 ♊ 45 R
63	1 ♌ 37	0 ♍ 13	14 ♏ 27 R	13 ♉ 4	7 ♉ 2	11 ♓ 29	29 ♉ 10
64	7 ♒ 45	18 ♐ 10	5 ♈ 48	12 ♒ 0	4 ♈ 14	23 ♒ 40	22 ♈ 16
65	4 ♋ 13	22 ♑ 17	20 ♋ 13	19 ♌ 29	6 ♊ 43	28 ♓ 40	7 ♉ 10
66	7 ♈ 24	7 ♋ 12	14 ♐ 57 R	20 ♉ 12	3 ♒ 18	21 ♋ 4	27 ♊ 16
67	6 ♋ 44	7 ♊ 1	28 ♓ 30	8 ♋ 11	14 ♒ 32 R	29 ♋ 53	2 ♋ 11
68	24 ♒ 10	27 ♊ 47	18 ♉ 15	6 ♉ 54	17 ♍ 24	13 ♉ 54	27 ♉ 17
69	15 ♋ 8	8 ♒ 47 R	24 ♈ 54 R	28 ♍ 41	2 ♏ 39	11 ♊ 8	9 ♊ 37
70	25 ♊ 46	10 ♋ 24	4 ♋ 47	2 ♏ 49 R	17 ♏ 55 R	14 ♊ 30	10 ♊ 41
71	20 ♒ 50	8 ♍ 14	20 ♈ 26	19 ♈ 50	3 ♑ 14	2 ♑ 40	29 ♓ 0
72	28 ♋ 43	17 ♋ 16	21 ♊ 43	21 ♐ 58 R	24 ♋ 24	21 ♈ 42 R	18 ♉ 47 R
73	7 ♈ 30	0 ♈ 30	9 ♈ 30	17 ♈ 0	3 ♑ 30	3 ♑ 30 R	28 ♓ 30
74	13 ♌ 56 R	13 ♊ 30	28 ♎ 5	29 ♍ 51	13 ♎ 19	23 ♏ 30	8 ♓ 30
75	0 ♈ 23	0 ♊ 50	1 ♉ 4	9 ♎ 26 R	9 ♏ 53 R	8 ♊ 58	8 ♊ 1
76	27 ♉ 28	8 ♉ 25	22 ♈ 46	8 ♋ 30	23 ♉ 20	21 ♓ 23	4 ♉ 6
77	9 ♒ 58	0 ♈ 39	9 ♒ 46	1 ♈ 26	9 ♉ 48 R	20 ♍ 45 R	28 ♋ 21 R
78	5 ♌ 29	10 ♍ 38	26 ♏ 33	3 ♓ 28 R	22 ♌ 17	5 ♉ 0 R	22 ♉ 21
79	11 ♐ 9	21 ♍ 57	12 ♒ 50	24 ♑ 44	20 ♐ 49	2 ♋ 55 R	18 ♊ 20 R
80	23 ♌ 5	22 ♊ 38	15 ♐ 2 R	29 ♉ 43	12 ♉ 24	13 ♑ 19 R	2 ♉ 39
81	0 ♈ 49	15 ♑ 0	8 ♊ 8	4 ♓ 30	12 ♈ 30	28 ♒ 34	24 ♈ 30
82	23 ♏ 26	0 ♑ 42	24 ♑ 28	13 ♊ 27 R	14 ♉ 8 R	13 ♓ 10 R	1 ♉ 31 R
83	19 ♋ 30	26 ♌ 8	1 ♌ 1	12 ♊ 45	24 ♍ 1	21 ♉ 26	0 ♊ 36
84	11 ♐ 8 R	20 ♐ 1	27 ♊ 8 R	20 ♉ 37 R	23 ♍ 14	16 ♉ 33 R	28 ♉ 48 R
85	3 ♉ 54	15 ♌ 40	6 ♓ 4	19 ♏ 39 R	6 ♋ 39	14 ♈ 24	15 ♉ 0
86	0 ♎ 50	10 ♑ 13	5 ♊ 20 R	26 ♒ 16 R	1 ♑ 1	10 ♋ 24 R	22 ♊ 28 R
87	15 ♒ 43 R	21 ♉ 6	13 ♎ 15 R	20 ♈ 27	23 ♑ 42	16 ♋ 46	25 ♊ 25
88	25 ♓ 49	10 ♐ 27	21 ♓ 38	29 ♍ 16 R	6 ♏ 5 R	6 ♊ 16 R	6 ♊ 49
89	28 ♒ 52	0 ♑ 34	22 ♉ 55	25 ♎ 03 R	15 ♏ 20	10 ♊ 46	8 ♊ 47 R
90	20 ♓ 3 R	2 ♉ 0	4 ♉ 17	21 ♒ 30	7 ♈ 40	25 ♒ 30	23 ♈ 8
91	15 ♓ 34	16 ♎ 16	29 ♒ 5	3 ♒ 14	24 ♐ 50	1 ♋ 4 R	17 ♊ 40 R
92	3 ♑ 9	18 ♐ 0	29 ♎ 0	2 ♎ 30	16 ♎ 0	24 ♏ 30	7 ♓ 30
93	16 ♌ 50	15 ♍ 30	28 ♓ 26 R	0 ♒ 46 R	4 ♈ 23 R	21 ♒ 17 R	23 ♈ 30 R
94	16 ♏ 55	3 ♑ 19	8 ♐ 6	11 ♉ 47 R	4 ♉ 53 R	8 ♓ 52	29 ♈ 57 R
95	11 ♎ 30 R	15 ♉ 12 R	18 ♋ 25	7 ♓ 28 R	16 ♈ 36 R	28 ♒ 0 R	26 ♈ 30 R
96	7 ♉ 0	24 ♉ 30	5 ♑ 0 R	22 ♎ 0 R	22 ♎ 0 R	28 ♏ 30 R	12 ♓ 30 R
97	11 ♎ 57	6 ♏ 54	11 ♏ 37	18 ♐ 24	5 ♐ 2	27 ♊ 2 R	16 ♊ 34 R
98	29 ♈ 24 R	26 ♓ 24	17 ♑ 50 R	4 ♊ 11	7 ♒ 30	23 ♋ 30	28 ♊ 30
99	4 ♉ 2	1 ♒ 3	4 ♎ 35 R	10 ♒ 16	6 ♐ 46 R	20 ♐ 35	22 ♓ 30
100	19 ♑ 30	23 ♉ 0	20 ♓ 0	27 ♍ 30	15 ♒ 30	25 ♑ 30	9 ♈ 0

	10	11	12	Asc.	2	3	☉	☽	☿
	°	°	°	° ′	°	°	° ′	° ′	° ′
101	♍ 10	♎ 11	♏ 8	29 ♏ 47	♑ 0	♒ 5	9 ♓ 36	7 ♑ 59	13 ♓ 0
102	♍ 22	♎ 21	♏ 12	28 ♏ 0	♑ 1	♒ 13	23 ♓ 28	0 ♈ 30	26 ♒ 14
103	♓ 23	♉ 1	♊ 13	19 ♋ 0	♌ 6	♌ 26	18 ♌ 30	9 ♎ 15	9 ♍ 30
104	♑ 8	♒ 1	♒ 30	14 ♈ 19	♉ 22	♊ 17	6 ♌ 57	4 ♓ 31	28 ♍ 36
105	♐ 28	♑ 19	♒ 20	25 ♓ 1	♉ 9	♊ 6	15 ♍ 34	0 ♐ 54	9 ♎ 32
106	♏ 13	♐ 3	♐ 22	10 ♑ 20	♓ 2	♈ 18	25 ♓ 45	25 ♋ 16	28 ♒ 9
107	♓ 18	♈ 24	♊ 5	11 ♋ 2	♌ 1	♌ 21	18 ♌ 25	6 ♓ 50	9 ♌ 45
108	♐ 16	♑ 6	♑ 28	1 ♓ 50	♈ 22	♉ 24	7 ♓ 38	15 ♌ 57	11 ♒ 40
109	♓ 0	♈ 3	♉ 13	23 ♊ 6	♋ 14	♌ 5	21 ♏ 24	20 ♐ 55	12 ♐ 31
110	♋ 23	♌ 28	♍ 26	17 ♎ 0	♏ 13	♐ 16	18 ♓ 30	16 ♈ 44	21 ♒ 58
111	♉ 19	♊ 26	♌ 0	28 ♌ 0	♍ 19	♎ 15	6 ♎ 0	5 ♋ 30	4 ♎ 0
112	♏ 22	♐ 6	♐ 24	27 ♑ 30	♓ 27	♉ 4	10 ♒ 20	27 ♏ 1	11 ♒ 9
113	♎ 11	♏ 6	♏ 25	10 ♐ 0	♑ 15	♓ 3	19 ♓ 8	10 ♐ 30	26 ♓ 11
114	♐ 20	♑ 7	♑ 27	3 ♓ 8	♉ 3	♊ 1	7 ♓ 1	7 ♈ 30	23 ♓ 30
115	♊ 19	♋ 25	♌ 27	21 ♍ 30	♎ 14	♏ 14	3 ♈ 19	15 ♈ 56	18 ♈ 13
116	♑ 13	♒ 2	♓ 3	4 ♉ 0	♊ 7	♊ 26	4 ♑ 30	9 ♊ 45	0 ♑ 30
117	♓ 9	♈ 14	♉ 29	8 ♋ 35	♋ 26	♌ 15	8 ♉ 46	26 ♒ 41	23 ♉ 46
118	♓ 3	♈ 6	♉ 18	27 ♊ 20	♋ 17	♌ 8	5 ♌ 30	0 ♋ 30	2 ♍ 24
119	♌ 4	♍ 7	♎ 6	28 ♎ 49	♏ 28	♐ 30	23 ♊ 38	2 ♋ 22	15 ♋ 0
120	♍ 21	♎ 21	♏ 13	2 ♐ 0	♑ 4	♒ 13	18 ♑ 40	1 ♉ 46	16 ♑ 30
121	♈ 9	♉ 18	♋ 0	2 ♌ 0	♌ 19	♍ 10	1 ♌ 0	4 ♏ 56	28 ♌ 1
122	♑ 20	♒ 14	♓ 17	6 ♉ 3	♊ 7	♊ 29	20 ♌ 28	9 ♑ 2	24 ♌ 0
123	♈ 22	♉ 28	♋ 4	5 ♌ 0	♌ 25	♍ 20	8 ♌ 51	7 ♈ 49	4 ♍ 4
124	♑ 10	♑ 28	♒ 26	25 ♈ 25	♊ 3	♊ 23	16 ♉ 16	24 ♐ 14	21 ♈ 55
125	♑ 25	♒ 19	♓ 26	24 ♉ 45	♊ 20	♋ 8	18 ♓ 52	25 ♋ 30	2 ♈ 50
126	♏ 10	♐ 2	♐ 19	6 ♑ 55	♒ 25	♈ 10	16 ♒ 4	29 ♍ 50	28 ♑ 40
127	♓ 13	♈ 18	♊ 3	10 ♋ 43	♋ 29	♌ 18	7 ♈ 30	15 ♓ 43	9 ♓ 50
128	♉ 12	♊ 18	♋ 21	20 ♌ 30	♍ 12	♎ 9	7 ♏ 15	23 ♒ 22	21 ♏ 0
129	♉ 4	♊ 11	♋ 16	14 ♌ 30	♍ 7	♎ 2	13 ♍ 53	23 ♋ 30	1 ♍ 40
130	♌ 27	♍ 28	♎ 23	14 ♏ 26	♐ 14	♑ 18	16 ♍ 56	5 ♋ 5	9 ♍ 37
131	♎ 12	♏ 7	♏ 26	12 ♐ 20	♑ 20	♓ 5	0 ♏ 9	28 ♓ 45	15 ♎ 32
132	♓ 24	♉ 3	♊ 19	25 ♋ 0	♌ 10	♌ 28	23 ♏ 26	1 ♐ 30	25 ♏ 6
133	♓ 5	♈ 9	♉ 26	7 ♋ 0	♋ 24	♌ 12	22 ♌ 30	19 ♉ 20	11 ♍ 0
134	♊ 12	♋ 19	♌ 21	16 ♍ 8	♎ 7	♏ 5	1 ♉ 20	25 ♒ 57	16 ♈ 47
135	♍ 19	♎ 18	♏ 8	24 ♏ 18	♐ 26	♒ 8	6 ♌ 45	8 ♋ 4	20 ♌ 38
136	♓ 12	♈ 17	♊ 5	14 ♋ 30	♌ 1	♌ 18	10 ♊ 25	29 ♓ 45	17 ♉ 26
137	♏ 29	♐ 17	♑ 4	25 ♑ 15	♓ 25	♉ 5	11 ♌ 2	10 ♒ 14	2 ♌ 19
138	♓ 28	♉ 7	♊ 23	27 ♋ 30	♌ 13	♍ 2	0 ♉ 25	10 ♋ 30	3 ♈ 30
139	♓ 9	♈ 13	♉ 23	1 ♋ 30	♋ 21	♌ 13	29 ♉ 17	22 ♎ 45	14 ♉ 21
140	♊ 28	♌ 5	♍ 5	28 ♍ 30	♎ 21	♏ 21	15 ♓ 17	11 ♎ 15	7 ♓ 31
141	♎ 13	♏ 9	♏ 27	11 ♐ 55	♑ 20	♓ 7	17 ♉ 4	1 ♈ 37	21 ♉ 44
142	♎ 22	♏ 17	♐ 8	26 ♐ 0	♒ 5	♓ 17	18 ♓ 30	18 ♍ 15	26 ♒ 44
143	♒ 8	♓ 7	♈ 13	23 ♉ 37	♊ 20	♋ 14	9 ♐ 34	15 ♉ 37	15 ♐ 12
144	♓ 14	♈ 20	♊ 7	15 ♋ 56	♌ 2	♌ 20	3 ♉ 9	10 ♐ 40	8 ♈ 55
145	♉ 16	♊ 24	♋ 28	25 ♌ 47	♍ 17	♎ 13	11 ♍ 31	24 ♑ 2	8 ♎ 11
146	♒ 18	♓ 17	♉ 4	24 ♊ 30	♋ 11	♋ 28	4 ♐ 30	2 ♌ 52	25 ♐ 30
147	♋ 3	♌ 6	♍ 5	2 ♎ 38	♎ 29	♏ 29	2 ♑ 1	29 ♑ 45	16 ♐ 5
148	♒ 11	♓ 10	♈ 19	3 ♊ 10	♊ 27	♋ 18	29 ♓ 15	27 ♒ 8	16 ♈ 58
149	10 ♑	♒ 3	♓ 4	17 ♈ 44	♉ 23	♊ 18	21 ♊ 21	28 ♊ 9	9 ♋ 17
150	♍ 15	♎ 15	♏ 9	28 ♏ 41	♑ 0	♒ 7	17 ♓ 32	7 ♍ 13	26 ♒ 47

	♀	♂	♃	♄	♅	♆	♇
	° ′	° ′	° ′	° ′	° ′	° ′	° ′
101	25 ♒ 0 R	18 ♍ 19 R	4 ♎ 0 R	1 ♋ 27 R	7 ♎ 0 R	23 ♉ 0	1 ♊ 6
102	9 ♓ 0	16 ♌ 15 R	19 ♈ 8	17 ♐ 2	13 ♋ 24 R	16 ♈ 8	15 ♉ 20
103	2 ♎ 30	2 ♍ 45	17 ♒ 14 R	3 ♍ 0	12 ♒ 16 R	22 ♑ 55 R	10 ♈ 30 R
104	9 ♎ 39	6 ♈ 23 R	21 ♍ 59	22 ♈ 41 R	17 ♑ 25	18 ♋ 35	26 ♊ 36
105	29 ♍ 40	6 ♊ 32	21 ♏ 57	16 ♎ 47	29 ♊ 14	7 ♈ 32 R	13 ♉ 3 R
106	23 ♒ 15	18 ♎ 55 R	18 ♓ 0	23 ♊ 32	17 ♉ 59	18 ♓ 10	2 ♉ 53
107	17 ♋ 44	15 ♈ 50	27 ♍ 18	21 ♍ 17	19 ♊ 53	3 ♈ 30 R	11 ♉ 15
108	20 ♒ 4	27 ♐ 45	29 ♐ 36	10 ♓ 20	22 ♌ 1 R	3 ♉ 5	22 ♉ 37
109	24 ♎ 11	17 ♏ 36	27 ♈ 54 R	7 ♎ 5	18 ♒ 45	27 ♑ 0	11 ♈ 30
110	14 ♒ 24	20 ♎ 28 R	16 ♓ 11	23 ♊ 16	17 ♉ 43	17 ♓ 52	2 ♉ 53
111	20 ♌ 0	4 ♏ 30	16 ♓ 0 R	10 ♈ 30 R	25 ♐ 30	28 ♐ 0	28 ♓ 0
112	5 ♓ 30 R	19 ♐ 59	21 ♉ 45	25 ♎ 10	15 ♏ 12	10 ♊ 55 R	8 ♊ 49 R
113	18 ♒ 53	16 ♊ 20	14 ♐ 37	15 ♉ 53	2 ♒ 4	21 ♋ 7	26 ♊ 56
114	13 ♈ 2	24 ♒ 6	17 ♓ 13	5 ♐ 27	9 ♋ 1 R	13 ♈ 25	14 ♉ 4
115	13 ♉ 56	0 ♑ 19	15 ♋ 29	19 ♌ 51 R	4 ♊ 30	27 ♓ 4	7 ♉ 15
116	5 ♑ 0	24 ♑ 30	27 ♉ 30 R	3 ♉ 30 R	7 ♑ 30	4 ♑ 30	28 ♓ 30
117	3 ♉ 26	16 ♌ 0	9 ♌ 3	14 ♒ 15 R	7 ♓ 43	8 ♒ 10	16 ♈ 0
118	21 ♊ 22	18 ♏ 22	1 ♊ 25	1 ♓ 18 R	0 ♑ 56 R	8 ♋ 57	22 ♊ 12
119	22 ♋ 0	30 ♊ 0	23 ♍ 0	14 ♒ 0 R	9 ♌ 0	0 ♉ 11	20 ♉ 10
120	3 ♓ 30	1 ♐ 56	27 ♍ 30	22 ♍ 30 R	13 ♊ 4 R	29 ♓ 6	8 ♉ 30
121	15 ♊ 30	3 ♍ 30	4 ♉ 0	24 ♍ 13	21 ♒ 30 R	28 ♑ 0 R	13 ♈ 30 R
122	27 ♌ 0	7 ♏ 0	9 ♈ 0 R	10 ♋ 0	25 ♉ 0	20 ♓ 0 R	5 ♉ 32
123	17 ♍ 37	5 ♊ 6	25 ♑ 48 R	6 ♏ 4	6 ♋ 15	12 ♈ 47 R	15 ♉ 1
124	1 ♊ 57 R	16 ♋ 32	20 ♈ 8	21 ♍ 29	22 ♒ 24	29 ♑ 23 R	11 ♈ 47
125	4 ♉ 30	14 ♏ 20	23 ♌ 43 R	29 ♑ 30	2 ♌ 12 R	24 ♈ 40	18 ♉ 56
126	8 ♑ 47	2 ♊ 10	10 ♐ 59	13 ♉ 44	0 ♒ 22	21 ♋ 45 R	27 ♊ 12 R
127	1 ♓ 6	25 ♑ 20	20 ♍ 30 R	17 ♍ 53 R	12 ♊ 58	1 ♈ 34	9 ♉ 5
128	25 ♍ 20	24 ♒ 30	17 ♈ 35	7 ♎ 26	6 ♏ 26	10 ♊ 40 R	9 ♊ 10 R
129	17 ♎ 29	13 ♍ 24	1 ♊ 11	11 ♎ 58	7 ♏ 51	13 ♊ 32	10 ♊ 40 R
130	2 ♏ 55	4 ♋ 4	13 ♎ 20	6 ♐ 25	29 ♏ 59	24 ♊ 33 R	15 ♊ 35 R
131	15 ♍ 5	3 ♎ 4	25 ♓ 14 R	0 ♒ 58	3 ♈ 16 R	20 ♒ 55 R	22 ♈ 47 R
132	2 ♐ 30	4 ♒ 54	5 ♋ 30 R	25 ♐ 6	19 ♏ 30	10 ♐ 30	16 ♓ 30
133	13 ♋ 30	9 ♒ 30 R	25 ♈ 0 R	28 ♍ 22	2 ♏ 30	11 ♊ 5	9 ♊ 30
134	4 ♈ 34	28 ♊ 35	5 ♏ 47 R	22 ♒ 0 R	10 ♐ 49 R	21 ♐ 53 R	23 ♓ 30
135	12 ♍ 16	11 ♍ 56	4 ♑ 37 R	17 ♓ 30R	16 ♐ 25 R	24 ♐ 3 R	26 ♓ 30 R
136	11 ♉ 31	28 ♊ 23	15 ♓ 57	10 ♍ 39	27 ♎ 47 R	6 ♊ 40	7 ♊ 21
137	24 ♍ 14	14 ♋ 53	28 ♎ 24	28 ♋ 6	9 ♎ 21	29 ♉ 50	4 ♊ 45
138	13 ♊ 30	6 ♑ 30	11 ♏ 0 R	14 ♋ 30	2 ♒ 12	18 ♑ 30	6 ♈ 30
139	27 ♈ 30	20 ♊ 30	14 ♓ 30	10 ♍ 20	28 ♎ 10 R	6 ♊ 43	7 ♊ 3
140	28 ♓ 30 R	9 ♓ 32	4 ♑ 33	27 ♎ 49 R	25 ♎ 6 R	0 ♐ 30 R	11 ♓ 30
141	1 ♋ 13	11 ♊ 6	4 ♋ 20	7 ♑ 42 R	21 ♏ 35 R	12 ♐ 42 R	19 ♓ 30
142	4 ♉ 33	6 ♒ 31	13 ♌ 53 R	26 ♓ 52	20 ♈ 23	3 ♓ 30	26 ♈ 30
143	22 ♎ 53	22 ♑ 36	14 ♓ 26	5 ♒ 9	24 ♐ 52	5 ♋ 14 R	19 ♊ 50 R
144	17 ♓ 12	18 ♒ 27	4 ♊ 20	20 ♎ 57 R	13 ♏ 46 R	11 ♊ 49	9 ♊ 23
145	21 ♍ 33	17 ♏ 14	3 ♌ 34	7 ♊ 38	11 ♑ 54 R	6 ♑ 52 R	1 ♈ 30 R
146	21 ♑ 30	8 ♍ 48	1 ♎ 30	7 ♋ 10 R	6 ♎ 30	23 ♉ 51 R	1 ♊ 58 R
147	1 ♐ 10	10 ♍ 15	24 ♐ 13	6 ♑ 47	13 ♐ 52	27 ♊ 42 R	16 ♊ 16 R
148	9 ♉ 1	28 ♐ 4	15 ♋ 19	20 ♌ 3 R	4 ♊ 22	26 ♓ 55	8 ♉ 55
149	26 ♉ 51	13 ♉ 34	26 ♓ 30	3 ♋ 55	15 ♒ 28 R	28 ♋ 45	1 ♋ 5
150	3 ♉ 46	5 ♒ 50	14 ♌ 0 R	26 ♓ 43	20 ♈ 19	3 ♓ 1	25 ♈ 45

	10	11	12	Asc.	2	3	☉	☽	☿
	°	°	°	° ′	°	°	° ′	° ′	° ′
151	♉ 11	♊ 15	♋ 18	17 ♌ 16	♍ 10	♎ 8	11 ♉ 7	28 ♑ 8	17 ♈ 7
152	♈ 29	♊ 9	♋ 17	17 ♌ 0	♍ 4	♍ 28	7 ♐ 47	20 ♌ 30	29 ♏ 0
153	♌ 14	♍ 17	♎ 13	2 ♏ 30	♐ 0	♑ 4	20 ♏ 38	14 ♒ 32	28 ♏ 52
154	♊ 10	♋ 14	♌ 15	12 ♍ 44	♎ 7	♏ 6	13 ♈ 53	25 ♓ 5	2 ♈ 21
155	♒ 7	♓ 3	♈ 16	12 ♊ 30	♋ 2	♋ 19	29 ♒ 1	12 ♉ 30	2 ♒ 30
156	♌ 20	♍ 23	♎ 18	7 ♏ 30	♐ 6	♑ 11	29 ♓ 0	11 ♎ 5	9 ♈ 0R
157	♓ 17	♈ 23	♊ 2	9 ♋ 3	♋ 28	♌ 20	12 ♈ 37	19 ♉ 38	16 ♓ 4
158	♏ 0	♏ 25	♐ 16	8 ♑ 30	♒ 17	♓ 27	2 ♏ 41	6 ♋ 40	15 ♏ 59
159	♑ 3	♑ 22	♒ 17	8 ♈ 0	♉ 22	15 ♊	17 ♐ 40	5 ♈ 39	0 ♐ 32
160	♑ 28	♒ 24	♈ 0	15 ♉ 18	♊ 14	♋ 6	24 ♈ 6	4 ♒ 22	29 ♈ 5R
161	♓ 12	♈ 19	♊ 10	19 ♋ 0	♌ 3	♌ 19	15 ♍ 20	10 ♌ 5	5 ♎ 9
162	♎ 15	♏ 12	♐ 3	23 ♐ 15	♒ 0	♓ 10	27 ♏ 50	26 ♍ 35	25 ♏ 47
163	♊ 15	♋ 19	♌ 20	17 ♍ 30	♎ 13	♏ 13	12 ♒ 0	14 ♓ 40	20 ♑ 1
164	♈ 24	♉ 27	♊ 29	29 ♋ 0	♌ 24	♍ 22	7 ♊ 49	13 ♌ 9	0 ♋ 17
165	♐ 0	♐ 21	♑ 12	8 ♒ 30	♓ 27	♉ 4	15 ♍ 7	28 ♏ 40	23 ♍ 4R
166	♏ 1	♏ 26	♐ 17	8 ♑ 0	♒ 18	♓ 29	4 ♎ 56	22 ♈ 14	26 ♎ 30
167	♑ 1	♑ 18	♒ 13	1 ♈ 0	♉ 18	♊ 12	16 ♊ 35	16 ♍ 0	12 ♊ 0
168	♑ 7	♑ 26	♒ 23	18 ♈ 0	♉ 28	♊ 19	7 ♑ 9	16 ♈ 18	19 ♑ 30
169	♑ 15	♒ 6	♓ 7	6 ♉ 0	♊ 8	♊ 27	17 ♊ 0	27 ♐ 30	4 ♊ 0
170	♌ 1	♍ 6	♎ 2	21 ♎ 47	♏ 18	♐ 21	2 ♐ 18	8 ♒ 28	12 ♏ 28
171	♏ 23	♐ 13	♑ 2	25 ♑ 0	♓ 15	♈ 26	19 ♌ 0	20 ♐ 7	2 ♍ 32
172	♉ 7	♊ 7	♋ 13	18 ♌ 0	♍ 16	♎ 11	21 ♎ 53	19 ♐ 0	8 ♏ 8
173	♐ 14	♑ 5	♑ 29	2 ♓ 10	♈ 17	♉ 20	19 ♐ 26	8 ♏ 1	0 ♐ 6
174	♑ 4	♑ 25	♒ 21	7 ♈ 0	♉ 19	♊ 13	7 ♋ 13	23 ♌ 15	27 ♋ 25
175	♎ 3	♏ 0	♏ 18	4 ♐ 0	♑ 9	♒ 24	6 ♒ 30	3 ♐ 30	12 ♑ 30
176	♋ 22	♌ 27	♍ 25	17 ♎ 0	♏ 13	♐ 14	12 ♒ 0	7 ♉ 30	7 ♒ 30
177	♒ 20	♓ 20	♉ 2	15 ♊ 0	♋ 6	♋ 27	23 ♊ 6	24 ♊ 14	14 ♋ 5
178	♓ 7	♈ 11	♉ 22	0 ♋ 4	♋ 21	♌ 12	6 ♓ 59	13 ♒ 7	10 ♓ 20
179	♍ 19	♎ 20	♏ 15	4 ♐ 55	♑ 7	♒ 13	4 ♊ 2	19 ♑ 32	1 ♊ 33
180	♋ 12	♌ 15	♍ 15	9 ♎ 42	♏ 6	♐ 7	10 ♎ 38	21 ♓ 36	22 ♍ 54
181	♓ 24	♉ 4	♊ 18	22 ♋ 40	♌ 10	♌ 30	15 ♋ 57	4 ♉ 42	8 ♌ 30
182	♌ 18	♍ 21	♎ 17	9 ♏ 37	♐ 8	♑ 12	19 ♍ 24	2 ♌ 51	1 ♍ 56
183	♋ 20	♌ 26	♍ 24	14 ♎ 20	♏ 9	♐ 11	12 ♐ 4	0 ♋ 1	2 ♑ 50
184	♉ 18	♊ 22	♋ 25	25 ♌ 23	♍ 17	♎ 15	28 ♓ 23	12 ♉ 25	11 ♓ 43
185	♌ 12	♍ 16	♎ 13	4 ♏ 30	♐ 3	♑ 6	28 ♑ 18	13 ♓ 15	5 ♑ 10
186	♒ 22	♓ 23	♉ 10	28 ♊ 16	♋ 15	♌ 2	15 ♋ 53	12 ♉ 55	1 ♋ 3
187	♏ 2	♏ 20	♐ 8	25 ♐ 6	♒ 8	♓ 20	27 ♓ 33	20 ♉ 7	29 ♒ 53
188	♏ 15	♐ 8	♐ 29	22 ♑ 46	♓ 6	♈ 15	6 ♒ 51	16 ♏ 7	28 ♑ 9R
189	♑ 28	♒ 23	♈ 29	15 ♉ 31	♊ 14	♋ 6	11 ♈ 31	20 ♑ 26	27 ♓ 3
190	♋ 15	♌ 19	♍ 8	13 ♎ 50	♏ 9	♐ 10	24 ♑ 0	3 ♊ 30	7 ♑ 30
191	♈ 28	♊ 7	♋ 15	15 ♌ 30	♍ 3	♍ 26	26 ♈ 40	4 ♏ 29	17 ♈ 9
192	♊ 20	♋ 25	♌ 26	21 ♍ 30	♎ 16	♏ 16	16 ♏ 30	12 ♒ 37	24 ♏ 3R
193	♋ 3	♌ 10	♍ 9	2 ♎ 0	♎ 26	♏ 26	22 ♋ 30	7 ♑ 14	16 ♌ 13
194	♋ 20	♌ 22	♍ 22	18 ♎ 30	♏ 16	♐ 17	24 ♌ 8	29 ♋ 36	5 ♌ 31
195	♈ 13	♉ 22	♋ 3	5 ♌ 15	♌ 22	♍ 14	22 ♏ 25	0 ♉ 27	6 ♏ 57
196	♍ 1	♎ 3	♎ 26	13 ♏ 28	♐ 13	♑ 21	16 ♏ 22	16 ♓ 52	2 ♐ 6
197	♏ 10	♐ 11	♑ 1	23 ♑ 47	♓ 9	♈ 19	17 ♈ 58	24 ♉ 9	6 ♉ 6
198	♈ 29	♊ 5	♋ 10	10 ♌ 31	♍ 1	♍ 27	3 ♑ 29	29 ♋ 33	14 ♐ 27
199	♈ 14	♉ 17	♊ 20	19 ♋ 0	♌ 14	♍ 12	20 ♌ 46	25 ♒ 29	12 ♍ 55
200	♌ 6	♍ 10	♎ 7	28 ♎ 27	♏ 26	♐ 29	24 ♒ 20	19 ♊ 51	26 ♒ 52

	♀	♂	♃	♄	♅	♆	♇
	° ′	° ′	° ′	° ′	° ′	° ′	° ′
151	5 ♈ 41	6 ♌ 52	4 ♏ 34 R	23 ♐ 0 R	7 ♐ 3 R	22 ♊ 56	14 ♊ 20
152	28 ♎ 3	22 ♌ 37	18 ♌ 4	11 ♏ 30	1 ♓ 0	4 ♒ 0	15 ♈ 0
153	27 ♐ 37	0 ♒ 1	19 ♊ 44 R	12 ♌ 14	1 ♊ 56 R	22 ♓ 15 R	6 ♉ 22 R
154	2 ♈ 14	9 ♌ 0	8 ♌ 5 R	16 ♏ 0	6 ♓ 38	8 ♒ 0	15 ♈ 30
155	13 ♓ 10	14 ♉ 12	6 ♒ 30	28 ♌ 20 R	11 ♒ 30	23 ♑ 48	8 ♈ 30
156	12 ♓ 30	14 ♓ 30	4 ♈ 30	14 ♈ 30	3 ♑ 0	3 ♑ 0	27 ♓ 30
157	3 ♓ 15	28 ♑ 54	20 ♍ 1 R	17 ♍ 30 R	13 ♊ 8	1 ♈ 44	9 ♉ 12
158	0 ♐ 21	1 ♑ 37	7 ♐ 40	19 ♌ 9	18 ♎ 24	1 ♊ 40 R	5 ♊ 25 R
159	1 ♏ 32	20 ♈ 26	2 ♏ 15	8 ♒ 36	7 ♐ 50	18 ♐ 30	20 ♓ 30
160	24 ♉ 48	19 ♒ 37	4 ♓ 3	8 ♈ 6	0 ♍ 19 R	8 ♉ 53	25 ♉ 10
161	3 ♌ 8	12 ♋ 0	8 ♌ 0	2 ♏ 5	2 ♓ 3 R	3 ♒ 36 R	15 ♈ 0 R
162	20 ♎ 25	21 ♐ 32	26 ♈ 59 R	0 ♌ 33	16 ♒ 02	4 ♌ 51 R	2 ♋ 29
163	14 ♓ 1	4 ♐ 30	19 ♓ 30	29 ♍ 42 R	6 ♏ 3 R	6 ♊ 19 R	6 ♊ 54 R
164	18 ♋ 50	22 ♋ 33	8 ♋ 45	1 ♏ 32 R	17 ♏ 6 R	15 ♊ 12	11 ♊ 5
165	15 ♎ 37	21 ♒ 7 R	10 ♉ 44 R	13 ♒ 31 R	9 ♈ 12 R	23 ♒ 58 R	24 ♈ 32 R
166	5 ♎ 30 R	6 ♎ 20	0 ♏ 30	8 ♎ 9	25 ♊ 8	4 ♈ 42 R	11 ♉ 50 R
167	3 ♊ 30	8 ♊ 30	10 ♏ 30 R	18 ♐ 37 R	20 ♓ 30	15 ♒ 0 R	19 ♈ 0
168	28 ♑ 30	12 ♓ 4	26 ♒ 6	25 ♑ 46	28 ♓ 30	19 ♒ 38	20 ♈ 55
169	1 ♊ 3	28 ♓ 5	7 ♋ 5	7 ♌ 0	23 ♍ 19	15 ♏ 0 R	5 ♓ 30 R
170	15 ♐ 11	9 ♐ 8	15 ♋ 8 R	0 ♏ 17	26 ♒ 50	1 ♒ 31	14 ♈ 30
171	12 ♍ 0	11 ♎ 0	27 ♌ 0	11 ♏ 6	7 ♓ 15 R	6 ♒ 29 R	17 ♈ 0 R
172	3 ♐ 51	8 ♎ 31	0 ♊ 23 R	16 ♎ 38	9 ♏ 53	13 ♊ 20 R	10 ♊ 25 R
173	3 ♏ 0	3 ♎ 0	23 ♏ 25	6 ♌ 1 R	16 ♎ 28	28 ♉ 6 R	3 ♊ 44 R
174	22 ♉ 42	0 ♏ 52	28 ♌ 27	1 ♒ 2 R	4 ♌ 24	28 ♈ 17	18 ♉ 19
175	23 ♐ 30	26 ♐ 0	28 ♒ 20	14 ♍ 14 R	14 ♒ 30	25 ♑ 30	9 ♈ 30
176	26 ♒ 0	0 ♓ 30	5 ♏ 30	17 ♋ 19 R	12 ♎ 24 R	25 ♉ 2	2 ♊ 1 R
177	21 ♋ 11	29 ♊ 14	22 ♍ 50	13 ♒ 51 R	8 ♌ 4	0 ♉ 10	21 ♉ 51
178	23 ♈ 28	12 ♏ 2	25 ♌ 10 R	28 ♑ 28	2 ♌ 34 R	24 ♈ 19	18 ♉ 48
179	19 ♉ 14	27 ♓ 55	21 ♏ 15 R	11 ♎ 38 R	23 ♊ 58	7 ♈ 47	12 ♉ 30
180	25 ♌ 0	14 ♏ 6	27 ♌ 25	24 ♊ 14	29 ♍ 19	22 ♉ 58 R	1 ♊ 53
181	19 ♌ 30	15 ♋ 0	25 ♍ 0	13 ♒ 0 R	9 ♌ 30	0 ♉ 30	22 ♉ 10
182	6 ♎ 44	24 ♉ 50	6 ♓ 11	14 ♈ 5 R	5 ♍ 33	11 ♉ 52 R	24 ♉ 30
183	21 ♏ 57	5 ♐ 15	4 ♑ 2	7 ♏ 30	2 ♋ 47 R	7 ♈ 51 R	12 ♉ 40 R
184	15 ♓ 43	11 ♑ 14	2 ♑ 2	12 ♓ 47	21 ♌ 16 R	3 ♉ 9	23 ♉ 51
185	6 ♒ 21	29 ♍ 20	18 ♎ 22	7 ♐ 29	10 ♓ 7	9 ♒ 42	14 ♈ 30
186	10 ♌ 52 R	1 ♊ 3	24 ♋ 39	28 ♎ 37	4 ♓ 10	5 ♒ 8 R	16 ♈ 0 R
187	14 ♓ 5	15 ♌ 43 R	20 ♈ 4	17 ♐ 6	13 ♋ 23 R	16 ♈ 17	15 ♉ 20
188	22 ♓ 21	12 ♊ 14	8 ♍ 38 R	29 ♏ 18	28 ♏ 29	17 ♊ 47 R	11 ♊ 45 R
189	29 ♒ 14	15 ♓ 3	24 ♊ 33	23 ♉ 31	20 ♍ 27 R	17 ♉ 10	28 ♉ 37
190	22 ♐ 30	23 ♑ 30	20 ♓ 30	8 ♈ 0	0 ♑ 30	1 ♑ 30	27 ♓ 30
191	18 ♉ 2 R	13 ♉ 20	8 ♑ 10	13 ♌ 30	19 ♎ 40 R	0 ♊ 30	4 ♊ 35
192	0 ♑ 42	21 ♎ 30	21 ♍ 40	20 ♍ 11	15 ♊ 28 R	29 ♓ 5 R	9 ♉ 10 R
193	3 ♋ 0	13 ♍ 36	7 ♓ 0 R	17 ♏ 30 R	9 ♋ 30	15 ♈ 5	15 ♉ 50
194	2 ♎ 47	23 ♋ 44	0 ♏ 9	29 ♋ 50	9 ♎ 59	0 ♊ 1	4 ♊ 49
195	16 ♎ 32	20 ♐ 57	29 ♐ 55	5 ♍ 16	29 ♊ 55 R	14 ♎ 8	16 ♌ 33
196	29 ♐ 50	22 ♑ 16	5 ♎ 38	5 ♋ 43 R	20 ♑ 49	12 ♑ 30	3 ♈ 30
197	14 ♉ 36 R	24 ♏ 55 R	7 ♉ 1	29 ♒ 34	4 ♑ 14	5 ♋ 31	19 ♊ 53
198	19 ♒ 22	25 ♏ 12	22 ♉ 14 R	23 ♎ 40	15 ♏ 0	11 ♊ 35 R	9 ♊ 10 R
199	8 ♌ 39	13 ♌ 31	14 ♋ 27	16 ♌ 33	7 ♊ 24	26 ♓ 38 R	8 ♉ 26 R
200	8 ♑ 17	11 ♋ 19 R	16 ♒ 56	23 ♏ 52	4 ♋ 39 R	10 ♈ 52	13 ♉ 13

	10 °	11 °	12 °	Asc. ° ′	2 °	3 °	☉ ° ′	☽ ° ′	☿ ° ′
201	♊ 4	♋ 12	♌ 15	10 ♍ 30	♎ 2	♎ 29	3 ♓ 26	11 ♎ 58	20 ♒ 52
202	♓ 22	♉ 1	♊ 20	25 ♋ 0	♌ 9	♌ 27	17 ♈ 57	18 ♉ 37	23 ♈ 18
203	♋ 6	♌ 11	♍ 11	5 ♎ 0	♎ 29	♐ 0	24 ♈ 30	3 ♍ 30	29 ♓ 30
204	♊ 15	♋ 17	♌ 17	16 ♍ 7	♎ 14	♏ 15	29 ♌ 23	22 ♑ 50	18 ♍ 20
205	♈ 12	♉ 18	♊ 24	26 ♋ 59	♌ 17	♍ 11	12 ♈ 40	25 ♒ 27	15 ♓ 21
206	♏ 25	♐ 13	♑ 0	19 ♑ 50	♓ 17	♈ 29	8 ♐ 7	4 ♍ 31	17 ♏ 45
207	♓ 0	♈ 3	♉ 13	23 ♊ 6	♋ 14	♌ 5	23 ♎ 7	0 ♍ 20	27 ♎ 40
208	♉ 21	♊ 27	♋ 30	27 ♌ 26	♍ 20	♎ 17	8 ♋ 1	1 ♋ 57	20 ♊ 32
209	♒ 28	♈ 0	♉ 14	27 ♊ 0	♋ 16	♌ 5	5 ♎ 35	15 ♓ 15	19 ♎ 45
210	♓ 20	♈ 26	♊ 6	11 ♋ 30	♌ 1	♌ 23	27 ♓ 53	17 ♌ 30	5 ♓ 12
211	♐ 2	♐ 19	♑ 4	24 ♑ 11	♈ 0	♉ 9	21 ♏ 39	3 ♑ 23	11 ♏ 37
212	♓ 22	♈ 27	♊ 6	10 ♋ 4	♌ 1	♌ 24	2 ♋ 15	24 ♋ 17	21 ♊ 42
213	♎ 23	♏ 15	♐ 2	18 ♐ 0	♑ 29	♓ 18	12 ♐ 0	27 ♌ 0	26 ♏ 0
214	♉ 25	♋ 3	♌ 7	3 ♍ 45	♍ 24	♎ 21	20 ♒ 44	0 ♓ 10	25 ♑ 7
215	♍ 4	♎ 5	♎ 28	16 ♏ 0	♐ 15	♑ 24	11 ♐ 30	12 ♏ 3	18 ♐ 30
216	♑ 29	♒ 25	♓ 2	21 ♉ 20	♊ 18	♋ 8	16 ♒ 53	10 ♉ 14	24 ♒ 31
217	♓ 13	♈ 19	♊ 10	19 ♋ 5	♌ 3	♌ 20	4 ♋ 19	29 ♓ 28	19 ♋ 30
218	♓ 12	♈ 18	♊ 4	13 ♋ 30	♋ 29	♌ 18	10 ♉ 30	6 ♑ 40	25 ♉ 12
219	♉ 29	♋ 3	♌ 5	3 ♍ 5	♍ 27	♎ 26	27 ♊ 34	24 ♈ 20	5 ♊ 24
220	♊ 19	♋ 21	♌ 22	18 ♍ 57	♎ 16	♏ 16	2 ♏ 11	8 ♒ 11	22 ♏ 55
221	♊ 2	♋ 8	♌ 10	6 ♍ 42	♎ 0	♎ 29	12 ♋ 49	29 ♊ 53	23 ♋ 56
222	♍ 26	♎ 26	♏ 21	11 ♐ 51	♑ 14	♒ 20	22 ♍ 11	9 ♋ 27	18 ♎ 6
223	♏ 29	♐ 20	♑ 11	6 ♒ 56	♓ 25	♉ 2	17 ♏ 41	11 ♈ 12	8 ♐ 31
224	♓ 3	♈ 6	♉ 16	24 ♊ 25	♋ 15	♌ 7	23 ♉ 58	6 ♎ 36	29 ♈ 47
225	♏ 8	♏ 29	♐ 18	6 ♑ 29	♒ 22	♈ 7	7 ♓ 30	0 ♈ 3	10 ♒ 35
226	♐ 3	♐ 24	♑ 16	14 ♒ 33	♓ 29	♉ 5	7 ♑ 14	16 ♉ 13	20 ♑ 31
227	♌ 28	♎ 1	♎ 25	12 ♏ 25	♐ 12	♑ 20	24 ♐ 3	13 ♊ 34	5 ♐ 50
228	♒ 11	♓ 9	♈ 19	3 ♊ 28	♊ 29	♋ 19	24 ♈ 59	26 ♋ 20	2 ♈ 11
229	♒ 18	♓ 18	♈ 27	10 ♊ 10	♋ 4	♋ 25	26 ♌ 14	17 ♍ 9	20 ♍ 45
230	♊ 22	♋ 29	♌ 29	24 ♍ 0	♎ 16	♏ 15	0 ♎ 37	28 ♌ 05	17 ♍ 30
231	♍ 18	♎ 17	♏ 9	25 ♏ 0	♐ 27	♒ 8	26 ♊ 30	14 ♒ 30	9 ♊ 21
232	♋ 8	♌ 12	♍ 12	6 ♎ 0	♏ 2	♐ 3	12 ♉ 9	20 ♐ 22	26 ♉ 23
233	♌ 4	♍ 7	♎ 6	29 ♎ 30	♏ 27	♐ 29	16 ♐ 0	11 ♓ 9	6 ♑ 12
234	♑ 2	♑ 19	♒ 13	4 ♈ 5	♉ 22	♊ 14	23 ♉ 52	6 ♋ 26	15 ♊ 48
235	♏ 13	♐ 1	♐ 15	0 ♑ 28	♒ 24	♓ 14	16 ♍ 14	16 ♒ 44	29 ♌ 51
236	♏ 12	♐ 6	♐ 25	17 ♑ 25	♓ 1	♈ 13	9 ♉ 40	3 ♉ 56	26 ♉ 52
237	♓ 27	♉ 6	♊ 20	25 ♋ 0	♌ 11	♍ 1	14 ♏ 56	21 ♓ 9	6 ♐ 48
238	♌ 17	♍ 21	♎ 14	1 ♏ 20	♏ 27	♑ 4	23 ♒ 26	8 ♒ 30	29 ♑ 4
239	♈ 11	♉ 21	♋ 4	5 ♌ 0	♌ 22	♍ 12	21 ♑ 12	14 ♈ 4	29 ♐ 57
240	♉ 2	♊ 9	♋ 15	13 ♌ 56	♍ 5	♍ 30	7 ♊ 51	8 ♓ 1	21 ♊ 41
241	♍ 0	♎ 2	♎ 28	19 ♏ 11	♐ 19	♑ 23	7 ♋ 27	23 ♏ 26	19 ♊ 27
242	♊ 12	♋ 17	♌ 18	15 ♍ 0	♎ 9	♏ 8	27 ♊ 31	21 ♈ 5	5 ♊ 21
243	♈ 1	♉ 6	♊ 14	17 ♋ 28	♌ 8	♍ 1	20 ♉ 13	2 ♈ 36	23 ♉ 28
244	♑ 19	♒ 13	♓ 16	5 ♉ 0	♊ 6	♊ 28	21 ♓ 15	14 ♐ 50	24 ♒ 8
245	♌ 22	♍ 24	♎ 21	13 ♏ 0	♐ 12	♑ 16	28 ♈ 52	17 ♒ 10	7 ♉ 59
246	♊ 15	♋ 19	♌ 20	16 ♍ 55	♎ 12	♏ 11	23 ♌ 27	2 ♐ 2	5 ♌ 34
247	♊ 9	♋ 15	♌ 17	13 ♍ 0	♎ 6	♏ 5	24 ♌ 30	23 ♋ 2	6 ♍ 30
248	♌ 23	♍ 26	♎ 21	12 ♏ 0	♐ 11	♑ 16	23 ♉ 0	23 ♎ 0	28 ♈ 30
249	♈ 11	♉ 20	♋ 0	2 ♌ 0	♌ 20	♍ 12	24 ♏ 43	0 ♌ 2	5 ♐ 30
250	♊ 0	♋ 9	♌ 13	8 ♍ 30	♍ 28	♎ 24	21 ♈ 38	15 ♏ 38	22 ♈ 26

	♀	♂	♃	♄	♅	♆	♇
	° ′	° ′	° ′	° ′	° ′	° ′	° ′
201	28 ♒ 21	2 ♈ 30	23 ♈ 12	14 ♐ 32	14 ♏ 16 R	8 ♐ 40	15 ♓ 30
202	24 ♈ 23	6 ♋ 36	12 ♑ 14	13 ♓ 17	20 ♐ 4 R	26 ♐ 30 R	22 ♓ 30
203	13 ♈ 29	24 ♋ 58	23 ♒ 0	22 ♏ 30 R	4 ♋ 50	12 ♈ 57	14 ♉ 8
204	28 ♍ 45	14 ♋ 0	12 ♍ 37	5 ♋ 24	1 ♎ 14	25 ♉ 35	2 ♊ 57 R
205	0 ♓ 8	24 ♐ 20	28 ♎ 30 R	22 ♒ 54	11 ♌ 18 R	29 ♈ 48	21 ♉ 20
206	21 ♐ 51 R	16 ♎ 48	23 ♎ 40	9 ♒ 37	15 ♌ 16 R	28 ♈ 26 R	21 ♉ 20 R
207	8 ♍ 24	17 ♒ 21	19 ♈ 31 R	5 ♎ 41	5 ♏ 34	11 ♊ 2 R	9 ♊ 20 R
208	22 ♉ 40	24 ♌ 31	5 ♍ 48	24 ♏ 46 R	25 ♏ 29 R	20 ♊ 41	13 ♊ 40
209	28 ♌ 43	15 ♐ 0	14 ♐ 3	27 ♐ 8	22 ♓ 0 R	14 ♒ 30 R	20 ♈ 0 R
210	12 ♓ 9	7 ♌ 29	8 ♌ 31 R	16 ♏ 43 R	5 ♓ 48	7 ♒ 29	15 ♈ 0
211	7 ♎ 46	7 ♏ 36	10 ♏ 48	13 ♎ 41	24 ♊ 20 R	3 ♈ 35 R	11 ♉ 1 R
212	0 ♌ 25 R	18 ♋ 13	23 ♏ 7 R	8 ♓ 3 R	17 ♌ 29	4 ♉ 46	23 ♉ 50
213	7 ♐ 0	7 ♑ 0	0 ♊ 30	4 ♉ 30	6 ♑ 30	4 ♑ 30	28 ♊ 30 R
214	4 ♑ 3	10 ♈ 42	23 ♒ 44	15 ♍ 32 R	1 ♏ 24 R	4 ♊ 30	5 ♊ 51 R
215	1 ♏ 0	21 ♐ 30	14 ♓ 30	7 ♈ 0 R	28 ♐ 0	29 ♐ 45	26 ♓ 30
216	2 ♈ 47	16 ♑ 30	15 ♈ 48	23 ♈ 46	12 ♍ 46	11 ♉ 36	26 ♉ 20
217	10 ♊ 30	26 ♐ 30	22 ♎ 0	26 ♒ 0 R	14 ♌ 0	2 ♉ 30	22 ♉ 55
218	25 ♉ 32	22 ♋ 25	13 ♍ 14 R	14 ♈ 36	27 ♈ 7	6 ♓ 41	27 ♈ 10
219	28 ♋ 11	7 ♍ 13	4 ♌ 56	15 ♊ 30	24 ♍ 9	22 ♉ 9	1 ♊ 12
220	9 ♐ 48	18 ♏ 38	12 ♒ 56	2 ♋ 13 R	7 ♒ 43	0 ♌ 26	2 ♋ 2 R
221	9 ♋ 34	0 ♋ 10	4 ♌ 35	18 ♑ 22 R	0 ♌ 21	26 ♈ 12	17 ♉ 49
222	8 ♏ 30	1 ♑ 17	21 ♎ 17	8 ♎ 20	11 ♎ 12 R	17 ♌ 2	11 ♋ 1 R
223	25 ♎ 22	22 ♋ 53	14 ♑ 28	16 ♊ 43 R	3 ♒ 56	28 ♋ 13 R	28 ♊ 50 R
224	28 ♈ 29 R	15 ♍ 7 R	15 ♏ 47	2 ♓ 12	3 ♑ 42 R	6 ♋ 19	20 ♊ 38
225	23 ♈ 56	3 ♈ 1	11 ♈ 39	7 ♋ 23 R	21 ♉ 26	19 ♓ 38	3 ♉ 43
226	6 ♐ 24	17 ♑ 39	5 ♍ 46 R	19 ♊ 27 R	2 ♎ 54	20 ♉ 50 R	0 ♊ 24 R
227	16 ♑ 41	1 ♑ 47	27 ♏ 56	25 ♐ 54	9 ♐ 16	25 ♊ 37	15 ♊ 30 R
228	6 ♉ 21 R	15 ♉ 29	9 ♍ 35 R	19 ♍ 0 R	8 ♓ 15	10 ♌ 58 R	6 ♋ 35 R
229	9 ♎ 50	20 ♊ 51	9 ♎ 13	5 ♐ 44	29 ♏ 23	24 ♊ 22	15 ♊ 26
230	29 ♍ 38	9 ♍ 27	21 ♋ 35	21 ♌ 31	7 ♊ 43 R	25 ♓ 36 R	8 ♉ 30 R
231	9 ♊ 30	10 ♈ 12	27 ♓ 9	9 ♍ 30	18 ♒ 16 R	26 ♑ 30 R	11 ♈ 30
232	24 ♈ 18	19 ♉ 10	14 ♈ 59	20 ♒ 21	29 ♐ 37 R	3 ♋ 48	19 ♊ 18
233	16 ♑ 13	0 ♏ 3	10 ♓ 8	29 ♍ 13 R	4 ♏ 21	7 ♊ 25	7 ♊ 30 R
234	29 ♊ 29	29 ♋ 55	13 ♍ 9	16 ♈ 8	27 ♈ 53	6 ♓ 54	29 ♈ 24
235	11 ♍ 28	0 ♍ 12	19 ♋ 20	19 ♌ 50	7 ♊ 46	26 ♓ 1 R	6 ♉ 11 R
236	23 ♓ 39	29 ♈ 14	27 ♉ 51	28 ♐ 7 R	18 ♋ 29	20 ♈ 2	17 ♉ 11
237	26♏ 1	29 ♏ 52	28 ♒ 1	25 ♏ 18	12 ♋ 47 R	12 ♈ 53 R	14 ♉ 50 R
238	2 ♒ 20	18 ♐ 30	27 ♐ 20	8 ♓ 35	22 ♌ 35 R	2 ♉ 48	21 ♉ 30
239	15 ♐ 34	14 ♓ 52	12 ♊ 34 R	10 ♌ 17 R	29 ♉ 48 R	22 ♓ 32 R	5 ♉ 34 R
240	7 ♉ 45	29 ♈ 34	5 ♋ 0	0 ♊ 40	19 ♍ 13	19 ♉ 16	29 ♉ 49
241	24 ♋ 9	20 ♓ 14	9 ♍ 20	22 ♈ 7	19 ♑ 35 R	16 ♋ 28	25 ♊ 35
242	28 ♋ 11	7 ♍ 13	4 ♌ 56	15 ♊ 30	24 ♍ 9	22 ♉ 8	1 ♊ 16
243	4 ♉ 32	25 ♉ 12	16 ♈ 54	20 ♒ 40	29 ♐ 23 R	4 ♋ 2	19 ♊ 23
244	13 ♈ 2	1 ♊ 43	26 ♎ 3 R	3 ♎ 2 R	16 ♊ 50	3 ♈ 6	9 ♉ 45
245	27 ♉ 53	11 ♉ 37	23 ♈ 51	8 ♋ 48	23 ♉ 34	21 ♓ 31	4 ♉ 47
246	15 ♌ 43	7 ♑ 28	29 ♋ 42	26 ♓ 16 R	9 ♑ 9 R	13 ♋ 52	24 ♊ 28
247	16 ♋ 30	23 ♌ 15	23 ♏ 30	5 ♓ 28 R	20 ♌ 30	5 ♉ 30	24 ♉ 30
248	3 ♉ 30	21 ♉ 30	13 ♏ R	20 ♐ 18 R	20 ♓ 30	15 ♒ 30 R	19 ♈ 30
249	7 ♐ 30	6 ♐ 30	28 ♒ 30	26 ♏ 30	12 ♋ 30 R	12 ♈ 30 R	14 ♉ 48 R
250	26 ♉ 5	6 ♉ 16	22 ♈ 4	8 ♋ 19	23 ♉ 11	21 ♓ 19	3 ♉ 55

	10	11	12	Asc.	2	3	☉	☽	☿
	°	°	°	° ′	°	°	° ′	° ′	° ′
251	♎ 17	♏ 13	♐ 4	22 ♐ 40	♒ 0	♓ 12	13 ♑ 26	16 ♑ 4	2 ♒ 10
252	♎ 17	♏ 13	♐ 3	22 ♐ 42	♒ 0	♓ 12	15 ♈ 59	18 ♊ 15	20 ♓ 12
253	♋ 12	♌ 16	♍ 15	10 ♎ 13	♏ 7	♐ 8	11 ♏ 35	10 ♍ 53	29 ♏ 41
254	♒ 4	♓ 2	♈ 10	25 ♉ 13	♊ 21	♋ 12	29 ♌ 40	2 ♉ 23	20 ♍ 25
255	♎ 8	♏ 15	♐ 6	26 ♐ 30	♒ 3	♓ 14	24 ♈ 4	9 ♏ 26	10 ♈ 28 R
256	♏ 1	♏ 26	♐ 7	7 ♑ 50	♒ 17	♓ 28	4 ♍ 19	16 ♏ 30	22 ♍ 30 R
257	♊ 22	♋ 23	♌ 23	22 ♍ 0	♎ 21	♏ 21	19 ♌ 30	1 ♎ 9	10 ♍ 26
258	♊ 21	♋ 13	♌ 10	15 ♍ 0	♏ 7	♏ 28	11 ♌ 3	9 ♍ 11	4 ♌ 23
259	♐ 2	♐ 21	♑ 9	2 ♒ 30	♓ 28	♉ 9	0 ♐ 10	9 ♈ 5	3 ♐ 12
260	♈ 19	♉ 29	♋ 8	9 ♌ 0	♌ 26	♍ 19	18 ♊ 30	11 ♓ 0	4 ♊ 30 R
261	♈ 1	♉ 9	♊ 21	24 ♋ 15	♌ 12	♍ 3	2 ♓ 2	29 ♈ 58	3 ♓ 20 R
262	♊ 4	♋ 5	♌ 6	4 ♍ 40	♎ 2	♏ 2	10 ♌ 46	29 ♈ 25	3 ♍ 8
263	♐ 1	♐ 19	♑ 7	29 ♑ 0	♓ 28	♉ 7	28 ♑ 50	15 ♋ 12	14 ♑ 4
264	♓ 24	♉ 0	♊ 9	12 ♋ 0	♌ 3	♌ 26	2 ♋ 50	24 ♋ 39	13 ♋ 10 R
265	♒ 0	♒ 26	♈ 3	21 ♉ 0	♊ 17	♋ 9	3 ♉ 0	1 ♏ 15	6 ♈ 30
266	♉ 8	♊ 17	♋ 23	21 ♌ 8	♍ 10	♎ 5	7 ♓ 55	7 ♑ 20	20 ♒ 12
267	♑ 11	♑ 26	♒ 23	20 ♈ 30	♊ 7	♊ 27	21 ♎ 27	22 ♏ 3	7 ♏ 41 R
268	♒ 29	♈ 1	♉ 13	24 ♊ 10	♋ 14	♌ 5	20 ♉ 37	20 ♓ 7	5 ♉ 49
269	♋ 16	♌ 22	♍ 20	11 ♎ 30	♏ 6	♐ 7	14 ♑ 59	29 ♏ 40	3 ♒ 51
270	♓ 27	♉ 4	♊ 15	18 ♋ 57	♌ 8	♌ 29	27 ♎ 12	21 ♌ 54	3 ♏ 53
271	♌ 1	♍ 5	♎ 3	25 ♎ 30	♏ 24	♐ 26	3 ♈ 15	14 ♎ 16	6 ♓ 59
272	♊ 0	♋ 8	♌ 11	7 ♍ 30	♍ 28	♎ 25	3 ♒ 37	21 ♏ 3	19 ♒ 8 R
273	♒ 15	♓ 14	♈ 25	8 ♊ 47	♋ 2	♋ 22	18 ♋ 25	14 ♏ 34	11 ♋ 57
274	♌ 14	♍ 17	♎ 13	3 ♏ 0	♐ 1	♑ 5	18 ♒ 8	15 ♐ 7	22 ♑ 21
275	♊ 17	♋ 21	♌ 22	19 ♍ 0	♎ 14	♏ 13	18 ♐ 41	3 ♏ 10	22 ♐ 34
276	♉ 4	♊ 15	♋ 23	21 ♌ 0	♍ 8	♎ 1	2 ♋ 40	20 ♏ 16	12 ♊ 25
277	♉ 18	♊ 29	♌ 4	0 ♍ 12	♍ 19	♎ 14	1 ♊ 49	5 ♌ 9	23 ♊ 31
278	♊ 5	♋ 12	♌ 15	11 ♍ 9	♎ 2	♏ 0	5 ♑ 50	14 ♍ 0	14 ♑ 10 R
279	♎ 15	♏ 11	♐ 2	20 ♐ 20	♑ 27	♓ 10	24 ♒ 16	9 ♓ 53	11 ♓ 42
280	♒ 2	♒ 28	♈ 7	27 ♉ 23	♊ 22	♋ 12	6 ♊ 20	29 ♏ 5	23 ♊ 8
281	♊ 22	♋ 26	♌ 26	23 ♍ 0	♎ 18	♏ 18	12 ♐ 30	9 ♎ 10	27 ♏ 30
282	♍ 23	♎ 21	♏ 13	28 ♏ 20	♑ 1	♒ 13	29 ♐ 16	28 ♌ 0	13 ♑ 0
283	♑ 9	♑ 27	♒ 25	21 ♈ 56	♊ 1	♊ 22	25 ♒ 55	17 ♋ 16	29 ♑ 40
284	♈ 23	♊ 1	♋ 10	9 ♌ 38	♌ 28	♍ 21	11 ♎ 9	9 ♓ 30	7 ♎ 53
285	♒ 25	♓ 27	♉ 7	17 ♊ 37	♋ 7	♌ 1	23 ♐ 33	26 ♈ 6	2 ♑ 38
286	♈ 6	♉ 15	♊ 27	0 ♌ 0	♌ 17	♍ 8	21 ♒ 20	23 ♒ 1	18 ♒ 3
287	♑ 14	♒ 8	♓ 10	27 ♈ 0	♊ 0	♊ 24	17 ♈ 6	12 ♌ 58	4 ♉ 3
288	♉ 0	♊ 6	♋ 11	10 ♌ 54	♍ 2	♍ 28	3 ♉ 6	2 ♒ 5	29 ♈ 31 R
289	♏ 20	♐ 11	♑ 1	23 ♑ 0	♓ 11	♈ 22	1 ♈ 30	10 ♒ 24	13 ♓ 34
290	♑ 24	♒ 18	♓ 24	15 ♉ 37	♊ 14	♋ 4	9 ♌ 9	12 ♓ 30	7 ♌ 30
291	♒ 10	♓ 5	♈ 24	22 ♊ 20	♋ 8	♋ 23	0 ♊ 37	0 ♒ 39	5 ♉ 24
292	♍ 20	♎ 20	♏ 14	4 ♐ 37	♑ 7	♒ 13	4 ♑ 56	25 ♍ 31	24 ♑ 27
293	♈ 12	♉ 14	♊ 16	14 ♋ 0	♌ 11	♍ 9	12 ♈ 13	1 ♈ 8	1 ♉ 12
294	♋ 11	♌ 14	♍ 14	9 ♎ 30	♏ 7	♐ 7	3 ♍ 50	28 ♑ 32	0 ♎ 12
295	♓ 17	♈ 22	♊ 5	11 ♋ 14	♌ 0	♌ 21	17 ♏ 39	6 ♒ 8	29 ♎ 46
296	♐ 9	♐ 29	♑ 18	17 ♒ 0	♈ 2	♉ 16	15 ♎ 50	19 ♓ 15	14 ♎ 50
297	♊ 5	♋ 11	♌ 14	10 ♍ 16	♎ 3	♏ 1	20 ♈ 4	16 ♑ 22	9 ♉ 20
298	♊ 14	♋ 18	♌ 19	16 ♍ 0	♎ 11	♏ 11	29 ♏ 30	28 ♈ 30	21 ♐ 30
299	♈ 26	♊ 5	♋ 14	13 ♌ 5	♍ 1	♍ 25	0 ♌ 31	28 ♉ 58	22 ♋ 51
300	♐ 12	♑ 0	♑ 19	22 ♒ 15	♈ 18	♉ 21	15 ♓ 12	28 ♑ 30	1 ♈ 58

	♀	♂	♃	♄	♅	♆	♇
	° ′	° ′	° ′	° ′	° ′	° ′	° ′
51	25 ♒ 53	12 ♊ 41 R	10 ♍ 6 R	27 ♏ 27	27 ♏ 34	18 ♊ 16 R	11 ♊ 55 R
52	29 ♉ 52	29 ♉ 20	3 ♌ 37	2 ♈ 9	16 ♑ 48	12 ♋ 7	23 ♊ 5
53	13 ♐ 5	11 ♏ 54	16 ♐ 48	2 ♊ 6 R	29 ♑ 46	26 ♋ 1 R	29 ♊ 50 R
54	21 ♌ 52	29 ♊ 22	23 ♋ 46	9 ♊ 19	22 ♍ 14	21 ♉ 6 R	1 ♊ 4
55	23 ♉ 30	11 ♏ 53 R	21 ♌ 20 R	2 ♒ 5	1 ♌ 50	25 ♈ 57	19 ♉ 40
56	22 ♋ 59	28 ♍ 30	19 ♐ 30	26 ♎ 30	3 ♋ 12	10 ♈ 6 R	14 ♉ 4 R
57	15 ♍ 45	18 ♓ 36 R	23 ♐ 53 R	18 ♓ 57 R	24 ♌ 44	7 ♉ 35 R	25 ♉ 20
58	14 ♌ 46	1 ♏ 45	9 ♈ 9 R	8 ♋ 37	24 ♉ 44	20 ♓ 3 R	5 ♉ 32 R
59	18 ♐ 6	11 ♒ 44	6 ♒ 57	16 ♍ 5	29 ♎ 6	5 ♊ 33	7 ♊ 0 R
60	16 ♋ 30	2 ♐ 12 R	12 ♒ 1 R	28 ♌ 30	22 ♎ 30 R	5 ♊ 0	6 ♊ 30
61	4 ♈ 59	16 ♒ 37	6 ♋ 1 R	5 ♏ 14 R	0 ♓ 36	4 ♒ 33	13 ♈ 17
62	18 ♌ 2	22 ♋ 27	29 ♈ 45	18 ♒ 12 R	26 ♐ 23 R	6 ♋ 59	21 ♊ 14
63	17 ♐ 43	16 ♋ 3 R	10 ♒ 50	22 ♏ 30	5 ♋ 30 R	10 ♈ 17	13 ♉ 6
64	17 ♌ 45	8 ♌ 46	14 ♋ 30	0 ♏ 35 R	16 ♏ 10 R	16 ♊ 12	11 ♊ 40
65	14 ♉ 30	18 ♓ 30	14 ♉ 30	5 ♎ 30 R	26 ♒ 30	1 ♒ 30 R	12 ♈ 0
66	29 ♒ 15 R	16 ♉ 30	26 ♑ 47	21 ♓ 10	26 ♌ 58 R	5 ♉ 17	23 ♉ 32
67	6 ♐ 32	8 ♏ 3	1 ♋ 23	25 ♉ 0 R	20 ♍ 59	18 ♉ 7 R	29 ♉ 46 R
68	10 ♊ 7	6 ♊ 15	21 ♍ 51 R	14 ♒ 12	6 ♌ 50	29 ♈ 6	21 ♉ 10
69	0 ♐ 24	14 ♐ 20	21 ♏ 20	17 ♎ 40	22 ♊ 12 R	3 ♈ 28	10 ♉ 19 R
70	3 ♏ 14	26 ♍ 25	24 ♋ 27	24 ♌ 4	7 ♊ 14 R	24 ♓ 54 R	7 ♉ 36 R
71	22 ♒ 52	4 ♈ 25	9 ♒ 45	26 ♑ 14	21 ♐ 17	28 ♊ 44	16 ♊ 40
72	17 ♒ 10	12 ♎ 58	23 ♒ 40	0 ♒ 35	23 ♐ 50	1 ♋ 30 R	17 ♊ 54 R
73	2 ♊ 50	1 ♍ 8	7 ♍ 36	24 ♏ 23 R	25 ♏ 14 R	21 ♊ 5	13 ♊ 58
74	16 ♓ 30	7 ♈ 40	26 ♊ 25 R	4 ♑ 25	23 ♏ 14	12 ♐ 31	17 ♓ 30
75	16 ♐ 18	5 ♈ 33	20 ♑ 30	1 ♍ 39	7 ♒ 45	21 ♑ 17	8 ♈ 0
76	2 ♌ 44	8 ♉ 34	0 ♒ 25 R	5 ♏ 49 R	4 ♋ 3	12 ♈ 43	14 ♉ 40
77	9 ♋ 57	15 ♋ 40	18 ♎ 11 R	28 ♍ 48 R	19 ♊ 43	5 ♈ 31	11 ♉ 10
78	17 ♒ 30	21 ♎ 15	20 ♈ 30 R	18 ♒ 9	0 ♑ 28	6 ♋ 49 R	20 ♊ 18 R
79	17 ♑ 0	27 ♎ 55	4 ♐ 13	1 ♌ 26 R	17 ♎ 1 R	27 ♉ 17	2 ♊ 49
80	24 ♈ 17	26 ♉ 13	13 ♎ 32 R	28 ♒ 5	29 ♈ 35	9 ♍ 37	23 ♋ 4
81	29 ♑ 47	8 ♑ 30	15 ♑ 30	14 ♑ 41	16 ♐ 50	0 ♋ 30 R	17 ♊ 35 R
82	22 ♏ 30	19 ♌ 6	25 ♏ 28	15 ♎ 5	21 ♎ 31	27 ♏ 30	7 ♓ 30
83	12 ♈ 35	16 ♊ 10	6 ♍ 28 R	0 ♐ 20	28 ♏ 57	17 ♊ 33 R	11 ♊ 41
84	25 ♌ 49	12 ♒ 48	21 ♈ 3 R	4 ♎ 17	4 ♏ 53	11 ♊ 12 R	9 ♊ 30 R
85	2 ♒ 26	18 ♊ 19 R	10 ♍ 2	25 ♏ 26	26 ♏ 33	18 ♊ 47 R	12 ♊ 30 R
86	13 ♑ 10	28 ♉ 15	17 ♓ 30	12 ♈ 6	7 ♍ 30	9 ♉ 30	25 ♉ 13 R
87	1 ♊ 2	13 ♑ 51	4 ♈ 57	25 ♏ 14 R	4 ♏ 47 R	6 ♊ 58	7 ♊ 12
88	24 ♈ 35	20 ♑ 37	0 ♌ 16	19 ♑ 22	26 ♏ 55 R	15 ♐ 9 R	20 ♓ 30
89	15 ♉ 34	21 ♈ 4	17 ♈ 10	7 ♋ 27	22 ♉ 13	20 ♓ 33	3 ♉ 41
90	24 ♍ 7	29 ♌ 30	20 ♎ 30	1 ♎ 30	23 ♊ 30	5 ♈ 58 R	12 ♉ 10
91	27 ♈ 7	18 ♊ 27	25 ♊ 50	7 ♌ 10	3 ♊ 22	26 ♓ 45	5 ♉ 55
92	21 ♒ 18	8 ♈ 53	11 ♑ 53	14 ♓ 58	29 ♌ 16 R	4 ♉ 52 R	23 ♉ 45 R
93	28 ♒ 57	14 ♉ 10	16 ♊ 17	5 ♌ 26 R	0 ♊ 46	25 ♓ 15	6 ♉ 26
94	9 ♎ 30	9 ♏ 20	20 ♋ 49	3 ♑ 30 R	29 ♋ 9	23 ♈ 51 R	19 ♉ 46
95	2 ♑ 12	16 ♐ 25	15 ♉ 46 R	15 ♐ 59	21 ♋ 59 R	17 ♈ 24 R	16 ♉ 50 R
96	18 ♎ 55	19 ♍ 12	23 ♋ 30	23 ♌ 7	7 ♊ 30 R	25 ♓ 30 R	7 ♉ 58 R
97	16 ♓ 19	7 ♈ 30	8 ♑ 0	26 ♎ 30 R	24 ♎ 30 R	29 ♏ 30 R	12 ♓ 30
98	4 ♑ 56	24 ♏ 18	20 ♐ 30	0 ♊ 42 R	0 ♒ 20	25 ♋ 52 R	29 ♊ 32 R
99	3 ♍ 30	21 ♉ 3	6 ♍ 24	5 ♍ 46	3 ♎ 45	19 ♏ 30	7 ♓ 30 R
00	14 ♓ 45	10 ♒ 33	4 ♉ 1	9 ♎ 5 R	23 ♒ 47	0 ♒ 45	12 ♈ 20

	10 °	11 °	12 °	Asc. ° ′	2 °	3 °	☉ ° ′	☽ ° ′	☿ ° ′
301	♑ 15	♒ 9	♓ 11	26 ♈ 12	♉ 29	♊ 23	5 ♊ 57	12 ♈ 42	13 ♉ 10
302	♐ 21	♑ 9	♒ 0	8 ♓ 24	♉ 3	♊ 1	11 ♐ 53	16 ♊ 25	11 ♐ 19
303	♉ 13	♊ 20	♋ 24	23 ♌ 0	♍ 14	♎ 10	9 ♎ 58	19 ♌ 30	23 ♍ 36
304	♎ 9	♏ 8	♐ 2	23 ♐ 16	♑ 27	♓ 5	16 ♌ 52	25 ♐ 55	29 ♌ 58
305	♒ 2	♒ 28	♈ 5	23 ♉ 0	♊ 19	♋ 10	2 ♌ 28	12 ♊ 20	12 ♌ 53
306	♒ 12	♓ 10	♈ 23	14 ♊ 0	♋ 4	♋ 22	15 ♒ 17	2 ♌ 20	20 ♑ 30
307	♋ 26	♍ 1	♍ 29	18 ♎ 30	♏ 14	♐ 16	17 ♌ 59	4 ♉ 30	0 ♌ 58
308	♎ 19	♏ 15	♐ 7	26 ♐ 10	♒ 3	♓ 15	23 ♋ 57	16 ♒ 13	15 ♌ 47
309	♐ 15	♐ 26	♑ 17	15 ♒ 0	♈ 5	♉ 10	7 ♋ 30	16 ♐ 10	26 ♋ 0
310	♋ 27	♍ 4	♍ 29	18 ♎ 0	♏ 12	♐ 15	28 ♋ 19	18 ♊ 46	13 ♌ 25
311	♈ 25	♊ 6	♋ 16	14 ♌ 40	♍ 1	♍ 24	21 ♊ 42	15 ♏ 45	29 ♉ 33
312	♌ 13	♍ 16	♎ 13	5 ♏ 0	♐ 4	♑ 7	23 ♒ 0	7 ♑ 15	20 ♒ 0
313	♏ 2	♏ 24	♐ 11	27 ♐ 37	♒ 12	♈ 0	16 ♏ 54	29 ♍ 27	1 ♐ 42
314	♈ 6	♉ 13	♊ 21	23 ♋ 32	♌ 13	♍ 6	11 ♊ 26	1 ♍ 48	21 ♉ 32
315	♌ 10	♍ 13	♎ 9	29 ♎ 0	♏ 26	♑ 0	29 ♏ 6	28 ♑ 4	16 ♐ 24
316	♊ 15	♋ 21	♌ 23	18 ♍ 30	♎ 12	♏ 10	3 ♑ 0	27 ♏ 45	19 ♑ 30
317	♌ 3	♍ 7	♎ 4	24 ♎ 50	♏ 22	♐ 25	11 ♌ 35	20 ♏ 24	6 ♌ 23
318	♏ 26	♐ 15	♑ 2	21 ♑ 18	♓ 18	♉ 0	0 ♉ 12	12 ♌ 9	4 ♈ 39
319	♐ 17	♑ 4	♑ 24	27 ♒ 30	♈ 26	♉ 26	13 ♒ 1	5 ♒ 23	20 ♑ 57
320	♊ 22	♋ 26	♌ 26	23 ♍ 15	♎ 18	♏ 18	3 ♊ 25	3 ♌ 59	24 ♊ 53
321	♊ 1	♋ 5	♌ 7	4 ♍ 50	♍ 28	♎ 27	26 ♉ 15	18 ♍ 56	7 ♊ 9R
322	♉ 14	♊ 19	♋ 21	20 ♌ 26	♍ 13	♎ 11	14 ♉ 24	27 ♈ 8	28 ♈ 21
323	♈ 10	♉ 22	♋ 6	7 ♌ 0	♌ 22	♍ 11	6 ♈ 17	28 ♋ 4	9 ♓ 36
324	♏ 12	♐ 5	♐ 25	17 ♑ 35	♓ 1	♈ 12	16 ♈ 38	21 ♒ 53	5 ♉ 46
325	♉ 29	♋ 8	♌ 11	6 ♍ 55	♍ 28	♎ 25	1 ♊ 50	1 ♎ 28	22 ♊ 39
326	♈ 17	♉ 23	♊ 29	1 ♌ 13	♌ 21	♍ 16	2 ♊ 8	19 ♐ 13	20 ♊ 51
327	♌ 11	♍ 14	♎ 11	4 ♏ 12	♐ 2	♑ 5	16 ♐ 47	7 ♏ 42	20 ♐ 16
328	♐ 17	♑ 7	♑ 28	3 ♓ 0	♈ 25	♉ 26	14 ♏ 0	19 ♌ 15	2 ♐ 38
329	♐ 2	♐ 25	♑ 19	16 ♒ 44	♓ 29	♉ 4	12 ♍ 29	29 ♎ 45	24 ♍ 9
330	♋ 26	♌ 28	♍ 28	24 ♎ 17	♏ 23	♐ 24	21 ♒ 49	21 ♏ 30	26 ♒ 37
331	♒ 1	♒ 27	♈ 5	23 ♉ 15	♊ 19	♋ 10	9 ♓ 56	21 ♋ 45	27 ♒ 33
332	♋ 17	♌ 21	♍ 20	13 ♎ 0	♏ 9	♐ 11	11 ♒ 0	16 ♉ 30	7 ♒ 0
333	♏ 15	♐ 8	♐ 28	20 ♑ 37	♓ 5	♈ 16	14 ♉ 19	28 ♐ 9	20 ♈ 51
334	♏ 9	♐ 0	♐ 17	5 ♑ 0	♒ 23	♈ 9	6 ♒ 59	21 ♍ 37	23 ♒ 19
335	♎ 15	♏ 15	♐ 5	21 ♐ 54	♒ 0	♓ 14	6 ♍ 42	22 ♒ 30	25 ♌ 59
336	♒ 17	♓ 17	♉ 3	22 ♊ 0	♋ 10	♋ 28	4 ♌ 40	11 ♈ 15	2 ♌ 4
337	♏ 1	♏ 19	♐ 6	23 ♐ 34	♒ 6	♓ 9	19 ♑ 6	3 ♌ 12	13 ♑ 4R
338	♈ 22	♊ 4	♋ 14	13 ♌ 30	♍ 0	♍ 21	23 ♑ 30	16 ♐ 30	29 ♐ 30
339	♉ 19	♊ 24	♋ 26	25 ♌ 10	♍ 18	♎ 16	29 ♋ 50	0 ♊ 22	13 ♋ 8
340	♓ 5	♈ 8	♉ 17	24 ♊ 10	♋ 16	♌ 8	1 ♈ 50	20 ♒ 55	4 ♓ 6
341	♏ 26	♐ 16	♑ 6	29 ♑ 56	♓ 20	♈ 29	2 ♎ 18	4 ♉ 23	24 ♎ 50
342	♐ 22	♑ 10	♒ 3	11 ♓ 0	♉ 3	♊ 2	22 ♈ 26	3 ♍ 47	8 ♈ 53
343	♏ 22	♐ 10	♐ 26	13 ♑ 5	♓ 12	♈ 27	28 ♊ 52	4 ♌ 20	20 ♊ 24
344	♓ 12	♈ 16	♉ 28	6 ♋ 30	♋ 25	♌ 16	9 ♎ 5	18 ♑ 25	22 ♍ 49
345	♑ 28	♓ 0	♈ 1	1 ♉ 40	♊ 1	♊ 29	16 ♈ 8	23 ♎ 36	12 ♈ 35
346	♋ 28	♍ 0	♎ 0	24 ♎ 50	♏ 24	♐ 24	27 ♎ 18	2 ♉ 46	22 ♏ 27
347	♍ 12	♎ 13	♏ 8	27 ♏ 0	♐ 28	♒ 5	7 ♌ 7	10 ♒ 53	3 ♌ 10
348	♋ 18	♌ 21	♍ 21	15 ♎ 45	♏ 13	♐ 14	12 ♋ 7	5 ♋ 30	23 ♋ 39
349	♋ 19	♌ 22	♍ 21	17 ♎ 10	♏ 15	♐ 16	4 ♐ 40	13 ♐ 26	18 ♐ 9R
350	♋ 4	♌ 10	♍ 10	3 ♎ 0	♎ 27	♏ 27	19 ♑ 30	20 ♈ 30	5 ♒ 30

	♀	♂	♃	♄	♅	♆	♇
	° ′	° ′	° ′	° ′	° ′	° ′	° ′
301	21 ♈ 41	13 ♋ 21	7 ♒ 10 R	1 ♈ 1	25 ♌ 36	8 ♉ 21	25 ♉ 5
302	26 ♏ 55 R	25 ♒ 6	8 ♏ 16	17 ♎ 28	9 ♓ 46	18 ♌ 8 R	10 ♋ 38 R
303	26 ♏ 36	0 ♑ 47	21 ♊ 32	10 ♌ 1	3 ♊ 6 R	23 ♓ 5 R	6 ♉ 55 R
304	7 ♋ 16	10 ♎ 45	5 ♉ 1	23 ♋ 41	17 ♒ 45 R	2 ♌ 57	3 ♋ 45
305	17 ♊ 44	10 ♍ 10	10 ♍ 18	24 ♏ 8 R	25 ♏ 2 R	21 ♊ 34	14 ♊ 11
306	29 ♒ 9	8 ♎ 2	16 ♊ 27 R	5 ♑ 40	23 ♋ 42	19 ♈ 25	16 ♉ 56
307	16 ♋ 16	27 ♊ 30	14 ♈ 9 R	29 ♏ 6	15 ♋ 18	17 ♈ 14 R	16 ♉ 56
308	8 ♌ 54	12 ♊ 44	28 ♈ 22	26 ♈ 17	0 ♑ 12 R	1 ♑ 3 R	28 ♓ 30
309	23 ♋ 45	22 ♍ 25	8 ♑ 15 R	13 ♑ 31 R	13 ♐ 58 R	29 ♊ 18	17 ♊ 34
310	22 ♊ 38	6 ♎ 58	21 ♑ 52 R	11 ♊ 57	16 ♉ 18	15 ♓ 41 R	3 ♉ 37 R
311	9 ♉ 15	14 ♌ 26	3 ♍ 22	25 ♏ 42 R	26 ♏ 1 R	20 ♊ 3	13 ♊ 20
312	7 ♓ 0	1 ♑ 11	7 ♊ 0	2 ♓ 30	12 ♈ 0	28 ♒ 0	24 ♈ 8
313	19 ♎ 14	15 ♑ 14	21 ♐ 28	0 ♑ 9	20 ♓ 37	14 ♒ 19	19 ♈ 30 R
314	21 ♋ 23	10 ♒ 51	17 ♈ 14	23 ♍ 22	2 ♏ 35 R	8 ♊ 52	8 ♊ 20
315	10 ♐ 2	4 ♌ 13	11 ♒ 6	24 ♓ 0 R	23 ♐ 10	27 ♐ 12	25 ♓ 30 R
316	21 ♒ 0	17 ♑ 0	18 ♍ 39	24 ♏ 35	5 ♓ 17	6 ♒ 30	15 ♈ 0
317	8 ♋ 3	26 ♊ 17	1 ♐ 3	29 ♐ 6 R	8 ♐ 32 R	28 ♊ 20	17 ♊ 25
318	13 ♓ 57	20 ♒ 58	22 ♒ 31	24 ♏ 27 R	27 ♓ 22	22 ♌ 2 R	12 ♋ 44
319	28 ♐ 17	1 ♈ 8	11 ♊ 4 R	8 ♌ 3 R	29 ♉ 31 R	23 ♓ 7	5 ♉ 38
320	27 ♈ 19	7 ♌ 39	26 ♍ 1	13 ♍ 54	7 ♎ 59 R	22 ♏ 5 R	7 ♓ 0
321	11 ♈ 43	10 ♋ 5	4 ♎ 55 R	0 ♉ 6	25 ♑ 5	17 ♋ 14	25 ♊ 26
322	28 ♉ 44	14 ♏ 9 R	4 ♍ 28	20 ♊ 10	24 ♑ 3 R	13 ♑ 30	4 ♈ 30
323	1 ♉ 8	9 ♈ 18	22 ♒ 30	10 ♊ 50	14 ♉ 29	16 ♓ 25	1 ♉ 56
324	1 ♓ 14	16 ♍ 3 R	8 ♊ 48	7 ♌ 37	26 ♒ 30	4 ♌ 19	3 ♋ 28
325	18 ♉ 48	0 ♈ 37	3 ♌ 58	14 ♏ 36 R	22 ♏ 5 R	17 ♊ 10	11 ♊ 53
326	0 ♉ 38	25 ♈ 8	3 ♋ 43	29 ♉ 59	19 ♍ 13	19 ♉ 3	29 ♉ 40
327	3 ♒ 54	6 ♈ 56	10 ♎ 43	16 ♈ 29 R	19 ♑ 14	18 ♋ 45 R	26 ♊ 0 R
328	16 ♎ 16	13 ♑ 30	21 ♐ 0	30 ♐ 0	21 ♓ 0 R	14 ♒ 30	20 ♈ 0 R
329	5 ♌ 31	21 ♌ 15	25 ♍ 51	26 ♍ 3	7 ♓ 27 R	14 ♌ 34	9 ♋ 49
330	16 ♑ 11	3 ♏ 41	12 ♌ 1 R	9 ♍ 35 R	1 ♓ 7	9 ♌ 50 R	5 ♋ 48 R
331	11 ♓ 49	0 ♋ 37	20 ♉ 3	8 ♉ 0	16 ♍ 49 R	14 ♉ 8	27 ♉ 20
332	25 ♓ 0	28 ♎ 30	14 ♐ 0	29 ♐ 30	18 ♓ 30	14 ♒ 30	18 ♈ 5
333	27 ♈ 42	16 ♋ 34	13 ♐ 36 R	22 ♉ 17	3 ♒ 28	21 ♋ 20	27 ♊ 30
334	22 ♐ 0	24 ♑ 45	21 ♊ 56 R	19 ♉ 19	22 ♍ 58 R	16 ♉ 2 R	28 ♉ 14
335	8 ♎ 19	20 ♉ 4	7 ♓ 52 R	14 ♈ 52 R	4 ♍ 44	12 ♉ 1 R	27 ♉ 15
336	15 ♌ 58 R	11 ♊ 7	27 ♎ 44	29 ♍ 33	13 ♎ 14	23 ♏ 30	9 ♓ 30
337	10 ♑ 3	5 ♑ 12	9 ♎ 55	8 ♐ 23	2 ♐ 7	20 ♊ 24	13 ♊ 0 R
338	12 ♑ 58	5 ♑ 5	13 ♑ 30	11 ♏ 9	1 ♋ 4 R	8 ♈ 0	12 ♉ 15 R
339	14 ♊ 41	19 ♋ 51	0 ♑ 9 R	20 ♌ 40	18 ♎ 11	4 ♊ 0	6 ♊ 32
340	28 ♈ 25	11 ♊ 57	27 ♊ 45	6 ♏ 13 R	19 ♏ 37 R	13 ♊ 13	9 ♊ 50
341	23 ♎ 12	20 ♊ 39	29 ♌ 30	16 ♏ 12	21 ♏ 50	20 ♊ 19	13 ♊ 30
342	19 ♉ 1 R	10 ♉ 11	8 ♑ 1	13 ♌ 26 R	19 ♎ 51 R	0 ♊ 35	4 ♊ 26
343	13 ♋ 4	5 ♓ 19	8 ♍ 4	21 ♈ 31	19 ♑ 55 R	16 ♋ 8	25 ♊ 20
344	9 ♎ 51	19 ♋ 38	28 ♎ 7	2 ♉ 32 R	3 ♉ 21 R	7 ♉ 1 R	29 ♈ 56 R
345	27 ♈ 44	11 ♐ 30	7 ♒ 35	27 ♌ 28 R	25 ♎ 3 R	2 ♊ 34	5 ♊ 19
346	6 ♏ 58	4 ♒ 54	11 ♌ 6	21 ♓ 41 R	9 ♑ 11	14 ♋ 53	24 ♊ 37 R
347	22 ♍ 16	28 ♌ 7	20 ♎ 26	1 ♎ 33	23 ♊ 34	6 ♈ 1 R	12 ♉ 13
348	12 ♌ 10	8 ♏ 0	10 ♍ 0	28 ♊ 0	22 ♑ 30 R	12 ♑ 38	5 ♈ 30 R
349	3 ♐ 3	8 ♑ 33	26 ♎ 31	22 ♋ 1 R	11 ♎ 20	26 ♉ 10 R	2 ♊ 54 R
350	3 ♓ 30	3 ♒ 0	11 ♉ 1	23 ♐ 0	20 ♋ 2 R	16 ♈ 50	16 ♉ 1 R

	10	11	12	Asc.	2	3	☉	☽	☿
	°	°	°	° ′	°	°	° ′	° ′	° ′
351	♋ 2	♌ 6	♍ 7	2 ♎ 0	♎ 27	♏ 27	24 ♌ 44	21 ♌ 59	7 ♍ 44
352	♌ 13	♍ 17	♎ 14	5 ♏ 40	♐ 4	♑ 7	12 ♐ 33	13 ♊ 50	28 ♐ 27
353	♐ 28	♑ 17	♒ 3	25 ♓ 0	♉ 22	♊ 3	29 ♏ 30	1 ♏ 30	18 ♐ 30
354	♉ 19	♊ 28	♌ 3	30 ♌ 0	♍ 20	♎ 16	26 ♐ 50	18 ♐ 9	9 ♑ 16
355	♍ 26	♎ 24	♏ 14	0 ♐ 0	♑ 3	♒ 16	24 ♎ 14	15 ♓ 15	7 ♎ 57
356	♏ 18	♐ 5	♐ 20	5 ♑ 30	♓ 3	♈ 21	12 ♊ 35	20 ♌ 30	1 ♋ 30
357	♎ 13	♏ 8	♏ 26	11 ♐ 30	♑ 19	♓ 6	16 ♉ 25	28 ♐ 58	21 ♉ 35
358	♐ 16	♑ 4	♑ 24	26 ♒ 0	♈ 25	♉ 25	5 ♎ 40	10 ♈ 19	21 ♍ 2
359	♓ 28	♉ 6	♊ 19	23 ♋ 5	♌ 16	♍ 1	15 ♉ 56	9 ♊ 56	27 ♉ 4
360	♈ 0	♉ 6	♊ 15	19 ♋ 5	♌ 8	♍ 1	28 ♌ 33	26 ♊ 7	25 ♍ 23
361	♊ 22	♋ 26	♌ 26	23 ♍ 10	♎ 18	♏ 18	12 ♒ 30	23 ♋ 50	20 ♒ 38
362	♋ 0	♌ 7	♍ 7	0 ♎ 0	♎ 23	♏ 23	23 ♊ 51	26 ♉ 24	1 ♊ 15
363	♋ 9	♌ 12	♍ 12	7 ♎ 56	♏ 5	♐ 6	18 ♉ 46	27 ♑ 0	27 ♉ 11
364	♎ 0	♎ 27	♏ 17	3 ♐ 0	♑ 7	♒ 21	21 ♌ 10	11 ♒ 45	5 ♌ 35
365	♋ 11	♌ 17	♍ 16	8 ♎ 17	♏ 3	♐ 4	27 ♒ 40	27 ♐ 4	15 ♓ 30
366	♌ 9	♍ 13	♎ 10	1 ♏ 0	♏ 29	♑ 3	12 ♈ 23	22 ♋ 11	16 ♈ 30
367	♌ 2	♍ 4	♎ 4	1 ♏ 25	♐ 1	♑ 0	8 ♎ 54	20 ♌ 16	3 ♏ 45
368	♒ 11	♓ 6	♈ 28	28 ♊ 30	♋ 11	♋ 25	25 ♍ 15	20 ♉ 45	8 ♍ 0
369	♑ 20	♒ 9	♓ 13	27 ♉ 20	♊ 20	♋ 5	1 ♓ 56	22 ♉ 35	5 ♒ 21
370	♑ 23	♒ 14	♓ 22	22 ♈ 25	♊ 17	♋ 6	10 ♈ 30	24 ♊ 16	29 ♓ 50
371	♊ 28	♌ 1	♍ 2	28 ♍ 0	♎ 24	♏ 24	26 ♏ 16	19 ♉ 50	29 ♏ 45
372	♓ 13	♈ 18	♊ 2	10 ♋ 55	♋ 28	♌ 17	18 ♊ 48	29 ♐ 3	0 ♋ 8R
373	♋ 15	♌ 17	♍ 17	13 ♎ 40	♏ 12	♐ 12	0 ♐ 16	6 ♋ 15	18 ♏ 30
374	♐ 14	♑ 5	♑ 28	0 ♓ 45	♈ 18	♉ 20	13 ♒ 30	6 ♑ 36	27 ♑ 36
375	♉ 30	♋ 8	♌ 11	7 ♍ 9	♍ 28	♎ 25	8 ♓ 27	10 ♓ 52	25 ♓ 0
376	♊ 21	♋ 28	♌ 29	23 ♍ 10	♎ 16	♏ 15	17 ♈ 37	15 ♏ 30	15 ♈ 38
377	♊ 16	♋ 19	♌ 20	17 ♍ 52	♎ 13	♏ 12	12 ♎ 11	25 ♉ 35	21 ♎ 3
378	♋ 7	♌ 12	♍ 11	5 ♎ 0	♎ 29	♐ 0	8 ♊ 15	6 ♑ 6	4 ♊ 5R
379	♎ 3	♏ 1	♏ 23	12 ♐ 0	♑ 16	♒ 26	8 ♉ 3	6 ♎ 15	11 ♈ 21
380	♈ 28	♊ 10	♋ 19	17 ♌ 50	♍ 5	♍ 27	2 ♑ 53	6 ♏ 25	9 ♑ 40
381	♊ 11	♋ 15	♌ 16	13 ♍ 17	♎ 8	♏ 8	26 ♋ 42	21 ♌ 30	22 ♋ 40
382	♑ 0	♑ 20	♒ 14	2 ♈ 5	♉ 17	♊ 13	12 ♊ 25	0 ♎ 52	18 ♉ 38
383	♌ 7	♍ 10	♎ 7	27 ♎ 20	♏ 24	♐ 28	21 ♐ 54	24 ♏ 47	18 ♐ 15
384	♍ 22	♎ 22	♏ 16	5 ♐ 0	♑ 8	♒ 16	3 ♎ 35	20 ♒ 35	17 ♍ 4
385	♓ 5	♈ 9	♉ 21	29 ♊ 51	♋ 19	♌ 10	29 ♉ 2	17 ♋ 22	4 ♉ 27
386	♉ 3	♊ 9	♋ 14	13 ♌ 15	♍ 5	♎ 1	0 ♌ 5	1 ♓ 6	18 ♌ 56
387	♐ 23	♑ 15	♒ 10	17 ♓ 15	♉ 1	♊ 0	21 ♐ 37	14 ♒ 4	5 ♐ 21
388	♊ 6	♋ 13	♌ 16	11 ♍ 53	♎ 3	♏ 1	17 ♑ 19	6 ♉ 47	28 ♐ 47
389	♏ 13	♐ 2	♐ 18	4 ♑ 30	♒ 26	♈ 15	7 ♑ 18	0 ♎ 8	6 ♑ 31
390	♑ 29	♒ 22	♈ 2	3 ♊ 24	♊ 24	♋ 11	1 ♒ 51	8 ♒ 41	19 ♒ 19
391	♑ 29	♒ 22	♈ 2	3 ♊ 0	♊ 24	♋ 11	10 ♈ 11	17 ♈ 32	29 ♓ 56
392	♓ 5	♈ 9	♉ 23	3 ♋ 0	♋ 22	♌ 11	20 ♉ 50	2 ♐ 35	0 ♊ 39
393	♉ 28	♋ 3	♌ 5	2 ♍ 44	♍ 26	♎ 25	25 ♊ 48	17 ♍ 25	19 ♋ 37
394	♈ 8	♉ 18	♊ 29	1 ♌ 30	♌ 18	♍ 10	7 ♏ 0	2 ♑ 0	0 ♏ 30
395	♏ 26	♐ 17	♑ 8	3 ♒ 34	♓ 20	♈ 29	7 ♋ 22	19 ♒ 0	26 ♊ 26
396	♓ 22	♈ 30	♊ 15	21 ♋ 34	♌ 7	♌ 26	9 ♈ 40	20 ♐ 44	25 ♈ 30
397	♋ 4	♌ 9	♍ 9	3 ♎ 0	♎ 28	♏ 29	4 ♑ 0	11 ♑ 0	12 ♐ 30
398	♑ 0	♑ 18	♒ 13	0 ♈ 0	♉ 17	♊ 12	8 ♒ 30	1 ♉ 2	17 ♑ 05
399	♍ 11	♎ 12	♏ 4	23 ♏ 0	♐ 24	♒ 2	22 ♑ 9	15 ♏ 38	1 ♑ 30
400	♒ 26	♓ 27	♉ 10	21 ♊ 24	♋ 12	♌ 2	6 ♊ 5	21 ♎ 42	28 ♊ 45

	♀	♂	♃	♄	♅	♆	♇
	° ′	° ′	° ′	° ′	° ′	° ′	° ′
351	23 ♋ 50	2 ♈ 2 R	8 ♑ 25 R	22 ♌ 9	7 ♒ 48 R	20 ♑ 30 R	9 ♈ 30 R
352	7 ♏ 4	14 ♓ 48	15 ♈ 2 R	10 ♎ 50	8 ♏ 35	9 ♊ 49 R	8 ♊ 36 R
353	30 ♐ 0	24 ♍ 30	29 ♏ 30	21 ♐ 30	16 ♓ 30 R	12 ♒ 30	19 ♈ 0 R
354	11 ♏ 40	24 ♉ 58 R	2 ♐ 1	13 ♉ 58 R	27 ♑ 36	23 ♋ 5 R	27 ♊ 11
355	8 ♎ 59 R	16 ♎ 18	12 ♒ 39	11 ♍ 10	10 ♒ 33 R	22 ♑ 15	10 ♈ 0
356	11 ♉ 0	16 ♐ 11 R	27 ♒ 15	25 ♑ 9 R	2 ♈ 0	21 ♒ 30	23 ♈ 0
357	5 ♊ 2	29 ♋ 3	3 ♊ 30	15 ♉ 45	14 ♍ 30 R	16 ♉ 17	28 ♉ 21
358	19 ♌ 31	7 ♏ 27	21 ♏ 41	17 ♉ 11 R	7 ♉ 42 R	9 ♓ 24 R	29 ♈ 30 R
359	25 ♈ 56	3 ♎ 25 R	29 ♓ 30	27 ♊ 30	20 ♉ 36	19 ♓ 49	2 ♉ 58
360	18 ♌ 4	24 ♊ 59	20 ♎ 3	4 ♉ 18 R	4 ♉ 22 R	8 ♓ 7 R	0 ♉ 38
361	20 ♑ 42	9 ♍ 58 R	2 ♑ 52	11 ♑ 22	15 ♐ 54	26 ♊ 45 R	15 ♊ 47 R
362	6 ♌ 33	29 ♍ 39	4 ♋ 56	7 ♑ 33 R	24 ♋ 52	23 ♈ 37	19 ♉ 2
363	24 ♊ 30	19 ♍ 36	27 ♊ 1	9 ♑ 33 R	23 ♋ 13	22 ♈ 51	18 ♉ 20
364	9 ♌ 48	2 ♎ 9	4 ♓ 6 R	17 ♏ 52	11 ♋ 10	14 ♈ 55 R	15 ♉ 59
365	27 ♓ 30	1 ♍ 30 R	26 ♈ 30	22 ♈ 33	6 ♑ 30	4 ♑ 30	29 ♓ 30
366	7 ♓ 30	4 ♈ 46	10 ♍ 26 R	28 ♏ 18 R	10 ♓ 23	10 ♒ 0	16 ♈ 0
367	16 ♏ 29	18 ♏ 24	20 ♉ 10 R	12 ♐ 20	21 ♋ 46	18 ♈ 26 R	17 ♉ 31 R
368	20 ♌ 0	17 ♐ 2	6 ♊ 25	27 ♒ 40 R	0 ♑ 17	10 ♋ 14	22 ♊ 39
369	12 ♒ 55	24 ♐ 0	28 ♐ 42	9 ♓ 38	22 ♌ 16 R	2 ♉ 57	22 ♉ 32
370	21 ♉ 50	27 ♈ 57	19 ♈ 21	7 ♋ 44	22 ♉ 37	20 ♓ 54	3 ♉ 41
371	13 ♎ 53	7 ♏ 42	15 ♒ 11	13 ♍ 55	10 ♒ 54	22 ♑ 46	9 ♈ 30 R
372	10 ♋ 2	18 ♐ 55 R	9 ♎ 0 R	0 ♎ 51	13 ♓ 34	13 ♌ 46	8 ♋ 57
373	16 ♑ 17	25 ♐ 48	14 ♉ 2 R	17 ♐ 22	21 ♋ 46 R	17 ♈ 8 R	16 ♉ 48 R
374	18 ♓ 55	12 ♒ 59	18 ♌ 11 R	27 ♑ 43	16 ♈ 7	7 ♍ 14 R	20 ♋ 35 R
375	21 ♑ 48	4 ♋ 38	3 ♊ 19	22 ♎ 33 R	27 ♒ 14	2 ♒ 39	13 ♈ 0
376	29 ♈ 35	11 ♐ 46	7 ♒ 58	27 ♌ 25 R	25 ♎ 0 R	2 ♊ 36	5 ♊ 25
377	27 ♏ 30	15 ♍ 4	10 ♋ 9	9 ♓ 25 R	4 ♑ 43	12 ♋ 37	23 ♊ 39 R
378	14 ♊ 15	25 ♒ 30	1 ♑ 30 R	19 ♓ 30	21 ♌ 1	6 ♉ 15	24 ♉ 17
379	6 ♉ 54	19 ♊ 20	7 ♉ 59	7 ♎ 23 R	8 ♏ 46 R	9 ♊ 46	8 ♊ 36
380	20 ♒ 7	1 ♈ 38	0 ♉ 50 R	16 ♒ 1	6 ♈ 22 R	23 ♒ 50	22 ♈ 58 R
381	4 ♍ 0	29 ♏ 28	8 ♒ 39 R	2 ♍ 10	22 ♎ 45	6 ♊ 6	7 ♊ 24
382	9 ♉ 40	5 ♌ 30	25 ♐ 40 R	24 ♎ 5 R	28 ♊ 38	10 ♈ 10	13 ♉ 18
383	5 ♏ 48	1 ♐ 13	8 ♌ 36 R	14 ♏ 45	22 ♏ 9	16 ♊ 32 R	12 ♊ 0 R
384	19 ♏ 58	13 ♋ 46	16 ♎ 56	7 ♐ 27	0 ♐ 34	24 ♊ 48	15 ♊ 33 R
385	16 ♉ 26	25 ♋ 24	12 ♐ 1 R	24 ♉ 17	3 ♒ 24 R	21 ♋ 38	27 ♊ 46
386	4 ♍ 57	25 ♉ 0	4 ♊ 47	5 ♎ 45	25 ♒ 31 R	0 ♒ 9 R	14 ♈ 0 R
387	14 ♐ 18 R	24 ♎ 53	25 ♎ 57	10 ♒ 43	15 ♌ 6 R	28 ♈ 13 R	21 ♉ 5 R
388	2 ♓ 52	16 ♍ 50	8 ♑ 20	25 ♉ 11 R	8 ♉ 40 R	11 ♓ 31	0 ♉ 44
389	18 ♐ 58	19 ♒ 31	15 ♈ 35	9 ♐ 54	13 ♏ 10	7 ♐ 40	14 ♓ 30
390	8 ♑ 9	8 ♐ 13	13 ♍ 41 R	5 ♈ 16	17 ♑ 52	15 ♋ 17 R	24 ♊ 9 R
391	23 ♉ 36	23 ♓ 56	10 ♐ 51 R	4 ♑ 53	12 ♐ 24 R	24 ♊ 24	14 ♊ 48
392	6 ♋ 3	18 ♌ 16	28 ♋ 20	10 ♊ 30	24 ♍ 11 R	20 ♉ 47	0 ♊ 11
393	18 ♊ 54	15 ♎ 42	28 ♏ 29 R	4 ♌ 25	13 ♎ 8 R	0 ♊ 46	4 ♊ 51
394	11 ♎ 4	13 ♏ 30	0 ♎ 30	0 ♐ 16	28 ♏ 0	23 ♊ 0 R	15 ♊ 0 R
395	8 ♌ 7	16 ♏ 13	7 ♊ 57	28 ♋ 40	1 ♊ 33	24 ♓ 55 R	6 ♉ 54
396	28 ♓ 8	26 ♊ 10	24 ♐ 16	16 ♉ 58	6 ♉ 57	12 ♓ 13	0 ♉ 13
397	10 ♑ 0	1 ♒ 30	1 ♏ 30	20 ♋ 17	12 ♎ 16	25 ♉ 30	3 ♊ 0 R
398	21 ♓ 30	27 ♉ 30	27 ♓ 30	28 ♍ 0 R	18 ♒ 0	27 ♑ 30	11 ♈ 0
399	25 ♐ 11	9 ♈ 57	16 ♈ 52	12 ♎ 43	10 ♏ 15	8 ♊ 51 R	8 ♊ 7 R
400	20 ♋ 56	0 ♉ 49	15 ♋ 52	29 ♎ 35 R	4 ♓ 27	5 ♒ 55 R	15 ♈ 30

	10	11	12	Asc.	2	3	☉	☽	☿
	°	°	°	° ′	°	°	° ′	° ′	° ′
401	♒ 6	♓ 1	♈ 15	11 ♊ 20	♋ 0	♋ 18	29 ♓ 37	2 ♌ 54	26 ♓ 0
402	♒ 26	♓ 27	♉ 13	28 ♊ 20	♋ 16	♌ 4	25 ♊ 30	4 ♐ 15	2 ♊ 30
403	♒ 14	♓ 11	♉ 1	26 ♊ 30	♋ 12	♋ 26	17 ♓ 21	28 ♈ 56	16 ♓ 50
404	♌ 9	♍ 12	♎ 9	29 ♎ 20	♏ 26	♑ 0	22 ♑ 26	12 ♐ 2	0 ♒ 6R
405	♍ 19	♎ 19	♏ 13	2 ♐ 37	♑ 8	♒ 12	14 ♊ 31	14 ♒ 1	14 ♊ 18
406	♑ 19	♒ 12	♓ 16	2 ♉ 40	♊ 4	♊ 27	6 ♉ 36	26 ♋ 0	18 ♈ 28
407	♉ 5	♊ 11	♋ 16	15 ♌ 35	♍ 6	♎ 2	6 ♋ 7	22 ♍ 28	21 ♊ 1R
408	♈ 3	♉ 9	♊ 18	22 ♋ 20	♌ 12	♍ 4	13 ♓ 31	16 ♉ 23	22 ♓ 29
409	♍ 29	♎ 26	♏ 16	1 ♐ 30	♑ 5	♒ 20	6 ♒ 46	21 ♏ 31	12 ♑ 57
410	♎ 0	♎ 29	♏ 21	9 ♐ 38	♑ 14	♒ 24	16 ♓ 27	1 ♒ 15	2 ♓ 21
411	♋ 17	♌ 20	♍ 20	14 ♎ 44	♏ 12	♐ 13	23 ♍ 57	0 ♋ 20	19 ♎ 58
412	♐ 9	♑ 0	♑ 22	22 ♒ 20	♈ 10	♉ 15	7 ♈ 10	20 ♓ 30	25 ♈ 15
413	♉ 26	♋ 9	♌ 13	7 ♍ 45	♍ 26	♎ 20	24 ♊ 51	0 ♍ 22	3 ♊ 23
414	♑ 28	♒ 17	♈ 0	16 ♊ 0	♋ 1	♋ 15	19 ♏ 10	27 ♏ 10	0 ♏ 50
415	♊ 1	♋ 10	♌ 13	9 ♍ 0	♍ 29	♎ 26	18 ♊ 58	20 ♎ 30	4 ♊ 22
416	♎ 13	♏ 7	♏ 24	8 ♐ 15	♑ 16	♓ 6	11 ♌ 23	3 ♌ 45	8 ♍ 48
417	♌ 4	♍ 8	♎ 6	27 ♎ 58	♏ 26	♐ 29	28 ♐ 1	15 ♈ 8	17 ♑ 30
418	♓ 17	♈ 17	♊ 11	19 ♋ 0	♌ 4	♌ 22	0 ♋ 53	18 ♒ 30	29 ♋ 52R
419	♏ 24	♐ 11	♐ 25	12 ♑ 0	♓ 15	♈ 29	28 ♊ 35	22 ♏ 3	23 ♋ 11
420	♋ 18	♌ 18	♍ 19	19 ♎ 39	♏ 20	♐ 19	0 ♌ 11	25 ♒ 18	16 ♌ 53
421	♍ 27	♎ 24	♏ 13	27 ♏ 30	♑ 0	♒ 16	7 ♌ 34	22 ♋ 58	26 ♋ 52
422	♈ 4	♉ 10	♊ 18	20 ♋ 55	♌ 12	♍ 5	21 ♒ 15	28 ♋ 30	4 ♒ 13
423	♓ 24	♉ 2	♊ 19	24 ♋ 0	♌ 10	♌ 28	26 ♈ 38	21 ♏ 15	0 ♈ 31
424	♎ 1	♏ 0	♏ 23	12 ♐ 49	♑ 17	♒ 24	16 ♊ 32	16 ♐ 19	29 ♊ 21R
425	♎ 27	♏ 21	♐ 11	29 ♐ 1	♒ 10	♓ 23	27 ♓ 0	25 ♒ 48	8 ♓ 18R
426	♒ 10	♓ 7	♈ 22	18 ♊ 0	♋ 6	♋ 22	11 ♌ 4	30 ♏ 0	0 ♍ 30
427	♐ 23	♑ 15	♒ 11	19 ♓ 8	♉ 2	♊ 1	23 ♈ 59	17 ♉ 13	29 ♓ 45
428	♑ 15	♒ 8	♓ 10	26 ♈ 10	♊ 2	♊ 24	8 ♋ 1	18 ♏ 19	20 ♋ 52
429	♏ 3	♏ 25	♐ 12	27 ♐ 20	♒ 12	♈ 1	8 ♐ 9	5 ♍ 50	18 ♏ 2
430	♐ 13	♑ 4	♑ 27	29 ♒ 30	♈ 17	♉ 14	10 ♏ 30	2 ♉ 45	17 ♏ 50
431	♈ 9	♉ 18	♊ 29	1 ♌ 30	♌ 19	♍ 10	11 ♊ 46	10 ♋ 41	1 ♊ 42
432	♋ 2	♌ 8	♍ 8	1 ♎ 0	♎ 26	♏ 26	16 ♍ 40	11 ♌ 5	6 ♎ 30
433	♋ 0	♌ 3	♍ 4	0 ♎ 0	♎ 26	♏ 27	12 ♓ 21	21 ♈ 8	28 ♒ 37
434	♉ 2	♊ 8	♋ 12	11 ♌ 48	♍ 3	♍ 30	27 ♌ 4	3 ♏ 36	1 ♍ 44
435	♏ 6	♏ 29	♐ 19	9 ♑ 30	♒ 22	♈ 5	2 ♍ 0	14 ♓ 45	16 ♍ 0R
436	♑ 8	♑ 28	♒ 27	17 ♈ 13	♉ 26	♊ 20	29 ♏ 52	1 ♒ 30	10 ♐ 8
437	♊ 26	♌ 0	♍ 1	26 ♍ 10	♎ 21	♏ 21	11 ♊ 31	3 ♉ 16	19 ♊ 55R
438	♐ 23	♑ 11	♒ 3	3 ♓ 0	♉ 6	♊ 4	4 ♐ 3	17 ♍ 31	22 ♐ 6R
439	♒ 3	♓ 0	♈ 8	26 ♉ 30	♊ 22	♋ 12	8 ♈ 11	15 ♒ 30	3 ♈ 30
440	♊ 10	♋ 13	♌ 15	12 ♍ 35	♎ 7	♏ 6	16 ♎ 30	11 ♉ 4	4 ♏ 30
441	♌ 25	♍ 27	♎ 24	15 ♏ 0	♐ 15	♑ 19	10 ♎ 41	0 ♊ 21	4 ♏ 17
442	♍ 24	♎ 24	♏ 18	9 ♐ 46	♑ 12	♒ 18	10 ♊ 36	6 ♒ 3	2 ♊ 52R
443	♋ 15	♌ 18	♍ 18	13 ♎ 0	♏ 10	♐ 11	29 ♊ 34	19 ♋ 53	15 ♋ 22
444	♒ 4	♓ 1	♈ 9	23 ♉ 50	♊ 20	♋ 12	8 ♉ 44	17 ♍ 40	18 ♉ 30
445	♏ 2	♏ 21	♐ 2	16 ♐ 40	♒ 4	♈ 0	0 ♓ 30	3 ♐ 4	10 ♒ 38
446	♒ 4	♓ 14	♈ 23	5 ♊ 25	♊ 29	♋ 21	12 ♌ 28	9 ♈ 45	25 ♌ 49
447	♍ 26	♎ 24	♏ 14	28 ♏ 43	♑ 2	♒ 16	12 ♒ 31	23 ♋ 19	20 ♒ 25
448	♈ 29	♊ 5	♋ 10	10 ♌ 24	♍ 1	♍ 27	8 ♒ 7	15 ♒ 48	13 ♑ 12
449	♈ 14	♉ 24	♊ 7	8 ♌ 27	♌ 24	♍ 14	0 ♌ 14	4 ♌ 56	21 ♌ 9
450	♋ 16	♌ 21	♍ 20	12 ♎ 10	♏ 7	♐ 9	4 ♊ 10	9 ♊ 0	9 ♊ 40

	♀	♂	♃	♄	♅	♆	♇
	° ′	° ′	° ′	° ′	° ′	° ′	° ′
401	15 ♒ 47	8 ♉ 37	2 ♓ 53	12 ♍ 33 R	0 ♏ 35	4 ♊ 21	6 ♊ 0
402	20 ♋ 18	15 ♌ 30	9 ♑ 44 R	18 ♓ 9	17 ♐ 50 R	25 ♐ 30 R	26 ♓ 30
403	1 ♒ 8	26 ♈ 13	13 ♊ 5	6 ♌ 11 R	29 ♉ 53	24 ♓ 18	5 ♉ 49
404	10 ♐ 27	25 ♒ 36	20 ♓ 0	9 ♒ 0	27 ♐ 37	4 ♋ 4 R	19 ♊ 3 R
405	23 ♊ 32	14 ♋ 1	16 ♉ 48	6 ♎ 2 R	7 ♏ 17 R	11 ♊ 8	9 ♊ 20
406	22 ♓ 47	23 ♌ 56	11 ♉ 33	0 ♉ 41	7 ♑ 17 R	5 ♑ 7 R	1 ♈ 0
407	0 ♌ 1 R	20 ♋ 49	22 ♏ 50 R	8 ♓ 0 R	17 ♌ 41	4 ♉ 52	24 ♉ 54
408	29 ♈ 24	13 ♏ 22	24 ♌ 25 R	29 ♑ 4	2 ♌ 22 R	24 ♈ 29	18 ♉ 56
409	23 ♐ 42	26 ♓ 16	11 ♊ 41 R	9 ♌ 2 R	29 ♉ 34 R	22 ♓ 57	5 ♉ 35
410	0 ♒ 57	29 ♈ 13	29 ♒ 50	13 ♍ 35 R	0 ♏ 59 R	4 ♊ 9	5 ♊ 54
411	19 ♍ 55	0 ♑ 27	18 ♒ 50 R	19 ♑ 14 R	0 ♈ 34 R	19 ♒ 12 R	21 ♈ 48 R
412	19 ♉ 50	8 ♑ 30	2 ♈ 32	26 ♍ 0 R	5 ♏ 10 R	6 ♊ 43	7 ♊ 4
413	22 ♋ 20	16 ♏ 25 R	5 ♊ 1	27 ♋ 6	0 ♊ 52	24 ♓ 53	6 ♉ 54
414	21 ♐ 47	27 ♏ 30	0 ♋ 30 R	22 ♉ 58 R	22 ♍ 30	17 ♉ 30 R	29 ♉ 11 R
415	20 ♉ 7	1 ♋ 20	0 ♋ 6	8 ♌ 51	4 ♊ 30	27 ♓ 3	6 ♉ 4
416	16 ♌ 33	20 ♋ 5	11 ♌ 10	16 ♑ 13 R	2 ♌ 11	26 ♈ 2 R	20 ♉ 38
417	11 ♏ 44	2 ♒ 59	28 ♋ 8 R	10 ♑ 37	0 ♌ 28 R	21 ♈ 19 R	18 ♉ 8 R
418	23 ♊ 3	11 ♎ 19	7 ♈ 2	3 ♋ 17	23 ♉ 13	20 ♓ 27 R	5 ♉ 11
419	9 ♋ 10	20 ♋ 15	23 ♌ 10	4 ♍ 26	13 ♊ 9	1 ♈ 36	9 ♉ 30
420	14 ♋ 41	2 ♌ 22	17 ♓ 37	14 ♍ 21	27 ♎ 26	8 ♊ 23	8 ♊ 25
421	10 ♌ 19	29 ♎ 42	9 ♈ 11 R	8 ♋ 11	24 ♉ 40	20 ♓ 7 R	3 ♉ 17
422	26 ♓ 4	10 ♐ 23	21 ♓ 37	29 ♍ 16R	6 ♏ 5 R	6 ♊ 16 R	6 ♊ 49
423	20 ♉ 57 R	10 ♓ 3	1 ♉ 7	1 ♉ 21	10 ♍ 2 R	13 ♉ 21	27 ♉ 2
424	26 ♋ 6	7 ♋ 32	24 ♏ 40 R	7 ♓ 58	16 ♌ 45	4 ♉ 21	23 ♉ 33
425	15 ♓ 47	24 ♌ 54 R	10 ♑ 15	15 ♑ 12	16 ♐ 54	26 ♊ 29	15 ♊ 42
426	29 ♌ 45	3 ♎ 0	26 ♏ 30	11 ♎ 30	17 ♎ 30	25 ♏ 30	11 ♓ 0
427	0 ♈ 23	20 ♎ 56 R	5 ♐ 36 R	29 ♋ 45	14 ♎ 50 R	28 ♉ 26	3 ♊ 30
428	22 ♌ 46	14 ♈ 45	12 ♓ 43	15 ♈ 5	1 ♍ 18	11 ♉ 30	26 ♉ 35
429	21 ♐ 49 R	16 ♎ 52	23 ♎ 40	9 ♒ 30	15 ♌ 16 R	28 ♈ 30 R	21 ♉ 35 R
430	12 ♎ 50	13 ♏ 2	27 ♐ 30	4 ♏ 1	3 ♋ 45 R	8 ♈ 30 R	13 ♉ 12 R
431	27 ♉ 23	4 ♊ 35	10 ♏ 35 R	18 ♐ 57 R	20 ♓ 11	14 ♒ 49 R	19 ♈ 30
432	2 ♏ 6	14 ♎ 5	28 ♊ 51	26 ♉ 11 R	18 ♍ 48	18 ♉ 45 R	0 ♊ 3 R
433	5 ♈ 31	22 ♑ 40	14 ♏ 33 R	2 ♉ 52	27 ♑ 50	18 ♋ 58 R	26 ♊ 41
434	13 ♋ 4	20 ♍ 32	5 ♉ 35	27 ♍ 1	20 ♒ 19 R	27 ♑ 13 R	12 ♈ 40 R
435	13 ♎ 30	4 ♏ 30	17 ♎ 30	4 ♐ 0	15 ♓ 0 R	11 ♒ 0 R	19 ♈ 30 R
436	23 ♏ 33	9 ♍ 11	11 ♎ 33	1 ♐ 12	8 ♓ 33	7 ♒ 58	17 ♈ 30 R
437	12 ♉ 22	2 ♉ 26	5 ♋ 49	1 ♊ 10	19 ♍ 14	19 ♉ 24	29 ♉ 54
438	22 ♐ 6	17 ♐ 1	23 ♏ 41	23 ♐ 34	8 ♐ 1 R	26 ♊ 12 R	15 ♊ 48 R
439	15 ♉ 8	3 ♋ 5	1 ♍ 30 R	0 ♐ 30 R	29 ♏ 0 R	18 ♊ 0	11 ♊ 51
440	1 ♍ 54	7 ♌ 50	8 ♐ 14	29 ♐ 34	9 ♐ 30	29 ♊ 15 R	18 ♊ 8 R
441	20 ♍ 56	22 ♏ 14	6 ♊ 23 R	8 ♉ 40 R	3 ♑ 34	2 ♑ 30	26 ♓ 0
442	17 ♊ 18	26 ♒ 38	1 ♑ 4 R	19 ♓ 36	21 ♌ 6	6 ♉ 20	24 ♉ 17
443	3 ♌ 51	0 ♒ 11 R	28 ♋ 5	22 ♌ 15	9 ♊ 11	29 ♓ 8	8 ♉ 59
444	11 ♊ 30	0 ♋ 53	20 ♎ 30 R	29 ♍ 30	18 ♊ 30	4 ♈ 51	10 ♉ 35
445	16 ♈ 52	11 ♊ 33	24 ♐ 38	0 ♏ 13 R	25 ♊ 32 R	6 ♈ 41	11 ♉ 15
446	23 ♍ 14	4 ♐ 8	6 ♒ 34 R	4 ♍ 5	23 ♎ 8	6 ♊ 28	7 ♊ 35
447	20 ♑ 30	9 ♍ 58 R	2 ♑ 50	11 ♑ 22	15 ♐ 53	26 ♊ 45 R	14 ♊ 35 R
448	22 ♓ 32	4 ♊ 27	20 ♐ 52	0 ♏ 10	26 ♊ 0 R	6 ♈ 4	11 ♉ 15 R
449	14 ♊ 34	5 ♍ 46	20 ♐ 3 R	24 ♎ 6	1 ♋ 35	10 ♈ 35 R	14 ♉ 2
450	18 ♋ 6	8 ♋ 58	26 ♉ 8	0 ♓ 35	13 ♈ 5	28 ♒ 9	25 ♈ 30

	10	11	12	Asc.	2	3	☉	☽	☿
	°	°	°	° ′	°	°	° ′	° ′	° ′
451	♎ 10	♏ 3	♐ 2	6 ♑ 0	♑ 29	♓ 1	18 ♈ 29	13 ♉ 41	29 ♓ 42R
452	♈ 29	♊ 8	♋ 15	15 ♌ 0	♍ 3	♍ 27	15 ♉ 52	17 ♏ 52	8 ♉ 4R
453	♐ 25	♑ 10	♒ 0	13 ♓ 38	♉ 14	♊ 8	16 ♌ 16	14 ♋ 17	0 ♌ 21
454	♑ 5	♑ 23	♒ 20	13 ♈ 0	♉ 25	♊ 17	28 ♎ 47	6 ♓ 30	11 ♎ 30
455	♑ 19	♒ 7	♓ 10	20 ♉ 56	♊ 16	♋ 3	20 ♋ 26	14 ♐ 17	16 ♌ 20
456	♌ 29	♎ 1	♎ 25	13 ♏ 0	♐ 12	♑ 26	2 ♒ 7	4 ♊ 44	25 ♑ 45
457	♎ 15	♏ 12	♐ 5	26 ♐ 0	♒ 1	♓ 10	11 ♒ 13	28 ♑ 30	23 ♒ 45
458	♈ 9	♉ 17	♊ 29	2 ♌ 50	♌ 19	♍ 10	24 ♏ 14	25 ♏ 45	6 ♏ 4
459	♏ 28	♐ 16	♑ 2	22 ♑ 30	♓ 23	♉ 4	8 ♎ 45	23 ♋ 46	18 ♎ 30
460	♐ 20	♑ 11	♒ 5	11 ♓ 13	♈ 27	♉ 27	21 ♈ 50	19 ♐ 43	6 ♉ 8
461	♎ 10	♏ 8	♐ 1	22 ♐ 0	♑ 22	♓ 5	8 ♉ 30	22 ♍ 30	22 ♈ 30
462	♌ 1	♍ 5	♎ 3	24 ♎ 16	♏ 22	♐ 25	0 ♉ 49	6 ♑ 42	25 ♈ 42
463	♊ 27	♌ 1	♍ 2	27 ♍ 25	♎ 23	♏ 23	26 ♈ 1	20 ♑ 40	0 ♈ 17
464	♎ 4	♏ 2	♏ 25	13 ♐ 58	♑ 19	♒ 28	18 ♒ 5	4 ♐ 29	21 ♒ 10
465	♋ 1	♌ 8	♍ 8	0 ♎ 44	♎ 24	♏ 24	29 ♈ 28	21 ♑ 50	9 ♈ 31
466	♑ 5	♑ 24	♒ 22	12 ♈ 0	♉ 23	♊ 16	10 ♓ 58	28 ♉ 49	23 ♓ 25
467	♉ 25	♋ 2	♌ 6	3 ♍ 39	♍ 23	♎ 20	14 ♋ 5	1 ♎ 11	16 ♋ 30
468	♒ 5	♓ 2	♈ 11	26 ♉ 55	♊ 23	♋ 13	8 ♉ 32	11 ♌ 6	27 ♉ 47
469	♏ 2	♏ 28	♐ 20	12 ♑ 15	♒ 20	♓ 29	14 ♒ 10	19 ♈ 14	23 ♑ 24
470	♋ 3	♌ 10	♍ 9	2 ♎ 30	♎ 26	♏ 26	23 ♈ 25	20 ♌ 30	29 ♓ 10
471	♌ 8	♍ 11	♎ 9	1 ♏ 35	♐ 0	♑ 3	18 ♓ 30	7 ♎ 30	4 ♈ 43
472	♉ 18	♊ 24	♋ 27	25 ♌ 30	♏ 18	♎ 15	20 ♓ 47	12 ♍ 49	4 ♓ 11
473	♈ 6	♉ 15	♊ 28	0 ♌ 43	♌ 17	♍ 8	27 ♍ 50	22 ♑ 18	8 ♎ 23
474	♒ 3	♒ 29	♈ 7	25 ♉ 55	♊ 21	♋ 11	18 ♌ 20	7 ♌ 12	0 ♌ 3
475	♎ 25	♏ 21	♐ 12	3 ♑ 5	♒ 12	♓ 22	10 ♑ 53	9 ♓ 37	5 ♑ 47
476	♋ 25	♌ 27	♍ 27	23 ♎ 12	♏ 22	♐ 21	24 ♎ 14	11 ♉ 49	27 ♎ 0R
477	♑ 9	♒ 2	♓ 1	16 ♈ 0	♉ 25	♊ 18	11 ♊ 35	28 ♐ 32	7 ♊ 2R
478	♉ 11	♊ 17	♋ 21	19 ♌ 58	♍ 12	♎ 8	15 ♎ 2	9 ♑ 55	4 ♏ 15
479	♈ 16	♉ 28	♋ 10	10 ♌ 30	♌ 28	♍ 17	27 ♓ 3	25 ♈ 14	9 ♈ 30
480	♏ 23	♐ 14	♑ 3	27 ♑ 0	♓ 15	♈ 26	16 ♈ 20	4 ♐ 18	21 ♓ 29
481	♏ 24	♐ 16	♑ 7	1 ♒ 0	♓ 18	♈ 27	0 ♓ 13	25 ♑ 18	4 ♒ 57
482	♋ 20	♌ 23	♍ 23	17 ♎ 15	♏ 15	♐ 16	10 ♑ 47	7 ♎ 25	19 ♑ 47
483	♋ 13	♌ 16	♍ 16	11 ♎ 17	♏ 8	♐ 9	28 ♊ 35	14 ♑ 50	1 ♋ 27
484	♎ 29	♏ 23	♐ 14	3 ♑ 11	♒ 14	♓ 26	21 ♓ 37	1 ♍ 40	15 ♓ 3
485	♐ 25	♑ 12	♒ 3	16 ♓ 0	♉ 12	♊ 7	28 ♊ 30	14 ♉ 30	14 ♊ 15
486	♊ 6	♋ 10	♌ 12	10 ♍ 1	♎ 4	♏ 3	21 ♈ 40	13 ♍ 45	29 ♈ 47
487	♌ 14	♍ 17	♎ 13	4 ♏ 0	♐ 1	♑ 6	7 ♓ 40	25 ♐ 3	25 ♓ 23
488	♈ 29	♊ 5	♋ 9	10 ♌ 0	♍ 2	♎ 1	8 ♎ 37	20 ♉ 5	20 ♍ 50
489	♒ 27	♓ 29	♉ 12	25 ♊ 0	♋ 15	♌ 4	24 ♓ 0	29 ♑ 45	3 ♓ 30
490	♓ 0	♈ 2	♉ 16	28 ♊ 0	♋ 17	♌ 6	22 ♍ 40	14 ♐ 30	23 ♍ 0R
491	♑ 1	♑ 23	♒ 20	1 ♈ 20	♉ 13	♊ 10	22 ♏ 1	28 ♑ 19	13 ♐ 34
492	♓ 11	♈ 16	♊ 4	13 ♋ 44	♋ 29	♌ 17	13 ♉ 30	6 ♐ 30	27 ♉ 10
493	♉ 13	♊ 18	♋ 22	20 ♌ 24	♍ 13	♎ 10	3 ♓ 50	25 ♈ 44	21 ♈ 28
494	♌ 4	♍ 7	♎ 6	28 ♎ 38	♏ 27	♐ 29	3 ♐ 39	0 ♌ 6	1 ♐ 47
495	♏ 8	♏ 27	♐ 12	26 ♐ 30	♒ 16	♈ 8	7 ♍ 46	25 ♓ 30	2 ♎ 30
496	♓ 10	♓ 29	♉ 16	17 ♋ 15	♌ 13	♌ 27	16 ♉ 8	13 ♈ 13	21 ♈ 37
497	♌ 12	♍ 16	♎ 12	1 ♏ 0	♏ 29	♑ 4	18 ♒ 0	19 ♋ 9	22 ♑ 30
498	♏ 21	♐ 13	♑ 4	27 ♑ 30	♓ 14	♈ 23	16 ♎ 30	6 ♌ 30	22 ♎ 6R
499	♋ 28	♍ 1	♍ 30	23 ♎ 35	♏ 22	♐ 24	0 ♒ 13	7 ♎ 3	18 ♒ 24
500	♓ 12	♈ 16	♉ 27	4 ♋ 15	♋ 24	♌ 15	12 ♍ 2	24 ♋ 44	28 ♋ 30

	♀	♂	♃	♄	♅	♆	♇
	° ′	° ′	° ′	° ′	° ′	° ′	° ′
451	11 ♉ 57 R	7 ♓ 31	16 ♑ 44	1 ♊ 21	7 ♒ 5	23 ♋ 13	28 ♊ 25
452	5 ♊ 50	5 ♈ 50	1 ♎ 1 R	10 ♐ 42 R	2 ♐ 14 R	20 ♊ 55	13 ♊ 28
453	0 ♎ 35	15 ♋ 25	29 ♒ 11 R	26 ♊ 32	20 ♉ 44	17 ♓ 37 R	4 ♉ 32 R
454	27 ♍ 20	22 ♎ 15	5 ♏ 50	11 ♎ 7	24 ♊ 57 R	4 ♈ 4 R	11 ♉ 30 R
455	14 ♊ 52	6 ♎ 2	29 ♍ 37	13 ♋ 8	4 ♎ 2	27 ♉ 12	4 ♊ 0
456	5 ♑ 1	11 ♈ 48	24 ♌ 30 R	8 ♍ 30 R	8 ♊ 16 R	27 ♓ 11	7 ♉ 25 R
457	14 ♓ 38	14 ♈ 55	8 ♌ 15 R	24 ♓ 31	14 ♑ 27	12 ♋ 45 R	25 ♊ 0
458	8 ♎ 8	12 ♏ 10	9 ♌ 2	11 ♏ 40	20 ♌ 30	17 ♊ 17 R	12 ♊ 0 R
459	10 ♎ 33 R	15 ♉ 30	18 ♋ 30	7 ♓ 30 R	16 ♈ 35 R	28 ♒ 0 R	26 ♈ 30 R
460	18 ♈ 12	12 ♈ 51	11 ♉ 52	23 ♋ 56	22 ♒ 51	2 ♌ 5	2 ♋ 40
461	8 ♉ 30	26 ♌ 30	13 ♑ 3	16 ♑ 23 R	16 ♐ 18 R	27 ♊ 10	16 ♊ 15
462	16 ♉ 41 R	16 ♉ 24	8 ♑ 15	13 ♌ 27	19 ♎ 30 R	0 ♊ 51	4 ♊ 35
463	11 ♉ 58	22 ♋ 56	17 ♒ 46	14 ♊ 44	11 ♒ 14	25 ♋ 27	29 ♊ 36
464	10 ♑ 15	11 ♑ 23	2 ♌ 21 R	18 ♏ 47	24 ♏ 20	15 ♊ 21	11 ♊ 0 R
465	22 ♉ 59	10 ♏ 15 R	21 ♌ 28	2 ♒ 18	1 ♌ 51	26 ♈ 9	19 ♉ 40
466	17 ♈ 47	27 ♒ 15	18 ♓ 10	5 ♐ 30	8 ♋ 57 R	13 ♈ 30	14 ♉ 15
467	6 ♊ 30	8 ♌ 30	4 ♒ 30 R	2 ♈ 51	27 ♌ 3	9 ♉ 30	25 ♉ 58
468	9 ♉ 28	25 ♈ 53	15 ♉ 53	24 ♋ 43	23 ♒ 22	2 ♋ 10	2 ♌ 40
469	17 ♓ 16	6 ♐ 2	20 ♓ 3	29 ♍ 36 R	6 ♏ 4	6 ♊ 18 R	6 ♊ 52
470	12 ♓ 22	24 ♋ 30	29 ♒ 45	22 ♏ 48 R	4 ♋ 48	12 ♈ 55	14 ♉ 14
471	4 ♉ 0	6 ♏ 0	18 ♐ 37	2 ♑ 9	20 ♓ 11	15 ♒ 43	19 ♈ 0
472	0 ♉ 21	2 ♌ 30 R	24 ♋ 38 R	4 ♊ 25	26 ♍ 21 R	18 ♉ 48	29 ♉ 14
473	14 ♏ 12	3 ♍ 1	9 ♎ 0	8 ♒ 2 R	13 ♌ 44	0 ♉ 13 R	22 ♉ 26
474	29 ♍ 25	7 ♌ 13	0 ♎ 45	10 ♒ 26 R	11 ♌ 25	0 ♉ 49 R	22 ♉ 34
475	18 ♑ 31	0 ♉ 28	30 ♊ 0	5 ♏ 37	18 ♏ 44	13 ♊ 42 R	10 ♊ 10 R
476	13 ♎ 49	26 ♌ 52	7 ♒ 44	21 ♑ 35	18 ♐ 24	3 ♋ 41 R	19 ♊ 37 R
477	7 ♋ 51	4 ♐ 30 R	12 ♒ 9 R	28 ♌ 3	22 ♒ 56 R	4 ♊ 33	6 ♊ 30
478	2 ♎ 10	21 ♌ 20	7 ♒ 27	21 ♑ 20	18 ♐ 3	3 ♋ 43 R	19 ♊ 0 R
479	14 ♓ 5	10 ♑ 30	1 ♑ 55	12 ♓ 30	21 ♌ 18 R	3 ♉ 30	23 ♉ 0
480	26 ♈ 48	11 ♉ 27	24 ♍ 26 R	12 ♒ 29	6 ♌ 31 R	27 ♈ 49	20 ♉ 30
481	13 ♒ 30	2 ♓ 10	1 ♉ 7	24 ♋ 43	20 ♒ 19	2 ♌ 47	2 ♋ 20
482	7 ♐ 47	5 ♑ 0	24 ♊ 28 R	19 ♉ 36 R	23 ♍ 21 R	16 ♉ 12 R	28 ♉ 30 R
483	19 ♊ 44	10 ♎ 20	6 ♈ 44	2 ♋ 55	23 ♉ 5	20 ♓ 36	5 ♉ 11
484	17 ♈ 1	29 ♑ 31	14 ♏ 19 R	3 ♉ 50	28 ♑ 15	18 ♋ 51 R	25 ♊ 25
485	16 ♉ 40	15 ♌ 30	23 ♐ 30 R	23 ♎ 30 R	29 ♊ 30	10 ♈ 30	13 ♉ 30
486	8 ♓ 45	5 ♒ 14	19 ♍ 4 R	16 ♍ 58 R	13 ♊ 28	2 ♈ 4	9 ♉ 30
487	2 ♓ 57	1 ♒ 2	29 ♌ 59 R	3 ♍ 47 R	6 ♎ 12 R	21 ♏ 36	5 ♓ 30
488	29 ♍ 25 R	3 ♐ 31	26 ♋ 40	3 ♑ 45	0 ♌ 42	23 ♈ 3 R	19 ♉ 30 R
489	2 ♉ 0	7 ♉ 30	13 ♓ 35	4 ♒ 14	2 ♈ 0	22 ♒ 30	22 ♈ 30
490	11 ♎ 35	20 ♌ 15	29 ♈ 3 R	15 ♒ 15 R	26 ♐ 1	8 ♋ 0	21 ♊ 36
491	25 ♐ 47	19 ♏ 3	18 ♐ 58	1 ♊ 17 R	0 ♒ 4	25 ♋ 57 R	27 ♊ 45
492	6 ♊ 0 R	19 ♉ 30	5 ♌ 30	8 ♊ 0	20 ♑ 0 R	12 ♑ 0 R	3 ♈ 30
493	29 ♈ 44	4 ♒ 29	29 ♒ 45	5 ♈ 27	0 ♍ 55 R	8 ♉ 10	24 ♉ 41
494	8 ♑ 50	25 ♊ 35	8 ♍ 51	23 ♏ 12	25 ♏ 21	19 ♊ 21 R	13 ♊ 0 R
495	10 ♎ 30	11 ♏ 55	21 ♋ 30	3 ♑ 30 R	29 ♋ 30	23 ♈ 47 R	19 ♉ 30
496	27 ♈ 42	14 ♋ 18	7 ♈ 40	22 ♈ 14	4 ♍ 52 R	11 ♉ 56	26 ♉ 30
497	22 ♓ 0	21 ♒ 30	17 ♍ 0 R	28 ♏ 30	7 ♓ 30	8 ♒ 30	14 ♈ 0
498	29 ♍ 1	21 ♓ 30 R	9 ♑ 57	28 ♌ 30	6 ♒ 30 R	20 ♑ 2	8 ♈ 30 R
499	15 ♐ 40	9 ♎ 55	3 ♋ 3 R	16 ♉ 59	12 ♑ 45	7 ♑ 56	1 ♈ 0
500	16 ♎ 40	12 ♉ 43	14 ♋ 40	9 ♓ 20 R	17 ♈ 34 R	28 ♒ 36 R	27 ♈ 35 R

	10 °	11 °	12 °	Asc. ° ′	2 °	3 °	☉ ° ′	☽ ° ′	☿ ° ′
501	♎ 23	♏ 19	♐ 12	3 ♑ 30	♒ 10	♓ 19	12 ♓ 44	0 ♋ 56	1 ♓ 34
502	♓ 28	♉ 4	♊ 13	16 ♋ 57	♌ 7	♌ 29	15 ♎ 42	11 ♉ 29	5 ♎ 43
503	♒ 4	♓ 1	♈ 9	25 ♉ 54	♊ 22	♋ 13	4 ♏ 18	29 ♊ 27	19 ♏ 38
504	♋ 29	♍ 4	♌ 1	23 ♎ 30	♏ 20	♐ 22	12 ♎ 40	27 ♉ 23	0 ♏ 13
505	♈ 9	♉ 11	♊ 11	10 ♋ 0	♌ 7	♍ 7	24 ♐ 13	16 ♌ 14	18 ♐ 40
506	♓ 4	♈ 7	♉ 26	8 ♊ 53	♋ 24	♌ 11	19 ♋ 4	20 ♏ 40	7 ♌ 34
507	♌ 22	♍ 24	♎ 20	11 ♏ 34	♐ 11	♑ 15	10 ♒ 29	27 ♊ 18	26 ♒ 10
508	♐ 10	♑ 1	♑ 23	24 ♒ 0	♈ 12	♉ 15	23 ♓ 54	20 ♊ 20	23 ♓ 38
509	♌ 18	♍ 20	♎ 17	10 ♏ 8	♐ 9	♑ 12	8 ♎ 50	16 ♌ 34	3 ♏ 1
510	♌ 5	♍ 8	♎ 6	29 ♎ 35	♏ 27	♑ 0	9 ♒ 42	8 ♐ 20	16 ♑ 17
511	♒ 22	♓ 22	♉ 9	28 ♊ 0	♋ 14	♌ 1	9 ♉ 20	12 ♍ 5	18 ♉ 59
512	♐ 11	♑ 0	♑ 20	20 ♒ 0	♈ 15	♉ 18	3 ♌ 20	15 ♉ 35	13 ♋ 48
513	♈ 3	♉ 8	♊ 14	16 ♋ 2	♌ 9	♍ 3	14 ♑ 30	24 ♍ 25	28 ♐ 27
514	♍ 5	♎ 7	♏ 3	25 ♏ 37	♐ 26	♑ 29	6 ♋ 8	18 ♓ 30	0 ♌ 14
515	♏ 10	♐ 3	♐ 23	14 ♑ 15	♒ 28	♈ 9	12 ♉ 8	28 ♌ 43	23 ♉ 19
516	♋ 4	♋ 22	♌ 19	10 ♎ 14	♏ 24	♐ 16	12 ♓ 44	3 ♉ 54	9 ♓ 42
517	♓ 18	♈ 25	♊ 15	21 ♋ 50	♌ 6	♌ 23	29 ♐ 8	29 ♏ 55	14 ♐ 53
518	♉ 20	♊ 28	♌ 3	1 ♍ 30	♍ 20	♎ 16	14 ♎ 50	0 ♓ 50	2 ♏ 30
519	♈ 25	♊ 4	♋ 13	13 ♌ 30	♍ 0	♍ 23	28 ♐ 2	15 ♍ 30	2 ♑ 47
520	♒ 27	♓ 29	♉ 11	21 ♊ 49	♋ 12	♌ 3	29 ♊ 9	3 ♍ 53	10 ♋ 11
521	♐ 25	♑ 9	♑ 25	9 ♓ 10	♉ 18	♊ 10	28 ♋ 24	13 ♑ 47	20 ♌ 1
522	♐ 29	♑ 24	♒ 23	28 ♓ 33	♉ 5	♊ 4	13 ♋ 32	14 ♓ 49	2 ♋ 45
523	♐ 12	♐ 29	♑ 8	16 ♒ 45	♈ 17	♉ 22	23 ♍ 30	11 ♌ 0	7 ♍ 0
524	♐ 17	♑ 8	♒ 1	5 ♓ 20	♈ 23	♉ 25	8 ♎ 33	21 ♐ 10	23 ♍ 37
525	♓ 21	♈ 25	♉ 29	0 ♋ 32	♋ 25	♌ 21	8 ♑ 55	15 ♊ 45	24 ♐ 8R
526	♊ 23	♋ 25	♌ 25	23 ♍ 23	♎ 21	♏ 21	10 ♓ 57	5 ♊ 49	7 ♓ 3
527	♑ 10	♑ 28	♒ 26	29 ♈ 35	♊ 5	♊ 24	2 ♋ 3	26 ♐ 8	14 ♊ 55
528	♑ 28	♒ 20	♈ 0	5 ♊ 50	♊ 26	♋ 12	8 ♋ 47	8 ♊ 54	26 ♊ 27
529	♐ 10	♑ 4	♒ 0	1 ♓ 36	♈ 10	♉ 13	8 ♒ 33	8 ♌ 47	15 ♒ 40
530	♓ 16	♈ 19	♊ 0	6 ♋ 14	♋ 27	♌ 19	2 ♌ 26	5 ♏ 30	5 ♌ 21
531	♐ 6	♐ 21	♑ 6	25 ♑ 35	♈ 8	♉ 16	12 ♓ 3	18 ♏ 30	26 ♓ 1
532	♏ 29	♐ 25	♑ 21	20 ♒ 0	♓ 27	♉ 0	20 ♉ 47	25 ♐ 12	28 ♉ 40
533	♎ 11	♏ 19	♐ 1	22 ♐ 0	♑ 27	♓ 6	24 ♏ 16	24 ♋ 59	16 ♐ 30
534	♋ 22	♌ 19	♍ 22	4 ♏ 0	♐ 5	♐ 29	17 ♎ 0	21 ♍ 30	2 ♎ 0
535	♏ 24	♐ 19	♑ 14	11 ♒ 30	♓ 20	♈ 25	18 ♍ 55	13 ♐ 30	13 ♍ 30
536	♉ 19	♊ 25	♋ 28	26 ♌ 42	♍ 18	♎ 16	18 ♉ 20	4 ♌ 45	4 ♊ 30
537	♈ 15	♊ 9	♋ 14	15 ♌ 0	♌ 27	♍ 16	28 ♏ 15	24 ♉ 15	10 ♐ 31
538	♑ 24	♒ 19	♓ 24	12 ♉ 40	♊ 11	♋ 3	19 ♐ 30	1 ♑ 14	16 ♐ 30
539	♓ 21	♈ 28	♊ 13	19 ♋ 8	♌ 6	♌ 25	6 ♒ 57	19 ♌ 14	22 ♒ 53
540	♓ 11	♈ 16	♊ 1	9 ♋ 40	♋ 27	♌ 16	16 ♏ 31	2 ♌ 6	11 ♏ 37
541	♐ 7	♑ 0	♑ 24	25 ♒ 8	♈ 6	♉ 10	10 ♌ 51	10 ♏ 58	6 ♌ 54
542	♏ 18	♐ 12	♑ 5	1 ♒ 14	♓ 11	♈ 18	13 ♎ 47	7 ♍ 24	25 ♎ 35
543	♎ 20	♏ 15	♐ 5	23 ♐ 8	♒ 2	♓ 15	10 ♑ 3	0 ♑ 18	18 ♐ 28
544	♍ 14	♎ 15	♏ 10	0 ♐ 7	♑ 1	♒ 8	16 ♍ 27	6 ♊ 15	15 ♍ 18
545	♑ 19	♒ 11	♓ 15	11 ♉ 0	♊ 11	♋ 1	22 ♈ 30	24 ♈ 30	5 ♈ 28
546	♑ 5	♑ 22	♒ 16	15 ♈ 0	♉ 29	♊ 19	8 ♏ 30	20 ♏ 6	2 ♏ 23
547	♊ 7	♋ 0	♋ 23	23 ♌ 20	♎ 6	♏ 11	0 ♑ 5	2 ♓ 30	9 ♑ 30
548	♊ 7	♋ 11	♌ 13	10 ♍ 23	♎ 5	♏ 4	13 ♓ 55	2 ♉ 24	1 ♈ 28
549	♉ 27	♋ 5	♌ 8	4 ♍ 43	♍ 26	♎ 23	17 ♎ 53	21 ♏ 44	14 ♎ 8
550	♉ 10	♊ 16	♋ 19	18 ♌ 40	♍ 10	♎ 7	21 ♍ 2	12 ♑ 5	17 ♍ 37

	♀	♂	♃	♄	♅	♆	♇
	° ′	° ′	° ′	° ′	° ′	° ′	° ′
01	13 ♒ 11	18 ♊ 36	19 ♌ 29 R	19 ♊ 49	5 ♊ 1	3 ♎ 25 R	6 ♌ 51 R
02	13 ♍ 36	10 ♊ 29	16 ♏ 40	19 ♉ 2 R	25 ♑ 25	23 ♋ 43	28 ♊ 52 R
03	17 ♐ 32	23 ♋ 18	24 ♑ 49	13 ♏ 45	8 ♋ 22 R	10 ♈ 52 R	14 ♉ 16 R
04	21 ♍ 7 R	25 ♌ 2	9 ♏ 5	4 ♌ 54	12 ♎ 52	29 ♉ 47 R	4 ♊ 22 R
05	15 ♑ 10	7 ♓ 30	21 ♏ 0	21 ♒ 30	19 ♌ 50 R	0 ♉ 26 R	22 ♉ 1 R
06	3 ♊ 34	12 ♏ 9	28 ♉ 24	2 ♓ 15 R	1 ♑ 33 R	8 ♐ 20	21 ♊ 48
07	5 ♒ 14	27 ♊ 2 R	16 ♉ 54	6 ♉ 4	17 ♍ 56 R	13 ♉ 47	27 ♉ 29 R
08	20 ♒ 28	20 ♑ 10	26 ♉ 37	23 ♎ 52	15 ♏ 6 R	10 ♊ 55	8 ♊ 52
09	0 ♏ 50	14 ♐ 15	3 ♐ 8	17 ♌ 14	17 ♎ 4	2 ♊ 8 R	5 ♊ 44 R
10	25 ♓ 44	7 ♏ 33	23 ♈ 30	21 ♒ 0	2 ♑ 20	5 ♋ 55 R	19 ♊ 48
11	9 ♉ 45	13 ♒ 35	4 ♍ 30 R	16 ♈ 24	21 ♑ 4 R	14 ♋ 39	24 ♊ 27
12	17 ♋ 33	21 ♐ 22	23 ♎ 48	24 ♒ 12 R	14 ♌ 50	3 ♉ 3	23 ♉ 15
13	4 ♐ 14	11 ♏ 36	4 ♋ 57 R	10 ♓ 44	8 ♑ 55	11 ♋ 10 R	22 ♊ 19 R
14	2 ♋ 5	15 ♌ 32	16 ♈ 48	27 ♈ 22	5 ♍ 47	13 ♉ 48	28 ♉ 0
15	27 ♊ 23	14 ♊ 0	29 ♏ 3 R	6 ♓ 21	15 ♌ 55	3 ♉ 6	22 ♉ 10
16	21 ♈ 19	23 ♐ 28	26 ♓ 35	27 ♍ 53 R	5 ♏ 52 R	6 ♊ 20	6 ♊ 50
17	20 ♑ 3	5 ♏ 2	22 ♋ 51 R	25 ♌ 52 R	4 ♊ 49 R	24 ♓ 55 R	6 ♉ 24
18	8 ♍ 22	15 ♐ 40	23 ♏ 30	4 ♓ 15 R	4 ♉ 16 R	15 ♍ 28	27 ♋ 13
19	3 ♑ 16	0 ♎ 20	16 ♒ 2	26 ♑ 30	21 ♐ 52	2 ♋ 30 R	19 ♊ 0
20	0 ♌ 14	24 ♌ 28	13 ♊ 54	21 ♉ 19	14 ♍ 49	17 ♉ 51	28 ♉ 58
21	0 ♌ 19	29 ♌ 54	18 ♈ 58	28 ♈ 35	6 ♍ 51	14 ♉ 7	28 ♉ 0
22	17 ♌ 22	2 ♍ 58	17 ♊ 7	22 ♉ 47	15 ♍ 16	18 ♉ 14	29 ♉ 30
23	1 ♍ 0	21 ♍ 19	16 ♊ 30	26 ♒ 33 R	13 ♈ 30 R	26 ♒ 30 R	25 ♈ 17 R
24	6 ♍ 18	24 ♎ 10	24 ♍ 36	27 ♏ 22	26 ♏ 27	22 ♊ 34 R	15 ♊ 0 R
25	25 ♐ 5	24 ♐ 28	10 ♑ 6	10 ♏ 9	1 ♋ 39 R	7 ♈ 49	2 ♉ 25 R
26	27 ♒ 33	15 ♉ 51	15 ♑ 45	14 ♏ 15 R	20 ♓ 22	20 ♌ 40 R	11 ♋ 33 R
27	0 ♌ 56	22 ♌ 46	15 ♍ 51	19 ♈ 41	29 ♈ 40	7 ♓ 0 R	27 ♈ 20
28	2 ♋ 40	14 ♎ 27	7 ♈ 50	4 ♋ 18	23 ♉ 35	20 ♓ 26 R	3 ♉ 8
29	28 ♐ 28	23 ♎ 58	2 ♐ 19	2 ♌ 36	17 ♎ 13 R	27 ♉ 18	2 ♊ 39 R
30	11 ♍ 7	0 ♐ 50	7 ♒ 53 R	2 ♍ 51	22 ♎ 52	6 ♊ 15	7 ♊ 29
31	8 ♒ 7	8 ♊ 9	22 ♓ 30	14 ♈ 0	6 ♍ 30 R	9 ♉ 47	25 ♉ 30
32	28 ♊ 26	11 ♋ 50	5 ♋ 14	2 ♏ 40 R	17 ♏ 49 R	14 ♊ 34	10 ♊ 40
33	20 ♏ 2	0 ♑ 53	24 ♎ 27	22 ♋ 22 R	10 ♎ 57	26 ♉ 28 R	4 ♊ 0 R
34	11 ♍ 30	4 ♍ 30	6 ♍ 0	22 ♊ 0	16 ♑ 30	10 ♑ 0	3 ♈ 30
35	5 ♎ 5	3 ♎ 15	17 ♈ 44 R	28 ♈ 5 R	10 ♍ 1	14 ♉ 10	28 ♉ 13
36	3 ♉ 1 R	24 ♋ 30	0 ♍ 30	28 ♏ 13 R	27 ♏ 30 R	18 ♊ 50	12 ♊ 35
37	29 ♐ 26	5 ♒ 37	18 ♊ 52 R	12 ♌ 19	1 ♊ 38 R	22 ♓ 10 R	6 ♉ 22 R
38	11 ♐ 30 R	19 ♐ 17	27 ♊ 15 R	20 ♉ 30 R	23 ♍ 13	16 ♉ 30 R	29 ♉ 0 R
39	15 ♒ 16	19 ♒ 21	26 ♉ 35	3 ♉ 42	9 ♑ 12	6 ♑ 4	29 ♓ 23
40	12 ♐ 9	28 ♏ 48	14 ♒ 2	1 ♋ 46 R	7 ♒ 54	0 ♌ 27 R	0 ♋ 34 R
41	7 ♋ 54	25 ♊ 46	1 ♐ 4	29 ♐ 8 R	8 ♐ 32 R	28 ♊ 19	17 ♊ 6
42	23 ♏ 41	2 ♎ 53	0 ♊ 59 R	15 ♎ 33	9 ♏ 23	13 ♊ 26 R	9 ♊ 37 R
43	19 ♑ 20	9 ♒ 33	10 ♋ 52 R	27 ♌ 47 R	25 ♒ 12	8 ♌ 40 R	5 ♋ 27 R
44	4 ♎ 39 R	8 ♌ 28	3 ♏ 53	2 ♌ 28	11 ♌ 33	0 ♊ 5 R	5 ♊ 0
45	15 ♈ 20	16 ♌ 50	26 ♈ 4	16 ♐ 55 R	13 ♋ 36	17 ♈ 14	15 ♉ 52
46	6 ♐ 1	18 ♊ 20 R	1 ♐ 52	23 ♎ 10	29 ♊ 14 R	6 ♈ 6 R	12 ♉ 10 R
47	27 ♏ 10	14 ♏ 15	16 ♐ 30	3 ♓ 14	23 ♌ 33 R	2 ♉ 38 R	23 ♉ 30
48	23 ♈ 10	3 ♓ 10	10 ♐ 4	3 ♑ 44	12 ♐ 24	24 ♊ 13 R	14 ♊ 39
49	28 ♏ 7	14 ♌ 25	23 ♍ 13	8 ♋ 20	4 ♎ 16	25 ♉ 6 R	2 ♊ 42 R
50	7 ♍ 49	4 ♎ 39	17 ♈ 30 R	27 ♈ 59 R	10 ♍ 8	14 ♉ 8 R	28 ♉ 15

	10	11	12	Asc.	2	3	☉	☽	☿
	°	°	°	° ′	°	°	° ′	° ′	° ′
551	♓ 21	♉ 0	♊ 19	25 ♋ 50	♌ 9	♌ 26	11 ♌ 27	8 ♏ 6	19 ♌ 53
552	♓ 11	♈ 18	♉ 9	18 ♋ 0	♌ 2	♌ 18	14 ♐ 30	11 ♑ 50	26 ♏ 30
553	♊ 11	♋ 15	♌ 17	14 ♍ 5	♎ 7	♏ 6	6 ♋ 19	14 ♈ 6	15 ♊ 29
554	♒ 6	♓ 1	♈ 15	11 ♊ 20	♋ 0	♋ 18	23 ♌ 30	10 ♐ 10	15 ♌ 0
555	♐ 3	♐ 20	♑ 5	25 ♑ 40	♈ 2	♉ 10	24 ♑ 50	19 ♒ 0	22 ♑ 42
556	♎ 16	♏ 11	♐ 0	16 ♐ 30	♑ 25	♓ 10	5 ♍ 48	27 ♒ 8	1 ♎ 12
557	♑ 11	♒ 6	♓ 6	17 ♈ 15	♉ 22	♊ 18	26 ♉ 26	20 ♈ 26	5 ♉ 57
558	♋ 9	♌ 12	♍ 12	7 ♎ 48	♏ 4	♐ 5	15 ♐ 1	18 ♌ 31	7 ♐ 5
559	♍ 23	♎ 22	♏ 14	1 ♐ 14	♑ 14	♒ 14	19 ♑ 3	2 ♐ 55	8 ♒ 21
560	♏ 8	♏ 29	♐ 16	2 ♑ 25	♒ 20	♈ 8	20 ♑ 53	11 ♑ 33	27 ♐ 20
561	♐ 25	♑ 13	♒ 6	18 ♓ 0	♉ 8	♊ 5	26 ♒ 0	21 ♉ 30	17 ♐ 30
562	♐ 24	♑ 15	♒ 10	18 ♓ 30	♉ 3	♊ 2	7 ♈ 30	8 ♒ 30	15 ♈ 10
563	♊ 27	♌ 2	♍ 3	27 ♍ 30	♎ 22	♏ 22	12 ♏ 20	4 ♒ 17	5 ♐ 31
564	♉ 18	♊ 29	♌ 5	1 ♍ 18	♍ 19	♎ 15	16 ♏ 26	4 ♉ 15	25 ♏ 45
565	♉ 5	♊ 13	♋ 18	17 ♌ 10	♍ 7	♎ 3	23 ♐ 41	28 ♑ 46	11 ♐ 37
566	♍ 8	♎ 9	♏ 1	17 ♏ 15	♐ 18	♑ 27	20 ♈ 40	10 ♌ 3	17 ♈ 30
567	♊ 4	♋ 9	♌ 11	9 ♍ 0	♎ 2	♏ 0	11 ♓ 30	2 ♒ 46	18 ♒ 25
568	♉ 16	♊ 25	♋ 29	27 ♌ 36	♍ 17	♎ 12	14 ♌ 53	15 ♈ 22	20 ♌ 11
569	♋ 22	♌ 26	♍ 25	17 ♎ 0	♏ 12	♐ 14	15 ♈ 41	7 ♑ 1	26 ♈ 48
570	♍ 21	♎ 20	♏ 11	28 ♏ 0	♑ 0	♒ 11	19 ♈ 20	2 ♍ 15	21 ♓ 45
571	♑ 5	♑ 14	♒ 2	12 ♈ 30	♊ 11	♊ 26	10 ♏ 30	14 ♌ 30	13 ♏ 15
572	♉ 5	♊ 14	♋ 21	20 ♌ 0	♍ 9	♎ 2	17 ♈ 38	7 ♈ 7	23 ♈ 31
573	♈ 28	♊ 5	♋ 10	10 ♌ 43	♍ 1	♍ 26	16 ♊ 48	19 ♋ 31	5 ♋ 11
574	♎ 13	♏ 10	♐ 2	23 ♐ 35	♑ 29	♓ 8	11 ♐ 10	9 ♊ 29	18 ♐ 19
575	♐ 15	♑ 6	♑ 29	2 ♓ 19	♈ 20	♉ 21	3 ♐ 8	19 ♎ 18	2 ♐ 51
576	♌ 29	♎ 1	♎ 27	18 ♏ 0	♐ 18	♑ 23	22 ♒ 59	15 ♓ 52	21 ♒ 2
577	♎ 7	♏ 2	♏ 19	0 ♐ 37	♑ 6	♒ 26	24 ♋ 32	11 ♎ 16	8 ♋ 30
578	♈ 13	♉ 20	♊ 28	0 ♌ 14	♌ 19	♍ 13	28 ♉ 21	19 ♍ 15	4 ♉ 23
579	♐ 10	♑ 2	♑ 25	25 ♒ 15	♈ 12	♉ 15	23 ♒ 29	27 ♑ 13	10 ♓ 21
580	♊ 21	♋ 24	♌ 25	21 ♍ 45	♎ 17	♏ 17	0 ♋ 18	8 ♋ 16	15 ♋ 49
581	♍ 20	♎ 19	♏ 13	2 ♐ 55	♑ 5	♒ 13	14 ♒ 45	25 ♐ 55	2 ♓ 57
582	♉ 21	♊ 28	♌ 2	29 ♌ 30	♍ 21	♎ 18	27 ♎ 41	19 ♐ 50	10 ♎ 55
583	♊ 5	♋ 8	♌ 9	7 ♍ 10	♎ 3	♏ 2	7 ♌ 0	7 ♊ 0	28 ♌ 41
584	♐ 10	♐ 26	♑ 13	9 ♒ 30	♈ 13	♉ 18	27 ♑ 16	24 ♐ 30	12 ♒ 30
585	♓ 10	♈ 16	♊ 4	14 ♋ 30	♋ 29	♌ 17	13 ♎ 10	25 ♑ 45	28 ♎ 13
586	♉ 7	♊ 13	♋ 17	17 ♌ 0	♍ 8	♎ 4	20 ♊ 2	4 ♎ 46	5 ♊ 26
587	♐ 12	♑ 3	♑ 26	27 ♒ 14	♈ 15	♉ 18	13 ♎ 13	1 ♓ 50	8 ♏ 30
588	♉ 23	♊ 28	♌ 1	29 ♌ 0	♍ 21	♎ 19	27 ♊ 22	11 ♐ 23	3 ♋ 35
589	♒ 18	♓ 18	♈ 29	10 ♊ 30	♋ 3	♋ 25	22 ♑ 10	16 ♌ 14	3 ♒ 11
590	♉ 12	♊ 16	♋ 18	17 ♌ 40	♍ 11	♎ 10	7 ♍ 10	15 ♈ 29	19 ♌ 55
591	♈ 4	♉ 9	♊ 16	17 ♋ 38	♌ 10	♍ 4	15 ♉ 16	9 ♈ 44	5 ♊ 22
592	♍ 7	♎ 9	♏ 4	24 ♏ 25	♐ 25	♒ 1	8 ♑ 35	19 ♊ 30	14 ♑ 20
593	♒ 16	♓ 14	♉ 5	28 ♊ 30	♋ 13	♋ 28	12 ♏ 30	14 ♑ 7	9 ♏ 13
594	♌ 2	♍ 6	♎ 4	25 ♎ 40	♏ 23	♐ 26	24 ♑ 5	5 ♒ 41	9 ♒ 48
595	♓ 23	♉ 0	♊ 12	18 ♋ 0	♌ 5	♌ 26	8 ♑ 30	4 ♋ 30	17 ♑ 30
596	♓ 8	♈ 12	♉ 27	7 ♋ 0	♋ 25	♌ 13	1 ♍ 36	4 ♊ 1	26 ♍ 34
597	♈ 4	♉ 9	♊ 16	17 ♋ 30	♌ 9	♍ 4	21 ♉ 57	11 ♑ 51	17 ♉ 19
598	♐ 8	♐ 21	♑ 13	9 ♒ 20	♈ 10	♉ 17	1 ♓ 25	19 ♍ 39	8 ♓ 45
599	♑ 25	♒ 20	♓ 25	14 ♉ 0	♊ 13	♋ 4	3 ♓ 11	6 ♒ 30	15 ♒ 13
600	♑ 16	♒ 10	♓ 12	29 ♈ 24	♊ 3	♊ 26	22 ♓ 22	17 ♑ 45	9 ♓ 4R

	♀	♂	♃	♄	♅	♆	♇
	° ′	° ′	° ′	° ′	° ′	° ′	° ′
551	9 ♋ 54	7 ♋ 0	19 ♊ 4	22 ♐ 19 R	23 ♋ 30	21 ♈ 50 R	18 ♉ 48
552	28 ♐ 6	19 ♎ 49	21 ♍ 30	20 ♍ 0	15 ♊ 30 R	29 ♓ 8 R	9 ♉ 20 R
553	13 ♊ 37	21 ♉ 24	11 ♋ 35	4 ♊ 22	19 ♍ 40	20 ♉ 15	1 ♊ 0
554	3 ♍ 7	13 ♏ 43	27 ♏ 17	11 ♌ 49	14 ♎ 27	2 ♊ 13	6 ♊ 0
555	12 ♐ 25	18 ♎ 53	0 ♐ 8	3 ♌ 45	17 ♎ 14	27 ♉ 25 R	3 ♊ 0 R
556	9 ♎ 56	10 ♏ 30	21 ♋ 12	3 ♑ 21 R	29 ♋ 16	23 ♈ 49 R	19 ♉ 46 R
557	19 ♊ 21	14 ♈ 12	0 ♎ 30 R	9 ♐ 56 R	1 ♐ 46 R	21 ♊ 19	13 ♊ 45
558	28 ♎ 26	26 ♏ 36	8 ♌ 57 R	14 ♏ 3	21 ♏ 44	16 ♊ 42 R	11 ♊ 37 R
559	27 ♒ 58	22 ♈ 49	13 ♎ 57	16 ♈ 47	21 ♑ 3	17 ♋ 55 R	25 ♊ 25
560	8 ♐ 59	1 ♌ 47 R	7 ♏ 29	18 ♐ 49	6 ♐ 29	22 ♊ 39	14 ♊ 5 R
561	7 ♓ 30	19 ♍ 10 R	28 ♑ 6	10 ♏ 30	0 ♏ 16	2 ♐ 30	11 ♓ 30
562	28 ♒ 25	5 ♊ 33	2 ♒ 14	24 ♓ 51	25 ♌ 51 R	6 ♉ 8	23 ♉ 20
563	18 ♎ 49	21 ♋ 38	13 ♑ 29	17 ♊ 4 R	3 ♒ 49	28 ♋ 14 R	0 ♋ 23
564	9 ♏ 58	29 ♎ 20	0 ♒ 40	26 ♓ 26 R	3 ♍ 50	8 ♉ 10 R	25 ♉ 19
565	7 ♏ 23	13 ♉ 2 R	6 ♓ 23	8 ♈ 59	9 ♍ 0 R	9 ♉ 36 R	25 ♉ 50 R
566	7 ♓ 30	14 ♈ 30	23 ♉ 20	28 ♐ 30	18 ♋ 2	19 ♈ 18	16 ♉ 40
567	8 ♓ 20	8 ♈ 33	24 ♈ 48	14 ♐ 53	14 ♏ 12 R	8 ♐ 45	15 ♓ 30
568	18 ♋ 21 R	20 ♒ 0 R	8 ♌ 25	27 ♌ 36	11 ♊ 27	29 ♓ 4 R	9 ♉ 21 R
569	24 ♈ 46	2 ♐ 1	18 ♉ 30	21 ♋ 35	26 ♉ 53	23 ♓ 12	5 ♉ 37
570	6 ♓ 9	18 ♋ 21	9 ♊ 30	20 ♎ 0 R	29 ♒ 30	3 ♒ 37	13 ♈ 30
571	25 ♐ 7	14 ♐ 31	9 ♑ 13	11 ♑ 45	15 ♐ 0	1 ♋ 15 R	18 ♊ 0 R
572	8 ♈ 7	2 ♈ 27	24 ♐ 27	16 ♉ 53	7 ♉ 16	12 ♓ 29	0 ♉ 5
573	5 ♉ 11	0 ♊ 52	17 ♒ 15 R	27 ♑ 3 R	19 ♐ 24 R	0 ♋ 38	17 ♊ 0
574	24 ♎ 33	23 ♑ 51	14 ♓ 27	5 ♒ 17	24 ♐ 58	5 ♋ 11 R	19 ♊ 47 R
575	19 ♐ 49	17 ♌ 39	4 ♌ 31 R	6 ♊ 56 R	27 ♍ 28	19 ♉ 18 R	0 ♊ 5
576	15 ♑ 9	29 ♉ 0	17 ♓ 53	12 ♈ 14	7 ♍ 33	9 ♉ 25	25 ♉ 11
577	26 ♋ 29	10 ♉ 22	14 ♌ 16	12 ♏ 27	20 ♏ 32 R	18 ♊ 7	13 ♊ 6
578	26 ♈ 58	15 ♌ 22	2 ♏ 29 R	22 ♐ 1 R	6 ♐ 22	23 ♊ 20	14 ♊ 43
579	7 ♈ 29	25 ♎ 29	22 ♓ 6	3 ♐ 10	9 ♏ 40	6 ♐ 30	14 ♓ 30
580	2 ♌ 22	7 ♋ 13	21 ♊ 35	15 ♓ 1	6 ♑ 46 R	9 ♋ 44	22 ♊ 28
581	1 ♓ 8 R	26 ♒ 27	29 ♑ 28	21 ♑ 44	20 ♐ 12	29 ♊ 0 R	16 ♊ 0 R
582	0 ♏ 15	16 ♑ 59	6 ♋ 14	22 ♐ 28	17 ♏ 55	9 ♐ 24	16 ♓ 10
583	23 ♋ 23	6 ♌ 55	17 ♓ 11 R	15 ♍ 5	27 ♎ 34	8 ♊ 33	8 ♊ 29
584	5 ♒ 40	1 ♉ 1	26 ♎ 30	5 ♎ 30 R	17 ♊ 18 R	1 ♈ 30	9 ♉ 30
585	16 ♎ 8	7 ♏ 30	28 ♒ 10 R	21 ♏ 47	12 ♋ 52	13 ♈ 42 R	15 ♉ 8 R
586	7 ♉ 24	8 ♏ 32 R	22 ♉ 3	2 ♓ 54	2 ♑ 46 R	7 ♋ 12	21 ♊ 9
587	28 ♌ 28	27 ♍ 57	4 ♍ 59	6 ♈ 14 R	13 ♑ 0	17 ♋ 4	24 ♊ 41 R
588	17 ♉ 44	8 ♊ 37	16 ♒ 57 R	26 ♑ 27 R	18 ♐ 57 R	1 ♋ 3	18 ♊ 19
589	19 ♒ 28	27 ♓ 18	26 ♏ 6	24 ♒ 30	19 ♌ 1 R	0 ♉ 16	21 ♉ 40 R
590	8 ♎ 59	8 ♍ 53	0 ♊ 47	11 ♎ 11	7 ♏ 33	13 ♊ 29	10 ♊ 37
591	29 ♓ 36	3 ♋ 1	5 ♎ 38 R	28 ♈ 43	25 ♑ 13 R	16 ♋ 57	25 ♊ 45
592	23 ♏ 50	12 ♐ 50	7 ♌ 14 R	16 ♏ 20	22 ♏ 59	16 ♊ 3 R	12 ♊ 0 R
593	11 ♐ 10	17 ♊ 40 R	2 ♐ 30	23 ♎ 30	29 ♊ 9 R	6 ♈ 2 R	12 ♉ 12 R
594	12 ♑ 35	18 ♊ 30 R	23 ♍ 0 R	2 ♈ 40	22 ♈ 27	3 ♓ 2	26 ♈ 50
595	11 ♑ 30	25 ♍ 0	17 ♎ 0	5 ♐ 30	9 ♓ 30	9 ♒ 0	17 ♈ 0
596	28 ♍ 39	24 ♒ 0 R	11 ♉ 0	14 ♒ 24 R	9 ♈ 39 R	24 ♒ 30 R	25 ♈ 0 R
597	14 ♊ 38	5 ♌ 57	21 ♒ 0	17 ♊ 44	11 ♒ 37	25 ♋ 48	0 ♋ 5
598	14 ♑ 42	11 ♋ 12	18 ♒ 29	24 ♏ 0	4 ♋ 32 R	11 ♈ 2	13 ♉ 13
599	17 ♑ 14	7 ♒ 38	3 ♒ 33	18 ♓ 45	23 ♐ 55	28 ♐ 0	25 ♓ 30
600	13 ♈ 51	28 ♓ 27	19 ♒ 32	9 ♊ 52	13 ♉ 51	15 ♓ 53	2 ♉ 29

	10	11	12	Asc.	2	3	☉	☽	☿
	°	°	°	° ′	°	°	° ′	° ′	° ′
601	♈ 21	♊ 0	♋ 0	10 ♌ 10	♌ 28	♍ 20	21 ♓ 3	12 ♒ 0	0 ♓ 1
602	♎ 15	♏ 9	♏ 27	13 ♐ 20	♑ 21	♓ 8	22 ♑ 30	5 ♎ 30	5 ♒ 0
603	♉ 8	♊ 18	♋ 25	22 ♌ 52	♍ 11	♎ 5	20 ♏ 0	6 ♊ 30	22 ♏ 7
604	♈ 3	♉ 12	♊ 26	29 ♋ 0	♌ 15	♍ 6	19 ♈ 30	0 ♎ 21	8 ♉ 30
605	♐ 29	♑ 19	♒ 14	26 ♓ 32	♉ 12	♊ 9	27 ♎ 6	4 ♒ 55	2 ♏ 52
606	♍ 23	♎ 26	♏ 16	2 ♐ 0	♑ 6	♒ 20	25 ♎ 30	5 ♍ 10	11 ♏ 50
607	♐ 26	♑ 13	♒ 4	19 ♓ 0	♉ 14	♊ 8	7 ♌ 3	20 ♌ 15	4 ♍ 16
608	♒ 0	♒ 23	♈ 3	3 ♊ 23	♊ 25	♋ 12	2 ♒ 19	5 ♐ 51	19 ♒ 2
609	♐ 29	♑ 20	♒ 17	26 ♓ 27	♉ 8	♊ 4	4 ♎ 18	8 ♐ 44	25 ♍ 20
610	♎ 12	♏ 7	♏ 25	12 ♐ 0	♑ 19	♓ 5	9 ♏ 17	1 ♒ 8	24 ♏ 0 R
611	♈ 2	♉ 11	♊ 24	28 ♋ 0	♌ 14	♍ 4	3 ♊ 6	28 ♋ 23	24 ♊ 15
612	♐ 16	♑ 3	♑ 22	25 ♒ 0	♈ 25	♉ 26	14 ♋ 22	29 ♒ 57	22 ♋ 16
613	♏ 20	♐ 14	♑ 7	0 ♒ 38	♓ 13	♈ 21	7 ♏ 50	6 ♋ 17	20 ♎ 25
614	♑ 8	♒ 2	♓ 2	13 ♈ 30	♉ 20	♊ 16	6 ♒ 9	27 ♋ 32	23 ♑ 25
615	♍ 5	♎ 7	♏ 3	23 ♏ 23	♐ 24	♑ 29	23 ♏ 58	12 ♉ 43	16 ♐ 17
616	♓ 26	♉ 4	♊ 20	25 ♋ 53	♌ 10	♌ 29	12 ♋ 3	22 ♒ 30	3 ♋ 12
617	♊ 17	♋ 20	♌ 22	18 ♍ 39	♎ 14	♏ 14	10 ♐ 34	2 ♒ 12	0 ♑ 59
618	♈ 10	♉ 22	♋ 6	8 ♌ 0	♌ 22	♍ 12	19 ♎ 20	6 ♐ 30	26 ♎ 23
619	♑ 7	♑ 26	♒ 24	18 ♈ 20	♉ 28	♊ 20	5 ♍ 0	10 ♋ 30	9 ♍ 0 R
620	♍ 21	♎ 20	♏ 10	24 ♏ 43	♐ 28	♑ 10	9 ♊ 28	26 ♈ 26	1 ♋ 51
621	♉ 1	♊ 7	♋ 12	11 ♌ 53	♍ 3	♍ 29	27 ♌ 2	29 ♊ 17	28 ♌ 2
622	♒ 5	♒ 29	♈ 14	17 ♊ 0	♋ 4	♋ 18	26 ♊ 30	26 ♈ 30	14 ♋ 30
623	♊ 25	♋ 28	♌ 29	25 ♍ 35	♎ 22	♏ 25	29 ♒ 50	29 ♏ 5	4 ♒ 3
624	♎ 9	♏ 6	♏ 25	10 ♐ 36	♑ 17	♓ 3	14 ♐ 5	7 ♍ 10	6 ♐ 50
625	♈ 19	♊ 1	♋ 12	11 ♌ 32	♌ 27	♍ 18	18 ♓ 58	6 ♍ 33	24 ♒ 30
626	♐ 25	♑ 10	♒ 0	12 ♓ 15	♉ 11	♊ 6	27 ♑ 0	14 ♉ 47	14 ♒ 51
627	♋ 8	♌ 12	♍ 12	6 ♎ 55	♏ 4	♐ 5	9 ♒ 40	5 ♒ 33	27 ♒ 59
628	♎ 10	♏ 4	♏ 22	6 ♐ 30	♑ 13	♓ 1	21 ♒ 15	7 ♊ 4	6 ♑ 50
629	♊ 21	♋ 29	♍ 0	23 ♍ 0	♎ 15	♏ 14	7 ♏ 30	5 ♒ 4	23 ♎ 59
630	♑ 27	♒ 17	♓ 26	6 ♊ 30	♊ 26	♋ 10	21 ♉ 59	29 ♓ 54	12 ♊ 54
631	♍ 3	♎ 5	♎ 29	20 ♏ 0	♐ 20	♑ 26	16 ♎ 17	20 ♈ 40	29 ♎ 36
632	♏ 2	♏ 23	♐ 9	22 ♐ 38	♒ 2	♈ 3	24 ♉ 30	26 ♋ 14	5 ♉ 4
633	♌ 26	♍ 28	♏ 7	16 ♐ 0	♑ 9	♒ 0	4 ♒ 44	25 ♌ 53	19 ♒ 50
634	♍ 11	♎ 11	♏ 4	21 ♏ 9	♐ 22	♒ 1	5 ♍ 50	27 ♎ 35	15 ♍ 15
635	♋ 17	♌ 23	♍ 21	12 ♎ 0	♏ 7	♐ 9	18 ♊ 15	3 ♍ 36	12 ♋ 30
636	♉ 7	♊ 17	♋ 23	21 ♌ 55	♍ 10	♎ 4	6 ♉ 30	26 ♋ 40	12 ♉ 7 R
637	♋ 25	♌ 28	♍ 27	21 ♎ 30	♏ 19	♐ 21	28 ♉ 55	3 ♈ 9	14 ♊ 52
638	♊ 15	♋ 23	♌ 24	18 ♍ 55	♎ 11	♏ 9	15 ♊ 19	20 ♋ 36	9 ♋ 2
639	♑ 4	♒ 11	♓ 13	10 ♈ 0	♉ 25	♊ 17	25 ♈ 26	20 ♌ 30	15 ♈ 9
640	♌ 26	♍ 27	♏ 8	19 ♐ 55	♑ 11	♒ 1	21 ♎ 6	13 ♒ 16	15 ♏ 30
641	♌ 19	♍ 21	♎ 18	11 ♏ 0	♐ 10	♑ 13	23 ♏ 3	16 ♌ 33	10 ♏ 16
642	♈ 13	♉ 22	♋ 3	5 ♌ 0	♌ 22	♍ 14	11 ♐ 48	17 ♐ 28	6 ♐ 21
643	♓ 12	♈ 17	♊ 0	7 ♋ 15	♋ 26	♌ 17	4 ♉ 56	25 ♌ 50	9 ♈ 30
644	♑ 4	♑ 22	♒ 17	11 ♈ 30	♉ 25	♊ 17	27 ♌ 58	24 ♋ 45	24 ♍ 50
645	♋ 4	♌ 10	♍ 11	3 ♎ 0	♎ 26	♏ 27	4 ♋ 30	13 ♒ 19	17 ♋ 49
646	♎ 16	♏ 11	♏ 30	15 ♐ 15	♑ 24	♓ 10	5 ♏ 36	8 ♏ 2	7 ♏ 27
647	♈ 0	♉ 6	♊ 15	19 ♋ 5	♌ 9	♍ 1	19 ♐ 44	25 ♎ 35	14 ♐ 59
648	♐ 29	♑ 19	♒ 15	27 ♓ 55	♉ 13	♊ 9	3 ♉ 32	19 ♊ 3	13 ♉ 20
649	♎ 16	♏ 12	♐ 4	22 ♐ 38	♑ 29	♓ 11	6 ♌ 36	7 ♌ 5	29 ♌ 35
650	♓ 29	♉ 4	♊ 12	15 ♋ 0	♌ 6	♌ 29	17 ♏ 45	8 ♈ 27	19 ♏ 45

	♀	♂	♃	♄	♅	♆	♇
	° ′	° ′	° ′	° ′	° ′	° ′	° ′
601	6 ♓ 33	6 ♑ 27	1 ♑ 16	11 ♓ 56	21 ♌ 30 R	3 ♉ 30	22 ♉ 30
602	27 ♐ 0	2 ♐ 2	14 ♍ 14 R	4 ♈ 37	17 ♑ 19	15 ♋ 31 R	24 ♊ 0 R
603	26 ♎ 46	22 ♏ 46	2 ♎ 53	1 ♐ 45	28 ♏ 44	21 ♊ 58 R	15 ♊ 0 R
604	24 ♉ 30	4 ♋ 50	28 ♐ 57	27 ♎ 30 R	26 ♊ 4	8 ♈ 30	12 ♉ 3
605	10 ♐ 57	11 ♏ 59	1 ♋ 25 R	24 ♉ 39	21 ♍ 13	17 ♉ 58 R	29 ♉ 42 R
606	12 ♎ 30	8 ♈ 48 R	11 ♎ 46	29 ♍ 30	20 ♊ 30 R	1 ♈ 50 R	10 ♉ 30 R
607	21 ♋ 7	4 ♌ 10	11 ♋ 26	14 ♌ 40	6 ♊ 57	26 ♓ 55 R	8 ♉ 13
608	15 ♒ 34	12 ♎ 36	23 ♒ 20	0 ♒ 30	23 ♐ 47	1 ♋ 32 R	17 ♊ 57
609	18 ♌ 27	10 ♒ 32	21 ♈ 58 R	3 ♎ 25	4 ♏ 28	11 ♊ 16 R	9 ♊ 38
610	26 ♐ 0	11 ♋ 22	27 ♍ 30	18 ♍ 0	9 ♎ 30	21 ♏ 0	5 ♓ 30
611	26 ♈ 48	7 ♌ 25	26 ♍ 1	13 ♍ 54	7 ♎ 59 R	22 ♏ 5 R	9 ♓ 0
612	20 ♌ 9	21 ♉ 11	2 ♎ 36	6 ♐ 33 R	29 ♏ 57	23 ♊ 6	14 ♊ 50
613	29 ♍ 41	28 ♎ 19	7 ♏ 45	12 ♎ 10	24 ♊ 46 R	3 ♈ 51 R	11 ♉ 18 R
614	25 ♐ 12	22 ♉ 2	14 ♓ 9	10 ♈ 46	8 ♍ 13 R	9 ♉ 17	25 ♉ 21 R
615	9 ♐ 39	9 ♐ 40	21 ♏ 28	22 ♐ 28	7 ♐ 25	26 ♊ 26 R	16 ♊ 0 R
616	15 ♌ 30	2 ♍ 10	16 ♊ 46	22 ♉ 30	15 ♍ 14	18 ♉ 13	2 ♊ 0
617	9 ♑ 32 R	10 ♒ 22	9 ♎ 42	4 ♋ 22 R	22 ♑ 0	12 ♑ 40	2 ♈ 30 R
618	5 ♐ 30	17 ♋ 15	23 ♑ 20	12 ♏ 0	8 ♋ 26	11 ♈ 13 R	14 ♉ 20 R
619	17 ♎ 0	3 ♐ 0	20 ♍ 28	4 ♋ 0	21 ♑ 0 R	11 ♑ 30 R	4 ♈ 30 R
620	25 ♉ 35	4 ♎ 47	3 ♈ 58	0 ♋ 23	22 ♉ 2	20 ♓ 17	3 ♉ 3
621	28 ♋ 48	18 ♈ 2	29 ♍ 2	22 ♍ 17	20 ♊ 11	3 ♈ 22 R	11 ♉ 17 R
622	10 ♌ 30	4 ♌ 30	13 ♋ 0	1 ♏ 0 R	16 ♏ 30 R	16 ♊ 0	12 ♊ 0
623	5 ♈ 22	5 ♌ 55 R	25 ♋ 51 R	3 ♊ 25	27 ♍ 12 R	18 ♉ 25	29 ♉ 12 R
624	23 ♐ 15	0 ♋ 56 R	21 ♍ 30	1 ♈ 10	22 ♈ 38 R	2 ♓ 13	27 ♈ 30 R
625	5 ♉ 2	11 ♈ 36	14 ♈ 13	7 ♋ 17 R	21 ♉ 46	20 ♓ 4	4 ♉ 10
626	14 ♐ 41	17 ♑ 10	22 ♊ 43 R	19 ♉ 16 R	23 ♍ 11 R	16 ♉ 3 R	28 ♉ 30 R
627	27 ♐ 17	18 ♏ 22	5 ♒ 54	19 ♑ 24	25 ♓ 44	18 ♒ 37	20 ♈ 1
628	11 ♓ 46 R	27 ♒ 57	13 ♉ 9	26 ♐ 4	18 ♋ 45 R	17 ♈ 30	15 ♉ 57
629	28 ♎ 5	1 ♍ 13	26 ♊ 1 R	25 ♐ 11	26 ♋ 30	19 ♈ 58 R	18 ♉ 1 R
630	28 ♊ 1	9 ♋ 30	18 ♎ 57 R	29 ♍ 2 R	19 ♊ 9	5 ♈ 30	11 ♉ 1
631	15 ♍ 5	10 ♍ 8	1 ♑ 31	0 ♍ 15	21 ♎ 59	4 ♊ 17 R	6 ♊ 40 R
632	8 ♉ 13	19 ♋ 26	9 ♈ 28	23 ♈ 14	4 ♍ 51	12 ♉ 14	26 ♉ 42
633	3 ♓ 21 R	18 ♒ 38	27 ♑ 9	20 ♑ 36	19 ♐ 45	29 ♊ 11 R	16 ♊ 0 R
634	9 ♌ 51	19 ♈ 7	0 ♎ 52	23 ♍ 22	20 ♊ 25	3 ♈ 12 R	11 ♉ 10 R
635	20 ♉ 20	1 ♑ 40 R	21 ♎ 53 R	26 ♒ 4 R	12 ♌ 19	2 ♉ 13	22 ♉ 30
636	21 ♊ 2	7 ♌ 30	19 ♏ 52	7 ♉ 20	4 ♉ 30	10 ♓ 51	29 ♈ 59 R
637	7 ♋ 50	16 ♋ 43	6 ♋ 48	2 ♏ 6 R	17 ♏ 30 R	14 ♊ 52	10 ♉ 52
638	16 ♉ 35	2 ♑ 25 R	21 ♎ 59 R	26 ♒ 5	12 ♌ 11	2 ♉ 8	22 ♉ 35
639	29 ♓ 48	8 ♎ 5 R	24 ♓ 59	25 ♊ 27	19 ♉ 27	19 ♓ 15	3 ♉ 58
640	16 ♏ 18	23 ♐ 50	5 ♐ 23	18 ♌ 19	17 ♎ 53	1 ♊ 55 R	5 ♊ 30 R
641	0 ♏ 30	2 ♎ 30	7 ♑ 38	3 ♍ 9	24 ♎ 15	3 ♊ 26 R	6 ♊ 0 R
642	28 ♑ 46	4 ♑ 24	12 ♉ 44 R	18 ♐ 41	21 ♋ 28 R	16 ♈ 57 R	16 ♉ 22
643	20 ♉ 12	24 ♉ 58	22 ♍ 39 R	13 ♒ 30	6 ♌ 30	23 ♈ 30	20 ♉ 35
644	12 ♎ 50	25 ♊ 45	11 ♋ 59	5 ♑ 34 R	15 ♈ 0 R	3 ♍ 7	20 ♋ 19
645	12 ♊ 30	5 ♍ 45	0 ♏ 19 R	19 ♐ 19 R	4 ♐ 52 R	24 ♊ 53	15 ♊ 36
646	14 ♏ 59	3 ♒ 39	10 ♏ 42	19 ♒ 27 R	19 ♌ 41	1 ♉ 33 R	22 ♉ 50 R
647	3 ♏ 26	29 ♏ 33	8 ♌ 45 R	14 ♏ 29	22 ♏ 1	16 ♊ 35 R	12 ♊ 0 R
648	17 ♊ 55	6 ♌ 18	20 ♏ 13 R	6 ♉ 56	4 ♉ 21	10 ♓ 48	29 ♈ 59 R
649	4 ♋ 16	23 ♌ 10	1 ♒ 40 R	2 ♈ 43 R	28 ♌ 21	15 ♊ 7 R	24 ♉ 20
650	12 ♏ 41	15 ♏ 48	22 ♈ 13 R	5 ♋ 43 R	0 ♏ 26	9 ♉ 45	11 ♊ 3 R

	10	11	12	Asc.	2	3	☉	☽	☿
	°	°	°	° ′	°	°	° ′	° ′	° ′
651	♈ 20	♉ 25	♋ 1	2 ♌ 12	♌ 23	♍ 18	29 ♈ 8	20 ♋ 17	7 ♈ 49
652	♌ 19	♍ 22	♎ 17	5 ♏ 52	♐ 3	♑ 9	19 ♌ 59	5 ♏ 25	2 ♍ 30
653	♒ 27	♓ 29	♉ 18	2 ♋ 40	♋ 19	♌ 6	13 ♋ 49	5 ♈ 34	7 ♌ 45
654	♐ 7	♐ 25	♑ 14	10 ♒ 28	♈ 9	♉ 14	13 ♉ 55	10 ♉ 56	3 ♊ 30
655	♊ 28	♌ 3	♍ 4	28 ♍ 0	♎ 21	♏ 2	6 ♉ 0	26 ♒ 10	26 ♉ 0
656	♐ 6	♐ 24	♑ 12	6 ♒ 0	♈ 6	♉ 14	5 ♊ 34	8 ♓ 12	29 ♉ 3
657	♍ 10	♎ 10	♏ 3	21 ♏ 30	♐ 22	♒ 0	17 ♓ 21	10 ♑ 2	19 ♒ 55
658	♐ 25	♑ 17	♒ 13	21 ♓ 38	♉ 4	♊ 2	2 ♈ 6	0 ♊ 45	16 ♈ 30
659	♐ 7	♐ 27	♑ 17	14 ♒ 28	♈ 7	♉ 13	20 ♉ 51	10 ♊ 2	22 ♉ 20
660	♊ 11	♋ 18	♌ 20	15 ♍ 35	♎ 8	♏ 6	3 ♐ 49	24 ♌ 30	24 ♏ 1
661	♊ 16	♋ 22	♌ 24	19 ♍ 13	♎ 12	♏ 11	12 ♌ 30	6 ♋ 30	17 ♌ 42
662	♓ 16	♈ 21	♊ 5	13 ♋ 0	♌ 1	♌ 20	14 ♋ 10	29 ♎ 18	17 ♋ 50
663	♐ 12	♑ 0	♑ 19	17 ♒ 30	♈ 18	♉ 21	9 ♓ 53	4 ♎ 31	23 ♒ 28 R
664	♊ 13	♋ 16	♌ 16	14 ♍ 1	♎ 11	♏ 11	10 ♍ 41	7 ♑ 58	23 ♍ 55
665	♒ 25	♓ 26	♉ 9	22 ♊ 27	♋ 12	♌ 2	26 ♋ 35	13 ♊ 50	14 ♌ 35
666	♒ 19	♓ 19	♉ 1	16 ♊ 0	♋ 7	♋ 26	7 ♋ 37	29 ♓ 24	2 ♌ 35
667	♏ 17	♐ 13	♑ 8	5 ♒ 0	♓ 11	♈ 16	6 ♓ 22	7 ♏ 20	24 ♓ 16
668	♋ 29	♍ 1	♎ 1	28 ♎ 25	♏ 28	♐ 28	29 ♎ 5	29 ♋ 30	22 ♏ 54
669	♓ 28	♉ 8	♊ 25	29 ♋ 18	♌ 13	♍ 2	29 ♓ 50	24 ♓ 49	12 ♓ 12
670	♓ 0	♈ 3	♉ 15	26 ♊ 0	♋ 16	♌ 6	1 ♍ 25	2 ♈ 0	1 ♍ 40
671	♒ 3	♓ 0	♈ 6	23 ♉ 34	♊ 20	♋ 11	20 ♍ 38	8 ♑ 3	17 ♍ 0
672	♋ 5	♌ 7	♍ 8	3 ♎ 29	♏ 0	♐ 0	0 ♓ 25	25 ♒ 22	4 ♒ 10
673	♋ 22	♌ 26	♍ 26	21 ♎ 24	♏ 18	♐ 19	2 ♒ 36	0 ♒ 46	23 ♑ 49 R
674	♐ 17	♑ 4	♑ 22	25 ♒ 30	♈ 25	♉ 26	29 ♏ 39	22 ♏ 30	7 ♐ 56
675	♓ 12	♈ 20	♊ 16	24 ♋ 0	♌ 6	♌ 21	12 ♌ 48	29 ♒ 5	23 ♋ 45
676	♐ 24	♑ 13	♒ 5	16 ♓ 0	♉ 7	♊ 4	4 ♎ 9	12 ♍ 24	28 ♎ 1
677	♉ 27	♋ 1	♌ 3	1 ♍ 39	♍ 25	♎ 24	17 ♏ 31	12 ♏ 27	0 ♐ 28 R
678	♋ 8	♌ 12	♍ 12	6 ♎ 30	♏ 3	♐ 3	1 ♏ 15	15 ♌ 30	14 ♏ 20 R
679	♐ 8	♐ 26	♑ 14	10 ♒ 0	♈ 11	♉ 16	30 ♍ 0	20 ♐ 0	18 ♎ 36
680	♋ 19	♌ 26	♍ 24	13 ♎ 20	♏ 8	♐ 10	7 ♊ 4	4 ♒ 30	15 ♊ 0
681	♍ 9	♎ 10	♏ 6	28 ♏ 16	♐ 29	♒ 3	11 ♑ 7	23 ♑ 10	26 ♐ 50
682	♒ 3	♒ 28	♈ 6	25 ♉ 52	♊ 20	♋ 11	21 ♓ 22	7 ♎ 46	23 ♒ 55
683	♑ 9	♒ 0	♒ 29	20 ♈ 30	♉ 28	♊ 20	21 ♒ 9	15 ♉ 47	2 ♒ 30
684	♒ 11	♓ 9	♈ 22	13 ♊ 30	♋ 4	♋ 21	10 ♎ 57	19 ♊ 13	20 ♎ 27
685	♍ 22	♎ 21	♏ 14	4 ♐ 30	♑ 6	♒ 15	2 ♈ 49	19 ♓ 54	10 ♓ 1
686	♋ 25	♌ 29	♍ 27	19 ♎ 5	♏ 15	♐ 17	10 ♐ 19	21 ♊ 18	9 ♐ 0
687	♑ 28	♒ 20	♈ 0	3 ♊ 30	♊ 24	♋ 11	8 ♋ 5	27 ♍ 36	16 ♊ 30
688	♊ 6	♋ 15	♌ 17	12 ♍ 51	♎ 3	♏ 0	28 ♈ 52	29 ♎ 30	5 ♉ 30 R
689	♐ 1	♐ 17	♑ 2	20 ♑ 30	♓ 27	♉ 8	18 ♓ 26	14 ♎ 47	24 ♒ 35
690	♍ 18	♎ 17	♏ 7	22 ♏ 0	♐ 23	♒ 6	5 ♎ 15	3 ♈ 55	8 ♎ 5 R
691	♍ 22	♎ 22	♏ 15	4 ♐ 0	♑ 7	♒ 16	7 ♍ 52	10 ♏ 30	3 ♎ 32
692	♓ 14	♈ 19	♊ 2	9 ♋ 0	♋ 28	♌ 18	0 ♐ 52	15 ♒ 40	24 ♏ 18
693	♌ 15	♍ 18	♎ 15	6 ♏ 30	♐ 5	♑ 9	16 ♐ 16	19 ♏ 55	11 ♐ 24
694	♎ 26	♏ 21	♐ 13	5 ♑ 0	♒ 13	♓ 22	12 ♐ 45	12 ♎ 50	27 ♏ 57
695	♋ 7	♌ 13	♍ 12	5 ♎ 21	♎ 29	♐ 0	13 ♈ 40	3 ♑ 30	29 ♓ 30
696	♐ 12	♑ 3	♑ 25	26 ♒ 35	♈ 15	♉ 18	27 ♈ 30	14 ♍ 30	29 ♈ 30
697	♒ 3	♓ 0	♈ 8	25 ♉ 0	♊ 20	♋ 11	14 ♍ 56	8 ♑ 2	8 ♍ 0
698	♒ 20	♓ 19	♉ 6	24 ♊ 40	♋ 12	♋ 29	15 ♉ 15	3 ♐ 23	28 ♉ 12 R
699	♊ 3	♋ 10	♌ 13	8 ♍ 55	♎ 1	♎ 29	26 ♎ 36	7 ♐ 56	9 ♎ 36
700	♐ 22	♑ 13	♒ 7	13 ♓ 58	♉ 1	♊ 1	23 ♏ 31	15 ♌ 55	15 ♐ 41

	♀	♂	♃	♄	♅	♆	♇
	° ′	° ′	° ′	° ′	° ′	° ′	° ′
651	6 ♈ 42	18 ♎ 57 R	5 ♐ 13 R	29 ♋ 54	14 ♎ 39 R	28 ♉ 37	3 ♊ 34
652	0 ♎ 15	23 ♍ 30	24 ♍ 6	20 ♈ 54 R	0 ♉ 20 R	6 ♓ 5 R	29 ♈ 31
653	17 ♌ 13	13 ♋ 40	25 ♍ 4	12 ♒ 57 R	9 ♌ 14	0 ♉ 37	21 ♉ 49
654	27 ♉ 30	20 ♋ 48	12 ♑ 57 R	15 ♓ 49	19 ♐ 30 R	25 ♐ 20 R	26 ♓ 30
655	11 ♉ 0 R	18 ♋ 0	0 ♍ 12 R	29 ♏ 7 R	28 ♏ 0 R	18 ♊ 26	12 ♊ 30
656	3 ♉ 30	15 ♌ 30	6 ♓ 2	19 ♏ 40 R	6 ♋ 36	14 ♈ 22	11 ♉ 0
657	18 ♓ 17	27 ♊ 5	18 ♍ 17 R	7 ♈ 53	24 ♈ 6	4 ♓ 59	27 ♈ 40
658	21 ♓ 34	25 ♉ 54	29 ♈ 18	10 ♎ 2 R	10 ♏ 8 R	8 ♊ 51	7 ♊ 57
659	8 ♊ 4	3 ♊ 15	22 ♑ 40 R	14 ♑ 9 R	27 ♓ 15	19 ♒ 15	21 ♈ 3
660	20 ♑ 12	28 ♐ 49	13 ♉ 33 R	17 ♐ 50	21 ♋ 41 R	17 ♈ 4 R	16 ♉ 30 R
661	20 ♍ 55	18 ♍ 40	22 ♍ 37	20 ♈ 59 R	0 ♉ 21 R	6 ♓ 18 R	29 ♈ 41 R
662	8 ♋ 0	23 ♈ 30	28 ♓ 30	11 ♍ 0	18 ♒ 0 R	26 ♑ 30 R	4 ♈ 26
663	21 ♒ 4	19 ♌ 30 R	15 ♈ 57	16 ♐ 35	13 ♋ 35 R	15 ♈ 42	15 ♉ 14
664	15 ♌ 56	19 ♈ 13 R	1 ♎ 54	23 ♍ 59	20 ♊ 30	3 ♈ 5 R	11 ♉ 10 R
665	10 ♊ 58	3 ♍ 31	20 ♐ 19 R	23 ♎ 58	1 ♋ 25	10 ♈ 36 R	13 ♉ 55
666	20 ♋ 53	26 ♋ 34	24 ♌ 53	5 ♍ 14	13 ♊ 43	1 ♈ 38 R	7 ♉ 25
667	22 ♒ 47 R	7 ♑ 54	24 ♉ 3	29 ♎ 45 R	15 ♏ 19 R	10 ♊ 35	8 ♊ 47 R
668	18 ♎ 30	27 ♈ 21 R	6 ♋ 20	28 ♎ 4	14 ♏ 35	15 ♊ 32 R	11 ♊ 22 R
669	7 ♈ 17	7 ♐ 13	5 ♒ 0	28 ♌ 14 R	25 ♎ 43 R	2 ♊ 10	5 ♊ 5
670	13 ♍ 30	18 ♏ 45	27 ♏ 59	12 ♌ 55	14 ♎ 58	2 ♊ 17	6 ♊ 0
671	7 ♎ 11	4 ♎ 17	17 ♈ 37 R	28 ♈ 0 R	10 ♍ 8	14 ♉ 9 R	28 ♉ 14 R
672	0 ♓ 31	25 ♏ 31	29 ♑ 5	0 ♍ 30	26 ♎ 32	1 ♊ 47	4 ♊ 53
673	9 ♑ 40	10 ♒ 45	27 ♈ 10	26 ♋ 42 R	18 ♒ 44	3 ♌ 33 R	2 ♋ 48
674	13 ♐ 8	10 ♌ 48	9 ♏ 4	28 ♈ 43 R	1 ♉ 22 R	6 ♓ 28 R	29 ♈ 30 R
675	16 ♋ 12 R	24 ♊ 26	14 ♈ 14	29 ♏ 4	15 ♋ 0	17 ♈ 16 R	16 ♉ 53
676	5 ♎ 20	13 ♑ 30	3 ♏ 54	20 ♒ 0 R	18 ♌ 30	2 ♉ 24 R	23 ♉ 20 R
677	20 ♐ 52	16 ♑ 19	14 ♍ 33	22 ♍ 11	1 ♓ 45 R	13 ♌ 45	8 ♋ 40 R
678	5 ♎ 35	22 ♍ 20	6 ♎ 14	2 ♎ 6	5 ♓ 54 R	15 ♌ 49	9 ♋ 58 R
679	13 ♌ 35	24 ♋ 35	10 ♈ 28 R	1 ♐ 3	17 ♋ 4	16 ♈ 22 R	16 ♉ 48 R
680	12 ♊ 0	6 ♋ 5	20 ♌ 0	3 ♍ 10	12 ♊ 0	1 ♈ 17	9 ♉ 30
681	22 ♒ 25	20 ♐ 32	10 ♈ 57	22 ♈ 10	13 ♍ 42 R	11 ♉ 38 R	26 ♉ 26 R
682	0 ♉ 36	8 ♉ 48	1 ♐ 56	1 ♓ 17	16 ♌ 39 R	1 ♉ 16	21 ♉ 48
683	5 ♑ 9	7 ♈ 8	11 ♊ 34	8 ♌ 0 R	29 ♉ 31	23 ♓ 19	5 ♉ 39
684	20 ♍ 23	0 ♎ 1	25 ♍ 6	24 ♑ 12	29 ♏ 48	15 ♐ 22	21 ♓ 55
685	13 ♉ 37	14 ♓ 28	23 ♓ 26	5 ♐ 39 R	8 ♋ 52	14 ♈ 20	14 ♉ 33
686	3 ♏ 30	1 ♏ 30	12 ♐ 30	2 ♓ 3	24 ♌ 45 R	2 ♉ 57 R	23 ♉ 30 R
687	23 ♌ 16	10 ♎ 41	23 ♓ 2	8 ♒ 1 R	23 ♐ 2 R	3 ♋ 30	19 ♊ 30
688	11 ♉ 4 R	23 ♏ 30 R	9 ♉ 30	0 ♓ 30	4 ♑ 12	5 ♋ 30	20 ♊ 0
689	23 ♓ 1	3 ♐ 9	2 ♒ 50	29 ♌ 5	26 ♎ 6 R	1 ♊ 58	4 ♊ 59
690	21 ♍ 40	3 ♑ 2	2 ♒ 20	10 ♍ 50	25 ♎ 43	7 ♊ 0 R	7 ♊ 30
691	12 ♌ 58	24 ♋ 46	23 ♊ 24	21 ♐ 56	25 ♋ 0	21 ♈ 28 R	18 ♉ 28 R
692	22 ♎ 7	25 ♎ 34	10 ♐ 12	1 ♓ 40	24 ♌ 44	3 ♉ 13 R	23 ♉ 21 R
693	13 ♐ 28 R	16 ♐ 55	27 ♊ 7 R	20 ♉ 53 R	23 ♍ 10	16 ♉ 30 R	29 ♉ 0 R
694	0 ♒ 1	8 ♑ 42	15 ♑ 27	14 ♑ 43	16 ♐ 51	0 ♋ 33 R	17 ♊ 0 R
695	21 ♈ 30	8 ♋ 30	15 ♍ 4 R	11 ♈ 12	25 ♈ 33	5 ♓ 54	28 ♈ 20
696	19 ♈ 0	12 ♌ 9	8 ♌ 21	15 ♏ 5 R	7 ♓ 30	8 ♒ 30	15 ♈ 30
697	10 ♍ 0	18 ♏ 0	0 ♓ 55 R	19 ♏ 14	12 ♋ 10	14 ♈ 28 R	16 ♉ 0 R
698	20 ♊ 14	19 ♍ 17	26 ♊ 19	9 ♑ 39 R	23 ♋ 7	22 ♈ 25	18 ♉ 9
699	28 ♎ 4	16 ♑ 20	6 ♋ 13	22 ♐ 30	17 ♏ 49	9 ♐ 30	17 ♓ 30 R
700	22 ♐ 46	21 ♍ 8	28 ♏ 9	20 ♐ 38	16 ♓ 32	12 ♒ 13	18 ♈ 19 R

	10	11	12	Asc.	2	3	☉	☽	☿
	°	°	°	° ′	°	°	° ′	° ′	° ′
701	♏ 3	♏ 25	♐ 12	28 ♐ 0	♒ 14	♈ 1	3 ♈ 0	15 ♍ 30	11 ♈ 30R
702	♉ 25	♋ 3	♌ 7	4 ♍ 0	♍ 24	♎ 21	25 ♏ 11	17 ♈ 30	18 ♏ 27
703	♑ 28	♒ 20	♈ 0	5 ♊ 50	♊ 26	♋ 12	14 ♏ 42	3 ♉ 35	5 ♏ 40
704	♋ 26	♍ 0	♍ 28	18 ♎ 0	♏ 14	♐ 16	23 ♌ 0	28 ♓ 21	17 ♍ 30
705	♊ 18	♋ 24	♌ 25	20 ♍ 37	♎ 14	♏ 13	29 ♍ 23	3 ♌ 59	29 ♍ 20R
706	♉ 2	♉ 26	♊ 17	7 ♋ 15	♌ 18	♍ 29	5 ♎ 22	5 ♈ 57	7 ♎ 0 R
707	♋ 9	♌ 12	♍ 12	8 ♎ 0	♏ 5	♐ 6	10 ♑ 30	22 ♍ 0	18 ♐ 0
708	♎ 10	♏ 4	♏ 22	5 ♐ 30	♑ 12	♓ 1	21 ♍ 16	16 ♉ 30	10 ♎ 30
709	♐ 6	♐ 25	♑ 14	11 ♒ 0	♈ 6	♉ 12	18 ♐ 45	25 ♊ 7	19 ♐ 45
710	♍ 5	♎ 7	♏ 1	21 ♏ 0	♐ 22	♑ 28	6 ♌ 0	9 ♊ 15	5 ♌ 33
711	♌ 12	♍ 15	♎ 13	4 ♏ 59	♐ 4	♑ 7	22 ♓ 24	16 ♌ 50	19 ♓ 53R
712	♏ 27	♐ 20	♑ 13	9 ♒ 8	♓ 23	♉ 0	10 ♏ 55	18 ♋ 56	20 ♏ 30
713	♒ 13	♓ 12	♈ 26	18 ♊ 0	♋ 6	♋ 23	28 ♓ 53	1 ♒ 45	10 ♓ 8
714	♏ 15	♐ 6	♐ 23	13 ♑ 20	♓ 2	♈ 16	29 ♈ 46	24 ♒ 41	2 ♈ 32
715	♉ 4	♊ 12	♋ 18	18 ♌ 0	♍ 7	♎ 2	25 ♋ 21	21 ♈ 1	7 ♋ 40
716	♊ 26	♌ 0	♍ 0	26 ♍ 35	♎ 22	♏ 22	26 ♒ 14	13 ♑ 15	9 ♓ 37R
717	♍ 28	♎ 27	♏ 21	10 ♐ 50	♑ 14	♒ 22	28 ♌ 30	5 ♋ 16	12 ♍ 1
718	♑ 17	♒ 9	♓ 11	6 ♉ 0	♊ 7	♊ 28	1 ♏ 42	20 ♓ 30	21 ♏ 46
719	♍ 8	♎ 9	♏ 0	16 ♏ 0	♐ 15	♑ 26	4 ♑ 0	2 ♈ 15	21 ♑ 14
720	♈ 5	♉ 11	♊ 19	22 ♋ 14	♌ 12	♍ 5	3 ♐ 35	3 ♒ 30	18 ♏ 57
721	♉ 29	♋ 12	♌ 15	9 ♍ 30	♍ 28	♎ 23	27 ♉ 46	9 ♈ 0	1 ♊ 30
722	♍ 26	♎ 24	♏ 15	0 ♐ 30	♑ 4	♒ 17	22 ♎ 11	9 ♐ 30	4 ♎ 10
723	♈ 22	♊ 4	♋ 9	9 ♌ 47	♌ 28	♏ 20	9 ♓ 55	1 ♋ 14	13 ♒ 30
724	♏ 28	♐ 20	♑ 12	8 ♒ 30	♓ 24	♉ 1	2 ♐ 13	1 ♓ 11	26 ♏ 30
725	♈ 15	♉ 23	♋ 4	6 ♌ 26	♌ 23	♍ 15	13 ♍ 1	3 ♊ 29	2 ♎ 52R
726	♎ 19	♏ 12	♏ 29	15 ♐ 0	♑ 24	♓ 13	23 ♋ 12	24 ♈ 36	8 ♌ 18
727	♋ 20	♌ 24	♍ 22	15 ♎ 0	♏ 11	♐ 13	3 ♋ 30	4 ♓ 0	20 ♋ 51R
728	♈ 25	♊ 5	♋ 13	12 ♌ 20	♍ 1	♍ 25	25 ♓ 30	17 ♎ 30	4 ♈ 30
729	♈ 28	♊ 7	♋ 14	13 ♌ 30	♍ 2	♍ 26	30 ♈ 0	17 ♈ 55	24 ♈ 55R
730	♈ 27	♊ 15	♋ 15	14 ♌ 45	♍ 2	♍ 26	19 ♈ 36	29 ♎ 27	10 ♉ 47R
731	♐ 9	♑ 3	♑ 28	29 ♒ 40	♈ 8	♉ 12	29 ♒ 16	6 ♏ 19	8 ♒ 14
732	♊ 16	♋ 20	♌ 22	17 ♍ 49	♎ 13	♏ 12	18 ♏ 42	28 ♒ 34	10 ♐ 21
733	♌ 9	♍ 12	♎ 10	2 ♏ 56	♐ 1	♑ 4	25 ♋ 9	23 ♊ 40	21 ♌ 31
734	♍ 17	♎ 16	♏ 6	20 ♏ 30	♐ 20	♒ 4	15 ♌ 40	7 ♌ 16	11 ♍ 0
735	♋ 28	♍ 1	♎ 0	24 ♎ 0	♏ 21	♐ 23	10 ♌ 30	1 ♏ 0	6 ♍ 0
736	♊ 7	♋ 14	♌ 16	11 ♍ 52	♎ 4	♏ 2	8 ♎ 15	2 ♊ 37	1 ♏ 17
737	♈ 11	♉ 25	♋ 10	11 ♌ 0	♌ 23	♍ 12	23 ♏ 11	10 ♏ 50	5 ♏ 3
738	♌ 22	♍ 24	♎ 23	16 ♏ 5	♐ 16	♑ 18	15 ♐ 51	25 ♓ 27	5 ♐ 23
739	♋ 11	♌ 14	♍ 14	9 ♎ 40	♏ 6	♐ 7	15 ♏: 25	28 ♋ 56	0 ♏ 4
740	♉ 20	♊ 25	♋ 28	26 ♌ 25	♍ 19	♎ 17	23 ♎ 30	12 ♓ 18	16 ♏ 35
741	♏ 3	♏ 24	♐ 11	25 ♐ 53	♒ 14	♈ 1	15 ♎ 56	15 ♏ 13	1 ♎ 40
742	♓ 13	♈ 19	♊ 6	14 ♋ 20	♌ 0	♌ 18	17 ♒ 50	22 ♐ 17	5 ♓ 42
743	♌ 9	♍ 14	♎ 8	26 ♎ 0	♏ 20	♐ 26	1 ♒ 0	11 ♌ 38	5 ♒ 30
744	♋ 8	♌ 12	♍ 12	6 ♎ 25	♏ 2	♐ 3	27 ♏ 23	1 ♈ 36	19 ♐ 29
745	♍ 24	♎ 24	♏ 17	6 ♐ 30	♑ 10	♒ 17	24 ♉ 31	25 ♎ 37	0 ♉ 23
746	♎ 3	♏ 0	♏ 19	5 ♐ 1	♑ 10	♒ 24	4 ♋ 55	6 ♒ 41	2 ♋ 32R
747	♐ 14	♑ 2	♑ 20	21 ♒ 0	♈ 22	♉ 24	22 ♋ 0	16 ♍ 35	29 ♋ 0
748	♉ 22	♊ 23	♋ 22	21 ♌ 56	♍ 19	♎ 20	17 ♍ 30	9 ♐ 40	2 ♍ 13
749	♐ 23	♑ 11	♒ 2	12 ♓ 23	♉ 6	♊ 4	5 ♓ 52	1 ♉ 30	20 ♏ 15
750	♑ 4	♑ 30	♒ 30	5 ♈ 4	♉ 10	♊ 9	12 ♒ 56	18 ♓ 30	17 ♒ 33

	♀	♂	♃	♄	♅	♆	♇
	° ′	° ′	° ′	° ′	° ′	° ′	° ′
701	7 ♈ 0	24 ♒ 19	8 ♉ 0	8 ♎ 0 R	25 ♒ 0	1 ♒ 0	11 ♈ 0
702	28 ♐ 32	27 ♊ 51 R	7 ♍ 58	22 ♏ 10	24 ♏ 50	19 ♊ 33 R	12 ♊ 59 R
703	7 ♏ 4	5 ♍ 4	25 ♊ 32 R	25 ♐ 52	26 ♋ 38 R	19 ♈ 48 R	17 ♉ 57 R
704	11 ♋ 0	23 ♍ 30	14 ♍ 30	24 ♏ 30	25 ♏ 5	22 ♊ 7	14 ♊ 30
705	24 ♌ 30	17 ♎ 57	22 ♍ 41	26 ♏ 34	26 ♏ 3	22 ♊ 34	14 ♊ 55 R
706	21 ♏ 48	3 ♑ 6	2 ♒ 20	10 ♍ 51	25 ♎ 43	6 ♊ 43 R	7 ♊ 42 R
707	24 ♐ 30	22 ♐ 0	26 ♈ 0	10 ♎ 30	20 ♒ 0	28 ♑ 30	13 ♈ 0
708	5 ♌ 30	13 ♍ 30	0 ♍ 30	7 ♈ 57 R	12 ♑ 58 R	16 ♋ 46	24 ♊ 44
709	14 ♑ 25 R	16 ♎ 30	23 ♉ 28 R	17 ♐ 25	16 ♏ 38•	9 ♐ 30	15 ♓ 30
710	21 ♋ 22	13 ♊ 9	18 ♋ 34	7 ♊ 34	20 ♍ 52	20 ♉ 55	0 ♊ 54
711	6 ♉ 56	13 ♒ 7	22 ♈ 55	27 ♈ 05	11 ♍ 17 R	12 ♉ 14	26 ♉ 30
712	27 ♍ 31	2 ♐ 27	28 ♏ 58	14 ♉ 45 R	6 ♉ 18 R	8 ♓ 47 R	0 ♉ 26 R
713	12 ♒ 3	4 ♐ 38	27 ♉ 20	26 ♐ 28	18 ♏ 35 R	11 ♐ 0 R	16 ♓ 30
714	2 ♈ 35	29 ♈ 53	9 ♓ 30	20 ♏ 22 R	3 ♏ 6 R	3 ♐ 50 R	14 ♓ 30
715	19 ♊ 31	6 ♈ 27	23 ♍ 6	18 ♍ 50	18 ♊ 49	3 ♈ 51 R	11 ♉ 11
716	24 ♒ 35	27 ♊ 51	18 ♉ 15	6 ♉ 56	17 ♍ 24 R	13 ♉ 54	27 ♉ 17
717	17 ♋ 28	9 ♌ 26	28 ♐ 27	24 ♌ 20	19 ♎ 15	4 ♊ 30	6 ♊ 48
718	16 ♎ 30	13 ♎ 30	29 ♍ 24	24 ♑ 45	0 ♐ 53	16 ♐ 30	20 ♓ 30 R
719	2 ♐ 30	15 ♑ 5	5 ♍ 42 R	19 ♊ 42 R	2 ♎ 52.	20 ♉ 53 R	0 ♊ 30 R
720	29 ♏ 54	9 ♈ 25	19 ♎ 18	3 ♎ 20	19 ♊ 21 R	1 ♈ 10 R	8 ♉ 22
721	12 ♋ 30	28 ♈ 0	6 ♈ 0	3 ♐ 0 R	10 ♋ 30	16 ♈ 0	17 ♉ 0
722	6 ♍ 25	27 ♍ 56	26 ♓ 2 R	0 ♒ 47	3 ♈ 35 R	20 ♒ 53 R	23 ♈ 0 R
723	12 ♓ 25	29 ♏ 41	1 ♒ 6	29 ♌ 45 R	26 ♎ 20 R	1 ♊ 51	4 ♊ 55
724	23 ♎ 30	26 ♎ 30	10 ♐ 30	1 ♓ 30	24 ♌ 30	3 ♉ 10 R	23 ♉ 15 R
725	10 ♎ 46 R	15 ♏ 34	22 ♋ 36	3 ♑ 16 R	29 ♋ 39	23 ♈ 41 R	19 ♉ 42 R
726	7 ♊ 36	1 ♍ 9	20 ♐ 39 R	23 ♎ 52	1 ♋ 13	10 ♈ 36 R	13 ♉ 57
727	17 ♉ 52	4 ♋ 30	12 ♍ 30	19 ♍ 2	9 ♓ 30 R	12 ♌ 2	8 ♋ 20
728	6 ♉ 0	1 ♑ 0	29 ♓ 30	27 ♍ 0 R	5 ♏ 30 R	6 ♊ 30	7 ♊ 0
729	2 ♊ 3	24 ♒ 4	5 ♓ 12	8 ♈ 46	0 ♍ 13 R	9 ♉ 8	25 ♉ 14
730	27 ♊ 55	13 ♓ 28	8 ♏ 24 R	11 ♉ 3	29 ♑ 20 R	19 ♋ 14	26 ♊ 56
731	19 ♓ 24	13 ♑ 9	14 ♏ 23	1 ♉ 42	27 ♑ 11	19 ♋ 11	26 ♊ 40
732	3 ♐ 7	5 ♐ 38	20 ♏ 16	21 ♐ 53	7 ♐ 5	26 ♊ 34 R	16 ♊ 24 R
733	3 ♍ 9	24 ♋ 17	27 ♊ 25	14 ♓ 39	5 ♑ 44 R	10 ♋ 42	23 ♊ 0
734	25 ♍ 30	27 ♍ 51	15 ♊ 49	3 ♌ 48	3 ♊ 7	24 ♓ 30 R	7 ♉ 30 R
735	12 ♌ 30	10 ♉ 0	28 ♓ 30 R	14 ♍ 0	17 ♒ 0 R	25 ♑ 30 R	11 ♈ 30 R
736	17 ♏ 28	21 ♏ 16	4 ♑ 50	10 ♑ 2	13 ♐ 34	1 ♋ 30	18 ♊ 33 R
737	7 ♎ 15	11 ♏ 40	8 ♌ 59	11 ♏ 34	20 ♏ 28	17 ♊ 8 R	12 ♊ 0 R
738	0 ♐ 52	19 ♎ 20	14 ♎ 18	6 ♎ 13	5 ♓ 56	15 ♌ 52 R	9 ♋ 26 R
739	3 ♎ 53	15 ♎ 45	6 ♐ 50	1 ♓ 23	24 ♌ 32	3 ♉ 36 R	23 ♉ 38 R
740	18 ♏ 56	24 ♐ 54	5 ♐ 51	18 ♌ 31	18 ♎ 0	1 ♊ 52 R	5 ♊ 24 R
741	2 ♐ 27	4 ♑ 56	21 ♊ 36	10 ♌ 32	3 ♊ 8 R	22 ♓ 55 R	6 ♉ 52 R
742	24 ♑ 55	27 ♌ 53 R	11 ♈ 38	15 ♐ 19	14 ♋ 10 R	15 ♈ 4	15 ♉ 2
743	1 ♑ 10	6 ♈ 30	8 ♐ 30	1 ♌ 0 R	2 ♒ 30	18 ♑ 30	5 ♈ 30
744	2 ♑ 16	22 ♏ 45	20 ♐ 16	0 ♊ 52 R	0 ♒ 14	25 ♋ 53 R	29 ♊ 34 R
745	9 ♈ 9	10 ♍ 18	26 ♍ 8	5 ♋ 54	3 ♎ 53 R	25 ♉ 15	2 ♊ 15
746	18 ♋ 10	17 ♑ 30	12 ♉ 58	12 ♐ 18 R	16 ♋ 53	19 ♈ 26	17 ♉ 30
747	26 ♌ 24	18 ♏ 49	11 ♊ 9	0 ♌ 35	2 ♊ 15	25 ♓ 51 R	7 ♉ 20
748	2 ♎ 55	14 ♌ 3	19 ♌ 13	14 ♑ 41 R	4 ♌ 17	25 ♈ 55 R	20 ♉ 35 R
749	26 ♍ 15	25 ♉ 6 R	2 ♓ 51 R	10 ♈ 30 R	8 ♍ 3	10 ♉ 48 R	26 ♉ 30
750	28 ♓ 31	13 ♑ 35	15 ♈ 7	23 ♈ 29	12 ♍ 55 R	11 ♉ 33	26 ♉ 17 R

	10	11	12	Asc.	2	3	☉	☽	☿
	°	°	°	° ′	°	°	° ′	° ′	° ′
751	♉ 3	♊ 13	♋ 21	19 ♌ 49	♍ 7	♎ 0	12 ♋ 52	25 ♍ 16	12 ♋ 11R
752	♎ 16	♏ 11	♐ 0	17 ♐ 30	♑ 25	♓ 10	1 ♍ 0	19 ♎ 0	28 ♍ 30
753	♌ 3	♍ 7	♎ 4	26 ♎ 0	♏ 23	♐ 26	5 ♑ 0	18 ♊ 0	1 ♑ 0
754	♈ 21	♉ 28	♋ 3	4 ♌ 30	♌ 25	♍ 20	21 ♒ 19	26 ♊ 30	0 ♓ 0R
755	♐ 19	♑ 5	♑ 23	27 ♒ 47	♉ 2	♊ 1	28 ♐ 52	11 ♎ 44	4 ♑ 38
756	♎ 10	♏ 6	♏ 24	10 ♐ 0	♑ 17	♓ 3	18 ♏ 5	27 ♉ 20	10 ♐ 31
757	♒ 17	♓ 16	♉ 2	22 ♊ 9	♋ 10	♋ 27	5 ♓ 40	4 ♋ 46	1 ♓ 30
758	♑ 0	♑ 7	♑ 15	26 ♓ 25	♊ 10	♊ 22	20 ♍ 30	22 ♎ 46	13 ♍ 55
759	♉ 18	♊ 23	♋ 26	25 ♌ 2	♍ 18	♎ 16	16 ♉ 18	14 ♊ 56	27 ♉ 46
760	♑ 14	♒ 3	♓ 2	9 ♉ 37	♊ 11	♊ 28	13 ♑ 10	5 ♎ 33	27 ♐ 2
761	♎ 12	♏ 8	♏ 27	12 ♐ 9	♑ 21	♓ 6	4 ♉ 54	27 ♐ 15	2 ♉ 45
762	♈ 29	♊ 0	♋ 6	12 ♌ 30	♍ 9	♎ 4	12 ♍ 30	11 ♋ 21	9 ♎ 12
763	♋ 8	♌ 13	♍ 13	6 ♎ 41	♏ 2	♐ 3	10 ♑ 0	29 ♌ 30	8 ♑ 30
764	♌ 29	♎ 1	♎ 24	13 ♏ 45	♐ 12	♑ 19	15 ♎ 47	13 ♏ 2	1 ♎ 31
765	♎ 20	♏ 16	♐ 8	28 ♐ 0	♒ 5	♓ 16	13 ♒ 5	3 ♈ 50	21 ♑ 54
766	♋ 20	♌ 24	♍ 23	16 ♎ 0	♏ 12	♐ 14	8 ♒ 30	17 ♒ 30	22 ♑ 5R
767	♐ 2	♐ 22	♑ 13	9 ♒ 14	♈ 2	♉ 6	19 ♈ 56	18 ♍ 18	4 ♉ 30
768	♋ 23	♌ 28	♍ 26	17 ♎ 8	♏ 14	♐ 16	13 ♑ 22	29 ♑ 52	0 ♑ 42R
769	♈ 0	♉ 7	♊ 18	21 ♋ 45	♌ 10	♍ 2	9 ♊ 35	18 ♍ 39	11 ♊ 18R
770	♓ 12	♈ 16	♉ 28	5 ♋ 0	♋ 24	♌ 15	12 ♓ 16	29 ♉ 54	16 ♒ 30
771	♏ 17	♐ 7	♐ 25	14 ♑ 35	♓ 5	♈ 18	27 ♌ 48	20 ♎ 34	12 ♌ 46
772	♏ 19	♐ 13	♑ 5	0 ♒ 35	♓ 12	♈ 20	0 ♐ 30	26 ♓ 7	18 ♍ 33
773	♈ 16	♉ 23	♋ 0	2 ♌ 0	♌ 21	♍ 15	4 ♈ 0	26 ♍ 22	11 ♈ 0R
774	♌ 2	♍ 5	♎ 4	27 ♎ 31	♏ 26	♐ 28	14 ♉ 33	19 ♍ 16	1 ♉ 4
775	♐ 21	♑ 11	♒ 5	11 ♓ 50	♉ 0	♊ 0	2 ♏ 28	25 ♍ 2	23 ♎ 45
776	♋ 21	♌ 27	♍ 24	15 ♎ 27	♏ 11	♐ 12	20 ♍ 30	29 ♒ 30	29 ♍ 2
777	♈ 26	♊ 4	♋ 11	11 ♌ 0	♍ 0	♍ 24	25 ♑ 16	21 ♑ 16	23 ♑ 0
778	♎ 18	♏ 14	♐ 6	25 ♐ 30	♒ 3	♓ 13	21 ♏ 45	13 ♋ 37	10 ♐ 41
779	♉ 10	♊ 21	♋ 26	24 ♌ 0	♍ 13	♎ 8	7 ♏ 30	12 ♓ 58	27 ♎ 29R
780	♊ 13	♋ 13	♌ 13	12 ♍ 35	♎ 12	♏ 13	25 ♌ 54	1 ♉ 5	22 ♍ 28
781	♌ 9	♍ 11	♎ 12	10 ♏ 5	♐ 9	♑ 9	23 ♏ 35	6 ♑ 20	22 ♏ 50
782	♑ 6	♑ 25	♒ 23	14 ♈ 30	♉ 25	♊ 18	22 ♊ 25	21 ♑ 39	13 ♊ 11
783	♓ 14	♈ 18	♉ 29	5 ♋ 0	♋ 27	♌ 18	16 ♒ 48	17 ♉ 41	21 ♑ 38
784	♈ 4	♉ 11	♊ 23	26 ♋ 13	♌ 13	♍ 5	16 ♍ 21	16 ♈ 19	2 ♍ 26
785	♎ 4	♎ 29	♏ 17	1 ♐ 0	♑ 6	♒ 24	28 ♋ 12	9 ♉ 29	10 ♋ 12
786	♎ 29	♏ 21	♐ 8	24 ♐ 0	♒ 8	♓ 26	1 ♋ 30	11 ♌ 7	23 ♊ 0
787	♒ 9	♓ 7	♈ 16	1 ♊ 20	♊ 26	♋ 16	8 ♍ 31	4 ♋ 54	3 ♍ 40
788	♏ 26	♐ 17	♑ 1	1 ♒ 0	♓ 21	♉ 0	22 ♎ 6	8 ♊ 30	15 ♎ 42
789	♏ 2	♏ 23	♐ 11	26 ♐ 20	♒ 11	♓ 29	13 ♋ 34	6 ♋ 9	5 ♌ 29
790	♈ 19	♉ 28	♋ 9	8 ♌ 50	♌ 26	♍ 18	10 ♉ 20	4 ♏ 8	13 ♈ 35
791	♋ 8	♎ 12	♍ 12	6 ♎ 46	♏ 3	♐ 4	19 ♎ 51	22 ♒ 13	9 ♎ 34
792	♌ 15	♍ 18	♎ 15	8 ♏ 22	♐ 7	♑ 10	15 ♎ 9	14 ♌ 32	0 ♎ 20
793	♓ 5	♈ 10	♊ 5	17 ♋ 20	♋ 29	♌ 14	27 ♓ 42	20 ♓ 30	9 ♓ 20
794	♋ 21	♌ 24	♍ 24	18 ♎ 30	♏ 16	♐ 17	4 ♑ 22	15 ♌ 4	15 ♐ 16
795	♐ 9	♐ 27	♑ 16	12 ♒ 0	♈ 12	♉ 17	7 ♑ 43	16 ♊ 50	27 ♑ 11
796	♓ 4	♈ 16	♉ 25	0 ♋ 0	♋ 22	♌ 15	20 ♐ 54	7 ♒ 45	29 ♏ 49
797	♉ 13	♊ 18	♋ 20	19 ♌ 0	♍ 13	♎ 10	23 ♉ 2	20 ♏ 24	17 ♉ 55
798	♊ 5	♋ 13	♌ 16	11 ♍ 20	♎ 2	♏ 0	5 ♊ 9	0 ♍ 16	10 ♊ 43R
799	♑ 15	♒ 7	♓ 10	27 ♈ 0	♊ 2	♊ 23	16 ♋ 15	23 ♊ 5	29 ♋ 30
800	♒ 6	♓ 3	♈ 12	28 ♉ 0	♊ 23	♋ 14	20 ♌ 57	28 ♍ 30	17 ♍ 40

	♀	♂	♃	♄	♅	♆	♇
	° ′	° ′	° ′	° ′	° ′	° ′	° ′
751	14 ♋ 5 R	28 ♋ 14	15 ♌ 14	9 ♈ 57	15 ♑ 0 R	14 ♋ 32	24 ♊ 50
752	2 ♌ 0	17 ♎ 30	23 ♍ 0	23 ♏ 0	11 ♓ 0 R	8 ♒ 30 R	17 ♈ 30 R
753	6 ♑ 0	25 ♑ 0	28 ♉ 0 R	3 ♉ 30 R	7 ♑ 30	5 ♑ 0	0 ♈ 30
754	6 ♑ 0	24 ♍ 30	8 ♒ 37	20 ♑ 40	26 ♓ 16	19 ♒ 4	20 ♈ 0
755	6 ♒ 29	10 ♒ 31	0 ♈ 26	11 ♋ 37 R	21 ♉ 41 R	17 ♓ 45	3 ♉ 31
756	16 ♐ 6	18 ♍ 4	26 ♏ 58	20 ♐ 4	16 ♓ 35 R	12 ♒ 11	19 ♈ 0 R
757	5 ♓ 16	6 ♒ 6	22 ♑ 30	12 ♏ 19 R	29 ♊ 58 R	9 ♈ 1	13 ♉ 0
758	25 ♎ 20	17 ♍ 30	1 ♊ 23	12 ♎ 43	8 ♏ 10	13 ♊ 30	10 ♊ 39 R
759	26 ♈ 10	3 ♎ 23 R	29 ♓ 36	27 ♊ 32	20 ♉ 38	19 ♓ 50	4 ♉ 20
760	11 ♐ 50	29 ♓ 5	26 ♌ 16 R	9 ♍ 21 R	8 ♊ 47 R	26 ♓ 48	7 ♉ 25 R
761	11 ♈ 50	5 ♎ 23 R	27 ♓ 7	26 ♊ 18	19 ♉ 57	19 ♓ 33	2 ♉ 58
762	11 ♍ 15	3 ♍ 11	14 ♏ 7	18 ♎ 13	15 ♓ 42 R	18 ♌ 50	12 ♋ 4
763	11 ♑ 45	28 ♑ 30	27 ♉ 30 R	3 ♉ 30 R	8 ♑ 0	5 ♑ 30	29 ♓ 30
764	2 ♐ 12	4 ♑ 49	21 ♊ 36	10 ♌ 30	3 ♊ 8 R	22 ♓ 55 R	6 ♉ 55 R
765	15 ♓ 48	5 ♐ 23	19 ♓ 48	29 ♍ 38 R	6 ♏ 3	6 ♊ 18 R	6 ♊ 52 R
766	9 ♓ 30	13 ♌ 30 R	28 ♋ 30 R	3 ♊ 14 R	27 ♍ 51 R	18 ♉ 17 R	29 ♉ 12 R
767	4 ♊ 21	15 ♑ 33	5 ♈ 42	25 ♍ 0 R	4 ♍ 39 R	7 ♊ 1	7 ♊ 14
768	9 ♐ 2	16 ♍ 54	6 ♌ 37 R	10 ♑ 45	26 ♏ 29	14 ♐ 12	18 ♓ 30
769	11 ♉ 27 R	11 ♊ 39	3 ♉ 38	12 ♋ 52	26 ♉ 0	22 ♓ 30	4 ♉ 1
770	19 ♈ 47	2 ♉ 30	1 ♐ 30	0 ♓ 13	16 ♌ 58 R	1 ♉ 1	21 ♉ 45
771	20 ♋ 24	19 ♑ 19	11 ♌ 22	29 ♌ 18	11 ♊ 46	28 ♓ 46 R	9 ♉ 18 R
772	14 ♐ 34	6 ♌ 52	29 ♎ 3	13 ♐ 5	3 ♐ 30	24 ♊ 0 R	15 ♊ 0 R
773	8 ♈ 0	25 ♒ 0	8 ♉ 0	8 ♎ 0 R	25 ♒ 0	1 ♒ 8	11 ♈ 0
774	5 ♊ 19	2 ♌ 2	20 ♒ 16	16 ♊ 49	11 ♒ 34	25 ♋ 40	0 ♋ 5
775	19 ♐ 12	9 ♏ 37	7 ♑ 51	11 ♓ 52 R	17 ♐ 40	25 ♐ 24	24 ♓ 30
776	0 ♍ 30	4 ♉ 59	3 ♋ 30	23 ♎ 36	12 ♏ 34	15 ♊ 49	11 ♊ 38
777	5 ♓ 0	17 ♎ 18	16 ♓ 11	1 ♐ 17	9 ♏ 19	5 ♐ 30	13 ♓ 30
778	3 ♐ 55	11 ♎ 51	26 ♋ 15 R	25 ♌ 35	6 ♊ 20 R	24 ♓ 30 R	6 ♉ 44
779	1 ♐ 24	0 ♏ 2	17 ♏ 47	17 ♒ 30	9 ♐ 36	20 ♐ 30	22 ♓ 30 R
780	28 ♋ 18	5 ♍ 51	29 ♑ 16 R	1 ♈ 53 R	29 ♌ 35	9 ♉ 49 R	26 ♉ 22
781	19 ♐ 37 R	6 ♒ 55	5 ♒ 57	15 ♍ 39	28 ♎ 43	5 ♊ 44 R	7 ♊ 1 R
782	25 ♋ 38	14 ♒ 19	19 ♈ 17	23 ♍ 37	2 ♏ 16 R	9 ♊ 17	8 ♊ 35
783	3 ♓ 55	4 ♑ 8	13 ♏ 45	0 ♉ 50	26 ♑ 31	19 ♋ 28 R	26 ♊ 6
784	7 ♌ 24	6 ♐ 12	13 ♍ 2	26 ♑ 28 R	8 ♌ 40	28 ♈ 12 R	21 ♉ 37 R
785	12 ♊ 45	18 ♋ 30	0 ♑ 30 R	20 ♌ 30	18 ♎ 10	3 ♊ 57	6 ♊ 30
786	4 ♌ 0	11 ♉ 30	1 ♎ 30	7 ♐ 30 R	0 ♐ 30 R	22 ♊ 30	15 ♊ 0
787	5 ♍ 1	10 ♑ 45	2 ♌ 49	25 ♓ 14 R	8 ♑ 513 R	14 ♋ 17	24 ♊ 36
788	9 ♎ 20	13 ♎ 2	28 ♑ 6	27 ♓ 48 R	2 ♍ 55	8 ♉ 51 R	25 ♉ 50 R
789	27 ♋ 55	8 ♊ 30	16 ♐ 36 R	27 ♉ 39	11 ♉ 51	13 ♓ 37 R	0 ♉ 15
790	9 ♉ 50	21 ♊ 6	8 ♉ 31	7 ♎ 12	8 ♏ 38 R	9 ♊ 52	8 ♊ 40
791	26 ♎ 24	24 ♍ 30	8 ♓ 53 R	24 ♍ 7	1 ♏ 1	8 ♊ 48 R	8 ♊ 33
792	0 ♐ 47	9 ♑ 40	2 ♒ 30	12 ♍ 1	26 ♎ 19	6 ♊ 35 R	7 ♊ 39 R
793	6 ♉ 15	9 ♉ 45	14 ♓ 30	4 ♒ 34	1 ♈ 59	22 ♒ 30	22 ♈ 0
794	20 ♒ 0	25 ♏ 32	22 ♉ 11 R	23 ♎ 51	14 ♏ 2	11 ♊ 34	10 ♊ 0 R
795	23 ♐ 1	24 ♎ 41	5 ♉ 57 R	26 ♋ 14 R	25 ♉ 48 R	20 ♓ 7	4 ♉ 29 R
796	7 ♒ 5	16 ♏ 51	23 ♉ 19 R	22 ♎ 52	13 ♏ 24	11 ♊ 55 R	10 ♊ 0 R
797	7 ♉ 15 R	0 ♈ 50	7 ♉ 37	4 ♉ 46	9 ♍ 38 R	14 ♉ 21	27 ♉ 40
798	20 ♊ 57	6 ♐ 50	12 ♒ 8	27 ♌ 41	23 ♎ 7 R	4 ♊ 19	6 ♊ 15
799	1 ♍ 8	6 ♎ 15	10 ♎ 30	4 ♐ 28 R	16 ♓ 18 R	11 ♒ 57 R	19 ♈ 0
800	1 ♍ 12	29 ♋ 30	0 ♉ 10	17 ♒ 23 R	26 ♐ 9	7 ♋ 17	21 ♊ 20

	10	11	12	Asc.	2	3	☉	☽	☿
	°	°	°	° ′	°	°	° ′	° ′	° ′
801	♒ 20	♓ 21	♈ 29	9 ♊ 0	♋ 3	♋ 25	22 ♋ 39	17 ♓ 21	6 ♌ 12
802	♓ 12	♈ 16	♉ 25	0 ♋ 30	♋ 23	♌ 15	12 ♏ 15	16 ♋ 47	29 ♏ 36
803	♎ 3	♏ 2	♏ 24	13 ♐ 45	♑ 18	♒ 27	0 ♎ 21	8 ♒ 30	11 ♎ 52
804	♍ 19	♎ 19	♏ 13	3 ♐ 0	♑ 5	♒ 12	18 ♎ 34	19 ♋ 0	2 ♎ 35
805	♊ 9	♋ 12	♌ 14	11 ♍ 26	♎ 6	♏ 5	11 ♒ 6	5 ♋ 43	27 ♒ 9
806	♎ 23	♏ 19	♐ 10	29 ♐ 25	♒ 7	♓ 19	3 ♏ 57	11 ♋ 40	2 ♏ 20
807	♋ 9	♌ 11	♍ 12	8 ♎ 15	♏ 6	♐ 6	11 ♈ 17	4 ♓ 40	1 ♈ 20R
808	♐ 29	♑ 17	♒ 11	28 ♓ 0	♉ 16	♊ 11	16 ♉ 0	5 ♒ 30	21 ♈ 0
809	♑ 28	♒ 21	♈ 0	24 ♉ 50	♊ 22	♋ 10	13 ♐ 0	25 ♌ 30	13 ♐ 52
810	♎ 12	♏ 8	♏ 27	13 ♐ 30	♑ 21	♓ 5	2 ♈ 8	24 ♒ 38	4 ♓ 24
811	♒ 1	♒ 26	♈ 5	29 ♉ 18	♊ 23	♋ 12	28 ♌ 27	27 ♑ 43	25 ♍ 30
812	♐ 8	♐ 28	♑ 20	19 ♒ 20	♈ 9	♉ 14	13 ♏ 24	15 ♒ 20	24 ♏ 21R
813	♐ 12	♐ 30	♑ 18	16 ♒ 19	♈ 18	♉ 21	18 ♒ 47	26 ♋ 51	24 ♑ 46
814	♉ 28	♋ 3	♌ 6	3 ♍ 15	♍ 27	♎ 25	12 ♐ 23	25 ♑ 19	23 ♏ 54
815	♌ 16	♍ 19	♎ 16	7 ♏ 45	♐ 7	♑ 10	13 ♊ 20	6 ♉ 9	29 ♊ 16R
816	♋ 27	♍ 1	♍ 29	20 ♎ 5	♏ 18	♐ 19	15 ♎ 15	13 ♉ 48	8 ♏ 56
817	♋ 21	♌ 27	♍ 24	15 ♎ 15	♏ 10	♐ 13	27 ♋ 36	17 ♋ 14	22 ♋ 56
818	♐ 17	♑ 6	♑ 28	27 ♒ 0	♈ 27	♉ 28	9 ♋ 44	26 ♈ 44	18 ♊ 30
819	♐ 15	♑ 3	♑ 25	28 ♒ 0	♈ 20	♉ 22	29 ♒ 45	5 ♑ 30	3 ♒ 51
820	♎ 0	♎ 26	♑ 15	0 ♐ 23	♑ 4	♒ 20	25 ♎ 1	0 ♏ 40	7 ♎ 5
821	♉ 3	♊ 9	♋ 14	13 ♌ 30	♍ 5	♎ 1	21 ♍ 7	16 ♒ 30	17 ♎ 30
822	♓ 1	♈ 4	♉ 10	14 ♊ 46	♋ 10	♌ 4	21 ♍ 14	8 ♋ 40	2 ♎ 30R
823	♏ 12	♐ 5	♐ 26	17 ♑ 59	♓ 1	♈ 11	23 ♐ 59	9 ♓ 40	2 ♑ 1
824	♈ 16	♉ 27	♋ 7	8 ♌ 0	♌ 25	♍ 16	8 ♓ 30	18 ♎ 53	19 ♒ 30
825	♒ 8	♓ 6	♈ 14	28 ♉ 32	♊ 23	♋ 15	8 ♍ 23	7 ♏ 18	19 ♍ 6
826	♋ 14	♌ 8	♍ 10	23 ♎ 45	♏ 27	♐ 22	18 ♓ 10	3 ♓ 11	15 ♓ 53
827	♒ 2	♒ 24	♈ 6	10 ♊ 0	♊ 29	♋ 14	9 ♒ 58	25 ♓ 6	28 ♒ 11
828	♎ 10	♏ 5	♏ 28	9 ♐ 0	♑ 15	♓ 2	18 ♈ 0	6 ♐ 30	26 ♓ 0
829	♎ 5	♏ 1	♏ 20	5 ♐ 30	♑ 10	♒ 26	4 ♎ 30	28 ♍ 12	23 ♍ 30
830	♓ 1	♈ 5	♊ 4	19 ♋ 0	♋ 29	♌ 13	16 ♏ 24	8 ♋ 12	8 ♐ 59
831	♑ 7	♑ 25	♒ 22	19 ♈ 30	♉ 29	♊ 20	22 ♉ 10	11 ♊ 30	10 ♉ 30
832	♏ 9	♐ 0	♐ 17	3 ♑ 0	♒ 22	♈ 9	17 ♊ 29	0 ♍ 30	3 ♋ 51R
833	♑ 15	♒ 6	♓ 8	4 ♉ 37	♊ 7	♊ 27	24 ♊ 18	12 ♍ 5	16 ♋ 38
834	♏ 25	♐ 17	♑ 8	3 ♒ 5	♓ 19	♒ 27	29 ♒ 29	18 ♎ 13	13 ♓ 56R
835	♊ 7	♋ 15	♌ 17	12 ♍ 56	♎ 4	♏ 2	3 ♎ 41	26 ♒ 29	26 ♍ 28
836	♑ 22	♒ 17	♓ 21	7 ♉ 19	♊ 8	♋ 0	11 ♈ 43	26 ♌ 23	3 ♈ 41
837	♍ 23	♎ 21	♏ 10	25 ♏ 0	♐ 27	♑ 12	2 ♎ 30	7 ♎ 30	28 ♎ 20
838	♒ 12	♓ 8	♈ 29	27 ♊ 30	♋ 11	♋ 25	15 ♑ 32	18 ♏ 5	5 ♑ 47R
839	♑ 13	♒ 0	♓ 0	9 ♉ 10	♊ 10	♊ 27	15 ♉ 49	27 ♏ 43	19 ♈ 50
840	♍ 24	♎ 22	♏ 12	28 ♏ 0	♑ 1	♒ 14	26 ♒ 17	2 ♒ 54	5 ♓ 27
841	♎ 13	♏ 9	♏ 29	16 ♐ 59	♑ 24	♓ 7	12 ♒ 40	24 ♍ 36	1 ♒ 3R
842	♒ 22	♓ 23	♉ 11	29 ♊ 35	♋ 16	♌ 2	3 ♌ 5	21 ♉ 2	18 ♋ 1
843	♎ 5	♏ 3	♏ 26	15 ♐ 59	♑ 20	♒ 29	28 ♎ 1	23 ♊ 23	23 ♎ 40
844	♋ 12	♌ 16	♍ 15	9 ♎ 48	♏ 8	♐ 6	16 ♌ 48	11 ♓ 35	1 ♍ 35
845	♌ 11	♍ 14	♎ 12	4 ♏ 50	♐ 4	♑ 6	27 ♍ 27	7 ♋ 16	11 ♍ 44
846	♐ 29	♑ 25	♒ 24	28 ♓ 40	♉ 3	♊ 3	10 ♓ 19	22 ♐ 0	22 ♓ 56
847	♊ 26	♌ 0	♍ 0	26 ♍ 30	♎ 22	♏ 22	11 ♉ 43	21 ♈ 39	27 ♈ 57R
848	♐ 13	♑ 2	♑ 23	23 ♒ 35	♈ 18	♉ 20	11 ♉ 40	6 ♓ 25	16 ♉ 24
849	♋ 9	♌ 16	♍ 15	6 ♎ 30	♎ 30	♐ 1	10 ♑ 30	25 ♓ 35	14 ♑ 30
850	♏ 3	♏ 27	♐ 18	8 ♑ 10	♒ 19	♈ 0	8 ♑ 56	27 ♉ 45	19 ♐ 41

	♀ ° ′	♂ ° ′	♃ ° ′	♄ ° ′	♅ ° ′	♆ ° ′	♇ ° ′
801	7 ♍ 51	0 ♉ 27	4 ♏ 56	18 ♉ 14	27 ♑ 35 R	21 ♋ 20	27 ♊ 4
802	29 ♍ 51	22 ♉ 57 R	2 ♓ 56	10 ♈ 10 R	8 ♍ 17	10 ♉ 20 R	26 ♉ 30 R
803	22 ♎ 28	12 ♐ 29	5 ♍ 54	16 ♍ 58	2 ♓ 39	12 ♌ 59	8 ♋ 48
804	3 ♍ 38	19 ♏ 42	28 ♌ 51	24 ♊ 13 R	29 ♍ 49	22 ♉ 50 R	1 ♊ 45 R
805	6 ♒ 2	27 ♊ 1	16 ♉ 54	6 ♉ 6	17 ♍ 55 R	13 ♉ 47	28 ♉ 0 R
806	18 ♐ 0	17 ♑ 49	21 ♊ 7 R	11 ♌ 38	2 ♊ 36 R	22 ♓ 0 R	6 ♉ 55 R
807	28 ♒ 15	19 ♋ 48	27 ♒ 23	23 ♏ 26 R	4 ♋ 32	12 ♈ 29	15 ♉ 0
808	19 ♊ 34	1 ♓ 25	19 ♊ 0	11 ♓ 30	16 ♈ 30	0 ♓ 25	26 ♈ 0
809	9 ♐ 16	3 ♈ 1	19 ♑ 18	1 ♍ 46	7 ♒ 30	21 ♑ 10	9 ♈ 0
810	28 ♈ 48	12 ♊ 7	27 ♊ 47	6 ♏ 11 R	19 ♏ 36 R	13 ♊ 14	9 ♊ 53
811	10 ♎ 41	4 ♐ 32	17 ♊ 52	5 ♌ 29	3 ♊ 23	24 ♓ 12 R	7 ♉ 50 R
812	7 ♏ 15	23 ♈ 1 R	6 ♋ 5 R	29 ♎ 54	15 ♏ 32	15 ♊ 14 R	11 ♊ 4 R
813	5 ♑ 49	26 ♑ 35	0 ♒ 20	18 ♓ 0	23 ♐ 35	27 ♐ 56	25 ♓ 24
814	29 ♑ 14	8 ♏ 9	25 ♍ 12	21 ♍ 57	14 ♊ 28 R	28 ♓ 51 R	8 ♉ 47 R
815	1 ♉ 26	21 ♋ 8	4 ♎ 37	2 ♉ 6	24 ♑ 44	17 ♋ 44	25 ♊ 54
816	16 ♎ 21	5 ♏ 47	14 ♋ 53	24 ♎ 46	26 ♒ 58 R	1 ♒ 2	14 ♈ 0
817	11 ♊ 58	15 ♋ 27	12 ♉ 41	19 ♋ 10	28 ♉ 27	22 ♓ 31 R	4 ♉ 11
818	17 ♌ 15	22 ♉ 58	26 ♎ 4	27 ♍ 40	12 ♎ 38	23 ♏ 27	9 ♓ 40
819	14 ♑ 42	23 ♏ 30	23 ♉ 15	25 ♐ 1	18 ♏ 51 R	10 ♐ 45	16 ♓ 30
820	23 ♍ 28	12 ♍ 33	13 ♉ 10 R	27 ♋ 52	28 ♉ 31 R	20 ♓ 21 R	5 ♉ 50 R
821	19 ♍ 30	13 ♋ 4	27 ♋ 57	10 ♊ 5	23 ♍ 30	20 ♉ 54 R	1 ♊ 3 R
822	5 ♌ 51	0 ♏ 55	23 ♌ 37	23 ♊ 49	28 ♍ 6	23 ♉ 15 R	2 ♊ 1 R
823	7 ♏ 20	29 ♏ 33	17 ♏ 30	16 ♎ 35	23 ♊ 3 R	3 ♈ 19	10 ♉ 43 R
824	22 ♑ 30	23 ♈ 35	28 ♒ 0	14 ♍ 12 R	1 ♍ 10 R	4 ♊ 4 R	5 ♊ 50 R
825	23 ♋ 16	5 ♍ 5	27 ♌ 36	8 ♈ 51 R	13 ♑ 8 R	16 ♋ 27	24 ♊ 32
826	15 ♒ 2	4 ♈ 54	19 ♋ 58 R	19 ♑ 5	27 ♋ 30 R	22 ♈ 25	17 ♉ 58
827	10 ♓ 57	9 ♈ 50	28 ♏ 42	26 ♒ 22	18 ♌ 19 R	0 ♉ 23	21 ♉ 40 R
828	29 ♈ 30	15 ♋ 0	27 ♉ 0	12 ♉ 2	15 ♍ 15 R	15 ♉ 12	27 ♉ 47
829	1 ♍ 30	23 ♐ 30	6 ♊ 30 R	27 ♒ 5 R	0 ♑ 30	10 ♋ 30	22 ♊ 30
830	20 ♎ 52	19 ♑ 5	25 ♍ 15	27 ♑ 21	10 ♌ 35	26 ♈ 28 R	20 ♉ 40 R
831	19 ♈ 30	16 ♑ 3	9 ♋ 13	24 ♓ 55	12 ♑ 30 R	10 ♋ 30	22 ♊ 30
832	9 ♋ 24	19 ♊ 9	17 ♉ 30	11 ♐ 30 R	11 ♏ 36 R	7 ♐ 30 R	16 ♓ 30
833	3 ♋ 6	17 ♋ 19	22 ♌ 27	4 ♍ 7	12 ♊ 53	1 ♈ 34	9 ♉ 50
834	11 ♓ 42 R	29 ♐ 17	25 ♍ 20 R	20 ♍ 48 R	12 ♊ 21 R	0 ♈ 9	8 ♉ 30
835	28 ♍ 43 R	28 ♉ 8	4 ♓ 31 R	13 ♈ 1 R	6 ♍ 27	11 ♉ 36 R	27 ♉ 7 R
836	22 ♈ 10	10 ♐ 33	7 ♒ 3	27 ♌ 40 R	25 ♎ 17 R	2 ♊ 16	5 ♊ 14
837	28 ♌ 2	1 ♍ 30	29 ♐ 56	28 ♌ 30	21 ♎ 1	4 ♊ 30 R	7 ♊ 0 R
838	1 ♐ 4	16 ♒ 30	26 ♑ 6 R	12 ♑ 37	29 ♋ 48 R	21 ♈ 17	17 ♉ 49 R
839	1 ♋ 11	21 ♑ 7	19 ♋ 49	19 ♌ 24	6 ♊ 34	28 ♓ 35	8 ♉ 3
840	24 ♒ 16	4 ♈ 30	0 ♎ 25 R	7 ♒ 33	7 ♌ 49 R	26 ♈ 15	19 ♉ 45
841	19 ♑ 6	11 ♐ 34	25 ♐ 25	7 ♓ 20	23 ♌ 6 R	2 ♉ 38	22 ♉ 30
842	4 ♌ 35	27 ♎ 8	9 ♈ 10	7 ♋ 39	24 ♉ 33	20 ♓ 10 R	3 ♉ 13
843	6 ♏ 39	29 ♍ 51	8 ♓ 25 R	25 ♍ 3	1 ♏ 31	8 ♊ 39 R	8 ♊ 25 R
844	26 ♍ 50	2 ♏ 18	22 ♓ 7 R	5 ♒ 11 R	21 ♐ 49 R	5 ♋ 0	20 ♊ 0
845	8 ♍ 15	26 ♍ 44	27 ♑ 21 R	29 ♓ 38 R	1 ♍ 35	9 ♉ 26 R	26 ♉ 14 R
846	6 ♒ 1	7 ♊ 17	21 ♓ 57	14 ♈ 2 R	6 ♍ 49	9 ♉ 44	25 ♉ 20
847	3 ♉ 9 R	19 ♏ 39 R	12 ♉ 46	1 ♓ 30	4 ♑ 0 R	5 ♋ 58	20 ♊ 15
848	25 ♓ 37	4 ♉ 32	15 ♒ 31	27 ♑ 47	20 ♐ 43 R	29 ♊ 28	16 ♊ 0
849	27 ♒ 30	23 ♏ 0	29 ♐ 30	17 ♌ 30 R	5 ♒ 0	19 ♑ 30	7 ♈ 30
850	25 ♐ 43	28 ♒ 43	1 ♎ 20	2 ♒ 5	9 ♌ 45 R	25 ♈ 49 R	19 ♉ 50 R

	10	11	12	Asc.	2	3	☉	☽	☿
	°	°	°	° ′	°	°	° ′	° ′	° ′
851	♑ 23	♒ 18	♓ 23	6 ♉ 10	♊ 7	♋ 0	2 ♊ 30	23 ♓ 54	18 ♊ 6R
852	♍ 8	♎ 9	♏ 0	17 ♏ 0	♐ 17	♑ 27	26 ♋ 10	17 ♑ 5	27 ♋ 30
853	♌ 11	♍ 13	♎ 13	9 ♏ 25	♐ 9	♑ 9	12 ♐ 12	23 ♒ 30	23 ♍ 40
854	♍ 8	♎ 9	♏ 2	19 ♏ 0	♐ 20	♑ 28	8 ♑ 0	2 ♓ 30	18 ♐ 30
855	♏ 22	♐ 13	♑ 3	26 ♑ 54	♓ 13	♈ 23	8 ♒ 56	21 ♍ 19	14 ♑ 44
856	♏ 7	♏ 28	♐ 14	30 ♐ 0	♒ 18	♈ 7	7 ♉ 30	3 ♏ 0	17 ♈ 0
857	♍ 14	♎ 15	♏ 7	23 ♏ 10	♐ 25	♒ 4	8 ♊ 30	23 ♒ 30	4 ♊ 5
858	♐ 17	♑ 4	♑ 24	27 ♒ 15	♈ 26	♉ 26	0 ♋ 52	12 ♊ 52	10 ♊ 9
859	♏ 18	♐ 3	♐ 21	22 ♑ 20	♓ 18	♈ 28	11 ♑ 15	3 ♍ 30	19 ♐ 0
860	♎ 28	♏ 20	♐ 6	22 ♐ 0	♒ 4	♓ 24	8 ♒ 10	10 ♈ 30	2 ♒ 20
861	♉ 29	♋ 4	♌ 6	3 ♍ 50	♍ 27	♎ 25	13 ♋ 20	29 ♉ 9	6 ♌ 18
862	♑ 10	♒ 1	♓ 0	22 ♈ 30	♉ 29	♊ 21	19 ♉ 12	23 ♉ 30	23 ♈ 3
863	♈ 12	♉ 24	♋ 7	7 ♌ 50	♌ 23	♍ 13	13 ♋ 1	9 ♑ 36	5 ♋ 36R
864	♉ 3	♊ 12	♋ 19	18 ♌ 12	♍ 6	♎ 1	13 ♌ 3	2 ♌ 3	13 ♌ 20R
865	♌ 24	♍ 26	♎ 22	12 ♏ 0	♐ 11	♑ 16	9 ♓ 23	16 ♎ 53	27 ♓ 23
866	♐ 11	♐ 29	♑ 19	20 ♒ 0	♈ 15	♉ 18	26 ♈ 10	12 ♊ 30	11 ♈ 50
867	♈ 19	♉ 28	♋ 9	8 ♌ 11	♌ 26	♍ 18	19 ♈ 0	0 ♎ 47	8 ♉ 36
868	♊ 10	♋ 14	♌ 16	12 ♍ 40	♎ 7	♏ 7	10 ♐ 5	23 ♏ 10	3 ♐ 43
869	♐ 16	♑ 1	♑ 18	18 ♒ 0	♈ 28	♉ 28	20 ♏ 51	8 ♓ 10	12 ♏ 2
870	♐ 23	♑ 11	♒ 3	12 ♓ 0	♉ 7	♊ 3	23 ♒ 30	4 ♋ 19	5 ♒ 30R
871	♊ 1	♋ 5	♌ 7	5 ♍ 0	♍ 29	♎ 28	15 ♈ 30	9 ♓ 0	2 ♈ 0R
872	♐ 29	♑ 17	♒ 11	27 ♓ 40	♉ 15	♊ 10	27 ♈ 48	1 ♓ 4	0 ♈ 29
873	♊ 28	♌ 3	♍ 4	28 ♍ 30	♎ 22	♏ 22	11 ♍ 15	6 ♋ 30	20 ♍ 8
874	♓ 19	♈ 25	♊ 9	16 ♋ 0	♌ 3	♌ 23	20 ♊ 30	6 ♍ 54	29 ♉ 34
875	♌ 11	♍ 15	♎ 11	1 ♏ 28	♏ 29	♑ 3	29 ♍ 37	6 ♓ 24	12 ♍ 31
876	♋ 14	♌ 19	♍ 18	10 ♎ 54	♏ 6	♐ 7	19 ♍ 38	18 ♉ 50	29 ♍ 47
877	♌ 1	♍ 5	♎ 3	23 ♎ 3	♏ 20	♐ 23	22 ♉ 28	2 ♋ 50	25 ♉ 59
878	♊ 1	♋ 6	♌ 8	5 ♍ 30	♍ 29	♎ 28	4 ♎ 30	21 ♌ 23	29 ♏ 50
879	♋ 14	♌ 15	♍ 16	13 ♎ 57	♏ 13	♐ 13	12 ♏ 8	16 ♐ 40	16 ♏ 54
880	♎ 23	♏ 21	♐ 16	10 ♑ 0	♒ 14	♓ 20	19 ♏ 35	9 ♑ 23	10 ♐ 40
881	♌ 27	♍ 29	♎ 25	16 ♏ 5	♐ 16	♑ 20	26 ♏ 42	14 ♓ 47	19 ♏ 37
882	♏ 11	♐ 1	♐ 17	3 ♑ 10	♒ 24	♈ 12	25 ♒ 55	28 ♏ 41	10 ♓ 15R
883	♎ 8	♏ 6	♏ 28	16 ♐ 20	♑ 22	♓ 2	6 ♈ 36	6 ♎ 30	24 ♈ 51
884	♐ 19	♑ 6	♑ 26	1 ♓ 55	♉ 0	♊ 0	15 ♈ 30	14 ♈ 0	5 ♈ 0
885	♍ 1	♎ 3	♎ 27	13 ♏ 0	♐ 13	♑ 21	10 ♋ 13	2 ♋ 20	17 ♋ 9R
886	♌ 20	♍ 23	♎ 20	11 ♏ 55	♐ 11	♑ 14	22 ♍ 34	22 ♌ 9	16 ♎ 29
887	♑ 14	♒ 16	♓ 12	20 ♈ 10	♉ 2	♊ 3	16 ♉ 19	13 ♈ 3	29 ♉ 51
888	♎ 18	♏ 14	♐ 6	27 ♐ 0	♒ 3	♓ 13	27 ♐ 43	1 ♓ 50	6 ♐ 19
889	♎ 18	♏ 13	♐ 2	18 ♐ 30	♑ 27	♓ 13	29 ♍ 50	26 ♏ 30	25 ♎ 40
890	♋ 14	♌ 17	♍ 17	6 ♎ 6	♏ 9	♐ 10	6 ♌ 29	13 ♈ 44	22 ♋ 21
891	♒ 24	♓ 24	♉ 19	8 ♋ 30	♋ 21	♌ 5	16 ♉ 40	28 ♋ 50	20 ♈ 30
892	♓ 0	♈ 3	♉ 12	19 ♊ 40	♋ 12	♌ 4	0 ♎ 53	24 ♑ 10	25 ♎ 58
893	♒ 15	♓ 12	♈ 29	23 ♊ 0	♋ 10	♋ 26	13 ♌ 2	13 ♊ 21	25 ♋ 13
894	♋ 11	♌ 17	♍ 17	9 ♎ 0	♏ 4	♐ 5	18 ♌ 46	26 ♊ 24	15 ♍ 50
895	♑ 16	♒ 7	♓ 10	4 ♉ 0	♊ 6	♊ 27	17 ♋ 48	13 ♎ 57	28 ♊ 7
896	♑ 13	♒ 13	♓ 3	2 ♉ 0	♊ 6	♊ 26	27 ♈ 7	0 ♈ 51	6 ♉ 3
897	♐ 23	♑ 14	♒ 9	16 ♓ 0	♉ 2	♊ 1	23 ♒ 22	22 ♏ 30	27 ♑ 24
898	♌ 11	♍ 14	♎ 12	4 ♏ 41	♐ 3	♑ 6	17 ♈ 27	17 ♌ 32	4 ♉ 8
899	♋ 6	♌ 12	♍ 12	4 ♎ 0	♎ 29	♏ 29	0 ♏ 10	14 ♈ 57	19 ♏ 14R
900	♐ 22	♑ 14	♒ 12	15 ♓ 30	♈ 28	♉ 28	25 ♏ 8	11 ♈ 43	18 ♏ 23

	♀	♂	♃	♄	♅	♆	♇
	° ′	° ′	° ′	° ′	° ′	° ′	° ′
851	17 ♈ 45	16 ♉ 54	3 ♊ 30	26 ♐ 53 R	19 ♋ 24	20 ♈ 53	17 ♉ 30
852	26 ♋ 10	6 ♉ 40	17 ♏ 45	12 ♎ 19	27 ♊ 8	8 ♈ 22 R	13 ♉ 0
853	13 ♐ 10	22 ♈ 24	3 ♋ 42 R	3 ♏ 7	17 ♏ 17	14 ♊ 28 R	10 ♊ 22 R
854	16 ♑ 0	6 ♒ 0	2 ♏ 4	20 ♋ 0 R	12 ♎ 21	25 ♉ 22 R	2 ♊ 31 R
855	28 ♐ 1	4 ♓ 36	28 ♋ 3 R	15 ♑ 20	28 ♋ 50 R	21 ♈ 29	17 ♉ 50
856	21 ♊ 30	3 ♌ 30	15 ♓ 0	8 ♈ 0	28 ♐ 30 R	1 ♑ 0 R	28 ♓ 30
857	26 ♉ 30	28 ♋ 8	12 ♈ 30	24 ♈ 53	5 ♍ 0	12 ♉ 46	27 ♉ 30
858	28 ♋ 14 R	9 ♍ 8	5 ♌ 37	15 ♊ 56	24 ♍ 12	22 ♉ 14	1 ♊ 17
859	26 ♏ 30	14 ♉ 46	9 ♓ 17	9 ♈ 30	8 ♍ 51 R	9 ♉ 21 R	25 ♉ 44 R
860	21 ♓ 30	27 ♎ 10	13 ♐ 25	28 ♐ 58	18 ♓ 7	14 ♒ 20	18 ♈ 4
861	24 ♊ 20	13 ♑ 25 R	20 ♋ 26	27 ♓ 27	10 ♑ 37 R	12 ♋ 24	23 ♊ 39
862	15 ♈ 30	11 ♌ 0	3 ♏ 30	22 ♐ 30 R	6 ♐ 30 R	23 ♊ 12	15 ♊ 0
863	28 ♉ 28	5 ♉ 15	22 ♌ 18	7 ♈ 49	26 ♈ 2	4 ♓ 37 R	29 ♈ 0
864	19 ♌ 12	9 ♍ 33	19 ♈ 32	28 ♈ 57	7 ♍ 42	14 ♉ 18	28 ♉ 13
865	20 ♒ 47	6 ♉ 55	19 ♌ 52 R	5 ♍ 53 R	8 ♊ 8	28 ♓ 19	7 ♉ 40
866	19 ♈ 55	17 ♌ 30	26 ♈ 55	16 ♐ 48 R	13 ♋ 41	17 ♈ 30	15 ♉ 55
867	24 ♉ 58	5 ♋ 0	29 ♐ 0	27 ♎ 35 R	26 ♊ 4	8 ♈ 28	12 ♉ 5
868	26 ♑ 57	3 ♑ 9	12 ♉ 54 R	18 ♐ 30	21 ♋ 31 R	16 ♈ 58 R	16 ♉ 30 R
869	29 ♐ 11	25 ♏ 33	13 ♎ 25	15 ♈ 9 R	27 ♈ 29 R	4 ♓ 16 R	27 ♈ 38 R
870	11 ♓ 7 R	29 ♒ 40	13 ♉ 23	26 ♐ 15	18 ♋ 41 R	17 ♈ 23	15 ♉ 58
871	22 ♈ 30	4 ♓ 10	10 ♉ 31	7 ♎ 0 R	25 ♒ 19	1 ♒ 23	12 ♈ 30
872	29 ♉ 52	29 ♈ 21	1 ♏ 25 R	16 ♋ 28	9 ♎ 42 R	26 ♉ 26	2 ♊ 40
873	28 ♋ 17	23 ♏ 56	24 ♈ 14 R	28 ♏ 8	6 ♏ 41	4 ♐ 10	15 ♓ 0
874	10 ♊ 19	10 ♈ 36	19 ♏ 22 R	11 ♎ 20	24 ♊ 59	8 ♈ 7	16 ♊ 35
875	6 ♏ 4	3 ♌ 25	19 ♍ 18	7 ♋ 41	3 ♎ 8	25 ♉ 26 R	3 ♊ 0 R
876	11 ♌ 50	23 ♊ 51	26 ♉ 14	12 ♉ 7 R	14 ♍ 33	16 ♉ 25 R	29 ♊ 9 R
877	10 ♊ 7	4 ♊ 24	22 ♑ 39 R	14 ♑ 6 R	27 ♈ 18	19 ♒ 15	21 ♈ 4
878	18 ♍ 34	14 ♌ 45	7 ♒ 29 R	21 ♑ 12	17 ♐ 42	3 ♋ 42	19 ♊ 35 R
879	24 ♏ 20	8 ♎ 49	8 ♓ 8	26 ♍ 31	2 ♏ 23	8 ♊ 21 R	8 ♊ 11 R
880	25 ♐ 32	27 ♋ 48	26 ♑ 52	15 ♏ 34	8 ♋ 6 R	10 ♈ 27 R	14 ♉ 2 R
881	11 ♎ 13	11 ♏ 1	11 ♏ 53	14 ♎ 13	24 ♊ 9 R	3 ♈ 30 R	11 ♉ 18 R
882	12 ♑ 29	25 ♊ 18	4 ♎ 58 R	18 ♍ 56 R	11 ♎ 31 R	24 ♏ 0	6 ♓ 30
883	23 ♒ 59	23 ♋ 40	8 ♏ 42 R	23 ♐ 39	7 ♐ 56 R	22 ♊ 8	13 ♊ 40
884	4 ♈ 0	9 ♌ 15	8 ♌ 30	16 ♏ 0 R	7 ♓ 0	8 ♒ 0	15 ♈ 30
885	18 ♊ 17	24 ♐ 52	22 ♎ 1	25 ♒ 32 R	13 ♌ 25	2 ♉ 45	23 ♉ 4
886	13 ♌ 56	22 ♌ 4	15 ♉ 47 R	25 ♋ 0	29 ♉ 15 R	22 ♓ 0 R	6 ♉ 18 R
887	15 ♉ 2	22 ♊ 5	17 ♌ 55	2 ♍ 41	10 ♊ 39	0 ♈ 46	8 ♉ 57
888	29 ♏ 27	1 ♏ 51	7 ♋ 6 R	9 ♓ 32	7 ♑ 59	11 ♋ 37 R	23 ♊ 0 R
889	13 ♌ 45	16 ♍ 20	27 ♏ 56	2 ♓ 52 R	22 ♌ 47	4 ♉ 48 R	24 ♉ 30 R
890	28 ♌ 27	6 ♎ 11	18 ♉ 13	10 ♐ 44 R	18 ♋ 54	19 ♈ 36 R	17 ♉ 44
891	25 ♈ 32	16 ♉ 5	13 ♏ 30 R	20 ♐ 30 R	19 ♓ 30	14 ♒ 49	18 ♈ 30
892	23 ♎ 44	26 ♊ 3	9 ♉ 28	13 ♐ 37	5 ♈ 36 R	0 ♍ 4	18 ♋ 18
893	27 ♊ 25	6 ♏ 1	25 ♈ 0	27 ♏ 14	6 ♏ 0	4 ♐ 6 R	15 ♓ 30 R
894	20 ♋ 23	5 ♎ 38	14 ♏ 47	17 ♉ 38	8 ♉ 30	10 ♓ 40 R	29 ♈ 10 R
895	14 ♋ 49	18 ♎ 58	8 ♈ 34	5 ♋ 37	23 ♉ 59	20 ♓ 22 R	5 ♉ 25
896	11 ♉ 35	13 ♐ 0	9 ♒ 20	27 ♌ 8 R	24 ♎ 34 R	2 ♊ 54	5 ♊ 30
897	9 ♓ 9	8 ♎ 5 R	16 ♊ 25	6 ♑ 36	23 ♋ 25 R	19 ♈ 36	17 ♉ 5
898	1 ♊ 27	14 ♑ 3	5 ♈ 4	25 ♍ 13 R	4 ♏ 47 R	6 ♊ 58	7 ♊ 11
899	29 ♍ 34	2 ♍ 25	22 ♒ 47	29 ♊ 56 R	19 ♉ 37 R	15 ♓ 42 R	2 ♉ 23 R
900	28 ♐ 30	27 ♊ 51 R	7 ♍ 55	22 ♏ 10	24 ♏ 50	19 ♊ 32 R	13 ♊ 0 R

	10 °	11 °	12 °	Asc. ° ′	2 °	3 °	☉ ° ′	☽ ° ′	☿ ° ′
901	♒ 16	♓ 16	♈ 26	9 ♊ 23	♋ 3	♋ 23	27 ♏ 18	9 ♓ 36	19 ♏ 4R
902	♊ 15	♋ 19	♌ 20	17 ♍ 7	♎ 12	♏ 11	13 ♋ 52	0 ♉ 20	9 ♌ 48
903	♐ 29	♑ 20	♒ 16	28 ♓ 0	♉ 10	♊ 7	5 ♌ 56	21 ♏ 30	26 ♌ 4R
904	♋ 6	♌ 9	♍ 10	5 ♎ 55	♏ 2	♐ 2	20 ♌ 42	8 ♋ 15	17 ♍ 36
905	♏ 4	♏ 27	♐ 16	5 ♑ 53	♒ 19	♈ 2	4 ♈ 50	28 ♏ 13	6 ♈ 39R
906	♏ 15	♐ 7	♐ 26	18 ♑ 40	♓ 4	♈ 15	15 ♈ 5	27 ♊ 4	26 ♊ 49R
907	♈ 4	♉ 10	♊ 19	22 ♋ 10	♌ 11	♍ 4	16 ♍ 16	18 ♍ 43	28 ♌ 30
908	♉ 0	♊ 6	♋ 10	10 ♌ 23	♍ 2	♍ 28	14 ♏ 43	22 ♌ 10	3 ♐ 38
909	♋ 20	♌ 23	♍ 23	17 ♎ 25	♏ 16	♐ 17	18 ♉ 41	5 ♏ 18	1 ♊ 16R
910	♏ 29	♐ 18	♑ 6	0 ♒ 38	♓ 24	♉ 3	16 ♉ 10	20 ♎ 33	18 ♉ 33
911	♎ 12	♏ 10	♐ 3	23 ♐ 37	♑ 29	♓ 7	0 ♑ 36	18 ♓ 54	15 ♐ 5
912	♈ 5	♉ 11	♊ 18	20 ♋ 25	♌ 11	♍ 5	6 ♎ 32	26 ♊ 25	24 ♎ 29R
913	♈ 8	♉ 15	♊ 23	25 ♋ 0	♌ 15	♍ 9	4 ♊ 4	8 ♐ 2	13 ♉ 22
914	♌ 17	♍ 20	♎ 17	9 ♏ 50	♐ 9	♑ 12	7 ♐ 34	15 ♈ 36	18 ♏ 48
915	♈ 17	♉ 29	♋ 11	11 ♌ 0	♌ 27	♍ 17	2 ♍ 30	29 ♊ 48	6 ♍ 16
916	♌ 14	♍ 18	♎ 13	3 ♏ 0	♐ 1	♑ 5	14 ♌ 25	26 ♉ 48	18 ♌ 57
917	♈ 22	♊ 0	♋ 7	7 ♌ 25	♌ 27	♍ 21	29 ♋ 6	27 ♊ 21	24 ♌ 59
918	♌ 19	♍ 21	♎ 16	6 ♏ 0	♐ 4	♑ 9	5 ♑ 24	4 ♏ 4	26 ♐ 11
919	♑ 0	♑ 19	♒ 15	0 ♈ 0	♉ 15	♊ 11	15 ♉ 25	7 ♎ 11	16 ♉ 30
920	♒ 21	♓ 21	♉ 7	23 ♊ 40	♋ 12	♌ 0	6 ♏ 56	4 ♊ 25	5 ♏ 24
921	♏ 25	♐ 11	♑ 1	24 ♑ 22	♓ 11	♈ 22	0 ♈ 2	4 ♑ 37	24 ♓ 33
922	♏ 6	♏ 27	♐ 15	1 ♑ 0	♒ 18	♈ 5	5 ♒ 6	23 ♉ 10	13 ♑ 30
923	♉ 27	♋ 5	♌ 8	5 ♍ 0	♍ 26	♎ 23	17 ♌ 0	29 ♋ 0	14 ♍ 0
924	♊ 12	♋ 17	♌ 19	15 ♍ 16	♎ 9	♏ 8	24 ♏ 13	17 ♈ 11	8 ♏ 29
925	♉ 19	♊ 23	♋ 25	24 ♌ 0	♍ 18	♎ 17	0 ♍ 12	16 ♉ 15	26 ♍ 45
926	♒ 17	♓ 16	♈ 29	14 ♊ 52	♋ 6	♋ 25	17 ♎ 5	27 ♈ 53	17 ♎ 46
927	♌ 21	♍ 24	♎ 19	8 ♏ 40	♐ 7	♑ 13	10 ♈ 15	24 ♌ 0	2 ♈ 0
928	♒ 16	♓ 15	♈ 26	15 ♊ 44	♋ 6	♋ 24	18 ♒ 47	14 ♏ 40	22 ♒ 43
929	♍ 25	♎ 24	♏ 16	4 ♐ 34	♑ 8	♒ 17	23 ♓ 20	15 ♓ 30	6 ♈ 15
930	♈ 27	♊ 3	♋ 9	8 ♌ 53	♍ 0	♍ 25	19 ♏ 35	28 ♒ 3	2 ♏ 23
931	♓ 20	♈ 27	♊ 12	19 ♋ 45	♌ 6	♌ 24	14 ♋ 36	28 ♑ 54	26 ♋ 52R
932	♉ 17	♊ 26	♌ 1	28 ♌ 16	♍ 18	♎ 14	20 ♍ 44	15 ♊ 5	20 ♍ 52
933	♒ 0	♒ 24	♈ 4	3 ♊ 25	♊ 25	♋ 12	2 ♊ 9	3 ♊ 23	8 ♉ 55
934	♐ 26	♑ 12	♒ 1	16 ♓ 30	♉ 16	♊ 10	0 ♏ 55	11 ♒ 24	24 ♏ 36
935	♉ 17	♊ 20	♋ 22	20 ♌ 16	♍ 16	♎ 15	19 ♒ 45	19 ♓ 43	27 ♒ 22
936	♊ 19	♋ 20	♌ 21	19 ♍ 11	♎ 19	♏ 18	11 ♎ 19	7 ♍ 20	27 ♍ 57R
937	♏ 2	♏ 29	♐ 24	18 ♑ 0	♒ 24	♈ 0	21 ♑ 38	12 ♎ 54	4 ♒ 9
938	♐ 4	♐ 25	♑ 17	16 ♒ 0	♈ 2	♉ 8	3 ♓ 4	25 ♋ 28	18 ♒ 32
939	♑ 29	♒ 23	♈ 2	1 ♊ 15	♊ 23	♋ 11	0 ♊ 30	15 ♒ 30	5 ♉ 35
940	♌ 18	♍ 21	♎ 17	10 ♏ 5	♐ 9	♑ 12	28 ♊ 36	10 ♈ 42	23 ♋ 39
941	♓ 9	♈ 14	♊ 1	12 ♋ 15	♋ 28	♌ 16	0 ♏ 53	15 ♎ 13	9 ♏ 46
942	♉ 25	♋ 4	♌ 8	5 ♍ 0	♍ 24	♎ 21	9 ♌ 30	27 ♎ 51	22 ♋ 53
943	♌ 19	♍ 22	♎ 17	6 ♏ 0	♐ 4	♑ 10	17 ♑ 0	30 ♏ 0	20 ♑ 5
944	♒ 3	♓ 0	♈ 8	24 ♉ 45	♊ 21	♋ 12	15 ♎ 12	19 ♏ 25	10 ♏ 10
945	♍ 14	♎ 15	♏ 10	29 ♏ 5	♑ 0	♒ 7	13 ♒ 35	28 ♓ 39	19 ♒ 8
946	♏ 11	♐ 4	♐ 25	17 ♑ 0	♒ 29	♈ 10	19 ♋ 30	18 ♓ 30	18 ♋ 0
947	♈ 13	♉ 17	♊ 20	20 ♋ 15	♌ 14	♍ 12	13 ♉ 9	2 ♈ 40	1 ♊ 20
948	♋ 10	♌ 11	♍ 11	10 ♎ 0	♏ 9	♐ 9	8 ♐ 45	7 ♈ 30	19 ♏ 57
949	♎ 19	♏ 14	♐ 4	23 ♐ 0	♒ 1	♓ 14	6 ♉ 0	24 ♐ 30	9 ♈ 0
950	♏ 1	♏ 26	♐ 18	10 ♑ 50	♒ 19	♓ 28	28 ♓ 32	21 ♋ 32	24 ♓ 1

	♀	♂	♃	♄	♅	♆	♇
	° ′	° ′	° ′	° ′	° ′	° ′	° ′
901	2 ♑ 42	24 ♑ 9	15 ♍ 53	22 ♍ 59	1 ♓ 47	13 ♌ 46 R	8 ♋ 31 R
902	28 ♌ 22	12 ♈ 50	2 ♋ 21	12 ♓ 47 R	18 ♈ 8	0 ♓ 0 R	26 ♈ 46
903	16 ♍ 10	1 ♌ 35	29 ♊ 48	14 ♓ 9 R	5 ♑ 20 R	11 ♋ 7	23 ♊ 0
904	3 ♎ 22	17 ♊ 7	8 ♎ 9	5 ♐ 40	29 ♏ 33	24 ♊ 14	16 ♊ 0
905	20 ♒ 48	17 ♋ 33	25 ♒ 57	23 ♏ 43 R	4 ♋ 26	12 ♈ 13	13 ♉ 37
906	29 ♉ 5	27 ♓ 48	10 ♐ 45 R	4 ♑ 59	12 ♐ 20 R	24 ♊ 29	14 ♊ 53
907	1 ♏ 45	29 ♊ 31	22 ♑ 34 R	8 ♏ 33	7 ♋ 55	12 ♈ 7 R	14 ♉ 55
908	1 ♎ 45	22 ♉ 10 R	3 ♓ 1	9 ♈ 59 R	8 ♍ 22	10 ♉ 32 R	24 ♉ 27
909	3 ♋ 59	17 ♌ 14	28 ♋ 6	10 ♊ 17	24 ♍ 13 R	20 ♉ 42	0 ♊ 16
910	22 ♊ 50	8 ♋ 56	4 ♋ 19	3 ♏ 0 R	18 ♏ 0 R	14 ♊ 25	13 ♊ 0
911	14 ♒ 51	25 ♑ 53	20 ♎ 1	13 ♒ 26	23 ♈ 31	12 ♍ 22	23 ♋ 50
912	28 ♎ 0	23 ♊ 0	0 ♍ 9	16 ♏ 38	22 ♏ 2	20 ♊ 19 R	13 ♊ 35 R
913	4 ♉ 6	18 ♌ 24	1 ♏ 54 R	21 ♐ 37 R	6 ♐ 7 R	23 ♊ 42	14 ♊ 55
914	21 ♐ 43	12 ♐ 57	14 ♋ 44 R	0 ♏ 52	26 ♒ 55	1 ♒ 39	13 ♈ 20
915	24 ♌ 51	27 ♐ 34	27 ♎ 55	21 ♒ 56 R	16 ♌ 40	2 ♉ 58 R	23 ♉ 30
916	28 ♍ 39	2 ♍ 57	21 ♎ 26	2 ♎ 16	23 ♊ 54	5 ♈ 54 R	12 ♉ 14 R
917	11 ♋ 35	15 ♒ 35	24 ♈ 2	25 ♍ 56	2 ♏ 3	10 ♊ 33	9 ♊ 21
918	22 ♒ 16	23 ♏ 12	27 ♍ 3	22 ♍ 41	13 ♊ 32 R	28 ♓ 55	8 ♉ 40 R
919	22 ♊ 0	8 ♋ 21	4 ♋ 9	3 ♏ 3 R	18 ♏ 2 R	14 ♊ 30	11 ♊ 0
920	27 ♍ 59	24 ♐ 10	29 ♋ 25	5 ♑ 27	1 ♌ 14	22 ♈ 17 R	19 ♉ 0 R
921	13 ♉ 40	3 ♌ 0	24 ♋ 30	5 ♊ 14	25 ♍ 6 R	19 ♉ 2	29 ♉ 26
922	27 ♑ 30	13 ♑ 30	16 ♑ 2	11 ♏ 47	0 ♋ 30 R	8 ♈ 12	12 ♉ 30
923	13 ♍ 0	5 ♋ 30	10 ♍ 0	5 ♋ 0	0 ♎ 30	25 ♉ 30	3 ♊ 0
924	9 ♑ 1	20 ♐ 55	14 ♉ 49 R	16 ♐ 41	21 ♋ 50	17 ♈ 15 R	16 ♉ 49 R
925	10 ♍ 5	28 ♉ 23	19 ♏ 57	15 ♎ 6	28 ♊ 46	7 ♈ 54 R	13 ♉ 7 R
926	22 ♏ 57	12 ♎ 15	2 ♍ 8	13 ♑ 3	25 ♏ 49	13 ♐ 30	20 ♓ 30
927	21 ♉ 0	18 ♉ 34	17 ♓ 30	5 ♒ 33	2 ♈ 41	23 ♒ 0	22 ♈ 0
928	18 ♓ 21	0 ♐ 31	15 ♏ 45	14 ♋ 28 R	29 ♑ 25	17 ♑ 30	5 ♈ 30
929	29 ♈ 35	18 ♋ 20	5 ♓ 25	2 ♈ 16	28 ♐ 39	27 ♐ 50	27 ♓ 30
930	4 ♑ 17	17 ♐ 50	15 ♉ 26 R	16 ♐ 11	21 ♋ 57 R	17 ♈ 22 R	16 ♉ 5 R
931	0 ♌ 5 R	3 ♊ 24	12 ♈ 59	29 ♏ 36 R	13 ♋ 15	17 ♈ 17	16 ♉ 38
932	5 ♌ 45	7 ♒ 39	23 ♈ 30 R	1 ♎ 43	3 ♏ 44	11 ♒ 19 R	9 ♊ 39 R
933	26 ♈ 30	17 ♈ 35	16 ♒ 57	28 ♓ 46	23 ♐ 20	27 ♐ 30	27 ♓ 30
934	22 ♍ 47	6 ♍ 4	13 ♏ 0	5 ♌ 59	14 ♎ 0	29 ♉ 24 R	4 ♊ 27 R
935	2 ♓ 19 R	26 ♐ 25	22 ♉ 24	25 ♎ 9 R	15 ♏ 19	10 ♊ 48 R	9 ♊ 0 R
936	19 ♏ 25	8 ♓ 30 R	26 ♐ 46	15 ♓ 8	27 ♌ 50	6 ♉ 51 R	4 ♊ 44 R
937	29 ♑ 32	28 ♈ 25	25 ♎ 59	5 ♎ 32	17 ♊ 27 R	1 ♈ 21	9 ♉ 20
938	14 ♒ 6 R	0 ♎ 51 R	2 ♊ 40	9 ♌ 24 R	24 ♒ 11	5 ♌ 0 R	3 ♋ 30 R
939	29 ♉ 42	3 ♒ 52	3 ♌ 41	18 ♑ 52 R	25 ♏ 45 R	14 ♐ 34 R	22 ♓ 0
940	15 ♉ 26	28 ♈ 36	15 ♉ 52	8 ♉ 55	10 ♍ 27	15 ♉ 31	28 ♉ 22
941	7 ♏ 52	28 ♍ 47	24 ♋ 42	24 ♌ 21	7 ♊ 7 R	24 ♓ 49 R	7 ♉ 58 R
942	7 ♋ 8	12 ♈ 54	25 ♍ 37	20 ♍ 17	19 ♊ 31	3 ♈ 42 R	11 ♉ 17 R
943	21 ♑ 0	4 ♒ 0	27 ♉ 0 R	3 ♉ 30	8 ♑ 1	5 ♑ 30	29 ♓ 0
944	8 ♏ 43	18 ♐ 28	4 ♐ 21	17 ♌ 46	17 ♎ 25	2 ♊ 2 R	5 ♊ 30 R
945	29 ♓ 29	14 ♑ 15	15 ♈ 14	23 ♈ 33	12 ♍ 53 R	11 ♉ 34	26 ♉ 20 R
946	10 ♊ 30	18 ♊ 30	15 ♍ 0	22 ♏ 21	12 ♓ 30 R	9 ♒ 30 R	18 ♈ 30
947	7 ♈ 28	10 ♈ 33	29 ♊ 54	27 ♉ 26	19 ♍ 26 R	18 ♉ 20	29 ♉ 17
948	19 ♏ 10	14 ♋ 19 R	18 ♉ 52 R	6 ♉ 43	18 ♍ 20	14 ♉ 31 R	28 ♉ 0 R
949	19 ♉ 30	21 ♓ 0	16 ♉ 0	5 ♎ 30 R	26 ♒ 30	2 ♒ 0	12 ♈ 0
950	14 ♒ 33	7 ♉ 50	2 ♓ 38	12 ♍ 38 R	0 ♏ 38 R	4 ♊ 20	6 ♊ 0

	10	11	12	Asc.	2	3	☉	☽	☿
	°	°	°	° ′	°	°	° ′	° ′	° ′
951	♍ 28	♎ 27	♏ 20	10 ♐ 1	♑ 13	♒ 21	7 ♏ 42	10 ♒ 48	1 ♐ 16
952	♓ 23	♉ 1	♊ 20	25 ♋ 10	♌ 10	♌ 28	29 ♉ 19	6 ♋ 16	18 ♊ 2
953	♍ 18	♎ 18	♏ 8	22 ♏ 50	♐ 24	♒ 7	3 ♑ 40	8 ♐ 30	12 ♑ 23
954	♍ 13	♎ 1	♏ 8	29 ♏ 5	♑ 0	♒ 6	11 ♊ 58	6 ♒ 12	19 ♉ 37
955	♐ 7	♐ 25	♑ 13	8 ♒ 20	♈ 9	♉ 15	28 ♍ 25	20 ♒ 40	19 ♍ 1
956	♏ 28	♐ 20	♑ 12	8 ♒ 0	♓ 24	♉ 1	11 ♈ 59	11 ♎ 23	11 ♈ 12
957	♓ 1	♈ 3	♉ 10	16 ♊ 2	♋ 10	♌ 4	10 ♑ 26	0 ♊ 3	7 ♑ 0
958	♎ 6	♏ 3	♏ 25	13 ♐ 49	♑ 19	♒ 29	13 ♎ 2	6 ♉ 35	12 ♎ 4
959	♐ 2	♐ 20	♑ 9	2 ♒ 30	♈ 1	♉ 8	0 ♒ 58	14 ♌ 34	16 ♑ 5
960	♌ 0	♍ 3	♎ 2	25 ♎ 25	♏ 23	♐ 25	11 ♊ 57	12 ♊ 48	0 ♊ 44
961	♒ 7	♓ 5	♈ 13	27 ♉ 55	♊ 23	♋ 14	11 ♍ 19	29 ♓ 46	4 ♍ 59
962	♊ 6	♋ 13	♌ 16	11 ♍ 30	♎ 3	♏ 1	7 ♉ 41	5 ♊ 30	28 ♉ 52
963	♌ 4	♍ 9	♎ 5	24 ♎ 1	♏ 20	♐ 24	28 ♐ 50	4 ♏ 36	10 ♐ 38
964	♑ 22	♒ 17	♓ 21	9 ♉ 0	♊ 9	♋ 1	17 ♏ 14	8 ♓ 14	8 ♐ 39
965	♐ 7	♐ 28	♑ 20	20 ♒ 0	♈ 7	♉ 12	7 ♈ 40	7 ♋ 53	26 ♓ 1
966	♏ 13	♐ 6	♐ 26	17 ♑ 30	♓ 2	♈ 13	24 ♐ 46	26 ♋ 33	4 ♐ 24
967	♉ 8	♊ 14	♋ 18	17 ♌ 30	♍ 9	♎ 6	28 ♍ 46	23 ♉ 54	17 ♎ 1
968	♊ 5	♋ 13	♌ 16	11 ♍ 24	♎ 2	♏ 0	21 ♎ 57	8 ♉ 31	26 ♎ 32
969	♐ 19	♑ 6	♒ 26	1 ♓ 55	♉ 0	♉ 29	8 ♍ 40	23 ♋ 9	23 ♌ 50
970	♎ 27	♐ 2	♑ 6	6 ♒ 0	♒ 28	♓ 25	8 ♏ 5	14 ♍ 23	10 ♏ 12
971	♍ 21	♎ 21	♏ 14	3 ♐ 0	♑ 6	♒ 14	5 ♎ 6	19 ♊ 0	21 ♍ 30
972	♓ 19	♈ 27	♊ 13	20 ♋ 0	♌ 5	♌ 29	7 ♒ 11	27 ♏ 14	13 ♑ 30
973	♊ 1	♋ 9	♌ 12	8 ♍ 0	♍ 28	♎ 25	11 ♋ 30	16 ♐ 15	5 ♌ 16
974	♓ 6	♈ 9	♉ 18	24 ♊ 24	♋ 17	♌ 19	17 ♓ 19	25 ♉ 25	20 ♒ 38
975	♑ 15	♒ 9	♓ 11	23 ♈ 49	♉ 27	♊ 22	27 f♌ 35	25 ♓ 44	25 ♌ 18
976	♏ 26	♐ 18	♑ 8	3 ♒ 30	♓ 21	♈ 29	29 ♒ 17	1 ♏ 30	16 ♒ 22
977	♉ 20	♊ 25	♋ 27	25 ♌ 30	♍ 19	♎ 17	12 ♎ 15	26 ♉ 30	21 ♎ 15
978	♎ 17	♏ 20	♐ 21	20 ♑ 59	♒ 17	♓ 15	25 ♒ 13	23 ♓ 26	5 ♓ 55
979	♍ 7	♎ 9	♏ 4	25 ♏ 25	♐ 26	♒ 1	22 ♎ 43	8 ♈ 53	24 ♎ 11
980	♋ 3	♌ 6	♍ 6	2 ♎ 40	♎ 29	♐ 0	7 ♑ 40	0 ♒ 3	17 ♑ 20
981	♒ 7	♓ 5	♈ 14	0 ♊ 15	♊ 25	♋ 15	17 ♈ 55	16 ♊ 16	23 ♈ 46
982	♈ 9	♉ 16	♊ 24	25 ♋ 47	♌ 16	♍ 9	28 ♊ 36	12 ♎ 3	16 ♊ 15
983	♐ 4	♐ 22	♑ 10	3 ♒ 10	♈ 3	♉ 11	2 ♋ 21	3 ♓ 56	27 ♋ 46
984	♉ 19	♊ 24	♋ 27	24 ♌ 0	♍ 17	♎ 15	22 ♒ 40	3 ♋ 45	3 ♓ 55
985	♒ 16	♓ 3	♈ 13	5 ♊ 30	♊ 27	♋ 16	14 ♍ 50	4 ♊ 19	27 ♌ 8
986	♐ 13	♑ 0	♑ 18	16 ♒ 33	♈ 20	♉ 23	14 ♊ 2	13 ♑ 30	28 ♉ 52
987	♒ 7	♓ 3	♈ 16	12 ♊ 0	♋ 1	♋ 18	12 ♓ 40	24 ♓ 20	15 ♒ 40
988	♓ 21	♈ 26	♊ 6	11 ♋ 6	♌ 1	♌ 23	29 ♑ 11	15 ♏ 35	14 ♒ 29
989	♓ 0	♈ 2	♉ 14	25 ♊ 0	♋ 15	♌ 5	20 ♋ 22	21 ♊ 51	0 ♋ 40
990	♐ 4	♐ 21	♑ 8	0 ♒ 0	♈ 2	♉ 2	23 ♊ 0	20 ♒ 0	4 ♊ 0
991	♋ 11	♌ 14	♍ 14	10 ♎ 0	♏ 7	♐ 8	7 ♍ 8	27 ♒ 5	25 ♌ 49
992	♓ 19	♈ 24	♊ 3	8 ♋	♋ 29	♌ 22	15 ♑ 2	15 ♌ 36	24 ♐ 23
993	♐ 8	♐ 24	♑ 9	1 ♒ 45	♓ 12	♉ 17	19 ♍ 40	4 ♑ 37	26 ♍ 13
994	♈ 13	♉ 24	♋ 7	7 ♌ 41	♌ 24	♍ 14	11 ♌ 45	2 ♊ 5	4 ♍ 47
995	♋ 29	♍ 2	♎ 1	25 ♎ 30	♏ 24	♐ 25	14 ♋ 30	16 ♉ 16	29 ♊ 22
996	♊ 9	♋ 13	♌ 14	11 ♍ 24	♎ 6	♏ 5	7 ♍ 43	5 ♌ 45	28 ♍ 35
997	♊ 10	♋ 16	♌ 18	14 ♍ 0	♎ 7	♏ 6	15 ♋ 40	26 ♑ 6	10 ♋5
998	♌ 26	♍ 28	♎ 23	12 ♏ 36	♐ 11	♑ 17	12 ♐ 25	23 ♉ 5	22 ♏ 9
999	♍ 26	♎ 25	♏ 16	2 ♐ 33	♑ 6	♒ 18	13 ♈ 16	17 ♈ 34	21 ♈ 39
1000	♑ 9	♑ 28	♒ 26	24 ♈ 5	♊ 2	♊ 2	11 ♑ 30	5 ♉ 22	0 ♒ 49

	♀	♂	♃	♄	♅	♆	♇
	° ′	° ′	° ′	° ′	° ′	° ′	° ′
951	26 ♍ 9	19 ♌ 18	12 ♐ 20	1 ♑ 6	10 ♐ 40	29 ♊ 2 R	17 ♊ 16 R
952	21 ♊ 42	6 ♌ 27	6 ♊ 29	17 ♉ 29	14 ♍ 25 R	16 ♉ 46	29 ♉ 0
953	12 ♒ 19	13 ♒ 59	0 ♈ 53	11 ♋ 15 R	21 ♉ 33 R	17 ♓ 50	3 ♉ 31 R
954	2 ♊ 19	11 ♊ 7	21 ♈ 36	21 ♒ 0 R	28 ♐ 38 R	4 ♋ 45	19 ♊ 55
955	14 ♏ 42	6 ♋ 29	22 ♑ 26	9 ♏ 42	8 ♋ 12	11 ♈ 48 R	15 ♉ 0
956	3 ♈ 59	2 ♊ 25	1 ♉ 38	9 ♎ 15 R	9 ♏ 48 R	9 ♊ 2	9 ♊ 0
957	28 ♐ 11	3 ♋ 50 R	16 ♉ 22 R	5 ♉ 35 R	18 ♍ 33 R	13 ♉ 55 R	27 ♉ 33 R
958	25 ♍ 30	4 ♎ 12	16 ♊ 40 R	24 ♒ 38 R	12 ♈ 15 R	25 ♒ 38 R	24 ♈ 34 R
959	18 ♐ 57	16 ♋ 19 R	11 ♎ 18	22 ♏ 40	5 ♋ 24 R	10 ♈ 19	13 ♉ 6
960	28 ♈ 46	16 ♍ 33	26 ♍ 12	8 ♋ 0	3 ♎ 37 R	25 ♉ 55	2 ♊ 40
961	5 ♎ 58 R	5 ♌ 6	2 ♏ 57	1 ♌ 54	10 ♎ 55	0 ♊ 5 R	4 ♊ 54 R
962	23 ♊ 3	12 ♌ 30	26 ♋ 42	8 ♊ 54	24 ♍ 30 R	20 ♉ 16	0 ♊ 4
963	20 ♑ 14	1 ♑ 57	2 ♓ 56	0 ♐ 26	11 ♋ 24 R	12 ♈ 18 R	14 ♉ 22 R
964	0 ♑ 58	26 ♌ 34	25 ♐ 14	29 ♉ 13 R	10 ♉ 20 R	10 ♓ 58 R	1 ♉ 2 R
965	17 ♈ 6	9 ♐ 30	6 ♒ 2	27 ♌ 51 R	25 ♎ 24 R	2 ♊ 21	5 ♊ 12
966	8 ♏ 14	23 ♑ 4	11 ♒ 18	17 ♏ 53	3 ♏ 45	3 ♐ 30	12 ♓ 30
967	21 ♌ 16	14 ♑ 38	21 ♌ 32	14 ♑ 38	4 ♌ 48	9 ♐ 0	17 ♉ 49
968	14 ♏ 56	19 ♐ 43	1 ♈ 50 R	14 ♋ 7	24 ♉ 14 R	18 ♓ 11 R	4 ♉ 46
969	22 ♍ 3	26 ♍ 24	18 ♈ 41 R	28 ♈ 34 R	9 ♍ 21	14 ♉ 17 R	28 ♉ 13
970	7 ♐ 35	5 ♑ 39	8 ♐ 47	19 ♌ 29	18 ♎ 55	1 ♊ 31 R	6 ♊ 0 R
971	16 ♎ 30 R	27 ♏ 30	24 ♎ 0	6 ♐ 0	14 ♓ 0 R	10 ♒ 0 R	18 ♈ 0 R
972	24 ♐ 1	27 ♓ 1	11 ♊ 41 R	9 ♌ 1 R	29 ♉ 34 R	22 ♓ 57	5 ♉ 34 R
973	16 ♌ 20	14 ♋ 57	24 ♊ 16	14 ♓ 59 R	6 ♑ 17 R	10 ♋ 11	22 ♊ 30
974	2 ♉ 42	13 ♈ 58	4 ♑ 50	14 ♌ 40 R	21 ♎ 16 R	29 ♉ 44	4 ♊ 30
975	17 ♋ 36	11 ♌ 26	22 ♍ 23	24 ♍ 12	8 ♓ 4 R	14 ♌ 2	9 ♋ 31
976	5 ♈ 21	15 ♐ 19	23 ♓ 27	28 ♍ 47 R	6 ♏ 3 R	6 ♊ 15	7 ♊ 0
977	27 ♏ 30	15 ♍ 8	10 ♋ 10	9 ♓ 26 R	4 ♑ 30	12 ♋ 30	23 ♊ 0 R
978	4 ♒ 22	24 ♌ 54 R	13 ♈ 7	15 ♐ 50	13 ♋ 54 R	15 ♈ 15	15 ♉ 2
979	16 ♏ 40	6 ♍ 5	25 ♌ 52	15 ♑ 13	5 ♌ 37	25 ♈ 0 R	20 ♉ 30 R
980	15 ♒ 55	16 ♒ 20	1 ♈ 18	10 ♋ 55 R	21 ♉ 28 R	17 ♓ 53	4 ♉ 3
981	16 ♉ 58	8 ♋ 31	0 ♍ 41 R	0 ♐ 4 R	28 ♏ 31 R	18 ♊ 0	12 ♊ 0
982	23 ♊ 6	21 ♈ 14	8 ♌ 49	12 ♏ 59 R	21 ♏ 7 R	18 ♊ 12	12 ♊ 33
983	23 ♉ 28	0 ♈ 23	18 ♊ 23	18 ♎ 25	11 ♏ 33 R	13 ♊ 53	10 ♊ 48
984	12 ♓ 25	25 ♉ 6	5 ♓ 47	6 ♐ 44	27 ♓ 24	25 ♌ 41 R	14 ♋ 10 R
985	8 ♎ 4 R	23 ♉ 16	6 ♓ 46 R	14 ♈ 24 R	5 ♍ 16	11 ♉ 56 R	27 ♉ 30
986	17 ♉ 7 R	3 ♌ 29	26 ♈ 20	21 ♍ 25	22 ♒ 32 R	29 ♑ 6 R	12 ♈ 30
987	0 ♓ 20 R	14 ♓ 40	16 ♉ 5	27 ♐ 30	18 ♋ 10 R	17 ♈ 55	16 ♉ 5
988	27 ♒ 51	2 ♈ 13	27 ♐ 11	25 ♒ 8	18 ♌ 46 R	0 ♉ 18	21 ♉ 40 R
989	5 ♍ 57	17 ♌ 10	18 ♎ 38	0 ♎ 12	22 ♊ 41	6 ♈ 7 R	9 ♉ 4
990	13 ♉ 0	12 ♌ 0	29 ♐ 0 R	24 ♎ 0 R	29 ♊ 0	10 ♈ 0	13 ♉ 30
991	8 ♎ 22	20 ♉ 16	7 ♓ 48 R	14 ♈ 50 R	4 ♍ 46	12 ♉ 1 R	27 ♉ 16 R
992	2 ♐ 17	24 ♉ 3	5 ♐ 39	13 ♉ 23 R	28 ♑ 35	22 ♋ 36 R	27 ♊ 37
993	22 ♎ 20	14 ♍ 16	10 ♍ 2	13 ♍ 45	16 ♊ 22	0 ♈ 31 R	10 ♉ 10 R
994	20 ♍ 41	25 ♏ 54	15 ♊ 7	3 ♌ 16	3 ♊ 0	24 ♈ 34 R	5 ♉ 9
995	0 ♌ 51	13 ♓ 6	26 ♐ 30	20 ♓ 19	22 ♌ 30	7 ♉ 15	24 ♉ 3
996	2 ♍ 47	27 ♌ 20	13 ♓ 45 R	18 ♍ 49	28 ♎ 39	9 ♊ 2	8 ♊ 43
997	6 ♊ 25	15 ♊ 30	14 ♍ 14	22 ♏ 26 R	12 ♓ 18 R	9 ♒ 39 R	18 ♈ 30
998	7 ♏ 27	4 ♍ 36	19 ♐ 50	4 ♑ 37	12 ♐ 41	28 ♊ 16 R	16 ♊ 40 R
999	13 ♓ 43	20 ♈ 43	17 ♏ 27 R	21 ♐ 43 R	17 ♓ 53	14 ♒ 21	18 ♈ 0
1000	13 ♐ 50	24 ♑ 28	25 ♈ 42	28 ♋ 22 R	17 ♒ 38	4 ♌ 5 R	2 ♋ 23

CHAPTER FOURTEEN

HOW TO MAKE A·HOROSCOPE

Needed for the calculation of a horoscope are (1) the date of the given birth or event, (2) the geographic latitude and longitude of the place of occurrence, (3) an astrological ephemeris of the planetary places during the particular year and (4) a proper Tables of Houses.

Needed for understanding the mathematical operations is an adequate visualization of the heavens in their astrological employment. Thus the earth is the center of the entire celestial vault in this perspective, which is known as geocentric in contrast with the astronomical or more literalistically correct view known as heliocentric. The horoscopic factors are created by the two more familiar motions of the earth. Its rotation on its axis establishes the celestial equator, as an extension of the terrestrial one, and this circle is divided into twelve equal pie-shaped segments that become the houses of the horoscope. The revolution of the earth around its orbit creates the ecliptic that is given astrological form in the zodiac, with again a division into twelve pie-shaped segments. These become the signs in which the planets are located for astrological purposes, and they are identified commonly by patterns that were described imaginatively in the fixed stars to be seen behind them at about the time of Hipparchus in the second century B.C. Measurement in the signs is by celes-

tial longitude in degrees and minutes, and in the other or
equatorial great circle by degrees of right ascension or
more customarily by hours and minutes of sidereal time.

The procedure in calculating a horoscope is simple, and
consists of two stages. First is the establishment of the
horoscopic wheel, and this is a matter of charting the position of the heavens as they are found or seen from the
earth at a particular moment in the globe's daily rotation.
An astrological ephemeris gives this position in sidereal
time, and most commonly for noon and at the meridian
of Greenwich or 0° of terrestrial longitude. In the case
of the chart on page 116 the sidereal time for December
2, 1942, is found to be 16h 42m 47s. Chicago is 87° 45′ in
longitude west from Greenwich, and this means a difference in mean time of 5h 51m. (Standard times are always
corrected to the local mean.) To adjust to the shifting
position of the noon point in the great circles of the
heavens, or the movement of the sun in the geocentric or
astrological mathematics, each mean-time hour of difference west from the 0° meridian requires the addition of
10s (9.86s exactly). Thus at Chicago 58s must be added to
the sidereal time of 16h 42m 47s. (Each such correction of
course is subtracted east of Greenwich.) When a birth or
event is not at the noon of its place of occurrence, the same
operation of correction from mean to sidereal time must
be repeated. The adjustment is by addition if the local
mean time is after noon, and by subtraction if before.
Many astrologers, however, always make their computations from a previous noon. In the instance of the horoscope on page 116 the time after noon, or 3h 1m, require
an added 30s in establishing the sidereal time of the mid-

heaven or symbolical noon-point of the given wheel-diagram, thus:

16h	42m	47s
		58
3	1	
		30
19	45	15

The houses of the horoscope that are established in the celestial equator in terms of degrees and minutes of right ascension or hours and minutes of sidereal time are shown almost universally by printed lines, as in this and the companion texts, and they are identified by number from one to twelve from an ascendant or first house at the horizon shown at the left hand and on counterclockwise through the midheaven or tenth house at the upper or individual noon-point. In addition and for a practical necessity in interpretation, each house is additionally identified in the zodiacal correspondence shown by notation at its cusp. The zodiacal correspondence is found in the Tables of Houses. In the tables computed by Joseph G. Dalton in 1893, which have a broad and long-time acceptability, a sidereal time of 19h 45m 15s corresponds to a midheaven at Capricorn 25°, an ascendant at Taurus 13° 50′ and the remaining cusps as seen on page 116.

The second stage in making a horoscope is the calculation of the positions of the planets in the zodiac at the moment of birth or event. The great zodiacal circle of the heavens, or the ecliptic as a factor completely distinct from the celestial equator, comprises not only the orbit of the earth but also and with only minor latitudinal deviations

mong them the orbits of all the other planets employed
n astrological measurement. By locating the houses in their
orrespondence to places in this second of the great circles,
he interrelations of all the horoscopic elements are
rought in virtually all normal practice to a single plane
f relationship. This fact contributes very significantly to
he almost illimitable facility of astrological analysis.

The astrological ephemeris shows the geocentric posi-
ion of each of the ten planets of usual employment in
odiacal degree and minutes. This most commonly is at
oon in Greenwich time, and an initial procedure is to
hange the local mean time to the Greenwich time of the
abulations. Since the sun rises at Greenwich before it does
n Chicago across the ocean to the west, the difference of
h 51m is added to the local 3:01 p.m. to obtain a Green-
vich 8:52 p.m. as the basis for calculation. The mathe-
natical operation is simple proportion. If as in the case
f the horoscope on page 116, and of the sun, the planet
noves 61' in the twenty-four hours from noon of Decem-
er 2d to the next noon, in a little short of nine hours out
f the twenty-four it will move from its noon position in
he ephemeris to approximately 9/24 of 61' farther. Many
strologers work with fractions in this computation, but
ewcomers to horoscopy may function better with a fixed
nethod that because invariable may prove simpler at the
tart. Such a method is readily available in the use of the
iurnal proportional logarithms usually found in the
phemeris. This is a mathematical short cut whereby the
1) propositional logarithm for the time from noon in
vhich a planet moves to its horoscopic position is added to
he (2) proportional logarithm of the distance it moves in

the whole twenty-four hours to obtain the (3) proportiona logarithm of the zodiacal distance from the noon position to the horoscopic place, thus:

Sun's daily motion:	61 (i.e., 1°1')	1.3730
Time from noon to event:	8h 52m	.4324
		1.8054

The nearest logarithm in the tables to 1.8054 is 1.7966 and this gives 23' to add to Sagittarius 9°41' and show the sun's horoscopic position to be Sagittarius 10°4'. The other planetary places are found similarly.

A very full exposition of the mathematical procedure in everyday horoscopy is provided in the author's *How to Learn Astrology* in which account is taken of the midnight base ephemeris and an alternate and equally recommended Tables of Houses together with other important detai passed over here. Considerable supplementary considera tion of the horoscopic mathematics is included in hi *Scope of Astrological Prediction*.

THE ASTROLOGICAL ESSENTIALS

THE TWELVE SIGNS OF THE ZODIAC

Name	Quadrature	Triplicity	Basic Keyword
♈ ARIES	Cardinal	Fire	Aspiration
♉ TAURUS	Fixed	Earth	Virility
♊ GEMINI	Common	Air	Vivification
♋ CANCER	Cardinal	Water	Expansion
♌ LEO	Fixed	Fire	Assurance
♍ VIRGO	Common	Earth	Assimilation
♎ LIBRA	Cardinal	Air	Equivalence
♏ SCORPIO	Fixed	Water	Creativity
♐ SAGITTARIUS	Common	Fire	Administration
♑ CAPRICORN	Cardinal	Earth	Discrimination
♒ AQUARIUS	Fixed	Air	Loyalty
♓ PISCES	Common	Water	Sympathy

The four signs established at the equinoctial and solstitial points are cardinal, and show the most direct impact of experience. The four immediately behind are common, and show experience in its greatest concern with people. The four which do not touch the basic points are fixed, and show experience as remote or as more concerned with ideas. This distinction is known as quadrature.

Each cardinal sign is related to a common and a fixed sign, to form a triangle in the zodiac, and this distinction is known as triplicity. The three fire signs stem from the vernal equinox, and show experience centered in personal identity. The three air signs stem from the autumnal equinox. They have a special sympathy with fire, and show experience in its concern over theoretical relations. The three water signs stem from the summer solstice, and show experience in its touch with universality. The three earth signs stem from the winter solstice. They have a special sympathy with water, and show experience in its concern over practical relations.

THE TWELVE HOUSES OF THE HOROSCOPE

Number	Axial Position	Distributive Function	Basic Keyword
1st	Angular	Personal impetus	Identity
2d	Succedent	Conditioned contact	Possession
3d	Cadent	Intimate relation	Environment
4th	Angular	Instinctive response	Home
5th	Succedent	Personal impetus	Offspring
6th	Cadent	Conditioned contact	Duty
7th	Angular	Intimate relation	Partnership·
8th	Succedent	Instinctive response	Regeneration
9th	Cadent	Personal impetus	Understanding
10th	Angular	Conditioned contact	Honor
11th	Succedent	Intimate relation	Friendship
12th	Cadent	Instinctive response	Confinement

The four houses established at the horizon and meridian points are angular, and show the immediate focus of circumstances. The four immediately behind are cadent, and show circumstantial elements which tend to sustain or buttress experience. The four which do not touch the basic axes are succedent, and they show circumstantial elements which tend to free or heighten experience.

Each angular house is related to a cadent and a succedent one, to form a triangle in the celestial equator, and this delineates a phase of everyday affairs. The houses which stem from the eastern horizon show details of a personal impact on life, and those which stem from the western horizon show details of intimate relations. Those which stem from the lower meridian show the ramification of a native's instinctive response, and those which stem from the upper meridian show the ramification of conditioned contact.

PRIMARY INDICATIONS OF THE TWELVE HOUSES

Number	Area of Experience
1st	Personality
2nd	Resources, money
3rd	Environment, brethren, communication, short trips
4th	Home, end of life, deeper-link parent
5th	Self-expression, speculation, children
6th	Servants, service, sickness
7th	Partnerships, competition, opportunity
8th	Legacies, regeneration, compulsive ideas, death
9th	Understanding, religion, long journeys
10th	Place in life, profession, outer-link parent
11th	Friends, hopes, objectives
12th	Hidden support and limitation, institutions

THE TEN PLANETS OF GENERAL RECOGNITION

Name	Department	Rulership	Basic Keyword
☉ THE SUN	Vitality	Leo	Purpose
☽ THE MOON	Vitality	Cancer	Feeling
♂ MARS	Efficiency	Aries, Scorpio	Initiative
♀ VENUS	Efficiency	Taurus, Libra	Acquisitiveness
☿ MERCURY	Efficiency	Gemini, Virgo	Mentality
♃ JUPITER	Motivation	Sagittarius, Pisces	Enthusiasm
♄ SATURN	Motivation	Capricorn, Aquarius	Sensitiveness
♅ URANUS	Significance	Aquarius in part	Independence
♆ NEPTUNE	Significance	Pisces in part	Obligation
♇ PLUTO	Significance	Scorpio in part	Obsession

The dragon's head ☊ and tail ☋, or moon's north and south nodes, are points of protection and temptation, and the Part of Fortune ⊕ is a point of effective self-interest.

PRINCIPAL PLANETARY ASPECTS

Major Aspects and Keywords				*Minor Aspects*	
☌	CONJUNCTION	0°	Emphasis	Semisextile	30°
✳	SEXTILE	60°	Encouragement	Semiquintile	36°
□	SQUARE	90°	Construction	Semisquare	45°
△	TRINE	120°	Momentum	Septile	51° 26′
☍	OPPOSITION	180°	Awareness	Quintile	72°
				Sesquiquadrate	135°
	Aspect in Declination			Biquintile	144°
P	PARALLEL	0°	Emphasis	Quincunx	150°

A house is ruled by the planet which rules the sign on its cusp. A planet DISPOSES of any other planet placed in a sign it rules. A planet in a sign opposite one it rules is in its DETRIMENT, and opposite one in which it is exalted is in its FALL. A planet in a sign which does not lie on the cusp of any house is INTERCEPTED. When a planet has an apparent backward movement in its orbit it is RETROGRADE. When apparently motionless, as it changes from forward to backward movement or the reverse, it is STATIONARY or in its STATION. The ORB of an aspect is the amount of permitted deviation from exactness. For major aspects this is 17° with the sun, 12° 30′ with the moon, and 10° when neither of the lights is involved, but otherwise 2°.

THE EXALTATIONS

Aries	☉	Cancer	♃	Libra	♄	Capricorn	♂
Taurus	☽	Leo	♆	Scorpio	♅	Aquarius	♅
Gemini	☋	Virgo	☿	Sagittarius	☊	Pisces	♀

INDEX TO SABIAN SYMBOLS

INDEX TO KEYWORDS

GENERAL INDEX

Absolutes, 23, 72, 74
Acuity tests, 22
Adverse aspects, 78
Ailment, 4
Air signs, 144
Allen, James Givens, viii
American Federation of Labor, 92
Anthropomorphic ways of understanding, 45, 331 ff
Apotheosis, 331
Aptitude test, 22
Aquarius, its indication, 23 f, 88, 90, 97, 101
Arabian astrological parts and points, 108, 126
Arabian Nights, 3
Arcturus, 16 f
Aries, its indication, 23 f 42, 91, 97, 108, 129
Aristotle, 15, 17, 331
Arizona, 97
Artist, true, 55, 59
Arts, 13
Ascendant, its astrological signficance, 124 ff
Aspects of planets, SEE adverse aspects, conjunction aspect, opposition aspect

Astrological analysis, its nature, 52, 114
Astrology, described, 16 ff, 19, 37, 48, 49
Astrology, How and Why It Works, 24
Astrology in Everyday Life, 127
Astrology, its mathematical inexactness, 36, 68
Astrology, its *modus operandi,* 18, 22, 35, 53, 75, 99
Astrology of Personality, 135
Astrology, unreliability of data, 148, 339
Astronomy, 36, 47
Atomic bomb, atomic energy, 87, 117, 121
Automaticities, the problem of, 46

Babylon, Babylonians, 37, 90
Baker, Hannah, 343
Balboa Park, 137, 333
Bank holiday, 84
Barber's brother, 3
Batchelor, Sylva, viii
Bears, caught by honey, 70
Bear, Great, 17

DATES TO WHICH REFERENCE IS MADE

HOROSCOPES AND DIAGRAMS

$\mathcal{M}$arc Edmund Jones created a solid foundation for contemporary scientific astrology in his many groundbreaking books and lectures. Methods he developed are integrated into the work of astrologers globally. Within his techniques are comprehensive principles which reach beyond astrology.

The Sabian Assembly implements the philosophical concepts developed by Marc Edmund Jones as the Solar path of initiation, basing knowledge on personal experience rather than external authority. Founded in 1923, the Assembly continues Dr. Jones' dedication to competent rather than superficial answers to the problems of life. To accomplish this the Assembly issues Dr. Jones' weekly lessons for each cycle. New students plunge directly into the flow of lessons all are currently receiving. Regular study groups, conferences and workshops offer opportunities for members to meet and learn together and share significant experiences.

To obtain more information about the ongoing fellowship known as the **Sabian Assembly** write to:

The SABIAN PUBLISHING SOCIETY
POST OFFICE BOX 7
STANWOOD, WA. 98292

The Marc Edmund Jones Literary Trust is devoted to keeping Dr. Jones' books in print. If you want to know more about this program or to contribute to its success, please write to the above address.